MICHIGAN CRIMINAL LAW & PROCEDURE

A Manual for Michigan Police Officers

2009

Kendall Hunt
publishing company

Cover image credits:
Police gun with holster: Jim Barber © 2009. Used under license from Shutterstock, Inc.
Handcuffs: Bliznetsov © 2009. Used under license from Shutterstock, Inc.
Finger print with magnifying glass: Bruce Rolff © 2009. Used under license from Shutterstock, Inc.
Police tape: JustASC © 2009. Used under license from Shutterstock, Inc.

All chapter opener photos are © Shutterstock, Inc.

Kendall Hunt
publishing company

www.kendallhunt.com
Send all inquiries to:
4050 Westmark Drive
Dubuque, IA 52004-1840

Copyright © 2009 by Michigan Department of State Police

ISBN 978-0-7575-6473-4

Kendall Hunt Publishing Company has the exclusive rights to reproduce this work, to prepare derivative works from this work, to publicly distribute this work, to publicly perform this work and to publicly display this work.

All rights reserved. No part of this publication may be reproduced, stored in a retrieval system, or transmitted, in any form or by any means, electronic, mechanical, photocopying, recording, or otherwise, without the prior written permission of the copyright owner.

Printed in the United States of America
10 9 8 7 6 5 4 3 2 1

ACKNOWLEDGMENTS AND REFERENCES

Several legal instructors throughout the state of Michigan contributed to the development of this and previous editions of this book in hopes that it will help police officers and police recruits comprehend the legal parameters that they operate within on a day-to-day basis. Their assistance is greatly appreciated, as any success this book has is a result of their insight and dedication.

This content of this edition was revised and edited by:

Matt W. Bolger, B.S.
Joseph E. Brodeur, J.D.
Matthew A. Church, J.D.
Thomas M. Deasy, J.D.
Christopher J. Hawkins, J.D.
Carl J. Lafata, Ph.D.
Gregory J. Zarotney, J.D.

The current content editors wish to thank David S. Greydanus, J.D. His leadership and dedication led to the first edition of this book more than a decade ago, and his insight and wisdom continue to drive the on-going development of this book. Without him, this book would not be the valuable resource it is today.

This book should be used for guidance only, and officers are encouraged to review issues with their local prosecutors for their interpretations. Many of the statutes in this book are broken down into basic elements or edited for clarity. For the complete text of any statute, officers should review the Michigan Complied Laws which can be accessed at the Michigan legislature's webpage (www.michiganlegislature.org).

The Michigan State Police legal resources website (www.michigan.gov/msp-legal) contains a variety of legal research tools and other materials that supplement this book. Additionally, the Executive Division publishes a legal update newsletter that describes changes to statutes and new court cases that impact the daily activities of police officers. To view current and past editions of the newsletter, or to subscribe to receive it via e-mail, visit the legal resources site.

CONTENTS

Acknowledgments and References   iii

Chapter 1 Constitutional Law

Declaration of Independence	1
U.S. Constitution	1
Three Branches of the Federal Government	2
Due Process	3
Equal Protection	3
Michigan Constitution and United States Constitution	3
Foot Soldiers of the Constitution	4

Chapter 2 Court Functions and Basic Legal Terminology

Organization and Function of State and Federal Courts	5
Roles within the Judicial System	6
Legal Terminology	6
Basic Concepts of Criminal Law	8
Sources of Michigan Law	10

Chapter 3 Inchoate Offenses

Aiding and Abetting	13
Accessory after the Fact	14
Attempts	14
Conspiracy	14
Solicitation to Commit a Felony	15

Chapter 4 Assault and Child Abuse

Assaults	17
Injury to Fetus or Embryo	22
Child Abuse	22
Violations Involving Minors	25

Chapter 5 Domestic Violence

Arrest Powers	29
Interim Bond	30
Substantive Crimes Associated with Domestic Violence	30
Michigan Personal Protection Orders (PPO)	31
Foreign Protection Order (FPO)	33
Authority to Enter Scene of Domestic Violence	34
Victim's Rights	35
Preparing a Domestic Violence Report	35
Liability	36

Chapter 6 Sex Offenses

Criminal Sexual Conduct	37
Crimes of Indecency	40
Prostitution	42
Registration of Sex Offenders	45

Chapter 7 Homicide & Kidnapping

Homicide	47
Kidnapping	49

Chapter 8 Robbery

Robbery	53
Carjacking	54
Extortion	55

Chapter 9 Crimes against Persons: Selected Statutes

Vulnerable Adult Abuse	57
Ethnic Intimidation	58
Stalking	59
Hazing	62
Eavesdropping	63
Obscene, Harassing, or Threatening Phone Calls	66
Identity Theft	66
Computer Crimes	69
Adulterated Food	73
Poisoning	73

Chapter 10 Destruction of Property

Arson	75
Malicious Destruction of Property	78

Chapter 11 Burglary

Breaking and Entering	81
Home Invasion	82
Entering without Breaking	82
Other Statutes of Interest	83

Chapter 12 Theft Crimes

Auto Theft	85
Larceny	88
Retail Fraud	93
Embezzlement	95

Chapter 13 Financial Crimes

Check Law Violations	97
Forgery	99
Uttering and Publishing	99
Counterfeiting	100
Defrauding an Innkeeper	101
Financial Transaction Device (FTD)	102

Chapter 14 Crimes against Property: Selected Statutes

Possession of Stolen Property	105
Trespass	106

Chapter 15 Controlled Substances

Schedules	111

Chapter 16 Explosives and Weapons

Explosives	119
Fireworks	121
Firearms	122

Chapter 17 Impersonation and Obstruction of Justice

Impersonation	137
False Representations	138
Bribery	139
False Reports	142
Escape	144
Perjury	146
Taking Weapons from an Officer	150
Resisting and Obstructing	151
Fleeing and Eluding	152
Peace Bonds	154

Chapter 18 Public Interest Crimes: Selected Statutes

Gambling	155
Body Armor	156
Liquor Law Violations	156
Police Scanners	161
Peddler License Violations	162
Cruelty to Animals	162
Disorderly Conduct	168
Riots	170
Littering	171

Chapter 19 Laws of Arrest

Laws of Arrest	173
Arrests Pursuant to Arrest Warrant	174
Arrests without a Warrant	175
Private Person's Authority to Arrest without a Warrant	178
Miscellaneous Information	178
Officer's Authority Outside Jurisdiction	179
Force Used to Effectuate Arrests	180
Fresh Pursuit	181
Persons Exempt from Arrest	181
Arrestee's Rights	181
Search Incident to Arrest	181
Bond	183
Custodial Traffic Arrests	184

Entry Into Residence to Make an Arrest 184
Knock and Announce 186

Chapter 20 Admissions and Confessions

Basic Considerations 189
The *Miranda* Warnings 190
Interrogation 193
Right to Remain Silent 195
"Fifth Amendment" Right to Counsel 196
Sixth Amendment Right to Counsel 198
Ambiguous or Limited Assertion of Rights 199
Advisement of Rights 200
Waiver of Rights 201
Voluntariness Standard 203
Juveniles 206
Questioning by Persons Other than
    Law Enforcement 207
Remedies for Violation of Rights 208

Chapter 21 Laws on Suspect Identification

Three Identification Methods 211
Corporeal Lineups 212
Photographic Lineups/ Photo Display 213
Show-Ups 215
Remedy for Improper Identification
    Procedures 216
Inanimate Objects 216

Chapter 22 Search and Seizure

The Fourth Amendment, U.S. Constitution 217
The Search Warrant Rule 217
The Exclusionary Rule 217
Difference between the Michigan Constitution
    and the United States Constitution 218
Applying the Fourth Amendment 218
Open View: No Expectation of Privacy 220
The Curtilage Surrounding a Residence
    Is Protected 223
Crime Scenes 224
Standing: Residence/Vehicle 225
Private Conversations 225
Pretext Stops 226
Pretext Arrests 226
Protective Sweeps 227
Fleeing from Police 228

48-Hour Rule	228
Search Warrant Requirements	228

Chapter 23 Warrantless Searches

Search Incident to a Lawful Arrest	239
Probable Cause and Exigent Circumstances	241
Plain View	244
Consent	246
Terry Encounters	250
Inventories	257
Emergencies	258
Hot Pursuit	259
Administrative Searches	261
Border Searches Exception	262

Chapter 24 Laws of Evidence

Introduction	263
Proof	264
Corpus Delicti	264
Res Gestae	264
Chain of Custody	265
Judicial Notice	265
Presumptions and Inferences	266
Admissibility of Evidence	266
Best Evidence Rule (Original Document Rule)	267
Hearsay Rule	267
Testimony	272
Opinion Evidence	272
Impeachment	273
Character Evidence	273
Privileges	275
Exclusionary Rule	277

Chapter 25 O.W.I. Law

O.W.I. Statute	279
Unlawful Bodily Alcohol Content (UBAC)	280
Impaired Driving	280
Operating with the Presence of Drugs (OWPD)	281
O.W.I. at the Scene of an Accident/Passed out behind the Wheel	281
Penalties	282
.02/Zero Tolerance	282
O.W.I., Impaired, or O.W.P.D. Causing Death	282
O.W.I., Impaired, or O.W.P.D. Causing Serious Impairment of a Body Function	283

Child Endangerment	284
Permitting Person Under Influence to Drive	284
Confiscation of Registration Plate	284
Immobilization	284
Ignition Interlocks	284
Registration Denial	285
Implied Consent	285
Preliminary Breath Tests (PBTs)	285
Chemical Tests	285
Dlad Hearing	287
Miranda Rights and the O.W.I. Arrest	287
Forcing Entry into the Residence	287

Chapter 26 Juvenile Law

Differences in Terminology	289
Jurisdiction of the Family Division of the Circuit Court	289
Custody	290
Waiver of Jurisdiction	291
Transfer of Jurisdiction	291
Rights of a Child	291
Fingerprinting, Photographing, Identification Procedures	292
Hearing Phases	292

Chapter 27 Laws on Use of Force

Michigan Standard	295
Federal Standard	295
Michigan Law on the Use of Deadly Force	296
Fleeing Felons	298
Private Citizen Use of Deadly Force	299
Use of Force in Self Defense	299

Chapter 28 Civil Law and Liability

Civil Law	301
Civil Litigation	301
Civil Liability	302
Intentional Torts	303
Negligence Torts	303
Constitutional torts	305

Chapter 29: Crime Victim's Rights Act

Definitions under the Crime Victim's Rights Act	307
Requirements under the Act for Law Enforcement	308

Appendix: Sample Forms — 311

Glossary — 333

Index — 347

CONSTITUTIONAL LAW

DECLARATION OF INDEPENDENCE

Under English rule, the American colonists experienced great unfairness:

- There were no trials.
- Fictitious charges were brought against people.
- The army was sent to compel compliance with the King's wishes.
- The army forced its way into homes.

With these concerns in mind, the Declaration of Independence was written.

We hold these truths to be self-evident, that all men are created equal, that they are endowed by their Creator with certain unalienable Rights, that among these are Life, Liberty and the pursuit of Happiness.—That to secure these rights, Governments are instituted among Men, deriving their just powers from the consent of the governed, That whenever any Form of Government becomes destructive of these ends, it is the Right of the People to alter or to abolish it, and to institute new Government, laying its foundation on such principles and organizing its powers in such form, as to them shall seem most likely to effect their Safety and Happiness. Prudence, indeed, will dictate that Governments long established should not be changed for light and transient causes; and accordingly all experience hath shown, that mankind are more disposed to suffer, while evils are sufferable, than to right themselves by abolishing the forms to which they are accustomed. But when a long train of abuses and usurpations, pursuing invariably the same Object evinces a design to reduce them under absolute Despotism, it is their right, it is their duty, to throw off such Government, and to provide new Guards for their future security.

U.S. CONSTITUTION

Three main provisions:

1. Establish the framework of government to ensure proper checks and balances.
2. Delegate and assign power to the government.
3. Restrain powers of governmental agents in order to protect individual rights.

Bill of Rights

The founding delegates would not ratify the Constitution until a bill of rights was written.

The Preamble to the Bill of Rights

Congress of the United States begun and held at the City of New York, on Wednesday the fourth of March, one thousand seven hundred and eighty nine. The Conventions of a number of the States, having at the time of their adopting the Constitution, expressed a desire, in order to prevent misconstruction or abuse of its powers, that further declaratory and restrictive clauses should be added: And as extending the ground of public confidence in the Government, will best ensure the beneficent ends of its institution.

The First Ten Amendments to the Constitution as Ratified by the States

Note: The following text is a transcription of the first ten amendments to the Constitution in their original form. These amendments were ratified December 15, 1791, and form what is known as the Bill of Rights.

Amendment I: Congress shall make no law respecting an establishment of religion, or prohibiting the free exercise thereof; or abridging the freedom of speech, or of the press; or the right of the people peaceably to assemble, and to petition the Government for a redress of grievances.

Amendment II: A well regulated Militia, being necessary to the security of a free State, the right of the people to keep and bear Arms, shall not be infringed.

Amendment III: No Soldier shall, in time of peace be quartered in any house, without the consent of the Owner, nor in time of war, but in a manner to be prescribed by law.

Amendment IV: The right of the people to be secure in their persons, houses, papers, and effects, against unreasonable searches and seizures, shall not be violated, and no Warrants shall issue, but upon probable cause, supported by Oath or affirmation, and particularly describing the place to be searched, and the persons or things to be seized.

Amendment V: No person shall be held to answer for a capital, or otherwise infamous crime, unless on a presentment or indictment of a Grand Jury, except in cases arising in the land or naval forces, or in the Militia, when in actual service in time of War or public danger; nor shall any person be subject for the same offence to be twice put in jeopardy of life or limb; nor shall be compelled in any criminal case to be a witness against himself, nor be deprived of life, liberty, or property, without due process of law; nor shall private property be taken for public use, without just compensation.

Amendment VI: In all criminal prosecutions, the accused shall enjoy the right to a speedy and public trial, by an impartial jury of the State and district wherein the crime shall have been committed, which district shall have been previously ascertained by law, and to be informed of the nature and cause of the accusation; to be confronted with the witnesses against him; to have compulsory process for obtaining witnesses in his favor, and to have the Assistance of Counsel for his defence.

Amendment VII: In suits at common law, where the value in controversy shall exceed twenty dollars, the right of trial by jury shall be preserved, and no fact tried by a jury, shall be otherwise reexamined in any Court of the United States, than according to the rules of the common law.

Amendment VIII: Excessive bail shall not be required, nor excessive fines imposed, nor cruel and unusual punishments inflicted.

Amendment IX: The enumeration in the Constitution, of certain rights, shall not be construed to deny or disparage others retained by the people.

Amendment X: The powers not delegated to the United States by the Constitution, nor prohibited by it to the States, are reserved to the States respectively, or to the people.

The Fourteenth Amendment

The Fourteenth Amendment establishes that persons in the United States have dual citizenship. They are citizens of both the United States and their individual states. The Bill of Rights establishes the basic rights that all citizens in the United States possess. The individual states may give more rights, but they cannot give less.

Amendment XIV (Passed by Congress June 13, 1866. Ratified July 9, 1868): All persons born or naturalized in the United States, and subject to the jurisdiction thereof, are citizens of the United States and of the State wherein they reside. No State shall make or enforce any law which shall abridge the privileges or immunities of citizens of the United States; nor shall any State deprive any person of life, liberty, or property, without due process of law; nor deny to any person within its jurisdiction the equal protection of the laws.

THREE BRANCHES OF THE FEDERAL GOVERNMENT

Legislative Branch (Article I) (lawmakers)

The **legislative branch** is bicameral, meaning it has two chambers, which are together called the Congress:

- The Senate: Two members from each state.
- The House of Representatives: 435 members apportioned based on population. No less than one per state.

Congress is responsible for passing laws. The following types of laws cannot be passed:

- No Bills of Attainder: Laws enacted naming individuals or an ascertainable group designed to punish them without a trial.
- No Ex Post Facto laws: Laws passed designed to punish conduct that occurred before the law was passed.

Executive Branch (Article II) (enforcement arm of government)

The **executive branch** is responsible for the following:

- Making treaties.
- Appointing federal judges.
- Enforcing laws (e.g., FBI, DEA, Secret Service).

Judicial Branch (Article III) (interprets laws and treaties)

The **judicial branch** has **jurisdiction** in the following areas:

- Reviews constitutional questions and treaties.
- Interprets the laws of the United States.
- Resolves controversies between states.

The Supreme Court held that it has the power to review the constitutional validity of actions taken by the other two branches of government as long as there is a case or controversy. The Supreme Court also has the power to declare acts of Congress as unconstitutional. This authority stems from *Marbury v. Madison*, 5 U.S. 137 (1803).

DUE PROCESS

Both the Fifth and Fourteenth Amendments discuss **due process** of law. The Fifth Amendment's due process clause is applicable to the federal government and the Fourteenth Amendment's clause is applicable to the states. *Black's Law Dictionary* states, "The essential elements of due process of law are notice and an opportunity to be heard. A person has the right to defend in orderly proceeding adapted to the nature of the case, and the guarantee of due process requires that every man have the protection of his day in court and the benefit of general law." Daniel Webster defined this phrase to mean, "A law that hears before it condemns and which proceeds on inquiry and renders judgment only after trial."

There are two types of due process. One is **substantive due process** and the other is **procedural due process**.

Substantive Due Process

- A Constitutional guarantee that no person will be arbitrarily or unreasonably deprived of life, liberty, or property without due process of law.
- The essence of substantive due process is the protection from arbitrary and unreasonable action. It is designed to protect individuals from unfair governmental power. The focus is on the limits that have been placed upon the government's ability to define conduct as criminal.

Procedural Due Process

Those safeguards to one's liberty and property mandated by the Constitution. Examples include:

- Right to counsel.
- Right to confrontation.
- Miranda warnings.

EQUAL PROTECTION

Under the Fourteenth Amendment, "no state shall . . . deny to any person within its jurisdiction the **equal protection** of the laws." This means that no person or class of persons shall be denied the same protection of the laws that is enjoyed by other persons or other classes in like circumstances in their lives, liberty, property, and in their pursuit of happiness. (*Black's Law Dictionary*)

MICHIGAN CONSTITUTION AND UNITED STATES CONSTITUTION

Generally, the Michigan Constitution closely follows the U.S. Constitution. The following are examples.

- Article I, Section 17 - *Self-Incrimination*: The self-incrimination provisions of both constitutions are nearly identical. Federal case law has largely influenced state interpretations of these provisions. Since the United States Supreme Court applies Miranda only to custodial interrogation, the Michigan Supreme Court has followed that application. *People v. Hill*, 429 Mich. 382 (1987).

- Article I, Section 11 - *Search and Seizure*: The Michigan Constitution has no exclusionary rule for narcotic drugs, firearms, bombs, or other dangerous weapons seized outside the curtilage of a dwelling. For example, a gun that was found illegally during a traffic stop would still be admissible under the Michigan Constitution.

  However, federal case law has developed the exclusionary rule that will suppress evidence that is seized in violation of the Fourth Amendment. In applying the standard set by the Fourth Amendment, the gun would be suppressed. The Bill of Rights provides basic protections to all people in the United States. States may grant more protections, but they cannot take away the basic rights found in the Constitution.

> The Michigan Supreme Court *cannot* impose a higher standard of scrutiny than that which would be imposed by the Supreme Court, under the Fourth Amendment, when reviewing the search of a police officer who is not within the **curtilage** of someone's dwelling, and who seizes narcotic drugs, firearms, bombs, or other dangerous weapons. *People v. Bullock*, 440 Mich. 15 (1992).

FOOT SOLDIERS OF THE CONSTITUTION

Police officers are the foot soldiers of the Constitution due to their role in preserving society's norms and values. It is the sense of "constitution" that prevents ethical breakdowns and strengthens a police officer's resolve to do right. As General Colin Powell once said:

> *I took an oath to support and defend the Constitution of the United States.... Our Constitution and our national conscience demand that every American be accorded dignity and respect, and receive the same treatment under the law.*

The Table 1.1 should remind police officers of the delicate balance that a democratic society requires.

TABLE 1.1

THE TWELEVE TABLES OF CITIZENSHIP

THE MORALITY OF DEMOCRACY & GOALS FOR CIVIC EDUCATION

THE OBLIGATIONS OF CITIZENSHIP		THE RIGHTS OF CITIZENSHIP	
Corrupted obligations of citizenship	True obligations of citizenship	True rights of citizenship	Corrupted rights of citizenship
Law Enforced Without Discretion	Justice	Freedom	Anarchy: Uncontrolled selfishness
Forced Mediocrity and Conformity: Stagnation	Equality	Diversity	Society Crippled by the Conflict between Parties
Totalitarianism	Authority	Privacy	Isolationism
Majority Rule without Individual Protections	Participation	Due process	Soft on Crime: Thinking that Everyone is a Victim and Everything is a Right
Unprecedented Regulations and Taxation: Excess Entitlements and Frivolous Liablitily	Honesty	Ownership	Monopolies: Capitalism Superior to Human Rights
Hatred of Outsiders: Racism; Discrimination; Cult-like Political Systems	Patriotism	Human rights	Cultural Relativism: Inablity to judge the morality of different customs and cultures - no concept of good and evil

DEMOCRATIC CITIZENSHIP

COURT FUNCTIONS AND BASIC LEGAL TERMINOLOGY

ORGANIZATION AND FUNCTION OF STATE AND FEDERAL COURTS

Federal Court System

- **Federal District Courts** are the trial courts for the federal system. They hear both civil and criminal matters.
- After adjudication at the district court level, the case may be appealed to the **Federal Circuit Court of Appeals** that has jurisdiction over the matter.
- The final court is the **United States Supreme Court**. The Supreme Court has appellate jurisdiction from the U.S. Courts of Appeal and may review constitutional issues from state supreme courts. The court also has original jurisdiction in suits between states.
- The appeal process in federal courts is from District Court to the Court of Appeals by right. Appeals to the Supreme Court are by *petition of certiorari*. (Discretionary on the part of the court on whether to hear the case).

State Court System

District Courts are responsible for the following:

- Small claims up to $3,000.
- Civil suits of $25,000 or less.
- Criminal trials for 1-year misdemeanors and all lesser offenses.
- **Arraignments.**
- Setting bail.
- Preliminary examinations for felonies and circuit court misdemeanors.
- Issuing search and arrest warrants.
- District Court magistrate (see below).

Circuit Courts are responsible for the following:

- Civil suits in excess of $25,000.
- Criminal felony and circuit court misdemeanor trials.
- **Personal Protection Orders.**
- Supervisory control over District Courts.
- The Family Law Division of the Circuit Court hears all matters concerning juveniles, excluding civil infractions.

The Court of Appeals hears appeals from the lower courts.

The Supreme Court hears appeals from Court of Appeals.

Appeal Process in State Court

Decisions from the district court are appealed by right to the circuit court. Circuit court decisions are appealed to the Court of Appeals. Felonies and circuit court misdemeanors are appealed as of right or automatic. Appeals to the Supreme Court are by application for leave to appeal. Cases involving constitutional issues may be appealed from the Michigan Supreme Court to the United States Supreme Court by petition of certiorari.

ROLES WITHIN THE JUDICIAL SYSTEM

Judges

Judges perform the following functions:

- Issue arrest warrants.
- Issue search warrants.
- Make legal rulings.
- Act as fact finders in bench trials only.
- Preside over all trials.

The Jury

- An accused has the right to trial by jury.
- The jury is the finder of fact.

Prosecuting Attorney

The prosecuting attorney is the chief law enforcement officer of a county, who:

- Authorizes complaints.
- Represents the county in all civil matters in those counties without corporation counsel.
- Represents the people in all criminal matters.

Defense Attorney

The defense attorney safeguards the guaranteed rights of the accused.

District Court Magistrate (MCL 600.8511)

- Hears informal civil infraction hearings.
- May issue search warrants.
- Sets bail and accepts bond in all cases.
- Issues warrants for arrest.
- Arraigns and sentences for limited violations upon pleas of guilty and nolo contendere.

LEGAL TERMINOLOGY

Jurisdiction: The types of cases a court has the power to hear.

Venue: The geographic areas a court may preside over, (e.g. Wayne County Circuit Court).

In-state prosecution for criminal offense (MCL 762.2):

(1) A person may be prosecuted for a criminal offense he or she commits while he or she is physically located within this state or outside of this state if any of the following circumstances exist:

(a) He or she commits a criminal offense wholly or partly within this state.

(b) His or her conduct constitutes an attempt to commit a criminal offense within this state.

(c) His or her conduct constitutes a conspiracy to commit a criminal offense within this state and an act in furtherance of the conspiracy is committed within this state by the offender, or at his or her instigation, or by another member of the conspiracy.

(d) A victim of the offense or an employee or agent of a governmental unit posing as a victim resides in this state or is located in this state at the time the criminal offense is committed.

(e) The criminal offense produces substantial and detrimental effects within this state.

(2) A criminal offense is considered under subsection (1) to be committed partly within this state if any of the following apply:

(a) An act constituting an element of the criminal offense is committed within this state.

(b) The result or consequences of an act constituting an element of the criminal offense occur within this state.

(c) The criminal offense produces consequences that have a materially harmful impact upon the system of government or the community welfare of this state, or results in persons within this state being defrauded or otherwise harmed.

Information and belief: The belief something is true but it is not based on firsthand knowledge.

Complaint and *warrant for arrest:* The complaint consists of the essential facts constituting the offense charged; the warrant for arrest is issued upon reasonable grounds to believe an offense has occurred.

Indictment: A formal written accusation issued by a grand jury or similar entity charging one or more people with a crime.

Arraignment: The first appearance of the defendant before a judge or magistrate following an arrest. The arraignment process consists of the following actions: The defendant is formally advised of charges. An attorney may be appointed. Bond is set.

Preliminary examination: A preliminary examination is held for felonies and circuit court misdemeanors. The purpose is to determine if probable cause exists to believe a crime has been committed and to determine if probable cause exists that defendant committed the offense. The prosecutor has the burden of proof.

Arraignment on the information: Occurs after bindover in a felony or circuit court misdemeanor.

Pretrial motions: Pretrial motions are presented to the judge in an attempt to exclude evidence. For example, during a Walker hearing, arguments are made to exclude confessions. Pretrial motions are also brought to exclude the admission of other types of evidence or to raise issues such as entrapment. The burden of proof in pretrial motions depends on the type of motion and who is bringing it. In a Walker hearing, the prosecutor has the burden, whereas in entrapment, the burden is on the defendant. The standard of proof is preponderance of the evidence.

Motion in limine: A written motion preventing certain prejudicial questions from being asked at trial.

Voir dire examination: Voir dire is the questioning of prospective jurors to determine their suitability to sit as jurors. A person has the right to an impartial jury of his or her peers. There are two times a juror may be disqualified from jury duty: (1) *Challenge for cause* is the exclusion of a prospective juror based on some prejudice or interest. For example, the juror may be a relative of the defendant. There is no limit to this type of challenge. (2) *Peremptory challenge* is the exclusion of a juror for no stated reason. The court rules have placed limits on this type of challenge. (MCR 6.412, MCR 2.510, and MCR 2.511)

Double jeopardy: The Fifth Amendment states, "Nor shall any person be subject for the same offense to be twice put in jeopardy of life or limb." Double jeopardy is being tried twice for the same crime. Double jeopardy does not preclude trial by state and federal courts because they are separate sovereigns.

> If there is a clear legislative intent to allow multiple punishments for a single wrong act, double jeopardy is not violated. *People v. Sturgis*, 427 Mich. 392 (1986).
>
> In determining whether the same act constitutes a violation of two different statutes, the test to be applied is whether each statute requires proof of an additional fact that the other does not. A defendant may be charged with home invasion in one county and possession of the property stolen from the home invasion in another county. The same "element test" for double jeopardy purposes replaced the same "criminal transaction" test. *People v. Nutt*, 469 Mich. 565 (2004).

Double jeopardy rights attach during different times in the judicial process. If the defendant is facing a jury trial, jeopardy attaches when the jury is impaneled and sworn. In a bench trial, jeopardy attaches when the first witness is sworn. If the defendant pleads guilty, jeopardy attaches when he or she is sentenced.

14-Day Rule (MCL 766.4): A preliminary examination must be held within 14 days of an arraignment. M.C.L. 766.7 states that a preliminary exam may be adjourned for good cause only.

180-Day Rule (MCL 780.131): Inmates of the Department of Corrections must be brought before the court for trial within 180 days. This allows a prisoner to serve his or her time concurrently if additional charges are brought against him or her. A good faith effort must be accomplished in bringing the inmate to trial within the time period.

Plea bargaining: The process where the accused and the prosecutor negotiate an agreement as to the disposition of a case. Defendant usually pleads guilty to a lesser charge or to one of a number of charges.

Pre-sentence investigation: Prior to sentencing, the probation department will review the defendant's criminal record, investigating officers' comments and other factors to make a recommendation to the judge for sentencing.

Sentencing requirements: Some sentences are set by statute—for example, first-degree murder, which is mandatory life in prison. Others are left more to the discretion of the judge who must sentence within guidelines.

Bond requirements: Under the Eighth Amendment, bail cannot be excessive. The judge sets bond by looking at such factors as the nature of the offense, community ties, prior record and flight risk. (MCR 6.106) Under MCL 766.7, there is no bond for murder or treason.

Probable cause: Facts and circumstances sufficient to cause a person of reasonable caution to suspect the person to be arrested is committing or has committed a crime, or that the place to be searched contains the evidence sought. It has been described as a "fair probability." Probable cause is also known as **reasonable cause**, sufficient cause, or reasonable grounds. For a more detailed discussion, see Chapter Nineteen on arrests.

Reasonable suspicion: An objective basis—supported by specific and articulable facts—for suspecting a person of committing a crime. This is a standard most commonly applied in the context of searches. For more information, see Chapter Twenty-Three.

Beyond a reasonable doubt: The belief that there is no real possibility that a defendant is not guilty. This is the standard for conviction in a criminal trial.

Clear and convincing evidence: Evidence indicating that something is substantially more likely true than not true.

Preponderance of the Evidence: Evidence sufficient to convince an impartial person to decide an issue one way rather than the other. This is often characterized as 51 percent. Thise is the burden of proof in civil trials and some evidentiary hearings.

Entrapment: Entrapment occurs if (1) the police engage in impermissible conduct that would induce an otherwise law-abiding person to commit a crime in similar circumstances, or (2) the police engage in conduct so reprehensible that it cannot be tolerated by the court.

> When examining whether governmental activity would impermissibly induce criminal conduct, several factors are considered: (1) whether there existed appeals to the defendant's sympathy as a friend, (2) whether the defendant had been known to commit the crime with which he or she was charged, (3) whether there were any long time lapses between the investigation and the arrest, (4) whether there existed any inducements that would make the commission of a crime unusually attractive to a hypothetical law-abiding citizen, (5) whether there were offers of excessive consideration or other enticement, (6) whether there was a guarantee that the acts alleged as crimes were not illegal, (7) whether, and to what extent, any government pressure existed, (8) whether there existed sexual favors, (9) whether there were any threats of arrest, (10) whether there existed any government procedures that tended to escalate the criminal culpability of the defendant, (11) whether there was police control over any informant, and (12) whether the investigation was targeted. *People v. Johnson*, 466 Mich. 491 (2002).

The outcome of court cases: There are essentially four terms that describe the end result of decisions made by the courts. They are often, but incorrectly, used interchangeably. Note that each has a distinct meaning:

- **Ruling:** The outcome of a court's decision on a specific point or a case as a whole.
- **Holding:** A court's determination of a matter of law, a specific legal principle contained in an opinion, or a court's ruling concerning a specific question.
- **Opinion:** A court's written statement explaining its decision in a case.
- **Finding:** A determination by a judge or jury of a fact.

BASIC CONCEPTS OF CRIMINAL LAW

Mens Rea

This is translated from the Latin to mean the guilty mind. To be guilty of most crimes, the defendant must have committed the act in a certain mental state. This is the *mens rea* and there are two types:

Specific Intent

- For specific intent, the prosecution must prove not only that the defendant did certain acts, but that he or she did the acts with the intent to cause a particular result. For example, larceny requires the prosecutor to prove that the defendant had the specific intent to permanently deprive the owner of the property.

- The defendant's intent may be proven by what he or she said, what he or she did, and how he or she did it, or by any other acts and circumstances in evidence. CJI2d 3.9.

General Intent

This is defined as the intent to do an act that the law prohibits. It is not necessary for the prosecution to prove that the defendant intended the precise harm or the precise result, which occurred. (*Black's Law Dictionary*)

Actus Reus

This term is translated as the guilty act. This is the wrongful deed that renders the actor criminally liable if combined with the mens rea. For example, the actus reus for larceny would be the taking of the property.

Corpus Delicti

This is another term translated from the Latin and means the "body of the crime," or the substance of the crime. It includes each element of the crime.

Definition of a Crime—MCL 750.5

"Crime" means an act or omission forbidden by law that is not designated as a civil infraction, and that is punishable upon conviction by any one or more of the following:

- Imprisonment.
- Fine not designated a civil fine.
- Removal from office.
- Disqualification to hold an office of trust, honor, or profit under the state.
- Other penal discipline.

Lesser Included Crimes—MCL 786.32

If a crime consists of different degrees, the fact finder may find the accused not guilty of the offense in the degree charged, but may find the accused person guilty of a lesser included offense, or of an attempt to commit that offense. For example, CSC third is a lesser included crime of CSC first.

Felony—MCL 761.1

"Felony" means a violation of a penal law of this state for which the offender may be punished by death or by imprisonment for more than one year or an offense expressly designated by law to be a felony.

> The term "felony" means an offense for which the offender may be punished by death, or by imprisonment in state prison. MCL 750.7.

Unless specifically stated otherwise, a felony is punishable in a state prison for four years. MCL 750.503.

Misdemeanor—MCL 761.1

"Misdemeanor" means a violation of a penal law of this state that is not a felony or a violation of an order, rule, or regulation of a state agency that is punishable by imprisonment or a fine that is not a civil fine.

Unless specifically stated otherwise, a misdemeanor is punishable in the county jail for not more than 90 days. (MCL 750.504)

Statute of Limitations—MCL 767.24

(1) An indictment for murder, conspiracy to commit murder, solicitation to commit murder, criminal sexual conduct in the first degree, or a violation of the Michigan anti-terrorism act, chapter LXXXIII-A of the Michigan penal code, 1931 PA 328, MCL 750.543a to 750.543z, or a violation of chapter XXXIII of the Michigan penal code, 1931 PA 328, MCL 750.200 to 750.212a, that is punishable by life imprisonment may be found and filed at any time.

(2) An indictment for a violation or attempted violation of section 145c, 520c, 520d, 520e, or 520g of the Michigan penal code, 1931 PA 328, MCL 750.145c, 750.520c, 750.520d, 750.520e, and 750.520g, may be found and filed as follows:

(a) Except as otherwise provided in subdivision (b), an indictment may be found and filed within 10 years after the offense is committed or by the alleged victim's twenty-first birthday, whichever is later.

(b) If evidence of the violation is obtained and that evidence contains DNA that is determined to be from an unidentified individual, an indictment against that individual for the violation may be found and filed at any time after the offense is committed. However, after the individual is identified, the indictment may be found and filed within 10 years after the individual is identified or by the alleged victim's twenty-first birthday, whichever is later.

(c) As used in this subsection:

(i) "DNA" means human deoxyribonucleic acid.

(ii) "Identified" means the individual's legal name is known and he or she has been determined to be the source of the DNA.

(3) An indictment for kidnapping, extortion, assault with intent to commit murder, attempted murder, manslaughter, or first-degree home invasion may be found and filed within 10 years after the offense is committed.

(4) An indictment for identity theft or attempted identity theft may be found and filed as follows:

(a) Except as otherwise provided in subdivision (b), an indictment may be found and filed within 6 years after the offense is committed.

(b) If evidence of the violation is obtained and the individual who committed the offense has not been identified, an indictment may be found and filed at any time after the offense is committed, but not more than 6 years after the individual is identified.

(c) As used in this subsection:

(i) "Identified" means the individual's legal name is known.

(ii) "Identity theft" means 1 or more of the following:

(A) Conduct prohibited in section 5 or 7 of the identity theft protection act, 2004 PA 452, MCL 445.65 and 445.67.

(B) Conduct prohibited under former section 285 of the Michigan penal code, 1931 PA 328.

(5) All other indictments may be found and filed within 6 years after the offense is committed.

(6) *Any period during which the party charged did not usually and publicly reside within this state is not part of the time within which the respective indictments may be found and filed.*

(7) *The extension or tolling, as applicable, of the limitations period provided in this section applies to any of those violations for which the limitations period has not expired at the time the extension or tolling takes effect.*

SOURCES OF MICHIGAN LAW

Michigan law is primarily gleaned from five sources:

1. Statutes.
2. Court opinions (case law).
3. Administrative rules.
4. Executive Orders.
5. Attorney General Opinions.

Statutes

Statutes are laws enacted by the legislature and governor or directly by the people. When the legislature enacts (passes) a law, both houses must approve it by majority vote; the legislature votes on items called bills. Once passed by both houses, a bill will become a public act only if approved by the governor. Public acts are then recorded as statutes in the Michigan Compiled Laws, which is a publication maintained by the legislature.

The statutes most commonly used by police officers typically do one of two things: They govern the conduct of the public, or they control the conduct of the government (i.e., police officers). Police officers enforce the statutes that govern the public within the rules established by the statutes that control the government.

The Michigan Compiled Laws (MCL) is divided into chapters that are loosely organized by related subject matter. Many chapters contain statutes that can be enforced by law enforcement officers. The most common are Chapter 750 (Penal Code), Chapter 257 (Vehicle Code), Chapter 333 (Public Health Code), and Chapter 324 (Natural Resources).

Generally, statutes enforced by police officers tell the public what they must not do or how to do something they are allowed to do, and they provide penalties for doing something that is prohibited or doing something incorrectly. Unless exceptions are listed in a statute, they almost never tell people what they are allowed to do. As a rule, if something is not expressly made illegal, it is legal. Police officers must never take action (e.g., arrest or citation) for something that is not illegal. Thus, knowing what is illegal (i.e., an act prohibited by law or a legal act done illegally) is paramount for all police officers.

Citations

Michigan statutes are identified by citations that begin with the designation "MCL" and identify the chapter and section in the MCL where the statute can be found. When appropriate, the subsection can also be included.

Example: Subsection 2 of section 227 of the Penal Code (chapter 750) makes it illegal for a person to possess a pistol in a vehicle without a license. That statute is properly cited as:

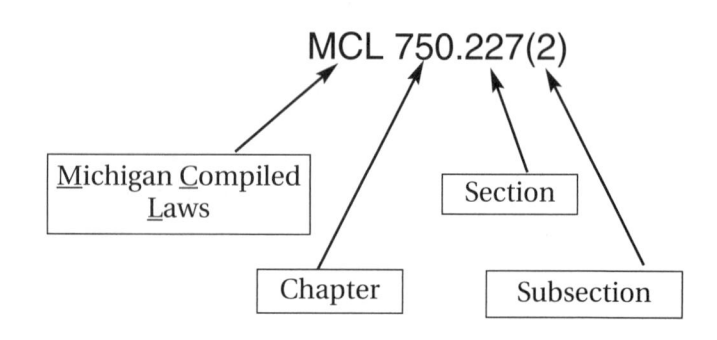

MCL 750.227(2)

- Michigan Compiled Laws
- Chapter
- Section
- Subsection

Court Opinions

Court opinions are written statements by a court explaining the decision in a particular case. Courts interpret and apply statutes, decide the constitutionality of statutes, and in some cases, make law. When an opinion contains a rule of law, police may be required to follow the rule if the opinion is binding. Whether an opinion is binding depends on which court issued the opinion and whether the opinion is published or unpublished.

Generally, court opinions are binding as follows:

Court	Effect of Opinion
United States Supreme Court	Binding on all lower courts—police must follow.
Michigan Supreme Court	Binding on all lower Michigan state courts—police in Michigan must follow.
Michigan Court of Appeals	Published opinions are binding, unpublished opinions are not binding—police must follow published opinions.
6th Circuit Court of Appeals	Binding on federal courts within the circuit and on Michigan in some circumstances.
Trial Courts	Binding only on that court for that case.

Citations

Court cases are cited by their name (which includes two parties separated by a "v" for versus) and reference to where they can be found (volume and page) in books in which the cases are published, followed by the year the decision was rendered and other clarifying information when needed (such as the name of the court when it is not obvious from the citation which court rendered the opinion). Those books are called "reporters."

For example, the United States Supreme Court case of *Terry versus Ohio*, decided in 1968, was published in volume 392 of the United States Reports beginning on page 1 of that volume. The citation looks like this:

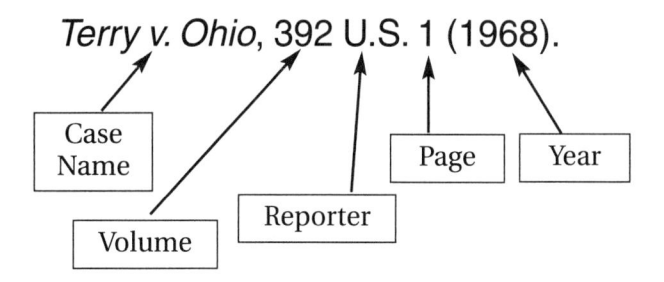

Terry v. Ohio, 392 U.S. 1 (1968).

- Case Name
- Volume
- Reporter
- Page
- Year

There are a variety of other ways in which court opinions may be properly cited (e.g., by docket number or by listing multiple cites). In this book you will generally find court cases cited to the official reporter. From time to time you may also see various citation formats, such as underlined case names instead of italicized, string cites (listing multiple reporters after the case name), and pinpoint cites (listing a second page number that points to a specific page within an opinion). In this book we do not generally string cite or pinpoint cite.

Court	Official Reporter	Other Common Reporters	Clarifying Information
United States Supreme Court	United States Reports (U.S.)	Supreme Court Reporter (S. Ct.)	None
United States Courts of Appeals	Federal Reporter (F., F.2d, or F.3d)	Federal Appendix (F.App'x)	The circuit will be identified by number at the end of the citation (e.g., "6th Cir.")
Michigan Supreme Court	Michigan Reports (Mich.)	North Western Reporter (N.W. or N.W.2d)	"Mich." will appear with the date when cited to N.W.
Michigan Court of Appeals	Michigan Appeals Reports (Mich. App.)	North Western Reporter (N.W. or N.W.2d)	"Mich. App." will appear with the date when cited to N.W.

Administrative Rules

Administrative rules are rules written and passed (promulgated) by executive branch agencies under authority of a statute. They have the same force and effect as a statute and can be found in the Michigan Administrative Code. Citations to rules appear much like statutes, with an "R" appearing where MCL would appear.

Executive Orders

Executive Orders are orders issued by the governor under authority granted by the Michigan Constitution. Executive Orders may (1) reorganize or rename departments or agencies within the executive branch; (2) reassign functions within the executive branch; (3) create or dissolve an executive body; or (4) proclaim or end a state of emergency. Executive Orders will eventually be codified as part of the MCL.

Citations

Executive Orders may be cited by their MCL section, by the designation E.O. (e.g., E.O. No. 2008-17), or by the designation E.R.O., which stands for Executive Reorganization Order (e.g., E.R.O. No. 2009-5). When cited as an E.O. or E.R.O., the citation includes the year issued and the sequential number of the order. An E.R.O. always starts as an E.O., but the sequential numbers may be different.

Attorney General Opinions

Attorney General Opinions are documents issued by the Michigan Attorney General that answer a specific question posed by a member of the executive branch or the legislature. AG Opinions may be formal or informal. Informal opinions only provide legal guidance and are not binding. Formal opinions are published as a matter of public record and are binding on the executive branch of state government. Formal opinions are given deference by the courts, but they are not binding on the courts.

Formal AG opinions are only binding as to the specific question answered.

Other Sources of Law

There are a number of other legal documents that affect law enforcement, although they may not require police officers to do anything during their day-to-day work. For example, the Michigan Supreme Court has created a number of rules that control the function of Michigan's courts, most notably the Michigan Rules of Evidence (cited as "MRE") and the Michigan Court Rules (cited as "MCR"). While these rules do not bind law enforcement, they impact police officers because they control how courts operate and what may be properly admitted as evidence in court proceedings.

Also worth noting are the Criminal Jury Instructions (cited as "CJI" or "CJI2d"). The CJI are used by judges to tell jurors what they must determine in order to find a defendant guilty. Although not binding law, they were created using statutes and case law and generally provide a concise description of the elements of a crime or defense.

INCHOATE OFFENSES

Inchoate offenses are incomplete crimes or a step toward another crime where the step itself is punishable as a crime (BLACK'S LAW DICTIONARY 885 Abridged 7th ed. 2000). Attempt, conspiracy, and solicitation are the crimes typically considered inchoate offenses. In this chapter we discuss those offenses and several others that are incident to, or part of, another offense. We have left for other chapters some offenses that might fit here, but are closely related to the subject of another chapter (e.g., assault with intent to maim appears in Chapter Four covering assaults).

AIDING AND ABETTING—MCL 767.39

Anyone who intentionally assists someone else in committing a crime is as guilty as the person who directly commits it and can be convicted of that crime as an aider and abettor.

Elements

1. The alleged crime was actually committed, either by the defendant or someone else. (It does not matter whether anyone else has been convicted of the crime.)
2. Before or during the crime, the defendant did something to assist in the commission of the crime.
3. The defendant must have intended the commission of the crime alleged or must have known that the other person intended its commission at the time of giving the assistance. CJI2d 8.3.

> Robinson agreed to assist Pannell in committing an aggravated assault. The assault was intended as an act of revenge after the victim threatened Pannell's family. After repeatedly punching and kicking the victim, Robinson told Pannell, "that's enough" and left the scene. After Robinson left, Pannell shot and killed the victim.
>
> The Court held that when a person aids another in the commission of one crime, he or she can be criminally liable for any other crime that is the "natural and probable" result of the original crime. Therefore, Robinson could properly be convicted of murder. *People v. Robinson*, 475 Mich. 1 (2006).

Inducement

It does not matter how much aid, advice, or encouragement the defendant gave. However, the defendant must have intended to assist another in committing the crime, and the help, advice, or encouragement actually helped the crime to occur. CJI2d 8.4.

Mere Presence Insufficient

Even if the defendant knew that the alleged crime was planned or was being committed, the mere fact that defendant was present when it was committed is not enough to prove that he or she assisted in committing it. CJI2d 8.5.

> Aiding and abetting describes all forms of assistance rendered to the perpetrator of a crime and comprehends all words or deeds that might support, encourage, or incite the commission of a crime. *People v. Bullis*, 262 Mich. App. 618 (2004).

ACCESSORY AFTER THE FACT— MCL 750.505 (felony)

An accessory after the fact is someone who knowingly helps a felon avoid discovery, arrest, trial, or punishment after the principal offense has occurred. This is one of a handful of common law offenses punishable under MCL 750.505, but not otherwise specifically addressed in a statute.

Elements

1. Someone else committed an offense that the defendant had knowledge of. (The prosecutor doesn't have to prove that the other person has been charged with or convicted of the offense, only that the offense was committed.)
2. The defendant knowingly helped the other person avoid discovery, arrest, trial or punishment.
3. The defendant intended to help the other person avoid discovery, arrest, trial, or punishment.

CJI2d 8.6.

> The person committing the original offense does not have to be convicted for an accessory to be convicted as an accessory, but the prosecutor must prove that the original crime did occur. *People v. Williams*, 117 Mich. App. 505 (1982).

Difference Between Aider and Abettor and Accessory After the Fact

If the prosecutor has proven beyond a reasonable doubt that before or during the offense the defendant gave encouragement or assistance intending to help another commit that crime, then the defendant may be found guilty of aiding and abetting the crime.

If the prosecutor has proven beyond a reasonable doubt that the defendant knew about the offense and helped the person who committed it avoid discovery, arrest, trial, or punishment after the crime ended, then the defendant may be found guilty of being an accessory after the fact. CJI2d 8.7.

> A person cannot be an aider and abettor and an accessory after the fact on the same crime. *People v. Lucas*, 402 Mich. 302 (1978).

ATTEMPTS—MCL 750.92

Elements

1. Defendant intended to commit a crime and took some action toward committing the offense but failed in completing it.
2. Preparations like planning and arranging are not enough. An attempt goes beyond mere preparation to the point where the crime would have been completed if it had not been interrupted by outside circumstances.

CJI2d 9.1

Impossibility Is Not a Defense

A person can be found guilty of attempting to commit a crime even if he or she could not finish the crime because circumstances turned out to be different than expected or he or she was stopped before the crime was completed. CJI2d 9.3.

CONSPIRACY—MCL 750.157a

Anyone who *knowingly agrees* with someone else to commit a crime is guilty of conspiracy.

Elements

1. The defendant and one or more persons knowingly agreed to commit a crime.
2. The defendant specifically intended to commit or help commit that crime.

CJI2d 10.2.

Agreement for Conspiracy

The agreement for conspiracy includes the following:

- An agreement is the coming together or meeting of the minds of two or more people, with each person intending and expressing the same purpose.

- It is not necessary for the people involved to have made a formal agreement to commit the crime or to write down how they were going to do it.

- In deciding whether there was an agreement to commit a crime, think about how all the members of the alleged conspiracy acted and what they said as well as all the other evidence.
- To find the defendant guilty of conspiracy, the judge or jury must be satisfied beyond a reasonable doubt that there was an agreement to commit a crime. However, it can be inferred that there was an agreement from the circumstances, such as how the members of the alleged conspiracy acted, but only if there is no other reasonable explanation for those circumstances.

Michigan is a "no one-man conspiracy" state. If two people are charged with a crime and one is acquitted and one is convicted, the conspiracy charges must be dropped. The charges do not have to be dropped if the indictment refers to unknown or unnamed conspirators and there is sufficient evidence to show the existence of a conspiracy between the convicted defendant and these other conspirators. *People v. Williams*, 240 Mich. App. 316 (2000).

Where police have frustrated a conspiracy's specific objective but conspirators (unaware of that fact) have neither abandoned the conspiracy nor withdrawn, the special conspiracy related dangers remain, as does the conspiracy's essence, the agreement to commit the crime. *United States v. Recio*, 537 U.S. 270 (2003).

SOLICITATION TO COMMIT A FELONY—MCL 750.157b

Elements

1. The defendant, through words or actions, offered, promised, or gave money, services, or anything of value (or forgave or promised to forgive a debt or obligation owed) to another person.
2. The defendant intended that what he or she said or did would cause the felony to be committed.
3. The prosecutor does not have to prove that the person the defendant solicited actually committed, attempted to commit, or intended to commit the crime. CJI2d 10.6.

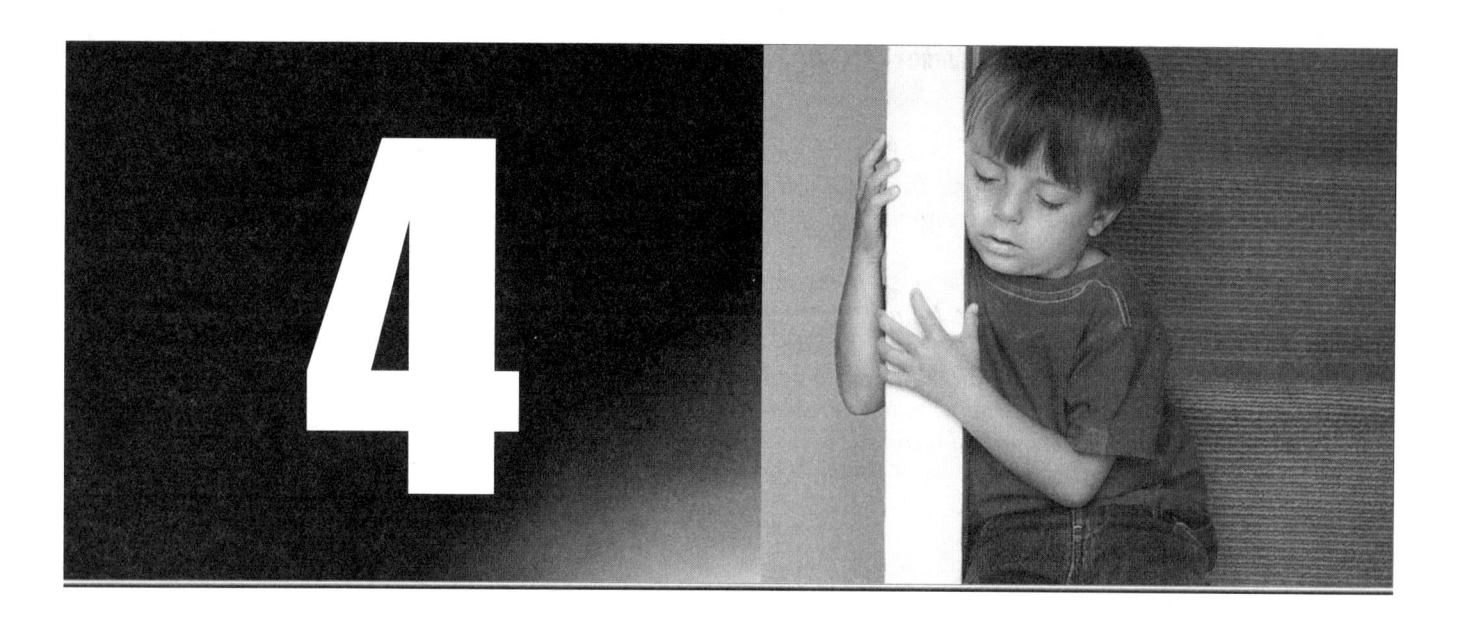

ASSAULT AND CHILD ABUSE

ASSAULTS

Assault and Battery—MCL 750.81 (93-day misdemeanor)

(1) Except as otherwise provided in this section, a person who assaults or assaults and batters an individual, if no other punishment is prescribed by law, is guilty of a misdemeanor punishable by imprisonment for not more than 93 days or a fine of not more than $500.00, or both.

(2) Except as provided in subsection (3) or (4), an individual who assaults or assaults and batters his or her spouse or former spouse, an individual with whom he or she has or has had a dating relationship, an individual with whom he or she has had a child in common, or a resident or former resident of his or her household, is guilty of a misdemeanor punishable by imprisonment for not more than 93 days or a fine of not more than $500.00, or both.

(3) An individual who commits an assault or an assault and battery in violation of subsection (2), and who has previously been convicted of assaulting or assaulting and battering his or her spouse or former spouse, an individual with whom he or she has or has had a dating relationship, an individual with whom he or she has had a child in common, or a resident or former resident of his or her household, under any of the following, may be punished by imprisonment for not more than 1 year or a fine of not more than $1,000.00, or both:

(a) This section or an ordinance of a political subdivision of this state substantially corresponding to this section.
(b) Section 81a, 82, 83, 84, or 86.
(c) A law of another state or an ordinance of a political subdivision of another state substantially corresponding to this section or section 81a, 82, 83, 84, or 86.

(4) An individual who commits an assault or an assault and battery in violation of subsection (2), and who has 2 or more previous convictions for assaulting or assaulting and battering his or her spouse or former spouse, an individual with whom he or she has or has had a dating relationship, an individual with whom he or she has had a child in common, or a resident or former resident of his or her household, under any of the following, is guilty of a felony punishable by imprisonment for not more than 2 years or a fine of not more than $2,500.00, or both:

(a) This section or an ordinance of a political subdivision of this state substantially corresponding to this section.
(b) Section 81a, 82, 83, 84, or 86.
(c) A law of another state or an ordinance of a political subdivision of another state substantially corresponding to this section or section 81a, 82, 83, 84, or 86.

(5) This section does not apply to an individual using necessary reasonable physical force in compliance with section 1312 of the revised school code, 1976 PA 451, MCL 380.1312.

(6) As used in this section, "dating relationship" means frequent, intimate associations primarily characterized by the expectation of affectional involvement. This term does not include a casual relationship or an ordinary fraternization between 2 individuals in a business or social context.

Assault—MCL 750.81 (93-day misdemeanor)

Elements

1. Defendant either attempts to commit a battery, or commits an illegal act that places the victim in reasonable apprehension or fear of an immediate battery.
2. Defendant intends to injure or to put the victim in reasonable fear or apprehension of an immediate battery.
3. Defendant, at the time, had the ability, appeared to have the ability, or thought he or she had the ability.

CJI2d 17.1.

> Placing hand in diaper bag and pointing at victim in threatening manner constituted assault even though no weapon was located. The assault element is satisfied where circumstances indicate that an assailant, by overt conduct, causes the victim to reasonably believe that he will do what is threatened. *People v. Reeves*, 458 Mich. 236 (1998).

Assault and Battery—MCL 750.81 (93-day misdemeanor)

Elements

1. Defendant committed a forceful battery.
2. The defendant intended either to commit the battery, or make the victim reasonably fear a battery.
3. The defendant committed the battery without the victim's consent.

CJI2d 17.2.

Battery defined:
Battery is a forceful, violent, or offensive touching of the person or something closely connected with the victim. The touching must not be accidental and must be against the victim's will. Injury is not required. CJI2d 17.2.

> Battery may involve striking with a closed fist or pushing another with an open hand. *People v. Solak*, 146 Mich. App. 659 (1985).

Domestic Assault and Battery

Elements

1. Defendant committed and assault or assault and battery.
2. Defendant and victim were in a domestic relationship.

CJI2d 17.2a.

Types of Domestic Relationships

Domestic relationships include the following:

- Spouse or former spouse.
- People who reside or formerly resided in the same household.
- Both parties have a child in common.
- Suspect and victim who have, or have had, a dating relationship.

Penalties:

1st offense	93-day misdemeanor
2nd offense	1 year misdemeanor
3rd offense	2 year felony

Aggravated Assault—MCL 750.81a (1 year misdemeanor)

(1) Except as otherwise provided in this section, a person who assaults an individual without a weapon and inflicts serious or aggravated injury upon that individual without intending to commit murder or to inflict great bodily harm less than murder is guilty of a misdemeanor punishable by imprisonment for not more than 1 year or a fine of not more than $1,000.00, or both.

(2) Except as provided in subsection (3), an individual who assaults his or her spouse or former spouse, an individual with whom he or she has or has had a dating relationship, an individual with whom he or she has had a child in common, or a resident or former resident of the same household without a weapon and inflicts serious or aggravated injury upon that individual without intending to commit murder or to inflict great bodily harm less than murder is guilty of a misdemeanor punishable by imprisonment for not more than 1 year or a fine of not more than $1,000.00, or both.

(3) *An individual who commits an assault and battery in violation of subsection (2), and who has 1 or more previous convictions for assaulting or assaulting and battering his or her spouse or former spouse, an individual with whom he or she has or has had a dating relationship, an individual with whom he or she has had a child in common, or a resident or former resident of the same household, in violation of any of the following, is guilty of a felony punishable by imprisonment for not more than 2 years or a fine of not more than $2,500.00, or both:*

(a) *This section or an ordinance of a political subdivision of this state substantially corresponding to this section.*
(b) *Section 81, 82, 83, 84, or 86.*
(c) *A law of another state or an ordinance of a political subdivision of another state substantially corresponding to this section or section 81, 82, 83, 84, or 86.*

(4) *As used in this section, "dating relationship" means frequent, intimate associations primarily characterized by the expectation of affectional involvement. This term does not include a casual relationship or an ordinary fraternization between 2 individuals in a business or social context.*

Elements

1. Defendant tried to physically injure another person (without a weapon).
2. Defendant intended to injure victim or make victim reasonably fear an immediate battery.
3. Defendant caused physical injury that requires immediate medical attention or that causes disfigurement or impairment.
CJI2d 17.6.

> Victim was rendered unconscious by a blow to the head and suffered injuries to his face, eye, and neck. *People v. Brown*, 97 Mich. App. 606 (1980).

Penalties:

1st offense	1 year misdemeanor
Previous conviction for domestic assault	2 year felony

Assault upon an FIA Worker—MCL 750.81c

Elements

1. A person who communicates to any person a threat that he or she will physically harm an employee of the Family Independence Agency and does so because of the employee's status with the agency = 1 year misdemeanor.
2. If a person assaults or assaults and batters an employee of the Family Independence Agency because of the employee's status with the agency.

Penalties:

Causes physical injury	2 year felony
Causes serious impairment of bodily function	5 year felony

Assaulting a Peace Officer, EMT, Firefighter, or Search and Rescue Team Performing Duties—MCL 750.81d (felony)

It is unlawful to assault, batter, wound, resist, obstruct, oppose, or endanger any of the following:

- Police officers, motor carrier officers, or capitol security officers.
- Federal conservation officers.
- Federal peace officers.
- Firefighters.
- Emergency medical service personnel.
- Search and rescue teams.

This section applies when the individual knows, or has reason to know, that any of the above are performing their duties.

Penalties:

Without injury	2 year felony
Causes bodily injury requiring medical attention	4 year felony
Causes serious impairment of bodily function	15 year felony
Causes death	20 year felony

> Where suspected drunk driver refused to cooperate with the execution of a search warrant for his blood by stating the word "No," there was sufficient evidence to convict for R and O. *People v. Philabaun*, 461 Mich. 255 (1999).

> Mere lies about one's identity are insufficient to trigger a violation of the R and O statute. *People v. Vasquez*, 465 Mich. 83 (2001).
>
> A person may not resist an arrest made by an officer when the person knows or has reason to know the officer is performing his or her duties. MCL 750.81d does not require a showing that a defendant's arrest was lawful. *People v. Ventura*, 262 Mich. App. 370 (2004).
>
> Serious impairment of a body function occurred where the officer lost the use of a leg for several weeks while he was on crutches and, to a more limited extent, during the several months that he was unable to return to work. *People v. Thomas*, 263 Mich. App. 70 (2004).

Killing, Harming, or Intefering with a Police or Search and Rescue Dog or Horse Performing Duties—MCL 750.50c

Penalties:

Killing the dog or horse	5 year felony
Causing physical harm to the dog or horse	1 year misdemeanor
Intentionally harassing or interfering with the dog or horse	1 year misdemeanor
Causing physical harm or harassing or interfering during commission of a crime	2 year felony

Assault with a Dangerous Weapon (Felonious Assault)—MCL 750.82 (felony)

A person who assaults another person with a gun, revolver, pistol, knife, iron bar, club, brass knuckles, or other dangerous weapon without intending to commit murder or to inflict great bodily harm less than murder is guilty of a felony punishable by imprisonment for not more than 4 years or a fine of not more than $2,000.00, or both.

Elements

1. Defendant either attempted to commit a battery or committed an illegal act that caused the victim to reasonably fear an immediate battery.
2. The defendant intended to injure or make the victim reasonably fear an immediate battery.
3. Defendant had the ability, appeared to have the ability, or thought he or she had the ability to commit a battery.
4. Defendant committed the assault with a dangerous weapon.

CJI2d 17.9.

- A dangerous weapon is any instrument that is used in a way that is likely to cause serious physical injury or death. CJI2d 17.8.
- A gun that is totally unusable as a firearm and cannot easily be made operable is not included here. CJI2d 17.13.

> Dangerous weapons:
> - Pellet gun. *People v. Jones*, 150 Mich. App. 440 (1986).
> - A dog. *People v. Kay*, 121 Mich. App. 438 (1982).
> - A broomstick thrown at head level or just below. *People v. Knapp*, 34 Mich. App. 325 (1971).
> - An automobile. *People v. Sheets*, 138 Mich. App. 794 (1984).
> - An unloaded gun. *People v. Smith*, 231 Mich. App. 50 (1998).
> - A starter pistol that could not fire was not a dangerous weapon for F.A. *People v. Stevens*, 409 Mich. 564 (1980).
> - Bare hands are not weapons under the statute. *People v. VanDriver*, 80 Mich. App. 352 (1977).

Assault with the Intent to Murder—MCL 750.83 (felony)

Any person who shall assault another with intent to commit the crime of murder, shall be guilty of a felony, punishable by imprisonment in the state prison for life or any number of years.

Elements

1. Defendant tried to physically injure another person.
2. When defendant committed the assault, he or she had the ability or at least believed he or she had the ability to cause an injury.
3. The defendant intended to kill the person assaulted.

CJI2d 17.3.

Assault with intent to murder is an assault where the suspect intended to kill the victim without justification.

> A choking where, had the choking continued, the victim would have died. *People v. Anderson*, 112 Mich. App. 640 (1981).

Assault with the Intent to Do Great Bodily Harm Less than Murder—MCL 750.84 (felony)

Any person who shall assault another with intent to do great bodily harm, less than the crime of murder, shall be guilty of a felony punishable by imprisonment in the state prison not more than 10 years, or by fine of not more than $5,00000.

Also included in this section is an assault with the intent to cause great bodily harm, although actual injury is not necessary.

> Beating and kicking the victim in her arms, face, head, and chest. *People v. Pena*, 224 Mich. App. 650 (1997).

Assault with the Intent to Maim—MCL 750.86 (felony)

Any person who shall assault another with intent to maim or disfigure his or her person by cutting out or maiming the tongue, putting out or destroying an eye, cutting or tearing off an ear, cutting or slitting or mutilating the nose or lips, or cutting off or disabling a limb, organ, or member, shall be guilty of a felony, punishable by imprisonment in the state prison not more than 10 years or by fine of not more than $5,000.00.

The following list gives examples of types of maiming:

- Assault with the intent to maim or disfigure
- Cutting out or maiming the tongue
- Putting out or destroying an eye
- Cutting, slitting, or mutilating the nose or lips
- Cutting off or disabling a limb, organ, or member

> Placing thumbs against the victim's eyes and stating that her eyes were going to be poked out. *People v. Ward*, 211 Mich. App. 489 (1997).

Assault with Intent to Commit a Felony—MCL 750.87 (felony)

Any person who shall assault another, with intent to commit any burglary, or any other felony, the punishment of which assault is not otherwise in this act prescribed, shall be guilty of a felony, punishable by imprisonment in the state prison not more than 10 years, or by fine of not more than $5,000.

Assault with the Intent to Rob; Unarmed—MCL 750.88 (felony)

Any person, not being armed with a dangerous weapon, who shall assault another with force and violence, and with intent to rob and steal, shall be guilty of a felony, punishable by imprisonment in the state prison not more than 15 years.

> Placing hand in a bag and pointing it at the victim in a menacing manner while saying, "What's more important, your job or your life?" *People v. Reeves*, 458 Mich. 236 (1998).

Assault to Rob; Armed—MCL 750.89 (felony)

Any person, being armed with a dangerous weapon, or any article used or fashioned in a manner to lead a person so assaulted reasonably to believe it to be a dangerous weapon, who shall assault another with intent to rob and steal shall be guilty of a felony, punishable by imprisonment in the state prison for life, or for any term of years.

Assault on a Third Person

If defendant intended to assault one person, but by mistake or accident assaulted another, the crime is the same as if the first person had been assaulted. CJI2d 17.17.

Torture—MCL 750.85 (felony)

A person who, with the intent to cause cruel or extreme physical or mental pain and suffering, inflicts great bodily injury or severe mental pain or suffering upon another person within his or her custody or physical control commits torture and is guilty of a felony punishable by imprisonment for life or any term of years.

"Cruel" means brutal, inhuman, sadistic, or that which torments.

"Custody or physical control" means the forcible restriction of a person's movements or forcible confinement of the person so as to interfere with that person's liberty, without that person's consent or without lawful authority.

"Great bodily injury" means either of the following:

> *(i) Serious impairment of a body function as that term is defined in section 58c of the Michigan vehicle code, 1949 PA 300, MCL 257.58c, or*

(ii) One or more of the following conditions: internal injury, poisoning, serious burns or scalding, severe cuts, or multiple puncture wounds.

"Severe mental pain or suffering" means a mental injury that results in a substantial alteration of mental functioning that is manifested in a visibly demonstrable manner caused by or resulting from any of the following:

(i) *The intentional infliction or threatened infliction of great bodily injury,*

(ii) *The administration or application, or threatened administration or application, of mind-altering substances or other procedures calculated to disrupt the senses or the personality,*

(iii) *The threat of imminent death,*

(iv) *The threat that another person will imminently be subjected to death, great bodily injury, or the administration or application of mind-altering substances or other procedures calculated to disrupt the senses or personality.*

Proof that a victim suffered pain is not an element of the crime under this section.

INJURY TO FETUS OR EMBRYO

Injury to a Fetus or Embryo—MCL 750.90a (felony)

The suspect either intentionally caused a miscarriage or stillbirth, or committed an act in wanton or willful disregard, which caused a miscarriage or stillbirth.

Intentionally Commits any Assault—MCL 750.81 to MCL 750.89 upon a Pregnant Individual—MCL 750.90b

Penalties:

Results in physical injury to embryo or fetus	93 day misdemeanor
Results in serious or aggravated injury to embryo or fetus	1 year misdemeanor
Results in great bodily harm to embryo or fetus	10 year felony
Results in miscarriage or stillbirth or death to embryo or fetus	15 year felony

Commits Gross Negligence to a Pregnant Individual—MCL 750.90c

Penalties:

Results in physical injury to embryo or fetus	93 day misdemeanor
Results in serious or aggravated injury to embryo or fetus	6 month misdemeanor
Results in great bodily harm to embryo or fetus	5 year felony
Results in miscarriage or stillbirth or death to embryo or fetus	15 year felony

Operating while Intoxicated (O.W.I.)—MCL 750.90d

Penalties:

Results in great bodily harm to embryo or fetus	5 year felony
Results in miscarriage or stillbirth or death to embryo or fetus	15 year felony

Operating a Vehicle in Careless or Reckless Manner—MCL 750.90e

Penalties:

Results in miscarriage or stillbirth or death to embryo or fetus	2 year misdemeanor

NOTE: Above sections do not apply to acts committed by the pregnant individual or lawful medical procedures.

CHILD ABUSE

Definitions—MCL 750.136b

Suspect must be one of the following:

- A parent or guardian of a child, or
- A person who had care, custody, or authority over the child.

Child: A person less than 18 years old.

Serious physical harm to a child: Any physical injury to a child that seriously impairs the child's health or physical well-being, including, but not limited to, brain damage, a skull or bone fracture, subdural hemorrhage or hematoma, dislocation, sprain, internal injury, poisoning, burn or scald, or severe cut.

Physical harm: Any injury to a child's physical condition.

Serious mental harm to a child: Injury to mental condition that results in visible signs of impairment in child's judgment, behavior, ability to recognize reality, or ability to cope with ordinary demands of life.

Omission: Willfully fail to provide food, clothing or shelter necessary for the welfare of the child or to abandon the child.

Cruel: Brutal, inhuman, sadistic, or that which torments.

First Degree—MCL 750.136b(2) (Felony)

The suspect knowingly or intentionally caused serious physical or mental harm.

> First-degree child abuse requires the prosecution to establish not only that defendant intended to commit the act, but also that defendant intended to cause serious physical harm or knew that serious physical harm would be caused by his or her act. *People v. Maynor*, 470 Mich. 289 (2004).

Second Degree—MCL 750.136b(3) (felony)

The suspect did one of the following:

- Performed a reckless act or omission that caused serious physical or mental harm.
- Knowingly or intentionally committed an act likely to cause serious physical harm or mental harm to a child, regardless of whether the harm resulted.
- Knowingly or intentionally committed an act that is cruel to a child, regardless of whether the harm resulted.

Third Degree—MCL 750.136b(5) (felony)

The suspect did one of the following:

- Either knowingly or intentionally caused physical injury to a child.
- Knowingly or intentionally committed an act that posed an unreasonable risk of harm or injury to a child, and the act resulted in physical harm to a child.

> Third degree child abuse occurred where the mother knew the child's susceptibility to bruising and still spanked her with enough force to dislodge a blood clot in her nose and cause substantial bruising. *People v. Sherman-Huffman*, 466 Mich. 39 (2002).

Fourth Degree—MCL 750.136b(7) (1 year misdemeanor)

The suspect did one of the following:

- Omission or reckless act caused physical harm to a child.
- Knowingly or intentionally committed an act that posed an unreasonable risk of harm or injury to a child, regardless of whether physical harm resulted.

Parental Discipline

Reasonable parental discipline is not against the law, including reasonable force.

> Blood blisters, bruises, and a hand-shaped welt on the side of a child's face that was still visible a week after the incident was not reasonable discipline. *People v. Gregg*, 206 Mich. App. 208 (1994).

Child Abandonment—MCL 750.135 (felony)

Any father or mother of a child under the age of 6 years, or any other person who shall expose such child in any street, field, house, or other place, with intent to injure or wholly to abandon it, shall be guilty of felony.

- Except for a situation involving actual or suspected child abuse or child neglect, it is an affirmative defense to a prosecution under subsection (1) that the child was not more than 72 hours old and was surrendered to an emergency service provider. A criminal investigation shall not be initiated solely on the basis of a newborn being surrendered to an emergency service provider.
- As used in this section, an "Emergency Service Provider" means an uniformed employee or contractor of a fire department, hospital, or police station when that individual is inside the premises and on duty.

Leaving Child Unattended in Vehicle—MCL 750.135a

A person who is responsible for the care or welfare of a child shall not leave that child unattended in a vehicle for a period of time that poses an unreasonable risk of harm or injury to the child or under circumstances that pose an unreasonable risk of harm or injury to the child. For the purposes of this statute, a child is a person under 6 and unattended means without supervision by a person 13 or older.

Penalties:

Results in no harm to the child	93 day misdemeanor
Results in physical harm other than serious physical harm	1 year misdemeanor
Results in serious physical harm to the child	10 year felony
Results in death of the child	15 year felony

Sale of Children—MCL 750.136c (felony)

(1) A person shall not transfer or attempt to transfer the legal or physical custody of an individual to another person for money or other valuable consideration, except as otherwise permitted by law.
(2) A person shall not acquire or attempt to acquire the legal or physical custody of an individual for payment of money or other valuable consideration to another person, except as otherwise permitted by law.
(3) A person who violates this section is guilty of a felony punishable by imprisonment for not more than 20 years or a fine of not more than $100,000.00, or both.

Requirements to Report Child Abuse or Neglect—MCL 722.623(1)

(1) An individual is required to report under this act as follows:
   (a) physician, dentist, physician's assistant, registered dental hygienist, medical examiner, nurse, person licensed to provide emergency medical care, audiologist, psychologist, marriage and family therapist, licensed professional counselor, social worker, licensed master's social worker, licensed bachelor's social worker, registered social service technician, social service technician, a person employed in a professional capacity in any office of the friend of the court, school administrator, school counselor or teacher, law enforcement officer, member of the clergy, or regulated child care provider who has reasonable cause to suspect child abuse or neglect shall make immediately, by telephone or otherwise, an oral report, or cause an oral report to be made, of the suspected child abuse or neglect to the department. Within 72 hours after making the oral report, the reporting person shall file a written report as required in this act. If the reporting person is a member of the staff of a hospital, agency, or school, the reporting person shall notify the person in charge of the hospital, agency, or school of his or her finding and that the report has been made, and shall make a copy of the written report available to the person in charge. A notification to the person in charge of a hospital, agency, or school does not relieve the member of the staff of the hospital, agency, or school of the obligation of reporting to the department as required by this section. One report from a hospital, agency, or school is adequate to meet the reporting requirement. A member of the staff of a hospital, agency, or school shall not be dismissed or otherwise penalized for making a report required by this act or for cooperating in an investigation.

Failure to Report Child Abuse/False Report of Child Abuse—MCL 722.633

(1) A person who is required by this act to report an instance of suspected child abuse or neglect and who fails to do so is civilly liable for the damages proximately caused by the failure.
(2) A person who is required by this act to report an instance of suspected child abuse or neglect and who knowingly fails to do so is guilty of a misdemeanor punishable by imprisonment for not more than 93 days or a fine of not more than $500.00, or both.
(3) Except as provided in section 7, a person who disseminates, or who permits or encourages the dissemination of, information contained in the central registry and in reports and records made as provided in this act is guilty of a misdemeanor punishable by imprisonment for not more than 93 days or a fine of not more than $100.00, or both, and is civilly liable for the damages proximately caused by the dissemination.
(4) A person who willfully maintains a report or record required to be expunged under section 7 is guilty of a misdemeanor punishable by imprisonment for not more than 93 days or a fine of not more than $100.00, or both.

(5) A person who intentionally makes a false report of child abuse or neglect under this act knowing that the report is false is guilty of a crime as follows:

(a) If the child abuse or neglect reported would not constitute a crime or would constitute a misdemeanor if the report were true, the person is guilty of a misdemeanor punishable by imprisonment for not more than 93 days or a fine of not more than $100.00, or both.

(b) If the child abuse or neglect reported would constitute a felony if the report were true, the person is guilty of a felony punishable by the lesser of the following:

(i) The penalty for the child abuse or neglect falsely reported.
(ii) Imprisonment for not more than 4 years or a fine of not more than $2,000.00, or both.

VIOLATIONS INVOLVING MINORS

Allowing Minor to Stay in Bar—MCL 750.141 (90-day misdemeanor)

A child under 17 years of age shall not be permitted to remain in any place where spirituous or alcoholic liquor, wine or beer is sold, given away or furnished for a beverage, unless the minor is accompanied by parent or guardian. A proprietor, keeper or manager who permits a minor child to remain, and a person who encourages or induces, in any way the minor child to enter the place or to remain therein, shall be deemed guilty of a misdemeanor.

Allowing Minor to Consume or Possess Alcoholic Liquor at Social Gathering or Allowing Someone to Possess Controlled Substances—MCL 750.141a (1st: 30-day, 2nd: 90-day misdemeanor)

The suspect is one of the following:

- Owner,
- Tenant, or
- Person in control

on one of the following:

- Premises,
- Residence, or
- Other real property.

The suspect knowingly allowed one of the following:

- A minor to consume or possess an alcoholic beverage, or
- An individual to consume or possess a controlled substance

without taking one of the following corrective actions:

- Demanding that the person leave,
- Reporting the violation to law enforcement, or
- Reporting the violation to someone with higher authority.

For an incident that occurred at a social gathering, it must involve two or more individuals not of the same household or immediate family.

Tobacco Violations

Furnishing Tobacco to a Person Under 18—MCL 722.641 (90-day misdemeanor)

A person shall not sell, give, or furnish a tobacco product to a minor. A person who violates this subsection is guilty of a misdemeanor punishable by a fine of not more than $50.00 for each violation

Possession by a Person Under 18—MCL 722.642 (90-day misdemeanor)

A minor shall not do any of the following:

(a) Purchase or attempt to purchase a tobacco product.

(b) Possess or attempt to possess a tobacco product.

(c) Use a tobacco product in a public place.

(d) Present or offer to an individual a purported proof of age that is false, fraudulent, or not actually his or her own proof of age for the purpose of purchasing, attempting to purchase, possessing, or attempting to possess a tobacco product.

Contributing to the Delinquency of a Minor— MCL 750.145 (90-day misdemeanor)

Any person who shall by any act, or by any word, encourage, contribute toward, cause or tend to cause any minor child under the age of 17 years to become neglected or delinquent so as to come or tend to come under the jurisdiction of the family division of the circuit court whether or not such child shall in fact be adjudicated a ward of the court, shall be guilty of a misdemeanor.

> Defendant promised minor girl a place to stay if she ran away from home and assisted her in the process. *People v. Owens*, 13 Mich. App. 469 (1968).

Soliciting Child for Immoral Purposes—MCL 750.145a (felony)

A person who accosts, entices, or solicits a child less than 16 years of age, regardless of whether the person knows the individual is a child or knows the actual age of the child, or an individual whom he or she believes is a child less than 16 years of age with the intent to induce or force that child or individual to commit an immoral act, to submit to an act of sexual intercourse or an act of gross indecency, or to any other act of depravity or delinquency, or who encourages a child less than 16 years of age, regardless of whether the person knows the individual is a child or knows the actual age of the child, or an individual whom he or she believes is a child less than 16 years of age to engage in any of those acts is guilty of a felony punishable by imprisonment for not more than 4 years or a fine of not more than $4,000.00, or both.

Soliciting a Minor to Commit a Felony—MCL 750.157c

A person 17 years of age or older who recruits, induces, solicits, or coerces a minor less than 17 years of age to commit or attempt to commit an act that would be a felony if committed by an adult is guilty of a felony and shall be punished by imprisonment for not more than the maximum term of imprisonment authorized by law for that act. The person may also be punished by a fine of not more than 3 times the amount of the fine authorized by law for that act.

> Defendant recruited a 15-year-old boy to help him kill and rape young children by offering the boy alcohol and cigarettes. This section applied even though the minor never planned to actually commit the act. *People v. Pfaffle*, 246 Mich. App. 282 (2001).

Child Sexually Abusive Material—MCL 750.145c

DEFINITIONS

Appears to include a child: The depiction appears to include, or conveys the impression that it includes, a person who is less than 18 years of age, and the depiction meets either of the following conditions:

- It was created using a depiction of any part of an actual person under the age of 18.
- It was not created using a depiction of any part of an actual person under the age of 18, but all of the following apply to that depiction:

  - The average individual, applying contemporary community standards, would find the depiction, taken as a whole, appeals to the prurient interest.
  - The reasonable person would find the depiction, taken as a whole, lacks serious literary, artistic, political, or scientific value.
  - The depiction depicts or describes a listed sexual act in a patently offensive way.

Child: Less than 18 years old who is not emancipated.

Child sexually abusive material: Any depiction, whether made or produced by electronic, mechanical, or other means, including a developed or undeveloped photograph, picture, film, slide, video, electronic visual image, computer diskette, computer or computer-generated image, or picture, or sound recording which is of a child or appears to include a child engaging in a listed sexual act; a book, magazine, computer, computer storage device, or other visual or print or printable medium containing such a photograph, picture, film, slide, video, electronic visual image, computer, or computer-generated image, or picture, or sound recording; or any reproduction, copy, or print of such a photograph, picture, film, slide, video, electronic visual image, book, magazine, computer, or computer-generated image, or picture, other visual or print or printable medium, or sound recording.

Child sexually abusive activity: Child engaged in a listed sexual act.

Commercial film or photographic print processor: A person or his or her employee who, for compensation, develops exposed photographic film into movie films, negatives, slides, or prints; makes prints from negatives or slides; or duplicates movie films or videotapes.

Contemporary community standards: The customary limits of candor and decency in this state at or near the time of the alleged violation of this section.

Erotic fondling: Touching a person's clothed or unclothed genitals, pubic area, buttocks, or, if the person is female, breasts, or if the person is a child, the developing or undeveloped breast area, for the purpose of real or simulated overt sexual gratification or stimulation of one or more of the persons involved. Erotic fondling does not include physical contact, even if affectionate, that is not for the purpose of real or simulated overt sexual gratification or stimulation of one or more of the persons involved.

Erotic nudity: The lascivious exhibition of the genital, pubic, or rectal area of any person. As used in this subdivision, "lascivious" means wanton, lewd, and lustful and tending to produce voluptuous or lewd emotions.

Listed sexual act: Sexual intercourse, erotic fondling, sadomasochistic abuse, masturbation, passive sexual involvement, sexual excitement or erotic nudity.

Masturbation: The real or simulated touching, rubbing, or otherwise stimulating of a person's own clothed or unclothed genitals, pubic area, buttocks, or, if the person is female, breasts, or if the person is a child, the developing or undeveloped breast area, either by manual manipulation or self-induced or with an artificial instrument, for the purpose of real or simulated overt sexual gratification or arousal of the person.

Passive sexual involvement: An act, real or simulated, that exposes another person to or draws another person's attention to an act of sexual intercourse, erotic fondling, sadomasochistic abuse, masturbation, sexual excitement, or erotic nudity because of viewing any of these acts or because of the proximity of the act to that person, for the purpose of real or simulated overt sexual gratification or stimulation of one or more of the persons involved.

Prurient interest: A shameful or morbid interest in nudity, sex, or excretion.

Sadomasochistic abuse: Abuse that is either of the following:

- Flagellation or torture, real or simulated, for the purpose of real or simulated sexual stimulation or gratification, by or upon a person.
- The condition, real or simulated, of being fettered, bound, or otherwise physically restrained for sexual stimulation or gratification of a person.

Sexual excitement: The condition, real or simulated, of human male or female genitals in a state of real or simulated overt sexual stimulation or arousal.

Sexual intercourse: Intercourse, real or simulated, whether genital-genital, oral-genital, anal-genital, or oral-anal, whether between persons of the same or opposite sex or between a human and an animal, or with an artificial genital.

Producing Child Sexually Abusive Material—MCL 750.145(c)(2) (felony)

The suspect does one of the following:

- Persuades, induces, entices, coerces, causes, or knowingly allows a child to engage in activity to produce child sexually abusive material.
- Prepares or conspires to arrange for, produce, make, or finance child sexually abusive material.

> Videotaping a 3-year-old girl performing fellatio on 1-year-old boy. *People v. Hack*, 219 Mich. App. 299 (1996).
>
> Erotic nudity occurred where a tape was edited to focus on, slow down, and replay a child's innocent exposure. *People v. Riggs*, 237 Mich. App. 584 (1999).
>
> Counts of sexually abusive material may be based on each picture taken. *People v. Harmon*, 248 Mich. App. 522 (2001).
>
> Downloading child pornography onto a CD is producing for the purposes of the statute. *People v. Hill*, 269 Mich. App. 505 (2006).
>
> The prosecution must prove that the defendant knew or should have known that the images were of children under 18. *People v. Girard*, 269 Mich. App. 15 (2005).
>
> Consent by the child is not a valid defense to producing sexually abusive material. *People v. Wilkens*, 267 Mich. App. 728 (2005).

Distribute or Promote Child Sexually Abusive Material—MCL 750.145(c)(3) (Felony)

The suspect does one of the following:

- Distributes, promotes, or finances the distribution or promotion of child sexually abusive material or activity.
- Receives for the purpose of distributing or promoting child sexually abusive material.
- Conspires, attempts, or prepares to distribute, receive, finance, or promote child sexually abusive material or activity.

> To "distribute" requires criminal intent to disseminate child sexually abusive material to others. *People v. Tombs*, 472 Mich. 446 (2005).

Exception: This section does not apply to parents or guardians who distribute explicit material to their child or ward unless the dissemination was for the sexual gratification of the parent or guardian.

Possession of Child Sexually Abusive Material—MCL 750.145(c)(4) (felony)

The suspect knowingly possessed child sexually abusive material. This applies to a person who knows, has reason to know, or should reasonably be expected to know the child is a child, or that person has not taken reasonable precautions to determine the age of the child.

This section does not apply to:

- A police officer acting within the scope of his or her duties.
- An employee or contract agent of the department of social services acting within the scope of his or her duties.
- A judicial officer or judicial employee acting within the scope of his or her duties.
- A party or witness in a criminal or civil proceeding acting within the scope of that criminal or civil proceeding.
- A physician, psychologist, limited license psychologist, professional counselor, or registered nurse licensed under the public health code, acting within the scope of practice for which he or she is licensed.
- A social worker registered in this state acting within the scope of practice for which he or she is registered.
- A commercial film or photographic print processor or computer technician acting within the scope of his or her professional capacity or employment.

Film Developers/Computer Technicians

If a commercial film or photographic print processor or computer technician reports to the local prosecuting attorney his or her knowledge or observation, within the scope of his or her professional capacity or employment, of a film, photograph, movie film, videotape, negative, or slide depicting a person that the processor has reason to know or reason to believe is a child engaged in a listed sexual act; furnishes a copy of the film, photograph, movie film, videotape, negative, or slide to the prosecuting attorney; or keeps the film, photograph, movie film, videotape, negative, or slide according to the prosecuting attorney's instructions, both of the following shall apply:

- The identity of the processor shall be confidential, subject to disclosure only with his or her consent or by judicial process.
- If the processor acted in good faith, he or she shall be immune from civil liability that might otherwise be incurred by his or her actions. This immunity extends only to acts described in this subsection.

> The prosecutor must prove that the defendant knew or should have known the pictures were those of children under 18. Expert testimony may be used but is not required if other evidence exists. *People v. Girard,* 269 Mich. App. 15 (2005).

DOMESTIC VIOLENCE

ARREST POWERS

General Arrest Powers: Non-Domestic-Relationship Incident

In non-domestic cases, a police officer's authority to make an arrest is governed by the general laws of arrest. Typically, that authority is limited to those circumstances briefly described below. For more information about an officer's general arrest authority, see Chapter Nineteen.

- Pursuant to a warrant.
- For a felony or misdemeanor punishable in excess of 92 days, officers may arrest on probable cause or if the offense is witnessed by an officer.
- For other misdemeanors, the offense generally must be committed in the officer's presence.
- Violation of parole or probation.

Domestic Violence Arrest Powers—MCL 764.15a

MCL 764.15a authorizes a peace officer to make an arrest if he or she has reasonable cause to believe or receives positive information that another officer has reasonable cause to believe both of the following:

Elements

1. An assault, assault and battery or aggravated assault has taken place or is taking place, and
2. The individual being arrested:
   - Is a spouse or former spouse of the victim,
   - Resides or has resided in the same household as the victim,
   - Has a child in common with the victim, or
   - Has or has had a dating relationship with the victim.

A **dating relationship** means frequent, intimate associations primarily characterized by the expectation of affectional involvement. This term does not include a casual relationship or an ordinary fraternization between two individuals in a business or social context.

The officer may make this arrest *without a warrant*, regardless of whether the offense was committed in the officer's presence. Officers should *not* arrest an individual if the officer has reasonable cause to believe the individual was acting in *lawful self-defense* or in the defense of another.

If an arrest is made, the officer may become the complainant under MCL 764.1a, which allows a magistrate to accept complaints of assault, assault, and battery or aggravated assault on a domestic victim where the complaint is signed based on information and belief by individuals other than the victim. The magistrate shall not refuse to accept a complaint on the grounds that the complaint is signed upon information and belief by an individual other than the victim.

Attorney General's Opinion No. 6822 (1994).

A peace officer may make a warrantless arrest for a misdemeanor of assault or assault and battery committed outside of the officer's presence, *in the absence of physical evidence of domestic abuse,* when there is other corroborating evidence sufficient to constitute probable cause to believe that the person to be arrested committed the offense.

INTERIM BOND—MCL 780.582a

A person arrested for domestic violence shall not be released on an interim bond or on his or her own recognizance until he or she can be arraigned or have interim bond set by a judge or district court magistrate.

SUBSTANTIVE CRIMES ASSOCIATED WITH DOMESTIC VIOLENCE

Misdemeanor Stalking—MCL 750.411h (1 year misdemeanor)

Stalking means a willful course of conduct involving repeated or continuing harassment of another individual that would

- Cause a reasonable person to feel terrorized, frightened, intimidated, threatened, harassed, or molested, *and*
- That actually causes the victim to feel terrorized, frightened, intimidated, threatened, harassed, or molested.

Harassment means conduct directed toward a victim that includes, but is not limited to, repeated or continuing unconsented contact that would

- Cause a reasonable individual to suffer emotional distress *and*
- That actually causes the victim to suffer emotional distress.

Harassment does *not* include constitutionally protected activity or conduct that serves a legitimate purpose.

Unconsented contact means any contact with another individual that is initiated or continued without that individual's consent or in disregard of that individual's expressed desire that the contact be avoided or discontinued. Unconsented contact includes, but is not limited to, any of the following:

- Following or appearing within the sight of that individual.
- Approaching or confronting that individual in any place.
- Appearing at that individual's workplace or residence.
- Entering onto or remaining on property owned, leased, or occupied by that individual.
- Contacting that individual by telephone.
- Sending mail or electronic communications to that individual.
- Placing an object on, or delivering an object to, property owned, leased, or occupied by that individual.

If the victim was less than 18 years of age at any time during the individual's course of conduct and the individual is five or more years older than the victim, the stalker is guilty of a felony punishable by not more than five years.

Aggravated Stalking—MCL 750.411i (felony)

An individual who engages in stalking is guilty of **aggravated stalking** if the violation involves any of the following circumstances:

- At least one of the actions constituting the offense is in violation of a restraining order and the individual has received actual notice of that restraining order or at least one of the actions is in violation of an injunction or preliminary injunction.
- At least one of the actions constituting the offense is in violation of a condition of probation, a condition of parole, a condition of pretrial release, or a condition of release on bond pending appeal.
- The course of conduct includes the making of one or more credible threats against the victim, a member of the victim's family, or another individual living in the same household as the victim.

Credible threat is a threat to kill another individual or inflict physical injury upon another individual that is made in any manner or context that causes the individual hearing or receiving the threat to reasonably fear for his or her safety or the safety of another individual.

- The individual has been *previously convicted* of a violation of aggravated stalking or misdemeanor stalking.

If the victim was less than 18 years of age at any time during the individual's course of conduct and the individual is five or more years older than the victim, the aggravated stalker is guilty of a felony punishable by not more than 10 years in prison.

Assault and Battery—MCL 750.81 (domestic relationship victim)

Penalties:

First offense	93 day misdemeanor
1 prior conviction	1 year misdemeanor
2 or more prior convictions	2 year felony

Aggravated Assault—MCL 750.81a (domestic relationship victim)

Penalties:

First offense	1 year misdemeanor
Previous conviction of domestic violence	2 year felony

The following laws are also commonly associated with domestic violence cases. See the appropriate chapter for a more detailed discussion of these laws.

Felonious Assault (MCL 750.82)

Assault with Intent to Do Great Bodily Harm Less than Murder (MCL 750.84)

Assault with Intent to Commit Murder (MCL 750.83)

Criminal Sexual Conduct (MCL 750.520b-g)

Kidnapping (MCL 750.349)

Child Abuse (MCL 750.136b)

Parental Kidnapping (MCL 750.350a)

Enticement (MCL 750.350)

MDOP (MCL 750.377a and 750.377b)

B & E, Home Invasion (MCL 750.110a)

Entering Without Permission (MCL 750.115)

Cruelty to Animals (MCL 750.50)

Local Ordinances

MICHIGAN PERSONAL PROTECTION ORDERS (PPO)—MCL 600.2950 AND 764.15b

A PPO is an injunctive order issued by the Circuit Court or the Family Division of Circuit Court restraining or enjoining activity and individuals from certain conduct. The two types of PPOs issued by Circuit Courts are:

- Domestic Relationship PPO and,
- A Nondomestic Stalking PPO

> While at a hockey game the victim was physically assaulted by another man who also threatened to kill him. The victim sought and obtained a stalking PPO against his attacker based on this one incident. The Court of Appeals terminated the PPO because for stalking the pattern of conduct must consist of two or more separate non-continuous acts evidencing a continuity of purpose. *Pobursky v. Gee*, 249 Mich. App. 44 (2001).

A person may seek to obtain a Domestic Relations PPO for the following relationships:

- A spouse or former spouse.
- An individual with whom he or she has had a child in common.
- An individual residing or having resided in the same household.
- An individual with whom he or she has or has had a dating relationship.

A *dating relationship* means frequent, intimate associations primarily characterized by the expectation of affectional involvement. This term does not include a casual relationship or an ordinary fraternization between two individuals in a business or social context.

Enforcement of PPO

A PPO is immediately enforceable anywhere in Michigan by any law enforcement agency or officer if the officer:

- Has received a true copy of the order,
- Is shown a true copy of the order (the victim may have a copy), or
- Has verified its existence in LEIN.

If an officer arrives at the scene of a call and the individual restrained or enjoined has been served the

PPO prior to the officer's arrival, and the individual is currently violating the PPO in the presence of the officer, the officer shall verify that the PPO is still valid. If the PPO is valid and LEIN verifies that the individual has received notice of the PPO, the officer may immediately arrest the individual who has been enjoined or restrained.

> To show actual knowledge of PPO by the defendant, the prosecutor need not show actual service but may show it by defendant's statements concerning evasion of service and conversations with the victim. *People v. Threatt*, 254 Mich. App. 504 (2002).

Serving a PPO

A law enforcement officer or court clerk may serve a PPO at any time (e.g., traffic stops). The officer does need to file proof of oral service with the court issuing the order.

If an officer arrives at the scene of a call and the individual restrained or enjoined *has not been served* the PPO, the law enforcement agency or officer responding to a call alleging a violation of a PPO shall:

- Serve the individual restrained or enjoined with a true copy of the PPO or
- Advise the individual restrained or enjoined about the existence of the PPO, *the specific conduct enjoined*, the penalties for violating the PPO, and where the individual restrained or enjoined may obtain a copy of the order.
- If the individual has not received prior notice of the PPO, the individual shall be given a reasonable opportunity to comply with the PPO before the law enforcement officer makes a custodial arrest for a violation of the PPO. Failure to immediately comply is grounds for custodial arrest.
- Immediately enter or cause to be entered into LEIN that the individual restrained or enjoined has actual notice of the PPO.
- File proof of service or proof of oral notice with the clerk of court issuing the PPO.

Arrest

For an arrest, the PPO must state on its face that a violation subjects the individual to immediate arrest and criminal contempt of court and, if found guilty, imprisonment for not more than 93 days or fine not more than $500. A police officer may arrest and take a person into custody when the officer has reasonable cause to believe that a valid PPO has been violated. A juvenile may be taken into custody without a court order upon reasonable cause to believe the minor is violating or has violated a personal protection order. An arrest can be made when:

- The personal protection order has been issued by a circuit court.
- The individual named in the personal protection order is violating or has violated the order. An individual is violating or has violated the order if that individual commits one or more of the following acts *and* the order specifically restrains or enjoins the individual from:
  - Entering onto premises.
  - Assaulting, attacking, beating, molesting, or wounding a named individual.
  - Threatening to kill or physically injure a named individual.
  - Removing minor children from the individual having legal custody of the children, except as otherwise authorized by a custody or parenting time order issued by a court of competent jurisdiction.
  - Purchasing or possessing a firearm.
  - Interfering with petitioner's efforts to remove petitioner's children or personal property from premises that are solely owned or leased by the individual to be restrained or enjoined.
  - Interfering with petitioner at petitioner's place of employment or education or engaging in conduct that impairs petitioner's employment or educational relationship or environment.
  - Having access to information in records concerning a minor child of both petitioner and respondent that will inform respondent about the address or telephone number of petitioner and petitioner's minor child or about petitioner's employment address.
  - Engaging in conduct that is prohibited under the stalking statutes, MCL 750.411h and 750.411i.
  - Any other specific act or conduct that imposes upon or interferes with personal liberty or that causes a reasonable apprehension of violence.

Bond / Court Appearance

A person arrested for violation of a PPO *shall not* be released on interim bond. The person must be brought before the circuit court within 24 hours of arrest. The circuit court where the violation occurred has primary jurisdiction. If the circuit court is not available, the person arrested shall be brought before the district court.

FOREIGN PROTECTION ORDER (FPO)—MCL 600.2950h-m

An FPO is an injunction or other court order issued by a court of another state, Indian tribe, or a United States Territory; it does not include foreign countries.

The order's purpose must be to prevent a person's violent or threatening acts against, harassment of, contact with, communication with, or physical proximity to another person.

The order must be issued against a spouse or intimate partner. A spouse or intimate partner includes:

- A spouse.
- A former spouse.
- A person with whom the petitioner has had a child in common.
- A person residing or having resided in the same household as the petitioner.
- A person with whom the petitioner has or has had a dating relationship.

The order may be a temporary or final order, and the order may be issued by a civil or criminal court:

- A civil FPO must be issued in response to a pleading filed or on behalf of the person seeking protection; mutual orders are not permitted.
- A criminal FPO may be either a conditional release order or a probation order.

A support or child custody order issued under divorce or custody laws is not an FPO.

Enforcement of FPO

Mutual Orders—MCL 600.2950k

An FPO that includes language restraining both the petitioner and the respondent is:

- Enforceable against the respondent.
- Enforceable against the petitioner *only* if all of the following are present:
    - The respondent filed a cross or counter petition.
    - The court made specific findings against the respondent.
    - The court determined that the respondent was entitled to relief.

Enforce All Provisions—MCL 600.2950j

The provisions of an FPO are enforceable even if they would not be available under Michigan law. This includes child custody or support provisions that are part of an FPO.

Copy of Order Available—MCL 600.2950l

An officer may rely upon a copy of an FPO received from any source if the FPO appears to contain all of the following:

- The names of the parties.
- The date the protection order was issued, which is prior to the date when enforcement is sought.
- The terms and conditions against respondent.
- The name of the issuing court.
- The signature of or on behalf of a judicial officer.
- No obvious indication that the order is invalid, such as an expiration date that is before the date enforcement is sought.

If a copy of an FPO cannot be verified on LEIN or the NCIC national protection order file, lack of verification is not grounds for an officer to refuse to enforce the terms of the order. An officer may rely on the statement of the petitioner that the FPO remains in effect and may rely on the statement of the petitioner or respondent that the respondent has received notice of the order.

Copy of Order Not Available; Attempt to Verify—MCL 600.2950l

If a copy of an FPO is not available, the officer must attempt to verify the order through LEIN, the NCIC protection order file, administrative messaging, by contacting the court that issued the FPO, by contacting the law enforcement agency in the issuing jurisdiction, by contacting the issuing jurisdiction's protection order registry, or by any other method the officer believes to be reliable. The officer must verify the existence of the order and:

- The names of the parties.
- The date the foreign protection order was issued, which is prior to the date when enforcement is sought.
- Terms and conditions against respondent.
- The name of the issuing court.
- No obvious indication that the foreign protection order is invalid, such as an expiration date that is before the date enforcement is sought.

If an officer verifies an FPO through this procedure, the FPO is enforceable.

No Copy of the Order and No Verification—MCL 600.2950l

If the officer is not shown a copy of the order and cannot verify the order through other means, the officer shall maintain the peace and take appropriate action with regard to any violation of criminal law.

No Notice of Order—MCL 600.2950l

If there is no evidence that respondent has been served with or received notice of the FPO, the law enforcement officer shall:

- Serve the respondent with a copy of the FPO if a copy is available.
- If a copy is not available, advise the respondent of the following:
  - The existence of the FPO.
  - The name of the issuing court.
  - The specific conduct enjoined.
  - The penalties for violating the order in Michigan.
  - The penalties for violating the order in the issuing jurisdiction if the officer is aware of those penalties.

If there is no evidence that the respondent has received notice of the FPO:

- The respondent shall be given an opportunity to comply before the officer makes a custodial arrest for violation of the order.
- Failure to comply immediately with the FPO is grounds for an immediate custodial arrest.

Proof of Service or Oral Notice—MCL 600.2950l

If the officer serves or provides oral notice of an FPO, the officer shall:

- Provide the petitioner with proof of service or proof of oral notice.
- Provide the issuing court with a proof of service or proof of oral notice, if the address of the issuing court is apparent on the face of the foreign protection order or otherwise is readily available to the officer.
- If the foreign protection order is entered into LEIN or the NCIC protection order file, provide that entity or the entering agency with a proof of service or proof of oral notice.

Other Enforcement Procedures; Civil FPO—MCL 600.2950l

A violation of a civil FPO is criminal contempt of court and the other enforcement procedures related to arrest, bond, court appearances, domestic violence reports, and fingerprinting are the same as for a Michigan PPO.

Other Enforcement Procedures, Criminal FPO—MCL 600.2950m; MCL 764.15

A violation of a criminal FPO (conditional release order or probation order) is a 93 day misdemeanor and may be enforced by:

- Warrantless arrest and a criminal prosecution, or
- Warrantless arrest and extradition.

Officers must complete a domestic violence report for a violation of a criminal FPO. (See section on report requirements).

Good Faith Immunity for Enforcement of FPO—MCL 600.2950l(10)

A law enforcement officer, prosecutor, or court personnel who act in good faith while enforcing a FPO are immune from civil and criminal liability in any action arising from the enforcement of the FPO.

AUTHORITY TO ENTER SCENE OF DOMESTIC VIOLENCE

Consent

> Consent must be freely and intelligently given without any duress or coercion on the part of the police. *People v. Malone*, 180 Mich. App. 347 (1989).
>
> A person must have actual or apparent authority over a premise to give consent. With apparent authority, police may rely in good faith on the apparent capability of an individual to consent to a search. *Illinois v. Rodriguez*, 497 U.S. 177 (1990).
>
> Consent by a third person is allowed where there is equal right to possession or control over the premises. *People v. Barbat*, 49 Mich. App. 519 (1973).
>
> The burden of proof is on the police to determine who has the authority to consent to an entry. *People v. Wagner*, 104 Mich. App. 169 (1981).

Emergency Circumstances

> Police may enter a dwelling without a warrant when they reasonably believe that a person within is in need of immediate aid. The police

must possess specific and articulable facts that lead to this conclusion and limit their entry to the justification. Police must do only that which is reasonably necessary to determine if a person is in need of assistance and render that assistance. *People v. Davis*, 442 Mich. 1 (1993).

A police officer may enter a dwelling without a warrant where it is reasonably believed that a person inside is in need of medical assistance. The entry must be limited to the reason for its justification. The officer must be motivated primarily by a perceived need to render assistance and may do no more than is reasonably necessary to determine whether assistance is required and render it. Once lawfully inside the residence, the officer may make an arrest without a warrant that is authorized by law and absent a reason for exclusion, evidence obtained is admissible. *People v. Ohlinger*, 438 Mich. 477 (1991).

VICTIM'S RIGHTS—MCL 764.15c

After intervening in a domestic violence dispute, the peace officer shall provide the following written information to the victim:

- The name and telephone number of the responding police agency.
- Name and badge number of responding officer.
- The following statement:

    "You may obtain a copy of the police incident report for your case by contacting this law enforcement agency at the telephone number provided.

    The domestic violence shelter program and other resources in your area are (include local information).

    Information about emergency shelter, counseling services, and the legal rights of domestic violence victims is available from these resources.

    Your legal rights include the right to go to court and file a petition requesting a personal protection order to protect you or other members of your household from domestic abuse, which could include restraining or enjoining the abuser from doing the following:

    (a) Entering onto premises.
    (b) Assaulting, attacking, beating, molesting, or wounding you.
    (c) Threatening to kill or physically injure you or another person.
    (d) Removing minor children from you, except as otherwise authorized by a custody or parenting time order issued by a court of competent jurisdiction.
    (e) Engaging in stalking behavior.
    (f) Purchasing or possessing a firearm.
    (g) Interfering with your efforts to remove your children or personal property from premises that are solely owned or leased by the abuser.
    (h) Interfering with you at your place of employment or education or engaging in conduct that impairs your employment relationship or your employment or educational environment.
    (i) Engaging in any other specific act or conduct that imposes upon or interferes with your personal liberty or that causes a reasonable apprehension of violence.
    (j) Having access to information in records concerning any minor child you have with the abuser that would inform the abuser about your address or telephone number, the child's address or telephone number, or your employment address.

    Your legal rights also include the right to go to court and file a motion for an order to show cause and a hearing if the abuser is violating or has violated a personal protection order and has not been arrested."

PREPARING A DOMESTIC VIOLENCE REPORT

Report Requirements—MCL 764.15c

- Officers shall prepare a domestic violence report after investigating or intervening at a domestic violence scene. Officers shall use the standard domestic violence incident form or a form substantially similar to that standard form to report a domestic violence incident.
- The report must be filed with prosecuting attorney within 48 hours after incident is reported to police.
- The report shall contain the following:
    - Address, date, time of incident.
    - VICTIM'S name, address, home and work telephone numbers, race, sex, and date of birth.
    - SUSPECT'S name, address, home and work telephone numbers, race, sex, date of birth, and whether a PPO covering the suspect exists.
    - WITNESS'S name, address, home and work telephone numbers, race, sex, date of birth, and relationship to victim and/or suspect.

- The name of the person WHO CALLED THE POLICE.
- The RELATIONSHIP of the victim and suspect.
- Whether ALCOHOL or CONTROLLED SUBSTANCE use was involved and by whom.
- A NARRATIVE describing the incident and the circumstances that led to it.
- Whether and how many times the suspect PHYSICALLY ASSAULTED the victim.
- A description of any WEAPON or object used.
- A description of all INJURIES sustained by the victim and how they were sustained.
- Information concerning MEDICAL ATTENTION, if sought by the victim, including where and how transported, admission to a hospital or clinic and name and address of the attending physician.
- A description of any PROPERTY DAMAGE reported or evident at the scene.
- PREVIOUS DOMESTIC VIOLENCE between the victim and the suspect.
- Date and time of report, name, badge number, and signature of officer completing the report.

Liability
42 U.S.C. 1983

For government officials to be liable under 1983 action, they must violate clearly established statutory or constitutional rights of which a reasonable person would have known. *Buckley v. Fitzsimmons*, 509 U.S. 259 (1993).

State Tort Actions

Before an individual can bring suit against a police officer for negligence, a special relationship must exist between the injured party and the officer. To demonstrate a special relationship, the plaintiff must show:

- The police officer *made assurances* of protection or assumed, by his or her actions, the protection of the individual.
- The police officer knew that without his or her action, harm could come to the victim.
- The police officer was in *direct contact* with the victim.
- The *victim relied* on the officer's assurances of protection.

White v. Beasley, 453 Mich. 308 (1996).

6

SEX OFFENSES

CRIMINAL SEXUAL CONDUCT
Definitions—MCL 750.520a

Sexual penetration: Sexual intercourse, cunnilingus, fellatio, anal intercourse or any other intrusion, however slight, of any part of a person's body or of any object into the genital or anal opening of another person's body, but emission of semen is not required.

Penetration occurred where defendant forced his finger into the vagina of his 9-year-old daughter through her underwear. *People v. Hammons*, 210 Mich. App. 554 (1995).

Each separate act of sexual penetration constitutes a separate act of CSC. *People v. Dowdy*, 148 Mich. App. 517 (1986).

Sexual contact: Includes the intentional touching of the victim's or actor's intimate parts or the intentional touching of the clothing covering the immediate area of the victim's or actor's intimate parts, if that intentional touching can reasonably be construed as being for the purpose of sexual arousal or gratification, done for a sexual purpose, or in a sexual manner for (i) revenge, (ii) to inflict humiliation, or (iii) out of anger.

Intimate part: The primary genital area, groin, inner thigh, buttock, or breast of a human being.

Personal injury: Bodily injury, disfigurement, mental anguish, chronic pain, pregnancy, disease, or loss or impairment of a sexual or reproductive organ.

Pregnancy and subsequent abortion. *People v. Woods*, 204 Mich. App. 472 (1994).

A neck injury where doctor testified that the neck was still tender several hours after the attack. *People v. Perry*, 172 Mich. App. 609 (1988).

Mental anguish: Extreme or excruciating pain, distress, or suffering of the mind that occurs either at the time of the incident or later as a result of the incident.

Mental anguish under the CSC statute may include threats of future harm and being forced to beg. *People v. Mackle*, 241 Mich. App. 583 (2000).

Mentally incapable: Person suffers from a mental disease or defect that renders that person temporarily or permanently incapable of appraising the nature of his or her conduct.

Mentally incapacitated: A person is temporarily incapable of appraising or controlling his or her conduct due to the influence of a narcotic anesthetic, or other substance administered to that person without his or her consent, or due to any other act committed upon that person without his or her consent.

CHAPTER 6 Sex Offenses

Mentally disabled: Person who has mental illness, is mentally retarded, or has a developmental disability.

Physically helpless: Person was unconscious, asleep, or for any other reason was physically unable to communicate an unwillingness to act.

Force or coercion: The defendant either used physical force or did something to make the victim reasonably afraid of present or future danger, including but not limited to any of the following circumstances:

- When the actor overcomes the victim through the actual application of physical force or physical violence.
- When the actor coerces the victim to submit by threatening to use force or violence on the victim, and the victim believes that the actor has the present ability to execute these threats.
- When the actor coerces the victim to submit by threatening to retaliate in the future against the victim, or any other person, and the victim believes that the actor has the ability to execute this threat. As used in this subdivision, "to retaliate" includes threats of physical punishment, kidnapping, or extortion.
- When the actor engages in the medical treatment or examination of the victim in a manner or for purposes that are medically recognized as unethical or unacceptable.
- When the actor, through concealment or by the element of surprise, is able to overcome the victim.

Coercion occurred where defendant took his 13-year-old babysitter to a remote and isolated location at night. *People v. McGill*, 131 Mich. App. 465 (1984).

Pinching victim's buttocks satisfied the force element. *People v. Premo*, 213 Mich. App. 406 (1995).

Force or coercion under the CSC statute may occur where the suspect is disguised. *People v. Crippen*, 242 Mich. App. 278 (2000).

The prohibited "force" for CSC encompasses the use of force against a victim to either induce the victim to submit to sexual penetration or to seize control of the victim in a manner to facilitate the accomplishment of sexual penetration without regard to the victim's wishes. *People v. Carlson*, 466 Mich. 130 (2002).

Degrees of affinity:

First degree	Parents and Children
Second degree	Grandparents, Brothers, Sisters, Grandchildren
Third degree	Great-Grandparents, Uncles, Aunts, Nephews, Nieces, Great-Grandchildren
Fourth degree	Great-great-grandparents, Great-Uncles, Great-Aunts, First Cousins, Grand-Nephews, Grand Nieces, Great-Great-Grandchildren

First Degree—MCL 750.520b (felony)
Elements

1. Sexual penetration and one of the following:

   - Victim's age is under 13
   - Victim's age is 13, 14 or 15, and one of following:
     - Same household. Same household refers to residing under one roof for any time other than a brief or chance encounter.

   The suspect and victim were members of the same household where the victim lived with the suspect for four months and the suspect was attempting to adopt the victim. *People v. Phillips*, 251 Mich. App. 100 (2002).

   - Related by blood or affinity to fourth degree.
   - Coerced victim through position of authority.
   - The actor is a teacher, substitute teacher, or administrator of the public or nonpublic school or school district in which the victim is enrolled.
   - The actor is an employee, contractual service provider, or non-student volunteer of the public or nonpublic school or school district and the actor uses his or her status to gain access to, or to establish a relationship with, that other person.
   - The actor is an employee of the state of Michigan or of a local unit of government of the state of Michigan or of the United States assigned to provide any service to that public or nonpublic school or school district and the actor uses his or her status to gain access to, or to establish a relationship with, that other person.

2. Weapon used or article fashioned in a manner to lead victim to believe it is a weapon.

3. During the commission of a felony.

> Subject could be charged with CSC first degree where he videotaped himself having sexual penetration with a 16 year-old female. The underlying felony was child sexually abusive material. *People v. Wilkins*, 267 Mich. App. 728 (2005).

4. Aided by one or more and one of the following:
   - Actor knows or has reason to know the victim is mentally incapacitated, mentally incapable, or physically helpless.
   - Force or coercion is used.
   - Force and coercion is used and victim suffers personal injury.
   - Victim suffers personal injury and actor knows or has reason to know victim is mentally incapacitated, mentally incapable, or physically helpless.
   - Victim is mentally incapacitated, mentally incapable, mentally disabled, or physically helpless and one of the following:
     - Related by blood and affinity to the fourth degree.
     - Actor is in a position of authority over the victim and used that authority to coerce the victim.

Second Degree—MCL 750.520c (felony)
Elements

1. Sexual contact and one of the following:
   - Victim's age is under 13.
   - Victim's age is 13, 14 or 15, and one of following:
     - Same household.
     - Related by blood or affinity to fourth degree.
     - Coerced victim through position of authority.

> A spiritual therapist was in a position of authority over a 14-year-old victim. *People v. Knapp*, 244 Mich. App. 361 (2001).

   - The actor is a teacher, substitute teacher, or administrator of the public or nonpublic school in which the victim is enrolled.
   - The actor is an employee, contractual service provider, or non-student volunteer of the public or nonpublic school or school district and the actor uses his or her status to gain access to, or to establish a relationship with, that other person.
   - The actor is an employee of the state of Michigan or of a local unit of government of the state of Michigan or of the United States assigned to provide any service to that public or nonpublic school or school district and the actor uses his or her status to gain access to, or to establish a relationship with, that other person.
2. Weapon used or article fashioned in a manner to lead victim to believe it is a weapon.
3. During the commission of a felony.
4. Aided by one or more and one of the following:
   - Actor knows or has reason to know victim is mentally incapacitated, mentally incapable, or physically helpless.
   - Force or coercion is used.
5. Force and coercion are used and victim suffers personal injury.
6. Victim suffers personal injury and actor knows or has reason to know victim is mentally incapacitated, mentally incapable, or physically helpless.
7. Victim is mentally incapacitated, mentally incapable, or physically helpless and one of the following:
   - Related by blood and affinity to the fourth degree.
   - Actor is in a position of authority over the victim and used that authority to coerce the victim.
8. Victim is under jurisdiction of the department of corrections and actor is employee or volunteers for the department and knows the victim's status.
9. Victim is in jail or on probation and the actor is employee or volunteers for the county and knows the victim's status.
10. Victim is being held pending a court hearing and actor is employee or volunteer of the facility holding the victim.

Third Degree—MCL 750.520d (felony)
Elements

1. Sexual penetration and one of the following:
   - Victim's age is 13, 14, or 15 years old (statutory rape).
   - Force or coercion is used.
   - Actor knows or reason to know victim is mentally incapacitated, mentally incapable, or physically helpless.
   - The two are related by blood or affinity to the third degree (incest).

It is an affirmative defense to a prosecution under this subdivision that the other person was in a position of authority over the defendant and used this authority to coerce the defendant, or the two are lawfully married to each other at the time of the incident.

> Term affinity includes relationship between stepbrother and stepsister. *People v. Armstrong*, 212 Mich. App. 121 (1995).
>
> Term affinity includes relationship between stepfather and stepdaughter. *People v. Goold*, 241 Mich. App. 333 (2000).

2. The victim is at least 16 years of age but less than 18 years of age (or less than 26 years of age if a special education student) and a student at a public or nonpublic school, and the actor is a teacher, substitute teacher, or administrator of that public or nonpublic school. This does not apply if the other person is emancipated or if both persons are lawfully married to each other at the time of the alleged violation.
3. The actor is an employee, contractual service provider, or non-student volunteer of the public or nonpublic school or school district and the actor uses his or her status to gain access to, or to establish a relationship with, that other person.
4. The actor is an employee of the state of Michigan or of a local unit of government of the state of Michigan or of the United States assigned to provide any service to that public or nonpublic school or school district and the actor uses his or her status to gain access to, or to establish a relationship with, that other person.

Fourth Degree—MCL 750.520e (2 year misdemeanor)

Elements

1. Sexual contact and one of the following:
    - Victim's age is 13, 14, or 15 and the actor is five or more years older.
    - Force or coercion is used.
    - Actor knows or has reason to know victim is mentally incapacitated, mentally incapable, or physically helpless.
    - Related by blood or affinity to the third degree (incest).

It is an affirmative defense to a prosecution under this subdivision that the other person was in a position of authority over the defendant and used this authority to coerce the defendant, or the two are lawfully married to each other at the time of the incident.

2. The actor is a mental health professional and the sexual contact occurs during or within two years after the period in which the victim is his or her client or patient and not his or her spouse. The consent of the victim is not a defense to a prosecution under this subdivision.
3. The victim is at least 16 years of age but less than 18 years of age (or less than 26 years of age if a special education student) and a student at a public or nonpublic school, and the actor is a teacher, substitute teacher, or administrator of that public or nonpublic school. This subdivision does not apply if the other person is emancipated or if both persons are lawfully married to each other at the time of the alleged violation.
4. The actor is an employee, contractual service provider, or non-student volunteer of the public or nonpublic school or school district and the actor uses his or her status to gain access to, or to establish a relationship with, that other person.
5. The actor is an employee of the state of Michigan or of a local unit of government of the state of Michigan or of the United States assigned to provide any service to that public or nonpublic school or school district and the actor uses his or her status to gain access to, or to establish a relationship with, that other person.

Resistance—MCL 750.520i

A victim need not resist the actor for prosecution of CSC.

Married Persons—MCL 750.520l

A person can be convicted of CSC even though the victim is his or her legal spouse.

CRIMES OF INDECENCY

Sodomy—MCL 750.158 (felony)

Any person who shall commit the abominable and detestable crime against nature either with mankind or with any animal shall be guilty of a felony, punishable by imprisonment in the state prison not more than 15 years, or if such person was at the time of the said offense a sexually delinquent person, may be punishable by imprisonment in the state prison for an indeterminate term, the minimum of which shall be 1 day and the maximum of which shall be life.

Bestiality, which is sexual conduct between man or woman and an animal, falls under this section. *People v. Carrier*, 74 Mich. App. 161 (1977).

Lewd and Lascivious Behavior—MCL 750.335 (1 year misdemeanor)

Any man or woman, not being married to each other, who lewdly and lasciviously associates and cohabits together, and any man or woman, married or unmarried, who is guilty of open and gross lewdness and lascivious behavior, is guilty of a misdemeanor punishable by imprisonment for not more than 1 year, or a fine of not more than $1,000.00. No prosecution shall be commenced under this section after 1 year from the time of committing the offense.

Includes the following:

- Any man or woman, not married, who shall lewdly and lasciviously associate and cohabit together, or
- Any man or woman who commits open and gross lewdness and lascivious behavior.

During a lap dance at a nightclub, a dancer allowed patrons to kiss and suck her breast. This was held to be lewd and lascivious behavior. *People v. Mell*, 459 Mich. 881 (1998).

Indecent Exposure—MCL 750.335a

(1) A person shall not knowingly make any open or indecent exposure of his or her person or of the person of another.

Elements

1. The defendant exposed a prohibited body part,
2. The defendant knew that the body part was being exposed,
3. The defendant "did this in a place under circumstances in which another person might reasonably have been expected to observe it and which created a substantial risk that someone might be offended or in a place where such exposure is likely to be an offense against your community's generally accepted standards of decency and morality[,]"
4. And, for the 2 year misdemeanor, the defendant was fondling his or her genital, pubic area, or buttocks, or her breasts.

CJ12d 20.33.

There is no requirement that defendant's exposure actually be witnessed by another person to constitute "open or indecent exposure," under this statute, as long as the exposure occurred in a public place under circumstances in which another person might reasonably have been expected to observe it. In this case, the defendant was masturbating in a parked car on a public street. *People v. Vronko*, 228 Mich. App. 649 (1998).

Indecent exposure occurred where defendant exposed his erect penis to a minor female while they were standing in his bedroom. The statute's focus is not the location of the exposure, but rather on defendant's conduct, his intent in making the exposure, and the reasonable reaction to the exposure by the viewer. Therefore, the statute does not require that the indecent exposure was made in a public place. *People v. Neal*, 266 Mich. App. 654 (2005).

Indecent exposure has been defined as "the exhibition of those private parts of the person which instinctive modesty, human decency or natural self-respect requires shall be customarily kept covered in the presence of others." *People v. Kratz*, 230 Mich. 334 (1925).

A "Sexually Delinquent Person" is defined by statute as: "any person whose sexual behavior is characterized by repetitive or compulsive acts which indicate a disregard of consequences or the recognized rights of others, or by the use of force upon another person in attempting sex relations of either a heterosexual or homosexual nature, or by the commission of sexual aggressions against children under the age of 16." MCL 750.10a.

Penalties

- A one-year misdemeanor unless another factor applies.
- Any person who was fondling his or her genitals, pubic area, or buttocks, or any female who was fondling her breasts, in violation of this statute is guilty of a 2 year misdemeanor.
- A person who violates this statute while being a sexually delinquent person faces a minimum sentence of one day to a maximum sentence of life.

Obscene Language—MCL 750.337 (90-day misdemeanor)

Any person who shall use any indecent, immoral, obscene, vulgar or insulting language in the presence or hearing of any woman or child shall be guilty of a misdemeanor.

> Law against using of profanity in front of women and children has been held to be unconstitutional. *People v. Boomer*, 250 Mich. App. 534 (2002).

Gross Indecency—MCL 750.338, 750.338a, and 750.33b (felony)

Any male person who, in public or in private, commits or is a party to the commission of or procures or attempts to procure the commission by any male person of any act of gross indecency with another male person shall be guilty of a felony, punishable by imprisonment in the state prison for not more than 5 years, or by a fine of not more than $2,500.00, or if such person was at the time of the said offense a sexually delinquent person, may be punishable by imprisonment in the state prison for an indeterminate term, the minimum of which shall be 1 day and the maximum of which shall be life.

There are three types of gross indecencies:

- Between males (MCL 750.338)
- Between females (MCL 750.338a)
- Between males and females (MCL 750.338b)

The suspect did one of the following:

- Committed an act of gross indecency with another.
- Procured or attempted to procure another for an act of gross indecency.

Most acts must occur in public, although this section can be applied to acts in private under certain circumstances.

> A public act of fellatio between males. *People v. Lino*, 447 Mich. 567 (1994).
>
> Attempting to procure oral, anal, or other sexual act with a person under the age of consent falls under gross indecency even if the act occurs in private. *People v. Lino*, 447 Mich. 567 (1994). (Note: this ruling is in reference to a co-appellant, Bashier, in a consolidated appeal.)

> Sexual intercourse between a male and female in a visitation room at a prison. *People v. Jones*, 222 Mich. App. 595 (1997).
>
> Oral sex in a closed room in a massage parlor could fall under the gross indecency statute, if there was a possibility the unsuspecting public could be exposed to or view the act. *People v. Brown*, 222 Mich. App. 586 (1997).
>
> Gross indecency includes an ultimate sex act, including masturbation, committed in a public place. In this case the act occurred between two males in a public restroom. *People v. Bono*, 249 Mich. App. 115 (2001).
>
> Gross indecency need not include an overtly sexual act. In one case, a defendant could be charged where he paid teenage females to beat him, spit on him, and provide him with urine and feces because he could reasonably be found to have received sexual gratification from these acts. *People v. Drake*, 246 Mich. App. 637 (2001).

PROSTITUTION

Soliciting for Prostitution—MCL 750.448 (93-day misdemeanor)

A person 16 years of age or older who accosts, solicits, or invites another person in a public place or in or from a building or vehicle, by word, gesture, or any other means, to commit prostitution or to do any other lewd or immoral act, is guilty of a crime punishable as provided in section 451.

Elements

Applies to the following:

1. Any person 16 year of age or older, who accosts, solicits, or invites another,
2. By word, gesture or other means, to commit prostitution or other lewd or immoral act,
3. While in public or from a building or vehicle.

Penalties:

First offense	93 day misdemeanor
Second offense	1 year misdemeanor
Third offense	2 year felony

Permitting a Place of Prostitution—MCL 750.449 (93-day misdemeanor)

A person 16 years of age or older who receives or admits or offers to receive or admit a person into a place, structure, house, building, or vehicle for the purpose of prostitution, lewdness, or assignation, or who knowingly permits a person to remain in a place, structure, house, building, or vehicle for the purpose of prostitution, lewdness, or assignation, is guilty of a crime punishable as provided in section 451.

Penalties:

First offense	93 day misdemeanor
Second offense	1 year misdemeanor
Third offense	2 year felony

Solicitor for Prostitution—MCL 750.449a (93-day misdemeanor)

Any male person who engages or offers to engage the services of a female person, not his wife, for the purpose of prostitution, lewdness, or assignation, by the payment in money or other forms of consideration, is guilty of a misdemeanor. Any person convicted of violating this section shall be subject to the provisions of Act No. 6 of the Public Acts of the Second Extra Session of 1942, being sections 329.201 to 329.208 of the Compiled Laws of 1948.

Note that this statute entails only a MALE person who solicits a FEMALE person.

Aiding and Abetting Prostitution—MCL 750.450 (93-day misdemeanor)

Any person 16 years of age or older who aids, assists, or abets another person to commit or offer to commit an act prohibited under section 448 or 449 is guilty of a crime punishable as provided in section 451.

Penalties:

First offense	93 day misdemeanor
Second offense	1 year misdemeanor
Third offense	2 year felony

Allowing Minor to Remain in House of Prostitution—MCL 750.462 (93-day misdemeanor)

A person who, for a purpose other than prostitution, takes or conveys to, or employs, receives, detains, or allows a person 16 years of age or less to remain in, a house of prostitution, house of ill-fame, bawdy-house, house of assignation, or any house or place for the resort of prostitutes or other disorderly persons is guilty of a crime punishable as provided in section 451.

Penalties:

First offense	93 day misdemeanor
Second offense	1 year misdemeanor
Third offense	2 year felony

Penalties for Prostitution—MCL 750.451

(1) Except as otherwise provided in this section, a person convicted of violating section 448, 449, 449a, 450, or 462 is guilty of a misdemeanor punishable by imprisonment for not more than 93 days or a fine of not more than $500.00, or both.

(2) A person 16 years of age or older who is convicted of violating section 448, 449, 449a, 450, or 462 and who has 1 prior conviction is guilty of a misdemeanor punishable by imprisonment for not more than 1 year or a fine of not more than $1,000.00, or both.

(3) A person convicted of violating section 448, 449, 449a, 450, or 462 and who has 2 or more prior convictions is guilty of a felony punishable by imprisonment for not more than 2 years, or a fine of not more than $2,000.00, or both.

Previous convictions can be proven by:

- A copy of the judgment of conviction,
- A transcript of the previous trial, plea, or sentencing,
- Information from the pre-sentencing report,
- The defendant's own statement.

Pandering—MCL 750.455 (felony)

Any person who shall procure a female inmate for a house of prostitution; or who shall induce, persuade, encourage, inveigle or entice a female person to become a prostitute; or who by promises, threats, violence or by any device or scheme, shall cause, induce, persuade, encourage, take, place, harbor, inveigle or entice a female person to become an inmate of a house of prostitution or assignation place, or any place where prostitution is practiced, encouraged or allowed; or any person who shall, by promises, threats, violence or by any device or scheme, cause, induce, persuade, encourage, inveigle or entice an inmate of a house of prostitution or place of assignation to remain therein as such inmate; or any person who by promises, threats, violence, by any device or scheme, by fraud or artifice, or by duress of person or goods, or by abuse of any position of confidence or authority, or having legal charge, shall take, place, harbor, inveigle, entice, persuade, encourage or procure any female person to enter any place within this state in which prostitution is practiced, encouraged or allowed, for the purpose of prostitution; or who shall inveigle, entice, persuade, encourage, or procure any female person to come into this state or to leave this state for the purpose of prostitution; or who upon the pretense of marriage takes or detains a female person for the purpose of sexual intercourse; or who shall receive or give or agree to receive or give any money or thing of value for procuring or attempting to procure any female person to become a prostitute or to come into this state or leave this state for the purpose of prostitution, shall be guilty of a felony, punishable by imprisonment in the state prison for not more than 20 years.

Elements

1. The defendant knowingly and intentionally,
2. Forced, persuaded, encouraged, or tricked another person to become a prostitute.

OR

1. The defendant knowingly and intentionally,
2. Took, agreed to take, gave, or agreed to give money or something of value for making or attempting to make another person become a prostitute.

CJ12d 20.34.

"A prostitute is a person who does sexual acts for money." CJ12d 20.34.

> This statute applies to a defendant who encourages someone to become a prostitute, but it does not apply to a defendant who encourages a current prostitute to engage in further acts of prostitution. Pandering requires that the defendant must have enticed or induced a woman "to become a prostitute." *People v. Morey*, 461 Mich. 325 (1999).

Pandering applies to any person who commits one of the following:

- Who shall induce, persuade, encourage, or entice a female person to become a prostitute.
- Procures a female inmate for a house of prostitution.
- Promises, threats, or uses violence or a scheme to cause, induce, encourage, take, place, harbor, or entice a female to become a prostitute.
- Uses promise, threat, violence, or scheme to keep a female in a place of prostitution.
- For any reason shall induce, persuade, encourage, inveigle, or entice a female to come into this state or leave this state for the purposes of prostitution.
- Takes or detains a female person for the purpose of sexual intercourse, upon the pretense of marriage.
- Who shall give money or anything of value for procuring or attempting to procure to become a prostitute or leave this state for the purpose of prostitution.

Accepting the Earnings of a Prostitute— MCL 750.457 (felony)

Any person who shall knowingly accept, receive, levy or appropriate any money or valuable thing without consideration from the proceeds of the earnings of any woman engaged in prostitution, or any person, knowing a female to be a prostitute, shall live or derive support or maintenance, in whole or in part, from the earnings or proceeds of the prostitution of said prostitute, or from moneys loaned or advanced to or charged against her by any keeper or manager or inmate of a house or other place where prostitution is practiced or allowed, shall be guilty of a felony, punishable by imprisonment in the state prison not more than 20 years. And such acceptance, receipt, levy or appropriation of such money or valuable thing, shall, upon any proceeding or trial for violation of this section, be presumptive evidence of lack of consideration.

Elements

1. The defendant received or took money or something of value from a prostitute,
2. The defendant knew that the woman was a prostitute,
3. The defendant knew that the money had been earned by prostitution, and
4. The defendant did not give the prostitute anything of value in exchange or made a profit from the exchange.

CJ12d 20.35

A person shall not knowingly accept the earnings of a prostitute.

> During an undercover investigation involving a massage parlor that the defendant owned, two women were sent to meet an officer. The defendant knew that the second was being sent for the purposes of sex. When they returned, she accepted the money they had received and was arrested and charged with accepting the earnings

of a prostitute and pandering. The pandering charges were dismissed because there was no evidence presented that the defendant enticed either woman to become a prostitute. The charge of accepting the earnings of a prostitute was upheld. *People v. Morey*, 461 Mich. 325 (1999).

"Prostitution" does not require actual sexual intercourse: the court found that the defendant had accepted earnings from prostitutes where the prostitutes manually stimulated a customer's genitals at a massage parlor. *People v. Warren*, 449 Mich. 341 (1995).

REGISTRATION OF SEX OFFENDERS—MCL 28.721 TO 28.732

Address Verification

Sex offenders must verify their address.

- Misdemeanor offenders—January 1–15 annually.
- Felons—First 15 days of January, April, July, October.

A valid ops or ID card may be used. Officers may request to see additional ID. DD-4 shall be completed and signed. Failure to sign is a misdemeanor. At the end of each verification period, LEIN shall make a list of those individuals who have not verified their addresses. An appearance ticket may be issued. If it is determined that the subject has moved, felony charges may be sought.

Institutes of Higher Learning

Registered sex offenders who attend and/or work at an institute of higher learning in Michigan must report the following information. Offenders must report this information if they are enrolled and/or work or volunteer at institutes of higher learning for 14 or more consecutive days, or 30 or more days in a calendar year.

- The name of the campus.
- The city where the campus is located.
- Proof of student and/or employment status such as but not limited to a W-2 form, pay stub, or written statement by an employer, a contract, a student identification card or a student transcript.
- Any changes of status within 10 days such as new employment, termination, dropping out of school, or new enrollment or any combination of the above.

- Students and temporary workers are required to register if they are present:
    - 14 or more consecutive days, or
    - 30 or more days in a calendar year.

Penalties:

Failure to sign DD-4 and DD-4A	93 day misdemeanor
Failure to verify address	93 day misdemeanor
Failure to verify address, 2nd offense	1 year misdemeanor
Failure to verify address, 3rd offense	felony
Failure to report change of address, or vacating residence, or failure to register, or use false information	felony

Where Can Prosecution Be Sought?

- Individual's last registered address.
- The individual's actual address.
- Where arrest was made.

Moving, Changing Schools or Place of Work, Parole

Within 10 days of moving, changing jobs or schools, or being paroled, the offender must report his or her new address to their local police.

Penalties:

First offense	4 year felony
Second offense	7 year felony
Third offense	10 year felony

Moving Out of State

Within 10 days of moving out of state, the offender must report his or her new address to his or her local state police post. A DD-4 must be completed and copy faxed to Investigative Resource Unit.

School Safety Zones—MCL 28.733 to 28.736

A registered sex offender may not work, loiter, or reside within 1,000 feet of school property.

Penalties:

First offense	1 year misdemeanor
Second offense	felony

HOMICIDE & KIDNAPPING

HOMICIDE

First Degree—MCL 750.316 (felony)
Elements

1. Defendant caused the death of the victim.
2. Defendant intended to kill the victim.
3. The intent to kill was premeditated, that is, thought out beforehand.
4. The killing was deliberate and premeditated. That is, the killing was not the result of sudden impulse; rather, the defendant had a chance to think twice about the intent to kill.
5. The killing was not justified, excused, or done under circumstances that reduce it to a lesser crime.

CJI2d 16.1.

> Time for a second look occurred where the victim was dragged to a secluded area and strangled. *People v. Johnson*, 460 Mich. 720 (1999).

Intervening Causes

> Defendant could be convicted of homicide even though the victim could have continued living on life support. *People v. Bowles*, 461 Mich. 555 (2000).

Felony Murder

Suspect committed murder while perpetrating or attempting to perpetrate one of the following:

- Arson
- CSC first, second, or third degrees
- Child abuse first degree
- Major controlled substance offense
- Robbery
- Breaking and entering of a dwelling
- Home invasion first or second degrees
- Larceny of any kind
- Extortion
- Kidnapping
- Aggravated stalking
- Torture
- Carjacking
- Vulnerable adult abuse (first and second degree).

> Assault with the intent to rob while unarmed falls under the offense of robbery under the felony murder statute. *People v. Ross*, 242 Mich. App. 241 (2000).

> Felony murder includes home invasion in the first degree. *People v. McCrady*, 244 Mich. App. 27 (2000).

> Felony murder occurred where underlying felony was child abuse in the first degree. *People v. Magyar*, 250 Mich. App. 408 (2002).

- Murder of a police officer or corrections employee
  - Officer must be performing lawful duties.
  - Suspect must know the victim was an officer.

> First degree murder for killing a police officer is upheld as constitutional. *People v. Clark*, 243 Mich. App. 424 (2000).
>
> This law applies to killing the manager of a prison store. *People v. Herndon*, 246 Mich. App. 371 (2001).

Second Degree Murder—MCL 750.317 (felony)
Elements

1. Defendant caused the death of the victim.
2. The defendant intended to kill, or intended to do great bodily harm to victim, or defendant knowingly created a very high risk of death or great bodily harm knowing that death or such harm would likely be the result of their actions.
3. The killing was not justified, excused, or done under circumstances that reduce it to a lesser crime.

CJI2d 16.5

> Defendant, with a BAC of 0.10, shot a man who was attacking his brother. *People v. Plummer*, 229 Mich. App. 293 (1998).
>
> A fatal accident where the driver was intoxicated, knew he was intoxicated, and was told by witnesses he should not be driving after backing into the same vehicle twice. *People v. Goecke*, 457 Mich. 442 (1998).

Delivery of a Controlled Substance Resulting in Death—MCL 750.317a

A person who delivers a schedule 1 or 2 controlled substance, other than marihuana, to another person in violation of section 7401 of the public health code, 1978 PA 368, MCL 333.7401, that is consumed by that person or any other person and that causes the death of that person or other person is guilty of a felony punishable by imprisonment for life or any term of years.

Manslaughter—MCL 750.321 (felony)

Any person who shall commit the crime of manslaughter shall be guilty of a felony punishable by imprisonment in the state prison, not more than 15 years or by fine of not more than 7,500 dollars, or both, at the discretion of the court.

Voluntary

For the crime of murder to be reduced to voluntary manslaughter, the following two things must be present:

- When the defendant acted, his or her thinking was disturbed by emotional excitement to the point that a reasonable person might have acted on impulse, without thinking twice, from passion instead of judgment. The emotional excitement must have been something that would cause a reasonable person to act rashly or on impulse.
- The killing itself must result from this emotional excitement. The defendant must have acted before a reasonable time had passed to calm down and return to reason.

CJI2d 16.9

> "Cooling-off" period of 24 hours was not reasonable where defendant had been threatened the day before, left, and returned 24 hours later with a gun. *People v. Wofford*, 196 Mich. App. 275 (1992).

Involuntary

The suspect did one of the following that resulted in death of another person:

- Acted in a grossly negligent manner.
- At the time of the act, the defendant had the intent to hurt or injure the deceased (e.g., assault and battery).

> Failing to stop for four red traffic lights causing a collision that resulted in the death of another. *People v. Moselar*, 202 Mich. App. 296 (1993).

Gross Negligence

Gross negligence means more than carelessness. It means willfully disregarding the results to others that might follow from an act or failure to act. In order to find that the defendant was grossly negligent, each of the following three things must exist beyond a reasonable doubt:

- First, that the defendant knew of the danger to another, that is, [he/she] knew that there was a situation that required [him/her] to take ordinary care to avoid injuring another.

- Second, that the defendant could have avoided injuring another by using ordinary care.
- Third, that the defendant failed to use ordinary care to prevent injuring another when, to a reasonable person, it must have been apparent that the result was likely to be serious injury.

CJI2d 16.18

Negligent Homicide—MCL 750.324 (2 year misdemeanor)

(NOTE: THIS SECTION IS REPEALED BY PUBLIC ACT 463 OF 2008 EFFECTIVE OCTOBER 31, 2010).

Any person who, by the operation of any vehicle upon any highway or upon any other property, public or private, at an immoderate rate of speed or in a careless, reckless or negligent manner, but not willfully or wantonly, shall cause the death of another, shall be guilty of a misdemeanor, punishable by imprisonment in the state prison not more than 2 years or by a fine of not more than $2,000.00, or by both such fine and imprisonment.

The suspect was operating a motor vehicle in a negligent manner, which caused an accident that resulted in the death of the victim.

> Falling asleep while driving. *People v. Robinson*, 253 Mich. 507 (1931).

Degrees of negligence (CJI2d 16.17 and 16.18)

Slight negligence	Doing something that is not usually dangerous, something that only an extremely careful person would have thought could cause injury.
Ordinary negligence	Not taking reasonable care under the circumstances. A sensible person would have known that the actions could have caused injury.
Gross negligence	The injury could have been avoided by using ordinary care. Willfully disregarding the dangerousness of the actions.

KIDNAPPING—MCL 750.349 (felony)

(1) A person commits the crime of kidnapping if he or she knowingly restrains another person with the intent to do 1 or more of the following:

  (a) Hold that person for ransom or reward.
  (b) Use that person as a shield or hostage.
  (c) Engage in criminal sexual penetration or criminal sexual contact with that person.
  (d) Take that person outside of this state.
  (e) Hold that person in involuntary servitude.

(2) As used in this section, "restrain" means to restrict a person's movements or to confine the person so as to interfere with that person's liberty without that person's consent or without legal authority. The restraint does not have to exist for any particular length of time and may be related or incidental to the commission of other criminal acts.

(3) A person who commits the crime of kidnapping is guilty of a felony punishable by imprisonment for life or any term of years or a fine of not more than $50,000.00, or both.

(4) This section does not prohibit the person from being charged with, convicted of, or sentenced for any other violation of law arising from the same transaction as the violation of this section.

Unlawful Imprisonment—MCL 750.349b (felony)

(1) A person commits the crime of unlawful imprisonment if he or she knowingly restrains another person under any of the following circumstances:

  (a) The person is restrained by means of a weapon or dangerous instrument.
  (b) The restrained person was secretly confined.
  (c) The person was restrained to facilitate the commission of another felony or to facilitate flight after commission of another felony.

(2) A person who commits unlawful imprisonment is guilty of a felony punishable by imprisonment for not more than 15 years or a fine of not more than $20,000.00, or both.

(3) As used in this section:

  (a) "Restrain" means to forcibly restrict a person's movements or to forcibly confine the person so as to interfere with that person's liberty without that person's consent or without lawful authority. The restraint does not have to exist for any particular length of time and may be related or incidental to the commission of other criminal acts.
  (b) "Secretly confined" means either of the following:
    (i) To keep the confinement of the restrained person a secret.
    (ii) To keep the location of the restrained person a secret.

(4) This section does not prohibit the person from being charged with, convicted of, or sentenced for any other violation of law that is committed by that person while violating this section.

Child Kidnapping—MCL 750.350 (felony)

(1) A person shall not maliciously, forcibly, or fraudulently lead, take, carry away, decoy, or entice away, any child under the age of 14 years, with the intent to detain or conceal the child from the child's parent or legal guardian, or from the person or persons who have adopted the child, or from any other person having the lawful charge of the child. A person who violates this section is guilty of a felony, punishable by imprisonment for life or any term of years.

(2) An adoptive or natural parent of the child shall not be charged with and convicted for a violation of this section.

The suspect maliciously, forcibly, fraudulently took or enticed away a child under 14 years of age with the intent to detain or conceal the child.

Parental Kidnapping—MCL 750.350a (felony)

(1) An adoptive or natural parent of a child shall not take that child, or retain that child for more than 24 hours, with the intent to detain or conceal the child from any other parent or legal guardian of the child who has custody or parenting time rights pursuant to a lawful court order at the time of the taking or retention, or from the person or persons who have adopted the child, or from any other person having lawful charge of the child at the time of the taking or retention.

(2) A parent who violates subsection (1) is guilty of a felony, punishable by imprisonment for not more than 1 year and 1 day, or a fine of not more than $2,000.00, or both.

(3) A parent who violates this section, upon conviction, in addition to any other punishment, may be ordered to make restitution to the other parent, legal guardian, the person or persons who have adopted the child, or any other person having lawful charge of the child for any financial expense incurred as a result of attempting to locate and having the child returned.

(4) When a parent who has not been convicted previously of a violation of section 349, 350, or this section, or under any statute of the United States or of any state related to kidnapping, pleads guilty to, or is found guilty of, a violation of this section, the court, without entering a judgment of guilt and with the consent of the accused parent, may defer further proceedings and place the accused parent on probation with lawful terms and conditions. Upon a violation of a term or condition of probation, the court may enter an adjudication of guilt and proceed as otherwise provided. Upon fulfillment of the terms and conditions of probation, the court shall discharge from probation and dismiss the proceedings against the parent. Discharge and dismissal under this subsection shall be without adjudication of guilt and is not a conviction for purposes of disqualifications or disabilities imposed by law upon conviction of a crime, including any additional penalties imposed for second or subsequent convictions. The department of state police shall retain a nonpublic record of an arrest and discharge and dismissal under this section. This record shall be furnished to a court or police agency upon request for the purpose of showing that a defendant in a criminal action has already availed himself or herself of this subsection.

(5) It is a complete defense under this section if a parent proves that his or her actions were taken for the purpose of protecting the child from an immediate and actual threat of physical or mental harm, abuse, or neglect.

The adoptive or natural parent took the child, or retained the child for more than 24 hours, with the intent to detain or conceal the child from:

- The parent or legal guardian who had legal custody or visitation at the time.
- The person who had adopted the child.
- The person who had lawful charge of the child at the time.

Defense: If the defendant took the child to protect the child from immediate and actual threat of physical and mental harm, abuse, or neglect.

Human Trafficking—MCL 750.462a-i (felony)

It is unlawful to knowingly subject or attempt to subject another person to forced labor or services by:

- Causing or threatening physical harm to another (MCL.462b)
- Physically restraining or threatening to physically restrain another person (MCL 750.462c)
- Abusing or threatening to abuse the law or legal process (750.462d)
- Destroying, concealing, removing, confiscating, or possessing an actual or purported passport or other government identification (MCL 750.462e)

- Using blackmail, threatening or causing financial harm, or exerting or threatening to exert financial control (MCL 750.462f)

Facilitating Human Trafficking—MCL 750.462h (felony)

It is unlawful to facilitate human trafficking, to benefit financially from human trafficking, or to receive anything of value from a venture engaged in human trafficking.

Penalties:

No injury	10 year felony
Injury to victim	15 year felony
Victim is a minor trafficked for purpose of sexually abusive activity.	20 year felony
Death of victim	Life felony

ROBBERY

ROBBERY

Larceny from the Person—MCL 750.357 (felony)

Any person who shall commit the offense of larceny by stealing from the person of another shall be guilty of a felony, punishable by imprisonment in the state prison not more than 10 years.

Elements

1. Defendant took someone else's property.
2. The property was taken without consent.
3. There was some movement of the property. It does not matter whether the defendant actually kept the property.
4. The property was taken from the victim's person or from the victim's immediate area of control or immediate presence.
5. At the time the property was taken, the defendant intended to permanently deprive the victim of the property.

CJI2d 23.3

Unarmed Robbery—MCL 750.530 (felony)

(1) A person who, in the course of committing a larceny of any money or other property that may be the subject of larceny, uses force or violence against any person who is present, or who assaults or puts the person in fear, is guilty of a felony punishable by imprisonment for not more than 15 years.

(2) As used in this section, "in the course of committing a larceny" includes acts that occur in an attempt to commit the larceny, or during commission of the larceny, or in flight or attempted flight after the commission of the larceny, or in an attempt to retain possession of the property.

Elements

1. Defendant used force or violence or assaulted victim.
2. Defendant did so while in the course of committing a larceny.
3. The victim was present while defendant was in the course of committing the larceny.

CJI2d 18.2.

Four men surrounded the victim, demanding money, and then assaulted him. *People v. Richardson*, 25 Mich. App. 117 (1970).

Unarmed robbery requires that the defendant took the purse by force or violence, or by assault, or putting the victim in fear. *People v. Hicks*, 259 Mich. App. 518 (2003).

Armed Robbery—MCL 750.529 (felony)

A person who engages in conduct proscribed under section 530 and who in the course of engaging in that conduct, possesses a dangerous weapon or an article used or fashioned in a manner to lead any person present to reasonably believe the article is a dangerous weapon, or who represents orally or otherwise that he or she is in possession of a dangerous weapon, is guilty of a felony punishable by imprisonment for life or for any term of years. If an aggravated assault or serious injury is inflicted by any person while violating this section, the person shall be sentenced to a minimum term of imprisonment of not less than 2 years.

Elements

1. Defendant used force or violence or assaulted victim.
2. Defendant did so while in the course of committing a larceny.
3. The victim was present while defendant was in the course of committing the larceny.
4. While in the course of committing the larceny the defendant:
   - Possessed a dangerous weapon.
   - Possessed any other object capable of causing death or serious injury.
   - Possessed an object used or fashioned in a manner to lead a person to believe it was a weapon.
   - Represented orally or otherwise that they were in possession of a weapon.

CJI2d 18.1.

The suspect was armed with a dangerous weapon, an article reasonably believed to be a weapon, or represented orally or otherwise that he or she was in possession of a dangerous weapon.

> A bulge in defendant's vest combined with threats to victim of being shot justified charges of armed robbery. *People v. Jolly*, 442 Mich. 458 (1993).
>
> Use of a knife. *People v. Rutherford*, 140 Mich. App. 272 (1985).
>
> Hand in paper bag and indication that armed. *People v. Kimble*, 109 Mich. App. 659 (1991).
>
> Armed robbery occurred where the defendant placed his hand under his clothing, the victim observed a bulge under the clothing and defendant announced, "this is a stick up." *People v. Taylor*, 245 Mich. App. 293 (2001).
>
> Each employee of an establishment may be a victim of armed robbery even though they do not all have access to the cash register since they

> have a superior right to the property than the suspect. *People v. Rodgers*, 248 Mich. App. 702 (2001).

CARJACKING—MCL 750.529a (felony)

(1) A person who in the course of committing a larceny of a motor vehicle uses force or violence or the threat of force or violence, or who puts in fear any operator, passenger, or person in lawful possession of the motor vehicle, or any person lawfully attempting to recover the motor vehicle, is guilty of carjacking, a felony punishable by imprisonment for life or for any term of years.

As used in this section, "in the course of committing a larceny of a motor vehicle" includes acts that occur in an attempt to commit the larceny, or during commission of the larceny, or in flight or attempted flight after the commission of the larceny, or in an attempt to retain possession of the motor vehicle.

Elements

1. Defendant used force or violence, or threatened force or violence, or assaulted victim.
2. Defendant did so while in the course of committing a larceny of a motor vehicle.
3. The victim was in lawful possession of the vehicle.

CJI2d 18.4a

> Jumping into the passenger side of a stopped automobile and aggressively moving over to the driver's side so that the driver exited. *People v. Terry*, 224 Mich. App. 447 (1997).
>
> Forcing gun into mouth of driver and demanding that she drive around the town. *People v. Green*, 228 Mich. App. 684 (1998).
>
> Defendant could only be charged with one count of carjacking, even though the vehicle had multiple occupants. *People v. Davis*, 468 Mich. 77 (2003).
>
> The Legislature did not intend to require "legal possession" as a prerequisite to all carjacking convictions. *People v. Small*, 467 Mich. 259 (2002).

EXTORTION—MCL 750.213 (felony)

Any person who shall, either orally or by a written or printed communication, maliciously threaten to accuse another of any crime or offense, or shall orally or by any written or printed communication maliciously threaten any injury to the person or property or mother, father, husband, wife or child of another with intent thereby to extort money or any pecuniary advantage whatever, or with intent to compel the person so threatened to do or refrain from doing any act against his will, shall be guilty of a felony, punishable by imprisonment in the state prison not more than 20 years or by a fine of not more than 10,000 dollars.

Elements

1. Suspect threatened to injure the victim, victim's property, victim's family (mother, father, husband, wife or child) or accused the victim of a crime.
2. The threat was stated or written down.
3. The suspect intended either to get money by making the threat, or makes the victim do something or refrain from doing something against his or her will.

> After assaulting the victim, the defendant stated to her, "You better not tell the cops." *People v. Pena*, 224 Mich. App. 650 (1997).

Threat for Extortion

A threat for the purpose of extortion is a written or spoken statement of an intent to injure another person or that person's property or family. A threat does not have to be said in certain words, but it can be made in general or vague terms without exactly what kind of injury is being threatened. It can be made by suggestion, but a threat must be definite enough to be understood by a person of ordinary intelligence as a threat of injury.

CJI2d 21.3

Completion of Extortion

It does not matter whether the threat was successful or whether the person threatened was afraid. It does not matter whether the victim actually did what the defendant wanted. The crime is complete when the threat is made, and it not a defense that the defendant later abandoned his intent to injure the victim. No act beside the threat is necessary.

CJI2d 21.5

CRIMES AGAINST PERSONS: SELECTED STATUTES

VULNERABLE ADULT ABUSE—MCL 750.145m

Definitions

Caregiver: An individual who directly cares for or has physical custody of a vulnerable adult.

Vulnerable adult: A person 18 years old or older who is one of the following:

- Because of age, developmental disability, mental illness, or physical handicap requires supervision or personal care or lacks the personal and social skills required for living independently.
- Is placed in an adult foster care family home or an adult foster care small group home.
- Is suspected of being or believed to be abused, neglected, or exploited.

Serious physical harm: A physical injury that threatens the life of a vulnerable adult, causes substantial bodily disfigurement, or seriously impairs the functioning or well-being of the vulnerable adult.

Serious mental harm: A mental injury that results in substantial alteration of mental functioning that is manifested in a visibly demonstrable manner.

Physical harm: Any injury to a vulnerable adult's physical condition.

Reckless act or reckless failure to act: Conduct that demonstrates a deliberate disregard of the likelihood that the natural tendency of the act or failure to act is to cause physical harm, serious physical harm, or serious mental harm.

> A foster care patient jumped or fell off the roof of a facility and subsequently complained of pain and paralysis, but the primary case manager failed to summon medical attention until the following day. This was sufficient evidence to establish the "reckless act or reckless failure to act" element of second-degree vulnerable adult abuse. *People v. DeKorte*, 233 Mich. App. 564 (1999).

First Degree (felony)

A caregiver intentionally caused serious physical harm or serious mental harm to a vulnerable adult.

Second Degree (felony)

The reckless act or reckless failure to act of a caregiver or other person with authority over a vulnerable adult, caused serious physical or mental harm to a vulnerable adult.

> To prove this charge, the prosecutor must introduce evidence that the defendant engaged in a reckless act or reckless failure to act causing the injuries to the victim. *People v. Hudson*, 241 Mich. App. 268 (2000).

Third Degree (2 year misdemeanor)

A caregiver intentionally caused physical harm to a vulnerable adult.

Fourth Degree (1 year misdemeanor)

The reckless act or reckless failure to act of a caregiver or other person with authority over a vulnerable adult, caused physical harm to a vulnerable adult.

THIS SECTION DOES NOT APPLY TO:
A caregiver or other person with authority over a vulnerable adult who is taking reasonable action to prevent a vulnerable adult from being harmed or harming others.

Vulnerable Adult Fraud—MCL 750.174a

This section creates penalties for a person who has a relationship of trust with a vulnerable adult and through fraud, deceit, misrepresentation, coercion, or unjust enrichment, used or attempted to obtain or use the vulnerable adult's money or property for his or her own direct or indirect benefit.

Penalties:

Less than $200	93 day misdemeanor
$200–$1,000 or less than $200 if, previously convicted	1 year misdemeanor
$1,000–$20,000 or $200 - $1,000 if, previously convicted	5 year felony
over $20,000 or $1,000–$20,000 if, previously convicted twice	10 year felony

Person in relationship of trust: A person who is a caregiver, relative by blood, marriage, or adoption, household member, court-appointed fiduciary, or other person entrusted with or has assumed responsibility for the management of the vulnerable adult's money or property.

ETHNIC INTIMIDATION—MCL 750.147b (felony)

(1) A person is guilty of ethnic intimidation if that person maliciously, and with specific intent to intimidate or harass another person because of that person's race, color, religion, gender, or national origin, does any of the following:

   (a) Causes physical contact with another person.
   (b) Damages, destroys, or defaces any real or personal property of another person.
   (c) Threatens, by word or act, to do an act described in subdivision (a) or (b), if there is reasonable cause to believe that an act described in subdivision (a) or (b) will occur.

(2) Ethnic intimidation is a felony punishable by imprisonment for not more than 2 years, or by a fine of not more than $5,000.00, or both.

(3) Regardless of the existence or outcome of any criminal prosecution, a person who suffers injury to his or her person or damage to his or her property as a result of ethnic intimidation may bring a civil cause of action against the person who commits the offense to secure an injunction, actual damages, including damages for emotional distress, or other appropriate relief. A plaintiff who prevails in a civil action brought pursuant to this section may recover both of the following:

   (a) Damages in the amount of 3 times the actual damages described in this subsection or $2,000.00, whichever is greater.
   (b) Reasonable attorney fees and costs.

The suspect MALICIOUSLY and with the specific intent to intimidate or harass, did one of the following because of the race, color, religion, gender or national origin of the victim

- Caused physical contact with the victim.
- Threatened to cause physical contact with the victim.
- Damaged, destroyed, or defaced property of the victim.
- Threatened by what he said or did to damage, destroy or deface property of the victim, and there was reasonable cause to believe that such an act would occur.

> Defendant started a heated argument over a trivial matter at a restaurant. He threw a punch at the victim. Defendant's act of throwing a

punch at the complainant provided reasonable cause to believe that physical contact would occur. He called the victim a "nigger" and stated that "you people should not be allowed in here." *People v. Stevens*, 230 Mich. App. 502 (1998).

Ethnic intimidation occurred where defendant and the victim were involved in a road rage incident and prior to an assault, defendant shouted racial slurs at the victim. Racial intent does not have to be the sole motivation for the crime. *People v. Schutter*, 265 Mich. App. 423 (2005).

STALKING

Misdemeanor Stalking—MCL 750.411h (1 year misdemeanor)

(1) As used in this section:

  (a) "Course of conduct" means a pattern of conduct composed of a series of 2 or more separate noncontinuous acts evidencing a continuity of purpose.

  (b) "Emotional distress" means significant mental suffering or distress that may, but does not necessarily, require medical or other professional treatment or counseling.

  (c) "Harassment" means conduct directed toward a victim that includes, but is not limited to, repeated or continuing unconsented contact that would cause a reasonable individual to suffer emotional distress and that actually causes the victim to suffer emotional distress. Harassment does not include constitutionally protected activity or conduct that serves a legitimate purpose.

  (d) "Stalking" means a willful course of conduct involving repeated or continuing harassment of another individual that would cause a reasonable person to feel terrorized, frightened, intimidated, threatened, harassed, or molested and that actually causes the victim to feel terrorized, frightened, intimidated, threatened, harassed, or molested.

  (e) "Unconsented contact" means any contact with another individual that is initiated or continued without that individual's consent or in disregard of that individual's expressed desire that the contact be avoided or discontinued. Unconsented contact includes, but is not limited to, any of the following:

    (i) Following or appearing within the sight of that individual.

    (ii) Approaching or confronting that individual in a public place or on private property.

    (iii) Appearing at that individual's workplace or residence.

    (iv) Entering onto or remaining on property owned, leased, or occupied by that individual.

    (v) Contacting that individual by telephone.

    (vi) Sending mail or electronic communications to that individual.

    (vii) Placing an object on, or delivering an object to, property owned, leased, or occupied by that individual.

  (f) "Victim" means an individual who is the target of a willful course of conduct involving repeated or continuing harassment.

(2) An individual who engages in stalking is guilty of a crime as follows:

  (a) Except as provided in subdivision (b), a misdemeanor punishable by imprisonment for not more than 1 year or a fine of not more than $1,000.00, or both.

  (b) If the victim was less than 18 years of age at any time during the individual's course of conduct and the individual is 5 or more years older than the victim, a felony punishable by imprisonment for not more than 5 years or a fine of not more than $10,000.00, or both.

(3) The court may place an individual convicted of violating this section on probation for a term of not more than 5 years. If a term of probation is ordered, the court may, in addition to any other lawful condition of probation, order the defendant to do any of the following:

  (a) Refrain from stalking any individual during the term of probation.

  (b) Refrain from having any contact with the victim of the offense.

  (c) Be evaluated to determine the need for psychiatric, psychological, or social counseling and if, determined appropriate by the court, to receive psychiatric, psychological, or social counseling at his or her own expense.

(4) In a prosecution for a violation of this section, evidence that the defendant continued to engage in a course of conduct involving repeated unconsented contact with the victim after having been requested by the victim to discontinue the same or a different form of unconsented contact, and to refrain from any further unconsented contact with the victim, gives rise to a rebuttable presumption that the continuation of the course of conduct caused the victim to feel terrorized, frightened, intimidated, threatened, harassed, or molested.

(5) A criminal penalty provided for under this section may be imposed in addition to any penalty that may be imposed for any other criminal offense arising from the same conduct or for any contempt of court arising from the same conduct.

Elements

Two or more willful, separate, and noncontinuous acts of unconsented contact with the victim that:

1. Would cause a reasonable individual to feel terrorized, frighten, intimidated, threatened, harassed or molested and
2. Caused the victim to feel terrorized, frighten, intimidated, threatened, harassed or molested.

Examples include the following:

- Following or appearing within sight of the victim.
- Approaching or confronting the person in public or private.
- Appearing at the workplace or residence of the victim.
- Entering upon the property of the victim.
- Contacting the victim by telephone.
- Sending mail or email.
- Placing an object or delivering an object to property owned or leased by the victim.

Aggravated Stalking—MCL 750.411i (felony)

(1) As used in this section:

(a) "Course of conduct" means a pattern of conduct composed of a series of 2 or more separate noncontinuous acts evidencing a continuity of purpose.

(b) "Credible threat" means a threat to kill another individual or a threat to inflict physical injury upon another individual that is made in any manner or in any context that causes the individual hearing or receiving the threat to reasonably fear for his or her safety or the safety of another individual.

(c) "Emotional distress" means significant mental suffering or distress that may, but does not necessarily, require medical or other professional treatment or counseling.

(d) "Harassment" means conduct directed toward a victim that includes, but is not limited to, repeated or continuing unconsented contact that would cause a reasonable individual to suffer emotional distress and that actually causes the victim to suffer emotional distress. Harassment does not include constitutionally protected activity or conduct that serves a legitimate purpose.

(e) "Stalking" means a willful course of conduct involving repeated or continuing harassment of another individual that would cause a reasonable person to feel terrorized, frightened, intimidated, threatened, harassed, or molested and that actually causes the victim to feel terrorized, frightened, intimidated, threatened, harassed, or molested.

(f) "Unconsented contact" means any contact with another individual that is initiated or continued without that individual's consent or in disregard of that individual's expressed desire that the contact be avoided or discontinued. Unconsented contact includes, but is not limited to, any of the following:

  (i) Following or appearing within the sight of that individual.
  (ii) Approaching or confronting that individual in a public place or on private property.
  (iii) Appearing at that individual's workplace or residence.
  (iv) Entering onto or remaining on property owned, leased, or occupied by that individual.
  (v) Contacting that individual by telephone.
  (vi) Sending mail or electronic communications to that individual.
  (vii) Placing an object on, or delivering an object to, property owned, leased, or occupied by that individual.

(g) "Victim" means an individual who is the target of a willful course of conduct involving repeated or continuing harassment.

(2) An individual who engages in stalking is guilty of aggravated stalking if the violation involves any of the following circumstances:

- *(a) At least 1 of the actions constituting the offense is in violation of a restraining order and the individual has received actual notice of that restraining order or at least 1 of the actions is in violation of an injunction or preliminary injunction.*
- *(b) At least 1 of the actions constituting the offense is in violation of a condition of probation, a condition of parole, a condition of pretrial release, or a condition of release on bond pending appeal.*
- *(c) The course of conduct includes the making of 1 or more credible threats against the victim, a member of the victim's family, or another individual living in the same household as the victim.*
- *(d) The individual has been previously convicted of a violation of this section or section 411h.*

(3) Aggravated stalking is a felony punishable as follows:

- *(a) Except as provided in subdivision (b), by imprisonment for not more than 5 years or a fine of not more than $10,000.00, or both.*
- *(b) If the victim was less than 18 years of age at any time during the individual's course of conduct and the individual is 5 or more years older than the victim, by imprisonment for not more than 10 years or a fine of not more than $15,000.00, or both.*

(4) The court may place an individual convicted of violating this section on probation for any term of years, but not less than 5 years. If a term of probation is ordered, the court may, in addition to any other lawful condition of probation, order the defendant to do any of the following:

- *(a) Refrain from stalking any individual during the term of probation.*
- *(b) Refrain from any contact with the victim of the offense.*
- *(c) Be evaluated to determine the need for psychiatric, psychological, or social counseling and, if determined appropriate by the court, to receive psychiatric, psychological, or social counseling at his or her own expense.*

(5) In a prosecution for a violation of this section, evidence that the defendant continued to engage in a course of conduct involving repeated unconsented contact with the victim after having been requested by the victim to discontinue the same or a different form of unconsented contact, and to refrain from any further unconsented contact with the victim, gives rise to a rebuttable presumption that the continuation of the course of conduct caused the victim to feel terrorized, frightened, intimidated, threatened, harassed, or molested.

(6) A criminal penalty provided for under this section may be imposed in addition to any penalty that may be imposed for any other criminal offense arising from the same conduct or for contempt of court arising from the same conduct.

Elements

For aggravated stalking, the elements for misdemeanor stalking must occur, including one of the following:

1. Suspect had a previous stalking conviction.
2. One of the acts was a violation of court order.
3. One of the threats involved a credible threat against:

- Victim.
- A member of the victim's family.
- Someone in victim's household.

Posting a Message—MCL 750.411s (felony)

A person shall not post a message through the use of any medium of communication, including the internet or a computer, computer program, computer system or computer network, or other electronic medium of communication, without the victim's consent, if all the following apply:

- The person knows or has reason to know that the posting could cause two or more separate noncontinuous acts of unconsented contact with the victim.
- Posting the message is intended to cause conduct that would make the victim feel terrorized, frightened, intimidated, threatened, harassed, or molested.
- Conduct arising from the posting would cause a reasonable person to suffer emotional distress and to feel terrorized, frightened, intimidated, threatened, harassed or molested.
- Conduct arising from the posting actually causes the victim to suffer emotional distress and to feel terrorized, frightened, intimidated, threatened, harassed, or molested.

Except as provided below, posting a message is a 2 year felony.

Posting a message is a 5 year felony if the act includes any of the following:

- Posting the message violates a restraining order and the person has received notice.
- Posting the message violates a condition of probation, parole or conditional release.
- The message results in a credible threat communicated to the victim or member of the victim's family or another individual living in the same household as the victim.
- The person has been previously convicted of stalking, MCL 750.145d, or MCL 752.796 or a law substantially similar from another state.
- The victim is less than 18 years of age and the person is 5 or more years older.

Prosecution may be sought if one of the following apply:

- The person posts the message while in this state.
- Conduct arising from posting the message occurs in this state.
- The victim is present in this state at the time the offense or any element of the offense occurs.
- The person posting the message knows that the victim resides in this state.

HAZING—MCL 750.411t

(1) *Except as provided in subsection (4), a person who attends, is employed by, or is a volunteer of an educational institution shall not engage in or participate in the hazing of an individual.*

(2) *A person who violates subsection (1) is guilty of a crime punishable as follows:*

(a) *If the violation results in physical injury, the person is guilty of a misdemeanor punishable by imprisonment for not more than 93 days or a fine of not more than $1,000.00, or both.*

(b) *If the violation results in serious impairment of a body function, the person is guilty of a felony punishable by imprisonment for not more than 5 years or a fine of not more than $2,500.00, or both.*

(c) *If the violation results in death, the person is guilty of a felony punishable by imprisonment for not more than 15 years or a fine of not more than $10,000.00, or both.*

(3) *A criminal penalty provided for under this section may be imposed in addition to any penalty that may be imposed for any other criminal offense arising from the same conduct.*

(4) *This section does not apply to an individual who is the subject of the hazing, regardless of whether the individual voluntarily allowed himself or herself to be hazed.*

(5) *This section does not apply to an activity that is normal and customary in an athletic, physical education, military training, or similar program sanctioned by the educational institution.*

(6) *It is not a defense to a prosecution for a crime under this section that the individual against whom the hazing was directed consented to or acquiesced in the hazing.*

(7) *As used in this section:*

(a) *"Educational institution" means a public or private school that is a middle school, junior high school, high school, vocational school, college, or university located in this state.*

(b) *"Hazing" means an intentional, knowing, or reckless act by a person acting alone or acting with others that is directed against an individual and that the person knew or should have known endangers the physical health or safety of the individual, and that is done for the purpose of pledging, being initiated into, affiliating with, participating in, holding office in, or maintaining membership in any organization. Subject to subsection (5), hazing includes any of the following that is done for such a purpose:*

(i) *Physical brutality, such as whipping, beating, striking, branding, electronic shocking, placing of a harmful substance on the body, or similar activity.*

(ii) *Physical activity, such as sleep deprivation, exposure to the elements, confinement in a small space, or calisthenics, that subjects the other person to an unreasonable risk of harm or that adversely affects the physical health or safety of the individual.*

(iii) *Activity involving consumption of a food, liquid, alcoholic beverage, liquor, drug, or other substance that subjects the individual to an unreasonable risk of harm or that adversely affects the physical health or safety of the individual.*

(iv) *Activity that induces, causes, or requires an individual to perform a duty or task that involves the commission of a crime or an act of hazing.*

(c) "Organization" means a fraternity, sorority, association, corporation, order, society, corps, cooperative, club, service group, social group, athletic team, or similar group whose members are primarily students at an educational institution.

(d) "Pledge" means an individual who has been accepted by, is considering an offer of membership from, or is in the process of qualifying for membership in any organization.

(e) "Pledging" means any action or activity related to becoming a member of an organization.

(f) "Serious impairment of a body function" means that term as defined in section 479a.

(8) This section shall be known and may be cited as "Garret's law".

EAVESDROPPING

Definitions—MCL 750.539a

As used in sections 539a to 539i:

(1) "Private place" means a place where one may reasonably expect to be safe from casual or hostile intrusion or surveillance but does not include a place to which the public or substantial group of the public has access.

(2) "Eavesdrop" or "eavesdropping" means to overhear, record, amplify or transmit any part of the private discourse of others without the permission of all persons engaged in the discourse. Neither this definition or any other provision of this act shall modify or affect any law or regulation concerning interception, divulgence or recording of messages transmitted by communications common carriers.

(3) "Surveillance" means to secretly observe the activities of another person for the purpose of spying upon and invading the privacy of the person observed.

(4) "Person" means any individual, partnership, corporation or association.

Trespassing for Purpose of Eavesdropping—MCL 750.539b (90-day misdemeanor)

A person who trespasses on property owned or under the control of any other person, to subject that person to eavesdropping or surveillance is guilty of a misdemeanor.

Eavesdropping upon Private Conversation—MCL 750.539c (felony)

Any person who is present or who is not present during a private conversation and who willfully uses any device to eavesdrop upon the conversation without the consent of all parties thereto, or who knowingly aids, employs or procures another person to do the same in violation of this section, is guilty of a felony punishable by imprisonment in a state prison for not more than 2 years or by a fine of not more than $2,000.00, or both.

Installation of Device for Observing, Photographing, or Eavesdropping in Private Place—MCL 750.539d (felony)

(1) Except as otherwise provided in this section, a person shall not do either of the following:

(a) Install, place, or use in any private place, without the consent of the person or persons entitled to privacy in that place, any device for observing, recording, transmitting, photographing, or eavesdropping upon the sounds or events in that place.

(b) Distribute, disseminate, or transmit for access by any other person a recording, photograph, or visual image the person knows or has reason to know was obtained in violation of this section.

(2) This section does not prohibit security monitoring in a residence if conducted by or at the direction of the owner or principal occupant of that residence unless conducted for a lewd or lascivious purpose.

(3) A person who violates or attempts to violate this section is guilty of a crime as follows:

(a) For a violation or attempted violation of subsection (1)(a):

(i) Except as provided in subparagraph (ii), the person is guilty of a felony punishable by imprisonment for not more than 2 years or a fine of not more than $2,000.00, or both.

(ii) If the person was previously convicted of violating or attempting to violate this section, the person is guilty of a felony punishable by imprisonment for not more than 5 years or a fine of not more than $5,000.00, or both.

(b) For a violation or attempted violation of subsection (1)(b), the person is guilty of a *felony punishable by imprisonment for not more than 5 years or a fine of not more than $5,000.00, or both.*

(4) *This section does not prohibit a person from being charged with, convicted of, or punished for any other violation of law committed by that person while violating or attempting to violate subsection (1)(a) or (b).*

> Eavesdropping could apply to a subject who hides a video camera in his bedroom to secretly videotape consensual sexual activity between himself and his girlfriends. *Lewis v. Legrow*, 258 Mich. App. 175 (2003).

Use or Divulgence of Information Unlawfully Obtained—MCL 750.539e (felony)

Any person who uses or divulges any information which he knows or reasonably should know was obtained in violation of sections 539b, 539c or 539d is guilty of a felony, punishable by imprisonment in a state prison not more than 2 years, or by a fine of not more than $2,000.00.

> Eavesdropping includes a person listening in on cordless phone conversations by means of a police scanner. *People v. Stone*, 463 Mich. 558 (2001).

Surveillance of Individual Having Reasonable Expectation of Privacy—MCL 750.539j (felony)

(1) *A person shall not do any of the following:*

(a) *Surveil another individual who is clad only in his or her undergarments, the unclad genitalia or buttocks of another individual, or the unclad breasts of a female individual under circumstances in which the individual would have a reasonable expectation of privacy.*

(b) *Photograph, or otherwise capture or record, the visual image of the undergarments worn by another individual, the unclad genitalia or buttocks of another individual, or the unclad breasts of a female individual under circumstances in which the individual would have a reasonable expectation of privacy.*

(c) *Distribute, disseminate, or transmit for access by any other person a recording, photograph, or visual image the person knows or has reason to know was obtained in violation of this section.*

(2) *A person who violates or attempts to violate this section is guilty of a crime as follows:*

(a) *For a violation or attempted violation of subsection (1)(a):*

(i) *Except as provided in subparagraph (ii), the person is guilty of a felony punishable by imprisonment for not more than 2 years or a fine of not more than $2,000.00, or both.*

(ii) *If the person was previously convicted of violating or attempting to violate subsection (1)(a), the person is guilty of a felony punishable by imprisonment for not more than 5 years or a fine of not more than $5,000.00, or both.*

(b) *For a violation or attempted violation of subsection (1)(b) or (c), the person is guilty of a felony punishable by imprisonment for not more than 5 years or a fine of not more than $5,000.00, or both.*

(3) *This section does not prohibit a person from being charged with, convicted of, or punished for any other violation of law committed by that person while violating or attempting to violate subsection (1)(a) to (c).*

(4) *This section does not prohibit security monitoring in a residence if conducted by or at the direction of the owner or principal occupant of that residence unless conducted for a lewd or lascivious purpose.*

(5) *This section does not apply to a peace officer of this state or of the federal government, or the officer's agent, while in the performance of the officer's duties.*

(6) *As used in this section, "surveil" means to subject an individual to surveillance as that term is defined in section 539a.*

Video Taping in Movie Theaters—MCL 750.465a (1 year misdemeanor)

(1) *A person who knowingly operates an audiovisual recording function of a device in a theatrical facility where a motion picture is being exhibited without the consent of the owner or lessee of that theatrical facility and of the licensor of the motion picture being exhibited is guilty of a crime as follows:*

(a) *Except as provided in subdivisions (b) and (c), the person is guilty of a misdemeanor*

punishable by imprisonment for not more than 1 year or a fine of not more than $10,000.00, or both.
  (b) *If the person has 1 prior conviction for violating this subsection, the person is guilty of a felony punishable by imprisonment for not more than 2 years or a fine of not more than $20,000.00, or both.*
  (c) *If the person has 2 or more prior convictions for violating this subsection, the person is guilty of a felony punishable by imprisonment for not more than 4 years or a fine of not more than $40,000.00, or both.*
(2) *This section does not prevent any lawfully authorized investigative, law enforcement, protective, or intelligence—gathering employee or agent, of this state or the United States, from operating the audiovisual recording function of a device in a theatrical facility where a motion picture is being exhibited as part of an investigative, protective, law enforcement, or intelligence-gathering activity.*
(3) *This section does not prohibit a person from being charged with, convicted of, or punished for any other violation of law that proscribes conduct described in this section and that provides a greater penalty.*
(4) *As used in this section:*
  (a) *"Audiovisual recording function" means the capability of a device to record or transmit a motion picture or any part of a motion picture by technological means.*
  (b) *"Theatrical facility" means a facility being used to exhibit a motion picture to the public, but does not include an individual's residence or a retail establishment.*

Tampering with Electronic Communication— MCL 750.540 (felony)

(1) *A person shall not willfully and maliciously cut, break, disconnect, interrupt, tap, or make any unauthorized connection with any electronic medium of communication, including the internet or a computer, computer program, computer system, or computer network, or a telephone.*
(2) *A person shall not willfully and maliciously read or copy any message from any telegraph, telephone line, wire, cable, computer network, computer program, or computer system, or telephone or other electronic medium of communication that the person accessed without authorization.*
(3) *A person shall not willfully and maliciously make unauthorized use of any electronic medium of communication, including the internet or a computer, computer program, computer system, or computer network, or telephone.*
(4) *A person shall not willfully and maliciously prevent, obstruct, or delay by any means the sending, conveyance, or delivery of any authorized communication, by or through any telegraph or telephone line, cable, wire, or any electronic medium of communication, including the internet or a computer, computer program, computer system, or computer network.*
(5) *A person who violates this section is guilty of a crime as follows:*
  (a) *Except as provided in subdivision (b), the person is guilty of a felony punishable by imprisonment for not more than 2 years or a fine of not more than $1,000.00, or both.*
  (b) *If the incident to be reported results in injury to or the death of any person, the person violating this section is guilty of a felony punishable by imprisonment for not more than 4 years or a fine of not more than $5,000.00, or both.*
(6) *As used in this section:*
  (a) *"Computer" means any connected, directly interoperable or interactive device, equipment, or facility that uses a computer program or other instructions to perform specific operations including logical, arithmetic, or memory functions with or on computer data or a computer program and that can store, retrieve, alter, or communicate the results of the operations to a person, computer program, computer, computer system, or computer network.*
  (b) *"Computer network" means the interconnection of hardwire or wireless communication lines with a computer through remote terminals, or a complex consisting of 2 or more interconnected computers.*
  (c) *"Computer program" means a series of internal or external instructions communicated in a form acceptable to a computer that directs the functioning of a computer, computer system, or computer network in a manner designed to provide or produce products or results from the computer, computer system, or computer network.*
  (d) *"Computer system" means a set of related, connected or unconnected, computer equipment, devices, software, or hardware.*

(e) "Internet" means that term as defined in section 230 of title II of the communications act of 1934, 47 USC 230, and includes voice over internet protocol services.

(7) This section does not prohibit a person from being charged with, convicted of, or punished for any other violation of law committed by that person while violating or attempting to violate this section.

OBSCENE, HARASSING, OR THREATENING PHONE CALLS

Malicious Use of Phones—MCL 750.540e (6 month misdemeanor)

A person is guilty of a misdemeanor who maliciously uses any service provided by a telecommunications service provider with intent to terrorize, frighten, intimidate, threaten, harass, molest or annoy any other person, or to disturb the peace and quiet of any other person by any of the following:

- Threatening physical harm or damage to any person or property.
- Falsely and deliberately reporting by telephone or telegraph message that any person has been injured, has suddenly taken ill, has suffered death, or has been the victim of a crime or accident.
- Deliberately refusing or failing to disengage a connection.
- Using any vulgar, indecent, obscene, or offensive language or suggesting any lewd or lascivious act in the course of a telephone conversation.
- Repeatedly initiating a telephone call and, without speaking, deliberately hanging up or breaking the telephone connection as or after the telephone call is answered.
- Making an unsolicited commercial telephone call that is received between the hours of 9 p.m. and 9 a.m.
- Deliberately engaging or causing to engage the use of a telecommunications service or device of another person in a repetitive manner that causes interruption in telecommunications service or prevents the person from utilizing his or her telecommunications service or device.

An offense is committed under this section if the communication either originates or terminates or both originates and terminates in this state and may be prosecuted at the place of origination or termination.

IDENTITY THEFT

Identity Protection Act—MCL 445.63

As used in this act:

(a) "Agency" means a department, board, commission, office, agency, authority, or other unit of state government of this state. The term includes an institution of higher education of this state. The term does not include a circuit, probate, district, or municipal court.

(b) "Breach of the security of a database" or "security breach" means the unauthorized access and acquisition of data that compromises the security or confidentiality of personal information maintained by a person or agency as part of a database of personal information regarding multiple individuals. These terms do not include unauthorized access to data by an employee or other individual if the access meets all of the following:

(i) The employee or other individual acted in good faith in accessing the data.
(ii) The access was related to the activities of the agency or person.
(iii) The employee or other individual did not misuse any personal information or disclose any personal information to an unauthorized person.

(c) "Child or spousal support" means support for a child or spouse, paid or provided pursuant to state or federal law under a court order or judgment. Support includes, but is not limited to, any of the following:

(i) Expenses for day-to-day care.
(ii) Medical, dental, or other health care.
(iii) Child care expenses.
(iv) Educational expenses.
(v) Expenses in connection with pregnancy or confinement under the paternity act, 1956 PA 205, MCL 722.711 to 722.730.
(vi) Repayment of genetic testing expenses, under the paternity act, 1956 PA 205, MCL 722.711 to 722.730.
(vii) A surcharge as provided by section 3a of the support and parenting time enforcement act, 1982 PA 295, MCL 552.603a.

(d) "Credit card" means that term as defined in section 157m of the Michigan penal code, 1931 PA 328, MCL 750.157m.

(e) "Data" means computerized personal information.
(f) "Depository institution" means a state or nationally chartered bank or a state or federally chartered savings and loan association, savings bank, or credit union.
(g) "Encrypted" means transformation of data through the use of an algorithmic process into a form in which there is a low probability of assigning meaning without use of a confidential process or key, or securing information by another method that renders the data elements unreadable or unusable.
(h) "Financial institution" means a depository institution, an affiliate of a depository institution, a licensee under the consumer financial services act, 1988 PA 161, MCL 487.2051 to 487.2072, 1984 PA 379, MCL 493.101 to 493.114, the motor vehicle sales finance act, 1950 (Ex Sess) PA 27, MCL 492.101 to 492.141, the secondary mortgage loan act, 1981 PA 125, MCL 493.51 to 493.81, the mortgage brokers, lenders, and servicers licensing act, 1987 PA 173, MCL 445.1651 to 445.1684, or the regulatory loan act, 1939 PA 21, MCL 493.1 to 493.24, a seller under the home improvement finance act, 1965 PA 332, MCL 445.1101 to 445.1431, or the retail installment sales act, 1966 PA 224, MCL 445.851 to 445.873, or a person subject to subtitle A of title V of the Gramm-Leach-Bliley act, 15 USC 6801 to 6809.
(i) "Financial transaction device" means that term as defined in section 157m of the Michigan penal code, 1931 PA 328, MCL 750.157m.
(j) "Identity theft" means engaging in an act or conduct prohibited in section 5(1).
(k) "Law enforcement agency" means that term as defined in section 2804 of the public health code, 1978 PA 368, MCL 333.2804.
(l) "Local registrar" means that term as defined in section 2804 of the public health code, 1978 PA 368, MCL 333.2804.
(m) "Medical records or information" includes, but is not limited to, medical and mental health histories, reports, summaries, diagnoses and prognoses, treatment and medication information, notes, entries, and x-rays and other imaging records.
(n) "Person" means an individual, partnership, corporation, limited liability company, association, or other legal entity.
(o) "Personal identifying information" means a name, number, or other information that is used for the purpose of identifying a specific person or providing access to a person's financial accounts, including, but not limited to, a person's name, address, telephone number, driver license or state personal identification card number, social security number, place of employment, employee identification number, employer or taxpayer identification number, government passport number, health insurance identification number, mother's maiden name, demand deposit account number, savings account number, financial transaction device account number or the person's account password, stock or other security certificate or account number, credit card number, vital record, or medical records or information.
(p) "Personal information" means the first name or first initial and last name linked to 1 or more of the following data elements of a resident of this state:

(i) Social security number.
(ii) Driver license number or state personal identification card number.
(iii) Demand deposit or other financial account number, or credit card or debit card number, in combination with any required security code, access code, or password that would permit access to any of the resident's financial accounts.

(q) "Public utility" means that term as defined in section 1 of 1972 PA 299, MCL 460.111.
(r) "Redact" means to alter or truncate data so that no more than 4 sequential digits of a driver license number, state personal identification card number, or account number, or no more than 5 sequential digits of a social security number, are accessible as part of personal information.
(s) "State registrar" means that term as defined in section 2805 of the public health code, 1978 PA 368, MCL 333.2805.
(t) "Trade or commerce" means that term as defined in section 2 of the Michigan consumer protection act, 1971 PA 331, MCL 445.902.
(u) "Vital record" means that term as defined in section 2805 of the public health code, 1978 PA 368, MCL 333.2805.

Unlawful Use—MCL 445.65

(1) A person shall not do any of the following:

(a) With intent to defraud or violate the law, use or attempt to use the personal identifying information of another person to do either of the following:

(i) Obtain credit, goods, services, money, property, a vital record, medical records or information, or employment.
(ii) Commit another unlawful act.

(b) By concealing, withholding, or misrepresenting the person's identity, use or attempt to use the personal identifying information of another person to do either of the following:

(i) Obtain credit, goods, services, money, property, a vital record, medical records or information, or employment.
(ii) Commit another unlawful act.

(2) A person who violates subsection (1)(b)(i) may assert 1 or more of the following as a defense in a civil action or as an affirmative defense in a criminal prosecution, and has the burden of proof on that defense by a preponderance of the evidence:

(a) That the person gave a bona fide gift for or for the benefit or control of, or use or consumption by, the person whose personal identifying information was used.
(b) That the person acted in otherwise lawful pursuit or enforcement of a person's legal rights, including an investigation of a crime or an audit, collection, investigation, or transfer of a debt, child or spousal support obligation, tax liability, claim, receivable, account, or interest in a receivable or account.
(c) That the action taken was authorized or required by state or federal law, rule, regulation, or court order or rule.
(d) That the person acted with the consent of the person whose personal identifying information was used, unless the person giving consent knows that the information will be used to commit an unlawful act.

Unlawfully Obtaining—MCL 445.67

A person shall not do any of the following:

(a) Obtain or possess, or attempt to obtain or possess, personal identifying information of another person with the intent to use that information to commit identity theft or another crime.
(b) Sell or transfer, or attempt to sell or transfer, personal identifying information of another person if the person knows or has reason to know that the specific intended recipient will use, attempt to use, or further transfer the information to another person for the purpose of committing identity theft or another crime.
(c) Falsify a police report of identity theft, or knowingly create, possess, or use a false police report of identity theft.

Penalties—MCL 445.69

(1) Subject to subsection (6), a person who violates section 5 or 7 is guilty of a felony punishable by imprisonment for not more than 5 years or a fine of not more than $25,000.00, or both.

(2) Sections 5 and 7 apply whether an individual who is a victim or intended victim of a violation of 1 of those sections is alive or deceased at the time of the violation.

(3) This section does not prohibit a person from being charged with, convicted of, or sentenced for any other violation of law committed by that person using information obtained in violation of this section or any other violation of law committed by that person while violating or attempting to violate this section.

(4) The court may order that a term of imprisonment imposed under this section be served consecutively to any term of imprisonment imposed for a conviction of any other violation of law committed by that person using the information obtained in violation of this section or any other violation of law committed by that person while violating or attempting to violate this section.

(5) A person may assert as a defense in a civil action or as an affirmative defense in a criminal prosecution for a violation of section 5 or 7, and has the burden of proof on that defense by a preponderance of the evidence, that the person lawfully transferred, obtained, or attempted to obtain personal identifying information of another person for the purpose of detecting, preventing, or deterring identity theft or another crime or the funding of a criminal activity.

(6) Subsection (1) does not apply to a violation of a statute or rule administered by a regulatory board, commission, or officer acting under authority of this state or the United States that confers primary jurisdiction on that regulatory board, commission, or officer to authorize, pro-

hibit, or regulate the transactions and conduct of that person, including, but not limited to, a state or federal statute or rule governing a financial institution and the insurance code of 1956, 1956 PA 218, MCL 500.100 to 500.8302, if the act is committed by a person subject to and regulated by that statute or rule, or by another person who has contracted with that person to use personal identifying information.

Venue for Prosecution of Identity Theft—MCL 762.10c

(1) Conduct prohibited under former section 750.285 of the Michigan penal code or a violation of the identity theft protection act, or a violation of law committed in furtherance of or arising from the same transaction as conduct prohibited under former section 285 of the Michigan penal code, 1931 PA 328, or a violation of the identity theft protection act, may be prosecuted in 1 of the following jurisdictions:

   (a) The jurisdiction in which the offense occurred.
   (b) The jurisdiction in which the information used to commit the violation was illegally used.
   (c) The jurisdiction in which the victim resides.

(2) If a person is charged with more than 1 violation of the identity theft protection act and those violations may be prosecuted in more than 1 jurisdiction, any of those jurisdictions is a proper jurisdiction for all of the violations.

Secretly Capturing Someone's ID—MCL 750.539k

(1) A person who is not a party to a transaction that involves the use of a financial transaction device shall not secretly or surreptitiously photograph, or otherwise capture or record, electronically or by any other means, or distribute, disseminate, or transmit, electronically or by any other means, personal identifying information from the transaction without the consent of the individual.
(2) This section does not prohibit the capture or transmission of personal identifying information in the ordinary and lawful course of business.
(3) This section does not apply to a peace officer of this state, or of the federal government, or the officer's agent, while in the lawful performance of the officer's duties.

(4) This section does not prohibit a person from being charged with, convicted of, or punished for any other violation of law committed by that person while violating or attempting to violate this section.
(5) A person who violates this section is guilty of a misdemeanor punishable by imprisonment for not more than 1 year or a fine of not more than $1,000.00, or both.
(6) As used in this section:

   (a) "Financial transaction device" means that term as defined in section 157m.
   (b) "Personal identifying information" means that term as defined in section 3 of the identity theft protection act, MCL 445.63.

COMPUTER CRIMES

Use of Computers to Commit Certain Crimes—MCL 750.145d (felony)

(1) A person shall not use the internet or a computer, computer program, computer network, or computer system to communicate with any person for the purpose of doing any of the following:

   (a) Committing, attempting to commit, conspiring to commit, or soliciting another person to commit conduct proscribed under section 145a, 145c, 157c, 349, 350, 520b, 520c, 520d, 520e, or 520g, or section 5 of 1978 PA 33, MCL 722.675, in which the victim or intended victim is a minor or is believed by that person to be a minor.
   (b) Committing, attempting to commit, conspiring to commit, or soliciting another person to commit conduct proscribed under section 411h or 411i.
   (c) Committing, attempting to commit, conspiring to commit, or soliciting another person to commit conduct proscribed under chapter XXXIII or section 327, 327a, 328, or 411a(2).

(2) A person who violates this section is guilty of a crime as follows:

   (a) If the underlying crime is a misdemeanor or a felony with a maximum term of imprisonment of less than 1 year, the person is guilty of a misdemeanor punishable by imprisonment for not more than 1 year or a fine of not more than $5,000.00, or both.

(b) If the underlying crime is a misdemeanor or a felony with a maximum term of imprisonment of 1 year or more but less than 2 years, the person is guilty of a felony punishable by imprisonment for not more than 2 years or a fine of not more than $5,000.00, or both.

(c) If the underlying crime is a misdemeanor or a felony with a maximum term of imprisonment of 2 years or more but less than 4 years, the person is guilty of a felony punishable by imprisonment for not more than 4 years or a fine of not more than $5,000.00, or both.

(d) If the underlying crime is a felony with a maximum term of imprisonment of 4 years or more but less than 10 years, the person is guilty of a felony punishable by imprisonment for not more than 10 years or a fine of not more than $5,000.00, or both.

(e) If the underlying crime is a felony punishable by a maximum term of imprisonment of 10 years or more but less than 15 years, the person is guilty of a felony punishable by imprisonment for not more than 15 years or a fine of not more than $10,000.00, or both.

(f) If the underlying crime is a felony punishable by a maximum term of imprisonment of 15 years or more or for life, the person is guilty of a felony punishable by imprisonment for not more than 20 years or a fine of not more than $20,000.00, or both.

(3) The court may order that a term of imprisonment imposed under this section be served consecutively to any term of imprisonment imposed for conviction of the underlying offense.

(4) This section does not prohibit a person from being charged with, convicted of, or punished for any other violation of law committed by that person while violating or attempting to violate this section, including the underlying offense.

(5) This section applies regardless of whether the person is convicted of committing, attempting to commit, conspiring to commit, or soliciting another person to commit the underlying offense.

(6) A violation or attempted violation of this section occurs if the communication originates in this state, is intended to terminate in this state, or is intended to terminate with a person who is in this state.

(7) A violation or attempted violation of this section may be prosecuted in any jurisdiction in which the communication originated or terminated.

(8) The court may order a person convicted of violating this section to reimburse this state or a local unit of government of this state for expenses incurred in relation to the violation in the same manner that expenses may be ordered to be reimbursed under section 1f of chapter IX of the code of criminal procedure, 1927 PA 175, MCL 769.1f.

(9) As used in this section:

(a) "Computer" means any connected, directly interoperable or interactive device, equipment, or facility that uses a computer program or other instructions to perform specific operations including logical, arithmetic, or memory functions with or on computer data or a computer program and that can store, retrieve, alter, or communicate the results of the operations to a person, computer program, computer, computer system, or computer network.

(b) "Computer network" means the interconnection of hardwire or wireless communication lines with a computer through remote terminals, or a complex consisting of 2 or more interconnected computers.

(c) "Computer program" means a series of internal or external instructions communicated in a form acceptable to a

(d) "Computer system" means a set of related, connected or unconnected, computer equipment, devices, software, or hardware.

(e) "Device" includes, but is not limited to, an electronic, magnetic, electrochemical, biochemical, hydraulic, optical, or organic object that performs input, output, or storage functions by the manipulation of electronic, magnetic, or other impulses.

(f) "Internet" means that term as defined in section 230 of title II of the communications act of 1934, chapter 652, 110 Stat. 137, 47 U.S.C. 230.

(g) "Minor" means an individual who is less than 18 years of age.

Access to Computer with Attempt to Defraud—MCL 752.794

A person shall not intentionally access or cause access to be made to a computer program, computer, computer system, or computer network to devise or execute a scheme or artifice with the intent to defraud or to obtain money, property, or a service by a false or fraudulent pretense, representation, or promise.

Prohibited Access to Computer—MCL 752.795

A person shall not intentionally and without authorization or by exceeding valid authorization do any of the following:

（a）*Access or cause access to be made to a computer program, computer, computer system, or computer network to acquire, alter, damage, delete, or destroy property or otherwise use the service of a computer program, computer, computer system, or computer network.*

（b）*Insert or attach or knowingly create the opportunity for an unknowing and unwanted insertion or attachment of a set of instructions or a computer program into a computer program, computer, computer system, or computer network, that is intended to acquire, alter, damage, delete, disrupt, or destroy property or otherwise use the services of a computer program, computer, computer system, or computer network. This subdivision does not prohibit conduct protected under section 5 of article I of the state constitution of 1963 or under the first amendment of the constitution of the United States.*

Committing Crime Using Computer—MCL 752.796

（1）*A person shall not use a computer program, computer, computer system, or computer network to commit, attempt to commit, conspire to commit, or solicit another person to commit a crime.*

（2）*This section does not prohibit a person from being charged with, convicted of, or punished for any other violation of law committed by that person while violating or attempting to violate this section, including the underlying offense.*

（3）*This section applies regardless of whether the person is convicted of committing, attempting to commit, conspiring to commit, or soliciting another person to commit the underlying offense.*

Penalties; Prior Convictions; Presumption; Reimbursement Order; Definition—MCL 752.797

（1）*A person who violates section 4 is guilty of a crime as follows:*

（a）*If the violation involves an aggregate amount of less than $200.00, the person is guilty of a misdemeanor punishable by imprisonment for not more than 93 days or a fine of not more than $500.00 or 3 times the aggregate amount, whichever is greater, or both imprisonment and a fine.*

（b）*If any of the following apply, the person is guilty of a misdemeanor punishable by imprisonment for not more than 1 year or a fine of not more than $2,000.00 or 3 times the aggregate amount, whichever is greater, or both imprisonment and a fine:*

（i）*The violation involves an aggregate amount of $200.00 or more but less than $1,000.00.*

（ii）*The person violates this act and has a prior conviction.*

（c）*If any of the following apply, the person is guilty of a felony punishable by imprisonment for not more than 5 years or a fine of not more than $10,000.00 or 3 times the aggregate amount, whichever is greater, or both imprisonment and a fine:*

（i）*The violation involves an aggregate amount of $1,000.00 or more but less than $20,000.00.*

（ii）*The person has 2 prior convictions.*

（d）*If any of the following apply, the person is guilty of a felony punishable by imprisonment for not more than 10 years or a fine of not more than 3 times the aggregate amount, or both imprisonment and a fine:*

（i）*The violation involves an aggregate amount of $20,000.00 or more.*

（ii）*The person has 3 or more prior convictions.*

（2）*A person who violates section 5 is guilty of a crime as follows:*

（a）*Except as provided in subdivision (b), the person is guilty of a felony punishable by imprisonment for not more than 5 years or a fine of not more than $10,000.00, or both.*

（b）*If the person has a prior conviction, the person is guilty of a felony punishable by imprisonment for not more than 10 years or a fine of not more than $50,000.00, or both.*

（3）*A person who violates section 6 is guilty of a crime as follows:*

（a）*If the underlying crime is a misdemeanor or a felony with a maximum term of imprisonment of 1 year or less, the person is guilty of a misdemeanor punishable by imprisonment for not more than 1 year or a fine of not more than $5,000.00, or both.*

(b) If the underlying crime is a misdemeanor or a felony with a maximum term of imprisonment of more than 1 year but less than 2 years, the person is guilty of a felony punishable by imprisonment for not more than 2 years or a fine of not more than $5,000.00, or both.

(c) If the underlying crime is a misdemeanor or a felony with a maximum term of imprisonment of 2 years or more but less than 4 years, the person is guilty of a felony punishable by imprisonment for not more than 4 years or a fine of not more than $5,000.00, or both.

(d) If the underlying crime is a felony with a maximum term of imprisonment of 4 years or more but less than 10 years, the person is guilty of a felony punishable by imprisonment for not more than 7 years or a fine of not more than $5,000.00, or both.

(e) If the underlying crime is a felony punishable by a maximum term of imprisonment of 10 years or more but less than 20 years, the person is guilty of a felony punishable by imprisonment for not more than 10 years or a fine of not more than $10,000.00, or both.

(f) If the underlying crime is a felony punishable by a maximum term of imprisonment of 20 years or more or for life, the person is guilty of a felony punishable by imprisonment for not more than 20 years or a fine of not more than $20,000.00, or both.

(4) The court may order that a term of imprisonment imposed under subsection (3) be served consecutively to any term of imprisonment imposed for conviction of the underlying offense.

(5) If the prosecuting attorney intends to seek an enhanced sentence under section 4 or section 5 based upon the defendant having a prior conviction, the prosecuting attorney shall include on the complaint and information a statement listing that prior conviction. The existence of the defendant's prior conviction shall be determined by the court, without a jury, at sentencing. The existence of a prior conviction may be established by any evidence relevant for that purpose, including, but not limited to, 1 or more of the following:

(a) A copy of the judgment of conviction.

(b) A transcript of a prior trial, plea-taking, or sentencing.

(c) Information contained in a presentence report.

(d) The defendant's statement.

(6) It is a rebuttable presumption in a prosecution for a violation of section 5 that the person did not have authorization from the owner, system operator, or other person who has authority from the owner or system operator to grant permission to access the computer program, computer, computer system, or computer network or has exceeded authorization unless 1 or more of the following circumstances existed at the time of access:

(a) Written or oral permission was granted by the owner, system operator, or other person who has authority from the owner or system operator to grant permission of the accessed computer program, computer, computer system, or computer network.

(b) The accessed computer program, computer, computer system, or computer network had a pre-programmed access procedure that would display a bulletin, command, or other message before access was achieved that a reasonable person would believe identified the computer program, computer, computer system, or computer network as within the public domain.

(c) Access was achieved without the use of a set of instructions, code, or computer program that bypasses, defrauds, or otherwise circumvents the pre-programmed access procedure for the computer program, computer, computer system, or computer network.

(7) The court may order a person convicted of violating this act to reimburse this state or a local unit of government of this state for expenses incurred in relation to the violation in the same manner that expenses may be ordered to be reimbursed under section 1f of chapter IX of the code of criminal procedure, 1927 PA 175, MCL 769.1f.

(8) As used in this section, "prior conviction" means a violation or attempted violation of section 145d of the Michigan penal code, 1931 PA 328, MCL 750.145d, or this act or a substantially similar law of the United States, another state, or a political subdivision of another state.

> Defendant's receipt of child sexually abusive material through the computer indicates that he communicated his desire to receive such material through the computer. *People v. Tombs*, 260 Mich. App. 201 (2003).

ADULTERATED FOOD— MCL 750.397.a (felony)

A person who places pins, needles, razor blades, glass, or other harmful objects in any food, or a person who places a harmful substance in any food, with intent to harm the consumer of the food, or who knowingly furnishes any food containing a harmful object or substance to another person, is guilty of a felony and shall be imprisoned for not more than 10 years, or fined not more than $10,000.00, or both.

Elements

1. The defendant intended to cause harm and
2. Knowingly placed pins, needles, razor blades, glass or any other harmful substance in food,

OR

1. The defendant intended to cause harm and,
2. Knowingly furnished food containing harmful substances to another.

> Stale urine can be a harmful substance under MCL 750.397a because expert testimony established that it can transmit disease through viruses or bacteria. *People v. Guthrie*, 262 Mich. App. 416 (2004).

POISONING—MCL 750.436 (felony)

A person shall not do either of the following:

(a) *Willfully mingle a poison or harmful substance with a food, drink, nonprescription medicine, or pharmaceutical product, or willfully place a poison or harmful substance in a spring, well, reservoir, or public water supply, knowing or having reason to know that the food, drink, nonprescription medicine, pharmaceutical product, or water may be ingested or used by a person to his or her injury.*

(b) *Maliciously inform another person that a poison or harmful substance has been or will be placed in a food, drink, nonprescription medicine, pharmaceutical product, spring, well, reservoir, or public water supply, knowing that the information is false and that it is likely that the information will be disseminated to the public.*

Elements

1. Willfully placed poison or a harmful substance into food, medicine, or a water supply,
2. Knowing or having reason to know that someone will ingest that item.

OR

1. Maliciously informed another person,
2. That poison or a harmful substance had been placed into food, medicine, or a water supply,
3. Knowing that this information is false, and
4. Knowing that this information is likely to be disseminated to the public.

> Defendants were convicted under this statute for placing a date rape drug into the victim's drink at a party. *People v. Holtschlag*, 471 Mich. 1 (2004).

> Defendant was convicted for making a false police report when he falsely told police that he had placed poison in his own milk to "get" the person who had been stealing his milk. *People v. Lay*, 336 Mich. 77 (1953).

> Defendant was convicted when she repeatedly placed ant poison in the victims' coffee. *People v. Belknap*, 146 Mich. App. 239 (1985).

DESTRUCTION OF PROPERTY

ARSON

Definition

Arson is defined as willfully or maliciously, without just cause or excuse, starting a fire or doing anything that could result in the starting of a fire. The property does not have to be completely burned, but there must be charring. Mere blackening by smoke is not enough. A person can be charged with arson for burning his or her own property.

CJI2d 31.2

> The careless throwing of matches on the floor is not sufficient for arson. *People v. McCarty,* 303 Mich. 629 (1942).
>
> Arson is not specific-intent crime under Michigan common law. *People v. Nowack,* 462 Mich. 392 (2000).
>
> The only intent required is that the suspect "intended to burn the dwelling or contents or intentionally committed an act that created a very high risk of burning the dwelling or contents and that, while committing the act, the defendant knew of that risk and disregarded it." CJI2d 31.2(4).

Dwelling House—MCL 750.72 (felony)

Any person who wilfully or maliciously burns any dwelling house, either occupied or unoccupied, or the contents thereof, whether owned by himself or another, or any building within the curtilage of such dwelling house, or the contents thereof, shall be guilty of a felony, punishable by imprisonment in the state prison not more than 20 years.

Elements

1. The suspect burned a building or its contents,
2. The building was a dwelling house at the time of the burning, and
3. The suspect intended the burning or intentionally acted in a manner that the suspect knew would create a high risk of a burning.

CJI2d 31.2.

A **dwelling house** is an occupied or unoccupied building that is actually lived in or could reasonably have been lived in at the time of the fire. Contents within the dwelling and any other buildings within the curtilage are included.

> A dilapidated abandoned building that had no utilities or running water was not a dwelling house under the arson statute where there was

no evidence that it was going to be restored in the near future. *People v. Reeves*, 448 Mich. 1 (1995).

A barn situated 15 yards from a dwelling house, with a public highway passing between them and a yard between the barn and the highway is not within the curtilage. *Carkendall v. People*, 36 Mich. 309 (1877).

A barn 80 feet from a dwelling house and in the back yard is within the curtilage. *People v. Taylor*, 2 Mich. 250 (1851).

Other Real Property—MCL 750.73 (felony)

Any person who wilfully or maliciously burns any building or other real property, or the contents thereof, other than those specified in the next preceding section of this chapter, the property of himself or another, shall be guilty of a felony, punishable by imprisonment in the state prison for not more than 10 years.

Elements

1. The suspect burned a building or its contents,
2. The suspect intended the burning or intentionally acted in a manner that the suspect knew would create a high risk of a burning, and
3. The building was not a dwelling house.

    CJI2d 31.3.

The suspect willfully or maliciously burned other real property. This includes buildings, other than a dwelling house, and contents. Examples include a bar, a barn (*People v. Jackson*, 211 Mich. App. 414 (1995)), gas station, store, etc.

A school construction site is real property under this statute. *People v. Smock*, 399 Mich. 282 (1975).

Personal Property—MCL 750.74

Elements

1. The suspect burned property,
2. The property was not a building or attached to a building,
3. The suspect intended the burning or intentionally acted in a manner that the suspect knew would create a high risk of a burning.

    CJI2d 31.4.

Personal property includes property that is not a building, in a building, or permanently attached to a building. This includes objects that are movable, such as cars, personal belongings, furniture, and tools.

Penalties:

Less than $200	93 day misdemeanor
$200 to less than $1,000 or less than $200, if previously convicted	1 year misdemeanor
$1,000 to less than $20,000 or $200 to less than $1,000, if previously convicted	5 year felony
Over $20,000 or $1,000 to less than $20,000, if previously convicted twice	10 year felony

Fair Market Value Test

The test for the value of property is the reasonable and fair market value of the property at the time and in the area when the crime was committed.

Fair market value is defined as the price the property would have sold for in the open market at that time and in that place if the following things were true: the owner wanted to sell but didn't have to, the buyer wanted to buy but didn't have to, the owner had a reasonable time to find a buyer, and the buyer knew what the property was worth and what it could be used for.

CJI2d 22.01

Insured Property—MCL 750.75 (felony)

Any person who shall willfully burn any building or personal property which shall be at the time insured against loss or damage by fire with intent to injure and defraud the insurer, whether such person be the owner of the property or not, shall be guilty of a felony, punishable by imprisonment in the state prison not more than 10 years.

Elements

1. The suspect burned property,
2. The property was insured against fire at the time of the burning,
3. The suspect knew that the property was insured when he or she burned it,
4. The suspect intentionally set the fire knowing that it would cause injury to another person or damage to property and the suspect did not have just cause or excuse,
5. The suspect intended to defraud the insurer when he or she burned the property.

    CJI2d 31.5.

This includes both buildings and personal property that are insured against loss due to fire. The suspect must have the intent to defraud or cheat the insurer at the time of the burning. There must be a valid insurance policy, but it is not necessary to prove that the defendant ever dealt with the insurance company.

> Intent to defraud may exist even if the defendant did not profit from the insurance claim and even if the defendant accepted an insurance payment that did not cover the entire loss. *People v. Rabin,* 317 Mich. 654 (1947).
>
> Convictions for burning a dwelling house (MCL 750.72) and burning insured property (MCL 750.75) during the course of the same fire does not violate the Double Jeopardy Clause. *People v. Ayers,* 213 Mich. App. 708 (1995).

Preparation to Burn—MCL 750.77

(1) A person who uses, arranges, places, devises, or distributes an inflammable, combustible, or explosive material, liquid, or substance or any device in or near a building or property described in section 72, 73, 74, or 75 with intent to willfully and maliciously set fire to or burn the building or property or who aids, counsels, induces, persuades, or procures another to do so is guilty of a crime as follows:

   (a) If the property intended to be burned is personal or real property, or both, with a combined value less than $200.00, the person is guilty of a misdemeanor punishable by imprisonment for not more than 93 days or a fine of not more than $500.00 or 3 times the combined value of the property intended to be burned, whichever is greater, or both imprisonment and a fine.

   (b) If any of the following apply, the person is guilty of a misdemeanor punishable by imprisonment for not more than 1 year or a fine of not more than $2,000.00 or 3 times the combined value of the property intended to be burned, whichever is greater, or both imprisonment and a fine:

   (i) The property intended to be burned is personal or real property, or both, with a combined value of $200.00 or more but less than $1,000.00.

   (ii) The person violates subdivision (a) and has 1 or more prior convictions for committing or attempting to commit an offense under this section or a local ordinance substantially corresponding to this section.

   (c) If any of the following apply, the person is guilty of a felony punishable by imprisonment for not more than 5 years or a fine of not more than $10,000.00 or 3 times the combined value of the property intended to be burned, whichever is greater, or both imprisonment and a fine:

   (i) The property intended to be burned is personal or real property, or both, with a combined value of $1,000.00 or more but less than $20,000.00.

   (ii) The person violates subdivision (b)(i) and has 1 or more prior convictions for violating or attempting to violate this section. For purposes of this subparagraph, however, a prior conviction does not include a conviction for a violation or attempted violation of subdivision (a) or (b)(ii).

   (d) If any of the following apply, the person is guilty of a felony punishable by imprisonment for not more than 10 years or a fine of not more than $15,000.00 or 3 times the combined value of the property intended to be burned, whichever is greater, or both imprisonment and a fine:

   (i) The property is personal or real property, or both, with a combined value of $20,000.00 or more.

   (ii) The person violates subdivision (c)(i) and has 2 or more prior convictions for committing or attempting to commit an offense under this section. For purposes of this subparagraph, however, a prior conviction does not include a conviction for committing or attempting to commit an offense for a violation or attempted violation of subdivision (a) or (b)(ii).

(2) The combined value of property intended to be burned in separate incidents pursuant to a scheme or course of conduct within any 12-month period may be aggregated to determine the total value of property intended to be burned.

Elements

1. The suspect placed a flammable or explosive device near the property,
2. The suspect intended to start a fire knowing that it would cause injury to a person or damage to property.
3. The suspect did not have just cause or excuse.

CJI2d 31.6.

CHAPTER 10 Destruction of Property

The suspect willfully and maliciously, without just cause or excuse, placed in or around property, a flammable or explosive device.

> This statute applies whether the suspect acted alone or persuaded someone else to act: a defendant was guilty under this section where he helped to make Molotov cocktails even though he was not present at the actual burning and the buildings that were burned were not the ones he thought were going to be burned. *People v. Davis*, 24 Mich. App 304 (1970).
>
> The prosecution must show evidence of the burned property's value in order to support a conviction under this section of law. *People v. Hill*, 257 Mich. App. 126 (2003).

Penalties

- Dwelling house and other real property (essentially always a felony due to the value of the real property).
- Personal property (either a misdemeanor or a felony, depending on the value of the property).

Less than $200	93 day misdemeanor
$200 to less than $1,000 or less than $200, if previously convicted	1 year misdemeanor
$1,000 to less than $20,000 or $200 to less than $1,000, if previously convicted	5 year felony
Over $20,000 or $1,000 to less than $20,000, if previously convicted twice	10 year felony

Willfully or Negligently Setting Fire to Woods, Prairies, or Grounds—MCL 750.78 (felony)

Any person who shall willfully or negligently set fire to any woods, prairies or grounds, not his property, or shall willfully permit any fire to pass from his own woods, prairies or grounds, to the injury or destruction of the property of any other person, shall be guilty of a felony.

This section applies to a person who does one of the following:

- Willfully or negligently sets fire to woods, prairies or grounds, or
- Willfully permits any fire to pass from his or her property to the property of another.

Disobeying a Firefighter or Persons Working during a Riot—MCL 750.241

(1) *Any person who, while in the vicinity of any fire, willfully disobeys any reasonable order or rule of the officer commanding any fire department at the fire, when the order or rule is given by the commanding officer or a firefighter there present, is guilty of a misdemeanor.*

(2) *During a riot or other civil disturbance, any person who knowingly and willfully hinders, obstructs, endangers, or interferes with any person who is engaged in the operation, installation, repair, or maintenance of any essential public service facility, including a facility for the transmission of electricity, gas, telephone messages, or water, is guilty of a felony.*

Elements

1. The suspect was in the vicinity of any fire,
2. And willfully disobeyed,
3. Any reasonable order or rule of the commanding officer of the fire department,
4. When the rule or order is given by the commanding officer or a firefighter.

ALSO it is a felony to:

1. Knowingly and willingly,
2. Hinder, obstruct, endanger, or interfere,
3. With a person operating, installing, or repairing any essential public service facility,
4. During a riot or other civil disturbance.

> The firefighter must be carrying out lawful duties to convict a defendant for disobeying a lawful order. Merely entering onto the defendant's property to extinguish a fire does not meet this requirement unless there is evidence that the fire was dangerous or that the firefighter has a statutory right to enter onto the property. *People v. Simpson*, 207 Mich. App. 560 (1994). However, this does not preclude an assault charge against the suspect if he or she assaults the firefighter.

MALICIOUS DESTRUCTION OF PROPERTY

Fair Market Value

Fair market value includes the reasonable and fair market value of repairing the damage or replacing the damaged property. The value will be considered at the time and in the place where the damage occurred.

CJI2d 32.1

> "Fair Market Value" is not necessarily the same as the actual cost incurred by the victim. For example, when the victim replaced a broken car window for $45 but several glass installers testified that it would cost $163 to $241 to replace the window, the court held that there was sufficient evidence to find that the damage was over $100. *People v. Hamblin*, 224 Mich. App. 87 (1997).

MDOP of Personal Property—MCL 750.377a

(1) A person who willfully and maliciously destroys or injures the personal property of another person is guilty of a crime as follows:

  (a) If any of the following apply, the person is guilty of a felony punishable by imprisonment for not more than 10 years or a fine of not more than $15,000.00 or 3 times the amount of the destruction or injury, whichever is greater, or both imprisonment and a fine:

   (i) The amount of the destruction or injury is $20,000.00 or more.
   (ii) The person violates subdivision (b)(i) and has 2 or more prior convictions for committing or attempting to commit an offense under this section. For purposes of this subparagraph, however, a prior conviction does not include a conviction for a violation or attempted violation of subdivision (c)(ii) or (d).

  (b) If any of the following apply, the person is guilty of a felony punishable by imprisonment for not more than 5 years or a fine of not more than $10,000.00 or 3 times the amount of the destruction or injury, whichever is greater, or both imprisonment and a fine:

   (i) The amount of the destruction or injury is $1,000.00 or more but less than $20,000.00.
   (ii) The person violates subdivision (c)(i) and has 1 or more prior convictions for committing or attempting to commit an offense under this section. For purposes of this subparagraph, however, a prior conviction does not include a conviction for a violation or attempted violation of subdivision (c)(ii) or (d).

  (c) If any of the following apply, the person is guilty of a misdemeanor punishable by imprisonment for not more than 1 year or a fine of not more than $2,000.00 or 3 times the amount of the destruction or injury, whichever is greater, or both imprisonment and a fine:

   (i) The amount of the destruction or injury is $200.00 or more but less than $1,000.00.
   (ii) The person violates subdivision (d) and has 1 or more prior convictions for committing or attempting to commit an offense under this section or a local ordinance substantially corresponding to this section.

  (d) If the amount of the destruction or injury is less than $200.00, the person is guilty of a misdemeanor punishable by imprisonment for not more than 93 days or a fine of not more than $500.00 or 3 times the amount of the destruction or injury, whichever is greater, or both imprisonment and a fine.

(2) The amounts of destruction or injury in separate incidents pursuant to a scheme or course of conduct within any 12-month period may be aggregated in determining the total amount of the destruction or injury.

Elements

1. The property belonged to someone other than the suspect,
2. The suspect destroyed or damaged the property,
3. The suspect did not have just cause or excuse, and
4. The suspect intended to cause the damage.

CJI2d 32.2.

This section applies to movable personal property and real estate.

The total amount can be aggregated over a 12-month eriod where there are separate incidents that are part of common scheme or plan. MCL 750.377(a)(2).

> MDOP is a specific intent crime. In a case where the defendant was intoxicated, the court remanded the case to the trial court because the trial court did not instruct the jury that voluntary intoxication could negate specific intent where the suspect cause $350 damage to the victim's vehicle. *People v. Ewing*, 127 Mich. App 582 (1983).

Penalties:

| Less than $200 | 93 day misdemeanor |
| $200 to less than $1,000 or less than $200, if previously convicted | 1 year misdemeanor |

$1,000 to less than $20,000 or $200 to less than $1,000, if previously convicted	5 year felony
Over $20,000 or $1,000 to less than $20,000, if previously convicted twice	10 year felony

MDOP to Real Property—MCL 750.380

The property must belong to someone other than the suspect, and this section includes real property such as houses, barns, stores, and other buildings. Otherwise, this statute is essentially the same as MDOP to personal property. With separate incidents that are part of common scheme or plan, the total amount can be aggregated over 12-month period for total.

Penalties:

Less than $200	93 day misdemeanor
$200 to less than $1,000 or less than $200, if previously convicted	1 year misdemeanor
$1,000 to less than $20,000 or $200 to less than $1,000, if previously convicted	5 year felony
Over $20,000 or $1,000 to less than $20,000, if previously convicted twice	10 year felony

MDOP to Police or Fire Department Property—MCL 750.377b (felony)

Any person who shall willfully and maliciously destroy or injure the personal property of any fire or police department, including the Michigan state police, shall be guilty of a felony.

Property must be the personal property of a police or fire department. The suspect willfully and maliciously, without just cause or excuse, destroyed or damaged the property.

Defendant was improperly convicted of MDOP to police property where he broke out the windows of a jail. This constitutes real property and MCL 750.377b applies to personal property. *People v. Fox,* 232 Mich. App. 541 (1998).

Perhaps the most common example of this statute, MDOP to the window of a police car, has been upheld even where there was no evidence offered as to which specific police car was damaged. *People v. Richardson,* 118 Mich. App. 492 (1982).

MDOP to School Bus—MCL 750.377c (felony)

(1) *If a person intentionally damages, destroys, or alters a school bus without the permission of the entity that owns that school bus and that damage, destruction, or alteration creates a health or safety hazard to any individual occupying that school bus or who may occupy that school bus, the person is guilty of a felony punishable by imprisonment for not more than 5 years, or a fine of not more than $5,000.00, or both.*

(2) *As used in this section, "school bus" means that term as defined in section 57 of the Michigan vehicle code, Act No. 300 of the Public Acts of 1949, being section 257.57 of the Michigan Compiled Laws. School bus includes a school transportation vehicle as that term is defined in section 57c of Act No. 300 of the Public Acts of 1949, being section 257.57c of the Michigan Compiled Laws, if that vehicle is clearly marked as a school transportation vehicle.*

The suspect damaged, destroyed, or altered a school bus without permission.

NOTE: The damage must create a health or safety hazard to an occupant or person who may have occupied the bus.

BURGLARY

BREAKING AND ENTERING
B and E—MCL 750.110 (felony)

A person who breaks and enters, with intent to commit a felony or a larceny therein, a tent, hotel, office, store, shop, warehouse, barn, granary, factory or other building, structure, boat, ship, shipping container, or railroad car is guilty of a felony, punishable by imprisonment for not more than 10 years.

Elements

1. The suspect broke into a building,
2. The suspect entered the building,
3. When the suspect broke and entered, he or she intended to commit a felony or a larceny.

   CJI2d 25.1.

Breaking: Some force must have been used but there is no requirement that anything was actually broken. Any amount of force is sufficient, including opening a door that is already partially open. *People v. Finney*, 113 Mich. App. 638 (1982). However, entering through a door or window that is already open does not constitute a sufficient amount of force.

CJI2d 25.1.

Entering: Any part of the suspect's body entering into the building is sufficient. *People v. Gillman*, 66 Mich. App. 419 (1976).

Intent: At the time, the suspect had the intent to commit a felony or larceny therein.

The mere act of committing the "breaking" and the "entering" does not create an assumption that the suspect intended to commit a larceny. *People v. Noel*, 123 Mich. App. 478 (1983).

Intent may be inferred by the suspect's actions before and during the breaking and entering. *People v. Uhl*, 169 Mich. App. 217 (1988).

Entry Without Owner's Permission (B and E / Unlawful Entry)—MCL 750.115 (90-day misdemeanor)

Any person who shall break and enter, or shall enter without breaking, any dwelling, house, tent, hotel, office, store, shop, warehouse, barn, granary, factory or other building, boat, ship, shipping container, railroad car or structure used or kept for public or private use, or any private apartment therein, or any cottage, clubhouse, boat house, hunting or fishing lodge, garage or the outbuildings belonging thereto, ice shanty with a value of $100.00 or more, or any other structure, whether occupied or unoccupied, *without first obtaining permission to enter from the owner or occupant, agent, or person having immediate control thereof, shall be guilty of a misdemeanor: Provided, That this section shall not apply to entering without breaking, any place which at the time of such entry was open to the public, unless such entry has been expressly denied.*

This section shall not apply in cases where the breaking and entering or entering without breaking were committed by a peace officer or someone under his direction in the lawful performance of his duties as such peace officer.

Elements

1. The suspect entered a building,
2. The suspect did not have the owner's permission.

CJI2d 25.4.

This is essentially breaking and entering without the "intent" element required by MCL 750.110. It includes unauthorized entries where the suspect intends to commit a misdemeanor but not a felony or a larceny.

HOME INVASION—MCL 750.110a

Definitions

Dwelling: A structure or shelter used permanently or temporarily as a place of abode, including a structure attached to it.

Dangerous weapons include any of the following:

1. Loaded or unloaded firearm, whether operable or not.
2. A knife, stabbing instrument, brass knuckles, **blackjack,** club, or other object specifically designed or customarily carried as a weapon.
3. An object that is likely to cause death or bodily injury when used and carried as a weapon.
4. Any object that is used or fashioned in such a manner as to lead one to believe it is one of the above.

First Degree (felony)

The suspect broke and entered into a dwelling, or entered without permission and:

- At the time, he or she intended to commit a felony, larceny, or assault, or
- While entering, present in, or exiting, committed a felony, larceny, or misdemeanor assault.

And when the suspect entered, was present in or leaving, one of the following occurred:

- The suspect was armed with a dangerous weapon, or
- A person was lawfully in the dwelling at the time.

> Fourth-degree CSC is an assault for the purposes of home invasion. *People v. Musser*, 259 Mich. App. 215 (2003).

Second Degree (felony)

The suspect broke and entered into a dwelling, or entered a dwelling without permission and:

- At the time, he or she intended to commit a felony, larceny, or assault, or
- He or she committed a felony, larceny or assault once inside.

Third Degree (felony)

The suspect broke and entered a dwelling or entered a dwelling without permission and:

- At the time, he or she intended to commit a misdemeanor, or
- He or she committed a misdemeanor once inside.
- He or she at any time while entering, present in, or exiting violated a court order.

ENTERING WITHOUT BREAKING—MCL 750.111 (felony)

Any person who, without breaking, enters any dwelling, house, tent, hotel, office, store, shop, warehouse, barn, granary, factory or other building, boat, ship, shipping container, railroad car or structure used or kept for public or private use, or any private apartment therein, with intent to commit a felony or any larceny therein, is guilty of a felony punishable by imprisonment for not more than 5 years or a fine of not more than $2,500.00.

This statute is essentially "breaking and entering" without the "breaking."

Elements

1. Entering a building,
2. Without breaking,
3. With the intent to commit a felony or a larceny.

CJI2d 25.3

OTHER STATUTES OF INTEREST

Possession of Burglary Tools—MCL 750.116 (felony)

Possession of burglar's tools—Any person who shall knowingly have in his possession any nitroglycerine, or other explosive, thermite, engine, machine, tool or implement, device, chemical or substance, adapted and designed for cutting or burning through, forcing or breaking open any building, room, vault, safe or other depository, in order to steal therefrom any money or other property, knowing the same to be adapted and designed for the purpose aforesaid, with intent to use or employ the same for the purpose aforesaid, shall be guilty of a felony, punishable by imprisonment in the state prison not more than 10 years.

Burglary Tools

1. Include any instruments or materials that are adapted and designed for breaking and entering.
2. "Adapted and designed" means that not only is the tool capable of being used to break and enter but it must also be designed or expressly planned for that purpose. CJI2d 25.5.

Elements

1. The instruments are burglary tools,
2. The suspect knowingly possessed them, and
3. When the suspect possessed the tools he intended to use them for a breaking and entering.

People v. Dorrington, 221 Mich. 571 (1923).

Examples of burglary tools include crowbars *People v. Gross*, 118 Mich. App. 161, (1982), and a chisel and flashlight *People v. Ross*, 39 Mich. App. 697 (1972).

A fiberglass antenna used in conjunction with a piece of metal that were used in an attempt to break into a car were found to be burglary tools. *People v. Wilson*, 180 Mich. App. 12 (1989).

Burglary Using Explosives—MCL 750.112 (felony)

Any person who enters any building, and for the purpose of committing any crime therein, uses or attempts to use nitroglycerine, dynamite, gunpowder or any other high explosive, shall be guilty of a felony, punishable by imprisonment in the state prison not less than 15 years nor more than 30 years.

Bank, Safe and Vault Robbery—MCL 750.531 (felony)

Bank, safe and vault robbery—Any person who, with intent to commit the crime of larceny, or any felony, shall confine, maim, injure or wound, or attempt, or threaten to confine, kill, maim, injure or wound, or shall put in fear any person for the purpose of stealing from any building, bank, safe or other depository of money, bond or other valuables, or shall by intimidation, fear or threats compel, or attempt to compel any person to disclose or surrender the means of opening any building, bank, safe, vault or other depository of money, bonds, or other valuables, or shall attempt to break, burn, blow up or otherwise injure or destroy any safe, vault or other depository of money, bonds or other valuables in any building or place, shall, whether he succeeds or fails in the perpetration of such larceny or felony, be guilty of a felony, punishable by imprisonment in the state prison for life or any term of years.

The defendant was not denied due process when the prosecutor chose to charge him with safe robbery (MCL 750.531, which is a potential life felony) rather than Burglary Using Explosives (MCL 750.112). *People v. Ferguson*, 60 Mich. App. 302 (1975).

Breaking and Entering or Opening a Coin or Depository Box—MCL 750.113 (6 month misdemeanor)

Any person who maliciously and willfully, by and with the aid and use of any key, instrument, device or explosive, blows or attempts to blow, or forces or attempts to force an entrance into any coin box, depository box or other receptacle established and maintained for the convenience of the public, or of any person or persons, in making payment for any article of merchandise or service, wherein is contained any money or thing of value, or extracts or obtains, or attempts to extract or obtain, therefrom any such money or thing of value so deposited or contained therein, shall be guilty of a misdemeanor, punishable by imprisonment in the county jail not more than 6 months or by a fine of not more than 250 dollars.

Breaking and Entering a Coin Operated Device—MCL 752.811 (felony)

A person shall be guilty of a felony punishable upon conviction by confinement in the state prison for a period not to exceed 3 years or by a fine of not more than $1,000.00 or both if he does either of the following:

(a) Enters or forces an entrance, alters or inserts any part of an instrument into any parking meter, vending machine dispensing goods or services, money changer or any other device designed to receive currency or coins with the intent to steal.
(b) Knowingly possesses a key or device, or a drawing, print or mold thereof, adapted and designed to open or break into any such machine with intent to steal money or other contents from it.

> Coin deposit boxes on a bus are not included under this statute. That type of coin box falls under the above-listed misdemeanor (MCL 750.113). *People v. Craig,* 131 Mich. App. 42 (1982).

THEFT CRIMES

AUTO THEFT

Definition of Motor Vehicle—MCL 750.412

The term "motor vehicle" as used in this chapter shall include all vehicles impelled on the public highways of this state by mechanical power, except traction engines, road rollers and such vehicles as run only upon rails or tracks.

> This includes motorcycles. *People v. Shipp*, 68 Mich. App. 452 (1976).

Unlawfully Driving Away an Automobile—MCL 750.413 (felony)

Any person who shall, willfully and without authority, take possession of and drive or take away, and any person who shall assist in or be a party to such taking possession, driving or taking away of any motor vehicle, belonging to another, shall be guilty of a felony, punishable by imprisonment in the state prison for not more than 5 years.

Elements

1. The vehicle belonged to someone else,
2. The suspect took possession of the vehicle and drove or took it away,
3. The suspect did not have the owner's permission,
4. The suspect intended to take the vehicle (it does not matter whether the suspect intended to keep the vehicle). CJI2d 24.1.

Unauthorized Use of an Automobile—MCL 750.414 (2 year misdemeanor)

Any person who takes or uses without authority any motor vehicle without intent to steal the same, or who is a party to such unauthorized taking or using, is guilty of a misdemeanor punishable by imprisonment for not more than 2 years or a fine of not more than $1,500.00. However, in case of a first offense, the court may reduce the punishment to imprisonment for not more than 3 months or a fine of not more than $ 500.00. However, this section does not apply to any person or persons employed by the owner of said motor vehicle or anyone else, who, by the nature of his or her employment, has the charge of or the authority to drive said motor vehicle if said motor vehicle is driven or used without the owner's knowledge or consent.

Elements

1. The suspect obtained lawful possession of a motor vehicle from its owner,
2. The suspect used the motor vehicle beyond the granted authority,
3. The suspect did so intentionally, and
4. The suspect knew he or she did not have authority to do so.

85

> This includes cases where the suspect had limited authority to possess the vehicle and knowingly acted beyond the scope of that authority. *People v. Hayward*, 127 Mich. App. 50 (1983).

Difference between UDAA and Unauthorized Use

For UDAA, the suspect must have physically taken possession of the vehicle without authority. For unauthorized use, the suspect had permission to use the vehicle but then used it in a way he or she knew was unauthorized. CJI2d 24.4.

> An automobile was stored at the defendant's garage. His possession of the car was lawful so his driving without authority from the owner was not UDAA, but falls under Unauthorized Use of an Automobile. *People v. Smith*, 213 Mich. 351 (1921).

Alteration of VINs—MCL 750.415

(1) A person who, without the intent to mislead another as to the identity of the vehicle, conceals or misrepresents the identity of a motor vehicle or of a mechanical device by removing or defacing the manufacturer's serial number or the engine or motor number on the motor vehicle, or by replacing a part of the motor vehicle or mechanical device bearing the serial number or engine or motor number of the vehicle with a new part upon which the proper serial number or engine or motor number has not been stamped, is guilty of a misdemeanor.

(2) A person who, with the intent to mislead another as to the identity of a vehicle, conceals or misrepresents the identity of a motor vehicle or of a mechanical device by removing or defacing the manufacturer's serial number or the engine or motor number on the motor vehicle, or by replacing a part of the motor vehicle or mechanical device bearing the serial number or engine or motor number of the vehicle with a new part upon which the proper serial number or engine or motor number has not been stamped, is guilty of a felony, and if the person is a licensed dealer, the dealer's license shall be revoked.

(3) In all prosecutions under this section, possession by a person of a motor vehicle or of a mechanical device with the manufacturer's serial number or the engine or motor number removed, defaced, destroyed or altered or with a part bearing the number or numbers replaced by one on which the proper number does not appear, shall be prima facie evidence of violation of this section.

(4) If the identification of a motor vehicle or a mechanical device has been removed, defaced, or altered as provided in this section and the real identity of the motor vehicle or mechanical device cannot be determined, the motor vehicle or mechanical device shall be subject to confiscation by the state and shall be sold at public auction, put to official use by the government agency seizing the vehicle, or rendered scrap. If the items are confiscated from a licensed vehicle dealer, the dealer's license shall be revoked.

(5) A person shall not knowingly possess, buy, deliver, or offer to buy, sell, exchange, or give away any manufacturer's vehicle identification number plate, federal safety certification label, antitheft label, posident die stamps, secretary of state vehicle identification label, rosette rivet, or any facsimile thereof. This subsection does not apply to a motor vehicle manufacturer, a motor vehicle parts supplier under contract with a motor vehicle manufacturer, or a law enforcement officer in the official performance of his or her duties or to a motor vehicle in which a manufacturer's vehicle identification plate and each of the applicable labels listed in this subsection have been installed as prescribed by law. A person who violates this subsection is guilty of a felony, punishable by imprisonment for not more than 4 years, a fine of not more than $10,000.00, or both. If the person who violates this subsection is a licensed dealer or repair facility, its license shall be revoked.

(6) A person shall not buy, receive, or obtain control of a motor vehicle or motor vehicle part with the intent to sell or otherwise dispose of the motor vehicle or motor vehicle part knowing that an identification number of that motor vehicle or motor vehicle part has been removed, obliterated, tampered with, or altered. This subsection does not apply to a motor vehicle obtained from or at the direction of a law enforcement agency. A person who violates this subsection is guilty of a felony punishable by imprisonment for not more than 10 years, a fine of not more than $20,000.00, or both.

(7) As used in this section:
  (a) "Antitheft label" means a label containing the vehicle identification number affixed to a motor vehicle by the manufacturer in accordance with subtitle VI of title 49 of the United States Code, 49 U.S.C. 30101 to 33118.
  (b) "Federal safety certification label" means a label affixed to a motor vehicle that certifies that the motor vehicle conforms to current safety standards at the time of production and displays the vehicle identification number.
  (c) "Motor vehicle" means a device in, upon, or by which a person or property is or may be transported or drawn upon a street, highway, or waterway, whether subject to or exempt from registration, except a device exclusively moved by human power or used exclusively upon stationary rails or tracks.
  (d) "Posident die stamps" means specially designed die stamps used by motor vehicle manufacturers to produce unique letters and numbers when stamping vehicle identification numbers upon vehicle identification plates, tags, and parts affixed to a motor vehicle.
  (e) "Rosette rivet" means a special rivet designed to prevent removal or tampering with a vehicle identification number plate affixed by the manufacturer to a motor vehicle and that, when used to affix a vehicle identification number plate, forms 5 or 6 petals at the rivet head.

With the Intent to Mislead (felony)
Elements

1. The suspect hid or misrepresented the identity of the vehicle (or vehicle part),
2. By either removing, damaging, or altering the VIN or by placing a replacement part on the vehicle that had a non-matching VIN, and
3. The suspect intended to mislead someone about the identity of the vehicle. CJ12d 24.8.

> Possession of an altered motor vehicle part is prima facie evidence of intent to mislead. *People v. Venticinque*, 459 Mich. 90 (1998).
>
> Convictions for receiving and concealing stolen property and for altering a VIN on the same piece of property does not violate the Double Jeopardy Clause. *People v. Griffis*, 218 Mich. App. 95 (1996).
>
> The defendant may be charged in any county where the defendant altered the VIN, misrepresented the VIN, or possessed the vehicle with the altered VIN. *People v. Belanger*, 120 Mich. App. 752 (1982).

Without intent to mislead (90-day misdemeanor)

The suspect hid or misrepresented the identity of the vehicle by removing or damaging the VIN number and replacing it with another without the intent to mislead anyone. This is a lesser included offense of the above-listed felony. CJ12d 24.9.

Tampering Or Meddling With A Motor Vehicle— MCL 750.416 (90-day misdemeanor)

Damaging or unauthorized tampering or meddling with motor vehicle—Any person shall be guilty of a misdemeanor, who shall:
Intentionally and without authority from the owner, start or cause to be started the motor of any motor vehicle, or maliciously shift or change the starting device or gears of a standing motor vehicle to a position other than that in which it was left by the owner or driver of said motor vehicle; or
Intentionally cut, mark, scratch or damage the chassis, running gear, body, sides, top, covering or upholstering of any motor vehicle, the property of another, or intentionally cut, mash, mark, destroy or damage such motor vehicle, or any of the accessories, equipment, appurtenances or attachments thereof, or any spare or extra parts thereon being or thereto attached, without the permission of the owner thereof; or Intentionally release the brake upon any standing motor vehicle, with intent to injure said machine or cause the same to be removed without the consent of the owner: Provided, That this section shall not apply in case of moving or starting of motor vehicles by the police under authority of local ordinance or by members of fire departments in case of emergency in the vicinity of a fire.

Elements

1. The suspect intentionally damaged a vehicle part, or
2. The suspect started the vehicle or maliciously shifted gears, or

3. The suspect released the brake either while the vehicle was stopped or with the intent of causing damage to the vehicle.

Note that the statute contains exceptions for police acting under authority of law and for firefighters acting under a fire emergency.

Chop Shop—MCL 750.535a (felony)

A person who knowingly owns, operates, or conducts a chop shop or who knowingly aids and abets another person in owning, operating, or conducting a chop shop is guilty of a felony punishable by imprisonment for not more than 10 years or a fine of not more than $250,000.00, or both.

Chop shop means any of the following: (i) Any area, building, storage lot, field, or other premises or place where one or more persons are engaged or have engaged in altering, dismantling, reassembling, or in any way concealing or disguising the identity of a stolen motor vehicle or of any major component part of a stolen motor vehicle.

For further definitions read entire statute.

LARCENY

Larceny—MCL 750.356

(1) *A person who commits larceny by stealing any of the following property of another person is guilty of a crime as provided in this section:*

    (a) Money, goods, or chattels.
    (b) A bank note, bank bill, bond, promissory note, due bill, bill of exchange or other bill, draft, order, or certificate.
    (c) A book of accounts for or concerning money or goods due, to become due, or to be delivered.
    (d) A deed or writing containing a conveyance of land or other valuable contract in force.
    (e) A receipt, release, or defeasance.
    (f) A writ, process, or public record.
    (g) Nonferrous metal.

(2) *If any of the following apply, the person is guilty of a felony punishable by imprisonment for not more than 10 years or a fine of not more than $15,000.00 or 3 times the value of the property stolen, whichever is greater, or both imprisonment and a fine:*

    (a) The property stolen has a value of $20,000.00 or more.
    (b) The person violates subsection (3)(a) and has 2 or more prior convictions for committing or attempting to commit an offense under this section. For purposes of this subdivision, however, a prior conviction does not include a conviction for a violation or attempted violation of subsection (4)(b) or (5).

(3) *If any of the following apply, the person is guilty of a felony punishable by imprisonment for not more than 5 years or a fine of not more than $10,000.00 or 3 times the value of the property stolen, whichever is greater, or both imprisonment and a fine:*

    (a) The property stolen has a value of $1,000.00 or more but less than $20,000.00.
    (b) The person violates subsection (4)(a) and has 1 or more prior convictions for committing or attempting to commit an offense under this section. For purposes of this subdivision, however, a prior conviction does not include a conviction for a violation or attempted violation of subsection (4)(b) or (5).

(4) *If any of the following apply, the person is guilty of a misdemeanor punishable by imprisonment for not more than 1 year or a fine of not more than $2,000.00 or 3 times the value of the property stolen, whichever is greater, or both imprisonment and a fine:*

    (a) The property stolen has a value of $200.00 or more but less than $1,000.00.
    (b) The person violates subsection (5) and has 1 or more prior convictions for committing or attempting to commit an offense under this section or a local ordinance substantially corresponding to this section.

(5) *If the property stolen has a value of less than $200.00, the person is guilty of a misdemeanor punishable by imprisonment for not more than 93 days or a fine of not more than $500.00 or 3 times the value of the property stolen, whichever is greater, or both imprisonment and a fine.*

(6) *If the property stolen is nonferrous metal, then, as used in this section, "the value of the property stolen" means the greatest of the following:*

    (a) The replacement cost of the stolen nonferrous metal.
    (b) The cost of repairing the damage caused by the larceny of the nonferrous metal.
    (c) The sum of subdivisions (a) and (b).

(7) *The values of property stolen in separate incidents pursuant to a scheme or course of conduct within any 12-month period may be*

aggregated to determine the total value of property stolen.

Elements

1. The suspect took someone else's property,
2. Without the owner's consent,
3. With some movement of the property,
4. Intending to permanently deprive the owner of the property. CJI2d 23.1.

> Any movement is sufficient to meet the "movement" element. For example, the court found that the movement was sufficient where the suspect picked up a tape deck, put it in a bag, then took it back out of the bag, and placed it on a table without ever leaving the premises. *People v. Wilbourne*, 44 Mich. App. 376 (1973).

Note: MCL 750.356(6) contains special provisions for "the value of the property stolen" for nonferrous metal.

The value of nonferrous metal is determined by the greatest of:

1. The replacement cost of the nonferrous metal,
2. The cost of repairing the damage done by the theft of the nonferrous metal,
3. A combination of the replacement cost and the repair cost.

> Nonferrous metal is defined as "a metal that does not contain significant quantities of ferrous metal but contains copper, brass, platinum-based metals, aluminum, bronze, lead, zinc, nickel, or alloys of those metals." MCL 750.356(10).

Penalties:

Less than $200	93 day misdemeanor
$200 to less than $1,000 or less than $200, if previously convicted	1 year misdemeanor
$1,000 to less than $20,000 or $200 to less than $1,000, if previously convicted	5 year felony
Over $20,000 or $1,000 to less than $20,000 if, previously convicted twice	10 year felony

When there are separate incidents that are part of common scheme or plan, the total amount can be aggregated over 12-month period for total.

Larceny in a Building—MCL 750.360 (felony)

Any person who shall commit the crime of larceny by stealing in any dwelling house, house trailer, office, store, gasoline service station, shop, warehouse, mill, factory, hotel, school, barn, granary, ship, boat, vessel, church, house of worship, locker room or any building used by the public shall be guilty of a felony.

Elements

Includes the same elements as larceny with the added element that the property be in a building. The value of the property is not an issue under this statute.

> This section applied to a metal shed, in which automobile tires were stored. The shed was bolted down to the cement and enclosed with overlapping padlocked doors. *People v. Williams*, 368 Mich. 494 (1962).
>
> The use of the structure determines if it is a building. A defendant's conviction for larceny in a building was upheld where the larceny occurred in a construction trailer that was being used as an office. *People v. Walters*, 186 Mich. App. 452 (1990).
>
> A conviction for larceny in a building was overturned where the defendant broke into a van that had four flat tires and was being used for storage because there was no evidence that the van was mechanically incapable of locomotion. *People v. Matusik*, 63 Mich. App. 347 (1975).
>
> Whether the theft of two chairs and a rug from the porch of a home is larceny in a building was found to be a jury issue. *People v. Thompson*, 114 Mich. App. 302 (1982).
>
> Larceny in building is complete when there is the slightest taking of property with the intent to steal. *People v. Cavanaugh*, 127 Mich. App. 632 (1983).

The difference between larceny in a building and retail fraud: Retail fraud is generally a lesser charge, but retail fraud requires that the item is OFFERED FOR SALE. Thus, it is larceny in a building (a felony) when the suspect steals cleaning or office supplies used by the store. Likewise, it is larceny in a building where one customer purchases an item, leaves it in the loading area of the store, and the suspect then steals it from the loading area.

> In cases where retail fraud is the appropriate charge, a suspect may not be charged with larceny in a building. *People v. Ramsey*, 218 Mich. App. 191 (1996).

Other Larcenies

Larceny at a Fire—MCL 750.358 (felony)

Any person who shall commit the offense of larceny by stealing in any building that is on fire, or by stealing any property removed in consequence of alarm caused by fire, shall be guilty of a felony, punishable by imprisonment in the state prison not more than 5 years or by a fine of not more than 2,500 dollars.

Larceny of Livestock—MCL 750.357a (felony)

Any person who shall commit the offense of larceny by stealing the livestock of another shall be guilty of a felony.

Livestock includes horses, stallions, colts, geldings, mares, sheep, rams, lambs, bulls, bullocks, steers, heifers, cows, calves, mules, jacks, jennets, burros, goats, kids, and swine.

> A defendant's conviction for larceny over $100 where he stole valuable "show" goats was remanded because the court reasoned that he should have been prosecuted under the more specific larceny of livestock statute. *People v. Patterson*, 212 Mich. App. 393 (1995).

Larceny of Firearms—MCL 750.357b (felony)

A person who commits larceny by stealing the firearm of another person is guilty of a felony, punishable by imprisonment for not more than 5 years or by a fine of not more than $2,500.00, or both.

Larceny From a Vacant Dwelling—MCL 750.359 (1 year misdemeanor)

Any person or persons who shall steal or unlawfully remove or in any manner damage any fixture, attachment, or other property belonging to, connected with, or used in the construction of any vacant structure or building, whether built or in the process of construction or who shall break into any vacant structure or building with the intention of unlawfully removing, taking therefrom, or in any manner damaging any fixture, attachment, or other property belonging to, connected with, or used in the construction of such vacant structure or building whether built or in the process of construction, is guilty of a misdemeanor punishable by imprisonment for not more than 1 year or a fine of not more than $1,000.00.

Elements

1. The suspect stole or damaged,
2. Any fixture, attachment, or property,
3. Belonging to, connected to, or used in the construction of,
4. Any vacant building, whether built or under construction.

OR

1. The suspect broke into a vacant building,
2. With the intent of committing larceny from a building.

> A defendant was convicted of breaking and entering into an occupied dwelling where the homeowner lived in Ohio during the week. The defendant argued that he should have been charged with larceny from a vacant building because the homeowner only stayed in the home on the weekends while completing its interior construction. The court held that, under the circumstances, the breaking and entering conviction was proper. *People v. McClain*, 105 Mich. App. 323 (1981).

Larceny From a Motor Vehicle—MCL 750.356a

Elements

1. The suspect took a wheel, tire, air bag, catalytic converter, radio, stereo, clock, telephone, computer, or other electronic device,
2. Without the owner's consent,
3. From a motor vehicle, house trailer, trailer, or semitrailer,
4. There was some movement of the property, and
5. The suspect intended to permanently keep the property (it does not matter whether or not the suspect actually kept the property). CJ12d 23.5.

Penalties:

- Steals a wheel, tire, air bag, radio, stereo, clock, telephone, computer, catalytic converter or other electronic device from motor vehicle, house trailer, trailer or semi trailer = 5 year felony.
- Damage: If the suspect causes damage to vehicle while trying to steal less than $1,000 = 5 year felony.
- Other property: Breaking or entering a vehicle and stealing property with one of the following dollar amounts:

Less than $200	93 day misdemeanor
$200 to less than $1,000 or less than $200, if previously convicted	1 year misdemeanor
$1,000 to less than $20,000 or $200 to less than $1,000, if previously convicted	5 year felony
Over $20,000 or $1,000 to less than $20,000 if, previously convicted twice	10 year felony

If separate incidents, but part of common scheme or plan, the total amount can be aggregated over 12-month period for total. MCL 750.356a(4).

Evidence that the defendant forced one of the ventilator windows open on an automobile, broke the glass, reached in to open the window, and entered with his head and shoulders, is sufficient to establish the charge. *People v. Hadesman*, 304 Mich. 481 1943).

Convictions for possession of burglary tools and attempted larceny from a motor vehicle arising from the same incident do not violate the Double Jeopardy Rule. *People v. Wilson*, 180 Mich. App. 12 (1989).

Larceny of Rental Property—MCL 750.362a (same property values as under larceny)
Elements

1. The suspect rented or leased a motor vehicle, trailer, or tangible property,
2. There was a written agreement providing for the item's time and place of return,
3. The time for return has expired,
4. The lessor made a demand for the item's return by registered or certified mail,
5. The suspect refuses or willfully neglects to return the item, and
6. The suspect intended to defraud the lessor.

This statute applies to a person who refuses or willfully neglects to return a rented motor vehicle, trailer, or other tangible property with the intent to defraud the lessor.

The rental or lease agreement must provide for its return to a particular place at a particular time. A notice in writing must be sent to the person after expiration of the agreement via registered or certified mail to the last known address.

There is no intent to permanently deprive, which separates it from larceny by conversion.

A defendant's conviction was overturned because a certified letter that stated that the vehicle was to be returned "as soon as possible" was insufficient under this statute. *People v. McKim*, 99 Mich. App. 829 1980).

Larceny by conversion—MCL 750.362 (same property values as under larceny)

Any person to whom any money, goods or other property, which may be the subject of larceny, shall have been delivered, who shall embezzle or fraudulently convert to his own use, or shall secrete with the intent to embezzle, or fraudulently use such goods, money or other property, or any part thereof, shall be deemed by so doing to have committed the crime of larceny and shall be punished as provided in the first section of this chapter.

Elements

1. Someone else's property was transferred to the suspect, either legally or illegally,
2. The suspect converted the property to his own use,
3. The owner did not consent to the suspect converting the property,
4. The property had value,
5. The suspect intended to defraud or cheat the owner out of the property permanently. *People v. Scott*, 72 Mich. App. 16 (1976).

Example: The property was given to the suspect to borrow. After taking the property, the suspect developed the intent to defraud or cheat the owner by converting the property to his or her own use.

The conversion constitutes the "unlawful taking" and the decision not to return the property is the "felonious intent."

Larceny by conversion is closely related to embezzlement. In both, the property is given to the suspect. However, in embezzlement there is a position of trust between the suspect and the owner. In larceny by conversion there is no such position of trust.

> Larceny by conversion occurred where a salesman placed a deposit into his personal account instead of his business account and without completing the sale. *People v. Mason*, 247 Mich. App. 64 (2001).
>
> Simply refusing to return the property upon demand is not sufficient to meet the elements of this crime. For example, a defendant's conviction was overturned because the prosecution could not prove felonious intent where the defendant borrowed a horse buggy and refused to return it. *People v. Taugher*, 102 Mich. 598, 601 (1894).

Larceny by Trick—MCL 750.356 (same property values as under larceny)

The suspect used some trick to obtain someone else's property.

Elements

1. The elements of larceny, plus,
2. The owner gave the suspect possession for a limited, special purpose without intending to give the suspect ownership, and
3. The suspect took the property in a manner that he knew was inconsistent with the limited, special purpose.

OR

1. The elements of larceny, plus,
2. The owner gave the property to the suspect due to some trick, and
3. The owner would not have given the property to the suspect if the suspect had not used the trick.

Larceny by trick is not a separate crime from larceny but describes the means used by the suspect to obtain the property. The victim relies on some representation by the accused and gives up possession of his or her property but not title or ownership.

The question to be asked is "Would the owner have given the property to the suspect had he or she known that the suspect was actually going to keep it?"

> Larceny by trick involves the criminal taking of property by means of fraudulent contrivances rather than by trespass when the true owner intends to give up possession but not ownership. *People v. Sykes*, 61 Mich. App. 233 (1975).

Larceny by False Pretense—MCL 750.218 (same property values as under larceny)

(1) A person who, with intent to defraud or cheat and by color of a false token or writing, by a false or bogus check or other written, printed, or engraved instrument, by counterfeit coin or metal that is intended to simulate a coin, or by any other false pretense does 1 or more of the following is guilty of a crime punishable as provided in this section:

   (a) Causes a person to grant, convey, assign, demise, lease, or mortgage land or an interest in land.
   (b) Obtains a person's signature on a forged written instrument.
   (c) Obtains from a person any money or personal property or the use of any instrument, facility, article, or other valuable thing or service.
   (d) By means of a false weight or measure obtains a larger amount or quantity of property than was bargained for.
   (e) By means of a false weight or measure sells or disposes of a smaller amount or quantity of property than was bargained for.

As used in this section, "false pretense" includes, but is not limited to, a false or fraudulent representation, writing, communication, statement, or message, communicated by any means to another person, that the maker of the representation, writing, communication, statement, or message knows is false or fraudulent. The false pretense may be a representation regarding a past or existing fact or circumstance or a representation regarding the intention to perform a future event or to have a future event performed.

Elements

1. The suspect used a pretense,
2. The suspect knew that the pretense was false,
3. The suspect intended to defraud or cheat,

4. Another person relied on the pretense,
5. The other person suffered some loss due to this reliance. (CJI2d 23.11)

Definition of pretense: To knowingly make someone believe something that is false, to keep someone from finding out something important about the property, to sell property while hiding a claim (e.g. a mortgage, an easement) against it, or to promise to do something while not intending to ever do it. CJ12d 23.9.

The suspect knowingly used a false pretense with the intent to cheat or defraud in order to obtain someone else's property. The victim relied on the pretense in giving up the property to the suspect (e.g., Charging for nonexistent repairs is a false pretense, but overcharging is not.)

This crime differs from larceny by trick in that the victim gives up title and ownership.

> False pretense occurred where the suspect short-changed two cashiers $10 each by creating confusion and distracting them and asking for various amounts of change thereby inducing them to give him the extra $10. *People v. Long*, 409 Mich. 346 (1980).
>
> When the victim realized that the defendant was lying during a "quick-change scheme," the proper charge was attempted larceny (not by false pretenses) because the victim never passed title. *People v. Jones*, 143 Mich. App. 775 (1985).

Lost Property—MCL 434.22

The Lost Property Act requires any person finding lost property to report the finding or deliver the property to a law enforcement agency in the jurisdiction where the property was found. If the finder converts the property to his or her own use, with the intent to permanently deprive the owner, he or she is guilty of larceny.

RETAIL FRAUD

Retail fraud occurs inside a store or in the immediate area around the store while it is *open to the public*. It only applies to property offered for sale. Concealment of the property is evidence of the intent.

Retail fraud applies to one of the following:

- *Theft:* The suspect took some property and moved it. It does not matter if the subject made it past the cashier.
- *False exchange*: The suspect exchanged or tried to exchange property that had not been paid for that belonged to the store. The exchange could be for money or other property.
- *Price switching*: The suspect altered or switched a price tag.

If separate incidents occur, but they are part of common scheme or plan, the value can be aggregated over a 12-month period for a total.

Retail Fraud In the First Degree—MCL 750.356c (felony)

Elements

1. The suspect took property that was OFFERED FOR SALE,
2. The suspect moved the property (any movement is enough),
3. The suspect intended to keep the property permanently,
4. Without the store's consent,
5. Inside or in the immediate area of the store while it is open to the public, and
6. One of the following:

   a. *$1,000 or more,*
   b. *$200 to less than $1,000* and previously convicted of one of the following:

      i. First or second degree retail fraud.
      ii. Larceny in a builhding.
      iii. Larceny by false pretenses, except section 218(2).
      iv. Larceny, except sections 356 4(b) or 5.

OR:

1. The suspect switched or altered the price tag,
2. Intending to pay less than the actual price (or nothing at all),
3. Inside or in the immediate area of the store while it is open to the public, and
4. One of the following:

   a. *$1,000 or more,*
   b. *$200 to less than $1,000* and previously convicted of one of the following:

      i. First or second-degree retail fraud.
      ii. Larceny in a building.
      iii. Larceny by false pretenses, except section 218(2).
      iv. Larceny, except sections 356 4(b) or 5.

OR

1. The suspect exchanged or attempted to exchange property that was not paid for and that belonged to the store,

2. The suspect intended to cheat or defraud the store,
3. Inside or in the immediate area of the store while it is open to the public, and
4. One of the following:
   a. *$1,000 or more,*
   b. *$200 to less than $1,000 and previously convicted of one of the following:*
      i. First or second-degree retail fraud.
      ii. Larceny in a building.
      iii. Larceny by false pretenses, except section 218(2).
      iv. Larceny, except sections 356 4(b) or 5.

Retail Fraud In The Second Degree and Third Degree—MCL 750.356d

(1) A person who does any of the following in a store or in its immediate vicinity is guilty of retail fraud in the second degree, a misdemeanor punishable by imprisonment for not more than 1 year or a fine of not more than $2,000.00 or 3 times the value of the difference in price, property stolen, or money or property obtained or attempted to be obtained, whichever is greater, or both imprisonment and a fine:

   (a) While a store is open to the public, alters, transfers, removes and replaces, conceals, or otherwise misrepresents the price at which property is offered for sale with the intent not to pay for the property or to pay less than the price at which the property is offered for sale if the resulting difference in price is $200.00 or more but less than $1,000.00.

   (b) While a store is open to the public, steals property of the store that is offered for sale at a price of $200.00 or more but less than $1,000.00.

   (c) With intent to defraud, obtains or attempts to obtain money or property from the store as a refund or exchange for property that was not paid for and belongs to the store if the amount of money or the value of the property obtained or attempted to be obtained is $200.00 or more but less than $1,000.00.

(2) A person who violates subsection (4) and who has 1 or more prior convictions for committing or attempting to commit an offense under this section, section 218, 356, 356c, or 360, or a local ordinance substantially corresponding to this section or section 218, 356, 356c, or 360 is guilty of retail fraud in the second degree.

(3) A person who commits retail fraud in the second degree shall not be prosecuted under section 360.

(4) A person who does any of the following in a store or in its immediate vicinity is guilty of retail fraud in the third degree, a misdemeanor punishable by imprisonment for not more than 93 days or a fine of not more than $500.00 or 3 times the value of the difference in price, property stolen, or money or property obtained or attempted to be obtained, whichever is greater, or both imprisonment and a fine:

   (a) While a store is open to the public, alters, transfers, removes and replaces, conceals, or otherwise misrepresents the price at which property is offered for sale, with the intent not to pay for the property or to pay less than the price at which the property is offered for sale, if the resulting difference in price is less than $200.00.

   (b) While a store is open to the public, steals property of the store that is offered for sale at a price of less than $200.00.

   (c) With intent to defraud, obtains or attempts to obtain money or property from the store as a refund or exchange for property that was not paid for and belongs to the store, if the amount of money, or the value of the property, obtained or attempted to be obtained is less than $200.00.

(5) A person who commits retail fraud in the third degree shall not be prosecuted under section 360.

(6) The values of the difference in price, property stolen, or money or property obtained or attempted to be obtained in separate incidents pursuant to a scheme or course of conduct within any 12-month period may be aggregated to determine the total value involved in the offense under this section.

Elements

The same as the elements for First Degree Retail Fraud except that the values are lower.

Retail Fraud In The Second Degree— MCL 750.356d (1 year misdemeanor)

$200 to less than $1,000 or, Less than $200 and previously convicted of one of the following:

- First or second degree retail fraud.
- Larceny in a building.
- Larceny by false pretenses.
- Larceny.

Retail Fraud In the Third Degree— MCL 750.356d (93-day misdemeanor)

Less than $200 = 93 day misdemeanor.

Possession of Device Used to Shield Merchandise From Detection—MCL 750.360a

(1) A person shall not do any of the following:

(a) Possess a laminated or coated bag or device that is intended to shield merchandise from detection by an electronic or magnetic theft detection device with the intent to commit or attempt to commit larceny.

(b) Manufacture, sell, offer for sale, or distribute, or attempt to manufacture, sell, offer for sale, or distribute, a laminated or coated bag or device that is intended to shield merchandise from detection by an electronic or magnetic theft detection device knowing or reasonably believing that the bag or device will be used to commit or attempt to commit larceny.

(c) Possess a tool or device designed to allow the deactivation or removal of a theft detection device from any merchandise with the intent to use the tool or device to deactivate a theft detection device on, or to remove a theft detection device from, any merchandise without the permission of the merchant or person owning or lawfully holding that merchandise with the intent to commit or attempt to commit larceny.

(d) Manufacture, sell, offer for sale, or distribute a tool or device designed to allow the deactivation or removal of a theft detection device from any merchandise without the permission of the merchant or person owning or lawfully holding that merchandise knowing or reasonably believing that the tool or device will be used to commit or attempt to commit larceny.

(e) Deactivate a theft detection device or remove a theft detection device from any merchandise in a retail establishment prior to purchasing the merchandise with the intent to commit or attempt to commit a larceny.

Penalties:

| First offense | 1 year misdemeanor |
| Second Offense | 4 year felony |

EMBEZZLEMENT
Embezzlement—MCL 750.174

A person who as the agent, servant, or employee of another person, governmental entity within this state, or other legal entity or who as the trustee, bailee, or custodian of the property of another person, governmental entity within this state, or other legal entity fraudulently disposes of or converts to his or her own use, or takes or secretes with the intent to convert to his or her own use without the consent of his or her principal, any money or other personal property of his or her principal that has come to that person's possession or that is under his or her charge or control by virtue of his or her being an agent, servant, employee, trustee, bailee, or custodian, is guilty of embezzlement.

Elements

1. The suspect had a relationship of trust with the victim,
2. Because of the relationship, the suspect obtained possession or control over money or property belonging to the victim,
3. The suspect converted the money or property into his or her own use or took it with the intent of converting it,
4. Without the victim's consent, and
5. The suspect had the intent to defraud.

The intent to return the property is no defense. *People v. Butts*, 128 Mich. 208 (1901). Unlawful use of the funds is the key factor.

The distinction between embezzlement and larceny is that in embezzlement, the taking is an unlawful appropriation of that which has come into one's possession rightfully. *People v. Bergman*, 246 Mich. 68 (1929).

Penalties:

Less than $200	93 day misdemeanor
Less than $200 with charity or nonprofit victim	1 year misdemeanor
$200 to less than $1,000 or less than $200 if, previously convicted	1 year misdemeanor
$200 to less than $1,000 with charity or nonprofit victim	5 year felony
$1,000 to less than $20,000 or $200 to less than $1,000 if, previously convicted	5 year felony
$1,000 to less than $20,000 with charity or nonprofit victim	10 year felony
$20,000 to less than $50,000 or two or more previous convictions	10 year felony
$50,000 to less than $100,000	15 year felony
More than $100,000	20 year felony

Embezzlement By A Public Official— MCL 750.175

Embezzlement by public officer, his agent, etc.—Any person holding any public office in this state, or the agent or servant of any such person, who knowingly and unlawfully appropriates to his own use, or to the use of any other person, the money or property received by him in his official capacity or employment, of the value of 50 dollars or upwards, shall be guilty of a felony, punishable by imprisonment in the state prison not more than 10 years or by fine of not more than 5,000 dollars.

In any prosecution under this section the failure, neglect or refusal of any public officer to pay over and deliver to his successor all moneys and property which should be in his hands as such officer, shall be prima facie evidence of an offense against the provisions of this section.

Elements

1. The suspect held a public office or worked for a public official,
2. The suspect received money or property in his or her official duties,
3. The suspect knew that the property or money was public property, and
4. The suspect used the property or money for an unauthorized purpose. CJI2d 27.3.

$50.00 or over is a felony.

Refusal by the suspect to deliver the money or property to his successor creates prima facie evidence of a violation of this statute. MCL 750.175.

"The intent of the statute [is] to prevent any public official from using money or property coming to [the suspect] in his official capacity for any other purpose than to which it was received." *People v. Warren*, 122 Mich. 504 (1899).

However, a demand for return of the money or property is not an element of this crime. A defendant's conviction was upheld where she repaid the money in question five days after she was charge with Embezzlement by a Public Official. *People v. Jones*, 182 Mich. App. 668 (1990).

Embezzlement By Police Officer—MCL 257.728

(c) At or before the completion of his or her tour of duty, a police officer taking a certificate or deposit of money shall deliver the certificate or deposit of money either to the magistrate named in the citation together with a report of the facts relating to the arrest, or to the police chief or person authorized by the police chief to receive certificates and deposits. The police chief or person authorized by the police chief shall deposit with the court the certificate or the money deposited and the citation in the same manner as prescribed for citations in section 728a. Failure to make a report and deliver the money deposited is embezzlement of public money.

Failure of police officer to deliver money obtained by a traffic bond to the court is embezzlement of public money.

FINANCIAL CRIMES

CHECK LAW VIOLATIONS
Non-Sufficient Funds (NSF)—MCL 750.131

(1) A person shall not make, draw, utter, or deliver any check, draft, or order for the payment of money, to apply on account or otherwise, upon any bank or other depository with intent to defraud and knowing at the time of the making, drawing, uttering, or delivering that the maker or drawer does not have sufficient funds in or credit with the bank or other depository to pay the check, draft, or order in full upon its presentation.

(2) A person shall not make, draw, utter, or deliver any check, draft, or order for the payment of money, to apply on account or otherwise, upon any bank or other depository with intent to defraud if the person does not have sufficient funds for the payment of the check, draft, or order when presentation for payment is made to the drawee. This subsection does not apply if the lack of funds is due to garnishment, attachment, levy, or other lawful cause and that fact was not known to the person when the person made, drew, uttered, or delivered the check, draft, or order.

(3) A person who violates this section is guilty of a crime as follows:

  (a) If the amount payable in the check, draft, or order is less than $100.00, as follows:

   (i) For a first offense, a misdemeanor punishable by imprisonment for not more than 93 days or a fine of not more than $500.00, or both.

   (ii) For an offense following 1 or more prior convictions under this section or a local ordinance substantially corresponding to this section, a misdemeanor punishable by imprisonment for not more than 1 year or a fine of not more than $1,000.00, or both.

  (b) If the amount payable in the check, draft, or order is $100.00 or more but less than $500.00, as follows:

   (i) For a first or second offense, a misdemeanor punishable by imprisonment for not more than 1 year or a fine of not more than $1,000.00 or 3 times the amount payable, whichever is greater, or both imprisonment and a fine.

   (ii) For an offense following 2 or more prior convictions under this section, a felony punishable by imprisonment for not more than 2 years or a fine of not more than $2,000.00, or both. For purposes of this subparagraph, however, a prior conviction does not include a conviction for a violation or attempted violation of subdivision (a).

  (c) If the amount payable in the check, draft, or order is $500.00 or more, a felony punishable by imprisonment for not more than 2 years or a fine of not more than $2,000.00

or 3 times the amount payable, whichever is greater, or both imprisonment and a fine.

Elements

1. There was drawing of a check for payment of money on a bank,
2. The suspect knew that the bank account had insufficient funds or credit to pay the check,
3. The suspect intended to defraud someone.

People v. Chappelle, 114 Mich. App. 364 (1982).

To prove that the defendant passed the check, it is necessary that the prosecution present evidence of identification. This can be done if the cashier remembers the person or verified who the person was by comparing a driver's license or any other form of ID. Other ways include if the suspect admits to the crime during an interview or by using handwriting analysis.

> The element of intent to defraud is lacking if at the time of the issuance of the check, the defendant has a reasonable expectation that the check will be paid on presentation. *People v. Bradford*, 144 Mich. App. 416 (1985).
>
> It is not possible to perpetrate a fraud if the check is accepted with full knowledge that there is not enough money in the account. *People v. Jacobson*, 248 Mich. 639 (1929).

Penalties:

Less than $100 – First offense	93 day misdemeanor
Less than $100 – Second offense or subsequent offense	1 year misdemeanor
$100 to less than $500 – First and second offense	1 year misdemeanor
$100 to less than $500 – Third or more offense	2 year felony
$500 or more	2 year felony

No Account Check—MCL 750.131a(1) (felony)

A person shall not, with intent to defraud, make, draw, utter, or deliver any check, draft, or order for the payment of money, to apply on an account or otherwise, upon any bank or other depository, if at the time of making, drawing, uttering, or delivering the check, draft, or order he or she does not have an account in or credit with the bank or other depository for the payment of the check, draft, or order upon presentation. A person who violates this subsection is guilty of a felony, punishable by imprisonment for not more than 2 years, or by a fine of not more than $500.00, or both.

Elements

1. The suspect signed the check on the date in question,
2. The check was drawn on a bank,
3. The suspect had no account or credit at that bank on that date,
4. The check was presented for payment, and
5. The suspect intended to defraud when he or she wrote or presented the check.

People v. Peach, 175 Mich. App. 419 (1989).

Presentation of an NSF check is prima facie evidence of intent to defraud so long as the suspect does not make good on the check within five days of receiving notice that the check was not honored. MCL 750.132.

> It is not necessary that the suspect receive payment on the check, only that he or she presented it for payment. *People v. Henson*, 18 Mich. App. 259 (1969).

Three NSF Checks within 10 Days— MCL 750.131a(2) (felony)

A person shall not, with intent to defraud, make, draw, utter, or deliver, within a period of not more than 10 days, 3 or more checks, drafts, or orders for the payment of money, to apply on account or otherwise, upon any bank or other depository, knowing at the time of making, drawing, uttering, or delivering each of the checks, drafts, or orders that the maker or drawer does not have sufficient funds or credit with the bank or other depository for the payment of the check, draft, or order in full upon its presentation. A person who violates this subsection is guilty of a felony, punishable by imprisonment for not more than 2 years, or by a fine of not more than $500.00, or both.

Elements

1. Suspect wrote or delivered three checks, drafts, or money orders within 10 days that were drawn on a bank.
2. The suspect knew he or she did not have enough money or credit to pay the amount in full and
3. The suspect intended to defraud or cheat someone.

> Where a person issued three checks within 10 days in three different counties, he may be prosecuted in any one of them. Op. Atty. Gen. 1945–1946, p. 175.

FORGERY
Forgery—MCL 750.248 (felony])

(1) A person who falsely makes, alters, forges, or counterfeits a public record, or a certificate, return, or attestation of a clerk of a court, register of deeds, notary public, township clerk, or any other public officer, in relation to a matter in which the certificate, return, or attestation may be received as legal proof, or a charter, deed, will, testament, bond, writing obligatory, letter of attorney, policy of insurance, bill of lading, bill of exchange, promissory note, or an order, acquittance [sic] of discharge for money or other property, or a waiver, release, claim or demand, or an acceptance of a bill of exchange, or indorsement [sic], or assignment of a bill of exchange or promissory note for the payment of money, or an accountable receipt for money, goods, or other property with intent to injure or defraud another person is guilty of a felony punishable by imprisonment for not more than 14 years.

(2) This section does not apply to a scrivener's error.

(3) The venue in a prosecution under this section may be in the county in which the forgery was performed; in a county in which a false, forged, altered, or counterfeit record, deed, instrument, or other writing is uttered and published with intent to injure or defraud; or in the county in which the rightful property owner resides.

Elements

1. A document was falsely made, altered, or forged,
2. By the suspect,
3. The forgery must expose someone to a risk of loss,
4. The suspect had the intent to defraud or cheat.

Prosecution may be sought where forgery was performed or where the forged document was executed. The crime is complete upon the making of the false writing.

> The signing of another's name to a document without authority constitutes forgery. *People v. Cook*, 223 Mich. 291 (1923).
>
> There is no requirement that the document be signed. *People v. Susalla*, 392 Mich. 387 (1974).
>
> While the forgery must expose someone to a risk of loss, there is no requirement that an actual loss occurred. *People v. Susalla*, 392 Mich. 387 (1974).

UTTERING AND PUBLISHING—MCL 750.249 (felony)

A person who utters and publishes as true a false, forged, altered, or counterfeit record, deed, instrument, or other writing listed in section 248 knowing it to be false, altered, forged, or counterfeit with intent to injure or defraud is guilty of a felony punishable by imprisonment for not more than 14 years.

Definitions

- **Uttering** is to offer a forged instrument.
- **Publishing** is to declare, by words or actions, that the forged document is genuine.

Elements

1. The suspect knew that the instrument was false,
2. The suspect intended to defraud,
3. The suspect presented the false instrument for payment.

People v. Hammond, 161 Mich. App. 837 (1987).

To utter and publish means to offer something as if it is real, whether or not anyone accepts it as real. CJI2d 22.22.

> Valid gifts certificates purchased with a stolen credit card have been found to be false instruments for Uttering and Publishing. *People v. Aguwa*, 245 Mich. App. 1 (2001).
>
> The crime of uttering and publishing includes a "copy" of a document. *People v. Cassadime*, 258 Mich. App. 395 (2003).

COUNTERFEITING

Possession of Counterfeit Bills—MCL 750.252

Any person who shall have in his possession at the same time, 10 or more similar false, altered, forged or counterfeit notes, bills of credit, bank bills or notes of this state, or any of its political subdivisions or municipalities, payable to the bearer thereof, or to the order of any person, such as are mentioned in the preceding sections of this chapter, knowing the same to be false, altered, forged or counterfeit, with intent to utter the same as true, and thereby to injure and defraud as aforesaid, shall be guilty of a felony, punishable by imprisonment in the state prison not more than 7 years.

Definition

"To **counterfeit** means to make an unauthorized copy, imitation or forgery of something with the intent to deceive or cheat someone by using the copy, imitation or forgery as it were real." CJI2d 22.13

Possession of Counterfeit Bills— MCL 750.254 (felony)

Any person who shall bring into this state, or shall have in his possession, any false, altered, forged or counterfeit bill or note in the similitude of the bills or notes payable to the bearer thereof, or to the order of any person issued by or for this state, or any of its political subdivisions or municipalities, or any bank or banking company, established in this state, or in any of the British provinces in North America, or in any other state or country, with intent to utter or pass the same, or to render the same current as true, knowing the same to be false, forged or counterfeit, shall be guilty of a felony, punishable by imprisonment in the state prison not more than 5 years, or by fine of not more than 2,500 dollars.

Elements

1. Possession of counterfeit bill,
2. With the intent to utter or pass,
3. While knowing that the bills are false, forged, or counterfeited.

10 or more bills fall under 750.252 (7-year felony).

Counterfeiting and Possession of Coins— MCL 750.260 (felony)

Any person who shall counterfeit any gold or silver coin, current by law or usage within this state, and every person who shall have in his possession, at the same time, 5 or more pieces of false money or coin, counterfeited in the similitude of any gold or silver coin current as aforesaid, knowing the same to be false and counterfeit, and with intent to utter or pass the same as true, shall be guilty of a felony, punishable by imprisonment in the state prison for life, or for any term of years.

Elements

1. The suspect counterfeited,
2. Any gold or silver coin used within the state.

OR

1. The suspect possessed,
2. Five or more pieces of false money or coins,
3. Knowing that the money or coins were false or counterfeit,
4. With the intent to utter or pass the money or coins as true.

Less than 5 coins falls under MCL 750.261 (10-year felony).

> In a case that preceded this statute, a suspect was found guilty of passing a counterfeit silver coin at a saloon. *People v. Clarkson*, 56 Mich. 164 (1885).

Tools for Counterfeiting Bills or Notes— MCL 750.255 (felony)

Any person who shall engrave, make or mend, or begin to engrave, make or mend, any plate, block, press or other tool, instrument or implement, or shall make or provide any paper or other material, adapted or designed for the forging and making any false or counterfeit note, certificate or other bill of credit in the similitude of the notes, certificates, bills of credit issued by lawful authority for any debt of this state, or any of its political subdivisions or municipalities, or any false or counterfeit note or bill in the similitude of the notes or bills issued by any bank or banking company established in this state, or within the United States, or in any of the British provinces in North America, or in any foreign state or country; and any person who shall have in his possession any such plate or block, engraved in whole or in part, or any press or other tool, instrument or implement, or any paper or other material, adapted and designed as aforesaid, with intent to use the same, or to cause or permit the same to be used in forging or making any such false or counterfeit certificates, bills or notes, shall be guilty of a felony, punishable by imprisonment in the state prison not more than 10 years or by fine of not more than 5,000 dollars.

Elements

1. The suspect made or began to make or provided to another person,
2. A tool designed for the forging of a bill or a note,
3. Where the bill or note is issued by a public entity.

OR

1. The suspect possessed,
2. A tool designed for the forging of a bill or a note,
3. Intending to use the tool or to cause the tool to be used to create a false bill or note,
4. Where the bill or note is issued by a public entity.

A community college district was found to be a public entity for purposes of this statute when the defendant possessed tools for creating forged Delta College checks. *People v. Egelston*, 114 Mich. App. 436 (1982).

Checks drawn on a county's commercial account meet the requirements for this statute. *People v. Beckner*, 92 Mich. App. 166 (1979). Likewise, checks drawn on a city's commercial account also meet the requirements of this statute. *People v. Jackson*, 92 Mich. App. 735 (1980).

Tools for Counterfeiting Coins—MCL 750.262 (felony)

Any person who shall cast, stamp, engrave, make or mend, or shall knowingly have in his possession, any mould, pattern, die, puncheon, engine, press or other tool or instrument, adapted and designed for coining or making any counterfeit coin, in the similitude of any gold or silver coin, current by law or usage in this state, with intent to use or employ the same, or to cause or permit the same to be used or employed in coining or making any such false and counterfeit coin as aforesaid, shall be guilty of a felony, punishable by imprisonment in the state prison not more than 10 years, or by a fine of not more than 5,000 dollars.

Elements

1. The suspect made or knowingly possessed,
2. A mold, pattern, die, puncheon, engine, press, or other tool,
3. Designed for coining or making a counterfeit coin,
4. Intending to use the tool or intending to permit its use in the making of a counterfeit coin.

DEFRAUDING AN INNKEEPER—MCL 750.292 (90-day misdemeanor)

Any person who shall put up at any hotel, motel, inn, restaurant or cafe as a guest and shall procure any food, entertainment or accommodation without paying therefor, except when credit is given therefor by express agreement, with intent to defraud such keeper thereof out of the pay for the same, or, who, with intent to defraud such keeper out of the pay therefor, shall obtain credit at any hotel, motel, inn, restaurant or cafe for such food, entertainment or accommodation, by means of any false show of baggage or effects brought thereto, is guilty of a misdemeanor. No conviction shall be had under the provisions of this section unless complaint is made within 60 days of the time of the violation hereof.

Applies to one of the following:

- The suspect, with the intent to defraud, stayed at a hotel, motel, inn, restaurant, or cafe as a guest and procured food, entertainment, or accommodation without paying and credit was not given by express agreement.

- The suspect, with the intent to defraud, obtained credit at a hotel, motel, inn, restaurant, or cafe for such food, entertainment, or accommodation, by means of a false show of baggage or effects.

No conviction shall be had under the provisions of this section unless complaint is made within 60 days of the time of the violation.

Refusal or neglect to pay is prima facie evidence of intent to defraud under this statute. MCL 750.293.

FINANCIAL TRANSACTION DEVICE (FTD)

Definition—750.157m

FTD means any of the following:

- Electronic funds card – ATM card.
- Credit card – e.g., Visa, JCPenney cards, health insurance cards.
- Debit card – e.g., gas cards, cards used in copy machines, long distance cards.
- Point of sale card – permits the purchase of goods and services where a deduction is made from an account at the time the goods/services are purchased.
- Any instrument, code number, PIN number, means of access to a credit or deposit
- Account, or a driver's license or identification card that can be used either alone or with another device, to:
  - Obtain money, cash, credit, goods, services, or anything else of value,
  - Certify or guarantee that the device holder has available funds on deposit to honor a draft or check, or
  - Provide the device holder with access to an account in order to deposit, withdraw, or transfer funds to obtain information about a deposit account. (MCL 750.157m)

A health insurance card is included as a FTD by statute. MCL 750.157m(f)(v).

A Mastercard check is not a FTD under this statute because the account is accessed by paper. *Peo.ple v. Kotesky*, 190 Mich. App. 330 (1991).

FTD Violations

Stealing, removing, or hiding an FTD— MCL 750.157n (felony])
Elements

1. The suspect obtained, retained, hid, or used someone else's FTD,
2. The suspect did so knowingly,
3. The suspect did so without the owner's consent,
4. The suspect intended to defraud or cheat (but see *People v. Cohen* below). CJ12d 30.3.

OR

1. The suspect possessed a fraudulent or altered FTD,
2. The suspect knew that the FTD was fraudulent or altered,
3. The suspect intended to defraud or cheat. CJ12d 30.4.

This was held to be a specific intent crime in *People v. Ainsworth*, 197 Mich. App. 321 (1991). However, in another case, a concurring opinion by Justice Corrigan of the Michigan Supreme Court stated that the intent required was that the suspect knowingly possessed someone else's FTD without that person's consent, which is general intent. *People v. Cohen*, 467 Mich. 874 (2002).

In *Cohen*, the suspect stole a wallet that contained three credit cards, and Justice Corrigan wrote that the suspect's conviction on three counts of possession of FTDs was appropriate even without a showing of intent to defraud or cheat. Justice Corrigan characterized the *Ainsworth* holding as to the intent element as dicta (i.e., non-binding).

A person could not be convicted under MCL 750.157n where she improperly used a company credit card that was issued in her name. Embezzlement would have been a more proper charge. *People v. Anderson*, 268 Mich. App. 410 (2005).

Possession of another's FTD with intent to use, deliver, circulate or sell—MCL 750.157p (felony)
Elements

1. The suspect knowingly possessed someone else's FTD,
2. The suspect did not have the owner's permission and knew that he did not have the owner's permission,

3. The suspect had the intent to use, deliver, circulate or sell the device,
4. With the intent to defraud or cheat. CJI2d 30.5.

Possession of fraudulent or altered FTD—MCL 750.157q (felony)

A person who delivers, circulates, or sells a financial transaction device which was obtained or held by that person under circumstances proscribed under section 157n, 157p, or 157v, or uses, permits, causes, or procures the financial transaction device to be used, delivered, circulated, or sold, knowing the device to have been obtained or held under circumstances proscribed under section 157n, 157p, or 157v is guilty of a felony.

> A defendant's conviction was upheld where she obtained a credit card that was never actually issued to the victim (the credit card was issued in the victim's name, but the victim never applied for or possessed the credit card). *People v. Collins*, 158 Mich. App. 508 (1987). This would include cases where the suspect used the victim's personal information to obtain credit cards in the victim's name.
>
> A defendant's conviction was upheld even though his attempted use of the FTD was not completed. The defendant argued that he was only guilty of an "attempt" crime, but the appellate court disagreed with him. *People v. Hillard*, 160 Mich. App. 484 (1987).

Fraud, forgery, material alteration, counterfeiting of FTD—MCL 750.157r (felony)

A person who, with intent to defraud, forges, materially alters, simulates, or counterfeits a financial transaction device is guilty of a felony.

Elements

1. The FTD was falsely made, materially altered, forged, counterfeited, or duplicated,
2. It was the suspect who falsely made, materially altered, forged, counterfeited, duplicated,
3. The suspect intended to defraud or cheat someone. CJI2d 30.6.

Use of a revoked or cancelled FTD with intent to defraud—MCL 750.157s

Elements

1. The FTD was revoked or cancelled by the issuer,
2. The suspect received notice and knew that the FTD was revoked or cancelled,
3. The suspect used the FTD to purchase something of value,
4. The holder intended to defraud or cheat someone.

Penalties:

Less than $100 – First offense	93 day misdemeanor
Less than $100 – Second offense or subsequent offense	1 year misdemeanor
$100 to less than $500 – First and second offense	1 year misdemeanor
$100 to less than $500 – Third or more offense	2 year felony
$500 or more	2 year felony

Use of FTD to defraud—MCL 750.157w

(1) A person who knowingly and with intent to defraud uses a financial transaction device to withdraw or transfer funds from a deposit account in violation of the contractual limitations imposed on the amount or frequency of withdrawals or transfers or in an amount exceeding the funds then on deposit in the account is guilty of a crime as follows:

(a) A misdemeanor punishable by imprisonment for not more than 93 days or a fine of not more than $500.00 or 3 times the amount of funds withdrawn or transferred, whichever is greater, or both imprisonment and a fine, if the amount of the funds withdrawn or transferred is less than $200.00.

(b) A misdemeanor punishable by imprisonment for not more than 1 year or a fine of not more than $2,000.00 or 3 times the amount of funds withdrawn or transferred, whichever is greater, or both imprisonment and a fine, if any of the following apply:

(i) The amount of the funds withdrawn or transferred is $200.00 or more but less than $1,000.00.

(ii) The person violates subdivision (a) and has 1 or more prior convictions for committing or attempting to commit an offense under this section or a local ordinance substantially corresponding to this section.

(c) A felony punishable by imprisonment for not more than 5 years or a fine of not more than $10,000.00 or 3 times the amount of funds withdrawn or transferred, whichever is greater, or both imprisonment and a fine, if any of the following apply:

(i) The amount of the funds withdrawn or transferred is $1,000.00 or more but less than $20,000.00.

(ii) The person violates subdivision (b)(i) and has 1 or more prior convictions for committing or attempting to commit an offense under this section. For purposes of this subparagraph, however, a prior conviction does not include a conviction for a violation or attempted violation of subdivision (a) or (b)(ii).

(d) A felony punishable by imprisonment for not more than 10 years or a fine of not more than $15,000.00 or 3 times the amount of funds withdrawn or transferred, whichever is greater, or both imprisonment and a fine, if any of the following apply:

(i) The amount of funds withdrawn or transferred is $20,000.00 or more.

(ii) The person violates subdivision (c)(i) and has 2 or more prior convictions for committing or attempting to commit an offense under this section. For purposes of this subparagraph, however, a prior conviction does not include a conviction for a violation or attempted violation of subdivision (a) or (b)(ii).

(2) The amounts of funds withdrawn or transferred in separate incidents pursuant to a scheme or course of conduct within any 12-month period may be aggregated to determine the total amount of funds withdrawn or transferred.

Elements

1. The suspect used a FTD to withdraw or transfer money,
2. The suspect did one of the following:
   - withdrew more money than he or she had on deposit,
   - withdrew more money than he or she was allowed to, or
   - withdrew money more often than allowed to.
3. The suspect did this knowingly, and
4. The suspect intended to defraud or cheat someone. CJ12d 30.11.

Penalties:

Less than $200	93 day misdemeanor
$200 to less than $1,000 or less than $200 if, previously convicted	1 year misdemeanor
$1,000 to less than $20,000 or $200 to less than $1,000 if, previously convicted	5 year felony
over $20,000 or $1,000 to less than $20,000 if, previously convicted twice	10 year felony

CRIMES AGAINST PROPERTY: SELECTED STATUTES

POSSESSION OF STOLEN PROPERTY
Possession of Stolen Property—MCL 750.535

(1) A person shall not buy, receive, possess, conceal, or aid in the concealment of stolen, embezzled, or converted money, goods, or property knowing the money, goods, or property is stolen, embezzled, or converted.

...

(6) The values of property purchased, received, possessed, or concealed in separate incidents pursuant to a scheme or course of conduct within any 12-month period may be aggregated to determine the total value of property purchased, received, possessed, or concealed.

(7) A person shall not buy, receive, possess, conceal, or aid in the concealment of a stolen motor vehicle knowing that the motor vehicle is stolen, embezzled, or converted. A person who violates this subsection is guilty of a felony punishable by imprisonment for not more than 5 years or a fine of not more than $10,000.00 or 3 times the value of the motor vehicle purchased, received, possessed, or concealed, whichever is greater, or both imprisonment and a fine. A person who is charged with, convicted of, or punished for a violation of this subsection shall not be convicted of or punished for a violation of another provision of this section arising from the purchase, receipt, possession, concealment, or aiding in the concealment of the same motor vehicle. This subsection does not prohibit the person from being charged, convicted, or punished under any other applicable law.

Elements

1. The property was stolen (or embezzled or converted) or was represented to the suspect as being stolen,
2. The suspect bought, received, possessed, concealed, or aided in the concealment of the property,
3. And the suspect knew or had reason to know the property was stolen.

CJ12d 26.1.

The suspect must have done one of the following:

- Bought,
- Received,
- Possessed,
- Concealed, or
- Aided in the concealment of the property.

Penalties:

Less than $200	93 day misdemeanor
$200 to less than $1,000 or less than $200, if previously convicted	1 year misdemeanor
$1,000 to less than $20,000 or $200 to less than $1,000, if previously convicted or the property is a motor vehicle	5 year felony
Over $20,000 or $1,000 to less than $20,000, if previously convicted twice	10 year felony

When there are separate incidents that are part of common scheme or plan, the total amount can be aggregated over 12-month period for a total.

> The value of stolen items is determined by the price that the item would be at the time and place the defendant received them *People v. Dandy*, 99 Mich. App. 166 (1980).
>
> Where thieves damaged slot machines while in the process of stealing them, their value was determined in light of their damaged state when the defendant received them (i.e., their value was not determined in light of their condition before the theft). *People v. Fishel*, 270 Mich. 82 (1935).
>
> Evidence was sufficient to show that a car was stolen where subject took his ex-girlfriend's vehicle without permission. *People v. Pratt*, 254 Mich. App. 425 (2002).
>
> The conviction was upheld where a defendant purchased two silver candelabras, later learned that they were stolen, and then retained the candelabras. *People v. Fortuin*, 143 Mich. App. 279 (1985).

Knowledge that property was stolen

Mere possession is not enough. There must be other facts or circumstances that show the defendant knew or should have known the property was stolen. Examples include the following:

- The circumstances surrounding the taking.
- The way the suspect acted.
- The price that was paid.
- What the suspect said about the property.
- The time between when the property had been taken and when it was found in the defendant's possession.
- Any other circumstances that would allow the person to know the property was stolen.

CJI2d 26.3.

Transporting or Concealing Stolen Firearms— MCL 750.535b (felony)

(1) A person who transports or ships a stolen firearm or stolen ammunition, knowing that the firearm or ammunition was stolen, is guilty of a felony, punishable by imprisonment for not more than 10 years or by a fine of not more than $5,000.00, or both.

(2) A person who receives, conceals, stores, barters, sells, disposes of, pledges, or accepts as security for a loan a stolen firearm or stolen ammunition, knowing that the firearm or ammunition was stolen, is guilty of a felony, punishable by imprisonment for not more than 10 years or by a fine of not more than $5,000.00, or both.

> Concealing or storing stolen firearms is a continuing crime and not barred from the statute of limitations during the concealment. *People v. Owen*, 251 Mich. App. 76 (2002).
>
> The defendant was a getaway driver in a breaking and entering. She was subsequently convicted of home invasion in Lapeer County and of receiving and concealing a stolen firearm (which was stolen during the Lapeer County breaking and entering) in Oakland County. The court held that the dual convictions were not a Double Jeopardy violation because the statutes do not contain the same elements. *People v. Nutt*, 469 Mich. 565 (2004).
>
> Convictions for receiving and concealing a stolen firearm and possession of a firearm during a felony ("felony-firearm") do not violate the Double Jeopardy Clause. *People v. Mitchell*, 456 Mich. 693 (1998).

TRESPASS

Trespass Upon the Land of Another—MCL 750.552 (30-day misdemeanor)

(1) A person shall not do any of the following:

(a) Enter the lands or premises of another without lawful authority after having been forbidden so to do by the owner or occupant or the agent of the owner or occupant.

(b) Remain without lawful authority on the land or premises of another after being

notified to depart by the owner or occupant or the agent of the owner or occupant.
  (c) Enter or remain without lawful authority on fenced or posted farm property of another person without the consent of the owner or his or her lessee or agent. A request to leave the premises is not a necessary element for a violation of this subdivision. This subdivision does not apply to a person who is in the process of attempting, by the most direct route, to contact the owner or his or her lessee or agent to request consent.
(2) A person who violates subsection (1) is guilty of a misdemeanor punishable by imprisonment in the county jail for not more than 30 days or by a fine of not more than $250.00, or both.

Elements

1. Suspect willfully entered upon,
2. The land of another,
3. After having been forbidden to do so.

OR

1. Was on the premises of another, and
2. After being notified to depart, refused to do so.

OR

1. Entered or remained on,
2. Without lawful authority,
3. The fenced or posted farmland,
4. Of another person
5. Without the landowner's consent.

> A refusal to leave is not a necessary element when the defendant had already been forbidden from being on the premises. *People v. Bell*, 182 Mich. App 181 (1989).
>
> A criminal trespass conviction was upheld where the defendants moved into a vacant city-owned house and made it habitable. *People v. Johnson*, 16 Mich. App. 745 (1969).

Trespassing on a State Correctional Facility—MCL 750.552b (felony)

(1) A person who willfully trespasses by entering or remaining upon the property of a state correctional facility without authority or permission to enter or remain is guilty of a felony punishable by imprisonment for not more than 4 years or a fine of not more than $2,000.00, or both.
(2) As used in this section, "state correctional facility" means a facility or institution that houses a prisoner population under the jurisdiction of the department of corrections. State correctional facility does not include a community corrections center or a community residential home.

Recreational Trespass—MCL 324.73102 (90-day misdemeanor)

(1) Except as provided in subsection (4), a person shall not enter or remain upon the property of another person, other than farm property or a wooded area connected to farm property, to engage in any recreational activity or trapping on that property without the consent of the owner or his or her lessee or agent, if either of the following circumstances exists:
  (a) The property is fenced or enclosed and is maintained in such a manner as to exclude intruders.
  (b) The property is posted in a conspicuous manner against entry. The minimum letter height on the posting signs shall be 1 inch. Each posting sign shall be not less than 50 square inches, and the signs shall be spaced to enable a person to observe not less than 1 sign at any point of entry upon the property.
(2) Except as provided in subsection (4), a person shall not enter or remain upon farm property or a wooded area connected to farm property for any recreational activity or trapping without the consent of the owner or his or her lessee or agent, whether or not the farm property or wooded area connected to farm property is fenced, enclosed, or posted.
(3) On fenced or posted property or farm property, a fisherman wading or floating a navigable public stream may, without written or oral consent, enter upon property within the clearly defined banks of the stream or, without damaging farm products, walk a route as closely proximate to the clearly defined bank as possible when necessary to avoid a natural or artificial hazard or obstruction, including, but not limited to, a dam, deep hole, or a fence or other exercise of ownership by the riparian owner.
(4) A person other than a person possessing a firearm may, unless previously prohibited in writing or orally by the property owner or his or her lessee or agent, enter on foot upon the property of another person for the sole purpose of retrieving a hunting dog. The person shall not remain on the property beyond the reasonable time necessary to retrieve the dog. In an action under section 73109 or 73110, the burden of showing that the property owner or his

or her lessee or agent previously prohibited entry under this subsection is on the plaintiff or prosecuting attorney, respectively.

(5) Consent to enter or remain upon the property of another person pursuant to this section may be given orally or in writing. The consent may establish conditions for entering or remaining upon that property. Unless prohibited in the written consent, a written consent may be amended or revoked orally. If the owner or his or her lessee or agent requires all persons entering or remaining upon the property to have written consent, the presence of the person on the property without written consent is prima facie evidence of unlawful entry.

Elements

1. The suspect entered or remained,
2. On someone else's property that is not farm property or woods connected to farm property,
3. To engage in recreational or trapping activities,
4. Without the owner's consent,
5. And if one of the following are in place:

   a. A fence or enclosure maintained so as to keep out intruders,
   b. Signs posted to keep out intruders that meet the statutory language.

There are exceptions for:

1. Fisherman wading or floating on a public stream who enter onto the property and walk directly to the road in order to avoid a natural or artificial hazard or obstruction
2. A person on foot who does not have a firearm may enter onto property to retrieve a hunting dog so long as that person has not been forbidden from being on the property.

> A defendant was convicted of recreational trespassing while fishing near a Consumer's Energy facility. He appealed to the Michigan Supreme Court and argued that subsection (3), which creates an exception allowing fishermen to exit public streams, should be applicable in his case. The Court denied the defendant's application for leave to appeal. *People v. Gatski*, 472 Mich. 887 (2005).

Trespass on Key Facilities—MCL 750.552c (felony)

(1) A person shall not intentionally and without authority or permission enter or remain in or upon premises or a structure belonging to another person that is a key facility if the key facility is completely enclosed by a physical barrier of any kind, including, but not limited to, a significant water barrier that prevents pedestrian access, and is posted with signage as prescribed under subsection (2). As used in this subsection, "key facility" means 1 or more of the following:

(a) A chemical manufacturing facility.
(b) A refinery.
(c) An electric utility facility, including, but not limited to, a power plant, a power generation facility peaker, an electric transmission facility, an electric station or substation, or any other facility used to support the generation, transmission, or distribution of electricity. Electric utility facility does not include electric transmission land or right-of-way that is not completely enclosed, posted, and maintained by the electric utility.
(d) A water intake structure or water treatment facility.
(e) A natural gas utility facility, including, but not limited to, an age station, compressor station, odorization facility, main line valve, natural gas storage facility, or any other facility used to support the acquisition, transmission, distribution, or storage of natural gas. Natural gas utility facility does not include gas transmission pipeline property that is not completely enclosed, posted, and maintained by the natural gas utility.
(f) Gasoline, propane, liquid natural gas (LNG), or other fuel terminal or storage facility.
(g) A transportation facility, including, but not limited to, a port, railroad switching yard, or trucking terminal.
(h) A pulp or paper manufacturing facility.
(i) A pharmaceutical manufacturing facility.
(j) A hazardous waste storage, treatment, or disposal facility.
(k) A telecommunication facility, including, but not limited to, a central office or cellular telephone tower site.
(l) A facility substantially similar to a facility, structure, or station listed in subdivisions (a) to (k) or a resource required to submit a risk management plan under 42 USC 7412(r).

(2) A key facility shall be posted in a conspicuous manner against entry. The minimum letter height on the posting signs shall be 1 inch. Each posting sign shall be not less than 50 square inches, and the signs shall be spaced to enable a

person to observe not less than 1 sign at any point of entry upon the property.

(3) A person who violates this section is guilty of a felony punishable by imprisonment for not more than 4 years or a fine of not more than $2,500.00, or both.

(4) This section does not prohibit and shall be not construed to prevent lawful assembly or a peaceful and orderly petition for the redress of grievances, including, but not limited to, a labor dispute between an employer and its employees.

CONTROLLED SUBSTANCES

SCHEDULES

Michigan and federal law both classify controlled substances, placing known chemical compounds on lists (called schedules) according to several factors. Substances are placed on Michigan's schedules as follows: (some substances may appear in multiple schedules depending on weight or mixture).

Schedule 1—MCL 333.7212

- High potential for abuse and has no accepted medical use.
- Examples: Mescaline, Cat, Peyote, GHB, Ecstacy, Psilocybin, Marihuana, Lysergic acid diethylamide

Schedule 2—MCL 333.7214

- High potential for abuse.
- Has accepted medical use.
- Abuse may lead to severe psychic or physical dependence.
- Examples: Opium, Morphine, Fentanyl, Methadone, Cocaine, Oxycodone

Schedule 3—MCL 333.7216

- Potential for abuse but less than schedules 1 and 2.
- The substance has currently accepted medical use.
- Abuse may lead to moderate or low physical dependence or high psychological dependence.
- Examples: Codeine, Lysergic acid, Opium or Morphine mixtures, Ketamine

Schedule 4—MCL 333.7218

- Low potential for abuse.
- Current medical use.
- Abuse may lead to limited physical dependence or psychological dependence compared to schedule 3.
- Examples: Phenobarbital, Diazepam

Schedule 5—MCL 333.7220

- Low potential for abuse.
- Current medical use.
- Limited physical dependence or psychological dependence compared to schedule 4.
- Examples: Opium or Codeine mixtures, Ephedrine

Manufacture, Delivery or Possession with the Intent to Deliver a Controlled Substance— MCL 333.7401 (felony)

Except as otherwise authorized by law, it is a felony to "manufacture, create, deliver, or possess with intent to manufacture, create, or deliver a controlled substance, a prescription form, or a counterfeit prescription form. A

Penalties:

Drug Type	Amount	Punishment
Schedule 1 or 2 narcotic or cocaine	1,000 grams or more	Felony – Life, $1,000,000 fine
	450 grams or more, but less than 1,000 grams	Felony – 30 years, $500,000 fine
	50 grams or more, but less than 450 grams	Felony – 20 years, $250,000 fine
	Less than 50 grams	Felony – 20 years, $25,000 fine
Ecstacy or Methampetamine	Any amount	Felony – 20 years, $25,000 fine
Any other schedule 1 or 2, or any schedule 3 (except marihuana)	Any amount	Felony – 7 years,
Schedule 4	Any amount	Felony – 4 years, $2,000 fine
Marijuana	45 kilograms or more, or 200 plants or more	Felony – 15 years, $10,000,000 fine
	5 kilograms or more, but less than 45 kilograms, or 20 plants or more, but less than 200 plants	Felony – 7 years, $500,000 fine
	Less than 5 kilograms or less than 20 plants	Felony – 4 years, $20,000 fine
Schedule 5	Any amount	Felony – 2 years, $2,000 fine
Prescription form or counterfeit form		Felony – 7 years, $5,000 fine

practitioner licensed by the administrator under this article shall not dispense, prescribe, or administer a controlled substance for other than legitimate and professionally recognized therapeutic or scientific purposes or outside the scope of practice of the practitioner, licensee, or applicant." MCL 333.7401(1).

Manufacture

- Producing or processing a controlled substance.

The conversion of powdered cocaine into crack cocaine constitutes manufacturing. *People v. Hunter*, 201 Mich. App. 671 (1994).

Delivery

- Transferred or attempted to transfer the substance to another person,
- Knowledge that it is a controlled substance,
- Intent to transfer said substance to another person.

Delivery does not include the use of cocaine by a pregnant woman, where the substance is passed unto her unborn child. *People v. Jones*, 162 Mich. App. 448 (1987).

Delivery includes the transferring of drugs during social sharing of drugs. *People v. Schultz*, 246 Mich. App. 695 (2001).

Two charges for delivery were proper where there was one delivery in the morning and another in the afternoon. Each delivery was also bargained for separately. *People v. Miller*, 182 Mich. App. 641 (1990).

"A defendant may be properly convicted of delivery of 225 grams or more but less than 650 grams of cocaine, even if he does not know the amount of drugs to be delivered. For conspiracy to deliver, the prosecutor must prove that the defendant knew the amount to be delivered." *People v. Mass*, 469 Mich. 615 (2001).

Attempt to deliver

- Intent to deliver a controlled substance or mixture of substance to someone else.
- In order to qualify as an attempt, the action must go beyond mere preparation, to the point where the crime would have been committed if it had not been interrupted by outside circumstances. Things like planning the crime or arranging how it will be committed are just preparations.

Possession with the intent to deliver

- Suspect knowingly possessed a controlled substance or mixture of the substance, with the intent to deliver the substance to someone else.

> Intent to deliver may be determined by circumstantial evidence. *People v. Tolbert*, 77 Mich. App 162 (1977). For example, the amount of substance, how it was packaged, and paraphernalia found with the substance are important considerations.

Includes controlled substance or mixture

- The amount determines the severity of the punishment.

> The term mixture precludes the weight of the controlled substance and filler material from being aggregated to punish the defendant more severely unless both the controlled substance and filler are mixed together to form a homogeneous or reasonably uniform mass. *People v. Hunter*, 201 Mich. App. 671 (1994).

Possession—MCL 333.7403

A person shall not knowingly or intentionally possess a controlled substance, a controlled substance analogue, or a prescription form unless the controlled substance, controlled substance analogue, or prescription form was obtained directly from, or pursuant to, a valid prescription or order of a practitioner while acting in the course of the practitioner's professional practice, or except as otherwise authorized by this article. MCL 333.7403(1).

Penalties:

LSD, peyote, mescaline, dimethyltryptamine, psilocyn, psilocybin, or controlled substances in schedule 5	1 year misdemeanor
Marijuana	1 year misdemeanor
Unlawful possession of an unofficial prescription form	1 year misdemeanor
Unlawful possession of an official prescription form	felony
Possession of schedule 1, 2, 3 or 4	felony

Knowingly possess

The suspect knowingly possessed a controlled substance or a mixture of a controlled substance for personal use. A person may be in possession even if the substance is in a different room. Also, more than one person may be in possession. It is not enough that the person merely knows about the substance, but he or she did possess the substance if he or she had control of it or the right to control it either alone or together with someone else.

> There was sufficient evidence for possession charges where the marijuana was found on the floor of defendant's automobile, in an area where defendant was observed bending down to, when the officer approached. *People v. Eaves*, 4 Mich. App. 457 (1966).
>
> Possession may be either actual or constructive. A person's presence where drugs are found is insufficient, by itself, to prove constructive possession. Some additional connection between the defendant and the contraband must be shown. *People v. Hardiman*, 466 Mich. 417 (2002).

Use—MCL 333.7404

A person shall not use a controlled substance or controlled substance analogue unless the substance was obtained directly from, or pursuant to, a valid prescription or order of a practitioner while acting in the course of the practitioner's professional practice, or except as otherwise authorized by this article. MCL 333.7404(1).

Penalties

Schedule 1, 2, 3, or 4	1 year misdemeanor
LSD, peyote, mescaline, dimethyltryptamine, psilocyn, psilocybin, or controlled substances in schedule 5	6 month misdemeanor
Marijuana	90 day misdemeanor

Additional Penalties for Manufacturing Substances—MCL 333.7401c

Except for violations involving only cocaine or marihuana (or both), it is a felony for a person to do any of the following:

(a) Own, possess, or use a vehicle, building, structure, place, or area that he or she knows or has reason to know is to be used as a location to manufacture a controlled substance in violation MCL 333.7401 or a counterfeit substance or a controlled substance analogue in violation of MCL 333.7402.

(b) Own or possess any chemical or any laboratory equipment that he or she knows or has reason to know is to be used for the purpose of manufacturing a controlled substance in violation of MCL 333.7401 or a counterfeit substance or a controlled substance analogue in violation of MCL 333.7402.

(c) Provide any chemical or laboratory equipment to another person knowing or having reason to know that the other person intends to use that chemical or laboratory equipment for the purpose of manufacturing a controlled substance in violation of MCL 333.7401 or a counterfeit substance or a controlled substance analogue in violation of MCL 333..7402.

For the purposes of this section only, the following definitions apply:

(a) "Laboratory equipment" means any equipment, device, or container used or intended to be used in the process of manufacturing a controlled substance, counterfeit substance, or controlled substance analogue.

(b) "Manufacture" means the production, preparation, propagation, compounding, conversion, or processing of a controlled substance, directly or indirectly by extraction from substances of natural origin, or independently by means of chemical synthesis, or by a combination of extraction and chemical synthesis. Manufacture does not include any of the following:

(i) The packaging or repackaging of the substance or labeling or relabeling of its container.

(ii) The preparation or compounding of a controlled substance by any of the following:

(A) A practitioner as an incident to the practitioner's administering or dispensing of a controlled substance in the course of his or her professional practice.

(B) A practitioner, or by the practitioner's authorized agent under his or her supervision, for the purpose of, or as an incident to, research, teaching, or chemical analysis and not for sale.

Date Rape Drugs—MCL 333.7401a (felony)

A person is guilty of violating this statute if they[sic], without an individual's consent, deliver a controlled substance or a substance described in MCL 333.7401b or cause a controlled substance or a substance described in MCL 333.7401b to be delivered to that individual to commit or attempt to commit criminal sexual conduct or assault with intent to commit criminal sexual conduct.

This section applies regardless of whether the person is convicted of a CSC violation or attempted violation.

Gamma Hydroxybutyrate (GHB)—MCL 333.7212

This date rape drug falls under Schedule 1.

Gamma-Butyrolactone (GBL)—MCL 333.7401b

GBL is a precursor to and can be readily converted to gamma hydroxybutyrate (GHB), also known as the "date rape drug" when taken orally. The manufacture, delivery, or possession of GBL for human consumption is prohibited. GBL can be possessed for use in a commercial application such as industrial solvent and floor stripper.

Penalties:

Penalty for manufacture, delivery, or intent to manufacture or deliver	7 year felony
Possession of GBL	2 year felony
GBL used to commit CSC	20 year felony

USE OR POSSESSION IN HOTELS—MCL 750.411g(2)(a) (90-day misdemeanor)

Suspect rented a room in a hotel or bed and breakfast with reason to know controlled sub- stance will be used or possessed.

Drug Paraphernalia—MCL 333.7453 (90-day misdemeanor)

A person shall not sell or offer for sale drug paraphernalia knowing that it is drug paraphernalia. Before a person can be arrested, the attorney general or prosecuting attorney shall notify the person in writing not less than two days before arrest for the violation.

Additional Penalty:

| If suspect is older than 18 and sells to a person less than 18 years old | 1 year misdemeanor |

> MCL 333.7457(d) specifically excludes from the definition of paraphernalia any item that may be used for the smoking of tobacco or herbs. Because anything designed for the smoking of marijuana, such as a dug-out pipe or a bong, may also be used to smoke tobacco, such items are not prohibited paraphernalia. *Gauthier v. Alpena County Prosecutor*, 267 Mich. App. 167 (2005).

Prescription Misuse—MCL 333.17766 (90-day misdemeanor)

This statue is violated when a person does any of the following:

(a) Obtains or attempts to obtain a prescription drug by giving a false name to a pharmacist or other authorized seller, prescriber, or dispenser.
(b) Obtains or attempts to obtain a prescription drug by falsely representing that he or she is a lawful prescriber, dispenser, or licensee, or acting on behalf of a lawful prescriber, dispenser, or licensee.
(c) Falsely makes, utters, publishes, passes, alters, or forges a prescription.
(d) Knowingly possesses a false, forged, or altered prescription.
(e) Knowingly attempts to obtain, obtains, or possesses a drug by means of a prescription for other than a legitimate therapeutic purpose, or as a result of a false, forged, or altered prescription.
(f) Possesses or controls for the purpose of resale, or sells, offers to sell, dispenses, or gives away, a drug, pharmaceutical preparation, or chemical that has been dispensed on prescription and has left the control of a pharmacist, or that has been damaged by heat, smoke, fire, water, or other cause and is unfit for human or animal use.
(g) Prepares or permits the preparation of a prescription drug, except as delegated by a pharmacist.
(h) Sells a drug in bulk or in an open package at auction, unless the sale has been approved in accordance with rules of the board.

Androgenic Anabolic Steroids—MCL 333.17766a

Penalties:

Use	90 day misdemeanor
Possession, 1st offense	90 day misdemeanor
Possession, 2nd offense	4 year felony
Delivery/Possession with intent to deliver	7 year felony

An athletic service provider shall place a warning notice of the dangers of steroid use and the above listed punishments.

Imitation Controlled Substance—MCL 333.7341

An imitation controlled substance is a substance that is not a controlled substance but by its color, shape, size, markings, or representation would lead a reasonable person to believe it is a controlled substance.

Penalties:

Use or possession with the intent to use, 1st offense	$100.00 fine
Use or possession with the intent to use, 2nd offense	90 day misdemeanor
Manufacture, distribute, and possess with intent to distribute	2 year felony
Advertise or solicit distribution of imitation controlled substance	1 year misdemeanor

Controlled Substance Analogue—MCL 333.7402 (felony)

An analogue has a similar chemical structure to that of a schedule 1 or 2 controlled substance and has a narcotic, stimulant, depressant, or hallucinogenic effect on the nervous system.

A person shall not manufacture, deliver, or possess with intent to deliver a controlled substance analogue intended for human consumption.

Counterfeit Substance—MCL 333.7402 (felony)

A counterfeit substance is a controlled substance that bears the trademark, trade name, or other identifying marks of a manufacturer other than the person who in fact manufactured the substance. MCL 333.7104(5).

A person shall not manufacture, deliver, or possess with intent to deliver a counterfeit substance intended for human consumption.

Possession of Ephedrine—MCL 333.17766c (felony)

It is unlawful to possess more than 12 grams of ephedrine or pseudoephedrine alone or in a mixture. This section does not apply to any of the following:

(a) A person who possesses ephedrine or pseudoephedrine pursuant to a license issued by this state or the United States to manufacture, deliver, dispense, possess with intent to manufacture or deliver, or possess a controlled substance, prescription drug, or other drug.
(b) An individual who possesses ephedrine or pseudoephedrine pursuant to a prescription.
(c) A person who possesses ephedrine or pseudoephedrine for retail sale pursuant to a license issued under the general sales tax act, 1933 PA 167, MCL 205.51 to 205.78.
(d) A person who possesses ephedrine or pseudoephedrine in the course of his or her business of selling or transporting ephedrine or pseudoephedrine to a person described in subdivision (a) or (c).
(e) A person who, in the course of his or her business, stores ephedrine or pseudoephedrine for sale or distribution to a person described in subdivision (a), (c), or (d).
(f) Any product that the state board of pharmacy, upon application of a manufacturer, exempts from this section because the product has been formulated in such a way as to effectively prevent the conversion of the active ingredient into methamphetamine.
(g) Possession of any pediatric product primarily intended for administration to children under 12 years of age according to label instructions.

Sale, Distribution, or Delivery of Ephedrine—MCL 333.7340 (felony)

It is unlawful to sell, distribute, deliver, or furnish ephedrine or pseudoephedrine through the use of the mail, internet, telephone, or other electronic means. This does not apply to pediatric products designed for children under 12, a liquid product in which ephedrine is not the only active ingredient, a product that cannot be converted into methamphetamine, products dispensed pursuant to a prescription, and products distributed by licensed manufacturers.

Unlawful Containers for Anhydrous Ammonia—MCL 750.502d (felony)

It is unlawful to transport or possess anhydrous ammonia in a container other than a container approved by law, or to unlawfully tamper with a container approved by law.

As used in this section, "container approved by law" means a container that was manufactured to satisfy the requirements for the storage and handling of anhydrous ammonia pursuant to R408.17801 of the Michigan administrative code or its successor rule.

Use of Inhalants—MCL 752.272 (90-day misdemeanor)

This statute makes it unlawful to do the following:

- For the purpose of causing a condition of intoxication, euphoria, excitement, exhilaration, stupefaction, or dulling senses,
- Intentionally smell, or inhale the fumes of a chemical agent or,
- Drink, eat, or otherwise introduce any chemical agent into one's respiratory or circulatory system.

This section does not prohibit inhaling anesthesia for medical or dental purposes.

Sale of Nitrous Oxide—MCL 752.272a

A person shall not sell or otherwise distribute to another person any device that contains any quantity of nitrous oxide (also known as laughing gas) for the purpose of causing a condition of intoxication, euphoria, excitement, exhilaration, stupefaction, or dulling of the senses or nervous system. Law targets novelty "head" shops, making it more difficult for persons to obtain the gas for recreational use.

Exemptions: Persons who sell or distribute catering supplies, persons who sell compressed gases for industrial or medical use, pharmacists or health care professionals, and persons licensed under the Food Processing Act of 1977.

Penalties:

First Violation	93 day misdemeanor
Second Violation	1 year misdemeanor
Two or more prior convictions	4 year felony

Licensing Requirement—MCL 333.7303

A person who manufactures, distributes, prescribes, or dispenses a controlled substance in this state or who proposes to engage in the manufacture, distribution, prescribing, or dispensing of a controlled substance in this state shall obtain a license issued by the administrator in accordance with the rules. The following persons need not be licensed and may lawfully possess controlled substances or prescription forms under this article:

- An agent or employee of a licensed manufacturer, distributor, prescriber, or dispenser of a controlled substance, if acting in the usual course of the agent's or employee's business or employment.
- A common or contract carrier or warehouseman or an employee thereof, whose possession of a controlled substance or prescription form is in the usual course of business or employment.
- An ultimate user or agent in possession of a controlled substance or prescription form pursuant to a lawful order of a practitioner or in lawful possession of a schedule 5 substance.
- The administrator may waive or include by rule the requirement for licensure of certain manufacturers, distributors, prescribers, or dispensers, if it finds the waiver or inclusion is consistent with public health and safety.
- A separate license is required at each principal place of business or professional practice where the applicant manufactures, distributes, prescribes, or dispenses controlled substances.

The requirement of licensure is waived for the following persons in the circumstances described:

- An officer or employee of the Drug Enforcement Administration while engaged in the course of official duties.
- An officer of the United States Customs Service while engaged in the course of official duties.
- An officer or employee of the United States Food and Drug Administration while engaged in the course of official duties.
- A federal officer who is lawfully engaged in the enforcement of a federal law relating to controlled substances, drugs, or customs and who is authorized to possess controlled substances in the course of that person's official duties.
- An officer or employee of this state, or a political subdivision or agency of this state who is engaged in the enforcement of a state or local law relating to controlled substances and who is authorized to possess controlled substances in the course of that person's official duties.
- An official exempted from licensure by this section, when acting in the course of that person's official duties, may possess a controlled substance and may transfer a controlled substance to any other official who is exempt and who is acting in the course of that person's official duties.
- An official exempted by this section may procure a controlled substance in the course of an administrative inspection or investigation or in the course of a criminal investigation involving the person from whom the substance was procured.
- A law enforcement officer exempted by this section may distribute a controlled substance to another person in the course of that officer's official duties as a means to detect criminal activity or to conduct a criminal investigation.

Drug-Free School Zones—MCL 333.7410

This statute provides enhanced sentences for the following:

- Delivery of a controlled substance by a person 18 or older to a person under 18 and at least 3 years younger than the person delivering the substance.
- Delivery, by a person 18 or older, of a schedule 1 or 2 narcotic drug or cocaine to any person on or within 1,000 feet of school property or a library.
- Possessing with intent to deliver, by a person 18 or older, a schedule 1 or 2 narcotic drug or cocaine to any person on or within 1,000 feet of school property or a library.
- Possession of any controlled substance on school property or a library.

"Library" means a library that is established by the state; a county, city, township, village, school district, or other local unit of government or authority or

combination of local units of government and authorities; a community college district; a college or university; or any private library open to the public.

"School property" means a building, playing field, or property used for school purposes to impart instruction to children in grades kindergarten through 12, when provided by a public, private, denominational, or parochial school, except those buildings used primarily for adult education or college extension courses.

This statute also provides that "A person who distributes marihuana without remuneration and not to further commercial distribution and who does not violate subsection (1) is guilty of a misdemeanor punishable by imprisonment for not more than 1 year or a fine of not more than $1,000.00, or both, unless the distribution is in accordance with the federal law or the law of this state."

Medical Marihuana—MCL 333.26421–333.26430; R 333.101–333.133

The Michigan Medical Marihuana Act is an exception to the statutes governing the use, delivery, and possession of marihuana. Patients registered with the Department of Community Health AND in possession of their registry identification card may legally use, grow, deliver, or possess marihuana, and their registered caregivers may grow, deliver, or possess marihuana. While not in use, all marihuana possessed under the Act must be stored in a closed, locked facility.

Each patient is limited to 2.5 ounces or 12 plants. Caregivers may be registered to assist up to five patients and may possess enough marihuana for those patients (i.e., 24 plants for 2 patients).

Limitations

The Act prohibits the following actions by patients or caregivers:

1. Smoking marihuana in public
2. Possession of marihuana at schools or correctional facilities
3. Operating a vehicle while under the influence of marihuana
4. Making a fraudulent claim of medical use or possession to law enforcement to avoid prosecution
5. Selling marijuana to someone other than a qualified patient

The Act prohibits the following actions by police:

1. Possession of a registry identification card cannot be used to justify a search.
2. Registered patients are permitted to use and possess paraphernalia. Statutes and ordinances to the contrary may not be enforced.

Affirmative Defense

The Act contains an affirmative defense that may be asserted by a person in any prosecution involving marihuana. The defense is not limited to registered patients and caregivers, so it may be asserted by anyone. Affirmative defenses have no impact on a decision to arrest. However, the charges will be dismissed if a person proves the following:

1. A physician has stated that the patient is likely to receive a medical benefit from marihuana use,
2. The person did not possess more than reasonably necessary to ensure uninterrupted availability for treating a patient, and
3. The possession, manufacture, or delivery was done for the purpose of treating the patient.

EXPLOSIVES AND WEAPONS

EXPLOSIVES

Concealment of Explosives as Baggage or Freight—MCL 750.201 (felony)

A person shall not send, order, or transport an explosive on any vehicle used for transporting passengers or articles of commerce.

Explosives as Implements of Terrorism—MCL 750.204 (felony)

A person shall not send or deliver to another person an explosive, or cause an explosive to be taken or received by any person, with one of the following intents:

- To frighten, terrorize, intimidate, injure or kill another person, or
- To damage or destroy property of another.

Penalties:

If no damage or injury	15 year felony
If causes damage	20 year felony
If causes physical injury	25 year felony
If causes serious injury	Up to life
If causes death	Mandatory life without possibility of parole

Sending Fake Bombs—MCL 750.204a (felony)

The suspect delivered, possessed, transported, sent, or placed a device constructed to represent or presented as an explosive with the intent to frighten, terrorize, harass, threaten, or annoy another person.

Placing Bombs—MCL 750.207 (felony)

A person shall not place an explosive substance in or near any real or personal property with the intent to frighten, terrorize, intimidate, threaten, harass, injure, or kill any person, or with the intent to damage or destroy any real or personal property without the permission of the property owner or, if the property is public property, without the permission of the governmental agency having authority over that property. MCL 750.207(1).

Penalties:

Placing bombs with the intent to frighten, threaten, or harass	15 year felony
If causes damage	20 year felony
If causes physical injury	25 year felony
If causes serious injury	Up to life
If causes death	Mandatory life without possibility of parole

Placing Offensive or Injurious Substances—MCL 750.209 (felony)

The suspect placed an offensive or injurious substance with one of the following intents:

- To injure or coerce another person, or
- To injure the property or business of another, or
- To interfere with the person's use or management of his or her property.

Penalties:

If the suspect places offensive or injurious substance in or near any real or personal property with intent to annoy or alarm	5 year felony
If no damage or injury	15 year felony
If causes damage	20 year felony
If causes physical injury	25 year felony
If causes serious injury	Up to life
If causes death	Mandatory life without possibility of parole.

Possessing Explosives in a Public Place—MCL 750.209a (felony)

This section covers possessing an explosive with an unlawful intent in a public place.

Possession of Substance with Explosive Capabilit—MCL 750.210 (felony)

The suspect possessed, with unlawful intent, a substance or compound that would become explosive when combined with another substance or compound.

Penalties:

If no damage or injury	15 year felony
If causes damage	20 year felony
If causes physical injury	25 year felony
If causes serious injury	Up to life
If causes death	Mandatory life without possibility of parole

Carry, Manufacture, Buy, Sell or Furnish Explosive Compounds with Intent to Frighten, Terrorize, Harass, and Injure—MCL 750.211a (felony)

Penalties:

If no damage or injury	15 year felony
If causes damage	20 year felony
If causes physical injury	25 year felony
If causes serious injury	Up to life
If causes death	Mandatory life without possibility of parole

Vulnerable Targets—MCL 750.212a

An additional 20-year penalty will be added if explosion occurs in or is directed at one of the following vulnerable targets and death or serious injury results:

- A child daycare center.
- A health care facility.
- A building open to the general public.
- A church or other place of religious worship.
- A school, K-12.
- A college or university.
- A stadium.
- Critical transportation infrastructures.
- Public service providers.

Possessing Information of Vulnerable Targets—MCL 750.543c (felony)

A person shall not obtain or possess a blueprint, an architectural or engineering diagram, security plan, or other similar information of a vulnerable target with the intent to commit a prohibited offense.

HARMFUL BIOLOGICAL, CHEMICAL, OR RADIOACTIVE SUBSTANCES OR DEVICES

Definitions—MCL 750.200h

Harmful biological substance—Bacteria, virus, or other microorganism or toxic substance derived from microorganism that can cause death, injury, or disease in humans, animals, or plants.

Harmful chemical substance—A solid, liquid, or gas that, alone or in combination with one or more other chemical substances, can cause death, injury, or disease in humans, animals, or plants.

Harmful radioactive material—Material that is radioactive that can cause death, injury, or disease in humans, animals, or plants.

Chemical irritant—A solid, liquid, or gas that, through its chemical or physical properties alone or in combination with other substances, can be used to produce an irritant effect in humans, animals, or plants.

For an unlawful purpose—To frighten, terrorize, intimidate, threaten, harass, injure, or kill any person. Damage or destroy any real or personal property without the permission of the property owner.

Manufacture, Deliver, Possess, Use—MCL 750.200i (felony)

A person shall not manufacture, deliver, possess, transport, use or release *for an unlawful purpose* any of the following:

- A harmful biological substance or device.
- A harmful chemical substance or device.
- A harmful radioactive material or device.

> Hot cooking oil used to injure another person is not a harmful substance under this statute because oil's chemical properties alone cannot cause injury, death, or disease. *People v. Blunt*, 282 Mich. App. 81 (2009).

Other Harmful Substances—MCL 750.200j (felony)

A person shall not manufacture, deliver, possess, transport, place, use, or release for an unlawful purpose any of the following:

(a) A chemical irritant or a chemical irritant device.
(b) A smoke device.
(c) An imitation harmful substance or device.

False Exposure to Harmful Substance—MCL 750.200l (felony)

A person shall not commit an act with the intent to cause an individual to falsely believe that the individual has been exposed to a harmful biological substance, harmful biological device, harmful chemical substance, harmful chemical device, harmful radioactive material, or harmful radioactive device.

The court also shall impose costs on a person who violates this subsection to reimburse any governmental agency for its expenses incurred.

Molotov Cocktails—MCL 750. 211a (felony)

A person shall not do either of the following:

(a) *Except as provided in subdivision (b), manufacture, buy, sell, furnish, or possess a Molotov cocktail or any similar device.*
(b) *Manufacture, buy, sell, furnish, or possess any device that is designed to explode or that will explode upon impact or with the application of heat or a flame or that is highly incendiary, with the intent to frighten, terrorize, intimidate, threaten, harass, injure, or kill any person, or with the intent to damage or destroy any real or personal property without the permission of the property owner or, if the property is public property, without the permission of the governmental agency having authority over that property.*

FIREWORKS—MCL 750.243a (90-day misdemeanor)

(1) *Definitions. As used in this chapter:*

(a) *"Fireworks" means a device made from explosive or flammable compositions used primarily for the purpose of producing a visible display or audible effect, or both, by combustion, deflagration, or detonation. Fireworks includes class B fireworks and class C fireworks.*

(b) *"Class B fireworks" means toy torpedoes, railway torpedoes, firecrackers or salutes that do not qualify as class C fireworks, exhibition display pieces, aeroplane flares, illuminating projectiles, incendiary projectiles, incendiary grenades, smoke projectiles or bombs containing expelling charges but without bursting charges, flash powders in inner units not exceeding 2 ounces each, flash sheets in interior packages, flash powder or spreader cartridges containing not more than 72 grains of flash powder each, and other similar devices.*

(c) *"Class C fireworks" means toy smoke devices, toy caps containing not more than .25 grains of explosive mixture, toy propellant devices, cigarette loads, trick matches, trick noise makers, smoke candles, smoke pots, smoke grenades, smoke signals, hand signal devices, very signal cartridges, sparklers, explosive auto alarms, and other similar devices.*

(2) *Sale, possession, transportation, use, prohibited.* Except as provided in subsection (3) and sections 243b, 243c, and 243d, a person, firm, partnership, or corporation shall not offer for sale, expose for sale, sell at retail, keep with intent to sell at retail, possess, give, furnish, transport, use, explode, or cause to explode any of the following:

  (a) A blank cartridge, blank cartridge pistol, toy cannon, toy cane, or toy gun in which explosives are used.
  (b) An unmanned balloon which requires fire underneath to propel it and is not moored to the ground while aloft.
  (c) Firecrackers, torpedoes, skyrockets, roman candles, daygo bombs, bottle rockets, whistling chasers, rockets on sticks, or other fireworks of like construction.
  (d) Fireworks containing an explosive or inflammable compound or a tablet or other device commonly used and sold as fireworks containing nitrates, fulminates, chlorates, oxalates, sulphides of lead, barium, antimony, arsenic, mercury, nitroglycerine, phosphorus, or a compound containing these or other modern explosives.

(3) *Exceptions.* A permit is not required for the following:

  (a) Flat paper caps containing not more than .25 of a grain of explosive content per cap, in packages labeled to indicate the maximum explosive content per cap.
  (b) Toy pistols, toy cannons, toy canes, toy trick noise makers, and toy guns of a type approved by the director of the department of state police in which paper caps as described in subdivision (a) are used and which are so constructed that the hand cannot come in contact with the cap when in place for the explosion and which are not designed to break apart or be separated so as to form a missile by the explosion.
  (c) Sparklers containing not more than .0125 pounds of burning portion per sparkler.
  (d) Flitter sparklers in paper tubes not exceeding 1/8 inch in diameter, cone fountains, and cylinder fountains.
  (e) Toy snakes not containing mercury, if packed in cardboard boxes with not more than 12 pieces per box for retail sale and if the manufacturer's name and the quantity contained in each box are printed on the box; and toy smoke devices.
  (f) Possession, transportation, sale, or use of signal flares of a type approved by the director of the department of state police, blank cartridges or blank cartridge pistols specifically for a show or theater, for the training or exhibiting of dogs, for signal purposes in athletic sports, for use by military organizations, and all items described in subsection (2) used by railroads for emergency signal purposes.
  (g) The sale of fireworks provided they are to be shipped directly out of state pursuant to regulations of the United States department of transportation covering the transportation of explosives and other dangerous articles by motor, rail, and water.

A person shall not possess, sell, furnish, or explode any of the following without a permit:

- A blank cartridge, toy cannon, toy cane, or toy gun in which explosives are used.
- An unmanned balloon, which requires fire underneath to propel it and is not moored to the ground.
- Firecrackers, torpedoes, skyrockets, roman candles, daygo bombs, bottle rockets, or other fireworks of like construction.
- Fireworks containing an explosive or inflammable compound.

Permits are not required for such things as paper caps, sparklers, toy snakes, toy trick noise makers, toy smoke devices, blank cartridges, and signal flares.

FIREARMS
Definitions—MCL 750.222

Firearm – Weapon from which a dangerous projectile may be propelled by an explosive or by gas or air. Firearm does not include a smooth bore rifle or handgun designed to shoot BBs not exceeding .177 caliber.

Pistol – Loaded or unloaded firearm, 30 inches or less in length, or by its construction or appearance conceals the fact that it is a firearm.

Purchaser – Person who receives a pistol by purchase, gift or loan.

Seller – A person who sells, loans or gives a pistol to another.

Shotgun – Firearm, designed and intended to be fired from the shoulder, fires a fixed shotgun shell, smooth bore, ball shot or single projectile with single pull of the trigger.

Rifle – Firearm, designed and intended to be fired from the shoulder, which fires a fixed metallic cartridge, rifle bore, or single projectile with single pull of trigger.

Possession of a Short Barreled Shotgun or Rifle—MCL 750.224b (felony)

Definitions

Short-barreled shotgun – A shotgun with 1 or more barrels less than 18 inches, or overall length less than 26 inches.

Short-barreled rifle – A rifle with 1 or more barrels less than 16 inches, or overall length less than 26 inches.

A person shall not manufacture, sell, offer for sale, or possess a short-barreled shotgun or short-barreled rifle.

Exceptions: Those which the Secretary of Treasury of the United States has found to be curios, relics, antiques, museum pieces, or collector's items, not likely to be used as a weapon.

Stun Gun—MCL 750.224a (felony)

(1) Except as otherwise provided in this section, a person shall not sell, offer for sale, or possess in this state a portable device or weapon from which an electrical current, impulse, wave, or beam may be directed, which current, impulse, wave, or beam is designed to incapacitate temporarily, injure, or kill.

(2) This section does not prohibit any of the following:

(a) The possession and reasonable use of a device that uses electro-muscular disruption technology by a peace officer, an employee of the department of corrections authorized in writing by the director of the department of corrections, a local corrections officer authorized in writing by the county sheriff, a probation officer, a court officer, a bail agent authorized under section 167b, a licensed private investigator, or an aircraft pilot or aircraft crew member, who has been trained in the use, effects, and risks of the device, while performing his or her official duties.

(b) Possession solely for the purpose of delivering a device described in subsection (1) to any governmental agency or to a laboratory for testing, with the prior written approval of the governmental agency or law enforcement agency and under conditions determined to be appropriate by that agency.

(3) A manufacturer, authorized importer, or authorized dealer may demonstrate, offer for sale, hold for sale, sell, give, lend, or deliver a device that uses electro-muscular disruption technology to a person authorized to possess a device that uses electro-muscular disruption technology and may possess a device that uses electro-muscular disruption technology for any of those purposes.

(4) A person who violates this section is guilty of a felony punishable by imprisonment for not more than 4 years or a fine of not more than $2,000.00, or both.

(5) As used in this section, "a device that uses electro-muscular disruption technology" means a device to which all of the following apply:

(a) The device is capable of creating an electro-muscular disruption and is used or intended to be used as a defensive device capable of temporarily incapacitating or immobilizing a person by the direction or emission of conducted energy.

(b) The device contains an identification and tracking system that, when the device is initially used, dispenses coded material traceable to the purchaser through records kept by the manufacturer.

(c) The manufacturer of the device has a policy of providing the identification and tracking information described in subdivision (b) to a police agency upon written request by that agency.

Unlawful Weapons—MCL 750.224 (felony)

A person is prohibited from manufacturing, selling or possessing the following weapons:

- A **machine gun,** which is a gun that fires more than one round with single pull of the trigger.
  - In a related section of law, MCL 750.224e prohibits knowingly manufacturing, selling, distributing, or possessing a device designed to convert a semi-automatic weapon into an automatic one. (felony)
  - Exceptions include police, armed forces, and a licensed dealer if the dealer had the device prior to March 28, 1991.
- A **muffler or silencer,** which is a device used to muffle the sound of a firing gun.
- A **bomb or bombshell,** which is a hollow container filled with gunpowder or other explosive designed to be set off with fuse or other device.
- A **blackjack,** which is a lead slug attached to a narrow strip, usually leather.

CHAPTER 16 Explosives and Weapons

> Does not apply to a fish billy carried as such. *People v. Battles*, 109 Mich. App. 384 (1981).
>
> A police nightstick or baton does not fall within this statute. *People v. Hassenfratz*, 99 Mich. App. 154 (1980).

- A **billy**, which is a small bludgeon that may be carried in a pocket.
- A **sand club or sandbag**, which is a narrow bag filled with sand and used as a bludgeon.
- A **bludgeon**, which is a short club usually weighted at one end or bigger at one end and designed to be a weapon.
- **Metallic knuckles**, which are pieces of metal designed to be worn over the knuckles in order to protect them in striking a blow or to make the blow more effective.
- A device that releases a gas or substance that renders a person temporarily or permanently disabled.
  - An exception to this is the **self-defense spray**, which is a device that contains not more than 35 grams of orthochlorobenzalmalonitrile and inert ingredients or not more than 2% oleoresin capsicum. Self-defense spray is allowed in the protection of a person or property under circumstances that would justify use of physical force. MCL 750.224d.
    - Unlawful use of self-defense spray is a two-year misdemeanor.
    - If used in the commission of another crime, the sentenced may be enhanced.
    - If sold to a minor, the penalty is a 90-day misdemeanor.

Carrying a Concealed Weapon (CCW)—MCL 750.227 (felony)

(1) A person shall not carry a dagger, dirk, stiletto, a double-edged non-folding stabbing instrument of any length, or any other dangerous weapon, except a hunting knife adapted and carried as such, concealed on or about his or her person, or whether concealed or otherwise in any vehicle operated or occupied by the person, except in his or her dwelling house, place of business or on other land possessed by the person.

(2) A person shall not carry a pistol concealed on or about his or her person, or, whether concealed or otherwise, in a vehicle operated or occupied by the person, except in his or her dwelling house, place of business, or on other land possessed by the person, without a license to carry the pistol as provided by law and if licensed, shall not carry the pistol in a place or manner inconsistent with any restrictions upon such license.

Pistol on a person

The suspect knowingly carried a pistol that was concealed on or about his or her person.

> For CCW, complete invisibility is not required. The weapon is concealed if it is not observed by those casually observing the suspect as people do in the ordinary and usual associations of life. *People v. Reynolds*, 38 Mich. App. 159 (1970).
>
> CCW laws apply to security guards licenses under the Private Security Guard Act. *People v. Biller*, 239 Mich. App. 590 (2000).
>
> The carrying of a pistol in a holster or belt outside the clothing is not CCW. However, carrying under a coat would constitute a violation. Op. Atty. Gen. 1945, O-3158. Note that it is legal to carry a visible pistol in public (often called "open carry").

Pistol in a vehicle

- The pistol was in a vehicle that the suspect was in and he knew or was aware that the pistol was there.
- The suspect took part in carrying or keeping the pistol in the vehicle.

> Participation in the act of carrying may be inferred from the fact that the defendant was found carrying ammunition usable in the gun in question. He was in close proximity to the weapon. He and others were engaged in a common, unlawful enterprise and the gun was being carried in furtherance of the enterprise. *People v. Stone*, 100 Mich. App. 24 (1980).
>
> CCW includes carrying a pistol hidden in a motorcycle. *People v. Nimeth*, 236 Mich. App. 616 (1999).

Operability

> It is an affirmative defense if it is proven that the pistol could not fire and could not be readily made to fire. *People v. Gardner*, 194 Mich. App. 652 (1992).
>
> Possession of a pistol, no matter how short the period of time, will satisfy the CCW statute.

> Momentary possession after disarming another person is not a defense. *People v. Hernandez-Garcia*, 477 Mich. 1039 (2007).

Other weapons under CCW

- Double-edged, non-folding stabbing instrument (Double-edged knives)
  - Does not include a knife, tool, implement, arrowhead, or artifact manufactured from stone by means of conchoidal fracturing (breaking of stone). The item cannot be transported in a vehicle, unless it is in a container and inaccessible to the driver. MCL 750.222a.
- Dirk, dagger, and stiletto
  - Dirk is a straight knife with a pointed blade.
  - Dagger is a knife with a short-pointed blade.
  - Stiletto is a small dagger with a slender, tapering blade.
- Dangerous Stabbing Instruments

A dangerous stabbing instrument is a stabbing weapon that is carried as a dangerous weapon and could cause serious physical injury or death. Some instruments are dangerous *per se*, others are left up to the jury to decide if they are dangerous. CJI2d 11.4.

> A homemade knife, which was pointed and ground down on both edges and discovered in possession of a prison inmate could properly be deemed a dangerous weapon per se. *People v. Grandberry*, 102 Mich. App. 769 (1980).

A person is not CCW under the following:

- In his or her house,

> Lawful ownership of the pistol is not required for the dwelling house exception. *People v. Pasha*, 466 Mich. 378 (2002).

- At his or her place of business, or
- On land he or she owns.

Exceptions to MCL 750.227(2) (CCW in a vehicle)— MCL 750.231a

CCW in a vehicle does not apply to the following:

(a) To a person holding a valid license to carry a pistol concealed upon his or her person issued by his or her state of residence except where the pistol is carried in nonconformance with a restriction appearing on the license.
(b) To the regular and ordinary transportation of pistols as merchandise by an authorized agent of a person licensed to manufacture firearms.
(c) To a person carrying an antique firearm as defined in subsection (2), completely unloaded in a closed case or container designed for the storage of firearms in the trunk of a vehicle.
(d) To a person while transporting a pistol for a lawful purpose that is licensed by the owner or occupant of the motor vehicle in compliance with section 2 of 1927 PA 372, MCL 28.422, and the pistol is unloaded in a closed case designed for the storage of firearms in the trunk of the vehicle.
(e) To a person while transporting a pistol for a lawful purpose that is licensed by the owner or occupant of the motor vehicle in compliance with section 2 of 1927 PA 372, MCL 28.422, and the pistol is unloaded in a closed case designed for the storage of firearms in a vehicle that does not have a trunk and is not readily accessible to the occupants of the vehicle.

The following definitions apply to this statute:

(a) "Antique firearm" means either of the following:
  (i) A firearm not designed or redesigned for using rimfire or conventional center fire ignition with fixed ammunition and manufactured in or before 1898, including a matchlock, flintlock, percussion cap, or similar type of ignition system or replica of such a firearm, whether actually manufactured before or after 1898.
  (ii) A firearm using fixed ammunition manufactured in or before 1898, for which ammunition is no longer manufactured in the United States and is not readily available in the ordinary channels of commercial trade.

(b) "Lawful purpose" includes the following:

   (i) While en route to or from a hunting or target shooting area.
   (ii) While transporting a pistol en route to or from his or her home or place of business and place of repair.
   (iii) While moving goods from 1 place of abode or business to another place of abode or business.
   (iv) While transporting a licensed pistol en route to or from a law enforcement agency or for the purpose of having a law enforcement official take possession of the weapon.
   (v) While en route to or from his or her abode or place of business and a gun show or places of purchase or sale.
   (vi) While en route to or from his or her abode to a public shooting facility or public land where discharge of firearms is permitted by law, rule, regulation, or local ordinance.
   (vii) While en route to or from his or her abode to a private property location where the pistol is to be used as is permitted by law, rule, regulation, or local ordinance.

> Where the evidence did not establish that the defendant intended to abandon his out-of-state domicile, his out-of-state CCW permit was valid in Michigan even though he had been here for three months. He still had his out-of-state driver's license and registration, had not sought gainful employment and was not renting or owning any real estate. *People v. Williams*, 226 Mich. App. 568 (1997).
>
> MCL 750.231a requires an out-of-state resident to still carry a permit in Michigan even if his or her state does not require a permit. *People v. Miller*, 238 Mich. App. 168 (1999).

Self-defense

Self-defense is not a defense for carrying a concealed weapon.

Concealed Pistol Lcenses (CPL)

A Michigan resident may obtain a license to carry a pistol concealed. The following is a brief review of some of the laws affecting Concealed Pistol License (CPL) holders.

Requirements of CPL holders when stopped by police—MCL 28.425f

- A CPL holder must disclose to a peace officer immediately when stopped that he or she has a CPL and that he or she possesses a concealed pistol on his or her person or in his or her vehicle. This requirement only applies when the CPL holder is actually in possession of a concealed pistol.

Penalties:

First offense	State civil infraction, $500 fine and 6 months CCW suspension, MCL 28.425f(5)(a)
Second Offense	State civil infraction, $1000 fine and CCW revocation, MCL 28.425f(5)(b)

- A CPL holder must possess his or her CPL when carrying a concealed pistol = $100 fine. MCL 28.425f(1).
- Failure to display CPL and Michigan driver's license or Michigan personal identification card when carrying a concealed pistol = $100 fine. MCL 28.425f(2).

Pistol-Free Zones

A person with a CPL may not carry a pistol in a pistol-free zone, which includes any of the following (parking lots are excluded):

- Schools or school property, except a parent or legal guardian who is dropping off or picking child up and pistol is kept in the vehicle.
- Public or private day care center.
- Sports arena or stadium.
- A bar or tavern where sale and consumption of liquor by the glass is the primary source of income.
- Any property or facility owned or operated by a church, synagogue, mosque, temple, or other place of worship, unless authorized by the presiding official.
- An entertainment facility that has a seating capacity of 2,500 or more.
- A hospital.
- A dormitory or classroom of a community college, college, or university.
- A casino.

Penalties:

First offense	State civil infraction, $500 fine CPL suspended 6 months
Second offense	Misdemeanor, $1000 fine, CPL revoked
Third and subsequent offenses	4-year felony, $5000 fine, CPL revoked

The pistol-free zones for CPL holders do not apply to the following when they are licensed:

- Retired police officers.
- Persons employed or contracted by a listed entity to provide security where carrying a concealed pistol in a term of employment.
- Licensed private detectives or investigators.
- Sheriff's department corrections officers.
- State police motor carrier officers or capitol security officers.
- Members of a sheriff's posse.
- Auxiliary or reserve officers of a police or sheriff's department.
- Parole or probation officers of the department of corrections.
- State court judges and retired state court judges.

Carrying while under the influence—MCL 28.425k

- Acceptance of a CPL constitutes implied consent to submit to a chemical test for violations of this law. A peace officer who has probable cause to believe an individual is carrying a concealed pistol in violation of this law may require a chemical test of breath, blood, or urine. The collection of a chemical test sample shall be conducted in the same manner as driving violations under the O.W.I./OUID law.

  If the person refuses the chemical test, the peace officer shall report the refusal to the licensing board. If the person takes the chemical test and the results prove any bodily content, the peace officer shall report the results to the licensing board.

- A person is not in violation of this section if he or she has bodily alcohol content and is a passenger in a vehicle and the pistol is locked up in a container in the trunk. If there is no trunk, the pistol must be unloaded and locked in a container and separated from the ammunition.

Penalties:

.02 -.079 BAC	State civil infraction and $100 fine, 1 year revocation
.08 -.099 BAC	93 day misdemeanor and $100 fine, 3 year revocation
.10 or more BAC	93 day misdemeanor and $100 fine, permanent revocation

Seizure of pistols—MCL 28.425g

A concealed pistol may be seized for any violation of the CPL statute *except*:

- The pistol should not be seized if the CPL holder is not in possession of his or her CPL but is in possession of his or her driver's license or Michigan personal identification card and the peace officer can verify through LEIN the existence of a valid CPL. If the license cannot be verified in LEIN, the pistol may be seized and the holder has 45 days to produce a license or the weapon may be forfeited.

Notice of suspension—MCL 28.428

The licensing board may suspend or revoke a CPL. That information shall immediately be placed in LEIN.

- If an officer locates an individual who has not received notice of a suspension, the officer should inform the person of the suspension and give him or her an opportunity to comply.
- The officer shall immediately enter into LEIN that notice was given.

Persons exempt from the requirement to obtain a concealed pistol license—MCL 28.432a

- Regularly employed police officers.
- MCOLES certified constables.
- Department of Corrections employees while performing duties, or going to or from those duties (must have written approval of MDOC director).
- Local corrections officers while on duty (must have written authorization of sheriff or police chief).
- Members of the military while on duty or while going to or from duty.
- A resident of another state licensed by that state of residence to carry a concealed pistol.
- Firearms manufacturers and their agents when the pistol is being transported as merchandise.
- A person transporting an unloaded pistol, in a wrapper or container, and in the trunk or, if the vehicle does not have a trunk, in a locked compartment or container and separate from ammunition (while moving goods or transporting to or from purchase or repair). (*see also*, MCL 750.231a).
- A Canadian police officer.

Carrying Dangerous Weapon with Unlawful Intent—MCL 750.226 (felony)

It is unlawful for a person, with intent to use the same unlawfully against the person of another, to go armed with a pistol or other firearm or dagger, dirk, razor, stiletto, or knife having a blade over 3 inches in length, or any other dangerous or deadly weapon or instrument.

The suspect is *armed with a dangerous weapon and has the intent* to use the weapon illegally against someone else.

- A dangerous weapon is any object that is likely to cause serious injury or death.
- Weapons under this statute include pistols, other firearms, daggers, dirks, stilettos, knives having a blade over 3 inches in length, or any other dangerous weapon.

> A weapon under this statute may be either a weapon designed and used to be dangerous or an object used as a dangerous weapon. *People v. Barkley*, 151 Mich. App. 234 (1986).
>
> Whether an object is a dangerous weapon does not depend on the victim's belief that the object is a dangerous weapon, but on the weapon itself and how it is used. *People v. Barkley*, 151 Mich. App. 234 (1986).

Difference between CCW and Carrying with Unlawful Intent

In CCW, the offense is carrying the weapon concealed and the reason for carrying it is immaterial. CCW is also restricted to pistols, double-edged knives, and other dangerous stabbing instruments. Under carrying with unlawful intent, the weapon could be any object that may be used as a dangerous weapon. The reason for carrying the weapon is material, as the suspect *must have unlawful intent.*

Mechanical Knife—MCL 750.226a (1 year misdemeanor)

It is unlawful for a person to sell or offer to sell, or have in his or her possession any knife having the appearance of a pocket knife, the blade or blades of which can be opened by the flick of a button, pressure on a handle or other mechanical contrivance.

The provisions of this section do not apply to any one-armed person carrying a knife on his person in connection with his living requirements.

> A switchblade concealed upon a person may be prosecuted under this statute or under CCW. *People v. Czerwinski*, 99 Mich. App. 304 (1980).

Long Gun Violations

Transporting loaded firearms in vehicles—MCL 750.227c (2 year misdemeanor)

Except as otherwise permitted by law, a person shall not transport or possess in or upon a sailboat or a motor vehicle, aircraft, motorboat, or any other vehicle propelled by mechanical means, a firearm, other than a pistol, which is loaded.

The suspect transported or possessed a loaded firearm, other than a pistol, in a motor vehicle. The term motor vehicle, under this section, includes a sailboat, motor vehicle, aircraft, motor boat, or other vehicle propelled by mechanical means.

> Knowledge that the weapon is loaded is not a necessary element. *People v. Quinn*, 440 Mich. 178 (1992).

Transporting unloaded firearms in vehicles—MCL 750.227d (90-day misdemeanor)

Except as otherwise permitted by law, a person shall not transport or possess in or upon a motor vehicle or any self-propelled vehicle designed for land travel a firearm, other than a pistol, unless the firearm is unloaded and is one or more of the following:

(a) Taken down.
(b) Enclosed in a case.
(c) Carried in the trunk of the vehicle.
(d) Inaccessible from the interior of the vehicle.

Exceptions to Weapons Violations—MCL 750.231

The following statutes do not apply to those persons or entities listed below: MCL 750.224 (unlawful weapons), MCL 750.224a (stun guns), MCL 750.224b (short-barreled rifles or shotguns), MCL 750.226a (mechanical knives), MCL 750.227 (CCW), MCL 750.227c and MCL 750.227d (transporting firearms in vehicles).

- A *police officer* of a duly authorized police agency of the United States, of this state, or of any political subdivision of this state, who is regularly employed and paid by the United States, this state, or a political subdivision of this state (including state police motor carrier officers and private police).
- *Department of Corrections* officers when given a letter from their director and when on official business (includes private vendors operating a correctional facility).
- *Military* when in performance of duties.

- An organization authorized by law to purchase or receive weapons from the United States or from this state.
- For stun gun use, the person must be trained on the use, effects, and risks of using a portable device or weapon.

Weapon-Free School Zone—MCL 750.237a

If a suspect violates sections 224, 224a, 224b, 224c, 224e, 226, 227, 227a, 227f, 234a, 234b, 234c or second offense 223(2) in a weapon-free school zone, the following apply:

- He or she is guilty of a *felony* (not more than maximum received for underlying violation).
- Community service for not more than *150 hours.*
- A fine of not more than *3 times* the maximum fine under the section.

If a suspect violates sections 223(1), 224d, 226a, 227c, 227d, 231c, 232a(1), or (4), 233, 234, 234e, 234f, 235, 236, 237 or second offense 223(2) in a weapon-free school zone, the following apply:

- He or she is guilty of a 93-day misdemeanor or the punishment for the underlying crime, whichever is greater.
- Community service for not more than 100 hours.
- Up to a $2,000 fine.

Under this section, the term "school" includes public, private, denominational, or parochial schools for grades kindergarten through 12. The school property includes buildings, playing fields, or property used for school purposes. Vehicles are also included if used to transport students to or from school property.

A parent may be guilty of a 93-day misdemeanor if he or she knew his or her child was violating a weapon-free school zone law and failed to notify law enforcement.

Altering, Removing, or Obliterating the Serial Number From a Firearm—MCL 750.230 (felony)

A person who shall willfully alter, remove, or obliterate the name of the maker, model, manufacturer's number, or other mark of identity of a pistol or other firearm, shall be guilty of a felony, punishable by imprisonment for not more than 2 years or fine of not more than $1,000.00. Possession of a firearm upon which the number shall have been altered, removed, or obliterated, other than an antique firearm as defined by section 231a(2)(a) or (b), shall be presumptive evidence that the possessor has altered, removed, or obliterated the same.

Presumptive evidence portion held to be unconstitutional. *People v. Moore*, 402 Mich. 538 (1978).

Brandishing a Firearm in Public—MCL 750.234e (90-day misdemeanor)

Except as provided below, a person shall not knowingly brandish a firearm in public.

This statute does not apply to any of the following:

(a) *A peace officer lawfully performing his or her duties as a peace officer.*
(b) *A person lawfully engaged in hunting.*
(c) *A person lawfully engaged in target practice.*
(d) *A person lawfully engaged in the sale, purchase, repair, or transfer of that firearm.*

"A person when carrying a handgun in a holster in plain view is not waving or displaying the firearm in a threatening manner. Thus, such conduct does not constitute brandishing a firearm in violation of section 234e of the Michigan Penal Code." Attorney General Opinion No. 7101.

Possession of Firearm by Person Under 18 Years Old—MCL 750.234f (90-day misdemeanor)

An individual less than 18 years of age shall not possess a firearm in public except under the direct supervision of an individual 18 years of age or older.

This section does not apply to the following:

- A person in possession of a valid hunting license and following DNR regulations.
- A person going to a target range and the firearm is enclosed in a case and locked in the trunk.

Selling Firearms and Ammunition—MCL 750.223

Selling pistol without complying with license to purchase requirements—MCL 750.223(1) (90-day misdemeanor)

Selling a firearm to a minor—MCL 750.223(2)

The suspect knowingly sold a firearm, longer than 30 inches in length, to a person less than 18 years old.

Penalties:

First offense	90 day misdemeanor
Second Offense	Felony

It is an affirmative defense to a prosecution under this subsection that the person who sold the firearm asked to see and was shown a driver's license or identification card issued by a state that identified the purchaser as being 18 years of age or older.

Selling firearm or ammunition under certain circumstances—MCL 750.223(3) (felony)

A seller shall not sell a firearm or ammunition if the buyer is under indictment for a felony or the person if prohibited from possessing a firearm under MCL 750.224f.

Prohibited Places to Possess Firearm—MCL 750.234d (90-day misdemeanor)

A person is prohibited from possessing a firearm in the following places:

- A depository financial institution (e.g., bank or credit union)
- A church or other place of religious worship.
- A court.
- A theatre.
- A sports arena.
- A day care center.
- A hospital.
- An establishment licensed under the Liquor Control Code.

This section does not apply to the following persons:

- The owner or a person hired as security (if the firearm is possessed for the purpose of providing security).
- A peace officer.
- A person with a valid CPL issued by any state.
- A person with permission of the owner.

Possession of Firearm During Commission Of Felony ("Felony Firearm")—MCL 750.227b (felony)

(1) A person who carries or has in his or her possession a firearm when he or she commits or attempts to commit a felony, except a violation of section 223, section 227, 227a or 230, is guilty of a felony, and shall be imprisoned for 2 years. Upon a second conviction under this section, the person shall be imprisoned for 5 years. Upon a third or subsequent conviction under this subsection, the person shall be imprisoned for 10 years.

(2) A term of imprisonment prescribed by this section is in addition to the sentence imposed for the conviction of the felony or the attempt to commit the felony, and shall be served consecutively with and preceding any term of imprisonment imposed for the conviction of the felony or attempt to commit the felony.

(3) A term of imprisonment imposed under this section shall not be suspended. The person subject to the sentence mandated by this section is not eligible for parole or probation during the mandatory term imposed pursuant to subsection (1).

(4) This section does not apply to a law enforcement officer who is authorized to carry a firearm while in the official performance of his or her duties, and who is in the performance of those duties. As used in this subsection, "law enforcement officer" means a person who is regularly employed as a member of a duly authorized police agency or other organization of the United States, this state, or a city, county, township, or village of this state, and who is responsible for the prevention and detection of crime and the enforcement of the general criminal laws of this state.

The suspect possessed or carried a firearm during the course of a felony or attempted felony.

> Felony firearm charges were upheld where officers located two handguns on top of a dresser and within three feet of a drawer that contained cocaine. *People v. Burgenmeyer*, 461 Mich. 431 (2000).
>
> First degree home invasion, where there is a larceny of a firearm, can be a predicate felony for a felony firearm conviction. *People v. Shipley*, 256 Mich. App. 367 (2003).

Spring Guns—MCL 750.236 (1 year misdemeanor)

Any person who shall set any spring or other gun, or any trap or device operating by the firing or explosion of gunpowder or any other explosive, and shall leave or permit the same to be left, except in the immediate presence of some competent person, shall be guilty of a misdemeanor, punishable by imprisonment in the county jail not more than 1 year, or by a fine of not more than 500 dollars, and the killing of any person by the firing of a gun or device so set shall be manslaughter.

A person shall not set up and leave or cause to be left a spring or other gun, or any trap or device operating by the firing or explosion of gunpowder or other explosive. This section does not apply if the weapon is left with a competent person.

If death results from a violation of this section, the suspect is guilty of manslaughter.

Possession of Firearm While Intoxicated—MCL 750.237 (93-day misdemeanor)

(1) An individual shall not carry, have in possession or under control, or use in any manner or discharge a firearm under any of the following circumstances:

   (a) The individual is under the influence of alcoholic liquor, a controlled substance, or a combination of alcoholic liquor and a controlled substance.
   (b) The individual has an alcohol content of 0.08 or more grams per 100 milliliters of blood, per 210 liters of breath, or per 67 milliliters of urine.
   (c) Because of the consumption of alcoholic liquor, a controlled substance, or a combination of alcoholic liquor and a controlled substance, the individual's ability to use a firearm is visibly impaired.

(5) A peace officer who has probable cause to believe an individual violated subsection (1) may require the individual to submit to a chemical analysis of his or her breath, blood, or urine. However, an individual who is afflicted with hemophilia, diabetes, or a condition requiring the use of an anticoagulant under the direction of a physician is not required to submit to a chemical analysis of his or her blood.

(6) Before an individual is required to submit to a chemical analysis under subsection (5), the peace officer shall inform the individual of all of the following:

   (a) The individual may refuse to submit to the chemical analysis, but if he or she refuses, the officer may obtain a court order requiring the individual to submit to a chemical analysis.
   (b) If the individual submits to the chemical analysis, he or she may obtain a chemical analysis from a person of his or her own choosing.

(7) The failure of a peace officer to comply with the requirements of subsection (6) does not render the results of a chemical analysis inadmissible as evidence in a criminal prosecution for violating this section, in a civil action arising out of a violation of this section, or in any administrative proceeding arising out of a violation of this section.

(8) The collection and testing of breath, blood, or urine specimens under this section shall be conducted in the same manner as O.W.I./OUID.

(9) Subject may be charged with other violations that arise out of the same transaction.

Penalties:

If causes no injury	93 day misdemeanor
If causes serious impairment of a body function of another individual.	5 year felony
If causes the death of another individual by the discharge or use in any manner of a firearm.	15 year felony

Hunting with Firearm While Intoxicated—MCL 750.167a (90-day misdemeanor)

The suspect was intoxicated while hunting with a firearm, and at the time, had a valid hunting license. Upon conviction, the firearm must be turned over to DNR and the person's hunting privileges must be suspended for 3 years.

Intentionally Aiming Firearm without Malice—MCL 750.233 (90-day misdemeanor)

The suspect intentionally aimed firearm at another without the intent to threaten or harm anyone. MCL 750.233, 750.234, 750.234a and b, 750.235, and 750.239 do not apply to the following:

- A peace officer of this state or another state, or of a local unit of government of this state or another state, or of the United States, performing his or her duties as a peace officer. As used in this section, "peace officer" means that term as defined in section 215.

Discharge of Firearm While Intentionally Aimed without Malice—MCL 750.234 (1 year misdemeanor)

The suspect pointed a firearm at or toward another person and, at the time, intended to point the firearm, but did not intend to threaten or harm anyone. The gun discharged.

Discharge of Firearm Causing Injury While Intentionally Aimed without Malice—MCL 750.235 (1 year misdemeanor)

The suspect pointed a firearm at or toward another person with the intent to point the firearm, but did not intend to threaten or harm anyone. The gun discharged and someone was injured.

Reckless or Wanton Use of Firearm—MCL 752.863a (90-day misdemeanor)

The suspect recklessly, heedlessly, willfully, or wantonly used, carried, handled, or fired a firearm without reasonable caution for the safety of property or others.

Discharge of Firearm at Dwelling or Occupied Structure—MCL 750.234b (felony)

Definitions

- *Dwelling*—Facility habitually used as a place of abode.
- *Occupied structure*—Facility where one or more persons are present.

The suspect intentionally discharged a firearm at a dwelling or occupied structure and knew or had reason to know that the building was a dwelling or occupied structure.

> MCL 750.234b applies where defendant shot above a house and the victim testified that she feared for her life and thought the house was being shot at. *People v. Wilson*, 230 Mich. App. 590 (1998).
>
> MCL 750.234b applies to a husband who, during an argument with his wife, fired a handgun into the bedroom wall. *People v. Henry*, 239 Mich. App. 140 (1999).

Discharge of a Firearm From a Motor Vehicle—MCL 750.234a (felony)

The suspect intentionally discharged a firearm from a motor vehicle, snowmobile, or off-road vehicle and endangered someone else.

Signaling Device—MCL 750.231c (90-day misdemeanor)

A person may possess an approved signaling device only under the following circumstances:

- If the possession is part of marketing or manufacturing and the device is unloaded.
- The device is on a vessel or airplane. (A vessel is a watercraft used for transportation on water).
- The device is at a person's residence.
- The person is en route from the place of purchase to his residence, vessel, or aircraft. The device must be unloaded and enclosed in a case and either in a trunk or not readily accessible to the occupants.

Discharge of a Firearm at an Emergency or Law Enforcement Vehicle—MCL 750.234c (felony)

(1) An individual who intentionally discharges a firearm at a motor vehicle that he or she knows or has reason to believe is an emergency or law enforcement vehicle is guilty of a felony, punishable by imprisonment for not more than 4 years, or a fine of not more than $2,000.00, or both.

(2) As used in this section, "emergency or law enforcement vehicle" means 1 or more of the following:

(a) A motor vehicle owned or operated by a fire department of a local unit of government of this state.

(b) A motor vehicle owned or operated by a police agency of the United States, of this state, or of a local unit of government of this state.

(c) A motor vehicle owned or operated by the department of natural resources that is used for law enforcement purposes.

(d) A motor vehicle owned or operated by an entity licensed to provide emergency medical services under part 192 of article 17 of the public health code, Act No. 368 of the Public Acts of 1978, being sections 333.20901 to 333.20979 of the Michigan Compiled Laws, and that is used to provide emergency medical assistance to individuals.

(e) A motor vehicle owned or operated by a volunteer employee or paid employee of an entity described in subdivisions (a) to (c) while the motor vehicle is being used to perform emergency or law enforcement duties for that entity.

Felon in Possession of Firearm—MCL 750.224f (felony)

(1) Except as provided in subsection (2), a person convicted of a felony shall not possess, use, transport, sell, purchase, carry, ship, receive, or distribute a firearm in this state until the expiration of 3 years after all of the following circumstances exist:

(a) The person has paid all fines imposed for the violation.

(b) The person has served all terms of imprisonment imposed for the violation.

(c) The person has successfully completed all conditions of probation or parole imposed for the violation.

(2) A person convicted of a specified felony shall not possess, use, transport, sell, purchase, carry, ship, receive, or distribute a firearm in this state until all of the following circumstances exist:

(a) The expiration of 5 years after all of the following circumstances exist:

   (i) The person has paid all fines imposed for the violation.
   (ii) The person has served all terms of imprisonment imposed for the violation.
   (iii) The person has successfully completed all conditions of probation or parole imposed for the violation.

(b) The person's right to possess, use, transport, sell, purchase, carry, ship, receive, or distribute a firearm has been restored pursuant to section 4 of Act No. 372 of the Public Acts of 1927, being section 28.424 of the Michigan Compiled Laws.

(3) A person who possesses, uses, transports, sells, purchases, carries, ships, receives, or distributes a firearm in violation of this section is guilty of a felony, punishable by imprisonment for not more than 5 years, or a fine of not more than $5,000.00, or both.

(4) This section does not apply to a conviction that has been expunged or set aside, or for which the person has been pardoned, unless the expunction, order, or pardon expressly provides that the person shall not possess a firearm.

(5) As used in this section, "felony" means a violation of a law of this state, or of another state, or of the United States that is punishable by imprisonment for 4 years or more, or an attempt to violate such a law.

(6) As used in subsection (2), "specified felony" means a felony in which 1 or more of the following circumstances exist:

   (a) An element of that felony is the use, attempted use, or threatened use of physical force against the person or property of another, or that by its nature, involves a substantial risk that physical force against the person or property of another may be used in the course of committing the offense.
   (b) An element of that felony is the unlawful manufacture, possession, importation, exportation, distribution, or dispensing of a controlled substance.
   (c) An element of that felony is the unlawful possession or distribution of a firearm.
   (d) An element of that felony is the unlawful use of an explosive.
   (e) The felony is burglary of an occupied dwelling, or breaking and entering an occupied dwelling, or arson.

The suspect possessed, used, transported, sold or received a firearm within certain time frames after being convicted of a felony punishable by 4 or more years. For all felonies, except those listed below, *three years* must have passed since all fines paid, all imprisonment served, and any terms of probation or parole have been completed.

A *five-year* time limit applies to the following felonies:

- Element of offense includes physical force, or substantial risk of physical force against the person or property of another.
- Controlled substance violation.
- Unlawful possession or distribution of firearm.
- Unlawful use of explosive.
- B and E of occupied dwelling.
- Arson.

Operability Requirements

A handgun need not be currently operable in order to qualify as a firearm for purposes of the felony-firearm statute. *People v. Brown*, 249 Mich. App. 382 (2002).

A firearm does not have to be operable in order to support a conviction for felon in possession or possession of a firearm during the commission of a felony. The relevant statute (MCL 750.222) does not require that a firearm be operable. Instead, it focuses on what the firearm was designed to do. *People v. Peals*, 476 Mich. 636 (2006).

Pistol Registration Requirements

Persons without a Concealed Pistol License—MCL 28.422

A person shall not purchase, carry, possess, or transport a pistol in Michigan without first having obtained a License to Purchase a Pistol from his or her local police or sheriff department. The license must be mailed or hand-delivered to the issuing department within 10 days of purchasing a pistol (failure to do so is a state civil infraction), and the purchaser must have a copy of the license with him or her for 30 days after purchase. Forging an application for a license is a 4 year felony.

Persons with a Concealed Pistol License—MCL 28.422a

CPL holders are not required to obtain a License to Purchase. Instead, they are required to sign a Pistol Sales Record completed by the seller when they purchase or otherwise acquire a pistol. The purchaser must mail or hand-deliver a copy of the record to his or her local police department within 10 days of purchasing a pistol (failure to do so is a state civil infraction), and the purchaser must have a copy of the license with him or her for 30 days after purchase.

Failure to have pistol registered or making false statement in application for license to purchase—MCL 750.232a

(1) Except as provided in subsection (2), a person who obtains a pistol in violation of section 2 of Act No. 372 of the Public Acts of 1927, as amended, being section 28.422 of the Michigan Compiled Laws, is guilty of a misdemeanor, punishable by imprisonment for not more than 90 days or a fine of not more than $100.00, or both.

(2) Subsection (1) does not apply to a person who obtained a pistol in violation of section 2 of Act No. 372 of the Public Acts of 1927 before the effective date of the 1990 amendatory act that added this subsection, who has not been convicted of that violation, and who obtains a license as required under section 2 of Act No. 372 of the Public Acts of 1927 within 90 days after the effective date of the 1990 amendatory act that added this subsection.

(3) A person who intentionally makes a material false statement on an application for a license to purchase a pistol under section 2 of Act No. 372 of the Public Acts of 1927, as amended, is guilty of a felony, punishable by imprisonment for not more than 4 years, or a fine of not more than $2,000.00, or both.

(4) A person who uses or attempts to use false identification or the identification of another person to purchase a firearm is guilty of a misdemeanor, punishable by imprisonment for not more than 90 days or a fine of not more than $100.00, or both.

Penalties:

Making a material false statement on application to purchase a pistol	felony
Use of false identification	90 day misdemeanor

Persons exempt from registration requirements—MCL 28.432

- Police and correctional agencies
- The United States Army, Air Force, Navy, or Marine Corps, including reserve and national guard components
- An organization authorized by law to purchase weapons from the United States of this state
- Police, corrections, and military while in the course of their duties or while going to or from those duties
- A United States citizen holding a concealed pistol license from another state
- Manufacturers and their agents while transporting pistols as merchandise
- Persons possessing antique firearms
- A Michigan CPL holder possessing a pistol properly registered to another person

Persons exempt from registration requirements—MCL 28.422

- Active duty members of the military are exempt for 30 days after returning to Michigan on leave
- Licensed dealers when buying a pistol from a wholesaler
- Non-residents if all of the following apply:
    - The person is licensed in his or her state of residence to purchase, carry, or transport a pistol
    - The person is in possession of that license
    - The person owns the pistol carried
    - The person possesses the pistol for a lawful purpose (see MCL 750.231a)
    - The person is in Michigan for fewer than 180 days and does not intend to establish residency
    - The person presents the license upon demand of a police officer (90 day misdemeanor)
- A resident under 18 possessing another person's pistol if all of the following apply:
    - The person is not otherwise prohibited from possessing the pistol
    - The person is at a recognized target range
    - The person possesses the pistol for target practice or instruction in safely using a pistol
    - The person's parent or guardian is physically present and supervising the use of the pistol
    - The owner of the pistol is physically present
    - Note: The age limit for this section is 21 if the owner of the pistol is a federally licensed dealer
- A resident 18 or older possessing another person's pistol if all of the following apply:
    - The person is not otherwise prohibited from possessing the pistol

- The person is at a recognized target range or shooting facility
- The person possesses the pistol for target practice or instruction in safely using a pistol
- The owner of the pistol is physically present and supervising the use of the pistol

Persons exempt from registration requirements—federal law

Notwithstanding state law, a person who is not prohibited from possessing a firearm under federal law is permitted to transport a firearm for any lawful purpose from any place where it may be lawfully possessed to any other place where it may be lawfully possessed. The firearm must be unloaded and neither the firearm nor ammunition may be directly accessible from the passenger compartment of the vehicle (if no trunk, firearm and ammunition must be locked in a closed container). 18 USC 926A.

Law enforcement officers and qualified retired law enforcement officers from any state may carry concealed pistols in Michigan without registering them or without a CPL. 18 USC 926B-C.

Forfeiture of Weapons—MCL 750.239)

All pistols, weapons, or devices carried, possessed or used in violation of the above sections shall be forfeited to the state.

Innocent owner—MCL 750.239a

- If the owner was not knowingly involved in the violation, and it is otherwise not illegal to possess, the weapon shall be returned to the owner.
- If the agency decides not to return the weapon, a person may appeal that decision to the circuit court within 30 days.
- If the owner is not alleged to be involved, he or she must be notified within 90 days of the completion of the criminal case of the status of the case and the possibility of obtaining the weapon.
- Prior to destruction of the weapon, the police must make reasonable efforts to notify the owner to determine if a claim is forthcoming.

IMPERSONATION AND OBSTRUCTION OF JUSTICE

IMPERSONATION
Impersonating a Police Officer—MCL 750.215

An individual who is not a peace officer or a medical examiner shall not do any of the following:

(a) *Perform the duties of a peace officer or a medical examiner.*
(b) *Represent to another person that he or she is a peace officer or a medical examiner for any unlawful purpose.*
(c) *Represent to another person that he or she is a peace officer or a medical examiner with the intent to compel the person to do or refrain from doing any act against his or her will.*

It is a 4 year felony if the person "performs the duties of a peace officer to commit or attempt to commit a crime or represents to another person that he or she is a peace officer to commit or attempt to commit a crime." All other violations are 1 year misdemeanors.

As used in this section, "peace officer" means any of the following:

(a) *A sheriff or deputy sheriff of a county of this state or another state.*
(b) *An officer of the police department of a city, village, or township of this state or another state.*
(c) *A marshal of a city, village, or township.*
(d) *A constable.*
(e) *An officer of the Michigan state police.*
(f) *A conservation officer.*
(g) *A security employee employed by the state pursuant to section 6c of 1935 PA 59, MCL 28.6c.*
(h) *A motor carrier officer appointed pursuant to section 6d of 1935 PA 59, MCL 28.6d.*
(i) *A police officer or public safety officer of a community college, college, or university who is authorized by the governing board of that community college, college, or university to enforce state law and the rules and ordinances of that community college, college, or university.*
(j) *A park and recreation officer commissioned pursuant to section 1606 of the natural resources and environmental protection act, 1994 PA 451, MCL 324.1606.*
(k) *A state forest officer commissioned pursuant to section 83107 of the natural resources and environmental protection act, 1994 PA 451, MCL 324.83107.*

(l) *A federal law enforcement officer.*
(m) *An investigator of the state department of attorney general.*

Unlawful Representation as Firefighter or EMT—MCL 750.217f (felony)

An individual who is not employed as a firefighter or emergency medical service personnel shall not inform another individual or represent to another individual by identification or any other means that he or she is employed in 1 of those capacities with intent to do 1 or more of the following:

(a) *Perform the duties of a firefighter or emergency medical service personnel.*
(b) *Represent to another person that he or she is a firefighter or emergency medical service personnel for any unlawful purpose.*
(c) *Compel a person to do or refrain from doing any act against his or her will.*
(d) *Gain or attempt to gain entry to a residence, building, structure, facility, or other property.*
(e) *Remain or attempt to remain in or upon a residence, building, structure, facility, or other property.*
(f) *Gain or attempt to gain access to financial account information.*
(g) *Commit or attempt to commit a crime.*
(h) *Obtain or attempt to obtain information to which the individual is not entitled.*
(i) *Gain access or attempt to gain access to a person less than 18 years of age or a vulnerable adult.*

Unauthorized Wearing of Badge or Uniform of State Police—MCL 750.216 (90-day misdemeanor)

A person who wears, exhibits, displays, or uses, for any purpose, the badge or uniform or a badge or uniform substantially identical to that prescribed by the department of state police for officers of the department, unless he or she is a member of the department, is guilty of a misdemeanor. However, this section shall not be construed to prohibit persons of the theatrical profession from wearing such badge or uniform in any playhouse or theatre while actually engaged in following that profession.

Disguising with Intent to Intimidate, Hinder, or Obstruct—MCL 750.217 (1 year misdemeanor)

Any person who shall, in any manner, disguise himself, with the intent to obstruct the due execution of the law, or with the intent to intimidate, hinder or interrupt any officer, or any other person, in the legal performance of his duty, or the exercise of his rights under the constitution and laws of this state, whether such intent be effective or not, shall be guilty of a 1 year misdemeanor.

> The giving of a false or fictitious name to a police officer by itself does not constitute obstruction by disguise under this statute. *People v. Jones*, 142 Mich. App. 819 (1985).

FALSE REPRESENTATIONS

Representation as Public Utility Employee—MCL 750.217b (felony)

An individual who is not employed by a public utility shall not inform another individual or represent to another individual by uniform, identification, or any other means that he or she is employed by that public utility with intent to do 1 or more of the following:

(a) *Gain or attempt to gain entry to a residence, building, structure, facility, or other property.*
(b) *Remain or attempt to remain in or upon a residence, building, structure, facility, or other property.*
(c) *Commit or attempt to commit a crime.*

As used in this section, "public utility" means a utility that provides steam, gas, heat, electricity, water, cable television, telecommunications services, or pipeline services, whether privately, municipally, or cooperatively owned.

Representation of an FIA Worker—MCL 750.217e (felony)

An individual who is not employed by the Family Independence Agency shall not inform another individual or represent to another individual by identification, or any other means that he or she is employed by the Family Independence Agency with intent to do 1 or more of the following:

(a) Gain or attempt to gain entry to a residence, building, structure, facility, or other property.
(b) Remain or attempt to remain in or upon a residence, building, structure, facility, or other property.
(c) Gain or attempt to gain access to financial account information.
(d) Commit or attempt to commit a crime.
(e) Obtain or attempt to obtain information to which the individual is not entitled under section 7 of the child protection law.
(f) Gain access or attempt to gain access to a person less than 18 years of age or a vulnerable adult.

Note: The Family Independence Agency is now the Department of Human Services.

Law Enforcement Badges, Patches, and Uniforms—MCL 750.216a (93-day misdemeanor)

A person shall not sell, furnish, possess, wear, exhibit, display, or use the badge, patch, or uniform, or facsimile of the badge, patch, or uniform, of any law enforcement agency.

Exceptions:

1. The person is authorized by the head of the law enforcement agency.
2. The person is a member of the agency.
3. The person is a retired law enforcement officer possessing a retirement badge.
4. The person is next-of-kin, child, or spouse of a deceased law enforcement officer.
5. The person is a collector (the badge, patch, uniform, or facsimile must be in a case when transported by a collector.
6. The person is in the "theatrical profession" and wears the item while actually engaged in the profession.
7. Bailiffs or court officers appointed pursuant to court rule.

A facsimile includes both an exact replica of an existing item and a close imitation of an existing item.

Law Enforcement Emblems, Insignia, Logos, Service Mark, or Idetification—MCL 750.216b (93-day misdemeanor)

This statute makes it unlawful for a person other than a police officer to wear or display the emblem, insignia, logo, service mark, or other law enforcement identification of any law enforcement agency, or a facsimile of any of those items, if either of the following applies:

(a) *The person represents himself or herself to another person as being a peace officer.*
(b) *The wearing or display occurs in a manner that would lead a reasonable person to falsely believe that the law enforcement agency whose emblem, insignia, logo, service mark, or other law enforcement identification or facsimile is being worn or displayed is promoting or endorsing a commercial service or product or a charitable endeavor.*

As used in this section, "law enforcement identification" means any identification that contains the words "law enforcement" or similar words, including, but not limited to, "agent", "enforcement agent", "detective", "task force", "fugitive recovery agent", or any other combination of names that gives the impression that the bearer is in any way connected with the federal government, state government, or any political subdivision of a state government. However, law enforcement identification does not include "bail agent" or "bondsman" when used by a bail agent or bondsman operating in accordance with the law.

This section does not apply to a person appointed by a court of this state to serve as a bailiff or court officer under the court rules.

Fire or EMS Badges, Patches, or Uniforms—MCL 750.217g (93-day misdemeanor)

This section parallels, and is substantially the same as, the corresponding statute governing police badges (MCL 750.216a) above.

Fire or EMS Emblems, Insignia, Logos, Service Mark, or Identification—MCL 750.217h (93-day misdemeanor)

This section parallels, and is substantially the same as, the corresponding statute governing police badges (MCL 750.216b) above.

BRIBERY

Bribery of a Public Official—MCL 750.117 (felony)

Any person who shall corruptly give, offer or promise to any public officer, agent, servant or employee, after the election or appointment of such public officer, agent, servant or employee and either before or after such public officer, agent, servant or employee shall have been qualified or shall take his seat, any gift, gratuity, money, property or other valuable thing, the intent or purpose of which is to influence the act, vote, opinion, decision or judgment of such public officer, agent, servant or employee, or his action on any matter, question, cause or proceeding, which may be pending or may by law be brought before him in his public capacity, or the purpose and intent of which is to influence any act or omission relating to any public duty of such officer, agent, servant or employee, shall be guilty of a felony.

Elements

1. The defendant intentionally and corruptly,
2. Gave, offered to give, or promised to give,
3. A gift, money, or other valuable thing,
4. To a public official,
5. With the intent of influencing that official to act or to fail to act.

> A defendant is not entitled to a jury instruction on the misdemeanor charge of an improper campaign contribution (MCL 169.241(1)) when he is properly charged with bribery. *People v. Hryshko*, 170 Mich. App. 368 (1988).

Public Official Accepting Bribe—MCL 750.118 (felony)

Any executive, legislative or judicial officer who shall corruptly accept any gift or gratuity, or any promise to make any gift, or to do any act beneficial to such officer, under an agreement, or with an understanding that his vote, opinion or judgment shall be given in any particular manner, or upon a particular side of any question, cause or proceeding, which is or may be by law brought before him in his official capacity, or that in such capacity, he shall make any particular nomination or appointment, shall forfeit his office, and be forever disqualified to hold any public office, trust or appointment under the constitution or laws of this state, and shall be guilty of a felony, punishable by imprisonment in the state prison not more than 10 years, or by fine of not more than 5,000 dollars.

Elements

1. A public official,
2. Accepted a gift, promise of a gift, or promise of an act that would benefit him or her,
3. With the understanding or agreement that his or her vote, opinion or judgment would be given in a particular manner, or that he or she would make a particular nomination or appointment.

> A city water commissioner was found to be a public official and not a mere employee under this statute because his position was created by an ordinance and he had discretionary authority. *People v. Clark*, 134 Mich. App. 324 (1984).
>
> A court clerk in the traffic division was not an *official* under this statute: rather, she was an employee who accepted bribes (MCL 750.125). *People v. Nankervis*, 330 Mich. 17 (1949).

Other Bribe Violations

Jurors, appraisers, executors, auditors, arbitrators —MCL 750.119 (felony)

(1) A person who corrupts or attempts to corrupt an appraiser, receiver, trustee, administrator, executor, commissioner, auditor, juror, arbitrator, or referee by giving, offering, or promising any gift or gratuity with the intent to bias the opinion or influence the decision of that appraiser, receiver, trustee, administrator, executor, commissioner, auditor, juror, arbitrator, or referee regarding any matter pending in a court, or before an inquest, or for the decision for which the appraiser, receiver, trustee, administrator, executor, commissioner, auditor, juror, arbitrator, or referee was appointed or chosen, is guilty of a crime as follows:

(a) Except as provided in subdivision (b), the person is guilty of a felony punishable by imprisonment for not more than 4 years or a fine of not more than $5,000.00, or both.

(b) If the violation is committed in a criminal case for which the maximum term of imprisonment for the violation is more than 10 years, or the violation is punishable by imprisonment for life or any term of years, the person is guilty of a felony punishable by imprisonment for not more than 10 years or a fine of not more than $20,000.00, or both.

Elements

1. The defendant gave, offered, or promised to give,

2. A gift,
3. Intending to,
4. Influence the decision of,
5. An appraiser, receiver, trustee, administer, executor, commissioner, auditor, juror, arbitrator, or referee.

Jurors, appraisers, executors, auditors, arbiters accepting bribes—MCL 750.120 (felony)

Any person summoned as a juror or chosen or appointed as an appraiser, receiver, trustee, administrator, executor, commissioner, auditor, arbitrator or referee who shall corruptly take anything to give his verdict, award, or report, or who shall corruptly receive any gift or gratuity whatever, from a party to any suit, cause, or proceeding, for the trial or decision of which such juror shall have been summoned, or for the hearing or determination of which such appraiser, receiver, trustee, administrator, executor, commissioner, auditor, arbitrator, or referee shall have been chosen or appointed, shall be guilty of a felony.

Elements

1. A juror, appraiser, executor, auditor, arbiter,
2. Took or received a gift or gratuity,
3. In exchange for a verdict, award, or report,
4. In the matter for which the juror, appraiser, executor, auditor, or arbiter was appointed.

Officials of public institutions by persons with contracts therewith—MCL 750.121 (felony)

Any person interested directly or indirectly in a contract with a state or municipal institution who shall corruptly give, offer or promise to any officer of such institution any bribe, gift, or gratuity whatever, with intent to improperly influence his official action under such contract, shall be guilty of felony.

Elements

1. The defendant was directly or indirectly interested in a contract,
2. With a state or municipal institution,
3. And gave, offered, or promised to give any bribe or gift,
4. With the intent of improperly influencing an official action under that contract.

Peace officers or others authorized to arrest offenders of criminal law—MCL 750.123 (6 month misdemeanor)

A sheriff, coroner, constable, peace officer, or any other officer authorized to serve process or arrest or apprehend offenders against criminal law who shall receive from a defendant or from any other person any money or other valuable thing or any service or promise to pay or give money or to perform or omit to perform any act as a consideration, reward, or inducement, for omitting or delaying to arrest any defendant, or to carry him or her before a magistrate, or for delaying to take any person to prison, or for postponing the sale of any property under an execution, or for omitting or delaying to perform any duty pertaining to his or her office, is guilty of a misdemeanor punishable by imprisonment for not more than 6 months or a fine of not more than $750.00. However, if that defendant is charged with an offense against the criminal laws of this state, an officer convicted under this section may be punished by any fine or by any term of imprisonment or both a fine and imprisonment, within the limits fixed by the statute that the defendant is charged with having violated.

Elements

1. The defendant is a police officer,
2. The defendant received consideration, reward, or inducement from another person,
3. The defendant omitted or delayed performance of a duty pertaining to his office.

People v. Bommarito, 11 Mich. App. 328 (1968).

> Prosecution of a police officer charged with accepting a bribe to refrain from making a complaint, which was his or her duty to make, should be brought under this section, instead of the general bribery statute. *People v. McDonald,* 216 Mich. 234 (1921).
>
> Defendants were property charged with felony extortion when they demanded a bribe in exchange for not reporting a bar owner for furnishing alcohol to minors because the charge of accepting a bribe is of an "entirely different nature." *People v. Percin,* 330 Mich. 94 (1951).

Athlete—MCL 750.124 (felony)

Any person who corruptly gives, offers or promises to any person engaged in amateur or professional baseball, boxing, wrestling or other competitive athletic pursuits, any gift, gratuity or valuable thing whatever, with intent to influence him to lose or try to lose, or to affect the result in any way of, any contest in which he is participating or expects to participate; or any person engaged in amateur or professional baseball, boxing, wrestling or other competitive athletic pursuits, who corruptly solicits or accepts a gift, gratuity or valuable thing, or a promise to make a gift or to do an act beneficial to himself, under an agreement or with the understanding that he shall lose or try to lose, or to affect the result in any way of, any contest in which he is participating or expects to participate, shall be guilty of a felony.

Bribery of employees to deceive employers—MCL 750.125 (1 year misdemeanor)

(1) A person shall not give, offer, or promise a commission, gift, or gratuity to an agent, employee, or other person or do or offer to do an act beneficial to an agent, employee, or other person with intent to influence the action of the agent or employee in relation to his or her principal's or employer's business.

(2) An agent or employee shall not request or accept a commission, gift, or gratuity, or a promise of a commission, gift, or gratuity, for the agent, employee, or another person or the doing of an act or offer of an act beneficial to the agent, employee, or another person according to an agreement or understanding between the agent or employee and any other person that the agent or employee shall act in a particular manner in relation to his or her principal's or employer's business.

(3) A person shall not use or give to an agent, employee, or other person, and an agent or employee shall not use, approve, or certify, with intent to deceive the principal or employer, a receipt, account, invoice, or other document concerning which the principal or employer is interested that contains a statement that is materially false, erroneous, or defective or omits to state fully any commission, money, property, or other valuable thing given or agreed to be given to the agent or employee.

(4) Evidence is not admissible in any proceeding or prosecution under this section to show that a gift or acceptance of a commission, money, property, or other valuable thing described in this section is customary in a business, trade, or calling. The customary nature of a transaction is not a defense in a proceeding or prosecution under this section.

(5) In a proceeding or prosecution under this section, a person shall not be excused from attending and testifying or from producing documentary evidence pursuant to a subpoena on the ground that the testimony or evidence may tend to incriminate him or her or subject him or her to a penalty or forfeiture. Truthful testimony, evidence, or other truthful information compelled under this section and any information derived directly or indirectly from that truthful testimony, evidence, or other truthful information shall not be used against the witness in a criminal case, except for impeachment purposes or in a prosecution for perjury or otherwise failing to testify or produce evidence as required.

(6) A person who violates this section is guilty of a misdemeanor punishable by imprisonment for not more than 1 year or a fine of not more than $1,000.00, or both.

A clerk of a traffic division of a court is a mere employee and should be prosecuted under this section. *People v. Nankervis*, 330 Mich. 17 (1949).

Bribing an assistant county purchasing agent should be prosecuted under the general statute punishing the bribery of a public official. *People v. Karoll*, 315 Mich. 423 (1946).

The defendant, who was the director of the city housing commission, was not a city employee under this statute because he did not represent the city in negotiations nor did he receive compensation for tasks under the city's direct control. Therefore, his conviction under this statute was overturned. *People v. Kirstein*, 6 Mich. App. 107 (1967).

FALSE REPORTS
False Police Report—MCL 750.411a

(1) Except as provided in subsection (2), a person who intentionally makes a false report of the commission of a crime, or intentionally causes a false report of the commission of a crime to be made, to a peace officer, police agency of this state or of a local unit of government, 9-1-1 operator, or any other governmental employee or contractor or employee of a contractor who is authorized to receive reports of a crime, knowing the report is false, is guilty of a crime as follows:

(a) If the report is a false report of a misdemeanor, the person is guilty of a misdemeanor punishable by imprisonment for

not more than 93 days or a fine of not more than $500.00, or both.

(b) If the report is a false report of a felony, the person is guilty of a felony punishable by imprisonment for not more than 4 years or a fine of not more than $2,000.00, or both.

(2) A person shall not do either of the following:

(a) Knowingly make a false report of a violation or attempted violation of chapter XXXIII or section 327, 328, 397a, or 436 and communicate or cause the communication of the false report to any other person, knowing the report to be false.

(b) Threaten to violate chapter XXXIII or section 327, 328, 397a, or 436 and communicate or cause the communication of the threat to any other person.

(3) A person who violates subsection (2) is guilty of a felony punishable as follows:

(a) For a first conviction under subsection (2), by imprisonment for not more than 4 years or a fine of not more than $2,000.00, or both.

(b) For a second or subsequent conviction under subsection (2), imprisonment for not more than 10 years or a fine of not more than $5,000.00, or both.

...

(6) As used in this section:

(a) "Local unit of government" means:

(i) A city, village, township, or county.
(ii) A local or intermediate school district.
(iii) A public school academy.
(iv) A community college.

(b) "State" includes, but is not limited to, a state institution of higher education.

Elements

1. The defendant reported to a police officer that a crime had been committed,
2. Either the crime had not occurred or the details that were reported were false,
3. The defendant knew that this was a falsehood, and
4. The defendant intended to make a false report.

CJI2d 13.19.

Penalties:

| False report of a misdemeanor | 93 day misdemeanor |
| False report of a felony | felony |

The defendant's conviction was upheld when he truthfully reported that he had been carjacked but he lied about where it had occurred. *People v. Chavis*, 468 Mich. 84 (2003). Under *Chavis*, the appropriate question is not whether the occurrence of the crime is false but whether there was falsity in the report.

The corpus delicti rule precludes the admission of a defendant's confession in the absence of some other evidence that the crime had occurred (the defendant could not be convicted when he reported that he had been carjacked but later admitted that he had "lost" his car). *People v. Borrelli*, 463 Mich. 930 (2000).

False Bomb Threat—MCL 750.411a(2) (felony)

The suspect knowingly and intentionally communicated to another person a false report about:

- A bombing,
- Attempted bombing, or
- Threat to bomb.

Ambulance—MCL 750.411d (1 year misdemeanor)

Suspect intentionally caused or requested the assistance of ambulance service with the intent not to use the assistance.

False Report to Police Dispatch Center—MCL 750.509 (1 year misdemeanor)

The suspect willfully made a false, misleading, or unfounded report to a radio broadcasting station operated by a law enforcement agency. The suspect had the purpose of interfering with the station's operation or intended to mislead a peace officer.

False Report of Abducted or Missing Child—MCL 28.754

(1) A person shall not intentionally make a false report of the abduction of a child, or intentionally

cause a false report of the abduction of a child to be made, to a peace officer, police agency of this state or of a local unit of government, 9-1-1 operator, or any other governmental employee or contractor or employee of a contractor who is authorized to receive the report, knowing the report is false. A person who violates this subsection is guilty of a felony punishable by imprisonment for not more than 4 years or a fine of not more than $2,000.00, or both.

(2) A person shall not intentionally make a false report that a child is missing who suffers from severe mental or physical disability that greatly impairs the child's ability to care for himself or herself, or intentionally cause such a report to be made, to a peace officer, police agency of this state or of a local unit of government, 9-1-1 operator, or any other governmental employee or contractor or employee of a contractor who is authorized to receive the report, knowing the report is false. A person who violates this subsection is guilty of a misdemeanor punishable by imprisonment for not more than 1 year or a fine of not more than $1,000.00, or both.

The difference between the felony and the misdemeanor:

- MCL 28.754(1) is a felony that entails the false report of an ABDUCTION.
- MCL 28.754(2) is a misdemeanor that entails a false report that a SEVERELY DISABLED child is MISSING.

ESCAPE

Aiding an Escape of a Prisoner—MCL 750.183
Elements

1. The suspect:
   a. Conveyed a disguise, weapon, or other object useful for escape,
   b. To a prisoner,
   c. Intending to assist the prisoner in escaping.

OR

   a. Assisted a prisoner in any way,
   b. In an attempt to escape, whether the prisoner actually escapes or not.

OR

   a. Forcibly rescues
   b. A prisoner.

Penalties:

| If the prisoner is being held on felony charges | 7 year felony |
| If the prisoner is being held on misdemeanor charges | 1 year misdemeanor |

This is a general intent crime. In a case where two inmates assaulted a guard during an escape, the defendant was properly convicted of aiding the other prisoner's escape even though the defendant claimed that he was only facilitating his own escape. *People v. Potts*, 55 Mich. App. 622 (1974).

By statute, the prisoner that the defendant aids must be lawfully detained at the time of the assistance. *People v. Gardineer*, 334 Mich. 663 (1952).

Aiding an Escape From an Officer—MCL 750.184 (1 year misdemeanor)

The suspect assisted a prisoner in an escape attempt from an officer or person who had lawful custody.

Escape From Juvenile Facility—MCL 750.186a (felony)

Suspect was placed in juvenile facility and did one of the following:

- Escaped, or attempted to escape, or
- Escaped or attempted to escape from an employee of the facility.

"Escape" means to leave without lawful authority or to fail to return to custody when required.

Escape From Prison—MCL 750.193 (felony)
Elements

1. The defendant was sentenced to imprisonment and was serving that sentence at the time,
2. The facility holding the defendant was a prison,
3. The defendant did one of the following:
   a. Escaped from prison,
   b. Attempted to escape from prison,
   c. Escaped from the custody of a guard or prison employee while outside of the prison,
   d. Left the prison without being legally discharged,
   e. Escaped from a mental health facility where he or she had been admitted from prison.

CJI2d 13.8.

Definition of prison: "a facility that houses prisoners committed to the jurisdiction of the department of corrections and includes the grounds, farm, shop, road camp, or place of employment operated by the facility or under control of the officers of the facility, the department of corrections, a police officer of this state, or any other person authorized by the department of corrections to have a prisoner under care, custody, or supervision, either in a facility or outside a facility, whether for the purpose of work, medical care, or any other reason." MCL 750.193(2).

> Escape is a general intent crime (*People v. Spalding*, 17 Mich. App. 73 (1969)), but attempted escape is a specific intent crime (*People v. Langworthy*, 416 Mich. 630 (1982)).
>
> Intentional violation of an electronic tether program may constitute an escape. *People v. Sheets*, 223 Mich. App. 651, (1997).
>
> This statute applies to any place authorized by the Department of Corrections to have inmates. This includes halfway houses (*People v. Mayes*, 95 Mich. App. 188 (1980)), community corrections centers (*People v. King*, 104 Mich. App. 459 (1981)) and hospitals to which prisoners are transferred for treatment (*People v. Smith*, 89 Mich. App. 478 (1979)).

Escape From Jail—MCL 750.195 (felony)

The suspect was placed in a county jail and did one of the following:

- Broke out of jail and escaped.
- Broke out of jail, though he did not actually escape,
- Left the jail without being legally discharged from it, or
- Attempted to escape from jail.

Definition of jail: "a facility that is operated by a local unit of government for the detention of persons charged with, or convicted of, criminal offenses or ordinance violations, or persons found guilty of civil or criminal contempt." MCL 750.195(4).

> A defendant who escapes before he is booked may be convicted of escaping from jail. In this case, the defendant asked to use the restroom; when the door opened he escaped through the open sally port door. *People v. Taylor*, 238 Mich. App. 259 (1999).

Day parole

Defendant is not guilty of escape from jail if he or she has been released to go to work, look for work, attend school, or obtain medical treatment, substance abuse treatment, medical health counseling, and was simply late in returning to jail. The prosecutor must prove beyond a reasonable doubt that defendant intended to escape.

> A defendant's conviction was overturned where she was released pending sentencing in order to ease jail overcrowding. However, the court held that she could be charged with violation of MCL 750.197a (see below), a misdemeanor. *People v. Jones*, 190 Mich. App. 509 (1991).

Breaking From County Work Farm, Factory or Shop—MCL 750.196 (misdemeanor)

Elements

1. The defendant was lawfully committed to a work farm, factory, or shop established by law for the confinement of persons sentenced there, and
2. Escaped or broke away with the intent to escape, or attempted by force, violence, or any other manner to escape.

    Punishable by double the term of the original sentence, to be served at the end of the original sentence.

Escape While Awaiting Court Hearing—MCL 750.197 (felony)

Suspect was awaiting examination, trial, arraignment, or sentence for a misdemeanor or a felony and escaped or attempted to escape.

Escape From Lawful Custody Under Any Criminal Process—MCL 750.197a (1 year misdemeanor)

Suspect escaped from lawful custody under any criminal process, including periods while at large on bail.

> This section does not apply to a person who was arrested without a warrant and escaped from the back seat of the police car because court action had not yet begun. *People v. Lawrence*, 246 Mich. App. 260 (2001).

> Defendant could be convicted of this crime for failing to appear for sentencing while out on bond. However, he could not be charged with absconding on a bond (a felony) because the crime that he was on bond for was not itself a felony. *People v. Williams*, 243 Mich. App. 333 (2000).

Concealing or Harboring a Fugitive—MCL 750.199

Knowingly and willfully concealing or harboring, for the purpose of concealment from a peace officer, another who is wanted on warrants:

Penalties:

Person wanted on misdemeanor arrest warrant, bench warrant in a civil case, criminal bench warrant in misdemeanor case	93 day misdemeanor
Person wanted on felony arrest warrant or bench warrant in felony case	4 year felony

Pursuit and Retaking of Escapee—MCL 764.23

If a person who has been lawfully arrested escapes, the person from whose custody he or she escaped may immediately pursue and retake him or her at any time and in any place within the state without a warrant.

If a prisoner escapes from a state correctional facility or willfully fails to remain within the extended limits of his or her confinement, the prisoner may be pursued and arrested, without a warrant, by a person who is either of the following:

- An employee of the department of corrections who is designated by the director of the department of corrections as having the authority to pursue and arrest escaped prisoners, or
- An employee of a private vendor that operates a youth correctional facility who is designated by the director of the department of corrections as having the authority to pursue and arrest escaped prisoners.

Cellular Telephone to Prisoner—MCL 800.283a (felony)

A person shall not sell, give, or furnish, or aid in the selling, giving, or furnishing of, a cellular telephone or other wireless communication device to a prisoner in a correctional facility, or dispose of a cellular telephone or other wireless communication device in or on the grounds of a correctional facility.

PERJURY

Perjury Under Statute—MCL 750.423 (felony)

Any person authorized by any statute of this state to take an oath, or any person of whom an oath shall be required by law, who shall willfully swear falsely, in regard to any matter or thing, respecting which such oath is authorized or required, shall be guilty of perjury, a felony, punishable by imprisonment in the state prison not more than 15 years.

Elements

1. The defendant took an oath to tell the truth,
2. The oath was authorized or required by law,
3. The defendant made a false statement while under oath, and
4. The defendant knew that the statement was false.

CJI2d 14.2.

> Types of oaths that are included:
> - An affidavit for a marriage license. *People v. Mankin*, 225 Mich. 246 (1923).
> - Signing of an application for a driver's license containing false and incorrect information. *People v. Thompson*, 193 Mich. App. 58 (1992).
> - But the signing of an Aid to Dependant Children application is not an oath. *People v. Ramos*, 430 Mich. 544 (1988).

Perjury in a Court of Justice—MCL 750.422 (felony)

Any person who, being lawfully required to depose the truth in any proceeding in a court of justice, shall commit perjury shall be guilty of a felony, punishable, if such perjury was committed on the trial of an indictment for a capital crime, by imprisonment in the state prison for life, or any term of years, and if committed in any other case, by imprisonment in the state prison for not more than 15 years.

Elements

1. The defendant was legally required to take an oath in a proceeding in a court of justice,
2. The defendant took the oath,
3. The defendant made a false statement while under oath,
4. The defendant knew that the statement was false when he or she made it.

CJI2d 14.1.

> A showing that the suspect had a good faith belief that his statement was true is not perjury. *Smith v. Hubbell*, 142 Mich. 637 (1906).
>
> Whether the false statement was about a material fact is not an element. *People v. Lively*, 470 Mich. 248 (2004).

Subornation of Perjury—MCL 750.424 (felony)

Any person who shall be guilty of subornation of perjury, by procuring another person to commit the crime of perjury, shall be punished as provided in the next preceding section.

The suspect persuaded another to make a false statement under a lawful oath that the suspect knew was false.

Attempted Subornation of Perjury—MCL 750.425 (felony)

Any person who shall endeavor to incite or procure any person to commit the crime of perjury, though no perjury be committed, shall be guilty of a felony, punishable by imprisonment in the state prison not more than 5 years.

Elements

1. The defendant tried to get another person to make a false statement under oath,
2. The defendant knew that the statement was false,
3. The other person made the false statement as a result of the defendant's actions,
4. The oath was authorized or required by law.

CJI2d 14.3.

> There is no requirement that witness knew that the statement was false, only that the defendant knew that the statement was false (i.e., the witness might not be committing perjury because he or she believes that the statement is true, but the defendant could still be charged with attempted subornation of perjury if the defendant knew that the statement was false). *People v. Mosley*, 338 Mich. 559 (1953).

Jury Tampering—MCL 750.120a

(1) *A person who willfully attempts to influence the decision of a juror in any case by argument or persuasion, other than as part of the proceedings in open court in the trial of the case, is guilty of a misdemeanor punishable by imprisonment for not more than 1 year or a fine of not more than $1,000.00, or both.*

(2) *A person who willfully attempts to influence the decision of a juror in any case by intimidation, other than as part of the proceedings in open court in the trial of the case, is guilty of a crime as follows:*

   (a) *Except as provided in subdivisions (b) and (c), the person is guilty of a felony punishable by imprisonment for not more than 4 years or a fine of not more than $5,000.00, or both.*

   (b) *If the intimidation is committed in a criminal case for which the maximum term of imprisonment for the violation is more than 10 years, or the violation is punishable by imprisonment for life or any term of years, the person is guilty of a felony punishable by imprisonment for not more than 10 years or a fine of not more than $20,000.00, or both.*

   (c) *If the intimidation involved committing or attempting to commit a crime or a threat to kill or injure any person or to cause property damage, the person is guilty of a felony punishable by imprisonment for not more than 15 years or a fine of not more than $25,000.00, or both.*

(3) *Subsections (1) and (2) do not prohibit any deliberating juror from attempting to influence*

other members of the same jury by any proper means.

(4) A person who retaliates, attempts to retaliate, or threatens to retaliate against another person for having performed his or her duties as a juror is guilty of a felony punishable by imprisonment for not more than 10 years or a fine of not more than $20,000.00, or both. As used in this subsection, "retaliate" means any of the following:

(a) Committing or attempting to commit a crime against any person.

(b) Threatening to kill or injure any person or threatening to cause property damage.

(5) This section does not prohibit a person from being charged with, convicted of, or punished for any other violation of law including any violation of law arising out of the same transaction as the violation of this section.

(6) The court may order a term of imprisonment imposed for violating subsection (2) or (4) to be served consecutively to a term of imprisonment imposed for any other violation of law including any violation of law arising out of the same transaction as the violation of this section.

Obstruction of Justice—MCL 750.483a

(1) A person shall not do any of the following:

(a) Withhold or refuse to produce any testimony, information, document, or thing after the court has ordered it to be produced following a hearing.

(b) Prevent or attempt to prevent through the unlawful use of physical force another person from reporting a crime committed or attempted by another person.

(c) Retaliate or attempt to retaliate against another person for having reported or attempted to report a crime committed or attempted by another person. As used in this subsection, "retaliate" means to do any of the following:

(i) Commit or attempt to commit a crime against any person.

(ii) Threaten to kill or injure any person or threaten to cause property damage.

(2) A person who violates subsection (1) is guilty of a crime as follows:

(a) Except as provided in subdivision (b), the person is guilty of a misdemeanor punishable by imprisonment for not more than 1 year or a fine of not more than $1,000.00, or both.

(b) If the violation involves committing or attempting to commit a crime or a threat to kill or injure any person or to cause property damage, the person is guilty of a felony punishable by imprisonment for not more than 10 years or a fine of not more than $20,000.00, or both.

(3) A person shall not do any of the following:

(a) Give, offer to give, or promise anything of value to any person to influence a person's statement to a police officer conducting a lawful investigation of a crime or the presentation of evidence to a police officer conducting a lawful investigation of a crime.

(b) Threaten or intimidate any person to influence a person's statement to a police officer conducting a lawful investigation of a crime or the presentation of evidence to a police officer conducting a lawful investigation of a crime.

(4) A person who violates subsection (3) is guilty of a crime as follows:

(a) Except as provided in subdivision (b), the person is guilty of a misdemeanor punishable by imprisonment for not more than 1 year or a fine of not more than $1,000.00, or both.

(b) If the violation involves committing or attempting to commit a crime or a threat to kill or injure any person or to cause property damage, the person is guilty of a felony punishable by imprisonment for not more than 10 years or a fine of not more than $20,000.00, or both.

(5) A person shall not do any of the following:

(a) Knowingly and intentionally remove, alter, conceal, destroy, or otherwise tamper with evidence to be offered in a present or future official proceeding.

(b) Offer evidence at an official proceeding that he or she recklessly disregards as false.

(6) A person who violates subsection (5) is guilty of a crime as follows:

(a) Except as provided in subdivision (b), the person is guilty of a felony punishable by imprisonment for not more than 4 years or a fine of not more than $5,000.00, or both.

(b) If the violation is committed in a criminal case for which the maximum term of imprisonment for the violation is more than 10 years, or the violation is punishable by imprisonment for life or any term of years,

the person is guilty of a felony punishable by imprisonment for not more than 10 years or a fine of not more than $20,000.00, or both.

(7) *It is an affirmative defense under subsection (3), for which the defendant has the burden of proof by a preponderance of the evidence, that the conduct consisted solely of lawful conduct and that the defendant's sole intention was to encourage, induce, or cause the other person to provide a statement or evidence truthfully.*

(8) *Subsections (1)(a), (3)(b), and (5)(b) do not apply to any of the following:*

(a) *The lawful conduct of an attorney in the performance of his or her duties, such as advising a client.*
(b) *The lawful conduct or communications of a person as permitted by statute or other lawful privilege.*

(9) *This section does not prohibit a person from being charged with, convicted of, or punished for any other violation of law arising out of the same transaction as the violation of this section.*

(10) *The court may order a term of imprisonment imposed for a violation of this section to be served consecutively to a term of imprisonment imposed for any other crime including any other violation of law arising out of the same transaction as the violation of this section.*

(11) *As used in this section:*

(a) *"Official proceeding" means a proceeding heard before a legislative, judicial, administrative, or other governmental agency or official authorized to hear evidence under oath, including a referee, prosecuting attorney, hearing examiner, commissioner, notary, or other person taking testimony or deposition in that proceeding.*
(b) *"Threaten or intimidate" does not mean a communication regarding the otherwise lawful access to courts or other branches of government, such as the lawful filing of any civil action or police report of which the purpose is not to harass the other person in violation of section 2907 of the revised judicature act of 1961, 1961 PA 236, MCL 600.2907.*

> The defendant used force to prevent the victim from making a felonious assault report. Even though the defendant was found not guilty of the original felonious assault, his obstruction conviction was upheld. *People v. Holley*, 480 Mich. 222 (2008).

Inhibiting a Witness—MCL 750.122 (felony)

(1) *A person shall not give, offer to give, or promise anything of value to an individual for any of the following purposes:*

(a) *To discourage any individual from attending a present or future official proceeding as a witness, testifying at a present or future official proceeding, or giving information at a present or future official proceeding.*
(b) *To influence any individual's testimony at a present or future official proceeding.*
(c) *To encourage any individual to avoid legal process, to withhold testimony, or to testify falsely in a present or future official proceeding.*

(2) *Subsection (1) does not apply to the reimbursement or payment of reasonable costs for any witness to provide a statement to testify truthfully or provide truthful information in an official proceeding as provided for under section 16 of the uniform condemnation procedures act, 1980 PA 87, MCL 213.66, or section 2164 of the revised judicature act of 1961, 1961 PA 236, MCL 600.2164, or court rule.*

(3) *A person shall not do any of the following by threat or intimidation:*

(a) *Discourage or attempt to discourage any individual from attending a present or future official proceeding as a witness, testifying at a present or future official proceeding, or giving information at a present or future official proceeding.*
(b) *Influence or attempt to influence testimony at a present or future official proceeding.*
(c) *Encourage or attempt to encourage any individual to avoid legal process, to withhold testimony, or to testify falsely in a present or future official proceeding.*

(4) *It is an affirmative defense under subsections (1) and (3), for which the defendant has the burden of proof by a preponderance of the evidence, that the conduct consisted solely of lawful conduct and that the defendant's sole intention was to encourage, induce, or cause the other person to testify or provide evidence truthfully.*

(5) Subsections (1) and (3) do not apply to any of the following:

(a) The lawful conduct of an attorney in the performance of his or her duties, such as advising a client.

(b) The lawful conduct or communications of a person as permitted by statute or other lawful privilege.

(6) A person shall not willfully impede, interfere with, prevent, or obstruct or attempt to willfully impede, interfere with, prevent, or obstruct the ability of a witness to attend, testify, or provide information in or for a present or future official proceeding.

(7) A person who violates this section is guilty of a crime as follows:

(a) Except as provided in subdivisions (b) and (c), the person is guilty of a felony punishable by imprisonment for not more than 4 years or a fine of not more than $5,000.00, or both.

(b) If the violation is committed in a criminal case for which the maximum term of imprisonment for the violation is more than 10 years, or the violation is punishable by imprisonment for life or any term of years, the person is guilty of a felony punishable by imprisonment for not more than 10 years or a fine of not more than $20,000.00, or both.

(c) If the violation involves committing or attempting to commit a crime or a threat to kill or injure any person or to cause property damage, the person is guilty of a felony punishable by imprisonment for not more than 15 years or a fine of not more than $25,000.00, or both.

(8) A person who retaliates, attempts to retaliate, or threatens to retaliate against another person for having been a witness in an official proceeding is guilty of a felony punishable by imprisonment for not more than 10 years or a fine of not more than $20,000.00, or both. As used in this subsection, "retaliate" means to do any of the following:

(a) Commit or attempt to commit a crime against any person.

(b) Threaten to kill or injure any person or threaten to cause property damage.

(9) This section applies regardless of whether an official proceeding actually takes place or is pending or whether the individual has been subpoenaed or otherwise ordered to appear at the official proceeding if the person knows or has reason to know the other person could be a witness at any official proceeding.

(10) This section does not prohibit a person from being charged with, convicted of, or punished for any other violation of law arising out of the same transaction as the violation of this section.

(11) The court may order a term of imprisonment imposed for violating this section to be served consecutively to a term of imprisonment imposed for the commission of any other crime including any other violation of law arising out of the same transaction as the violation of this section.

(12) As used in this section:

(a) "Official proceeding" means a proceeding heard before a legislative, judicial, administrative, or other governmental agency or official authorized to hear evidence under oath, including a referee, prosecuting attorney, hearing examiner, commissioner, notary, or other person taking testimony or deposition in that proceeding.

(b) "Threaten or intimidate" does not mean a communication regarding the otherwise lawful access to courts or other branches of government, such as the otherwise lawful filing of any civil action or police report of which the purpose is not to harass the other person in violation of section 2907 of the revised judicature act of 1961, 1961 PA 236, MCL 600.2907.

> "Defendant could be charged with M.C.L. 750.122(6) where he willfully attempted to interfere with the witness' intention to attend a hearing by telling her explicitly not to attend, playing to her feelings for him, and assuring her that the consequences would be minor, or nonexistent; and this interference attempted to affect her ability to attend the hearing by impairing her ability to choose to do the right thing, which was to obey the subpoena." *People v. Greene*, 255 Mich. App. 426 (2003).

TAKING WEAPONS FROM AN OFFICER—MCL 750.479b (felony)

(1) An individual who takes a weapon other than a firearm from the lawful possession of a peace officer or a corrections officer is guilty of a felony punishable by imprisonment for not more than 4 years or a fine of not more than $2,500.00, or both, if all of the following circumstances exist at the time the weapon is taken:

- (a) The individual knows or has reason to believe the person from whom the weapon is taken is a peace officer or a corrections officer.
- (b) The peace officer or corrections officer is performing his or her duties as a peace officer or a corrections officer.
- (c) The individual takes the weapon without consent of the peace officer or corrections officer.
- (d) The peace officer or corrections officer is authorized by his or her employer to carry the weapon in the line of duty.

(2) An individual who takes a firearm from the lawful possession of a peace officer or a corrections officer is guilty of a felony punishable by imprisonment for not more than 10 years or a fine of not more than $5,000.00, or both, if all of the following circumstances exist at the time the firearm is taken:

- (a) The individual knows or has reason to believe the person from whom the firearm is taken is a peace officer or a corrections officer.
- (b) The peace officer or corrections officer is performing his or her duties as a peace officer or a corrections officer.
- (c) The individual takes the firearm without the consent of the peace officer or corrections officer.
- (d) The peace officer or corrections officer is authorized by his or her employer to carry the firearm in the line of duty.

(3) This section does not prohibit an individual from being charged with, convicted of, or punished for any other violation of law that is committed by that individual while violating this section.

(4) A term of imprisonment imposed for a violation of this section may run consecutively to any term of imprisonment imposed for another violation arising from the same transaction.

(5) As used in this section:

- (a) "Corrections officer" means a prison or jail guard or other employee of a jail or a state or federal correctional facility, who performs duties involving the transportation, care, custody, or supervision of prisoners.
- (b) "Peace officer" means 1 or more of the following:
  - (i) A police officer of this state or a political subdivision of this state.
  - (ii) A police officer of any entity of the United States.
  - (iii) The sheriff of a county of this state or the sheriff's deputy.
  - (iv) A public safety officer of a college or university who is authorized by the governing board of that college or university to enforce state law and the rules and ordinances of that college or university.
  - (v) A conservation officer of the department of natural resources.
  - (vi) A conservation officer of the United States department of interior.

Elements

1. The defendant took a weapon,
2. From a police officer or corrections officer,
3. The defendant knew that the person was an officer,
4. The officer was performing his or her duties at the time,
5. The officer did not consent to the taking of the weapon, and
6. The officer was authorized to carry the weapon.

CJI2d 13.18.

RESISTING AND OBSTRUCTING

(For Obstructing a Police Officer, see Assaulting a Police Officer in Assault Chapter)

Obstructing Person Performing Lawful Duty— MCL 750.479 (felony)

(1) A person shall not knowingly and willfully do any of the following:

- (a) Assault, batter, wound, obstruct, or endanger a medical examiner, township treasurer, judge, magistrate, probation officer, parole officer, prosecutor, city attorney, court employee, court officer, or other officer or duly authorized person serving or attempting to serve or execute any process, rule, or order made or issued by lawful authority or otherwise acting in the performance of his or her duties.
- (b) Assault, batter, wound, obstruct, or endanger an officer enforcing an ordinance, law, rule, order, or resolution of the common council of a city board of trustees, the common council or village council of an incorporated village, or a township board of a township.

(2) Except as provided in subsections (3), (4), and (5), a person who violates this section is guilty

of a felony punishable by imprisonment for not more than 2 years or a fine of not more than $2,000.00, or both.

(3) A person who violates this section and by that violation causes a bodily injury requiring medical attention or medical care to an individual described in this section is guilty of a felony punishable by imprisonment for not more than 4 years or a fine of not more than $5,000.00, or both.

(4) A person who violates this section and by that violation causes serious impairment of a body function of an individual described in this section is guilty of a felony punishable by imprisonment for not more than 10 years or a fine of not more than $10,000.00, or both.

(5) A person who violates this section and by that violation causes the death of an individual described in this section is guilty of a felony punishable by imprisonment for not more than 20 years or a fine of not more than $20,000.00, or both.

(6) This section does not prohibit an individual from being charged with, convicted of, or punished for any other violation of law that is committed by that individual while violating this section.

(7) The court may order a term of imprisonment for a violation of this section to be served consecutively to any other term of imprisonment imposed for a violation arising out of the same criminal transaction as the violation of this section.

(8) As used in this section:

(a) "Obstruct" includes the use or threatened use of physical interference or force or a knowing failure to comply with a lawful command.

(b) "Serious impairment of a body function" means that term as defined in section 58c of the Michigan vehicle code, 1949 PA 300, MCL 257.58c.

Elements

1. The defendant assaulted, battered, wounded, obstructed, or endangered,
2. A medical examiner, township treasurer, judge, magistrate, probation officer, parole officer, prosecutor, city attorney, court employee, court officer, etc. who was performing his or her duties,
3. The defendant knew that the person was one of the persons listed above,
4. The defendant's actions were intentional.

CJI2d 13.2.

> A defendant's polite refusal to comply with a search warrant for his blood was held to be sufficient obstruction where the police officer did not force the defendant to comply. *People v. Philabaun*, 461 Mich. 255 (1999).

FLEEING AND ELUDING—MCL 750.479a (felony)

(1) A driver of a motor vehicle who is given by hand, voice, emergency light, or siren a visual or audible signal by a police or conservation officer, acting in the lawful performance of his or her duty, directing the driver to bring his or her motor vehicle to a stop shall not willfully fail to obey that direction by increasing the speed of the vehicle, extinguishing the lights of the vehicle, or otherwise attempting to flee or elude the police or conservation officer. This subsection does not apply unless the police or conservation officer giving the signal is in uniform and the officer's vehicle is identified as an official police or department of natural resources vehicle.

(2) Except as provided in subsection (3), (4), or (5), an individual who violates subsection (1) is guilty of fourth-degree fleeing and eluding, a felony punishable by imprisonment for not more than 2 years or a fine of not more than $2,000.00, or both.

(3) Except as provided in subsection (4) or (5), an individual who violates subsection (1) is guilty of third-degree fleeing and eluding, a felony punishable by imprisonment for not more than 5 years or a fine of not more than $5,000.00, or both, if 1 or more of the following circumstances apply:

(a) The violation results in a collision or accident.

(b) A portion of the violation occurred in an area where the speed limit is 35 miles an hour or less, whether that speed limit is posted or imposed as a matter of law.

(c) The individual has a prior conviction for fourth-degree fleeing and eluding, attempted fourth-degree fleeing and eluding, or fleeing and eluding under a current or former law of this state prohibiting substantially similar conduct.

(4) Except as provided in subsection (5), an individual who violates subsection (1) is guilty of second-degree fleeing and eluding, a felony punishable by imprisonment for not more than 10 years or a fine of not more than $10,000.00, or both, if 1 or more of the following circumstances apply:

(a) The violation results in serious impairment of a body function of an individual.
(b) The individual has 1 or more prior convictions for first-, second-, or third-degree fleeing and eluding, attempted first-, second-, or third-degree fleeing and eluding, or fleeing and eluding under a current or former law of this state prohibiting substantially similar conduct.
(c) The individual has any combination of 2 or more prior convictions for fourth-degree fleeing and eluding, attempted fourth-degree fleeing and eluding, or fleeing and eluding under a current or former law of this state prohibiting substantially similar conduct.

(5) If the violation results in the death of another individual, an individual who violates subsection (1) is guilty of first-degree fleeing and eluding, a felony punishable by imprisonment for not more than 15 years or a fine of not more than $15,000.00, or both.
(6) Upon a conviction for a violation or attempted violation under subsection (2) or (3), the secretary of state shall suspend the individual's operator's or chauffeur's license as provided in section 319 of the Michigan vehicle code, 1949 PA 300, MCL 257.319.
(7) Upon a conviction for a violation or attempted violation under subsection (4) or (5), the secretary of state shall revoke the individual's operator's or chauffeur's license as provided in section 303 of the Michigan vehicle code, 1949 PA 300, MCL 257.303.
(8) Except as otherwise provided, a conviction under this section does not prohibit a conviction and sentence under any other applicable provision for conduct arising out of the same transaction. A conviction under subsection (2), (3), (4), or (5) prohibits a conviction under section 602a of the Michigan vehicle code, 1949 PA 300, MCL 257.602a, for conduct arising out of the same transaction.
(9) As used in this section, "serious impairment of a body function" means that term as defined in section 58c of the Michigan vehicle code, 1949 PA 300, MCL 257.58c.

Fourth Degree—MCL 750.479a(2)
Elements

1. The law enforcement officer was in uniform and performing lawful duties,
2. The defendant was driving a motor vehicle,
3. The officer ordered the defendant to stop,
4. The defendant knew that he or she was being ordered to stop,
5. The defendant refused to obey the order by trying to flee.
CJ12d 13.6d.

The order to stop can be by hand, voice, siren, or emergency light.

The suspect was aware that he had been ordered to stop but refused to stop by trying to flee or avoid being caught, which could be evidenced by speeding up or turning off his lights among other things.

There was sufficient evidence to convict for fleeing and eluding where the officer in a fully marked police car activated his emergency equipment in an attempt to stop the defendant. The defendant refused to stop, drove approximately one mile at speeds of 25 to 30 mph, stopped his car and ran up to a house. *People v. Grayer*, 235 Mich. App. 737 (1999).

There is no requirement for fleeing and eluding that the officer be present in an officially identified vehicle. In this case, the uniformed officer was standing away from his car when he ordered the suspect to stop. *People v. Green*, 260 Mich. App. 710 (2004).

Third Degree—MCL 750.479a(3)

Same elements as in fourth degree plus one of the following:

- Violation results in collision or accident.
- A portion of the violation took part through a 35-mile-per-hour zone.
- Prior conviction of fourth degree.

There is "no requirement that the defendant's speeding exceed a certain level or that the speeding occur over a long distance in order for the elements of the statute to be met." *People v. Grayer*, 235 Mich. App. 737 (1999).

Since this is a general intent crime, voluntary intoxication is not a valid defense. *People v. Abramski*, 257 Mich. App. 71 (2003).

Second Degree—MCL 750.479a(4)

Same elements as in fourth degree plus one of the following:

- Violation results in *"serious impairment of a bodily function"* to another person.
- Suspect has one or more prior convictions for first, second, or third degree fleeing and eluding.
- Suspect has two or more convictions of fourth degree fleeing and eluding.

"Serious impairment of a body function" includes, but is not limited to, one or more of the following: loss of a limb or loss of use of a limb; loss of a foot, hand, finger, or thumb or loss of use of a foot, hand, finger, or thumb; loss of an eye or ear or loss of use of an eye or ear; loss or substantial impairment of a bodily function; serious visible disfigurement; a comatose state that lasts for more than 3 days; measurable brain or mental impairment; a skull fracture or other serious bone fracture; subdural hemorrhage or subdural hematoma; or loss of an organ. MCL 257.58c.

First Degree—MCL 750.479a(5)

The same elements as in fourth degree plus:

The violation results in the **death** of another person.

> In a case where a pursuing police officer lost control of his vehicle, crashed, and was killed, the court ruled that "results" is not the same as "causes," and the defendant's conviction for first-degree fleeing and eluding was upheld. *People v. Wood*, 276 Mich. App. 669 (2007).

PEACE BONDS—MCL 772.1

A district or municipal judge may cause all the laws made for the preservation of the public peace to be kept and, in the execution of this authority, may require a person to give security to keep the peace in the manner provided in this chapter.

Complaint—MCL 772.2

If a complaint is made in writing and on oath to the district court or a municipal court that a person has threatened to commit an offense against the person or property of another, the judge shall examine on oath the complainant and any witnesses who may be produced.

Issuance of a Warrant by the Court—MCL 772.3

If the judge determines from the examination that there is just reason to believe the person will commit an offense described in section 2 of this chapter, the judge may enter an order directing the person to appear on a date certain within 7 days. If the person fails to appear as ordered, the court shall issue a warrant. Alternatively, the court may issue a warrant directed to the sheriff or any peace officer, reciting the substance of the complaint and commanding that the person be promptly apprehended and brought before the court.

Arrest Authority—MCL 772.13a

If a peace officer has reason to believe that the conditions of a recognizance required under this chapter are being violated in his or her presence or were violated, the peace officer shall arrest the person and hold him or her for presentation to the court on the next day.

18

PUBLIC INTEREST CRIMES: SELECTED STATUTES

GAMBLING

Gambling—MCL 750.301 (1 year misdemeanor)

Any person or his or her agent or employee who, directly or indirectly, takes, receives, or accepts from any person any money or valuable thing with the agreement, understanding or allegation that any money or valuable thing will be paid or delivered to any person where the payment or delivery is alleged to be or will be contingent upon the result of any race, contest, or game or upon the happening of any event not known by the parties to be certain, is guilty of a misdemeanor punishable by imprisonment for not more than 1 year or a fine of not more than $1,000.00.

Money or other valuable items were directly or indirectly taken, received, or accepted from a person. The valuables were taken with the agreement and understanding that they would be paid or delivered to another person contingent upon the result of any race, contest, game, or upon the happening of any uncertain event.

Other Gambling Statutes

Keeping and occupying a gambling house—MCL 750.302 (1 year misdemeanor)

(1) *Except as provided in subsection (2), any person, or his or her agent or employee who, directly or indirectly, keeps, occupies, or assists in keeping or occupying any common gambling house or any building or place where gaming is permitted or suffered or who suffers or permits on any premises owned, occupied, or controlled by him or her any apparatus used for gaming or gambling or who shall use such apparatus for gaming or gambling in any place within this state, is guilty of a misdemeanor punishable by imprisonment for not more than 1 year or a fine of not more than $1,000.00.*

(2) *This section does not prohibit the manufacture of gaming or gambling apparatus or the possession of gaming or gambling apparatus by the manufacturer of the apparatus solely for sale outside of this state, or for sale to a gambling establishment operating within this*

state in compliance with the laws of this state, if applicable, and in compliance with the laws of the United States, provided the manufacturer meets or exceeds federal government requirements in regard to manufacture, storage, and transportation.

> The Michigan Supreme Court overturned the conviction of a landlord who leased property that was used by the tenant as a gambling house. The Court found that there was no evidence that the defendant controlled the premises. *People v. Johnson*, 323 Mich. 573 (1949).
>
> Video poker machines are not exempt under this statute unless they do not pay out money or something of value. *People v. Lopez*, 187 Mich. App. 305 (1991).

Selling pools and registered bets—MCL 750.304 (1 year misdemeanor)

Any person or his or her agent or employee who, directly or indirectly, keeps, maintains, operates, or occupies any building or room or any part of a building or room or any place with apparatus, books, or any device for registering bets or buying or selling pools upon the result of a trial or contest of skill, speed or endurance or upon the result of a game, competition, political nomination, appointment, or election or any purported event of like character or who registers bets or buys or sells pools, or who is concerned in buying or selling pools or who knowingly permits any grounds or premises, owned, occupied, or controlled by him or her to be used for any of the purposes aforesaid, is guilty of a misdemeanor punishable by imprisonment for not more than 1 year or a fine of not more than $1,000.00.

Frequenting or attending gaming places—MCL 750.309 (90-day misdemeanor

Any person who shall attend or frequent any place where gaming or gambling is suffered or permitted, or any place operated or occupied as a common gaming or gambling house or room, shall be guilty of a misdemeanor.

BODY ARMOR

Use of Body Armor During Crime—MCL 750.227f (felony)

(1) Except as provided in subsection (2), an individual who commits or attempts to commit a crime that involves a violent act or a threat of a violent act against another person while wearing body armor is guilty of a felony, punishable by imprisonment for not more than 4 years, or a fine of not more than $2,000.00, or both.

(2) Subsection (1) does not apply to either of the following:

(a) A peace officer of this state or another state, or of a local unit of government of this state or another state, or of the United States, performing his or her duties as a peace officer while on or off a scheduled work shift as a peace officer.

(b) A security officer performing his or her duties as a security officer while on a scheduled work shift as a security officer.

(3) As used in this section:

(a) "Body armor" means clothing or a device designed or intended to protect an individual's body or a portion of an individual's body from injury caused by a firearm.

(b) "Security officer" means an individual lawfully employed to physically protect another individual or to physically protect the property of another person.

Felons in Possession of Body Armor—MCL 750.227g (felony)

This statute prohibits anyone convicted of a violent felony from owning, possessing, or using body armor.

Exception: A person convicted of a felony may petition the chief of a local unit of government of the county sheriff for written permission to possess body armor. If the chief or sheriff does issue the written permission, the person must carry it at all times he or she is in possession of the body armor. Failure to carry the written permission is a 93 day misdemeanor.

LIQUOR LAW VIOLATIONS

License Requirement—MCL 436.1913

A person shall not maintain, operate, lease, or otherwise furnish to any person alcoholic liquor for consideration without a license.

Definitions

Consideration means any fee, cover charge, the storage of alcoholic liquor, the sale of food, ice, mixers, or other liquids used with alcoholic liquor drinks, or the furnishing of glassware or other containers for use in the consumption of alcoholic liquor in conjunction with the sale of food.

Alcoholic liquor is more than half of one percent of alcohol per volume. (MCL 436.1105 (2))

A **minor** is a person under 21 years of age.

Inspections

A licensed premise may be inspected during regular business hours, or when occupied by licensee or employee, by a LCC investigator or a law enforcement officer.

Furnishing Alcoholic Liquor to Minors—MCL 436.1701

(1) Alcoholic liquor shall not be sold or furnished to a minor. Except as otherwise provided in subsection (2) and subject to subsections (4), (5), and (6), a person who knowingly sells or furnishes alcoholic liquor to a minor, or who fails to make diligent inquiry as to whether the person is a minor, is guilty of a misdemeanor. A retail licensee or a retail licensee's clerk, agent, or employee who violates this subsection shall be punished in the manner provided for licensees in section 909 except that if the violation is the result of an undercover operation in which the minor received alcoholic liquor under the direction of the state police, the commission, or a local police agency as part of an enforcement action, the retail licensee's clerk, agent, or employee is responsible for a state civil infraction and may be ordered to pay a civil fine of not more than $100.00. Except as otherwise provided in subsection (2), a person who is not a retail licensee or a retail licensee's clerk, agent, or employee and who violates this subsection is guilty of a misdemeanor punishable by a fine of not more than $1,000.00 and imprisonment for not more than 60 days for a first offense, a fine of not more than $2,500.00 and imprisonment for not more than 90 days for a second or subsequent offense, and may be ordered to perform community service. A suitable sign describing the content of this section and the penalties for its violation shall be posted in a conspicuous place in each room where alcoholic liquor is sold. The signs shall be approved and furnished by the commission.

(2) A person who is not a retail licensee or the retail licensee's clerk, agent, or employee and who violates subsection (1) is guilty of a felony, punishable by imprisonment for not more than 10 years or a fine of not more than $5,000.00, or both, if the subsequent consumption of the alcoholic liquor by the minor is a direct and substantial cause of that person's death or an accidental injury that causes that person's death.

(3) If a violation occurs in an establishment that is licensed by the commission for consumption of alcoholic liquor on the licensed premises, a person who is a licensee or the clerk, agent, or employee of a licensee shall not be charged with a violation of subsection (1) or section 801(2) unless the licensee or the clerk, agent, or employee of the licensee knew or should have reasonably known with the exercise of due diligence that a person less than 21 years of age possessed or consumed alcoholic liquor on the licensed premises and the licensee or clerk, agent, or employee of the licensee failed to take immediate corrective action.

(4) If the enforcing agency involved in the violation is the state police or a local police agency, a licensee shall not be charged with a violation of subsection (1) or section 801(2) unless all of the following occur, if applicable:

   (a) Enforcement action is taken against the minor who purchased or attempted to purchase, consumed or attempted to consume, or possessed or attempted to possess alcoholic liquor.

   (b) Enforcement action is taken under this section against the person 21 years of age or older who is not the retail licensee or the retail licensee's clerk, agent, or employee who sold or furnished the alcoholic liquor to the minor.

   (c) Enforcement action under this section is taken against the clerk, agent, or employee who directly sold or furnished alcoholic liquor to the minor.

(5) If the enforcing agency is the commission and an appearance ticket or civil infraction citation has not been issued, then the commission shall recommend to a local law enforcement agency that enforcement action be taken against a violator of this section or section 703 who is not a licensee. However, subsection (4) does not apply if the minor against whom enforcement action

is taken under section 703, the clerk, agent, or employee of the licensee who directly sold or furnished alcoholic liquor to the minor, or the person 21 years of age or older who sold or furnished alcoholic liquor to the minor is not alive or is not present in this state at the time the licensee is charged.

Subsection (4)(a) does not apply under either of the following circumstances:

(a) The violation of subsection (1) is the result of an undercover operation in which the minor purchased or received alcoholic liquor under the direction of the person's employer and with the prior approval of the local prosecutor's office as part of an employer-sponsored internal enforcement action.

(b) The violation of subsection (1) is the result of an undercover operation in which the minor purchased or received alcoholic liquor under the direction of the state police, the commission, or a local police agency as part of an enforcement action.

(6) Any initial or contemporaneous purchase or receipt of alcoholic liquor by the minor under subsection (5)(a) or (b) must have been under the direction of the state police, the commission, or the local police agency and must have been part of the undercover operation.

(7) If a minor participates in an undercover operation in which the minor is to purchase or receive alcoholic liquor under the supervision of a law enforcement agency, his or her parents or legal guardian shall consent to the participation if that person is less than 18 years of age.

(8) In an action for the violation of this section, proof that the defendant or the defendant's agent or employee demanded and was shown, before furnishing alcoholic liquor to a minor, a motor vehicle operator's or chauffeur's license or a registration certificate issued by the federal selective service, or other bona fide documentary evidence of the age and identity of that person, shall be a defense to an action brought under this section.

(9) The commission shall provide, on an annual basis, a written report to the department of state police as to the number of actions heard by the commission involving violations of this section and section 801(2). The report shall include the disposition of each action and contain figures representing the following categories:

(a) Decoy operations.
(b) Off-premises violations.
(c) On-premises violations.
(d) Repeat offenses within the 3 years preceding the date of that report.

(10) As used in this section:

(a) "Corrective action" means action taken by a licensee or a clerk, agent, or employee of a licensee designed to prevent a minor from further possessing or consuming alcoholic liquor on the licensed premises. Corrective action includes, but is not limited to, contacting a law enforcement agency and ejecting the minor and any other person suspected of aiding and abetting the minor.

(b) "Diligent inquiry" means a diligent good faith effort to determine the age of a person, which includes at least an examination of an official Michigan operator's or chauffeur's license, an official Michigan personal identification card, or any other bona fide picture identification which establishes the identity and age of the person.

Minor in Possession of Alcoholic Liquor—MCL 436.1703

(1) A minor shall not purchase or attempt to purchase alcoholic liquor, consume or attempt to consume alcoholic liquor, possess or attempt to possess alcoholic liquor, or have any bodily alcohol content, except as provided in this section. A minor who violates this subsection is guilty of a misdemeanor punishable by the following fines and sanctions and is not subject to the penalties prescribed in section 909:

(a) For the first violation a fine of not more than $100.00, and may be ordered to participate in substance abuse prevention services or substance abuse treatment and rehabilitation services as defined in section 6107 of the public health code, 1978 PA 368, MCL 333.6107, and designated by the administrator of substance abuse services, and may be ordered to perform community service and to undergo substance abuse screening and assessment at his or her own expense as described in subsection (4).

(b) For a violation of this subsection following a prior conviction or juvenile adjudication for a violation of this subsection, section 33b(1) of former 1933 (Ex Sess) PA 8, or a local ordinance substantially corresponding to this subsection or section 33b(1) of former 1933 (Ex Sess) PA 8, by imprisonment for not more than 30 days but only if the minor has been found by the court to have violated an order of probation, failed to successfully complete any treatment, screening, or community service ordered by the court, or failed to pay any fine for that conviction or juvenile adjudication, a fine of not more than $200.00, or both, and may be ordered to participate in substance abuse prevention services or substance abuse treatment and rehabilitation services as defined in section 6107 of the public health code, 1978 PA 368, MCL 333.6107, and designated by the administrator of substance abuse services, to perform community service, and to undergo substance abuse screening and assessment at his or her own expense as described in subsection (4).

(c) For a violation of this subsection following 2 or more prior convictions or juvenile adjudications for a violation of this subsection, section 33b(1) of former 1933 (Ex Sess) PA 8, or a local ordinance substantially corresponding to this subsection or section 33b(1) of former 1933 (Ex Sess) PA 8, by imprisonment for not more than 60 days but only if the minor has been found by the court to have violated an order of probation, failed to successfully complete any treatment, screening, or community service ordered by the court, or failed to pay any fine for that conviction or juvenile adjudication, a fine of not more than $500.00, or both, and may be ordered to participate in substance abuse prevention services or substance abuse treatment and rehabilitation services as defined in section 6107 of the public health code, 1978 PA 368, MCL 333.6107, and designated by the administrator of substance abuse services, to perform community service, and to undergo substance abuse screening and assessment at his or her own expense as described in subsection (4).

(2) A person who furnishes fraudulent identification to a minor, or notwithstanding subsection (1) a minor who uses fraudulent identification to purchase alcoholic liquor, is guilty of a misdemeanor punishable by imprisonment for not more than 93 days or a fine of not more than $100.00, or both.

(3) When an individual who has not previously been convicted of or received a juvenile adjudication for a violation of subsection (1) pleads guilty to a violation of subsection (1) or offers a plea of admission in a juvenile delinquency proceeding for a violation of subsection (1), the court, without entering a judgment of guilt in a criminal proceeding or a determination in a juvenile delinquency proceeding that the juvenile has committed the offense and with the consent of the accused, may defer further proceedings and place the individual on probation upon terms and conditions that include, but are not limited to, the sanctions set forth in subsection (1)(a), payment of the costs including minimum state cost as provided for in section 18m of chapter XIIA of the probate code of 1939, 1939 PA 288, MCL 712A.18m, and section 1j of chapter IX of the code of criminal procedure, 1927 PA 175, MCL 769.1j, and the costs of probation as prescribed in section 3 of chapter XI of the code of criminal procedure, 1927 PA 175, MCL 771.3. Upon violation of a term or condition of probation or upon a finding that the individual is utilizing this subsection in another court, the court may enter an adjudication of guilt, or a determination in a juvenile delinquency proceeding that the individual has committed the offense, and proceed as otherwise provided by law. Upon fulfillment of the terms and conditions of probation, the court shall discharge the individual and dismiss the proceedings. Discharge and dismissal under this section shall be without adjudication of guilt or without a determination in a juvenile delinquency proceeding that the individual has committed the offense and is not a conviction or juvenile adjudication for purposes of this section or for purposes of disqualifications or disabilities imposed by law upon conviction of a crime, including the additional penalties imposed for second or subsequent convictions or juvenile adjudications under subsection (1)(b) and (c). There may be only 1 discharge or dismissal under this subsection as to an individual. The court shall maintain a nonpublic record of the matter while proceedings are deferred and the individual is on probation under this subsection. The secretary of state shall retain a nonpublic record of a plea and of the discharge and dismissal under this subsection. This record shall be furnished to any of the following:

(a) To a court, prosecutor, or police agency upon request for the purpose of determining if an individual has already utilized this subsection.

(b) To the department of corrections, a prosecutor, or a law enforcement agency, upon the department's, a prosecutor's, or a law enforcement agency's request, subject to all of the following conditions:

(i) At the time of the request, the individual is an employee of the department of corrections, the prosecutor, or the law enforcement agency, or an applicant for employment with the department of corrections, the prosecutor, or the law enforcement agency.

(ii) The record is used by the department of corrections, the prosecutor, or the law enforcement agency only to determine whether an employee has violated his or her conditions of employment or whether an applicant meets criteria for employment.

(4) The court may order the person convicted of violating subsection (1) to undergo screening and assessment by a person or agency as designated by the substance abuse coordinating agency as defined in section 6103 of the public health code, 1978 PA 368, MCL 333.6103, in order to determine whether the person is likely to benefit from rehabilitative services, including alcohol or drug education and alcohol or drug treatment programs.

(5) The secretary of state shall suspend the operator's or chauffeur's license of an individual convicted of violating subsection (1) or (2) as provided in section 319 of the Michigan vehicle code, 1949 PA 300, MCL 257.319.

(6) A peace officer who has reasonable cause to believe a minor has consumed alcoholic liquor or has any bodily alcohol content may require the person to submit to a preliminary chemical breath analysis. A peace officer may arrest a person based in whole or in part upon the results of a preliminary chemical breath analysis. The results of a preliminary chemical breath analysis or other acceptable blood alcohol test are admissible in a criminal prosecution to determine whether the minor has consumed or possessed alcoholic liquor or had any bodily alcohol content. A minor who refuses to submit to a preliminary chemical breath test analysis as required in this subsection is responsible for a state civil infraction and may be ordered to pay a civil fine of not more than $100.00.

(7) A law enforcement agency, upon determining that a person less than 18 years of age who is not emancipated under 1968 PA 293, MCL 722.1 to 722.6, allegedly consumed, possessed, purchased alcoholic liquor, attempted to consume, possess, or purchase alcoholic liquor, or had any bodily alcohol content in violation of subsection (1) shall notify the parent or parents, custodian, or guardian of the person as to the nature of the violation if the name of a parent, guardian, or custodian is reasonably ascertainable by the law enforcement agency. The notice required by this subsection shall be made not later than 48 hours after the law enforcement agency determines that the person who allegedly violated subsection (1) is less than 18 years of age and not emancipated under 1968 PA 293, MCL 722.1 to 722.6. The notice may be made by any means reasonably calculated to give prompt actual notice including, but not limited to, notice in person, by telephone, or by first-class mail. If an individual less than 17 years of age is incarcerated for violating subsection (1), his or her parents or legal guardian shall be notified immediately as provided in this subsection.

(8) This section does not prohibit a minor from possessing alcoholic liquor during regular working hours and in the course of his or her employment if employed by a person licensed by this act, by the commission, or by an agent of the commission, if the alcoholic liquor is not possessed for his or her personal consumption.

(9) This section does not limit the civil or criminal liability of the vendor or the vendor's clerk, servant, agent, or employee for a violation of this act.

(10) The consumption of alcoholic liquor by a minor who is enrolled in a course offered by an accredited postsecondary educational institution in an academic building of the institution under the supervision of a faculty member is not prohibited by this act if the purpose of the consumption is solely educational and is a requirement of the course.

(11) The consumption by a minor of sacramental wine in connection with religious services at a church, synagogue, or temple is not prohibited by this act.

(12) Subsection (1) does not apply to a minor who participates in either or both of the following:

(a) An undercover operation in which the minor purchases or receives alcoholic liquor under the direction of the person's employer and with the prior approval of the local prosecutor's office as part of an employer-sponsored internal enforcement action.

(b) An undercover operation in which the minor purchases or receives alcoholic liquor under the direction of the state police, the commission, or a local police agency as part of an enforcement action unless the initial or contemporaneous purchase or receipt of alcoholic liquor by the minor was not under the direction of the state police, the commission, or the local police agency and was not part of the undercover operation.

(13) The state police, the commission, or a local police agency shall not recruit or attempt to recruit a minor for participation in an undercover operation at the scene of a violation of subsection (1), section 801(2), or section 701(1).

(14) In a criminal prosecution for the violation of subsection (1) concerning a minor having any bodily alcohol content, it is an affirmative defense that the minor consumed the alcoholic liquor in a venue or location where that consumption is legal.

(15) As used in this section, "any bodily alcohol content" means either of the following:

(a) An alcohol content of 0.02 grams or more per 100 milliliters of blood, per 210 liters of breath, or per 67 milliliters of urine.

(b) Any presence of alcohol within a person's body resulting from the consumption of alcoholic liquor, other than consumption of alcoholic liquor as a part of a generally recognized religious service or ceremony.

Note: The constitutionality of the provisions of this statute requiring minors to submit to a PBT (subsection 6) has been called into question by the United States District Court for the Eastern District of Michigan. That Court has enjoined the Michigan State Police and the Thomas Township Police Department from enforcing that subsection. While that injunction only binds those two agencies, it is advisable that all officers consult with their prosecutors before enforcing that subsection. PBTs may still be administered with a minor's consent by any officer.

Authority to detain—MCL 436.1705

A peace officer may stop and detain a person and obtain satisfactory identification for a violation of MCL 436.1703.

Possessing or Consuming Alcoholic Liquor in Certain Places—MCL 436.1915 (90-day misdemeanor)

Alcoholic liquor shall not be consumed on public highways.

Alcoholic liquor may be consumed in public parks, public places of amusement, or publicly owned areas unless prohibited by local governments or state agencies with authority over the lands.

Consuming alcoholic liquor on school property—MCL 436.1904

A person shall not consume alcoholic liquor or possess with the intent to consume alcoholic liquor on school property.

Penalties:

1st offense	93 day misdemeanor/$250
2nd offense	93 day misdemeanor/$500
3rd offense or more	1 year misdemeanor/$1,000

Section does not apply to a recognized religious event or if allowed by the superintendent or administrator of the school.

This section does not prohibit additional charges arising out of the same transaction, except violations under MCL 436.1703.

Definitions

School: Public school kindergarten through 12th grade.

School property: Buildings, playing fields, vehicles, or other property used for functions and events sponsored by a school. Does not include a building primarily used for adult education or college extension courses.

POLICE SCANNERS—MCL 750.508

It is unlawful for a person to possess a police scanner in any of the following circumstances:

The person has been convicted of a felony within the preceding 5 years	1 year misdemeanor
The person is committing a crime punishable by at least 93 days but less than 1 year	1 year misdemeanor
The person is committing a crime punishable by 1 year or more	2 year felony

It is not a crime to possess a scanner while committing a crime punishable by less than 93 days.

PEDDLER LICENSE VIOLATIONS

Transient Merchant—MCL 445.372 (misdemeanor, fine only)

It is unlawful for any person, either as a principal or agent, to engage in a business as a transient merchant in the State of Michigan without having first obtained a license.

Transient merchant: Any person, firm, association, or corporation engaging temporarily in a retail sale of goods, wares, or merchandise, in any place in this state and who, for the purpose of conducting business, occupies any lot, building, room, or structure of any kind. The term shall not apply to any of the following:

- A person selling goods, wares, or merchandise of any description raised, produced, or manufactured by the individual offering the same for sale.
- A person soliciting orders by sample, brochure, or sales catalog for future delivery or making sales at residential premises pursuant to an invitation issued by the owner or legal occupant of the premises.
- A person handling vegetables, fruits, or perishable farm products at any established city or village market.
- A person operating a store or refreshment stand at a resort or having a booth on or adjacent to the property owned or occupied by him or her.
- A person operating a stand on any fairgrounds.
- A person selling at an art fair or festival or similar event at the invitation of the event's sponsor, if all of the following conditions are met:
  - The sponsor is a governmental entity or non-profit organization.
  - The person provides the sponsor with the person's sales tax license number.
  - The sponsor provides a list of the event's vendors and their sales tax license numbers to the county treasurer and the state treasurer.

Confiscation of goods: If the county sheriff or local law enforcement officer has probable cause to believe that a person is engaging in business as a transient merchant without having first obtained a license, the officer shall immediately impound all goods offered for sale until the matter has been adjudicated by court.

Restrictions on Items to be Sold at Flea Markets and Swap Meets—MCL 750.411r (93-day misdemeanor)

An unused property merchant is a person who sells, offers, displays, or exchanges tangible personal property at an unused property market, such as swap meets, indoor swap meets, or flea markets.

An unused property merchant may not sell one or more of the following:

- Food manufactured, packaged, and labeled specifically for sale or consumption by a child less than 2 years of age.
- A nonprescription drug that is past its expiration date.
- A medical device.

This section does not apply a merchant who has written authorization from the manufacturer of the product. Use of a false or forged authorization is a 93-day misdemeanor.

An unused property merchant shall retain for two years a purchase receipt for each new and unused property the merchant acquires. The following are a 93-day misdemeanors.

- Falsifying a receipt.
- Refusing or failing to make a receipt available for inspection by a law enforcement officer within a reasonable time after the request.
- Destroying the receipt before the end of the two-year period.

CRUELTY TO ANIMALS

Fighting Animals—MCL 750.49

For the purposes of this section, an "animal" is a vertebrate other than a human.

It is a felony for a person to knowingly do any of the following:

- Own, possess, use, buy, sell, offer to buy or sell, import, or export an animal for fighting or baiting, or as a target to be shot at as a test of skill in marksmanship.
- Be a party to or cause the fighting, baiting, or shooting of an animal.
- Rent or otherwise obtain the use of a building, shed, room, yard, ground, or premises for fighting, baiting, or shooting an animal.
- Permit the use of a building, shed, room, yard, ground, or premises belonging to him or her or under his or her control for any of the purposes prohibited by this statute.
- Organize, promote, or collect money for the fighting, baiting, or shooting of an animal.

- Be present at a building, shed, room, yard, ground, or premises where preparations are being made for an exhibition described above, or be present at the exhibition, knowing that an exhibition is taking place or about to take place.
- Breed, buy, sell, offer to buy or sell, exchange, import, or export an animal (or offspring) the person knows has been trained or used for fighting (except when animal is kept for agricultural purposes).
- Own, possess, use, buy, sell, offer to buy or sell, transport, or deliver any device or equipment intended for use in the fighting, baiting, or shooting of an animal.

It is also a felony to incite an animal trained or used for fighting, or an animal that is the first or second generation offspring of an animal trained or used for fighting, to attack a person (does not apply if the person attacked was committing a crime).

If an animal trained or used for fighting or an animal that is the first or second generation offspring of an animal trained or used for fighting attacks a person without provocation, the owner is guilty of a felony if the person dies and a 1 year misdemeanor if the person does not die (does not apply if the person attacked was committing a crime).

If an animal trained or used for fighting or an animal that is the first or second generation offspring of a dog trained or used for fighting goes beyond the property limits of its owner without being securely restrained, the owner is guilty of a 90 day misdemeanor.

If an animal trained or used for fighting or an animal that is the first or second generation offspring of a dog trained or used for fighting is not securely enclosed or restrained on the owner's property, the owner is guilty of a 90 day misdemeanor.

The statute contains exceptions for police dogs, leader dogs, or dogs used by licensed private security.

Confiscation and forfeiture

An animal that has been used to fight in violation of this section shall be confiscated as contraband by a law enforcement officer and shall not be returned to the owner, trainer, or possessor of the animal. The animal shall be taken to a local humane society or other animal welfare agency.

All animals being used or to be used in fighting, equipment, devices, and money involved shall be forfeited to the state. All other instrumentalities, proceeds, and substituted proceeds of a violation of subsection (2) are subject to forfeiture under chapter 47 of the revised judicature act of 1961, 1961 PA 236, MCL 600.4701 to 600.4709.

> This statute was not unconstitutionally vague where the defendant was observed training his two dogs to fight, and they subsequently escaped their pen and killed a person. *People v Beam*, 244 Mich. App 103 (2000).

Cruelty to Animals—MCL 750.50

(1) As used in this section and section 50b:
 (a) "Adequate care" means the provision of sufficient food, water, shelter, sanitary conditions, exercise, and veterinary medical attention in order to maintain an animal in a state of good health.
 (b) "Animal" means any vertebrate other than a human being.
 (c) "Animal protection shelter" means a facility operated by a person, humane society, society for the prevention of cruelty to animals, or any other nonprofit organization, for the care of homeless animals.
 (d) "Animal control shelter" means a facility operated by a county, city, village, or township to impound and care for animals found in streets or otherwise at large contrary to any ordinance of the county, city, village, or township or state law.
 (e) "Licensed veterinarian" means a person licensed to practice veterinary medicine under article 15 of the public health code, 1978 PA 368, MCL 333.16101 to 333.18838.
 (f) "Livestock" means that term as defined in the animal industry act of 1987, 1988 PA 466, MCL 287.701 to 287.747.
 (g) "Person" means an individual, partnership, limited liability company, corporation, association, governmental entity, or other legal entity.
 (h) "Neglect" means to fail to sufficiently and properly care for an animal to the extent that the animal's health is jeopardized.
 (i) "Sanitary conditions" means space free from health hazards including excessive animal waste, overcrowding of animals, or other conditions that endanger the animal's health. This definition does not include any condition resulting from a customary and reasonable practice pursuant to farming or animal husbandry.
 (j) "Shelter" means adequate protection from the elements and weather conditions suitable for the age, species, and physical condition of the animal so as to maintain the

animal in a state of good health. Shelter, for livestock, includes structures or natural features such as trees or topography. Shelter, for a dog, includes 1 or more of the following:

  (i) *The residence of the dog's owner or other individual.*
  (ii) *A doghouse that is an enclosed structure with a roof and of appropriate dimensions for the breed and size of the dog. The doghouse shall have dry bedding when the outdoor temperature is or is predicted to drop below freezing.*
  (iii) *A structure, including a garage, barn, or shed, that is sufficiently insulated and ventilated to protect the dog from exposure to extreme temperatures or, if not sufficiently insulated and ventilated, contains a doghouse as provided under subparagraph (ii) that is accessible to the dog.*

  (k) *"State of good health" means freedom from disease and illness, and in a condition of proper body weight and temperature for the age and species of the animal, unless the animal is undergoing appropriate treatment.*
  (l) *"Tethering" means the restraint and confinement of a dog by use of a chain, rope, or similar device.*
  (m) *"Water" means potable water that is suitable for the age and species of animal that is made regularly available unless otherwise directed by a licensed veterinarian.*

(2) *An owner, possessor, or person having the charge or custody of an animal shall not do any of the following:*

  (a) *Fail to provide an animal with adequate care.*
  (b) *Cruelly drive, work, or beat an animal, or cause an animal to be cruelly driven, worked, or beaten.*
  (c) *Carry or cause to be carried in or upon a vehicle or otherwise any live animal having the feet or legs tied together, other than an animal being transported for medical care, or a horse whose feet are hobbled to protect the horse during transport or in any other cruel and inhumane manner.*
  (d) *Carry or cause to be carried a live animal in or upon a vehicle or otherwise without providing a secure space, rack, car, crate, or cage, in which livestock may stand, and in which all other animals may stand, turn around, and lie down during transportation, or while awaiting slaughter. As used in this subdivision, for purposes of transportation of sled dogs, "stand" means sufficient vertical distance to allow the animal to stand without its shoulders touching the top of the crate or transportation vehicle.*
  (e) *Abandon an animal or cause an animal to be abandoned, in any place, without making provisions for the animal's adequate care, unless premises are vacated for the protection of human life or the prevention of injury to a human. An animal that is lost by an owner or custodian while traveling, walking, hiking, or hunting is not abandoned under this section when the owner or custodian has made a reasonable effort to locate the animal.*
  (f) *Negligently allow any animal, including one who is aged, diseased, maimed, hopelessly sick, disabled, or nonambulatory to suffer unnecessary neglect, torture, or pain.*
  (g) *Tether a dog unless the tether is at least 3 times the length of the dog as measured from the tip of its nose to the base of its tail and is attached to a harness or nonchoke collar designed for tethering.*

  …

(11) *This section does not prohibit the lawful killing or other use of an animal, including the following:*

  (a) *Fishing.*
  (b) *Hunting, trapping, or wildlife control regulated under the natural resources and environmental protection act, 1994 PA 451, MCL 324.101 to 324.90106.*
  (c) *Horse racing.*
  (d) *The operation of a zoological park or aquarium.*
  (e) *Pest or rodent control regulated under part 83 of the natural resources and environmental protection act, 1994 PA 451, MCL 324.8301 to 324.8336.*
  (f) *Farming or a generally accepted animal husbandry or farming practice involving livestock.*
  (g) *Activities authorized under rules promulgated under section 9 of the executive organization act of 1965, 1965 PA 380, MCL 16.109.*
  (h) *Scientific research under 1969 PA 224, MCL 287.381 to 287.395.*
  (i) *Scientific research under sections 2226, 2671, 2676, and 7333 of the public health code, 1978 PA 368, MCL 333.2226, 333.2671, 333.2676, and 333.7333.*

(12) This section does not apply to a veterinarian or a veterinary technician lawfully engaging in the practice of veterinary medicine under part 188 of the public health code, 1978 PA 368, MCL 333.18801 to 333.18838.

Penalties:

Injury to 1 animal	93 day misdemeanor
Injury of 2–3 animals *or* the death of any animal	1 year misdemeanor
Injury to 4–9 animals *or* a prior conviction under MCL 750.50	2 year felony
Injury to 10 or more animals *or* two or more prior convictions under MCL 750.50	4 year felony

Note: There are numerous exceptions for fishing, hunting, trapping, horse racing, zoos, aquariums, pest control, farming, scientific research, and lawful veterinary care.

> The defendants were the owner and the caretaker of 69 lice-ridden horses that did not have access to adequate food and water. The court held that there was sufficient evidence that a crime was committed, that the defendants had committed that crime, and that the prosecution is not required to prove that the defendants intended to harm the horses. *People v. Henderson*, 282 Mich. App. 307 (2009).

Beat or Impede Service Dog—MCL 750.50a (90-day misdemeanor)

(1) An individual shall not do either of the following:

   (a) Willfully and maliciously assault, beat, harass, injure, or attempt to assault, beat, harass or injure a dog that he or she knows or has reason to believe is a guide or leader dog for a blind individual, a hearing dog for a deaf or audibly impaired individual, or a service dog for a physically limited individual.

   (b) Willfully and maliciously impede or interfere with, or attempt to impede or interfere with duties performed by a dog that he or she knows or has reason to believe is a guide or leader dog for a blind individual, a hearing dog for a deaf or audibly impaired individual, or a service dog for a physically limited individual.

…

(5) As used in this section:

   (a) "Audibly impaired" means the inability to hear air conduction thresholds at an average of 40 decibels or greater in the individual's better ear.

   (b) "Blind" means having a visual acuity of 20/200 or less in the individual's better eye with correction, or having a limitation of the individual's field of vision such that the widest diameter of the visual field subtends an angular distance not greater than 20 degrees.

   (c) "Deaf" means the individual's hearing is totally impaired or the individual's hearing, with or without amplification, is so seriously impaired that the primary means of receiving spoken language is through other sensory input, including, but not limited to, lip reading, sign language, finger spelling, or reading.

   (d) "Harass" means to engage in any conduct directed toward a guide, leader, hearing, or service dog that is likely to impede or interfere with the dog's performance of its duties or that places the blind, deaf, audibly impaired, or physically limited individual being served or assisted by the dog in danger of injury.

   (e) "Injure" means to cause any physical injury to a dog described in subsection (1).

   (f) "Maliciously" means any of the following:

   (i) With intent to assault, beat, harass or injure a dog described in subsection (1).

   (ii) With intent to impede or interfere with duties performed by a dog described in subsection (1).

   (iii) With intent to disturb, endanger, or cause emotional distress to a blind, deaf, audibly impaired, or physically limited individual being served or assisted by a dog described in subsection (1).

   (iv) With knowledge that the individual's conduct will, or is likely to harass or injure a dog described in subsection (1).

   (v) With knowledge that the individual's conduct will, or is likely to impede or

interfere with duties performed by a dog described in subsection (1).

(vi) With knowledge that the individual's conduct will, or is likely to disturb, endanger, or cause emotional distress to a blind, deaf, audibly impaired, or physically limited individual being served or assisted by a dog described in subsection (1).

(g) "Physically limited" means having limited ambulatory abilities and includes but is not limited to having a temporary or permanent impairment or condition that does 1 or more of the following:

(i) Causes the individual to use a wheelchair or walk with difficulty or insecurity.
(ii) Affects sight or hearing to the extent that an individual is insecure or exposed to danger.
(iii) Causes faulty coordination.
(iv) Reduces mobility, flexibility, coordination, or perceptiveness.

Willfully Killing/Torturing Animal—MCL 750.50b (felony)

(1) As used in this section, "animal" means any vertebrate other than a human being.

(2) Except as otherwise provided in this section, a person shall not do any of the following without just cause:

(a) Knowingly kill, torture, mutilate, maim, or disfigure an animal.
(b) Commit a reckless act knowing or having reason to know that the act will cause an animal to be killed, tortured, mutilated, maimed, or disfigured.
(c) Knowingly administer poison to an animal, or knowingly expose an animal to any poisonous substance, with the intent that the substance be taken or swallowed by the animal.

...

(8) This section does not prohibit the lawful killing of livestock or a customary animal husbandry or farming practice involving livestock. As used in this subsection, "livestock" means that term as defined in section 5 of the animal industry act, 1988 PA 466, MCL 287.705.

(9) This section does not prohibit the lawful killing of an animal pursuant to any of the following:

(a) Fishing.
(b) Hunting, trapping, or wildlife control regulated under the natural resources and environmental protection act, 1994 PA 451, MCL 324.101 to 324.90106, and orders issued under that act.
(c) Pest or rodent control regulated under part 83 of the natural resources and environmental protection act, 1994 PA 451, MCL 324.8301 to 324.8336.
(d) Activities authorized under rules promulgated under section 9 of the executive organization act of 1965, 1965 PA 380, MCL 16.109.
(e) Section 19 of the dog law of 1919, 1919 PA 339, MCL 287.279.

(10) This section does not prohibit the lawful killing or use of an animal for scientific research under any of the following or a rule promulgated under any of the following:

(a) 1969 PA 224, MCL 287.381 to 287.395.
(b) Sections 2226, 2671, 2676, 7109, and 7333 of the public health code, 1978 PA 368, MCL 333.2226, 333.2671, 333.2676, 333.7109, and 333.7333.

(11) This section does not apply to a veterinarian or a veterinary technician lawfully engaging in the practice of veterinary medicine under part 188 of the public health code, 1978 PA 368, MCL 333.18801 to 333.18838.

This statute contains exceptions for farming, hunting, fishing, pest control, dog law, scientific research, and lawful veterinary practices.

A subject could be charged with animal cruelty when he threw firecrackers into a barn that subsequently caught on fire, killing 19 horses. Animal cruelty is a general intent crime. *People v Fennell*, 260 Mich. App. 261 (2004).

The defendant admitted shooting and killing his neighbor's dog because it was attacking his dogs. He argued that this shooting was justified under MCL 287.279, which allows a person to kill a dog that is attacking livestock,

> poultry, or person. The court held that dogs are not livestock so the defendant could be charged under 750.50b. *People v. Bugaiski*, 224 Mich. App. 241 (1997).

Police Animal—MCL 750.50c

(1) As used in this section:
   (a) "Dog handler" means a peace officer who has successfully completed training in the handling of a police dog pursuant to a policy of the law enforcement agency that employs that peace officer.
   (b) "Physical harm" means any injury to a dog's or horse's physical condition.
   (c) "Police dog" means a dog used by a law enforcement agency of this state or of a local unit of government of this state that is trained for law enforcement work and subject to the control of a dog handler.
   (d) "Police horse" means a horse used by a law enforcement agency of this state or of a local unit of government of this state for law enforcement work.
   (e) "Search and rescue dog" means a dog that is trained for, being trained for, or engaged in a search and rescue operation.
   (f) "Search and rescue operation" means an effort conducted at the direction of an agency of this state or of a political subdivision of this state to locate or rescue a lost, injured, or deceased individual.
   (g) "Serious physical harm" means any injury to a dog's or horse's physical condition or welfare that is not necessarily permanent but that constitutes substantial body disfigurement, or that seriously impairs the function of a body organ or limb.

(2) A person shall not intentionally kill or cause serious physical harm to a police dog or police horse or a search and rescue dog.
(3) A person shall not intentionally cause physical harm to a police dog or police horse or a search and rescue dog.
(4) A person shall not intentionally harass or interfere with a police dog or police horse or search and rescue dog lawfully performing its duties.

Penalties:

Injuring harassing, or interfering with a police dog, police horse, or search and rescue dog	1 year misdemeanor
Injuring, harassing, or interfering with a police dog, police horse, or search and rescue dog during the commission of another crime	2 year felony
Killing or seriously injuring a police dog, police horse, or search and rescue dog	5 year felony

Dog Bites—MCL 750.66 (93-day misdemeanor)

(1) If a person 18 years of age or older is responsible for controlling the actions of a dog or wolf-dog cross and the person knows or has reason to know that the dog or wolf-dog cross has bitten another person, the person shall immediately provide the person who was bitten with all of the following information:
   (a) His or her name and address and, if that person does not own the dog or wolf-dog cross, the name and address of the dog's or wolf-dog cross's owner.
   (b) Information, if known by that person, as to whether the dog or wolf-dog cross is current on all legally required vaccinations.
(2) A person who violates this section is guilty of a misdemeanor punishable by imprisonment for not more than 93 days or a fine of not more than $500.00, or both.
(3) This section does not apply if the person is bitten by a police dog. As used in this subsection, "police dog" means that term as defined in section 50c.
(4) As used in this section, "dog" and "wolf-dog cross" mean those terms as defined in section 2 of the wolf-dog cross act, 2000 PA 246, MCL 287.1002.

If a person who is responsible for a dog or wolf-dog knows or has reason to know that the animal has bitten another person, then he or she must immediately provide the bitten person with the following:

1. His or her name and address and the dog owner's name and address, and
2. Information on the dog's vaccinations.

DISORDERLY CONDUCT

Disorderly Person—MCL 750.167 (90-day misdemeanor)

Includes any of the following:

- A person with sufficient ability who refuses to or neglects to support his or her family.

> The prosecutor has discretion in charging this offense under the misdemeanor disorderly statute or under the felony desertion and non-support statute (MCL 750.161). Op. Att'y Gen., No. 0-2096 (April 13, 1944).
>
> Support includes sufficient funds to provide for shelter, clothing, and medical expenses, not just sufficient funds for food. *People v. Beckman*, 239 Mich. 590 (1927).

- A common prostitute.
- A window peeper.

> *Conduct:* At night the defendant left the sidewalk, proceeded to a lighted residence and stood six feet away. He then looked into the window where the shade was raised. *City of Grand Rapids v. Williams*, 112 Mich. 247 (1897).

- A person involved in illegal occupation or business.

> A defendant's conviction was upheld where he was running an illegal "mutuels" gaming system (i.e., a "numbers" lottery). *People v. Singer*, 304 Mich. 70 (1942).

- A person intoxicated in a public place who either:
  - Directly endangers the safety of another person or of property, or
  - Acts in a manner that causes a public disturbance.

> The public disturbance provision of the disorderly statute requires a finding that the accused, while intoxicated, directly endangered the safety of another person or another person's property. *People v. Gagnon*, 129 Mich. App. 678 (1983).
>
> Because the noise came from defendant's hotel room, he was not in a public place when he created the disturbance. Thus, his conduct did not fall within the definition of disorderly person even though the noise was heard in a public place. *People v. Favreau*, 252 Mich. App. 32 (2003).
>
> Preliminary Breath Test results were admissible to impeach defendants who claimed that they were not intoxicated when they were arrested for disorderly conduct at a wedding reception. *City of Westland v. Okopski*, 208 Mich. App. 66 (1994). Note: This case involves a Westland ordinance that mirrors MCL 750.167(1)(e).
>
> Whether the defendant is voluntarily or involuntarily intoxicated is immaterial. Therefore, a defendant's alcoholism is not an affirmative defense. *People v. Hoy*, 3 Mich. App. 666 (1966).

- A person engaged in indecent or obscene conduct in a public place.

Three convictions under this section require sex offender registration. (MCL 28.722(e)(iv)).

> A defendant who exposed himself to a 13-year-old female from his front porch was found to be in a public place, and his conviction was upheld. *People v. Devine*, 271 Mich. 635 (1935).
>
> However, a defendant who urinated in a national forest in view of a hidden United States Department of Agriculture Forest Service officer was not in a public place for purposes of this statute. The court reasoned that the defendant had no reason to believe that others might view him. *United States v. Whitmore*, 314 F. Supp. 2d 690 (E.D. Mich. 2004).

- A vagrant.

> Someone who is idle and is unwilling to work, although he or she is able to. The constitutionality of this portion is questionable because the statute punishes a status and not an action. *Papachristou v. City of Jacksonville*, 405 U.S. 156 (1972).
>
> Even early Michigan case law recognized that an arrest without a warrant for this violation should be rare since the offense generally will not involve a danger to public or private security where an immediate arrest is needed. *In re Way*, 41 Mich. 299 (1879).

- A person begging in a public place.
- Loitering in house of ill fame or prostitution.

> To establish this charge, it must be proven that the house was kept as a place for prostitution and that the person found loitering had no lawful purpose to be there. *People v. Cox*, 107 Mich. 435. (1895).

- Loitering in a place where an illegal occupation or business is being conducted.

> The court ruled that the defendants were properly convicted when they were present in a home where illegal drugs were being sold. This statute is not unconstitutionally vague nor does it infringe on the First Amendment. *People v. Dombe*, 133 Mich. App. 179 (1984).

- Soliciting legal services or services of sureties at police station, hospital, or court building.
- Jostling or roughly crowding people in a public place.

> This provision was aimed at pickpockets and those assisting them in a crowded area. *People v. O'Keefe*, 218 Mich. 1 (1922).
>
> A defendant's conviction was upheld where he grabbed the chief of police by the arm during attempts to disperse a disorderly crowd. *People v. Bishop*, 30 Mich. App. 204 (1971).

Disorderly Conduct at Funerals—MCL 750.167d (felony)

(1) A person shall not do any of the following within 500 feet of a building or other location where a funeral, memorial service, or viewing of a deceased person is being conducted or within 500 feet of a funeral procession or burial:

   (a) Make loud and raucous noise and continue to do so after being asked to stop.
   (b) Make any statement or gesture that would make a reasonable person under the circumstances feel intimidated, threatened, or harassed.
   (c) Engage in any other conduct that the person knows or should reasonably know will disturb, disrupt, or adversely affect the funeral, memorial service, viewing of the deceased person, funeral procession, or burial.

Penalties:

1st offense	2 year felony
2nd offense	4 year felony

Disturbing the Peace—MCL 750.170 (90-day misdemeanor)

Any person who shall make or excite any disturbance or contention in any tavern, store or grocery, manufacturing establishment or any other business place or in any street, lane, alley, highway, public building, grounds or park, or at any election or other public meeting where citizens are peaceably and lawfully assembled, shall be guilty of a misdemeanor.

Suspect made or excited a disturbance at one of the following:

- A business.
- An election place.
- A street, lane, alley, highway, public grounds, or park.
- A public building.
- A public meeting where citizens were peaceably and lawfully assembled.

In order to justify a conviction under this section, there must be a disturbance or contention. Two individuals merely jostling others at a bus stop did not fall under this section. Contention is actual or threatened violence.

The court held that "no reasonable officer would have found probable cause to arrest Leonard solely for uttering 'God damn' while addressing the township board...." *Leonard v. Robinson*, 477 F.3d 347 (6th Cir. 2007).

The court upheld a defendant's conviction under this statute where the defendant took part in a "sit-in" at a university. The court also held that this statute is not unconstitutionally vague. *People v. Mash*, 45 Mich. App. 459 (1973).

"Disturbance" means an interruption of peace and quiet, a violation of public order, or an interference with a person's lawful pursuit of his or her occupation or rights. Peacefully sitting on the floor in a business can constitute a disturbance. *People v. Weinberg*, 6 Mich. App. 345 (1967).

RIOTS

Riots—MCL 752.541 (felony)

It is unlawful and constitutes the crime of riot for 5 or more persons, acting in concert, to wrongfully engage in violent conduct and thereby intentionally or recklessly cause or create a serious risk of causing public terror or alarm.

Requires all of the following:
- Five or more persons working together who are engaging in violent conduct, and
- Intentionally or recklessly creating a serious risk of causing public terror or alarm.

Public terror or alarm is "caused any time a segment of the public is put in fear of injury either to their persons or their property." *People v. Garcia*, 31 Mich. App. 447 (1971).

Defendant and five others could be charged under MCL 752.541 when during a KKK rally they ran up the stairs of city hall and threw rocks at the police and the building. The riot statute does not require that the violent conduct at issue be directed toward the public at large, only that the conduct creates a risk of public alarm. *People v. Kim*, 245 Mich. App. 609 (2001).

Inciting to Riot—MCL 752.542 (felony)

It is unlawful and constitutes incitement to riot for a person or persons, intending to cause or to aid or abet the institution or maintenance of a riot, to do an act or engage in conduct that urges other persons to commit acts of unlawful force or violence, or the unlawful burning or destroying of property, or the unlawful interference with a police officer, peace officer, fireman or a member of the Michigan national guard or any unit of the armed services officially assigned to riot duty in the lawful performance of his duty.

Includes one of the following:
- Acts that encourage other people to riot.
- Aiding or abetting the maintenance of rioting.
- Unlawful interference with police officers, firemen, or military personnel assigned to riot duty.

Riotously Destroying Dwelling House or Other Property—MCL 750.528 (felony)

Any of the persons so unlawfully assembled, who shall demolish, pull down, destroy or injure, or who shall begin to demolish, pull down, destroy or injure any dwelling house or any other building, or any ship or vessel, shall be guilty of a felony, and shall be answerable to any person injured, to the full amount of the damage, in an action of trespass.

Elements

1. During an unlawful assembly,
2. The suspects demolished, pulled down, destroyed, or injured a dwelling house, other building, ship, or vessel.

Refusal to Aid Officer—MCL 750.523 (felony)

If any person present, being commanded by any of the magistrates or officers aforesaid, to aid and assist in seizing and securing such rioters, or persons so unlawfully assembled, or in suppressing such riot or unlawful assembly, shall refuse or neglect to obey such command, or when required by any such magistrate or officer to depart from the place of such riotous or unlawful assembly, shall refuse or neglect so to do, he shall be deemed to be 1 of the rioters or persons unlawfully assembled, and shall be liable to be prosecuted and punished accordingly.

If a person present at a riot refuses an order from an officer to assist in suppressing the riot, then that person will be considered to be one of the rioters.

Disobeying a Firefighter or Persons Working During a Riot—MCL 750.241

(1) Any person who, while in the vicinity of any fire, willfully disobeys any reasonable order or rule of the officer commanding any fire department at the fire, when the order or rule is given by the commanding officer or a firefighter there present, is guilty of a misdemeanor.

(2) During a riot or other civil disturbance, any person who knowingly and willfully hinders, obstructs, endangers, or interferes with any person who is engaged in the operation, installation, repair, or maintenance of any essential public service facility, including a facility for the transmission of electricity, gas, telephone messages, or water, is guilty of a felony.

- Penalties:
  - It is a misdemeanor to disobey a firefighter's reasonable order at a fire.
  - It is a felony to knowingly hinder a person operating or repairing an essential public service facility at a riot.

LITTERING

Littering—MCL 324.8902(1) (state civil infraction)

(1) A person shall not knowingly, without the consent of the public authority having supervision of public property or the owner of private property, dump, deposit, place, throw, or leave, or cause or permit the dumping, depositing, placing, throwing, or leaving of, litter on public or private property or water other than property designated and set aside for such purposes.

Definitions—MCL 324.8901

- "Litter" means rubbish, refuse, waste material, garbage, offal, paper, glass, cans, bottles, trash, debris, or other foreign substances or a vehicle that is considered abandoned under section 252a of the Michigan vehicle code, 1949 PA 300, MCL 257.252a.
- "Public or private property or water" includes, but is not limited to, any of the following:
  - The right-of-way of a road or highway, a body of water or watercourse, or the shore or beach of a body of water or watercourse, including the ice above the water.
  - A park, playground, building, refuge, or conservation or recreation area.
  - Residential or farm properties or timberlands.
- "Vehicle" means a motor vehicle registered or required to be registered under the Michigan vehicle code, 1949 PA 300, MCL 257.1 to 257.923.
- "Vessel" means a vessel registered under part 801.

A person shall not knowingly, without consent, leave litter on public or private property.

Penalties (state civil infraction):

If less than 1 cubic foot volume	$800 fine
If 1 to 3 cubic feet	Up to $1,500 fine
If over 3 cubic feet, 1st offense	$2,500 fine
If over 3 cubic feet, 2nd offense	$5,000 fine
If an abandoned vehicle	$500 - $2,500 fine

Presumptions

The following are presumed responsible for litter that comes from a vehicle:

- The driver of the vehicle
- The registered owner or lessee of the vehicle
- In the case of abandoned vehicles, the registered owner or lessee of the vehicle.

Wreckers—MCL 324.8902 (2) [State Civil Infraction])

(1) A person who removes a vehicle that is wrecked or damaged in an accident on a highway, road, or street shall remove all glass and other injurious substances dropped on the highway, road, or street as a result of the accident.

A person who removes a vehicle that is wrecked or damaged in an accident shall remove all glass and other injurious substances from the roadway.

Throwing Litter in Front of Vehicle—MCL 324.8903 (1 year misdemeanor)

(1) A person shall not knowingly cause litter or any object to fall or to be thrown into the path of or to hit a vehicle traveling upon a highway.

(2) A person who violates this section is guilty of a misdemeanor, punishable by imprisonment for not more than 1 year or a fine of not more than $500.00, or both.

Throwing Dangerous Objects at Vehicles—MCL 750.394

(1) *A person shall not throw, propel, or drop a stone, brick, or other dangerous object at a passenger train, sleeping car, passenger coach, express car, mail car, baggage car, locomotive, caboose, or freight train or at a street car, trolley car, or motor vehicle.*

Penalties:

Absent other factors	93 day misdemeanor
If property damage is caused	1 year misdemeanor
If injury to a person is caused	4 year felony
If serious impairment of person's bodily function is caused	10 year felony
If a person's death is caused	15 year felony

"Serious impairment of a body function" includes, but is not limited to, one or more of the following: loss of a limb or loss of use of a limb; loss of a foot, hand, finger, or thumb or loss of use of a foot, hand, finger, or thumb; loss of an eye or ear or loss of use of an eye or ear; loss or substantial impairment of a bodily function; serious visible disfigurement; a comatose state that lasts for more than 3 days; measurable brain or mental impairment; a skull fracture or other serious bone fracture; subdural hemorrhage or subdural hematoma; or loss of an organ, MCL 257.58c.

LAWS OF ARREST

LAWS OF ARREST
Fourth Amendment to the Constitution

The right of the people to be secure in their persons, houses, papers, and effects against unreasonable searches and seizures, shall not be violated and no warrants shall issue but upon probable cause, supported by oath or affirmation, and particularly describing the place to be searched and the persons and the things to be seized.

Three Levels of Contacts Between Police and Citizens

Informational/voluntary, where no level of suspicion is needed.

Investigatory detention, where the officer has **reasonable suspicion** that a crime is afoot.

Arrest, where the officer has **probable cause** to believe a crime has occurred and that the person being arrested committed the crime.

The Michigan Supreme Court in *People v. Freeman*, 413 Mich. 492 (1982), suppressed evidence located when officers approached a parked car and ordered the occupant to exit and produce ID. The Court held that, by ordering the occupant to exit, a detention occurred, which required reasonable suspicion that crime was afoot. Since there was no suspicion articulated by the officer, the seizure was unlawful, and therefore, the evidence suppressed. The Court of Appeals distinguished that case in *People v. Shankle*, 227 Mich. App. 690 (1998), where the officer "asked" for ID. "Unlike Freeman, the arresting officer did not order defendant from his car. There is nothing on the record to suggest that intimidating circumstances compelled defendant to cooperate." The record shows that the officer "merely made a voluntary request to defendant to produce identification." No suspicion was required for this contact. *Shankle* is further differentiated from *Freeman* because the officer in *Freeman* specifically told the defendant that he was not allowed to leave until he presented identification.

A witness saw three men moving something over a golf course at 3:00 a.m. When he confronted them, they ran. An officer responded and found a pile of equipment and three sets of prints leading toward an apartment complex. The officer radioed to another officer to watch out for three white males. The defendants were located and stopped. The investigating officer followed the tracks to a locker facility and found that it had been broken into. The officer then checked and found that the boots of the three defendants matched the tracks he had been following. This took 20 minutes. The initial detention was valid because the officers had reasonable suspicion that a crime was occurring. They also diligently investigated the facts to build up to probable cause to make an arrest within a reasonable amount of time. *People v. Chambers*, 195 Mich. App. 118 (1992)

Length of Detention During an Investigatory Stop

An investigative detention must be temporary and must last no longer than what is necessary to effectuate the purpose of the stop. In determining if the detention is too lengthy, the court must examine whether police diligently pursued a means of investigation that was likely to confirm or dispel their suspicions quickly. *United States v. Sharp*, 470 U.S. 675 (1985). In *Sharp*, the Court determined that a 20-minute traffic stop that led to a narcotics arrest was not too lengthy under the circumstances.

What Is Probable Cause?

Police have probable cause to arrest an individual when the facts and circumstances within their knowledge and of which they have reasonably trustworthy information are sufficient to cause a person of reasonable caution to believe the person to be arrested is committing or has committed a crime. *Brinegar v. United States*, 338 U.S. 160 (1949).

Probable cause is a practical, non-technical, common sense concept. *People v. Keller*, 479 Mich. 467 (2007).

Whether probable cause exists is reviewed by courts using an objective standard. *Scott v. United States*, 436 U.S. 128 (1978). That is, "what a *reasonable* officer would have believed under the circumstances, given the facts *actually known* to the arresting officer." *Richardson v. Bonds*, 860 F.2d 1427 (7th Cir. 1988).

Probable cause is not a point, but a zone in which reasonable mistakes can be made. MI Attorney General Opinion No. 6822.

Under Michigan law, probable cause and reasonable cause are the same standard.

Elements of a Valid Arrest

- **Authority:** The lawful authority granted to a peace officer.
- **Intent:** The arresting party must have the intent to arrest. The arrested subject should be so informed of this intent.
- **Force:** Some amount of force must be used, but only to the extent necessary to make the arrest. That force may be a verbal command or physical.
- **Custody:** Verbal or physical custody or control must be exercised by the arresting officer.
- **Submission:** There must be a submission to the arrest by the arrested subject. This may be voluntary or forced. Submission is present when custody or control is gained.

An arrest is the taking, seizing, or detaining of another person by either touching or putting hands on that person, or by any act that indicates an intention to take him or her into custody and subjects the person arrested to the actual control and will of the person making the arrest and must be so understood by the person arrested. *People v. Gonzales*, 356 Mich. 247 (1959).

ARRESTS PURSUANT TO ARREST WARRANT

Arrest Warrants

Steps for obtaining an arrest warrant:

1. During the investigation, the officer must establish probable cause that a crime was committed and that the suspect committed it.
2. A warrant request must be completed by the officer and submitted to the prosecutor.
3. The prosecutor authorizes, if criteria are met.
4. A complaint is prepared.
5. A complaint is presented to the judge.
6. An officer swears, under oath, that the facts presented are true to the best of his or her knowledge.
7. A judge reviews whether probable cause exists.
8. If the judge finds that there is probable cause, a warrant is issued with the judge's signature.
9. An arrest is made.
10. The suspect is processed (fingerprinting, photos, local paperwork).
11. The suspect is offered bond, if appropriate.
12. The suspect is lodged, if judge is unavailable for arraignment.
13. The suspect is brought before judge, without unnecessary delay.

A judge's command

Once issued, the warrant shall command an officer to arrest the person. MCL 764.1b.

Authority to enter residence

Officers may break the door of a suspect's residence to make an arrest, if there is reason to believe he or she is in the residence. (MCL 764.21) (See section on entry into residence for arrest.) This requires:

- Probable cause that the suspect lives there (*Steagald v. United States*, 451 U.S. 204 (1981), and
- Reasonable suspicion that the suspect is in the house. MCL 764.21.

Where can the arrest with a warrant be made?

An officer with a warrant may arrest anywhere in the state. MCL 764.2.

Possession of the warrant at the time of arrest

It shall not be necessary for the arresting officer to have the warrant in possession at the time of the arrest. The officer must, if possible, inform the person arrested of the warrant for his or her arrest and, after the arrest is made, shall show the person the warrant, if required, as soon as practicable. MCL 764.18.

The warrant is valid on its face

> An arrest warrant is valid on its face and will protect an officer from liability for false arrest and false imprisonment. If the officer should have known or doubted the validity of the warrant, the warrant will not shield the officer from liability. *Hollis v. Baker*, 45 Mich. App. 666 (1973).

ARRESTS WITHOUT A WARRANT

Arrests Without a Warrant—MCL 764.15

Basic crimes

- A felony, misdemeanor, or ordinance committed in the officer's presence.

> Offenses are committed in presence of the officer if ascertainable through sight, sound, smell, or touch. *People v. Wolfe*, 5 Mich. App. 543 (1973) (citing *Draper v. United States*, 358 U.S. 307 (1959)).

- A felony that is not committed in the officer's presence.
- A felony was committed and the officer has reasonable cause to believe the person committed it.

> Police may not arrest someone "for questioning in a homicide" unless there is reasonable cause to believe that the person to be questioned actually committed the homicide. *People v. Kelly*, 231 Mich. App. 627 (1998).

- The officer has reasonable cause to believe a felony was committed and reasonable cause to believe the person committed the felony.
- The officer has reasonable cause to believe a misdemeanor punishable by imprisonment for more than 92 days or a felony has been committed and reasonable cause to believe the person committed it.

> A defendant's "OUIL" arrest was upheld when he was found sleeping in his vehicle at a fairgrounds and he admitted to the officer that he had driven there. *People v. Stephen*, 262 Mich. App. 213 (2004).

- When the officer receives positive information from an authoritative source that another officer or a court holds a warrant for the person's arrest.
- The officer receives positive information by broadcast from a recognized police or other governmental radio station or teletype that affords the peace officer reasonable cause to believe a misdemeanor punishable by imprisonment for more than 92 days or a felony has been committed and reasonable cause to believe the person committed it.
- The peace officer has reasonable cause to believe the person is an escaped convict, has violated a condition of parole from a prison, has violated a condition of a pardon granted by the executive, or has violated one or more conditions of a conditional release order or probation order imposed by a court of this state, another state, Indian tribe, or United States territory.

Accidents and O.W.I.

- The officer has reasonable cause to believe that a person was at the time of an accident in this state, the operator of a vehicle involved in an accident and was in violation of MCL 257.625(1), (3), (6), (7) or 257.625m.

> See *People v. Ohlinger*, 438 Mich. 477 (1991), where the police officer was investigating a car-mailbox crash and saw the suspect lying unconscious and bleeding inside his bedroom. Also MCL 257.625a(1)(a) and MCL 764.15(1)(h).

- The person is found in the driver's seat of a vehicle parked or stopped on a highway or street and any part of the vehicle intrudes into the roadway and the officer has reasonable cause to believe the person was operating the vehicle in violation of 625(1), (3), (6) or (7). MCL 257.625a(1)(b) and MCL 764.15(i).
- The officer has reasonable cause to believe the person was the driver of a snowmobile and was intoxicated or OUID, when involved in an accident. MCL 324.82136(1) and MCL 764.15(1)(j).
- The officer has reasonable cause to believe the person was the driver of an off-road vehicle (ORV) and was intoxicated or OUID, when involved in an accident. MCL 324.81144 and MCL 764.15(1)(k).

Retail fraud

The officer has reasonable cause to believe a violation of MCL 750.356c and 750.356d has taken place or is taking place, and reasonable cause to believe that person committed or is committing the violation, regardless if it was committed in the officer's presence. MCL 764.15(1)(m).

School property

The officer has reasonable cause to believe a misdemeanor has taken place or is taking place on school property and reasonable cause to believe the person committed or is committing the violation, regardless of whether the violation was committed in the officer's presence. MCL 764.15(1)(n).

As used in this section, "school property" means a building, playing field, or property used for school purposes to impart instruction to children in grades kindergarten through 12, when provided by a public, private, denominational, or parochial school, except those buildings used primarily for adult education or college extension courses. MCL 333.7410.

Domestic violence—MCL 764.15a

A peace officer may arrest an individual for assault, assault and battery, and aggravated assault regardless of whether the peace officer has a warrant or whether the violation was committed in his or her presence, if the peace officer has or receives positive information that another peace officer has reasonable cause to believe both of the following:

- The violation occurred or is occurring, and
- The individual has had a child in common with the victim, resides or has resided in the same household as the victim, has or has had a dating relationship with the victim, or is a spouse or former spouse of the victim. As used in this subdivision, dating relationship means frequent, intimate associations primarily characterized by the expectation of affectional involvement. This term does not include a casual relationship or an ordinary fraternization between two individuals in a business or social context.

Narcotic arrests—MCL 333.7501

An arrest without a warrant may be made where the officer has reasonable cause that a one year misdemeanor or higher drug violation is being or has been committed. *People v. Jones*, 162 Mich. App. 675 (1987).

Personal protection orders—MCL 600.2950 and MCL 764.15b

A peace officer, without a warrant, may arrest and take into custody an individual, when the peace officer has or receives positive information that another peace officer has reasonable cause to believe all of the following apply:

- A personal protection order or valid foreign protection order has been issued.
- The individual named in the personal protection order is violating or has violated the order.

  - Assaulting, attacking, beating, molesting, or wounding a named individual.
  - Removing minor children from an individual having legal custody of the children, except as otherwise authorized by a custody or parenting time order issued by a court of competent jurisdiction.
  - Entering onto premises.
  - Engaging in stalking conduct.
  - Threatening to kill or physically injure a named individual.
  - Purchasing or possessing a firearm.
  - Interfering with petitioner's efforts to remove petitioner's children or personal property from premises that are solely owned or leased by the individual to be restrained or enjoined.
  - Interfering with petitioner at petitioner's place of employment or education or engaging in conduct that impairs petitioner's employment or educational relationship or environment.
  - Any other act or conduct specified by the court in the personal protection order.

- The person has *received notice*. A peace officer may serve a personal protection order at any time. If the officer responds to a violation and the LEIN reports that the subject had not yet

been served, the officer should serve the order by specifically stating what the order prohibits. After service, the suspect must be given a reasonable opportunity to comply. Failure to comply is grounds for immediate arrest. If the suspect does comply, the LEIN entry should be changed to show that service was completed.
- The personal protection order states on its face that a violation of its terms subjects the individual to immediate arrest *and* the following:
    - If the individual restrained or enjoined is 17 years of age or older, to criminal contempt of court and, if found guilty of criminal contempt, to imprisonment of not more than 93 days and a fine of not more than $500.00.
    - If the individual restrained or enjoined is less than 17 years of age, to the dispositional alternatives listed in section 18 of chapter XIIA of the probate code of 1939, 1939 PA 288, MCL 712A.18.
    - If the respondent violates the PPO in a jurisdiction other than this state, the respondent is subject to the enforcement procedures and penalties of that jurisdiction.
- An individual arrested under this section shall be brought before the family division of the circuit court having jurisdiction in the cause within 24 hours after arrest. If the circuit court judge is unavailable, then the individual must be brought before the district court judge. If the district court judge is unavailable, then the individual must be brought before the magistrate.

Violation of a condition of release—MCL 764.15e

A peace officer, without a warrant, may arrest and take into custody a suspect whom the peace officer has or receives positive information that another peace officer has reasonable cause to believe is violating or has violated a condition of release imposed by a court of this state, another state, Indian Tribe, or United States territory. The arresting officer must fill out a violation of condition of release report.

The officer must bring the defendant before the court within one business day. If the violation occurred outside the jurisdiction of the court that issued the order, the defendant must be brought before the court that has jurisdiction where the incident occurred.

If, in the opinion of the arresting police agency or officer in charge of the jail, it is safe to release the defendant before the defendant is brought before the court, that agency or officer may release the defendant on interim bond of not more than $500.00, requiring defendant to appear at the opening of court the next business day. If the defendant is held for more than 24 hours without being brought before the court under subsection (2), the officer in charge of the jail shall note in the jail records why it was not safe to release the defendant on interim bond under this subsection.

Violation of a child protective order—MCL 764.15f

A peace officer, without a warrant, may arrest and take into custody a person if the officer has reasonable cause to believe all of the following exist:

- A child protective order has been issued by the probate court before January 1, 1998 or the family division of circuit court on or after January 1, 1998.
- A true copy of the order and proof of service has been filed with the law enforcement agency having jurisdiction.
- The person named in the order *has received notice of the same.*
- The person named is acting in violation of the order.
- The order states on its face that a violation of its terms subjects the person to criminal contempt of court and, if found guilty, the person shall be imprisoned for not more than 90 days and may be fined not more than $500.00.
- If a peace officer arrests a person under this section, the peace officer shall do all of the following:
    - Prepare a complaint of a violation of a child protective order.
    - Provide one copy of the complaint to the person subject to the order and the original and one copy to the court that imposed the conditions. The law enforcement agency shall retain one copy.
    - Bring the person before the family division of circuit court having jurisdiction in the cause within 24 hours after arrest to answer a charge of contempt. If the circuit court judge is unavailable, then to the district court judge.

Protective custody—MCL 330.1427

A peace officer may take a person into custody if it is shown that he or she is requiring treatment.

- who can reasonably be expected in the near future to intentionally or unintentionally injure himself or another, and
- who has engaged in an act or made significant threats that are supportive of this expectation.

MCL 330.1401.

If a police officer observes a person conducting himself in such a manner so as to cause the officer to reasonably believe the person is a person "requiring treatment" as defined in MCL 330.1401, the officer may take the person into protective custody and transport him or her to a hospital or community mental health facility.

> Plaintiff sued defendant police officers alleging that he was a "person requiring treatment" when the defendants failed to take him into protective custody. The court dismissed the case for several reasons: because of immunity, because the defendants never determined that the plaintiff was a "person requiring treatment," and because taking a person into protective custody is permissive. *Hoffman v. Warden*, 184 Mich. App. 328 (1990).

An officer may use the same degree of force that would be lawful if the officer was arresting for a misdemeanor without a warrant. The officer may conduct a pat-down search to the extent necessary to remove dangerous weapons, but the pat-down may only be extensive enough to discover and seize weapons. The officer shall inform the person that he or she is in protective custody and not under arrest. Immunity will be granted to the officer unless grossly negligent or acting with willful and wanton misconduct. MCL 330.1427a.

PRIVATE PERSON'S AUTHORITY TO ARREST WITHOUT A WARRANT— MCL 764.16

A private person may make an arrest under the following circumstances:

- Felony committed in his or her presence.
- The suspect committed a felony, although not in the person's presence.
- When summoned by a peace officer to assist in making an arrest.
- If the private person is a merchant, is employed by a merchant, or works security for a merchant and has reasonable cause to believe the person to be arrested violated 750.356c or 750.356d, regardless of whether it was committed in the presence of the private person (retail fraud).

After an arrest, the private person must, without unnecessary delay, deliver the person to a peace officer.

> Bail bondsmen are considered private citizens and can be held liable for making an arrest of a subject listed on a warrant who was not the actual person who had committed the crime. The person they arrested had not actually committed a felony, and private citizens only have arrest powers if the person actually committed a felony. *Bright v. Littlefield*, 465 Mich. 770 (2002).

MISCELLANEOUS INFORMATION
When Can Arrest Be Made?

Arrests can be made anytime, day or night. MCL 764.17.

> Arrests with a warrant at night are frowned on unless good cause is shown. *Malcomson v. Scott*, 56 Mich. 459 (1885).

Prosecuting Certain Crimes

Any offense committed on a county boundary or within one mile of a boundary may be prosecuted in either county MCL 762.3.

Continuing crimes, i.e., kidnapping moving through state, may be prosecuted in any county the crime continues through MCL 762.3.

If fatal wound or poison is administered in one county and the victim dies in another county, prosecution may be held in either county MCL 762.5.

> A homicide conviction was upheld where the defendant claimed that the murder occurred 2/10 of mile into another county. *People v. Lundberg*, 364 Mich. 596 (1961).
>
> A defendant's homicide conviction was upheld where he assaulted the victim in Cass County, MI, but the victim died in an Indiana hospital. *People v. Duffield*, 387 Mich. 300 (1972).

RESISTING ARREST

A person may not resist an illegal arrest. Previously, a person could resist an illegal arrest:

> An unlawful arrest is nothing more than assault and battery against which a person sought to be restrained may defend himself as he would against any other unlawful intrusion upon his or her person or liberty. A person may resist an arrest up to, but not including, using deadly force. *People v. Eisenberg*, 72 Mich. 106 (1976).

Third parties may not resist an illegal arrest. In this case, friends of a person being unlawfully arrested tried to stop the arrest. Their charges for R and O were upheld. *People v. Wess*, 235 Mich. App. 241 (1999).

Even if the underlying charges are dismissed, an arrest is lawful if the officers have probable cause to believe a violation has occurred and the officers have the authority to make the arrest. *People v. Freeman*, 240 Mich. App 235 (2000).

However, the law has been changed:

A minor defendant resisted arrest on an MIP charge. The MIP charge was dismissed by a lower court, but the appellate court held that the defendant could still be convicted of resisting (MCL 750.81(d)). *People v. Ventura*, 262 Mich. App. 370 (2004).

Under MCL 750.81(d), which was new law when the above case was decided, "the lawfulness of an arrest is not an element under the amended assault chapter." *People v. Ventura*, 262 Mich. App. 370 (2004).

Fingerprint Requirement—MCL 28.243

Immediately upon the arrest of a person for a felony or for a misdemeanor violation of state law for which the maximum possible penalty exceeds 92 days' imprisonment or a fine of $1,000.00, or both, or for criminal contempt under MCL 600.2950 and 600.2950a, or criminal contempt for a violation of a foreign protection order that satisfies the conditions for validity provided in MCL 600.2950i, or for a juvenile offense, other than a juvenile offense for which the maximum possible penalty does not exceed 92 days imprisonment or a fine of $1,000.00, or both, the arresting law enforcement agency in this state shall take the person's fingerprints and forward the fingerprints to the department within 72 hours after the arrest.

A person who refuses to allow or resists the taking of his or her fingerprints if authorized or required under this act is guilty of a 90-day misdemeanor or $500.00 fine. MCL 28.243a.

Admissibility of Evidence

Evidence obtained as a result of an illegal arrest will not be admissible in court. *Wong Sun v. United States*, 371 U.S. 471 (1963).

LEIN Check Requirements—MCL 764.1g and MCL 764.15g

Police officers must conduct LEIN checks to determine whether a person is on parole when police make an arrest or prior to seeking an arrest warrant. If the person is found to be on parole, the officer must promptly notify the Department of Corrections of the person's identity, the fact that LEIN indicates the person is a parolee, and the charges for which the person has been arrested or the charges in the warrant. If a court delays entry of a warrant into LEIN, it becomes the court's responsibility to notify the Department of Corrections.

OFFICER'S AUTHORITY OUTSIDE JURISDICTION—MCL 764.2a

(1) *A peace officer of a county, city, village, township, or university of this state may exercise the authority and powers of a peace officer outside the geographical boundaries of the officer's county, city, village, township, or university under any of the following circumstances:*

   (a) *If the officer is enforcing the laws of this state in conjunction with the Michigan state police.*
   (b) *If the officer is enforcing the laws of this state in conjunction with a peace officer of any other county, city, village, township, or university in which the officer may be.*
   (c) *If the officer has witnessed an individual violate any of the following within the geographical boundaries of the officer's county, city, village, township, or university and immediately pursues the individual outside of the geographical boundaries of the officer's county, city, village, township, or university:*

      (i) *A state law or administrative rule.*
      (ii) *A local ordinance.*
      (iii) *A state law, administrative rule, or local ordinance, the violation of which is a civil infraction, municipal civil infraction, or state civil infraction.*

(2) *The officer pursuing an individual under subsection (1)(c) may stop and detain the person outside the geographical boundaries of the officer's county, city, village, township, or university for the purpose of enforcing that law, administrative rule, or ordinance or enforcing any other law, administrative rule, or ordinance before, during, or immediately after the detaining of the individual. If the violation or pursuit*

involves a vessel moving on the waters of this state, the officer pursuing the individual may direct the operator of the vessel to bring the vessel to a stop or maneuver it in a manner that permits the officer to come beside the vessel.

> A Mt. Morris Township police officer who was deputized by Genessee County could extend his authority to another Mt. Morris officer who made a traffic stop at the first officer's request. *People v. Oliver*, 192 Mich. App. 201 (1991).

FORCE USED TO EFFECTUATE ARRESTS

Caselaw on the Use of Force

The use of force must be *necessary*.

> The use of force is discretionary with the officer. *Firestones v. Rice*, 71 Mich. 377 (1888). But only that force *necessary* to effectuate the arrest is permissible. *People v. McCord*, 76 Mich. 200 (1889).
>
> An officer may use such force as he or she deems *necessary* in forcibly arresting an offender, or in preventing an escape after an arrest. *Werner v. Hartfelder*, 113 Mich. App. 747 (1982).
>
> An officer may use whatever force *necessary* to apprehend a criminal but neither law nor morality can tolerate the use of needless violence even upon the worst criminals. *People v. McCord*, 76 Mich. 200 (1889).
>
> A peace officer may use **deadly force:**
> - in defense of his or her own life,
> - in defense of another, or
> - in pursuit of a fleeing felon.
>
> *Jenkins v. Starkey*, 95 Mich. App. 685 (1980).
>
> The use of deadly force for a fleeing felon has been limited by the case of *Tennessee v. Garner*, which is discussed below.
>
> No one can be justified in taking a life in an attempt to arrest a subject on suspicion only, without incurring serious responsibilities, and thus where the life of a felon is taken by one who does not know, or believe in his or her guilt, the slaying involves criminal liability. *People v. Burt*, 51 Mich. 199 (1883).

What is deadly force?

Any force used by an officer that has a reasonable probability to cause death. (Michigan Law Enforcement Officer—Subject Control Continuum). A court must determine if the use of force was *objectively reasonable* under the circumstances.

> An officer's use of force will be judged in light of an objective reasonableness standard. Reasonableness will be determined by balancing the nature and quality of the intrusions with the countervailing govern-mental interests. The standard takes into consideration the severity of the crime, whether the suspect poses an immediate threat to the safety of the officers or others and whether the suspect is actively resisting arrest or attempting to evade arrest by flight. The reasonableness will be judged on the scene and at the moment the force was used, rather than from 20/20 hindsight, and will take into consideration the fact that police officers are often forced to make split-second decisions in circumstances that are tense, uncertain, and rapidly evolving. *Graham v. Connor*, 490 U.S. 386 (1989).

Deadly Force and Fleeing Felon

The suspect must have threatened the officer with a weapon, or the officer must have probable cause to believe that the suspect has committed a crime involving the infliction or threatened infliction of serious physical harm. If feasible, some warning must be given.

> "Where the officer has *probable cause* to believe that the suspect *poses a threat of serious physical harm*, either to the officer or others, it is not constitutionally unreasonable to prevent escape by using deadly force." However, the use of deadly force must be reasonably necessary to prevent the suspect's escape and alternative steps are not likely to lead to the safe control of the subject. *Tennessee v. Garner*, 471 U.S. 1 (1985).

An officer may not use fatal force to effect a misdemeanor arrest.

To retake an escapee, an officer may utilize that force authorized for the crime that person has escaped from. MCL 764.24.

FRESH PURSUIT
Fresh Pursuit—MCL 780.101

The **fresh pursuit** statute allows an officer from another state to pursue felons into Michigan and make the arrest with the same arrest powers as those of Michigan peace officers. Once arrested, the person must be brought before the magistrate in the judicial district where the arrest was made and extradition proceedings must be followed.

"Fresh pursuit shall not necessarily imply instant pursuit, but pursuit without unreasonable delay." MCL 780.105.

Police officers from adjacent states—MCL 764.2b

A law enforcement officer of an adjacent state (Indiana, Ohio, Minnesota, and Wisconsin) has the same authority and immunity as a law enforcement officer of Michigan if he or she is on duty, is authorized to arrest in his or her home state, and notifies a law enforcement agency of this state that he or she is in Michigan for one of the following reasons:

- The officer is engaged in pursuing, arresting, or attempting to arrest an individual for a violation of a law in an adjacent state.
- The officer is in Michigan at the request of a Michigan officer.
- The officer is working in conjunction with a Michigan officer.
- The officer is responding to an emergency.

PERSONS EXEMPT FROM ARREST

Diplomats, their families, official staff, and servants are immune from criminal arrest and civil proceedings. Vienna Convention on Diplomatic Relations and Optional Protocols arts. 29-37, Apr. 18, 1961, 23 U.S.T. 3227.

Consular officers, but not their families, have limited immunity from arrest, except for grave crimes. Vienna Convention on Consular Relations and Optional Protocol on Disputes art. 41, *done* Apr. 24, 1963, 21 U.S.T. 77.

Federal legislators are immune from arrest in all cases except treason, felony, and breach of peace, when they are in session or when going to and from session. U.S. CONST. art. I, § 6.

State legislators are immune from civil arrest and civil process during session and for five days before the commencement and five days after the termination of session. Mich. CONST., art. IV, § 11. However, they may be issued citations for civil infraction violations of the Michigan Vehicle Code. MCL 600.1865.

ARRESTEE'S RIGHTS
Arrest by a Private Person—MCL 764.14

A private person, who has made an arrest, shall, without unnecessary delay, deliver the person arrested to a peace officer. The officer shall, without unnecessary delay, take that person before a magistrate of the judicial district in which the offense charged is alleged to have been committed. The peace officer or private person shall present to the magistrate a complaint stating the charge against the person arrested. If arrested by a private person, the person arrested *must* be delivered to a peace officer.

Arrest by a Peace Officer

An arresting officer shall inform the suspect of his or her authority and the cause for the arrest at the time of the arrest unless the person is committing a crime, fleeing, or resisting arrest. MCL 764.19.

A peace officer who has arrested a person without a warrant shall, without unnecessary delay, take the person arrested before a magistrate of the judicial district in which the offense has been committed, and shall present to the magistrate a complaint stating the charge against the person arrested. MCL 764.13.

> A delay of more than 48 hours between a warrantless arrest and a judicial determination of probable cause if presumptively unreasonable. Conversely, when the delay is less than 48 hours the burden is on the plaintiff to prove that the delay was unreasonable. *County of Riverside v. McLaughlin*, 500 U.S. 44 (1991).

Notice to appear—MCL 764.9c

For minor offenses of 93-day misdemeanors or less an appearance ticket may be issued in lieu of custodial arrest except in cases of domestic violence and PPO violations.

SEARCH INCIDENT TO ARREST
Search Incident to Arrest—MCL 764.25

Any person making an arrest shall take from the person arrested all offensive weapons or incriminating articles that may be on his or her person. Case law has expanded the area to be searched to include the "wingspan" of the person being arrested.

182 CHAPTER 19 **Laws of Arrest**

> Officers arrested defendant at his home, based on a warrant, and searched the entire three-bedroom house, which included the attic, garage, and small workshop. During this search they found incriminating evidence. Under this circumstance, the search cannot go beyond areas outside the defendant's reach. Anything within the wingspan of control can be searched. *Chimel v California*, 395 U.S. 752 (1969).
>
> A search incident to arrest was upheld where a motorist was arrested on a warrant and officers located tinfoil packets containing heroin and cocaine in his mouth. *People v. Holloway*, 416 Mich. 288 (1982).

Accompanying arrestees into the dwelling

> Officers went to defendant's house with an arrest warrant. He answered the door wearing pajamas. It was suggested that he get dressed. When he approached his dresser to get socks, an officer checked the drawers and found a blackjack. Seizing the blackjack was valid as a search incident to arrest. *People v. Giacalone*, 23 Mich. App. 163 (1970).

Vehicles

> The defendant was arrested for driving while his license was suspended. After he was handcuffed and secured in a patrol car, officers searched the vehicle he had been driving and found cocaine. The Court held the search violated the Fourth Amendment, which required suppression of the cocaine. *Arizona v. Gant*, 556 U.S.—(2009).

The officers in *Gant* were presumably relying on the long-standing rule that allowed officers to search a vehicle without a warrant *every* time an occupant was arrested. With the Court's opinion in *Gant*, that is no longer the rule.

The rule only allows police to conduct a vehicle search incident to the arrest of an occupant when either of two circumstances exists:

First, officers may search if the arrestee is within "reaching distance of the passenger compartment." When the arrestee has been secured in a patrol car, he or she is not within reach of the vehicle.

Second, officers may search a vehicle incident to arrest if they reasonably believe the vehicle contains evidence of the crime for which the person was arrested. Gant had been arrested for DWLS, and the cocaine was not evidence of DWLS. It appears the Court would not have suppressed the cocaine had Gant been arrested for a drug crime.

What if the suspect voluntarily leaves the vehicle?

> A police officer observed a vehicle with improper license plates. Before the officer was able to stop the vehicle, the driver parked the car and began to walk away. The officer made contact with the driver and, after patting him down, located drugs on him. The officer then searched the vehicle the driver left and found a firearm.
>
> The court held that once a police officer makes a lawful custodial arrest of an automobile's occupant, the officer may search the vehicle's passenger compartment as a contemporaneous incident of arrest, even when an officer does not make contact until the person arrested has already left the vehicle. An arrestee is no less likely to attempt to lunge for a weapon or to destroy evidence if he is outside of, but still in control of, the vehicle. *Thornton v. United States*, 541 U.S. 615 (2004).
>
> NOTE: The authority to search in these instances is limited by the Court's holding in *Gant*. Therefore, officers may only search in this instance if the arrestee is within reaching distance of the passenger compartment, or the officer reasonably believes the vehicle contains evidence of the crime for which the person was arrested.

Strip Search—MCL 764.25a

A strip search includes the removal of clothing exposing underclothing, breasts, buttocks, or genitalia of another person.

- The person is lodged on a court order, or
- The officer has reasonable cause to believe the person is concealing a weapon, controlled substance, or evidence and only upon written authorization of the chief law enforcement officer of that agency or his designee.

The search must be conducted by an officer of the same sex and, if assisted, by an assistant of the same sex as the person searched. The search must be conducted privately so that others do not observe it. After completing the search, the officer must finish a report containing the following information:

- Name and sex of person searched, person conducting search, and person assisting.
- Date, time and place of search.

- Reason for search.
- List of items recovered.
- A copy of the written authorization.

Unauthorized strip searches are punishable as a **misdemeanor**.

Body Cavity Search (Mcl 764.25b)

A *body cavity*, under this section, includes the interior of the human body, stomach, rectal cavity, and vagina of females.

A **body cavity search** includes the physical intrusion into the body cavity to discover any object concealed therein.

Except as otherwise provided, a body cavity search shall not be conducted without a search warrant. Except for:

- A person serving a sentence for a criminal offense in a detention facility or a state correctional facility housing prisoners under the jurisdiction of the department of corrections, including a youth correctional facility operated by the department of corrections or a private vendor . . . , or
- Persons in mental institutions for that person's protection (self-destruction tendencies).
- A person who, as the result of a dispositional order entered after adjudication by the juvenile division of probate court before January 1, 1998 or by the family division of the circuit court on or after January 1, 1998, is residing in a juvenile detention facility. MCL 764.25b(3).

Note: for the exceptions listed above, the person conducting the search must have "prior written authorization from the chief administrative officer of the facility or from that officer's designee."

A body cavity search shall be conducted by a licensed physician, or any of the following under the direction of a licensed physician:

- Physician's assistant,
- LPN or RN, acting with permission of a physician, and
- If the search is conducted by a person of the opposite sex, a person of the same sex as the person searched must be present.

A report is required for searches conducted pursuant to a search warrant. The report must include:

- Copies of the search warrant.
- The name of the person who conducted the search.
- The time, date, and place of the search.
- A list of all items recovered.
- The name and sex of all law enforcement officers present at the search.

BOND
Interim Bond—MCL 780.581

If a person is arrested without a warrant for a misdemeanor or a violation of a city, village, or township ordinance punishable by imprisonment for not more than one year, or by a fine or both, the officer making the arrest shall take, without unnecessary delay, the person arrested before the most convenient magistrate of the county in which the offense was committed to answer to the complaint.

If a magistrate is not available or an immediate trial cannot be held, the person arrested may deposit an interim bond to guarantee his or her appearance. The bond shall be a sum of money, as determined by the officer who accepts the bond, not to exceed the amount of the maximum possible fine, but not less than 20 percent of the amount of the minimum possible fine that may be imposed for the offense for which the person was arrested. The person shall be given a receipt.

If, in the opinion of the arresting officer or department, the arrested person falls under one of the following, bond may be denied:

- The person is under the influence of alcoholic liquor, a controlled substance or a combination of both,
- The person is wanted by police authorities to answer to another charge,
- The person is unable to establish or demonstrate his or her identity,
- It is otherwise unsafe to release him or her.

If bond is denied, the suspect shall be held until he or she is in a proper condition to be released, or until the next session of court.

> The interim bond statute does not deprive the arresting officer of the ability to do a search subsequent to a lawful custodial arrest. *People v. Chapman*, 425 Mich. 245 (1986).
>
> Interim bond is violated when a search incident to incarceration occurs. *People v. Dixon*, 392 Mich. 691 (1974).

Exception to interim bond for domestic violence arrests—MCL 780.582a

(1) A person shall not be released on an interim bond as provided in section 1 or on his or her own recognizance as provided in section 3a, but shall be held until he or she can be arraigned or have interim bond set by a judge or district

court magistrate if either of the following applies:

(a) The person is arrested without a warrant under section 15a of chapter IV of the code of criminal procedure, 1927 PA 175, MCL 764.15a, or a local ordinance substantially corresponding to that section.

(b) The person is arrested with a warrant for a violation of section 81 or 81a of the Michigan penal code, 1931 PA 328, MCL 750.81 and 750.81a, or a local ordinance substantially corresponding to section 81 of that act and the person is a spouse or former spouse of the victim of the violation, has or has had a dating relationship with the victim of the violation, has had a child in common with the victim of the violation, or is a person who resides or has resided in the same household as the victim of the violation. As used in this subdivision, "dating relationship" means that term as defined in section 2950 of the revised judicature act of 1961, 1961 PA 236, MCL 600.2950.

CUSTODIAL TRAFFIC ARRESTS— MCL 257.727 AND MCL 257.728

Officers are authorized to make custodial arrests for the following traffic violations:

- Negligent homicide (MCL 750.324).
- O.W.I., UBAC, OUID, Impaired (MCL 257.625).
- Reckless driving (MCL 257.626).
- Failure to stop and identify at a serious injury accident or death (MCL 257.617).
- Failure to give aid and information at a personal injury accident (MCL 257.619).
- Failure to have a valid operator's or chauffeur's license in possession (MCL 257.727(d)).

ENTRY INTO RESIDENCE TO MAKE AN ARREST

Right to Break Open Inner or Outer Door— MCL 764.21

A private person, when making an arrest for a felony committed in his or her presence, or a peace officer or federal law enforcement officer, when making an arrest with a warrant or when making a felony arrest without a warrant as authorized by law, may break open an inner or outer door of a building in which the person to be arrested is located or is reasonably believed to be located if, after announcing his or her purpose, he or she is refused admittance.

This statute has been modified through case law that is discussed below.

Entry is Not Allowed for Routine Felony Arrests

The physical entry of the home is the chief evil against which the wording of the Fourth Amendment is directed. This is a substantial invasion to allow without a warrant, in the absence of exigent circumstances, even when it is accomplished under statutory authority and when probable cause is present.

For Fourth Amendment purposes, an arrest warrant founded on probable cause implicitly carries with it the limited authority to enter a dwelling in which the suspect lives, when there is reason to believe the suspect is within. *Payton v. New York*, 445 U.S. 573 (1980).

Officer Cannot Enter for Warrantless Misdemeanors

Officers chased subject into his house for fleeing and eluding, which was a misdemeanor at the time. The court held the arrest to be unlawful. While MCL 764.21 authorizes a peace officer to break and enter any outer or inner door of any building for purpose of making an arrest with a warrant or a felony without a warrant, this section does not authorize a nonconsensual entry into a person's home or other building for purpose of making a warrantless misdemeanor arrest. *People v. Reinhardt*, 141 Mich. App. 173 (1985).

Arrest Warrants Do Not Authorize Entry Into a Third Party Residence

DEA agents had an arrest warrant for a subject with the last name of Lyons. They had information that he was at Steagald's house. They went to the residence and entered, without a search warrant or consent. The officers did not find Lyons, but did seize cocaine and subsequently charged Steagald. The U.S. Supreme Court suppressed the evidence. When a magistrate issues a search warrant, the interest in privacy in the areas to be searched are directly considered. When issuing an arrest warrant, however, the magistrate does not generally consider third party interests. Therefore, the arrest warrant issued for Lyons offered no protection to Steagald's expectation of privacy and the entry was unlawful. *Steagald v. United States*, 451 U.S. 204 (1982).

Officers entered a third party residence to arrest a subject for outstanding warrants. The person with the warrants was not a resident of the house. A scuffle with the occupants broke out and the officers charged them with R and O. The charges were dismissed on the basis that the officers did not first seek a search warrant before entry into the house. *People v. Stark*, 120 Mich. App. 350 (1982).

Exigent Circumstances May Authorize Entry without a Warrant

Police suspected respondent Olson of being the driver of the getaway car used in a robbery and murder. After recovering the murder weapon and arresting the suspect, they surrounded the home of two women with whom they believed Olson had been staying. When police telephoned the home and told one of the women that Olson should come out, a male voice was heard saying, "Tell them I left." Without seeking permission and with weapons drawn, they entered the home, found Olson hiding in a closet, and arrested him. Shortly thereafter, he made an inculpatory statement. An entry may be justified by hot pursuit of a fleeing felon where there is the imminent destruction of evidence, the need to prevent a suspect's escape, or the risk of danger to police or others. In the absence of hot pursuit, there must be at least probable cause to believe that one or more of the other factors were present and, in assessing the risk of danger, the gravity of the crime and likelihood that the suspect is armed should be considered. Although a grave crime was involved, Olson was known not to be the murderer, the murder weapon had been recovered, and there was no suggestion of danger to the women. Several police squads surrounded the house, and it was evident that the suspect was going nowhere and that if he came out of the house he would have been promptly apprehended. Arrest held to be invalid as well as statement. *Minnesota v. Olson*, 495 U.S. 91 (1990).

An officer responded to a shooting at a hotel at 10:00 p.m. where two people had been murdered. Officers learned that the suspect had been staying in the motel. After completing their investigation at the scene, they informed the night manager to contact them if the suspect returned. At 4:00 a.m., the manager informed the officers that the suspect had returned and was in his room. The officers responded and after not receiving a response to their knocks, entered to make the arrest. The entry and arrest was valid. "Here, the police were justified in concluding that Snider's armed presence in the hotel endangered the lives of the other guests. Further, the police were justified in concluding that any delay in arresting Snider while obtaining an arrest warrant would be unreasonable in light of the danger that Snider posed to the other guests. Therefore, we find that there were exigent circumstances known to the police that excused them from taking time to obtain an arrest warrant. The police were confronted with what can only be classified as an emergency situation: a murder suspect, whom they had every reason to believe was armed, located in a hotel room under circumstances that very probably might put the lives and safety of others at risk." *People v. Snider*, 239 Mich. App. 393 (2000).

Officers were investigating a B&E and received a tip that Love may have been involved. There were no indications that the suspect was armed or that there was a danger to anyone. There was no concern that evidence would be lost or destroyed. Police entered the residence an hour after the crime. Based on these facts, there were no exigent circumstances for hot pursuit. Arrest held to be invalid as well as statement. *People v. Love*, 156 Mich. App. 568 (1986).

Police were dispatched to a robbery/murder that had just occurred. A tracking dog led officers to a nearby house. The officers entered and discovered defendant and the murder weapon.

The court held that the entry was valid because the dog track constituted probable cause and the entry was within minutes of the murder. *People v. Joyner*, 93 Mich. App. 554 (1979).

Protective Sweeps

Two men committed an armed robbery of a pizza restaurant, and one of them was wearing a red running suit.

Two days later, six or seven officers went to the suspect's home with an arrest warrant. One of the officers shouted into the basement and ordered that anyone in the basement come out. The defendant came out and was arrested." An officer went into the basement "in case there was someone else" down there. There was a red running suit in plain view, and the officer seized it.

The Court upheld the search as a protective sweep. "The Fourth Amendment permits a properly limited protective sweep in conjunction with an in-home arrest when the searching officer possesses a reasonable belief based on specific and articulable facts that the area to be swept harbors an individual posing a danger to those on the arrest scene." However, the Court also stated, "We should emphasize that such a protective sweep, aimed at protecting the arresting officers, if justified by the circumstances, is nevertheless not a full search of the premises, but may extend only to a cursory inspection of those spaces where a person may be found. The sweep lasts no longer than is necessary to dispel the reasonable suspicion of danger and in any event no longer than it takes to complete the arrest and depart the premises." *Maryland v. Buie*, 494 U.S. 325 (1990).

KNOCK AND ANNOUNCE—MCL 780.656

Officers may break in or out of a building after giving notice of their authority and purpose and being refused admittance.

Fourth Amendment Requires Knock and Announce

The Fourth Amendment requires that police officers must announce their identity and purpose before attempting forcible entry into a dwelling unless an unannounced entry is reasonable. *Wilson v. Arkansas*, 514 U.S. 927 (1995).

In order to justify a "no-knock" entry, the police must have a *reasonable suspicion* that knocking and announcing would be one of the following:

- Dangerous,
- Futile, or
- Inhibit the effective investigation of the crime (i.e., destruction of evidence). *Richard v. Wisconsin*, 520 U.S. 385 (1997). Note, however, that there is not a blanket exception allowing an unannounced entry with search warrants for drugs: An unannounced entry must be reasonable under the circumstances of the specific case.

Announce: There must be substantial compliance with the statute.

"Police officers, open up." *People v. Doane*, 33 Mich. App. 579 (1971) (Reversed on other grounds by *People v. Doane*, 387 Mich. 608 (1972)).

"Police officers. I have a search warrant. Open the door." *People v. Mayes*, 78 Mich. App. 618 (1977).

How long to wait

A warrant was properly served where an officer knocked on a door and clearly announced authority and purpose and waited long enough for inhabitants to reach the door from the room farthest away before kicking in the door. *People v. Harvey*, 38 Mich. App. 39 (1972).

The length of time is flexible and is determined by the "totality of the circumstances." In drug cases, the appropriate measure of how long to wait may be determined by how long it would take to dispose the evidence as opposed to how long it would take an occupant to get to the door. However, if the search warrant is for a piano then the officers may be required to wait until the occupants actually answer the door and refuse entry. *United States v. Banks*, 540 U.S. 31 (2003).

No exclusionary rule

The Court has held that the exclusionary rule does not apply when the police do not wait long enough under the knock and announce rule. Thus, evidence was not suppressed after police waited "three to five seconds" after announcing their presence. *Hudson v. Michigan*, 547 U.S. 586 (2006).

20

ADMISSIONS AND CONFESSIONS

The defendant's own confession is probably the most probative and damaging evidence that can be admitted against him.... The admissions of a defendant come from the actor himself, the most knowledgeable and unimpeachable source of information about his past conduct. Certainly, confessions have a profound impact on the jury. Bruton v. United States, 391 U.S. 123 (1968).

BASIC CONSIDERATIONS
The Fifth Amendment

No person shall be held to answer for a capital, or otherwise infamous crime, unless on a presentment or indictment of a Grand Jury, except in cases arising in the land or naval forces, or in the Militia, when in actual service in time of War or public danger; nor shall any person be subject for the same offence to be twice put in jeopardy of life or limb; nor shall be compelled in any criminal case to be a witness against himself, nor be deprived of life, liberty, or property, without due process of law; nor shall private property be taken for public use, without just compensation.

The Fifth Amendment is applicable to the states via the Fourteenth Amendment.

"Witness against himself"

The privilege only protects *testimonial evidence*. It does not include physical evidence, blood sample, voice exemplar, or handwriting sample.

An in-custody suspect does *not* have a Fifth Amendment right against self-incrimination that would allow him to refuse to stand in a lineup. If an in-custody suspect refuses to cooperate, this can be used at trial to show knowledge of guilt. *United States v. Wade*, 388 U.S. 218 (1967).

A suspect can be compelled to repeat words spoken by the culprit at the crime scene, as well as to make gestures or wear certain clothing, without violating the Fifth Amendment. *People v. Hall*, 396 Mich. 650 (1976); *United States v. Dionisio*, 410 U.S. 1 (1973).

The privilege protects a defendant from testifying against himself at a criminal trial.

A person may refuse to answer any official questions put to him in any other proceeding, whether criminal or civil, formal or informal, *if the answers might incriminate him* in future criminal proceedings. *Minnesota v. Murphy*, 465 U.S. 420 (1984).

189

The Difference between an Admission and a Confession

- An admission is a partial admittance to criminal involvement.
- A confession is the complete admittance to criminal involvement.

THE *MIRANDA* WARNINGS

The *Miranda* Case

In 1963, the Phoenix police arrested Ernesto Miranda for raping and kidnapping a mildly retarded 18-year-old woman. After two hours in a police interrogation room, Miranda signed a written confession, but he was not told that he had the right to remain silent, to have a lawyer, and to be protected against self-incrimination.

Despite his lawyer's objections, the confession was presented as evidence at Miranda's trial, and he was convicted and sentenced to 20 years. His appeal went all the way to the Supreme Court, where it was joined with three other similar cases. In a landmark ruling issued in 1966, the Court established that an accused has the right to remain silent and that prosecutors may not use statements made by defendants during custodial interrogations unless the police have advised them of their rights. The *Miranda* Court found custodial interrogations to be an *inherently coercive environment* where the suspect's rights must be explained and waived.

The *Miranda* Warnings Generally Include the Following:

- You have the right to remain silent and refuse to answer questions.
- Anything you do say may be used against you in a court of law.
- You have the right to consult with an attorney before speaking to the police and to have an attorney present during questioning now or in the future.
- If you cannot afford an attorney, one will be appointed for you before any questioning, if you wish.
- If you decide to answer questions without an attorney present, you will still have the right to stop answering at any time until you talk to an attorney.
- Knowing and understanding your rights as I have explained them to you, are you willing to answer my questions at this time?

When are *Miranda* Warnings Required?

For many years the Michigan courts followed a focus test for determining when *Miranda* warnings were required. *Miranda* warnings were to be given when an officer focused his or her attention on a person as a possible criminal suspect. This test was difficult to apply and the Michigan Supreme Court rejected it in the case of *People v. Hill*, 429 Mich. 382 (1987). The Court instead ruled that *Miranda* warnings have to be given when a person is in custody and subjected to interrogation.

Custody + Interrogation = *Miranda* warnings

Custody

Custody means:

- The person is under arrest, or
- The person's freedom has been deprived in any significant way. The question will be whether the defendant felt he was free to leave.

> A defendant was interviewed in his motel room. Though the police testified he would not have been able to walk out freely, this information was not relayed to the defendant. In fact, he was told that he was not under arrest. This was held not to be custodial and *Miranda* warnings did not have to be given. *People v. Zahn*, 234 Mich. App. 438 (1999).

Statements made at the *police station* may be noncustodial, especially when the suspect voluntarily goes to the station.

> A trooper asked Mathiason, a burglary suspect, to come into the post. Mathiason went to the post and was told that he was not under arrest. The officer told him that he wanted to talk about a burglary at which Mathiason's fingerprints were found (no prints were actually found). Mr. Mathiason confessed and left the post a half an hour later. The U.S. Supreme Court held that Mathiason was not in custody because his freedom was not restricted in any way. He had gone to the post voluntarily and was immediately informed that he was not under arrest. He then left within half an hour without hindrance. *Oregon v. Mathiason*, 429 U.S. 492 (1977).

A detective suspected that Stansbury had raped and killed a 10-year-old girl. He informed the suspect that he believed he may have *witnessed* the girl's disappearance. The officer asked the suspect to accompany him to the station. The suspect agreed. The United States Supreme Court held that "A police officer's *subjective view* that the individual under questioning is a suspect, if undisclosed, does not bear upon the question whether the individual is in custody for purposes of *Miranda*. An officer's knowledge or beliefs may bear upon the custody issue if they are conveyed, by word or deed, to the individual being questioned. The test for custody will be determined by the objective conditions surrounding the interrogation." *Stansbury v. California*, 511 U.S. 318 (1994).

The court found custody where officers picked up an individual they wanted to question about a murder. The officers did not have a warrant or probable cause to make an arrest. They informed the subject that he was *not under arrest, but he would be physically restrained* if he tried to leave. *Dunaway v. New York*, 442 U.S. 200 (1979).

Police suspected that Marbury had committed a murder. They went to his house and asked him to accompany them to the precinct. He voluntarily went with them to the station. The Court held this was not custody. The question to be asked is whether "*that person reasonably believed that he or she was not free to leave.*" *People v. Marbury*, 151 Mich. App. 159 (1986).

Police believed Williams had information about a recent murder. The officers went to his house and asked him to accompany them to the station for questioning. *The suspect was searched prior to entering the patrol car, but was not handcuffed.* He was questioned at the station, and there he gave an incriminating statement. As a result of the statement, the defendant was placed under arrest and read his *Miranda* rights. The court held that the defendant was not in custody prior to his arrest. *People v. Williams*, 171 Mich. App. 234 (1988).

There was no custody where the defendant picked the time for the interview, drove himself to the station, was unrestrained and alone for periods of time, and after giving a written statement, was allowed to leave. *People v. Mendez*, 225 Mich. App. 381 (1997).

The defendant was picked up for questioning on a homicide. At 2:23 p.m., he initially denied any involvement during his first statement. He was later confronted with a number of inconsistencies at 4:00 p.m. At this time he stated that the gun fell from the victim's hand and discharged when it hit the floor. He asked to talk to his father and was told he would be able to later. At 7:10 p.m. he was given a polygraph test. Prior to the test, he was advised of his *Miranda* rights. He waived his rights. During the exam, he was told that he was not being truthful. He then confessed to intentionally shooting the victim. He was then placed under arrest and again advised of his *Miranda* rights. He then gave a recorded statement at 11:35 p.m. During this time period, he was also told that he was not under arrest and was free to leave at any time. The Michigan Supreme Court upheld the confession. "The trial court found that defendant was treated fairly by the investigating officers throughout his interrogation. Defendant was provided with food and water and was told on at least two occasions that he was not under arrest and could leave at any time. Defendant himself testified that he was treated fairly by the officers and that he was not coerced in any manner into making the challenged statements. Defendant was also advised of his *Miranda* rights and voluntarily waived those rights before making the challenged statements. Although there was evidence that defendant suffers from an auditory processing disorder and that he has below average intelligence, the trial judge, who was in the best position to observe defendant's demeanor, noted that defendant, while testifying in this matter, understood the questions presented to him and responded to those questions in an appropriate manner. Finally, although the police failed to inform defendant that he had counsel available during his interrogation, failed to disclose defendant's whereabouts to defense counsel, and failed to heed defense counsel's demands that the interrogation be stopped, [we are] not prepared to say that, under the totality of the circumstances, these factors alone rendered defendant's otherwise voluntary statements involuntary." *People v. Sexton*, 461 Mich. 746 (2000).

Generally, questioning at the home or office is not considered custodial

The defendant was questioned while in his office. The defendant owned the building and was surrounded by people he was familiar with. The Michigan Supreme Court held that the defendant was not in custody, nor was his freedom significantly deprived. *People v. Hill*, 429 Mich. 382 (1987).

Four police officers standing around defendant's bed and pointing their guns at him constituted custody. *Orozco v. Texas*, 394 U.S. 324 (1969).

Generally, phone conversations do not constitute custody

A pre-arrest telephone conver-sation between a police officer and the defendant did not require *Miranda* warnings because the defendant was not in custody. The defendant had called the police officer and made incriminating statements. The court reasoned that there was no coercive police pressure and no custody when a suspect is on the phone at his home speaking with police. *People v. Fisher*, 166 Mich. App. 699 (1988).

Generally, traffic stops do not constitute custody because a traffic stop does not significantly deprive a person of his or her freedom

Roadside questioning during a traffic stop does not constitute custodial interrogation. But once an arrest is made, questioning about the driving requires *Miranda* warnings, even if the arrest is for a misdemeanor traffic violation. *Berkemer v. McCarty*, 468 U.S. 420 (1984).

Chinn was stopped as a suspected drunk driver. He had a strong odor of intoxicants on his breath. When asked how much he had to drink, he responded, "Too much." Warnings were not required and the statement was admissible. *People v. Chinn*, 141 Mich. App. 92 (1985).

On a traffic stop for a civil infraction, an officer asked the driver if there were any weapons in the car. The driver admitted to having a gun. The admission was admissible, as a traffic stop is not custody for purposes of *Miranda*. *People v. Edwards*, 158 Mich. App. 561 (1987).

A *traffic stop must be temporary* and last no longer than is necessary to effectuate the purpose of the stop. *Florida v. Royer*, 460 U.S. 491 (1983).

Generally, pat-down searches do not constitute custody

During a non-custodial pat-down, an officer felt a hard object in defendant's chest pocket. The officer believed the object to be a weapon and asked defendant what it was. Defendant replied that it was marijuana. The Court held that "The limited constraint placed upon defendant's freedom by the officer's conducting the pat-down search does not rise to the level of a custodial interrogation and precludes a finding that defendant's admission was compelled by police action." *People v. Harmelin*, 176 Mich. App. 524 (1989).

Generally, questioning at a hospital room does not constitute custody

During defendant's attempt to commit murder with a bomb, she was seriously injured when the bomb exploded. She lost her hands and was in the hospital when she was interviewed and made incriminating statements. She first argued that she should have been given her *Miranda* rights. The Court disagreed because she was not in custody. She also claimed that her statements were not voluntary because of the medicine she was on. The court disagreed by looking at the doctor's statements that her ability to remain silent was not impaired. *People v. Peerenboom*, 224 Mich. App. 195 (1997).

An arrest under a warrant will be custody, even if the suspect will soon be released on bond

Defendant was arrested on a warrant. She was told she would be released after posting bond. She was then questioned about drug paraphernalia found in her vehicle. She made a number of admissions. The court held that even though she was going to be released on bond, she was still in custody at the time of the questioning and *Miranda* warnings should have been given. *People v. Roark*, 214 Mich. App. 421 (1995).

An individual does not have to be arrested when sufficient probable cause exists

Hoffa was being investigated for jury tampering, but was not in custody. Hoffa made some incriminating statements and argued that he should have been taken into custody as soon as probable cause was established. The Court held that a defendant has no right to be arrested. Police do not have to stop the investigation and make an arrest the moment they have probable cause. *Hoffa v. United States*, 385 U.S. 293 (1966).

Custody and unrelated charges?

Miranda warnings are required to be given to a person incarcerated prior to potentially incriminating questions being asked, even when the questioning pertains to crimes unrelated to the offense for which the person is incarcerated. *Mathis v. United States*, 391 U.S. 1 (1968).

Evidence obtained in violation of *Miranda* does not automatically have to be suppressed if the confession was voluntarily made

Officers were investigating the defendant for a violation of a temporary restraining order. They also had information that he was a convicted felon and illegally possessing a pistol. The officers proceeded to his home and arrested him for violating the restraining order. One officer attempted to advise him of his rights when the defendant interrupted, asserting that he knew his rights. The officer then asked about the pistol and defendant told him where it was. The pistol was retrieved and the defendant was indicted for possession of a firearm by a convicted felon in violation of federal law. He argued on appeal that the firearm should be suppressed as a violation of *Miranda*.

The United States Supreme Court held that:

1. Failure to give suspect warnings does not require suppression of physical fruits of suspect's unwarned but voluntary statements;
2. Officers' failure to give warnings in conjunction with restraining-order arrest did not require suppression of weapon at firearms trial, since weapon was recovered based on defendant's voluntary statement that he possessed it. *United States v. Patane*, 542 U.S. 630 (2004).

INTERROGATION

Interrogation consists of one of the following:
- Express questioning, or
- Any words or actions that the police know or reasonably should know are likely to elicit an incriminating response.

Held to be Interrogation

The defendant was arrested in connection with the disappearance of a 10-year-old girl. He invoked his rights. As he rode in the police car, the detective began to converse with him. The detective knew that the defendant was deeply religious and so presented what is now known as the "Christian Burial Speech" in an attempt to recover the little girl's body. "Reverend, I want to give you something to think about while we're traveling down the road.... Number one, I want you to observe the weather conditions, it's raining, it's sleeting, it's freezing, driving is very treacherous, visibility is poor, it's going to be dark early this evening. They are predicting several inches of snow for tonight, and I feel that you yourself are the only person that knows where this little girl's body is, that you yourself have only been there once, and if you get a snow on top of it you yourself may be unable to find it. And, since we will be going right past the area on the way into Des Moines, I feel that we could stop and locate the body, that the parents of this little girl should be entitled to a Christian burial for the little girl who was snatched away from them on Christmas Eve and murdered. And I feel we should stop and locate it on the way in rather than waiting until morning and trying to come back out after a snow storm and possibly not being able to find it at all." The Court held this to be interrogation because the officer knew or should have known that the statements about the Christian burial would elicit incriminating statements. The officer knew defendant was deeply religious and used that to obtain the confession. *Brewer v. Williams*, 430 U.S. 387 (1977).

Held Not to be Interrogation

Two officers were transporting a murder suspect who they suspected had just killed a taxi cab driver with a shotgun. They were in the front seat and the suspect was sitting in the back. During the drive, the officers had a conversation that they knew was being overheard by the suspect. They mentioned that they wished they could find the missing gun because there was a school for handicapped children nearby, and it would be tragic if any of the children were injured. The suspect spoke up and told them he would show them where the gun was so the children would not be injured. The Court held that this did not constitute interrogation. There was no showing that the officers knew or should have known that their conversations would lead to incriminating statements. The officers did not know that the suspect had a "consciousness" for children's safety. *Rhode Island v. Innis*, 446 U.S. 291 (1980).

The suspect in this case killed his son and was being held in jail. He was very emotional and asked to speak to his wife. The wife talked to her husband in the presence of an officer who they knew was taping the conversation. There was no direct questioning or psychological ploys used, even though the officer knew that the suspect was in an emotional state making it likely he would confess. The Court held that this did not constitute interrogation. The officer did nothing that he knew or should have known may lead to incriminating response (Note: Any husband/wife privilege was lost when the husband talked to his wife in front of a third party, here the officer.) *Arizona v. Mauro*, 481 U.S. 520 (1987).

The suspect was taken to the booking room, where the officer informed him he was going to be fingerprinted. Defendant stated, "It was like a bad dream." The officer responded, "What was like a bad dream?" Defendant replied, "To shoot a man six times and see him still try to get up." The officer said nothing else. Another time, while in a patrol car, defendant mumbled something at which the officer asked, "What did you say?" The defendant responded, "How would you feel in my situation?" The officer said, "I'd probably feel pretty depressed." Defendant then stated, "I didn't mean to reload the gun, but I was afraid my dad was going to get me." The Court held the officer's questions were not interrogation. The questioning was not likely to elicit an incriminating response. *People v. Giuchici*, 118 Mich. App. 252 (1982).

Defendant was in custody and being transported from one county to another. During a conversation, the officers informed him that he was being taken to Monroe County to answer questions about a murder. Defendant said he would cooperate and then suddenly blurted out, "I shot him." The officers stopped the car and advised him of his *Miranda* warnings. He subsequently gave a full confession. Informing the defendant of the charges was not likely to elicit incriminating response, and thus there was no interrogation requiring *Miranda* warnings. *People v. Raper*, 222 Mich. App. 475 (1997).

Police Communication versus Interrogation

Co-defendants were being questioned separately about a shooting that had occurred at a gas station. After being advised of his *Miranda* rights, one defendant asked to speak to an attorney. The questioning immediately ceased. He was taken to another room and left alone. He had access to a phone, but was not free to leave. The defendant called a friend and asked for help in locating an attorney. His friend never called back. About an hour and a half later, the detective returned and informed him that the co-defendant had made a statement and asked him if he "would still like to talk to an attorney." The detective did not discuss the substance of the statement or what effect it had on the defendant. The defendant then told the detective, "If Ron doesn't want an attorney, than neither do I." He then gave a statement. He was then given his *Miranda* rights again and specifically asked if he wanted to talk to an attorney. He agreed to be interviewed and gave another statement. The Court of Appeals refused to apply the Supreme Court's decision of *Edwards v. Arizona*, 451 U.S. 477 (1981), to this case, distinguishing between police interrogation and police communication. The *Edwards* case does not "prohibit all communication between the police and a suspect who has requested an attorney. Rather, a careful reading of *Edwards* reveals that what is prohibited is further 'police-initiated custodial interrogation'. . . . We further conclude that Detective Lister's remark informing defendant that co-defendant Sands had given a statement did not constitute interrogation. The remark did not involve any express questioning, but merely described an event that transpired since Lister last saw the defendant. Significantly, Detective Lister made no attempt to discuss the substance of Sands' statement with defendant or to discuss what effect, if any, Sands' statement might have on defendant's case. In this context, the remark was not likely to elicit an incriminating response." *People v. Kowalski*, 230 Mich. App. 464 (1998).

Interrogation Does Not Apply to:

Voluntary statements not in response to police interrogation

Prompt, on the scene questions

General on-the-scene questioning as to the facts surrounding a crime or other general questioning of citizens in the fact-finding process is not affected by the holding of *Miranda*. *People v. Dunlap*, 82 Mich. App. 171 (1978).

Normal arrest and booking procedures

Sobriety questions could fall under *Miranda*, i.e. mathematical questions. *Pennsylvania v. Muniz*, 496 U.S. 582 (1990).

Miranda Warnings	
Right to Remain Silent	Right to an Attorney
Questioning must stop.	Questioning must stop.
Officers may reinitiate questioning after a reasonable period of time.	Officers may not reinitiate questioning on any crime.

RIGHT TO REMAIN SILENT

If a person invokes his or her right to remain silent, officers must stop questioning. Officers may reinitiate questioning, after a *reasonable time*, if they scrupulously honor the person's rights.

Once a suspect states he or she wishes to remain silent, the questioning must stop. This right must be *scrupulously* honored. But reinitiating questioning two hours later by a different police officer on an unrelated murder was permissible. *Michigan v. Mosley*, 423 U.S. 96 (1975).

A suspect was arrested for murder and was advised of her rights. She invoked her right to remain silent. Officers initiated questioning 22 hours later on the same charges. The court held that where the officers *scrupulously honor* the defendant's rights by stopping the questioning when she requested them to stop, officers could reinitiate questioning 22 hours later. The key is whether the "police scrupulously honored the assertion of the right to cut off questioning" and did not persist in "repeated efforts to wear down her resistance." *People v. Slocum*, 219 Mich. App. 695 (1996).

Tacit Admission

> A tacit admission is an acknowledgment of guilt inferred from silence. Silence in response to accusation of criminal activity is generally not admissible. *People v. Bobo*, 390 Mich. 355 (1973).
>
> A defendant was a Salvation Army truck driver who went to the victim's house to pick up a donation. The next day, the victim noticed a ring was missing. She reported the larceny and a detective called the defendant and requested him to come to the station. Defendant agreed, but never showed up. At trial, the prosecutor stated that the defendant must be guilty of the crime because he did not accept the invitation to discuss the crime with the detective. The conviction was reversed because of the statements made by the prosecutor. *People v. Greenwood*, 209 Mich. App. 470 (1995).

Silence and Demeanor During Custodial Interrogation

The Fifth Amendment does not preclude use of testimony concerning defendant's behavior and demeanor after a valid waiver of rights. When a defendant speaks after receiving his or her warnings, a momentary pause or even a failure to answer a question will not be construed as an assertion of the right to remain silent.

> If defendant refuses to say anything after being given *Miranda* warnings, testimony regarding the refusal would be improper. *People v. McReavy*, 436 Mich. 197 (1990).

"FIFTH AMENDMENT" RIGHT TO COUNSEL

Once the Fifth Amendment right to counsel has been invoked, all questioning must stop!

The right to an attorney cannot be found in the wording of the Fifth Amendment, but has been gleaned from the *Miranda* decision. The *Miranda* decision held that to protect a person from being compelled to incriminate him or herself during a custodial interrogation he or she must be informed of his right to an attorney. In the case of *United States v. Dickerson*, 530 U.S. 428 (2000), the U.S. Supreme Court held that the *Miranda* decision was based on the Constitution and that an act of Congress could not overturn it. For these reasons, a "Fifth Amendment right to counsel" during custodial interrogation was created.

Once a suspect has invoked his or her right to counsel under *Miranda*, the suspect may not be subjected to further interrogation until counsel is present, unless:

- The suspect voluntarily initiates further conversation, **and**
- Waives the previous request for counsel after a fresh set of warnings.

> After being arrested on a state criminal charge and after being informed of his *Miranda* rights, the suspect was questioned by the police on January 19, 1976, until he said that he wanted an attorney. Questioning then ceased, but on January 20, police officers came to the jail and, after stating that they wanted to talk to him and again informing petitioner of his *Miranda* rights, obtained his confession after he said that he was willing to talk. The Court held the use of the defendant's confession against him at his trial violated his right under the Fifth and Fourteenth Amendments to have counsel present during custodial interrogation, as declared in *Miranda*. Having exercised his right on January 19 to have counsel present during interrogation, petitioner did not validly waive that right on the 20th. *Edwards v. Arizona*, 451 U.S. 477 (1981).
>
> A suspect was arrested and advised of his *Miranda* rights prior to questioning. He requested an attorney and the questioning stopped. *Three days later*, a different officer advised defendant of his rights and questioned him about an unrelated crime. The officer was unaware of defendant's earlier request for counsel. During this interrogation, the suspect incriminated himself. The Court held that when a suspect in police custody requests an attorney after *Miranda, no further questioning can be conducted regarding the present charge or any other charge.* The right to the continued assistance of coun-

Reassertion of Rights

> A defendant who has waived his or her rights may reassert them at any time. *Miranda v. Arizona*, 384 U.S. 436 (1966).

VOLUNTARINESS STANDARD

Determination of Voluntariness

The privilege against self-incrimination protects compelled statements, not voluntary ones. The court, rather than the jury, will determine if a statement was voluntarily given by looking at the "totality of the circumstances." This is determined in a Walker hearing. The standard used is a preponderance of the evidence. The defendant may testify at a Walker hearing as to his or her version of the facts surrounding the alleged statements without waiving his or her right to remain silent at trial or any other right.

"Totality of the Circumstances"

In *People v. Cipriano*, 431 Mich. 315 (1988), the Michigan Supreme Court provided guidance to assist in determining if a statement is voluntary. The Court held that a trial court should consider the totality of the circumstances, which include the following:

- Age
- Education
- Intelligence
- Criminal experience
- Lack of advice of constitutional rights
- Unnecessary delay
- Injuries
- Intoxication/drugs
- Ill health
- Deprivation of food, sleep, or medical attention
- Physical abuse
- Threats of abuse

> At statement was voluntarily made where the evidence showed the defendant permitted the police officers to enter her apartment building and permitted them to enter her apartment. The officers did not display weapons, and the officer indicated that he informed the defendant several times that she was not under arrest. The officer also told defendant that if she wanted them to leave, they would go. Contrary to defendant's contention, her subjective belief that she was not free to leave (because the officer asked her about the murder) is not dispositive because an objective assessment of the totality of the circumstances indicates that she was not in custody or under arrest when she gave her oral statement. Defendant proceeded to give a statement, largely in narrative form, with little police questioning. She fully acknowledged that she was not compelled or coerced to give a statement. *People v. Coomer*, 245 Mich. App. 206 (2001).

Coercive Police Activity

> While defendant's mental condition may be a significant factor in determining voluntariness, it alone, without regard to official coercion, cannot violate the voluntariness standard. *Colorado v. Connelly* 479 U.S. 157 (1986).

> Coercive police activity is a necessary predicate to a finding that a confession is not voluntary. Coercive police conduct may be psychological, as well as physical. *People v. DeLisle*, 183 Mich. App. 713 (1990).

Pre-Arraignment Delay

> Where the purpose in delaying a suspect's arraignment is to obtain a confession, the confession will be suppressed. *People v. Hamilton*, 359 Mich. 410 (1960).

> If the totality of the circumstances indicates that the confession was voluntarily given, it should not be excluded from evidence solely because of pre-arraignment delay. *People v. Feldman*, 181 Mich. App. 523 (1989).

> A confession was still admissible under the totality of the circumstances where an 81-hour delay in arraignment was due to difficulty in getting the paperwork done and a change in the detective assignments due to vacations. Prior to getting the paperwork together, the suspect asked to talk to the officer in charge. The Court

held "The record indicates that suspect, who was 19 years old at the time of her arrest, received *Miranda* warnings prior to giving her inculpatory statement. She testified that she both read and understood her rights. She further testified that the police did not deprive her of food, water, or sleep. The detective testified that she did not appear to be under the influence of any drug or other intoxicant, and that she did not appear to need medical attention. Finally, we note that the suspect, rather than the police, initiated the discussion that resulted in her giving the inculpatory statement." *People v. Manning*, 244 Mich. App. 615 (2000).

Physical Abuse

Confession was inadmissible when obtained by whipping and hanging of the defendant. *Brown v. Mississippi*, 297 U.S. 278 (1936).

The defendant was convicted of two counts of armed robbery. He argued that the police obtained his confession by physical compulsion. The court held that, under the totality of the circumstances, the defendant made a voluntary confession to the police. The court reasoned that, although the police told the defendant that "rapists get kicked around in jail," there was no physical abuse by the police. *People v. Hardy*, 151 Mich. App. 605 (1986).

Injury

A detective interrogated Mincey while he was in the intensive care unit of a hospital. Mincey was wounded, had partial paralysis of his right leg, was receiving drugs, and had tubes in his mouth, arms, and bladder. Mincey was unable to talk, but could communicate with paper and pencil. The detective advised Mincey of his rights and continued to question him until midnight, ceasing questioning whenever Mincey would lose consciousness. The Court held that statements made by the defendant while he was in the hospital, in great pain, almost to the point of a coma, while he was encumbered by tubes, needles, and a breathing apparatus, were involuntary and could not be used against him. *Mincey v. Arizona*, 437 U.S. 385 (1978).

Threats

Confessions obtained by threats or playing on fears, real or imagined, are inadmissible (i.e., "If you don't talk, we'll see you lose your child.") *People v. Richter*, 54 Mich. App. 598 (1974).

A statement obtained from a defendant who was informed that his pregnant wife would be jailed if he did not confess, is inadmissible. *People v. Robinson*, 386 Mich. 551 (1972).

The defendant was charged with first degree murder. At a preliminary hearing, he wanted the court to suppress his oral and written confessions due to threats by police. Specifically, the defendant was told he "needed his ass beat for going around shooting people." The court held that under the totality of the circumstances, the confession the police obtained from defendant was involuntary and should be suppressed. *People v. Jordan*, 149 Mich. App. 568 (1986).

Promises

Statements are inadmissible if obtained by any direct or implied promises, however slight. *Bram v. United States*, 168 U.S. 532 (1897).

Promises made by someone acting with authority, which would lead a person to believe he will get off easier if he confesses, makes subsequent statements inadmissible. *People v. Cleveland*, 251 Mich. 542 (1930).

An officer's statement that he would do what he could to help and that cooperation was usually taken into account at sentencing, did not amount to an improper promise that would render the confession involuntary. *People v. Ewing*, 102 Mich. App. 81 (1980).

A promise to release a third person who is not a relative of the defendant's does not alone constitute coercion, which would render a confession inadmissible. To promise to release a relative, though, may result in a finding that the confession was involuntarily made. *People v. Smith*, 124 Mich. App. 723 (1983).

The two-part test for promises

- Did the suspect reasonably understand the statements by the police to be promises of leniency?
- Did the defendant rely upon the promise in deciding to make a confession and prompted by the promise to give the statement?

People v. Conte, 421 Mich. 704 (1984).

Plea Bargaining

- Statements made by the defendant to a prosecuting attorney during plea negotiations cannot be used if:
  - The defendant had an actual subjective expectation to negotiate a plea during the discussion, and
  - The expectation was reasonable given the totality of the objective circumstances. MRE 410; *People v. Dunn*, 446 Mich. 409 (1994)

Even though a plea bargain is the basis of a statement and the defendant violates the plea bargain, the statement will be inadmissible as it is involuntary under MRE 410. *People v. Conte*, 421 Mich. 704 (1984).

The rights under plea negotiations may be waived

The defendant may waive the protections under plea bargaining. An agreement, extracted as a condition of plea bargaining, may be used for impeachment purposes if the bargain fails, unless the defendant made the waiver without knowledge or under coercion. *United States v. Mezzanatto*, 513 U.S. 196 (1995).

During plea negotiations, defendant admitted to being involved in a robbery and murder. At each of the interviews, he was given warnings about the use of statements that he might make. A plea arrangement was reached, but when he was in front of the judge, he changed his mind and stated that he no longer wanted to take the plea bargain. The question then arose on whether the admissions he made during the plea negotiations could be used against him during the trial. The Michigan Supreme Court held that the statements could be used against him and possibly be introduced in the prosecutor's case-in-chief. MRE 410(4) provides that "any statement made in the course of plea discussions with a prosecutor is generally inadmissible at trial. However, the criminal defendant may waive this right as long as they are [sic] appropriately advised and as long as the statements are voluntarily, knowingly and understandingly made." *People v. Stevens*, 461 Mich. 655 (2000)

Deception, Trick, or Fraud

Use of deception, trick, or fraud to induce a statement will not alone render that statement inadmissible. KEY: If it tends to induce a *false* statement, that statement will be excluded. *People v. Dunnigan*, 163 Mich. 349 (1910).

Falsely telling the defendant that his co-conspirator had confessed would not in itself make a confession involuntary. *Frasier v. Cupp*, 394 U.S. 731 (1969).

The fact that the police misrepresented to defendant that his fingerprints were discovered on an article retrieved from the crime scene is insufficient, by itself, to render the statement involuntary. *People v. Hicks*, 185 Mich. App. 107 (1990).

During a custodial interrogation that lasted from midnight to 3 a.m., a detective lied to the suspect, first by telling him that a witness had placed him at the scene of the crime. The officer then showed the suspect phony charts and photographs purporting to indicate a fingerprint expert's determination that the suspect's prints were at the scene. Finally, the officer staged an identification by a female officer posing as the victim. The Court held the confession was admissible as voluntarily given and the trickery did not tend to induce a false statement. An officer must remember, though, that he or she will have to testify in court about the process used to obtain a statement. *Ledbetter v. Edwards*, 35 F.3d 1062 (6th Cir. 1994).

The defendant is entitled to have the jury hear the circumstances of the confession, even if the judge has determined it to be given voluntarily. *Crane v. Kentucky*, 476 U.S. 683 (1986).

Corpus Delecti

A confession by itself cannot establish the corpus delecti. A voluntary confession, made extrajudicially, is only received as evidence of guilt and by itself cannot establish guilt. The purpose of this rule is to prevent a person's confession from convicting him of a crime he did not commit. *People v. Ish*, 252 Mich. App. 115 (2002).

A woman disappeared without a trace in 1985. In 1990, police were investigating the defendant when he confessed to killing her. He stated that he had cut the body up and had thrown it into a dumpster. Besides the confession, there was no other evidence. The Court reversed the defendant's second-degree murder conviction and held there must be evidence independent of the confession to uphold the murder conviction. *People v. McMahan*, 451 Mich. 543 (1996).

JUVENILES—MCL 712A.14

A juvenile, under the age of 17, must, on being arrested, be immediately taken before the family division of the circuit court or released to a parent.

The court should look at the following when determining the *totality of the circumstances* as it relates to juvenile confessions:

- Whether the juvenile was advised of his or her rights and clearly understood those rights.
- The degree of police compliance with applicable statutes and juvenile rules (i.e., MCL 712A.14).
- The presence of an adult, parent, custodian, or guardian.
- The juvenile background.
- The juvenile's age, education, and intelligence level and extent of defendant's prior experience with police.
- The length of detention before statement is made.
- The repeated and prolonged nature of the questioning.
- Whether the juvenile was injured, intoxicated, in ill health, physically abused or threatened with abuse, or deprived of food, sleep, or medical attention.

People v. Good, 186 Mich. App. 180 (1990) and *People v. Hana*, 443 Mich. 202 (1993).

Police received a tip that the defendant was involved in an armed robbery. They interviewed him in a detention center where he was being held. Since he was 16 years old, the officers contacted his mother. She had no objections to the interview. The officers ascertained that the defendant could read and write and was not taking medication. He was then advised of his rights and signed a waiver that he would talk without an attorney. Initially, he denied involvement, but then asked if he could make a deal with the prosecutor. The officers said that his cooperation would be noted in their reports to the prosecutor. During the interview the officers asked if there was any way that the defendant's fingerprints could have been left on the cash register. In fact, no prints had been obtained. Defendant stated that this could have happened as he was reaching for one of the clerks that had been shot. He eventually confessed to the crime. The court upheld the confession under the "totality of the circumstances." His mother had given her permission to interview him. There was a determination that he could read and write and was not under the influence of anything. Also, there was no promise of leniency made. "We do not believe that the mere pledge to note defendant's cooperation in a police report, without more, could reasonably be considered a promise of leniency." Also, the statement about the fingerprints did not make defendant's statement involuntary. It may have been a misrepresentation, but it did not, under the totality of the circumstances make the confession involuntary. *People v. Givans*, 227 Mich. App. 113 (1997).

Defendant, an 11-year-old, was charged with first degree murder. During a police interrogation where his mother was present, defendant confessed to the shooting. The trial court suppressed the confession claiming that due, to his age, the defendant could not intelligently waive his rights. The Court of Appeals looked at the facts and disagreed. The Court held the officers asked the defendant to explain the rights they had read to him. In reference to his right to an attorney, he stated, "that-that when the police talk to me that I can talk with my lawyer with the police." Also, "If we don't got no money, the court give me one." Finally, as to the fact that his statements may be used against him, he replied "If you say something you go to court for it." In ruling the confession was admissible, the court also found as a matter of "great significance that defendant's mother was present for, and participated in, the entire *Miranda*-waiver process." *People v. Abraham*, 234 Mich. App. 640 (1999).

A 13-year-old boy was accused of sexually touching two girls ages four and seven. The officer asked the 13-year-old and his mother to come to the station. The officer first talked to the mother and advised her of the charges and asked to talk to the 13-year-old alone. The mother agreed. The officer also advised her that she could contact an attorney for her son if she wanted to but she declined. Without advising the 13-year-old of his rights, the officer interviewed him for thirty to forty minutes during which time the juvenile confessed to the charges. The trial court suppressed the statements but the Court of Appeals reversed. "A juvenile's confession is admissible if, under the totality of the circumstances, the statement was voluntarily made." Under these circumstances *Miranda* warnings were not required and failure to give them did not result in an involuntary statement. The court further noted that there was no claim made that either the statute or court rules pertaining to juveniles were violated. "In addition, we find that the separation of defendant from his mother, although potentially troublesome in an analysis of the voluntariness of a statement, under the totality of the circumstances here, does not merit a finding that defendant's statement was involuntary. Defendant knew his mother had consented to his talking alone with the officer and that she was readily available to him. No manipulation of defendant or his mother by the police is established by the circumstances. To the contrary, everything was done openly and with the knowledge and consent of defendant and his mother." *People v. SLL*, 246 Mich. App. 204 (2001).

A statement obtained in violation of M.C.L. 764.27 and MCR 5.934 is not subject to automatic suppression because of the violation. Rather, the violation is considered as part of the totality of the circumstances to determine whether the statement was voluntary. *People v. Hall*, 249 Mich. App. (2002).

QUESTIONING BY PERSONS OTHER THAN LAW ENFORCEMENT

Generally, questioning by persons other than law enforcement will not require *Miranda*, unless the individual is working with the police.

Security Guards

Private investigators are not officers of the law and therefore are not required to comply with *Miranda*. *People v. Omell*, 15 Mich. App. 154 (1968).

Incriminating statements made by a defendant to private retail security personnel may be admitted at trial as long as the security officer did not act at the instigation of the police nor function with their assistance or cooperation. *Grand Rapids v. Impens*, 414 Mich. 667 (1982).

Corrections Officers

Defendant was held in a juvenile facility in South Carolina. He was being held on a homicide that had occurred in Michigan. During his stay, he made a statement to a correction supervisor. The Court held that clearly, defendant was in custody, but the supervisor had no arrest or detention authority and was not shown to be acting at the behest of the police. *Miranda* warnings were not required. *People v. Anderson*, 209 Mich. App. 527 (1995).

Inmates

A jailed suspect is not entitled to *Miranda* warnings when he makes a voluntary statement to an undercover agent he believes to be another inmate. A police-dominated atmosphere and compulsion are not present. *Illinois v. Perkins*, 496 U.S. 292 (1990).

KEY: Undercover agent cannot ask questions about crime that defendant was charged, arraigned, and requested an attorney on. Mere listening is okay. *Kuhlmann v. Wilson*, 477 U.S. 436 (1986).

Protective Service Workers

Statements made by a defendant to a protective service worker are admissible where the worker was not acting at the behest of the police. *People v. Porterfield*, 166 Mich. App. 562 (1988).

REMEDIES FOR VIOLATION OF RIGHTS
Exclusionary Rule

A confession illegally obtained will be excluded. Also, any evidence obtained through that confession will also be excluded under the Fruit of the Poisonous Tree Doctrine. For example, in the Christian Burial case, the defendant was arrested in connection with the disappearance of a 10-year-old girl. He invoked his rights. As he rode in the police car, the detective began to converse with him. The detective knew that the defendant was deeply religious and so presented what is now called the "Christian Burial" speech in an attempt to recover the little girl's body. The defendant confessed and led the officer to the body. Not only was the confession suppressed, but also the body and all the evidence that was located through the unlawful confession. *Brewer v. Williams*, 430 U.S. 387 (1977).

"A seizure of the person within the meaning of the Fourth and Fourteenth Amendments occurs when, taking into account all of the circumstances surrounding the encounter, the police conduct would have communicated to a reasonable person that he was not at liberty to ignore the police presence and go about his business. In this case a 17-year-old boy was awakened in his bedroom at three in the morning by at least three police officers, one of whom stated we need to go and talk. He was taken out in handcuffs, without shoes, dressed only in his underwear in January, placed in a patrol car, driven to the scene of a crime and then to the sheriff's offices, where he was taken into an interrogation room and questioned. This evidence points to an arrest. Since he was arrested before he was questioned, and because the state does not even claim that the sheriff's department had probable cause to detain him at that point, well-established precedent requires suppression of the confession unless that confession was an act of free will sufficient to purge the primary taint of the unlawful invasion. *Miranda* warnings, alone and per se, cannot always break, for Fourth Amendment purposes, the causal connection between illegality of arrest and confession." *Kaupp v. Texas*, 538 U.S. 626 (2003).

Exceptions

Inevitable Discovery

Evidence obtained through an illegal confession may still be admissible if:

- Police were actively pursuing the evidence, and
- The evidence would have been found anyway as a result of an ongoing investigation. *People v. Kroll*, 179 Mich. App. 423 (1989) and *Nix v. Williams*, 467 U.S. 431 (1984).

Generally, the inevitable discovery rule will not apply to confessions taken after an unlawful arrest. *People v. Thomas*, 191 Mich. App. 576 (1991).

Public Safety

Officers were dispatched to a rape that had just occurred where the suspect had used a gun. As the officers were interviewing the victim, she saw the suspect enter a grocery store. The officers entered the store and attempted to arrest him. The suspect ran and officers lost sight of him for a few minutes before catching him and placing him under arrest. As they searched him, they found an empty holster. They immediately asked him where the gun was. He admitted to having a gun and told the officers where he threw it in the store. The Court held that where spontaneous questioning of a suspect results in the gaining of evidence against the defendant, the evidence will be admissible if accomplished to protect the public from harm. *New York v. Quarles*, 467 U.S. 649 (1984).

Officers obtained an arrest warrant for Mr. Attebury after he assaulted his wife with a pistol. They had also received information that he was suicidal and homicidal. He was arrested at his house as he was in the shower. While he was getting dressed, the officers asked him if there were any weapons in the house and he responded, "Not at this time." The officers then asked him where the weapon was that was used in the assault, and he indicated that it was at his brother's house. At no time prior to this conversation were *Miranda* rights advised. The Supreme Court was then asked if the public safety exception to *Miranda* warnings applied to this case. The Court held "Defendant easily could have hidden the weapon in one of the dresser drawers to which he had immediate access. The officers' initial attempts to ascertain the location of the gun were directly related to an objectively reasonable need to secure protection from the possibility of immediate danger associated with the gun. Moreover, the pre-*Miranda* questioning in the present case related solely to neutralizing this danger. The officers only asked about the whereabouts of the gun and not other broader questions relating to investigation of the crime. Here, once the officers were satisfied that defendant posed no immediate threat of danger to them, they informed defendant of the *Miranda* rights and began their general investigation. For all of these reasons, the pre-*Miranda* questioning at issue in this case falls squarely within the public safety exception to *Miranda*." *People v. Attebury*, 463 Mich. 662 (2001).

Harmless Error

The admission of an involuntary confession at trial is subject to the harmless error analysis. This means that if the confession is suppressed and the subject can still be convicted on the other evidence presented, the error was harmless and the conviction will be upheld. *Arizona v. Fulminante*, 499 U.S. 279 (1991).

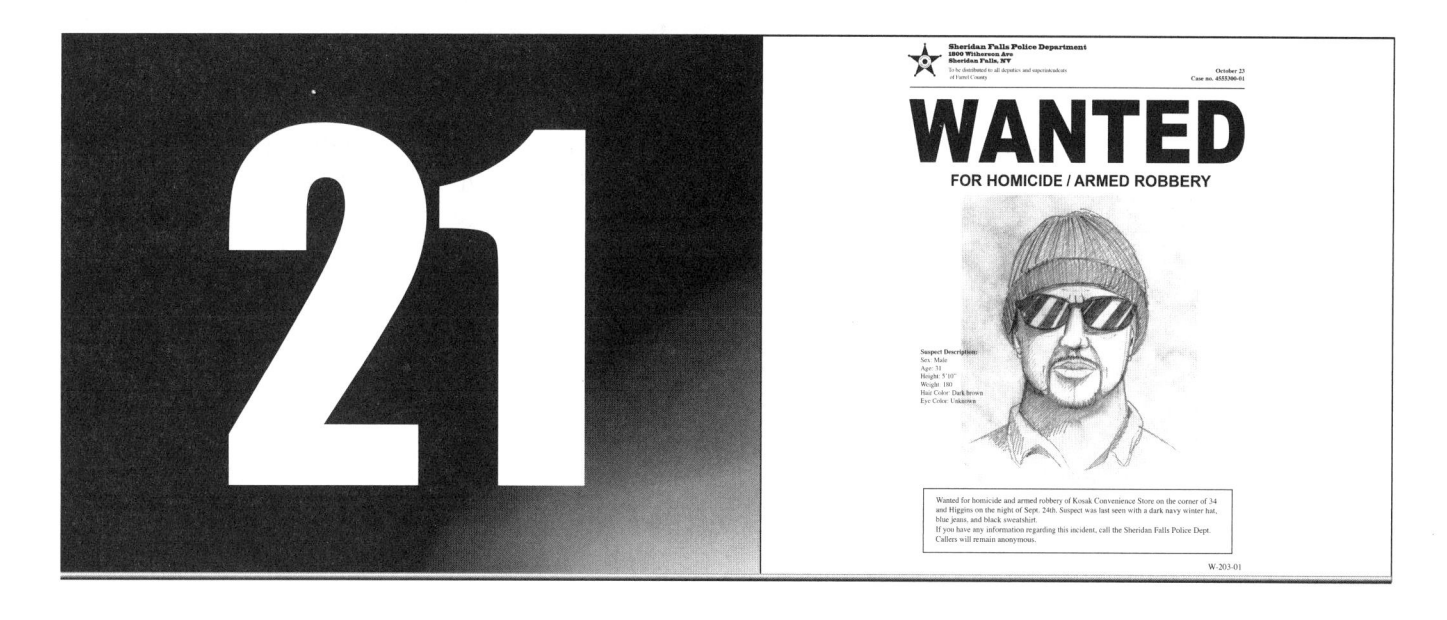

LAWS ON SUSPECT IDENTIFICATION

THREE IDENTIFICATION METHODS

The courts generally recognize three types of pretrial identification methods whereby witnesses identify suspects. The courts closely guard the identification process because of concerns over possible misidentification. Identification procedures are considered a critical stage since misidentification prior to trial will generally *cast the die and crystallize* the witnesses' opinion that the person identified was the culprit. The following methods are used:

- Corporeal Lineups
- Photo Displays
- Show-ups

Values Protected Through These Methods

Right to a fair trial

> "It is a matter of common experience that, once a witness has selected an accused out of a lineup, he is not likely to go back on his word later on...." *United States v. Wade*, 388 U.S. 218 (1966).
>
> Identification procedures that are impermissibly suggestive or conducive to misidentification violate an accused's right to due process of law. *Stovall v. Denno*, 388 U.S. 293 (1966).

> A happenstance or inadvertent encounter between a witness and the accused in the absence of counsel does not violate due process. *People v. Hampton*, 52 Mich. App. 71 (1974).
>
> To protect a person's right to a fair trial, a person who has been indicted generally has a right to counsel at any critical pretrial confrontation with an eyewitness. *California v. Gilbert*, 388 U.S. 263 (1966). (*See also Moore v. Illinois*, 434 U.S. 220 (1977): In-court identification at a preliminary hearing was found to be improper because the defendant was not represented by an attorney.)

Right to counsel

> The Michigan Supreme Court held that the right to counsel attaches only to corporeal identifications conducted at or after the initiation of adversarial judicial proceedings. The Court stated that the on-the-scene identification in this case was made before the initiation of any adversarial judicial criminal proceeding; thus, counsel

was not required. *People v. Hickman*, 470 Mich. 602 (2004). Note: In Michigan the accused has a right to counsel at photo lineups conducted while the accused is in custody. *People v. Anderson*, 389 Mich. 155 (1973).

CORPOREAL LINEUPS

A **corporeal lineup** is a police identification procedure by which the suspect in a crime is exhibited in person before the victim or witness to determine if he or she committed the offense.

It is generally recognized that a corporeal identification is superior to a photographic identification. *Simmons v. United States*, 390 US 377 (1968).

In *U.S. v. Wade*, 388 U.S. 218 (1966), the defendant was arrested for armed robbery. An attorney was appointed at his arraignment. Fifteen days later, he was place in a lineup without his counsel being notified. The Supreme Court suppressed the identification because the attorney was not present. Since the suspect was in custody, he had the right to an attorney at the lineup.

Exceptions to the right to counsel include:

- Intelligent waiver of counsel by the accused. *People v. Shipp*, 21 Mich. App. 415 (1970).
- Emergency situations requiring immediate identification. *People v. Adams*, 19 Mich. App. 131 (1969).
- Prompt on-the-scene corporeal identifications within minutes of the crime. Caution: See show-ups for the limits of this exception. *Russell v. United States*, 408 F.2d 1280 (D.C. Cir. 1969).

People v. Anderson, 389 Mich. 155 (1973).

A suspect should be advised of his or her right to have counsel at the lineup and should be encouraged to have counsel present or to have counsel appointed.

If counsel is present, then the defendant has the burden at trial of supporting any claim that the lineup was unfair or improper. If counsel is not present, the burden falls on the officer. *See People v. Haisha*, 111 Mich. App. 165 (1981) ("[W]here a criminal defendant is represented by counsel at a lineup, the burden rests upon the defendant to factually support his claim that the lineup was impermissibly suggestive."), and *People v. Young*, 21 Mich. App. 684 (1970) "([F]or identifications made at a confrontation out of the presence of defendant's attorney, the burden is on the prosecution to show fairness.").

Counsel's role at the lineup is merely that of an observer. The attorney cannot dictate how the lineup should be conducted.

The Right Against Self-Incrimination Does Not Apply To Lineups

An in-custody suspect does not have a Fifth Amendment right against selfincrimination, which allows him to refuse to stand in a lineup. If an in-custody suspect refuses to cooperate with a lineup, this can be used at trial to show knowledge of guilt. *U.S. v. Wade*, 388 U.S. 218 1926 (1966).

A suspect can be compelled to repeat words spoken by the culprit at the crime scene, as well as to make gestures or wear certain clothing. *People v. Hall*, 396 Mich. 650 (1976) (citing *U.S. v. Dionisio*, 410 U.S. 1 (1972)). NOTE: All subjects in the lineup must be asked to perform the same actions. For example in *Wade*, each person in the lineup had to put tape on his or her face and state, "Put the money in the bag."

Taking examples of defendant's handwriting did not violate the Fifth Amendment. Handwriting samples identify a physical characteristic that is not constitutionally protected. In this case, a bank robber wrote a note to the clerk. *Gilbert v. California*, 388 U.S. 263 (1966).

Fairness and Suggestibility of a Lineup Are to be Determined From the Totality of the Circumstances

Officers should use good judgment in selecting participants as to height, weight, complexion, hair, unique physical features, age, etc. A photo lineup may be necessary if the suspect is so unique that a fair physical lineup is not possible.

A suggestive lineup is not necessarily constitutionally defective. It is improper where, under the "totality of circumstances," there is a substantial likelihood of misidentification. *People v. Kurylczyk*, 443 Mich. 289 (1993) (Defendant's identification in a photo lineup was held to be admissible even though he was the only person pictured wearing a "trucker's wallet," his image was larger than the other images in the lineup, his image's background was of a different color, etc.)

The victim identified the defendant in a lineup. The defendant argued that he appeared in the lineup in the same clothing that he wore on the night of the incident. The court held that this does not automatically render the lineup impermissibly suggestive. *People v. Johnson*, 202 Mich. App. 281 (1993).

The victim identified the suspect in the lineup. The suspect asserted that the lineup was suggestive because his skin tone was darker than other participants in the lineup. The court stated that there was no indication from the victim's testimony that the tone of the defendant's skin was a factor in the identification. Nothing in the record showed that the defendant's skin tone was substantially distinguished from others in the lineup. *People v. Vaughn*, 200 Mich. App. 611 (1993) *rev'd on other grounds*, 447 Mich. 217 (1994).

During a lineup that included three people, the suspect was considerably taller than the other two and the only one wearing a leather coat similar to the one the victim stated the suspect had been wearing. The victim could not identify the suspect, so the police allowed the victim to confront the suspect "one-on-one." The victim was still not certain. Finally, the police conducted a third lineup where the suspect was the only person who was also part of the first lineup. The victim finally stated, "Yep, that is him." The Supreme Court suppressed the identification as overly suggestive. *Foster v. California*, 394 U.S. 440 (1968).

Identification procedure was overly suggestive where officers played an audiotape involving an interview of the primary suspect by two officers. The officers did not tell the witness which voice was the defendant, but the witness admitted that she knew which voices were the officers. *People v. Williams*, 244 Mich. App. 533 (2001).

Physical differences among lineup participants do not necessarily render the procedure defective. Such differences are significant only to the extent that they are apparent to the witness and substantially distinguish the defendant from the other participants. *People v. Hornsby*, 251 Mich. App. 462 (2002).

Right to a Line Up

Prior to a trial for assault, defendant's attorney requested a lineup. The trial court denied the request, and the Court of Appeals agreed.

"A right to a lineup arises when eyewitness identification has been shown to be a material issue and when there is a reasonable likelihood of mistaken identification that a lineup would tend to resolve. In the present case, eyewitness identification was a material issue; however, a lineup would not have resolved any 'mistaken identification.'" *People v. McAllister*, 241 Mich. App. 466 (2000).

PHOTOGRAPHIC LINEUPS/ PHOTO DISPLAY

Suspect Is in Custody

In-custody suspects have the same right to counsel at a photo lineup as they would at a physical lineup. Photographic lineups should not be used for suspects who are in custody, since photo lineups are inferior to physical lineups and are more likely to cause misidentification. *People v. Anderson*, 389 Mich. 155 (1973).

Exceptions to the rule. People v. Davis, 146 Mich. App. 537 (1985) (*citing People v. Anderson*, 389 Mich. 155 (1973)). Photo lineup may be used for in-custody suspects, if:

- *It is not possible to arrange a proper lineup.* For example, there are an insufficient number of persons with defendant's physical characteristics. Defend-ant was a 50-year-old, 6-foot tall black male and there were not enough persons available to make a fair lineup. *People v. Hider*, 135 Mich. App 147 (1984).

- *Nature of the case requires immediate identification*, such as a medical emergency where victim may die during surgery. *People v. Adams*, 19 Mich. App. 131 (1969).
- *Witnesses are <u>very</u> distant* from the in-custody accused. One possible example of this involved a defendant in a Michigan case who was lodged in Tennessee. *People v. Thornton*, 62 Mich. App. 763 (1975).
- *Subject refuses to participate* or acts to destroy the value of the identification procedure. *People v. Anderson*, 389 Mich. 155 (1973).
- *Protecting a child of tender years.* For example, a photo display was proper for identification by a 5-year-old rape victim. *People v. Currelley*, 99 Mich. App. 561 (1980).

A victim was robbed and brutally beaten. A suspect was arrested and a photo lineup was done in the hospital room before the victim went in for surgery. She was able to identify the suspect. The next day, another photo display was done after the victim's status had stabilized. Another identification was done three days before the preliminary examination. All of these were done without an attorney. The Court upheld the first identification because of exigency (it was unknown whether the victim would survive) but dismissed the other two. *People v. Anderson*, 389 Mich. 155 (1973).

Suspect Is <u>Not</u> In Custody

Corporeal lineups should be used instead of photographic displays when the suspect is not in custody but is *readily available*. A suspect is readily available when he or she could be legally compelled to appear, such as when the police have a warrant or P.C. to obtain a warrant.

Non-custodial, photographic identification procedure was used in a rape case. Police caught the suspect shortly after the crime in the victim's car as he was searching through the victim's purse. The court held that the photo display was improper since strong probable cause existed to arrest the defendant prior to the photo display and the purpose was to "build a case against the defendant by eliciting identification evidence, not to extinguish a case against innocent bystanders." *People v. Eaton*, 114 Mich. App. 330 (1982) (*citing People v. Kachar*, 400 Mich. 78 (1977)).

Some cases have held that the defendant is not readily available unless he is in custody.

People v. Harrison, 138 Mich. App. 74 (1984) ("Readily available has been construed in narrow terms. In the case at bar, while defendant was apparently cooperative and had talked with the police, we do not find he was available under the applicable case law. 'Readily available' has been strictly construed to mean subject to legal compulsion to appear at a line-up.")

Suspect has *no right to counsel at photo lineup during the pre-custody, pre-questioning, mere suspicion phase*. If counsel were required, every person in a mug book would need an attorney since they are all possible suspects. "In the case of photographic identifications, the right of counsel attaches with custody." *People v. Kurylczyk*, 443 Mich. 289 (1993).

NOTE: Defense counsel can always attack the fairness of the lineup on due process grounds, and it is the prosecution's duty to preserve the photographs. Therefore, the officer should preserve and record the lineup procedure. *People v. Wilson*, 96 Mich. App. 792 (1980).

An armed robbery suspect was arrested after a witness picked his photograph from an eight-photo display. Investigating officers viewed Lee as a possible suspect based on the similarity of his clothing to that worn by the robber. Lee had not yet been approached or questioned by the police and was not in custody. No right to counsel at this stage of the investigation. *People v. Lee*, 391 Mich. App. 618 (1974).

Defendant was a suspect in a bank robbery. His picture was included with that of five others in a photo lineup. Defendant's picture was identified, and he was arrested and placed in a corporeal lineup. Defendant argued that he should have had counsel present at the photo lineup.

A defendant is not entitled to counsel at a photo lineup merely because the investigation was focused on him. Once he was in custody, generally, a corporeal lineup is required. Where a corporeal lineup is not possible for an in-custody defendant, counsel is required for photographic lineup.

The Sixth Amendment right to counsel is not required at a photographic lineup unless the accused is in custody; only under unusual circumstances may a suspect who is not in custody have a right to counsel during a pretrial photographic lineup. *People v. Kurylczyk*, 443 Mich. 289 (1993).

Defendant is not entitled to counsel at a pre-custodial investigatory photographic lineup unless the circumstances underlying the investigation are unusual. *People v. McKenzie*, 205 Mich. App. 466 (1994).
    Examples of "unusual":

- Defendant was contacted or questioned and had been taken into custody and released before the lineup was conducted without counsel.
- Where the witness has previously made a positive identification and the clear intent of the lineup is to build a case against the defendant.

The photo should be as similar as possible, but the fact that five of the six pictures were horizontal shots and the suspect's was vertical did not make the display unduly suggestive. *People v. Dean*, 103 Mich. App. 1 (1981).

SHOW-UPS

Show-ups are one-on-one confrontations done either physically or by photograph.

Show-ups are considered highly suggestive and are likely to cause misidentification. They *should not* be used except in emergency situations (e.g., victim may die or public safety requires immediate identification) or subject to the on-the-scene exception listed below.

On-the-Scene Exception

- Justifications for the exception
    - Permits police to decide whom to arrest.
    - Prompt identification may exculpate an innocent person.
- A police officer may conduct an on-the-scene identification without counsel promptly after the crime.

Example of more than mere suspicion: Defendant entered a party store with a shotgun and stole a twelve-pack of Budweiser beer. The cashier informed the police of the type of beer that was stolen, a description of the robber, and a description of the vehicle, which included a partial license plate number. Officers observed a vehicle and driver that met the description. A chase ensued in which the suspect picked up and fired a shotgun. The suspect drove his vehicle into the police cars and was observed drinking Budweiser beer. Eventually, the suspect crashed and was arrested. The cashier was brought to the scene and identified the driver as the robber.

The court adopted the *Turner* holding and invalidated the identification. Defendant was already arrested for felonious assault on the police officer. The police may subject the defendant to an on-the-scene identification without counsel unless they have more than a mere suspicion that the suspect was responsible for the second crime. In this case, the officers had more than a mere suspicion and should have returned the defendant to the police station to conduct a lineup with counsel present. *People v. Miller*, 208 Mich. App. 495 (1995) (*citing People v. Turner*, 120 Mich. App. 23 (1982).

The victim was robbed at gunpoint by two black males in their twenties. One was wearing a tan cap and the other was wearing a black hood. After the robbery, the victim called 911 to make a report. That report was then broadcast out to surrounding agencies. Within minutes of the robbery, officers observed two subjects that met the description. They stopped the vehicle and brought the two back to the victim where an identification was made. The court believed that it may have been suggestive to bring the suspects to the victim. Further, the court felt that the fact that suspects were handcuffed during the show up also may have been suggestive. However, the court found this procedure to be reasonable and upheld the at-scene identification. *People v. Purofoy*, 116 Mich. App. 471 (1982).

The victim in this case was carjacked by two black males. The police were able to locate the car approximately one hour and 20 minutes later and a vehicle pursuit ensued. There were four occupants when the vehicle finally stopped, and two of them fled on foot. The two that fled were located by a canine unit approximately 20 minutes later. The victim was then brought to the scene where he identified the defendants. The on-scene identification occurred approximately two hours after the carjacking.

The defendants argued that too much time had elapsed between the crime and the identification. The Court of Appeals disagreed. "One of the main benefits of prompt on-the-scene identifications is to obtain reliability in the apprehension of suspects, which insures both that the police have the actual perpetrator and that any improvidently detained individual can be immediately released. Here, because the victim stated that only two males had been involved in the crime, police were confronted with the possibility that two of the four individuals apprehended from the car were not involved in the carjacking.

"Moreover, because the victim had just two hours earlier seen the perpetrators who had committed the crime upon him, it was still fresh in his mind. Hence, bringing him to the two locations where the individuals were being detained accomplished the dual purposes behind holding a prompt on-the-scene identification. The passage of almost two hours is simply not an unreasonable amount of time between the crime and the identification . . . under the facts presented in this case." *People v. Libbett*, 251 Mich. App. 353 (2002).

REMEDY FOR IMPROPER IDENTIFICATION PROCEDURES

Evidence of identification cannot be used at trial when obtained in violation of suspect's right to counsel or due process. If the witness identifies the suspect at trial after an improper identification, the prosecution must prove that the in-court identification is not tainted by the improper pretrial identification and has an independent basis.

Independent Basis Test: Whether the in-court identification is due to the perceptions of the witness at the time of the offense or due to the improper suggestiveness of the lineup or show-up.

A witness was asked to make photo identification several months after the crime. The photos were labeled with suspect's name, and the witness was aware of the suspect's name prior to the photo lineup. This was clearly a violation of due process and, thus, an in-court identification could not be used unless it had an independent basis. *People v. Kachar*, 400 Mich. 78 (1977).

Factors for the court to consider:

- Prior relationship or knowledge of the defendant.
- Opportunity to observe the offense.
- Length of time between offense and the identification procedure.
- Accuracy of pre-lineup descriptions.
- Any previous proper or improper identifications.
- Any previous identification of another person as the suspect by the witness.
- Nature of the offense and psychological state of the witness
- Idiosyncratic or special features of the defendant.

The Court held that the photo identification of the defendant in a kidnapping and sexual case assault was overly suggestive. However, the Court examined the independent basis factors and held that there was an independent basis for an in-court identification. The Court paid particular attention to the victim's previous identification of the defendant at a corporeal lineup and the length of time that she observed the crime. *People v. Gray*, 457 Mich. 107 (1998).

INANIMATE OBJECTS

Lineup procedures applicable to people are not applicable to the identification of objects. *People v. Miller*, 211 Mich. App. 30 (1995).

SEARCH AND SEIZURE

THE FOURTH AMENDMENT, U.S. CONSTITUTION

The right of the people to be secure in their persons, houses, papers, and effects, against unreasonable searches and seizures, shall not be violated, and no warrants shall be issued, but upon probable cause, supported by oath or affirmation and particularly describing the place to be searched and the persons or things to be seized.

THE SEARCH WARRANT RULE

A search warrant is required to conduct a search unless the search falls under one of the specifically stated exceptions. (*Katz v. United States*, 389 U.S. 347 [1967]) Put another way: The general rule is that police officers must have a warrant to conduct a search. There are exceptions to the general rule, which are discussed in the next chapter.

There are two policy reasons for the United States Supreme Court's interpretations requiring a search warrant. The first is to protect citizen's rights from overzealous police officers who are personally involved in the investigations. The second is to ensure that a neutral and detached magistrate makes the determination of probable cause. (*Coolidge v. New Hampshire*, 403 U.S. 443 [1971])

Minority view for search and seizure (*Robbins v. California*, 453 U.S. 420 [1981])

The dissent in Robbins argued that the Constitution only prohibits searches that are unreasonable. This view is difficult to apply because of different standards of reasonableness. Each officer may have a different level of reasonableness. Based on this, the majority of the courts have followed the requirement of the search warrant rule.

THE EXCLUSIONARY RULE

When evidence has been obtained in violation of the accused person's Constitutional rights, the evidence will be excluded (also called suppressed) from court proceedings. (*Mapp v. Ohio*, 367 U.S. 643 [1961]) This means that when officers violate the *Katz* rule, the seized evidence cannot be used against the defendant. The next chapter will discuss the exclusionary rule more fully. The purpose of this rule is to deter illegal police conduct. The rule has caused problems where the police officer was acting in good faith, but violated a technical rule, which resulted in the evidence being suppressed.

The Good Faith Exception

In the cases of *United States v. Leon*, 468 U.S. 897 (1984) and *Massachusetts v. Sheppard*, 468 U.S. 981 (1984), the United States Supreme Court recognized the good faith exception to the exclusionary rule. The Court held that the purpose of the exclusionary rule was to deter illegal police conduct. As long as the police did not act illegally and in good faith, the evidence should be admissible.

The Michigan Supreme Court has also adopted the good faith exception to the exclusionary rule in search warrant cases. The Court held that the purpose of the rule, i.e., deterring police misconduct, would not be served by applying the exclusionary rule in a case where the police officers' good faith reliance on the search warrant is objectively reasonable, even if the warrant itself was later held to be invalid. *People v. Goldston*, 470 Mich. 523 (2004).

Statutory Violations Do Not Require Evidence Suppression

Where there is no determination that a statutory violation constitutes an error of constitutional dimensions, application of the exclusionary rule is inappropriate unless the plain language of the statute indicates a legislative intent that the rule be applied. Michigan courts must determine the Legislature's intent from its words, not from its silence. *People v. Hawkins*, 468 Mich. 488 (2003).

DIFFERENCE BETWEEN THE MICHIGAN CONSTITUTION AND THE UNITED STATES CONSTITUTION

Article I, Section 11, Michigan Constitution

The person, houses, papers and possessions of every person shall be secure from unreasonable searches and seizures. No warrant to search any place or to seize any person or things shall issue without describing them, nor without probable cause, supported by oath or affirmation. The provisions of this section shall not be construed to bar from evidence in any criminal proceeding any narcotic drug, firearm, bomb, explosive or any other dangerous weapon, seized by a peace officer outside the curtilage of any dwelling house in this state.

The Michigan Constitution has no exclusionary rule for narcotic drugs, firearms, bombs, or other dangerous weapons seized outside the curtilage of a dwelling. For example, a gun that was found illegally during a traffic stop would still be admissible under the Michigan Constitution.

However, the courts have held that the protections of the Fourth Amendment and due process requirements of the Fourteenth Amendment provide that any evidence gained in violation of the U.S. Constitution will be barred by the exclusionary rule. Thus, the gun would be suppressed under the Fourth Amendment. *States can grant more protections but not fewer than those that are granted by the Bill of Rights.*

"The Michigan Supreme Court cannot impose a higher standard of scrutiny than that which would be imposed by the Supreme Court, under the Fourth Amendment, when reviewing the search of a police officer who is not within the curtilage of someone's dwelling, and who seizes narcotic drugs, firearms, bombs, or other dangerous weapons." *People v. Bullock*, 440 Mich. 15 (1992).

"Under state search and seizure law, a 'higher standard' is imposed under art. 1, § 11 of the 1963 Michigan Constitution. If, however, the item seized is, inter alia, a "narcotic drug ... seized by a peace officer outside the curtilage of any dwelling house in this state," art. 1, § 11 of the 1963 Michigan Constitution, then the seizure is governed by a standard identical to that imposed by the Fourth Amendment." *Michigan v. Long*, 463 U.S. 1032 (1983).

APPLYING THE FOURTH AMENDMENT

There Must Be Governmental Conduct

Governmental conduct for Fourth Amendment purposes generally involves a law enforcement officer or his or her agent. Actions by private citizens do not involve Fourth Amendment issues. The Bill of Rights was created to protect the people from the government and not from each other.

Besides law enforcement, another group that the courts have applied the Fourth Amendment to is public school teachers and school administrators.

> Teachers are governmental agents, but with the need to maintain order in the schools, they only need reasonable suspicion for a search. In this case a teacher found TLO in the bathroom and suspected that she had been smoking cigarettes. She was brought to the assistant principal's office where her purse was opened. The principal observed the cigarettes and after removing them observed some *Zig Zag* rolling papers commonly used for smoking marijuana. The principal then searched further and located the marijuana. The Court held that the principal was a governmental agent for Fourth Amendment purposes. However, due to the need to maintain order and safety in the school, a teacher needs the lower level of reasonable suspicion to conduct a search. In this case the teacher had the reasonable suspicion based on the *Zig Zag* papers. *New Jersey v. T.L.O.*, 469 U.S. 325 (1985).

Since the increased concern in school safety, statutes have also addressed the issue of school searches. For example, MCL 380.1306.

- A pupil who uses a locker that is property of a school district is presumed to have no expectation of privacy in that locker or that locker's contents.
- The school district must adopt a policy on searches of pupil's lockers and the locker contents taking into consideration the pupil's privacy rights in items that are not illegal or against school policy.
- A public school principal or his designee may search the pupil's locker or contents at any time in accordance with the policy.
- A law enforcement agency having jurisdiction of the school may assist school personnel in conducting a search if that assistance is at the request of the principal or his designee and in accordance with the policy.

There Must Be a Reasonable Expectation of Privacy in the Place Being Searched

A reasonable expectation of privacy is one that society and the courts are prepared to recognize as reasonable.

> Defendant used a telephone booth to make illegal bets. The FBI placed a listening device on the outside of the booth. The government argued that the listening device was on the outside, thus not in a place in which there was a reasonable expectation of privacy. The Supreme Court disagreed and held that the Fourth Amendment protects people, not places. What a person seeks to preserve in private, even in a place accessible to the public may have Fourth Amendment protections. *Katz v. United States*, 389 U.S. 347 (1967).

Physical Manipulation Invokes the Fourth Amendment

> As an officer was exiting a bus, he squeezed soft luggage that passengers had placed in the overhead storage space. In one bag he felt a brick-like object. He then asked the owner for consent to search the bag, which was given. The bag was opened and the officer located a brick of methamphetamine.
>
> The United States Supreme Court suppressed the evidence holding the search violated the owner's expectation of privacy. "Under this Court's Fourth Amendment analysis, a court first asks whether the individual, by his conduct, has exhibited an actual expectation of privacy; that is, whether he has shown that he sought to preserve something in private. Here, petitioner sought to preserve privacy by using an opaque bag and placing it directly above his seat. Second, a court inquires whether the individual's expectation of privacy is one that society is prepared to recognize as reasonable. Although a bus passenger clearly expects that passengers or bus employees may handle the bag, he does not expect that they will feel the bag in an exploratory manner. But this is exactly what the agent did here." *Bond v. United States*, 529 U.S. 334 (2000).
>
> The Sixth Circuit Court of Appeals distinguished a case from *Bond* where officers received reliable information from an informant that a subject was transporting drugs in his luggage. The Court reasoned that in the Bond case, the officers had no suspicion to believe the luggage that was handled contained controlled substances.

In this case, the officers received information that the defendant was a drug courier. "In other words, unlike the agent in Bond, the officers in this case had a reasonable belief that the luggage contained contraband before ever touching it." *U.S. v. Flowal*, 234 F.3d 932 6th Cir. (2000).

OPEN VIEW: NO EXPECTATION OF PRIVACY

What a person knowingly exposes to the public, even in his own home, is not protected under the Fourth Amendment. *Katz v. United States*, 389 U.S. 347 (1967) When something is visible to the public, the Fourth Amendment does not apply, thus neither does the search warrant rule. Open view is distinct from plain view, which is discussed in the next chapter.

Aiding Vision

An officer used a 300 mm zoom lens from 125 feet to get a picture of a defendant carrying glassine bags containing a white powder. The court held there was no expectation of privacy. *People v. Ward*, 107 Mich. App. 38 (1981).

An off-duty police officer used a pair of binoculars to see the license plate of a car parked in his neighbor's garage. He then requested a LEIN check, which indicated the vehicle as stolen. A search warrant was then obtained and executed. Defendant argued that the use of the binoculars constituted an unreasonable search and seizure. The Michigan Court of Appeals held that there is no protection for things a person knowingly exposes to the public such as the car parked in an open garage. *People v. Clark*, 133 Mich. App. 619 (1983).

Electronic Tracking Device

If attachment of the device requires entering a Fourth Amendment protected area, this would constitute a search (i.e., entering a garage or similar place to gain access to the vehicle). Also, if the installation requires entering into the vehicle the Fourth Amendment would be invoked.

An officer placed a tracking device inside a five-gallon container of chloroform that was purchased by the defendant. The defendant was followed by police, who were aided by the device, for over three days before he stopped at a cabin. A search warrant was obtained and executed.

The Supreme Court held the monitoring was neither a search nor seizure because it did not invade any legitimate expectation of privacy. "A person traveling in an automobile on public thoroughfares has no reasonable expectation of privacy in his movements from one place to another." *United States v. Knotts*, 460 U.S. 276 (1981).

The Supreme Court has held that monitoring a tracking device may sometimes be considered a search when monitoring it discloses information from inside a private residence, a location not open to visual surveillance.

But, attaching a device is not necessarily a Fourth Amendment activity because that act alone conveys no information at all and did not infringe any privacy interest.

The court noted that despite this holding, warrants for the installation and monitoring of a tracking device will obviously be desirable since it may be useful, even critical, to monitor the beeper to determine that it is actually located in a place not open to visual surveillance. *United States v. Karo*, 468 U.S. 705 (1984).

Standing on a Patrol Car

Acting on a tip, an officer stood on the bumper of his patrol car to look over a six-foot high fence. From his position he was able to see marijuana plants. The court held that the defendant could not have had expectation of privacy against someone standing on an object to look over the fence. *People v. Smola*, 174 Mich. App. 220 (1988).

Use of a Dog

A dog may sniff the outside of luggage without violating a person's expectation of privacy. (*U.S. v. Place*, 462 U.S. 696 [1983]).

After an Illinois state trooper stopped respondent for speeding and radioed in, a second trooper, overhearing the transmission, drove to the scene with his narcotics-detection dog and walked the dog around respondent's car while the first trooper wrote respondent a warning ticket. When the dog alerted at respondent's trunk, the officers searched the trunk, found marijuana, and arrested respondent. The United States Supreme Court held that a dog sniff conducted during a lawful traffic stop that reveals no information other than the location of a substance that no individual has any right to possess does not violate the Fourth Amendment. *Illinois v. Caballes*, 543 U.S. 405 (2005).

Garbage

Police suspected defendant of drug trafficking. They requested the trash collector to pick up defendant's trash and to keep it separate from the other trash. The collector then turned it over to the police. The trash had been left by the defendant at the curb for pick up. The court held that a person has no reasonable expectation of privacy in garbage left for collection outside the curtilage of residence. *California v. Greenwood*, 486 U.S. 35 (1988).

The *Greenwood* rule also applies when police, not the trash collector, pick up curbside trash. *People v. Pinnix*, 174 Mich. App. 445 (1989).

Vehicle Identification Numbers (VINs)

There is no expectation of privacy in the VIN plate and if it is obstructed from view by papers on the dashboard, the papers can be moved if there is no other way to see the VIN. *New York v. Class*, 475 U.S. 106 (1986).

A trooper stopped a motorcycle and discovered that the VIN number on the registration was not the same as on the cycle. The cycle was brought back to the post where two days later electrolysis was done to determine the actual VIN number, which corresponded to a stolen cycle. The court held there was no privacy interest in the number listed on the motorcycle's fork. Like the *Class* dashboard VIN, the fork serial number was originally in plain view. If defendant Class's efforts to obscure the dashboard VIN with papers, probably inadvertent, created no Fourth Amendment privacy interest, then neither did the guilty efforts of one who defaced the motorcycle fork. *People v. Dinsmore*, 166 Mich. App. 33 (1988) (vacated on other grounds).

There is no VIN exemption to the search warrant rule. Officers must rely on the "automobile exception," another exception, or a search warrant to search for *hidden* VINs within the vehicle. *People v. Wilson*, 257 Mich. App 337 (2003).

Helicopter, Airplane

A person has no reasonable expectation of privacy in activities that can be viewed from the air. Police in a helicopter descended to 400 feet and observed marijuana plants growing in the defendant's greenhouse. The court held that the search was valid because the helicopter was not violating any FAA rules. *Florida v. Riley*, 488 U.S. 445 (1989).

Thermal Imaging

Using sense-enhancing technology to obtain information regarding a home's interior that could not otherwise be obtained without physical intrusion is a search where the technology is not in general public use. *Kyllo v. United States*, 533 U.S. 27 (2001).

Rest Areas

The stall of the rest room is protected, but not the common areas. *People v. Lillis*, 181 Mich. App. 315 (1989).

Hospital Room

There is no expectation of privacy in a hospital room. A patient does maintain an expectation of privacy in the drawers and closets, but not in the room itself. *People v. Courts*, 205 Mich. App. 326 (1994).

Jail Cell

A search of defendant's jail cell did not violate his Fourth Amendment right to privacy. *People v. Phillips*, 219 Mich. App 159 (1996).

Includes prison cells. *People v. Herndon*, 246 Mich. App. 371 (2001).

Running Registration Plates

A police officer may properly run a computer check on a license plate number in open view even if the vehicle is not observed to violate any traffic law and there is no other information to suggest that a crime has been or is being committed. That is, there is no probable cause or articulable suspicion requirement to run a computer check of a license plate number in which there is no expectation of privacy. In the absence of evidence to the contrary, a police officer may reasonably suspect that a vehicle is being driven by its registered owner.

Where information gleaned from a computer check provides a basis for the arrest or further investigation of the registered owner of the vehicle, a police officer may initiate an investigatory stop to determine if the driver is the registered owner of the vehicle. In the course of the investigatory stop the officer may request identification and may act to reasonably secure his own safety. *People v. Jones*, 260 Mich. App. 424 (2004).

The Workplace

Defendant was convicted for possession of stolen property. He claimed his office was improperly searched because the officers did not on the basis that the office was shared with another person who could invite anyone into the office. The supervisor also had access to the work area. Also, security, the custodial staff, and one other person had keys to the office. Ultimately, the amount of control a person has over his or her work space will dictate whether he or she has a reasonable expectation of privacy in it; the more control the person has, the more likely a court will find he or she has an expectation of privacy there. *People v. Powell*, 235 Mich. App. 557 (1999).

Abandonment

While on patrol, officers observed a subject running from a dwelling. As they chased him, they observed him throw a bag away. The bag was retrieved and officers located cocaine inside. The court ruled that once the defendant abandoned the bag, he relinquished any reasonable expectation of privacy in the bag and its contents. *People v. Mamon*, 435 Mich. 1 (1990).

A person does not have to give up ownership in property for it to be abandoned for Fourth Amendment purposes. He or she simply needs to give up his or her reasonable expectation of privacy in it, e.g., placing it where anyone could have access to it and/or failing to assert a property interest in it while observing another search the property. *People v. Henry*, 477 Mich. 1123 (2007).

Entry into and contemporaneous search of an abandoned structure is presumptively reasonable because the owner no longer has an expectation of privacy in the property that he or she has abandoned. *People v. Taylor*, 253 Mich. App. 399 (2002).

Open Fields

Open fields beyond the curtilage are not protected by the Fourth Amendment, thus observation of those areas does not constitute a search. *United States v. Dunn*, 480 U.S. 294 (1987).

Even if real property located outside the curtilage of a home is posted against trespassing, officers entering the property and finding evidence have not conducted a search within the meaning of the Fourth Amendment. *Oliver v. United States*, 466 U.S. 170 (1984).

THE CURTILAGE SURROUNDING A RESIDENCE IS PROTECTED

DEA agents tracked large quantities of chemicals used for making controlled substances to a barn on defendant's ranch. The barn was behind the house. The house was completely surrounded by a barbed wire fence. The barn was outside the barbed-fence, but was inside a wooden fence. The agents jumped over the wooden fence and shined a flashlight through a window where they saw a drug laboratory. The agents then secured a warrant based on their observations.

The United States Supreme Court held that the barn was not within the curtilage of the home and thus not under the home's Fourth Amendment protection where it was located 50 yards from fence surrounding home and 60 yards from home itself, where the barn was not within area surrounding home that was enclosed by fence, where law enforcement officials possessed objective data indicating that barn was not being used for intimate activities of home, and where owner did little to protect barn from observation by those standing in open fields. *U.S. v. Dunn*, 480 U.S. 294 (1987).

Four Point Test for Determining Curtilage

1. Proximity of area to the home.
2. Whether the area is in an enclosure surrounding the home.
3. The nature of the area's use.
4. Steps taken to protect the area from observation.

Technical Trespass

Officers received a call that a car was being stripped and that the suspects were taking the parts to a garage located at the rear of a particular address. The police found a stripped auto and approached the garage. The officers entered the backyard from the alley and approached a door on the side of the garage. Through a window, the officers observed the defendants removing parts from a vehicle. Upon entry, they determined the vehicle to be stolen and the subjects were arrested.

The Michigan Supreme Court held that a technical trespass would not automatically make a search unreasonable and that what the police did here did not constitute a search. "The police did not enter defendant's home or peer into the windows of his home. Rather, they looked into an unattached garage, which abutted a public alley from a common access route, . . . *The route which any visitor to a residence would use is not private in the Fourth Amendment sense, and thus if police take the route for the purpose of making a general inquiry or for some other legitimate reason, they are free to keep their eyes open . . .* " *People v. Houze*, 425 Mich. 82 (1986).

Officers had reason to believe that a house contained controlled substances. The officers approached the residence and noticed that the window immediately to the left of the door had its inside blinds pulled up. With the aid of a flashlight, one officer observed what was in the house. Based on these observations, a search warrant was sought and executed. The Court of Appeals upheld the observations made by the officers. "Because the officer was properly present on defendant's porch when he observed the objects in defendant's window, his actions were entirely proper." The Court focused on the fact that the officer was lawfully on the front porch and that the homeowner left the blinds open. Thus, it was not reasonable for him to expect privacy when anyone on the porch could look though the window. *People v. Custer*, 248 Mich. App. 552 (2001).

Troopers learned that defendant was a suspect in the murders of two of his co-workers at the Michigan Department of Corrections prison facility and went to his house. The officers went to a door on an enclosed porch and knocked and received no answer. They then opened the unlocked porch door and entered through the porch to knock at the inner residence door. Looking through the window the officers observed defendant, slumped at a table with his back to the door. A rifle and ammunition were visible next to him. When he did not respond to loud knocking, the troopers entered the residence and took defendant into custody.

The Court held that defendant did not have a reasonable expectation of privacy in the enclosed porch of his parents' home. The porch appeared to be an entryway into the home. There was no doorbell located on the exterior door (which was a screen door), while there was a doorbell on the inner door. The porch did not have the characteristics of a living area. Rather, it was an unheated area used primarily as storage space. Like any other visitor desiring to speak to the occupant of the residence, the police simply entered the porch to access the inner door adjacent to the residence. Police conducting an investigation may go to places visitors may be expected to go (e.g., walkways, driveways, porches). Therefore, the police actions were reasonable and did not violate the Fourth Amendment. *People v. Tierney*, 266 Mich. App. 687 (2005).

CRIME SCENES

The United States Supreme Court has consistently held that there is no crime scene exception to the search warrant rule. A person still maintains an expectation of privacy in his residence even if he has committed a crime.

Undercover officers went to buy heroin from a house. While in the house, an altercation arose where an officer was shot and killed. Back-up officers arrived and entered the residence without a warrant to search for other victims. Homicide detectives then arrived and searched the residence for four days. During the search all drawers, cupboards, clothing, closets, etc., were examined and sections of carpet were removed. A total of two to three hundred items were seized as evidence.

The United States Supreme Court invalidated the search. "The police may make warrantless entries and searches when they reasonably believe that a person within is in need of immediate aid and that police officers may enter a homicide scene to see if there are other victims or if the killer is still on the premises. Any evidence found in plain view during these searches is admissible." The Court held, however, a search outside of these parameters is unconstitutional without a warrant. *Mincey v. Arizona*, 437 U.S. 385 (1978).

The defendant shot and killed her husband and then attempted suicide. She was unsuccessful before family and police found her. The responding officers transported her to the hospital and secured the scene. Thirty-five minutes later, two members of the homicide unit arrived and conducted a follow-up investigation and commenced a general exploratory search for evidence finding a suicide note from the wife that included a statement that she had killed her husband. The Supreme Court held that the police may make warrantless entry where they reasonably believe a person is in need of immediate attention, and they may make a prompt warrantless search of the area to see if there are other victims or if the killer is on the premise. However, there is no murder scene exception to the search warrant and once the scene was secured, the officers should have obtained a warrant before further searching. *Thompson v. Louisiana*, 469 U.S. 17 (1984).

Mr. and Mrs. Flippo were vacationing at a cabin in a state park. Mr. Flippo called 911 to report that they had been attacked. When the officers arrived, they located Mr. Flippo outside with wounds to his head and feet. They entered the cabin and discovered that Mrs. Flippo had been killed. The officers then secured the scene and Mr. Flippo was taken to the hospital. When investigators arrived, they entered the cabin and searched for over 16 hours. At one point they opened a briefcase and located pictures of a man who appears to be taking off his jeans. These pictures were entered into evidence to support the theory that Mr. Flippo murdered his wife. The United States Supreme Court suppressed the pictures. "This position squarely conflicts with *Mincey v. Arizona, supra,* where we rejected the contention that there is a 'murder scene exception' to the warrant clause of the Fourth Amendment. We noted that police may make warrantless entries onto premises if they reasonably believe a person is in need of immediate aid and may make prompt warrantless searches of a homicide scene for possible other victims or a killer on the premises, but we rejected any general 'murder scene exception' as 'inconsistent with the Fourth and Fourteenth Amendments.'" *Flippo v. West Virginia,* 528 U.S. 11 (1999).

STANDING: RESIDENCE/VEHICLE

In order to challenge a search, a person must have "standing," which means an expectation of privacy in the place being searched.

Police removed evidence from an apartment that was rented by defendant's mother after searching with an invalid warrant. Since defendant did not have an expectation of privacy in the apartment, he did not have standing to attack the search. It was the defendant's mother, not the defendant, who had a reasonable expectation of privacy in the apartment. *United States v. Salvucci,* 448 U.S. 83 (1980).

Neither legitimately being at a particular place nor possession of items seized automatically gives a defendant standing to challenge a search. *Rakas v. Illinois,* 439 U.S. 128 (1978).

Defendant was wanted on an armed robbery where a victim was killed. Police confirmed that defendant was an overnight guest at a duplex and later received a call that he was there. They surrounded the residence, entered without permission, and arrested the defendant. The Court held that the defendant had a reasonable expectation of privacy as an overnight guest. *Minnesota v. Olson,* 495 U.S. 91 (1990).

The defendants were invited to another person's house to package cocaine. A police officer observed them through a window. The officer stood 12 to 18 inches away from the apartment when he made his observations. The defendants were there approximately 2 1/2 hours. When they left, they were stopped and arrested for possessing 47 grams of cocaine. They argued that the observations of the police were illegal under the Fourth Amendment. The United States Supreme Court did not even answer that question because it held that the defendants did not have any standing to challenge the observations due to their short stay at the apartment. The Court made a distinction between this visit and an overnight guest who does have an expectation of privacy.

In reaching its decision the Court looked at the following factors:

- The purely commercial nature of the transaction.
- The relatively short period of time on the premises.
- The lack of any previous connection between the defendants and the householder. *Minnesota v. Carter,* 525 U.S. 83 (1998).

Defendant was a passenger in a vehicle where a .22 caliber pistol was located. The mere fact that defendant was in the car with the owner's permission immediately prior to the search did not endow him with a reasonable expectation of privacy in the area searched. *People v. Smith,* 106 Mich. App. 203 (1981).

PRIVATE CONVERSATIONS

If one party to a conversation consents to someone taping or listening into the conversation, a search warrant is not needed. Search warrants still are needed where neither party consents. *People v. Collins,* 438 Mich. 8 (1991).

PRETEXT STOPS

Undercover vice officers observed two subjects acting suspiciously in a vehicle. As the officers turned to investigate, the vehicle took off quickly and made a right turn without using a turn signal. The officers stopped the vehicle for failing to use a turn signal. When they approached the car, they observed a plastic baggie in the passenger's hands with a substance believed to be cocaine.

The Court held the stop to be valid. The justices refused to look at the officer's subjective reasons for making the stop and instead asked if the officer "could have" made the stop. Failing to use a signal when turning is a violation of law and thus the stop was reasonable. As long as the officers have probable cause that a violation has occurred, the stop will be reasonable under the Fourth Amendment. *Whren v. United States*, 517 U.S. 806 (1996)

Officers were waiting to obtain a narcotics search warrant for a residence when Mr. Haney approached. He exited his vehicle, went to the house, and exchanged money for a package. He returned to his car and drove off. A marked unit was called to stop him. He failed to use his turn signal and was stopped. When he failed to produce a license, he was arrested. A search subsequent to the arrest revealed narcotics. The court upheld the stop and search. Even though the stop was a pretext for the looking for drugs, the stop was lawful because the defendant failed to use his turn signal. *People v. Haney*, 192 Mich. App. 207 (1991).

Defendant was pulled over while driving his motor home. During a consent search, officers located marijuana. The basis of the stop was that the vehicle crossed the white line separating the emergency lane from the right-hand lane of traffic for an estimated twenty to thirty feet. The Tennessee code states that a vehicle "shall be driven as nearly as practicable entirely within a single lane." The prosecutor argued that the basis for the stop was probable cause to believe a traffic violation had occurred or a belief the driver was intoxicated. The court denied both these arguments and held the stop was unlawful.

The 6th Circuit Court of Appeals stated "We cannot agree that an isolated incident of a large motor home partially weaving into the emergency lane for a few feet and an instant time constitutes a failure to keep the vehicle within a single lane as nearly as practicable." Also, "the motor home's brief entry into the emergency lane does not constitute probable cause that the driver was intoxicated." *United States v. Freeman*, 209 F.3d 464 (6th Cir. 2000).

PRETEXT ARRESTS

Officers stopped defendant for speeding and having an improperly tinted windshield. Upon seeing Sullivan's driver's license, the officer recognized him from intelligence reports that reported Sullivan was involved in narcotics. Sullivan then opened his car door in an unsuccessful attempt to locate his registration and proof of insurance. At that point the officer observed a rusty roofing hatchet on the floorboard of the car. Sullivan was arrested for speeding, driving without his registration and insurance, carrying a weapon, and improper window tinting. A subsequent inventory search of the car revealed drugs and Sullivan was charged. Sullivan moved to suppress the evidence on the basis that the arrest was merely a pretext and sham to search his car. The Arkansas Supreme Court suppressed the evidence but the United States Supreme Court reversed in a per curiam decision based on the *Whren* decision.

The Supreme Court said, "The Arkansas Supreme Court's holding to that effect cannot be squared with our decision in *Whren*, in which we noted our unwillingness to entertain Fourth Amendment challenges based on the actual motivations of individual officers, and held unanimously that subjective intentions play no role in ordinary, probable-cause Fourth Amendment analysis. That *Whren* involved a traffic stop, rather than a custodial arrest, is of no particular moment; indeed, *Whren* itself relied on *United States v. Robinson*, 414 U.S. 218 (1973), for the proposition that a traffic-violation arrest will not be rendered invalid by the fact that it was 'a mere pretext for a narcotics search.'"

Officers should be aware of the concern of four Justices, who stated, "If experience demonstrates anything like an epidemic of unnecessary minor-offense arrests, (we) hope the Court will reconsider its recent precedent." (*Arkansas v. Sullivan*, 532 U.S. 769 [2001]).

PROTECTIVE SWEEPS

Officers may make a protective sweep of a residence where there is an articulable concern for officer safety.

On February 3, 1986, two men committed an armed robbery of a Godfather's Pizza restaurant in Prince George's County, Maryland. One of the robbers was wearing a red running suit. On February 5, the police executed an arrest warrant for Buie. They first had a police department secretary telephone Buie's house to verify that he was home. Six or seven officers then proceeded to Buie's house. Once inside, the officers fanned out through the first and second floors. With his weapon drawn, one officer shouted into the basement, ordering anyone down there to come out. Eventually, a pair of hands appeared around the bottom of the stairwell and Buie emerged from the basement. He was arrested, searched, and handcuffed. An officer entered the basement "in case there was someone else" down there. In the process he noticed a red running suit lying in plain view on a stack of clothing and seized it.

The Court upheld the search as a protective sweep. "The Fourth Amendment permits a properly limited protective sweep in conjunction with an in-home arrest when the searching officer possesses a reasonable belief based on specific and articulable facts that the area to be swept harbors an individual posing a danger to those on the arrest scene. We should emphasize that such a protective sweep, aimed at protecting the arresting officers, if justified by the circumstances, is nevertheless not a full search of the premises, but may extend only to a cursory inspection of those spaces where a person may be found. The sweep lasts no longer than is necessary to dispel the reasonable suspicion of danger and in any event no longer than it takes to complete the arrest and depart the premises." *Maryland v. Buie*, 494 U.S. 325 (1990).

Officers in a helicopter spotted marijuana near a mobile home. As they flew closer, a pickup drove up to the home and the driver, Randy Cartwright, jumped out and signaled the helicopter to go away. The helicopter dropped closer, and the driver gave an obscene hand gesture and ran into the trailer. A short time later a woman with some children emerged and fled in the truck. The driver exited the back of the residence with an object wrapped in a blanket. The officer radioed to the ground crew that the suspect had run into the woods with what might be a weapon. The first officer on the scene entered the residence to see if any more suspects were inside. During the 30 to 45 second sweep he observed marijuana and firearms laying in plain view. These observations were used to obtain a search warrant, which revealed that the Cartwrights were operating a marijuana operation.

The Court held that it was reasonable for the officer to be concerned that there were armed, hostile suspects in the area. One suspect had fled into the woods with what could have been a weapon, while another fled in the truck. It would be tactically unsound for the officer to watch the doors of the mobile home until a warrant arrived. His concern for safety justified the limited warrantless intrusion. *People v. Cartwright*, 454 Mich. 550 1997).

Officers went to Shaw's apartment to execute an arrest warrant for delivery of cocaine. The officers knew that another person was involved but were not sure of his identity. They knocked on the door and Shaw answered. After telling her about the warrant, she stepped back and they entered. They made a protective sweep of her apartment to see if anyone else was present. During the sweep they found a scale with what appeared to be cocaine residue. The court found the protective sweep to be reasonable and it could be completed without probable cause or reasonable suspicion. *People v. Shaw*, 188 Mich. App. 520 (1991).

When an arrest is made in a dwelling, those places immediately adjacent to the place of arrest may be searched for persons who may cause the officers harm; a search beyond these places requires reasonable suspicion. *People v. Gonzalez*, 256 Mich. App. 212 (2003).

FLEEING FROM POLICE

As officers approached a group of youths in a high crime area, the defendant took off running. As officers pursued, they saw him throw something away. They recovered the object and found it to be rock cocaine and defendant was arrested. The Court held that at the time Hodari threw the object down he was not seized for Fourth Amendment purposes. Since he was not seized for Fourth Amendment purposes, the cocaine was admissible because Hodari abandoned it and thus lost his expectation of privacy. A seizure occurs:

- Whenever, because of a police show of authority or force, a reasonable person would believe that he or she is not free to leave, and submits, or
- Custody of the individual is achieved through the application of physical force. *California v. Hodari D.* 499 U.S 621 (1991).

48-HOUR RULE

The defendant in this case was held for four days without a judicial determination of probable cause justifying his arrest. On the fourth day he confessed to the crime. The court was not impressed with this procedure. The Court stated, "We emphasize to police authorities across Michigan the importance of securing a judicial determination of probable cause within forty-eight hours of a warrantless arrest in all but the most extraordinary situations. Finally, this decision provides a warning that statements made by an accused person during a longer detainment may well be found inadmissible for purposes of securing a conviction at trial." *People v. Whitehead*, 238 Mich. App. 1 (1999) (Citing to *County of Riverside v. McLaughlin*, 500 U.S. 44 (1991)).

SEARCH WARRANT REQUIREMENTS

Search warrants are written court orders requiring a search of a particular place for particular things. Search warrants are issued by judges or magistrates after they have determined that probable cause exists to believe that the evidence sought will be found in the place to be searched.

There are three documents associated with all search warrants: The warrant itself, an affidavit, and a return and tabulation. Those documents will be discussed in the pages that follow.

Neutral and Detached Magistrate

Search warrants may only be issued by a magistrate or judge who is neutral and detached. That is, the issuing person must be impartial, having no stake in the outcome of the case, any bias related to the case, or any role in the investigation of the case.

A judge or district court magistrate may issue a written search warrant in person or by any electronic or electromagnetic means of communication, including by facsimile or over a computer network. MCL 780.651(3).

The magistrate was not neutral and detached where he had previously prosecuted the defendant and had been sued by him. *People v. Lowenstein*, 118 Mich. App. 475 (1982).

Officers executed a controlled buy, which was electronically monitored. After the delivery, the officers contacted other officers who were waiting in the magistrate's chambers. A search warrant was signed. The court upheld the warrant.

> "The mere fact that police wait in court does not mean that the magistrate has injected himself into the investigatory process." *People v. Tejeda*, 192 Mich. App. 635 (1992).

Judge's Signature on Warrant

> On a search warrant, the judge signed the actual search warrant and the copy for the prosecutor but failed to sign the one that was left for the defendant. The court refused to follow prior case law and found the warrant to be valid.
>
> The court instead followed the case of *People v. Mitchell*, 428 Mich. 364 (1987), which dealt with an unsigned affidavit. "Applying *Mitchell* to the issue presented here, we hold that the fact that a search warrant had not been signed by a magistrate or judge presents a presumption that the warrant is invalid. However, this presumption may be rebutted with evidence that, in fact, the magistrate or judge did make a determination that the search was warranted and did intend to issue the warrant prior to the search." (*People v. Barkley*, 225 Mich. App. 539 [1997]).

Affidavit for a Search Warrant—MCL 780.651

An **affidavit for a search warrant** is a written document prepared by a person called the affiant that contains facts by which the judge or magistrate may determine whether probable cause to search exists. The affiant (usually a police officer) must affirm under oath that the contents of the affidavit are true.

The magistrate's finding of reasonable or probable cause shall be based upon all the facts related within the affidavit made before him or her. An affidavit is an application for a search warrant. The affiant should list facts only, not conclusions. Conclusions are to be determined by magistrate.

> The affidavit must be signed before the magistrate; however, it is no longer invalid if affiant fails to sign. The burden falls on the prosecutor to show the affidavit is valid. *People v. Mitchell*, 142 Mich. App. 518 (1985).

"Four corners of the affidavit"

The facts establishing probable cause must fall within the "four corners of the affidavit."

> An officer sought a search warrant for blood on a suspected drunk driver. The affidavit for the warrant stated that, "It appears Robert Leonard Sloan is under the influence of alcoholic liquors." The officer seeking the warrant provided a sworn oral statement to the magistrate. After the statement, the magistrate issued the warrant.
>
> The Court held that a reviewing court may not consider sworn, yet unrecorded testimony, when examining an affidavit to determine if there was sufficient probable cause to issue a search warrant. The recording may take various forms, including handwritten notes, video or audiotapes, or formal or informal transcripts of testimony." *People v. Sloan*, 450 Mich. 160 (1995).

Administration of oath—MCL 600.1432

The affiant for a search warrant must swear or affirm that the information contained in the affidavit is true to the best of his or her belief while holding up his or her right hand.

> Failure to raise hand was cause for dismissal of case. *Dawson v. Austin*, 44 Mich. App. 390 (1973).

Showing of probable/reasonable cause

In determining if probable cause exists, the magistrate should review the facts in a "common sense" manner.

> It is not necessary to determine that the items sought are more likely than not in the place to be searched. It is only necessary that the affidavit enable the magistrate to conclude that it would be reasonable to seek the evidence in the place indicated. The courts must have a "common sense" reading of the affidavit. *People v. Russo*, 439 Mich. 584 (1992).
>
> The basis of a search warrant included the following:
>
> "On July 09, 1997, Affiant who is assigned to the Detroit Police Narcotic Division attempted a purchase of narcotics from 18072 Bloom. The above described seller asked the Affiant what the Affiant wanted, Affiant replied 'one' meaning one (1) pack heroin. The above described seller produced from his right front pocket a large bundle of blue folded small coin envelopes

wrapped in rubber bands. The seller looked at the Affiant and asked the Affiant who did Affiant know. Affiant was unable to convince the seller to sell illegal narcotics. The described seller stated come back with someone I know and I'll take care of you." The affidavit continued with information that the Affiant had participated in over 100 narcotics raids and had seen heroin in similar coin envelopes on numerous occasions. The lower courts suppressed the evidence obtained on the basis that the warrant established mere suspicion and not probable cause. The Michigan Supreme Court reversed.

The Michigan Supreme Court stated that "Considering these facts in a common sense and realistic manner, we are certain the magistrate had a substantial basis for finding probable cause to issue the search warrant because there was a fair probability that contraband or evidence of a crime would be found at the home where this conversation took place." *People v. Whitfield*, 461 Mich. 441 (2000).

The defendant was wanted on a federal indictment for delivery of cocaine. Surveillance on an apartment showed that defendant's vehicle was parked there on two different occasions. He was eventually arrested while he was driving in his car. He lied to the officer about were he lived and gave a different address. A search of the vehicle revealed a key to the apartment and a telephone bill to the defendant mailed to the apartment. A dog was also called and cocaine was located inside the vehicle. Based on this information a search warrant was obtained for the apartment and additional evidence was seized.

The Court stated that "Under the totality of these circumstances, a reasonably cautious person could conclude that there was a substantial basis for the magistrate's finding of probable cause. Indeed, defendant was arrested as a drug trafficker, cocaine was found in his vehicle, and there was abundant evidence that he resided at or habitually used the Kentwood apartment and had lied about this to the police. Defendant contends that the affidavit did not support a search of the Kentwood apartment because nothing in the affidavit tied the alleged drug activity to the apartment. However, defendant's denial that he lived at the Kentwood apartment, combined with the rea-

sonable inference that drug traffickers often keep evidence of illicit activity in their homes, provided a sufficient basis for the magistrate's finding of probable cause to search the apartment." *People v. Nunez*, 242 Mich. App. 610 2000).

Staleness

Probable cause must exist when the search warrant is sought and executed. The Michigan Supreme Court held in the case of *People v. Russo*, 439 Mich. 584 (1992), that probable cause could have existed where a woman reported that seven years earlier, when she was 8 years old, she had been photographed in sexually explicit pictures. Using studies on how pedophiles maintain the pictures for years, the Court held that probable cause existed even though there was a lapse of time. The question to be asked is whether it is reasonable to believe the items are still where the information placed them. If there is a continued criminal enterprise, there is a likelihood the items sought will remain for a longer time.

The probable cause may also become stale if the warrant is not executed within a reasonable time after it has been issued. For example, a search warrant for drugs should be executed immediately after it is obtained because the evidence may disappear if there is a delay. One exception to the rule that probable cause must exist when the search warrant is obtained is an anticipatory search warrant.

Anticipatory search warrants are constitutional

Officers intercepted a package that contained twenty-eight pounds of marijuana. They set up a delivery with an undercover officer. Prior to completing the delivery, they obtained an "anticipatory search warrant." The warrant specifically identified what would have to occur before it would become valid. "The search was subject to the successful delivery of the narcotics which was to be carried out by an undercover police officer. Further, the affidavit clearly indicated that the warrant would not be executed unless the marijuana was successfully delivered." Based on these facts, the court held that anticipatory search warrants are not unconstitutional per se. *People v. Kaslowski*, 239 Mich. App. 320 2000).

Anticipatory search warrants are constitutionally valid so long as the affidavit establishes probable cause that the triggering event will occur and probable cause that particular evidence will be found when the triggering event occurs. *United States v. Grubbs*, 547 U.S. 90 (2006).

Named or unnamed persons—MCL 780.653

The affidavit may be based upon information supplied by named or unnamed person if the affidavit contains one of the following:

- If the person is named, affirmative allegations from which the magistrate can conclude that the person spoke with personal knowledge of the information.

A mall manager reported to the police that he had received a number of complaints of homosexual activity in the restroom stalls. Based on this information, a warrant was sought. Problem: No personal knowledge. *People v. Kalchik*, 160 Mich. App. 40 (1987).

- If the person is unnamed, affirmative allegations from which the magistrate may conclude that the person spoke with personal knowledge of the information and either that the unnamed person is credible or that the information is reliable.

What Can Be Searched For—MCL 780.652

A warrant may be issued to search for and seize any of the following property:

- Stolen or embezzled in violation of any law of this state.
- Designed and intended for use or which is or has been used as the means of committing a criminal offense.
- Possessed, controlled, or used wholly or partially in violation of any law of this state.
- Evidence of crime or criminal conduct on the part of any person.
- Contraband.
- The bodies or persons of human beings or of animals, who may be the victims of a criminal offense.
- The objects of a search warrant under any other law of this state providing for the same. If a conflict exists between this act and any other search warrant law, this act shall be deemed controlling.
- A person who is wanted on an arrest warrant or a bench warrant in a criminal case.

Search warrant: Search and seizure of hair, tissue, blood, or other fluids—MCL 780.652a

If the court has probable cause to believe that an individual has violated one of the following CSC sections: 520b(1)(b)(ii) or (h)(i), 520c(1)(b)(ii) or (h)(i), 520d(1)(d), or 520e(1)(g) of the Michigan penal code, the court shall, upon proper petition for a search warrant, authorize the search and seizure of hair or tissue, or blood or other fluid samples from all of the following:

- Any individual whom the court has probable cause to believe committed that violation.
- If the court has probable cause to believe that the violation resulted in the birth of a child, that child.
- If the court has probable cause to believe that the violation resulted in a pregnancy that was terminated before the birth of a child, the remains of that unborn child.

This section does not prohibit the court from issuing a search warrant for other evidence as considered appropriate by the court.

Mistakes on a Warrant

Police executed a warrant where they had the proper address on the affidavit but due to a computer "error," the wrong address was printed on the warrant. Neither the officer nor the magistrate noticed the error. The officers executed the warrant at the proper residence. The court held that the error was harmless. "We conclude that the description in the affidavit of the property to be searched, as well as the relevant information known to by the executing officers, can be relied upon to validate the search warrant." *People v. Hampton*, 237 Mich. App. 143 (1999)

A search warrant that utterly failed to describe the persons or things to be seized was invalid on its face, notwithstanding that requisite particularized description was provided in search warrant application. A residential search that was conducted pursuant to this facially invalid warrant could not be regarded as "reasonable," though items to be seized were described in the search warrant application, and though officers conducting search exercised restraint in limiting scope of search to that indicated in the application. The officer who had prepared and executed warrant was not entitled to qualified immunity from liability. *Groh v. Ramirez*, 540 U.S. 551 (2004).

General Warrants

General warrants are unconstitutional because they are not specific enough. In this case the search warrant allowed the search of "persons or other individuals on or coming into the premises during the execution of the search warrant." Defendant arrived and was searched. The subsequent marijuana was suppressed because he was searched under a general warrant. *People v. Jackson*, 180 Mich. App. 339 (1989).

The Place to Be Searched

An officer executing the warrant must be able to reasonably identify the place to be searched. *Steele v. United States*, 267 U.S. 498 (1925).

The address on the warrant stated to search entire apartment located at 242 National, N.W., Apt. 2, City of Grand Rapids, County of Kent, State of Michigan, further described as being a "blue wooden framed 2 story multi-dwelling residence." In reality the defendant's apartment was No.1 in 246, next to 242. Both were painted blue.

When obtaining the warrant, the officers checked the address using the Secretary of State. The defendant had lived at 242, but failed to change his address.

Even though the address was incorrect, the court held that the description, along with the officer's knowledge and the information in the affidavit was adequate to define the premises. *People v. Westra*, 445 Mich. 284 (1994).

Other buildings within the curtilage to be searched must be included in the warrant.

Curtilage is the land, yard, or buildings adjacent to a house, usually within an enclosure, that is protected by the Fourth Amendment just as the house is.

Officers obtained a search warrant for a residence. During a search they also looked in a shed located near the house. "While it is recognized that rural property does not lend itself readily to precise description, property that is within the curtilage of any dwelling house must be described with specificity in a search warrant to justify a search of that property." *People v. Mackey*, 121 Mich. App. 748 (1982).

The test for determining sufficiency of description in a search warrant of the place to be searched is: (1) whether the place to be searched is described with sufficient particularity to enable executing officers to locate and identify the premises with reasonable effort, and (2) whether there is any reasonable probability that another premises might be mistakenly searched.

The search of a detached garage was within scope of a warrant authorizing a search of a residence, although trial court concluded that warrant specifically described areas contained within the home only, and that warrant did not say exterior storage areas, search warrant specifically mentioned home as well as "storage areas" accessible from property address. *People v. McGhee*, 255 Mich. App. 623 (2003).

Descriptions of a building should include:
- Type of structure, e.g. dwelling, apartment building, business, storage shed, etc.
- The number of floors or stories.
- The areas within to be searched.
- Type of construction; e.g., white brick, blue-gray aluminum, etc.
- The color of the exterior.

- Any other building within the curtilage to be searched.
- The street name and address.
- The side of the street the property is located.
- The intersecting roadways between which the property is located, e.g., on Canal between Lansing Road and Davis Highway.
- Any unique characteristics of the premises to be searched, e.g., with satellite dish located 20 feet south of dwelling house.
- The political subdivisions within which the premises are located, i.e., city, village or township; county; and the state of Michigan.

Descriptions of vehicles should include:

- Year, make, and model.
- Body style.
- Color.
- Registration plate number, year, and state where issued.
- VIN number.
- Any known owner, occupant, or operator of vehicle.
- The usual or probable location of the vehicle.

Objects of search

> A warrant that leaves the objects to be seized blank or open ended is invalid. The application must describe as specifically as possible the items to be seized. *LoJi Sales, Inc. v. New York*, 442 U.S. 319 (1979).

Example of how to describe an item on a search warrant:

> Evidence of the cultivation and/or manufacture of the controlled substance marijuana, including but not limited to, a quantity of marijuana, both live plants and processed marijuana; growing devices and supplies, such as grow lights, heaters, reflectors, fans and blowers, motors, timers, irrigation tubs, hoses, pumps, potting soil, nutrients, fertilizers, carbon dioxide exchangers and tanks, and pots or planters; paraphernalia for processing, packaging, and distribution, including dryers, heaters, scales, baggies, and/or other packaging materials; evidence of bills, canceled envelopes, drivers licenses, keys, and deeds or other documents showing ownership; United States Currency, including pre-recorded bills, fingerprints, and palm prints; and weapons to protect the cultivation.

Search Warrants for Blood

> PBT results may be utilized in an affidavit for a search warrant for blood of an O.W.I. suspect. *People v. Tracy*, 186 Mich. App. 171 (1990).

Search warrants for blood and pain compliance

> Defendant was stopped for speeding and admitted to drinking. He failed the sobriety tests and then refused to take a Breathalyzer. A search warrant was obtained, and he was taken to the hospital. At the hospital he refused to lie down on the table and evaded the lab technician's attempts to draw the blood. An officer then applied Do-Right sticks to the suspect's wrists, and he subsequently complied with the withdrawal of his blood.
>
> The Court upheld the action as reasonable. The Do-Right sticks were not used to punish the defendant but were used to subdue him and to ensure his safety as well as that of others. Because the contact was not severe, unnecessary, or unduly intrusive, the officer's actions were proper. *People v. Hanna*, 223 Mich. App. 466 (1997).

Knock and Announce

Officers can break in or out after notice of authority and purpose, and the police are refused admittance. MCL 780.656

Fourth amendment requirements

> The Fourth Amendment requires that police officers entering a dwelling must announce their identity and purpose before attempting forcible entry. *Wilson v. Arkansas*, 514 U.S. 927 (1995).

No blanket exception to knock and announce

> The Wisconsin Supreme Court concluded that officers are never required to knock and announce their presence when executing a search warrant in a felony drug investigation. The United States Supreme Court reversed and disallowed a blanket exception and required the courts to look at a case-by-case analysis.

In order to justify a "no-knock" entry, the police must have a reasonable suspicion that knocking and announcing under the particular circumstances:

- would be dangerous or futile, or
- would inhibit the effective investigation of the crime by, for example, allowing the destruction of evidence.

After reviewing the facts in the case, the Court did allow a no-knock entry because the defendant saw the police and ran back into his hotel room. *Richard v. Wisconsin*, 520 U.S. 385 (1997).

Actual knock not required

The ES Team assisted in executing a search warrant. They entered the driveway with a police vehicle. The emergency lights were activated and an officer announced on the PA system, "This is the police. We have a search warrant." The officers also had "Police" clearly written on their body armor. Once the team arrived at the door, they entered. The officers testified that it took 30 to 45 seconds to enter the residence after the announcements were made. They did not announce anything at the door. Defendant argued that the officers were required to knock on the door before entering. The Court of Appeals disagreed and upheld the entry as providing sufficient notice to the occupants of the officer's authority and purpose. *People v. Fetterley*, 229 Mich. App. 511 (1998).

Knock and announce violation will not result in suppression of evidence

Officers executed a search warrant at 12:32 a.m. There were no lights on, and they did not observe any activity or hear any footsteps. They knocked and announced, waited 11 seconds, and then broke the door down. Under these facts the Michigan Supreme Court agreed with the lower courts that the officers violated the knock and announce principles. The question presented, however, was whether the evidence found in the house should be suppressed.

The Court said that "The discovery of the evidence in the present case was inevitable, regardless of the illegalities on the police officer's entry into defendant's home. One of the purposes of the statute is to allow a defendant a brief opportunity to put his personal affairs in order before the police enter his home. . . . It is not meant to allow the defendant the time to destroy evidence. In the present case, the police did not exceed the scope of the search warrant. Therefore, they would have discovered the contested evidence, unless the defendant had been afforded the opportunity to destroy the evidence." *People v. Stevens*, 460 Mich. 626 (1999).

Officers should be mindful that a knock-and-announce violation may still result in civil litigation for violating the homeowner's Fourth Amendment rights.

Police obtained a search warrant for the defendant's residence and executed it by knocking, waiting for less than five seconds, and entering the residence. They found drugs and an illegally possessed gun. The Court held that the exclusionary rule does not apply to federal knock-and-announce violations. The exclusionary rule is designed to prevent the use of evidence that was found only because of a violation of the Constitution. However, when police have a warrant, they will find evidence lawfully, even when they did not follow the knock-and-announce rule; a rule violation does not lead to discovery of evidence, the warrant does. *Hudson v. Michigan*, 547 U.S. 586 (2006).

Examples of litigation

An undercover officer gave a suspect $20.00 to buy crack cocaine. When the suspect returned, he stated he had been robbed. The officers tried to arrest him and the subject took off running. He ran into a house and the officers chased him inside where an altercation arose with a number of the occupants. The officers initially arrested the wrong person and then later found the right suspect hiding in the house. The occupants of the house sued the officers for violating the Fourth Amendment rights because the officers failed to knock and announce their presence before entry. The officers argued that they had a right to enter the house under hot pursuit. The Sixth Circuit ruled that it would not give a blanket exception to hot pursuit. It remanded the case to the trial court to determine if to knock and announce would have been dangerous or futile or would have inhibited an investigation. *Ingram v. City of Columbus*, 185 F.3d 579 (6th Cir., 1999).

The need for damage does not increase the level needed for a no-knock entry.

While executing a warrant for a dangerous escaped prisoner, officers broke a single window and pointed a gun inside as they announced that they had a warrant and shouted "police." The defendant thought he was being burglarized and fired a shot from a pistol. He was then arrested. The lower courts dismissed the charges of being a felon in the possession of a firearm because there were insufficient exigent circumstances to allow a no-knock entry. The Supreme Court reversed.

The United States Supreme Court held that "The Fourth Amendment does not hold officers to a higher standard when a 'no-knock' entry results in the destruction of property. To prove a no-knock entry, the officers must have a reasonable suspicion that knocking and announcing would "be dangerous or futile, or . . . inhibit the effective investigation of the crime." Here the officers had sufficient reasonable suspicion because of a reliable informant's statement that he was there. This was confirmed by an officer, the defendant had a violent past and had vowed that he would not do federal time. Plus, breaking the window was reasonable as to discourage anyone from rushing to weapons. *United States v. Ramirez*, 523 U.S. 65 (1998).

Announce: Substantial compliance with the statute

"Police officers, open up." *People v. Doane*, 33 Mich. App. 579 (1971).

"Police officers. I have a search warrant. Open the door." *People v. Mayes*, 78 Mich. App. 618 (1977).

How long to wait

Officers went to Banks's apartment to execute a search warrant. They called out "police— search warrant" and knocked on the front door hard enough to be heard by officers at the back door. They waited for 15 to 20 seconds with no response and then broke open the door. Banks was in the shower and testified that he heard nothing until the crash of the door. Banks argued on appeal that the entry was unreasonable and that the evidence found should be suppressed.

The Court stated that "This case turns on the exigency revealed by the circumstances known to the officers after they knocked and announced, which the Government contends was the risk of losing easily disposable evidence. After 15 to 20 seconds without a response, officers could fairly have suspected that Banks would flush away the cocaine if they remained reticent. Each of Banks's counterarguments— that he was in the shower and did not hear the officers and that it might have taken him longer than 20 seconds to reach the door—rests on a mistake about the relevant inquiry. As to the first argument, the facts known to the police are what count in judging a reasonable waiting time, and there is no indication that they knew that Banks was in the shower and thus unaware of an impending search. As to the second, the crucial fact is not the time it would take Banks to reach the door but the time it would take him to destroy the cocaine. It is not unreasonable to think that someone could get in a position to destroy the drugs within 15 to 20 seconds. Once the exigency had matured, the officers were not bound to learn anything more or wait any longer before entering, even though the entry entailed some harm to the building." *United States v. Banks*, 540 U.S. 31 (2003).

A search warrant was properly served under MCL 780.656, where an officer knocked on the door and clearly announced authority and purpose and waited long enough for inhabitants to reach the door from the room farthest away before kicking in the door. *People v. Harvey*, 38 Mich. App. 39 (1972)

Police do not have to wait if they have a basis to conclude that:
- evidence will be destroyed, or
- lives will be endangered, or
- events indicate that knocking and announcing would be useless. *People v. Williams*, 198 Mich. App. 537 (1993).

Detention During Execution of Search Warrant

Officers are allowed to detain people during the execution of a search warrant for narcotics. The Court recognized the need to detain people for a safe execution of the warrant. For the safety of everyone, the officers need to be able to take command of the situation. *Michigan v. Summers*, 452 U.S. 692 (1981).

Detentions Pending the Issuance of a Search Warrant

Officers assisted a woman in keeping the peace as she removed some belongings from her residence. When she came outside after getting her possessions, she told one officer that her husband had marijuana under the couch. The officers made contact with the husband and requested permission to search the residence, but the husband refused. One officer then left to get a search warrant while the other officer waited with the husband. The husband was told that he could not enter the residence without being accompanied by the officer. A warrant was obtained and executed two hours later. Marijuana was located and the husband was charged with possession of marijuana and drug paraphernalia.

The United States Supreme Court upheld the detention as reasonable, stating, "In light of the following circumstances, considered in combination, the Court concludes that the restriction was reasonable, and hence lawful. First, the police had probable cause to believe that McArthur's home contained evidence of a crime and unlawful drugs. Second, they had good reason to fear that, unless restrained, he would destroy the drugs before they could return with a warrant. Third, they made reasonable efforts to reconcile their law enforcement needs with the demands of personal privacy by avoiding a warrantless entry or arrest and preventing McArthur only from entering his home unaccompanied. Fourth, they imposed the restraint for a limited period, which was no longer than reasonably necessary for them, acting with diligence, to obtain the warrant." *Illinois v. McArthur*, 531 U.S. 326 (2001).

Scope of the Search Under a Search Warrant

A lawful search extends to the entire area in which the object of the search may be found. *United States v. Ross*, 456 U.S. 798 (1982).

A warrant authorizing the search of a premises authorizes the search of containers within the premises that might contain the items listed in the warrant. *People v. Coleman*, 436 Mich. 124 (1990).

Cortez was the lessee of a single-family house. He rented rooms in the house to two individuals. One of the individuals was named in an affidavit for a search warrant. The affidavit further stated that this individual was selling drugs from the house. The warrant authorized the search of the house. During the search the police located drugs in Cortez's room. The Michigan Supreme Court held that the search was within the scope of the warrant. *People v. Cortez*, 451 Mich. 888 (1996).

Search of Persons at Scene

A search warrant authorizing the search of a particular building or premises does not give the officers the right to search all persons who may be found at that location. *People v. Krokker*, 83 Mich. App. 474 (1978).

During the execution of a search warrant, an officer at the back door heard a knock. He opened the door and admitted the person. He was immediately frisked and the officer located a gun. The court held frisks of this type should be allowed because people present during the execution of a search warrant pose a hazard to the officers. *People v. Jackson*, 188 Mich. App. 117 (1990).

Court allowed the search of purses where the search warrant was for controlled substances. *People v. Stewart*, 166 Mich. App. 263 (1988).

Taking Private Citizens on Search Warrant Executions

"It violates the Fourth Amendment rights of homeowners to bring members of the media or other third parties into their home during the execution of a warrant when the presence of the third parties in the home was not in aid of the warrant's execution." In this case the officers brought along the media. The exception to this rule is when the citizen is necessary to assist the police in their task (i.e., identify stolen property). *Wilson v. Layne*, 526 U.S. 603 (1999).

Tabulation and Receipt—MCL 780.655

The tabulation is a list of the items seized during the execution of a search warrant.

The Tabulation should be completed in the presence of the owner or occupant. If the owner or occupant is not available, tabulation must be taken in the presence of another person. The tabulation may be suppressed on order of the court.

Evidence seized in plain view must also be listed in the tabulation. *People v. Secrest*, 413 Mich. 521 (1982).

According to MCL 780.655 property seized during the execution of a search warrant must be tabulated in front of the person from whose possession or premises the property or thing was taken, if present, or in the presence of at least one other person. In applying the literal meaning to the facts of this case the court held that all money seized during the execution of a search warrant must be counted and tabulated before the officer leaves the scene and in front of the owner or another person. In addition, the court held that the money may not be deposited, but must be kept separate so that the defendants have an opportunity to do an independent analysis. *In re Forfeiture of $25,505*, 220 Mich. App. 572 (1996).

Leave Copy of the Warrant, Affadavit, and Tabulation at Location Searched—MCL 780.655

- The officer taking property or other things under the warrant shall give to the person from whom or from whose premises the property was taken a copy of the warrant and shall give to the person a copy of the tabulation upon completion, or shall leave a copy of the warrant and tabulation at the place from which the property or thing was taken. The officer is not required to give a copy of the affidavit to that person or to leave a copy of the affidavit at the place from which the property or thing was taken. MCL 780.655(1)
- Upon a showing that it is necessary to protect an ongoing investigation or the privacy or safety of a victim or witness, the magistrate may order that the affidavit be suppressed and not be given to the person whose property was seized or whose premises were searched until that person is charged with a crime or named as a claimant in a civil forfeiture proceeding involving evidence seized as a result of the search. MCL 780.654(3)
- On the fifty-sixth day following the issuance of a search warrant, the search warrant affidavit contained in any court file or court record retention system is public information unless, before the fifty-sixth day after the search warrant is issued a peace officer or prosecuting attorney obtains a suppression order from a magistrate upon a showing under oath that suppression of the affidavit is necessary to protect an ongoing investigation or the privacy or safety of a victim or witness. The suppression order may be obtained ex parte in the same manner that the search warrant was issued. An initial suppression order issued under this subsection expires on the fifty-sixth day after the order is issued. A second or subsequent suppression order may be obtained in the same manner as the initial suppression order and shall expire on a date specified in the order. This subsection does not affect a person's right to obtain a copy of a search warrant affidavit from the prosecuting attorney or law

enforcement agency under the freedom of information act, MCL 15.231 to 15.246. MCL 780.651(9).

File Tabulation with the Court—MCL 780.655

After executing a search warrant, officers must file the tabulation of property seized with the issuing court (often called the return). This must be done even if there was no property seized. The tabulation may be suppressed by order of the court until the final disposition of the case unless otherwise ordered.

Police Must Safe Keep Property for Trial—MCL 780.655

The property seized shall be safely kept by the officer so long as necessary for the purpose of being produced or used as evidence in trial.

> The defendant's blood was taken via a search warrant. The blood was held for two months and then destroyed accordingly to lab policy. Defendant argued that under MCL 780.655 the officers were required to "safe keep" the evidence until after trial for a test of his own. The Michigan Supreme Court disagreed. The Court held the statute in question protects evidence that will be presented to the jury at trial and the sample of blood will not be used for this purpose. Under this logic, there was no violation of MCL 780.655 or the Michigan or Federal Constitutions. *People v. Jagotka*, 461 Mich. 275 (1999).

Disposition of Property—MCL 780.655)

Property must be properly disposed of once the proceedings are complete. As soon as practicable, stolen or embezzled property shall be restored to the owner of the property.

Once the Search is Complete Under a Warrant, Officers Need a Second Warrant to Reenter

> Officers may take as long as "reasonably necessary" to execute the warrant and generally may continue to search the premises described in the warrant until they are satisfied that all available evidence has been located. Once the execution of the warrant is complete, the authority conferred by the warrant terminates. A single warrant might authorize more than one entry into a premise as long as the second entry is a "reasonable continuation" of the original search. *United States v. Keszthelyi*, 308 F.3d 557 (6th Cir., 2002).

Penalty for Exceeding Authority When Executing a Search Warrant—MCL 780.657

- $1,000 fine
- One year in jail

Penalty for Unlawfully Procuring a Search Warrant—MCL 780.658

- $1,000 fine
- One year in jail

23

WARRANTLESS SEARCHES

SEARCH INCIDENT TO A LAWFUL ARREST

Elements:

- A lawful, custodial arrest.
- The search is for weapons and evidence located within reach of the arrestee.
- The search must occur contemporaneously with the arrest.

Two rationales for the search incident arrest exception:

1. The need to disarm the suspect in order to take him or her into custody, and
2. The need to preserve evidence for later use at trial.

Arrest in a Home

Officers arrested defendant at his home based on a warrant. Based upon the lawful arrest, the officers searched the entire three-bedroom house including the attic, garage, and small workshop.

The court held that a warrantless search of defendant's entire house, incident to his arrest, was unreasonable. An arresting officer may search the person arrested, in order to remove any weapons and to seize evidence on the arrestee's person, an area into which arrestee might reach in order to grab a weapon or evidentiary items. Exceeding the scope of this exemption will result in evidence obtained being excluded. *Chimel v. California*, 395 U.S. 752 (1969)

Accompanying Arrestees into the Dwelling

Officers went to defendant's house with an arrest warrant. He answered the door wearing his pajamas. It was suggested that he get dressed. When he approached his dresser to get socks, an officer checked the drawers and found a blackjack. The court held the search of the drawer and seizure of the blackjack was valid, because an officer may search anywhere where an arrestee may reach in order to grab a weapon. The fact that the defendant was not in the area at the time of arrest has no bearing on the fact that he later had access to the area while still under arrest. *People v. Giacalone*, 23 Mich. App. 163 (1970).

Vehicles

The defendant was arrested for driving while his license was suspended. After he was handcuffed and secured in a patrol car, officers searched the vehicle he had been driving and found cocaine. The Court held the search violated the Fourth Amendment, which required suppression of the cocaine. *Arizona v. Gant*, 556 U.S. ___ (2009).

The officers in *Gant* were presumably relying on the long-standing rule that allowed officers to search a vehicle without a warrant *every* time an occupant was arrested. With the Court's opinion in *Gant*, that is no longer the rule.

The rule only allows police to conduct a vehicle search incident to the arrest of an occupant when either of two circumstances exists:

First, officers may search if the arrestee is within "reaching distance of the passenger compartment." When the arrestee has been secured in a patrol car, he or she is not within reach of the vehicle.

Second, officers may search a vehicle incident to arrest if they reasonably believe the vehicle contains evidence of the crime for which the person was arrested. Gant had been arrested for DWLS, and the cocaine was not evidence of DWLS. It appears the Court would not have suppressed the cocaine had Gant been arrested for a drug crime.

Suspect voluntarily leaving the vehicle

A police officer observed a vehicle with improper license plates. Before the officer was able to stop the vehicle, the driver parked the car and began to walk away. The officer made contact with the driver and, after patting him down, located drugs on him. The officer then searched the vehicle the driver left and found a firearm.

The court held that once a police officer makes a lawful custodial arrest of an automobile's occupant, the officer may search the vehicle's passenger compartment as a contemporaneous incident of arrest, even when an officer does not make contact until the person arrested has already left the vehicle. An arrestee is no less likely to attempt to lunge for a weapon or to destroy evidence if he is outside of, but still in control of, the vehicle. *Thornton v. United States*, 541 U.S. 615 (2004).

NOTE: The authority to search in these instances is limited by the Court's holding in *Gant*. Therefore, officers may only search in this instance if the arrestee is within reaching distance of the passenger compartment, or the officer reasonably believes the vehicle contains evidence of the crime for which the person was arrested.

Interim Bond

Defendant was arrested based on a warrant. Before offering him the opportunity to post bond, the officer completed a search and discovered a vial containing a controlled substance in the defendant's trousers. The court upheld the search as a search incident to arrest. *People v. Chapman*, 425 Mich. 245 (1986).

If statute requires an officer to offer interim bond to an arrestee in lieu of lodging him or her (i.e., certain traffic arrests), the officer must comply with the statute. Lodging the arrested person without offering him or her interim bond is not permitted and evidence located due to a search incident to incarceration would be excluded. *People v. Dixon*, 392 Mich. 691 (1974).

Search Subsequent to a Citation

Police officers in Iowa were authorized by statute to search vehicles where a citation was issued in lieu of arrest. The Iowa Supreme Court interpreted this statute to mean that officers had the authority to "conduct a full-blown search of an automobile and driver in those cases where police elect not to make a custodial arrest and instead issue a citation—that is, a search incident to citation." The United States Supreme Court found this practice to violate the Fourth Amendment.

Although the Court realized the dangerousness involved in traffic stops, a search incident to citation does not fall under either of the above rationales. The Court did suggest that where there is an articulable concern for safety, the officer is justified in performing a **Terry search**. *Knowles v. Iowa*, 525 U.S. 113 (1998).

Arrestee Swallowing Evidence

During an arrest, officers believed defendant was attempting to swallow something. He refused to open his mouth and continued to chew. Eventually pressure was applied to his jaws under the cheekbones, and nine tinfoil packets of heroin were seized from his mouth.

The court upheld the seizure and stated that the police may use a reasonable method and a reasonable amount of force to prevent the destruction of evidence of a crime. *People v. Holloway*, 416 Mich. 288 (1982).

The court of appeals upheld a seizure where the police were acting to save the defendant from harm as well as to obtain evidence of a crime. An officer arrested defendant after he put a baggie in his mouth. The officers and defendant went to the police station and officers awaited a warrant to search defendant's mouth. Before the warrant arrived, the defendant began to act as if he might lose consciousness. Defendant then collapsed, and the officer held defendant's nose closed and placed his hand over defendant's mouth, forcing him to spit out the bag. The court noted that police officers were content to wait until a proper warrant was issued and that the plan was aborted only after an apparent life-threatening situation arose. *Wayne County Prosecutor v. Recorder's Court Judge*, 149 Mich. App. 183 (1986).

An Officer Does Not Violate the Fourth Amendment if He or She Makes a Lawful Arrest of a Person with Probable Cause, Even if the Offense is Minor

An officer arrested a woman for not wearing her seatbelt, which was a misdemeanor punishable by fine only in the state of Texas. The warrantless arrest of anyone violating these provisions is expressly authorized by Texas law, but the police may issue citations in lieu of arrest. The question presented before the Court was whether the officer violated the woman's Fourth Amendment rights against unreasonable search and seizure. In a 5 to 4 decision, the Court held that the woman could not sue the officers.

The Court found that the woman's arrest satisfied constitutional requirements. It was undisputed that the officer had probable cause to believe that the woman committed a crime in his presence. Because she admitted that neither she nor her children were wearing seat belts, the officer was authorized (though not required) to make a custodial arrest without balancing costs and benefits or determining whether her arrest was in some sense required or necessary. Whether a search or seizure is "extraordinary" turns, above all else, on the manner in which it is executed. Atwater's arrest and subsequent booking, though surely humiliating, were no more harmful to her interests than a normal, custodial arrest." *Atwater v. City of Lago Vista*, 538 U.S. 318 (2001).

Probable Cause to Make an Arrest

At 3:16 a.m. a Baltimore County Police officer stopped a car for speeding. There were three occupants in the car. Pringle was the front-seat passenger. The officer asked the driver for his license and registration. When the driver opened the glove compartment to retrieve the vehicle registration, the officer observed a large amount of rolled-up money. A computer check did not reveal any violations, and the officer gave the driver a verbal warning. A second patrol car arrived, and the first officer asked the driver if he had any weapons or narcotics in the vehicle. The driver indicated that he did not, and he consented to a search of the vehicle. The search yielded $763 from the glove compartment and five plastic glassine baggies containing cocaine from behind the back-seat armrest. The officer questioned all three men about the ownership of the drugs and money and told them that if no one admitted to ownership of the drugs he was going to arrest them all. The men offered no information regarding the ownership of the drugs or money. All three were placed under arrest and transported to the police station. The front seat passenger, Mr. Pringle, admitted to owning the drugs while at the station.

The officer, upon recovering the suspected cocaine, had probable cause to believe a felony had been committed. To determine whether an officer had probable cause to make an arrest, a court must examine the events leading up to the arrest, and then decide whether these historical facts, viewed from the standpoint of an objectively reasonable police officer, amount to probable cause.

The Court held it was an entirely reasonable inference from these facts that any or all three of the occupants had knowledge of, and exercised dominion and control over, the cocaine. Thus, a reasonable officer could conclude that there was probable cause to believe Pringle committed the crime of possession of cocaine, either solely or jointly and his arrest was proper. *Maryland v. Pringle*, 540 U.S. 366 (2003).

PROBABLE CAUSE AND EXIGENT CIRCUMSTANCES

Elements:
- Probable cause that items sought are in a specific location.
- Exigent circumstances occur when a delay to get a warrant will result in the loss of evidence.

Vehicle-automobile exception

Exigent circumstances automatically occur with a vehicle due to its mobility.

> Police received reliable information that an individual known as "Bandit" was in front of a certain address and selling drugs from the trunk of his car. The informant stated that he had just purchased drugs from "Bandit" and that "Bandit" informed him that additional drugs were in the car. A detailed description of "Bandit" and the vehicle were also given. Officers responded to the address and observed the vehicle. A few minutes later, a man meeting "Bandit's" description was observed driving the vehicle away. The vehicle was stopped and officers searched the vehicle locating a gun in the glove compartment. The defendant was then arrested and the trunk was searched where officers located a brown bag containing heroin. The vehicle was taken to the station where a more thorough search revealed a red-leather pouch containing $32,000.
>
> The United States Supreme Court upheld the searches. Once officers have probable cause to believe a vehicle contains contraband, they may search it in the same manner as if they had a search warrant. The search may include closed containers if it is possible that the evidence being searched for could be hidden in those containers. *United States v. Ross*, 456 U.S. 798 (1982).
>
> The police may open and search any container placed or found in an automobile as long as they have the requisite probable cause with regard to the container, even if the probable cause focuses specifically on the container and arises before the container is placed in the automobile. *People v. Bullock*, 440 Mich. 15 (1992).
>
> If a car is readily mobile and probable cause exists to believe it contains contraband, the Fourth Amendment permits police to search the vehicle without more. *Pennsylvania v. Labron*, 518 U.S. 938 (1996).
>
> Two months after officers observed defendant use his vehicle to deliver cocaine, he was arrested on unrelated charges. At that time, his vehicle was seized under the forfeiture laws of Florida. Officers searched the vehicle, locating additional cocaine.
>
> The Court held that the police are not required to obtain a warrant before seizing an automobile from a public place when the police have probable cause to believe that the vehicle itself is forfeitable contraband. Applying this rule to the case, the court held that police were not required to obtain a warrant before seizing and searching the vehicle. The Court recognized the need to seize readily movable contraband before it is "spirited away." *Florida v. White*, 526 U.S. 559 (1999).
>
> During a traffic stop, a Wyoming Highway Patrol officer noticed a hypodermic syringe in the driver's shirt pocket. The driver admitted to taking drugs. The officer then searched the vehicle including a purse that belonged to the passenger. Drugs were found inside the purse.
>
> The Court held that with probable cause to search a car, a police officer may inspect passengers' belongings found in the car that are capable of concealing the object of the search, in this case drugs. *Wyoming v. Houghton*, 526 U.S. 295 (1999).
>
> Officers executed a search warrant on a residence and located a large amount of cash and illicit drugs. The owner of the residence attempted to flee the officers when initially contacted. After searching the residence, the officers also searched the defendant's vehicle, which was located outside the residence (the vehicle was not listed in the warrant). The defendant argued that the search of his vehicle was illegal because it was not listed on the warrant, and the officers had no other reason to search it.
>
> The Michigan Court of Appeals disagreed and examined the issue under the totality of the circumstances. The court found that the defendant's presence in a drug house with a large amount of cash was sufficient for concluding that the defendant was a drug dealer and that there was a fair probability that their search of defendant's vehicle would locate more contraband. The court found the police had probable cause, plus exigent circumstances to search the defendant's vehicle. *People v. Garvin*, 235 Mich. App. 90 (1999).

An anonymous tip may lead to probable cause if the information is corroborated by independent sources.

> An undercover officer received information from an informant that a drug transaction was going to occur at a specific residence. This information

was relayed to another officer who began surveillance forty-five minutes later. The officer verified the residence and the names of the two people that were supposed to be there. The officer was also familiar with the subject from previous dealings. The officer watched three vehicles arrive and three vehicles leave within a twenty-minute period. She then observed a man leave with dark clothing carrying a black bag, which he placed into the trunk of a car. A marked unit then stopped the vehicle and searched the trunk. Marijuana was located inside the bag.

In looking at the officer's training and experience, the Michigan Supreme Court held there was sufficient probable cause. The information provided by the undercover police officer was sufficiently corrobo-rated and supplemented by the officer's own investigation and observations to warrant a finding of probable cause. *People v. Levine*, 461 Mich. 172 (1999).

Vehicle destroyed by fire is still readily mobile

At approximately 4:00 a.m. a fire department extinguished an automobile fire. After examining the car, they determined that the fire had started in the engine compartment, and since they were unable to find any accidental cause of the fire, it was reported that the fire was of "suspicious" origin. At approxi-mately 8:00 p.m. on the same date, an expert arson investigator went to investigate defendant's burned car, which was still parked on the street. Without a search warrant, the arson investigator searched the vehicle and discovered evidence of arson. The defendant was subsequently charged. The lower courts dismissed the charges on the grounds that since the vehicle was not mobile the automobile exception no longer was applicable.

The Court of Appeals disagreed with the premise that defendant's vehicle was immobile. Although the motor of the automobile was inoperable after the fire, the vehicle was capable of mobility. During the time interval between the first and second search, defendant could have moved the automobile by summoning a tow truck. Defendant's automobile could have been hauled to any location while the police were preoccupied in court seeking a search warrant. *People v. Carter*, 250 Mich. App. 510 (2002).

Search at police station

If police have probable cause that evidence will be found in an automobile, the automobile can be taken to a station house and searched without a warrant. *Chambers v. Maroney*, 399 U.S. 42 (1970).

Where there is probable cause, the officers may conduct a search of a vehicle without a warrant even after it has been impounded and is in police custody. *People v. Wade*, 157 Mich. App. 481 (1987).

The defendant was arrested for a sexual battery. Police searched his vehicle at the time of his arrest and it was impounded. Eight hours later, a detective returned to the impound lot and searched the vehicle again. The detective had not obtained a search warrant. Additional evidence was seized.

The United States Supreme Court upheld the search because the vehicle was still readily mobile even though it was parked in an impound lot and the officer had probable cause to believe the vehicle contained evidence of the crime. *Florida v Meyers*, 466 U.S. 380 (1984).

Motor homes

The police had information that the defendant was exchanging marijuana for various sex acts from his motor home, parked in a parking lot. At the time, the defendant was using the motor home as his residence. An officer went to the motor home, entered it, and observed marijuana.

The Court held that since a motor home is readily mobile, exigent circumstances exist. So long as probable cause also exists, officers do not need a warrant. *California v. Carney*, 471 U.S. 386 (1985).

Residence

It is more difficult to establish exigent circumstances in a residence. The court developed a two-part test:

1. Is there probable cause?
2. For immediate entry, officers must show the existence of actual emergency and articulate specific and objective facts that reveal a necessity for immediate action.

More than a mere possibility of destruction or removal of evidence is necessary.

The threshold question is whether the police can produce specific facts supporting a reasonable and objective belief that there is imminent risk of the removal or destruction of evidence.

> If an officer enters a home under probable cause and exigent circumstances, the courts prefer the residence to be secured to prevent the removal or destruction of evidence. Officers should then obtain a search warrant before searching and seizing property. *People v. Blasius*, 435 Mich. 573 (1990).
>
> An officer responded to a shooting at a hotel. Upon arrival, he located a victim in the parking lot who was still responsive. The officer asked the victim who shot him, and the victim provided the name "Eric." When asked for a last name, the victim gave no reply. The officer asked where Eric lived, and the victim responded "here" and nodded toward the hotel. The officer also observed a white van with its doors open and located the body of a female who apparently died from a gunshot wound inside. The officer recovered a red spent 12-gauge shotgun shell near the driver's side front tire.
>
> The officer then went to the hotel's office and determined that "Eric Snider," in room 412, was the only Eric registered. He went back to the victim who was being loaded in the ambulance and asked if Eric Snider was the one who had shot him and the victim stated "yes." The officer then obtained a room key and entered room 412. No one was present, but he did observe a red 12 gauge shot gun shell that was similar to the one found near the van. The room was secured and a search warrant was obtained. The warrant was executed and officers recovered the shell, as well as Snider's identification.
>
> Officers then left the scene and informed the night clerk to call if Snider returned. At approximately 4:00 a.m. the clerk called and advised Snider had returned. The officers obtained the key and, after knocking and getting no response, they entered and found Snider sitting on the bed holding a shotgun. He was then arrested.
>
> The Court of Appeals upheld all three of the entries as reasonable under the Fourth Amendment. The initial warrantless entry into room 412 was justified under the exigent circumstances exception to the warrant requirement. The officer had probable cause to believe that a crime had just been committed and justification for a search of the room to prevent the destruction of any evidence, to protect the police or others, and to prevent Snider's escape or to determine if he were wounded. The search warrant was valid based on the officer's observations during his initial entry.
>
> The final entry without a warrant was also valid. The court held the police were justified in concluding that Snider's armed presence in the hotel endangered the lives of the other guests. Further, the police were justified in concluding that any delay in arresting Snider while obtaining an arrest warrant would be unreasonable in light of the danger that Snider posed to the other guests. Therefore, there were exigent circumstances known to the police that excused them from taking time to obtain an arrest warrant. The police were confronted with what can only be classified as an emergency situation: a murder suspect, whom they had every reason to believe was armed, located in a hotel room under circumstances that very probably might put the lives and safety of the others at risk. *People v. Snider*, 239 Mich. App. 393 (2000).

PLAIN VIEW

Elements:

- Police are lawfully in an area protected by the Fourth Amendment.
- While in the protected area, they locate items that they have probable cause to believe are contraband or evidence.
- The fact that the items may be contraband or evidence must be readily apparent to the officer.

> During a traffic stop at night, an officer shined his flashlight into the car and observed a green party balloon, knotted at the tip, fall from the driver's hand. Based on his training and experience, the officer knew that drugs were often carried in similar balloons. The officer then shined his flashlight into the glove compartment that the driver had opened. He noticed small plastic vials, loose powder, and an open bag of party balloons. The officer seized the knotted balloon, which seemed to contain a powdery substance.
>
> The Court held that if a police officer is lawfully performing his or her duties and observes an in-

criminating object for which he or she has probable cause to believe is contraband, that object may be seized. The seizure of property in plain view is not an invasion of privacy and was presumptively reasonable, assuming that there was probable cause to associate the property with criminal activity. In this case, the arresting officer had lawfully viewed the green balloon in connection with a lawful encounter by the officer. The officer also had probable cause to believe that the balloon was subject to seizure; therefore, the seizure was proper. The level needed to seize the item is merely probable cause, the officer need not be certain that the item is contraband. *Texas v. Brown*, 460 U.S. 730 (1983).

Defendant was stopped for a traffic violation. The officer observed several partially smoked marijuana cigarettes in the ashtray. The officer seized the evidence.

The court held that police have a right to look inside a properly stopped vehicle and to seize any evidence inside the vehicle that is in plain view. *People v. Julkowski*, 124 Mich. App. 379 (1983).

Officers stopped a car for speeding. Bending down in order to speak with the driver, one of the officers noticed "an alligator clip with a roach attached to it" between the two sun visors. He asked defendant to get out of the car, confiscated the item, and placed defendant under arrest for possession of marijuana. The officer on the passenger side testified that she also noticed the metal clip above the rearview mirror. She testified that she was not absolutely certain what the cigarette was but told her partner that it was possibly a controlled substance. After escorting defendant to the police vehicle and seating him in the back seat, the vehicle's passenger compartment was searched and a small black bag on the front passenger seat was located. The bag was opened and the officer located four small glass vials containing a powdery residue later determined to be cocaine.

The court upheld the search as a valid under the plain view exception. The police had probable cause to believe that the item contained marijuana. Therefore, the subsequent search that lead to the discovery of cocaine was justified as a search incident to lawful arrest. *People v. Alfafara*, 140 Mich. App. 551 (1985).

Plain view does not have to be inadvertent

Defendant and an accomplice used a stun gun and machine gun to commit an armed robbery. Jewelry and cash were taken. Police obtained a warrant to search for the jewelry at defendant's residence, knowing that they may also find the weapons used. During the search, the police discovered an Uzi, a .38 caliber revolver, and two stun guns. The court allowed the weapons into evidence under the plain view exception. The court held that discovery of evidence does not have to be inadvertent. *Horton v. California*, 496 U.S. 128 (1990).

Officers responded to a report of shots fired at a known drug house. When they knocked on the door, they observed a subject run downstairs with a package they believed from their training and experience to be a kilo of cocaine. The subject came back upstairs and opened the door. The officers entered and went directly downstairs. They were looking for shooting victims, but they were also aware that the defendant had taken a kilo of cocaine downstairs. They found the cocaine and seized it. The court held the cocaine was found in plain view. *People v. Moore*, 186 Mich. App. 551 (1990).

Moving objects do not fall under plain view

Police officers cannot move objects to develop probable cause under plain view. In this case, the officers moved some stereo components, turning them around, in order to read the serial numbers. The Court held that this was NOT plain view because the officer had to manipulate the items so they were not readily apparent contraband. *Arizona v. Hicks*, 480 U.S. 321 (1987).

Plain feel

An object that a police officer detects on a suspect during the course of a pat-down may be seized without a warrant, if the officer's sense of touch makes it readily apparent that the object, though not threatening in nature, is contraband.

An officer may not manipulate the item to determine what it is. The fact that it is contraband must be readily apparent. It was not plain feel where officer had to roll the object in his fingers before he could determine it was rock cocaine. *Minnesota v. Dickerson*, 508 U.S. 366 (1993).

During a valid pat-down, the officer felt a pill bottle in the subject's groin. The pill bottle was removed and the officer found cocaine inside. The Michigan Supreme Court upheld the search because the officer had probable cause to believe the pill bottle contained contraband. The probable cause consisted of the following:

- The defendant walked away from the officers as they approached,
- One of the officers knew defendant from previous drug and weapon convictions,
- The officers were in a high drug crime area,
- The defendant had his hands tucked inside the front of his sweat pants and refused to remove his hands after being requested to do so by the officers,
- The officer knew from his experience that controlled substances were often transported in pill bottles.

    KEY: Officers had probable cause to seize the object and arrest the subject. Opening the bottle was allowed as a search incident to arrest. *People v. Champion*, 452 Mich. 92 (1996).

During a valid pat-down, the officer felt what he believed to be blotter acid in defendant's pocket. He removed it and placed it on the roof of the car before completing the pat-down. He then retrieved the objects, which turned out to be three photographs facing down. He turned the pictures over and observed that they depicted a subject in a house containing large quantities of marijuana. The question presented was whether the officer could lawfully turn the pictures over under the plain feel doctrine.

The Michigan Supreme Court upheld the seizure of the pictures as valid under plain feel. "We conclude that the exterior of an item that is validly seized during a pat down search may be examined without a search warrant, even if the officer subsequently learns that the item is not the contraband the officer initially thought that it was before the seizure." *People v. Custer*, 465 Mich. 319 (2001).

Plain smell: Odor of marijuana

During a traffic stop, an officer testified that he detected "a very strong smell of marijuana emanating from the vehicle that was overpowering."

The officer further testified that he had previously participated in fifteen to twenty cases involving marijuana. The driver denied having any marijuana, and the officer then searched the car, locating a brick of marijuana in the trunk. The officer testified that the only basis for searching the trunk was the odor of marijuana.

The court upheld the search. "[T]he smell of marijuana alone by a person qualified to know the odor may establish probable cause to search a motor vehicle, pursuant to the motor vehicle exception to the warrant requirement." *People v. Kazmierczak*, 461 Mich. 411 (2000).

CONSENT

KEY: Voluntarily Given by a Proper Party
Test = Totality of the Circumstances

If a defendant consents to a search it may be conducted without probable cause or a warrant because the Fourth Amendment rights have been waived. The only requirement is that consent must be voluntary and under no threat or compulsion. *Schneckloth v. Bustamonte*, 412 U.S. 218 (1973).

The Fourth Amendment does not require that a lawfully seized defendant be advised that he is "free to go" before his consent to search will be recognized as voluntary. The Amendment's touchstone is reasonableness, which is measured in objective terms by examining the totality of the circumstances.

Defendant was stopped for speeding, 69 in a 45. He was given a verbal warning after the officer checked his license and found no previous violations. The officer returned his driver's license to him and asked "Are you carrying any illegal contraband in your car? Any weapons of any kind, drugs, anything like that?" Robinette answered no, and the officer asked for consent to search the car. Robinette agreed and the officer found drugs. The Court held that the police are not required to tell suspects that they are "legally free to go" before asking for consent to search. *Ohio v. Robinette*, 519 U.S. 33 (1996).

Plainclothes officers boarded a bus looking for drug couriers. Officers gave the passengers no reason to believe that they were required to answer questions or that they were not free to leave. The officers did not brandish weapons or make any intimidating movements; they left the aisle free so that passengers could exit, and spoke to them one by one in a polite, quiet voice. An officer asked the defendants first if they objected to a search. Even after arresting one defendant, the officer addressed the second defendant politely and gave no indication that he was required to answer questions or consent to a search. Although the officer did not inform the defendants of their right to refuse the search, he did request permission to search. The totality of the circumstances indicated that the consent was voluntary.

Officers need not always inform citizens of their right to refuse when seeking permission to conduct a warrantless consent search. Instead, the totality of the circumstances control, without giving extra weight to whether this type of warning was given. *United States v. Drayton*, 536 U.S. 194 (2002).

Scope of search

The scope of a search under a consent search turns on whether it is objectively reasonable for the officer to believe that the scope of the consent permits the officer to open a particular closed container.

The defendants were suspected of selling drugs from their car. They were stopped for not using a turn signal, and the officers asked for consent to search the car for drugs. The driver gave consent, and, during the search, the officer opened up a rolled paper bag, which was on the floor, and located a kilo of cocaine.

The Court held that, because the officers asked to search the car for drugs, the officers were allowed to open the bag as it was within the scope of the consented search. *Florida v. Jimeno*, 500 U.S. 248 (1991).

Troopers arrested a subject for a sex offender registration violation. The troopers obtained a signed consent form that authorized a complete search of his vehicle and any containers therein. The subject unlocked the vehicle and allowed the troopers access. A laptop computer was located and a cursory search of the computer files revealed child pornography. The computer was secured and a search warrant was obtained. The subject argued that he did not give consent to search the computer.

The Court of Appeals held that the scope of consent to search given by the defendant authorized the search of the computer. The word "complete" included the files. In addition, the defendant did not restrict the search when the computer was seized. *People v. Dagwan*, 269 Mich. App. 338 (2005).

An officer stopped a vehicle and obtained consent from the driver to search the vehicle. The officer did not ask the other occupants for consent, and during the search found marijuana in a backpack belonging to a passenger. The passenger who owned the backpack did not object, nor did she make any attempt to remove the bag from the car when she exited prior to the search.

The court held that when police have authority to search the entire passenger compartment of a vehicle, that authority extends to any unlocked containers within the vehicle. *People v. Labelle*, 478 Mich. 891 (2007).

Consent can be limited and revoked

A suspect can revoke his or her consent to a search at any time. Similarly, a suspect can limit the scope of a search at the beginning. If a person revokes consent given to a search, he or she can halt further police activity that relies on the consent.

An officer asked Powell if he was carrying any guns, knives, or drugs. When Powell said no, the officer asked if he could check. Powell agreed, but when the officer felt small bulges in his pocket and felt plastic baggies, Powell stepped back and told the officer, "No, you need a warrant for that." The officer nonetheless went into the pocket and retrieved the bag, which contained drugs. The court held that the seizure of the drugs was improper because the defendant limited the search and revoked consent. *People v. Powell*, 199 Mich. App. 492 (1993).

Joint access or control

One who possesses authority over premises or effects with one or more other persons has common authority to give consent. Property interest is not necessarily enough. There must be a showing of mutual use of the property by persons generally having joint access or control so that each person has a right to permit inspection in his or her own right. *United States v. Matlock*, 415 U.S. 164 (1974).

Officers suspected that a husband had killed his girlfriend. They learned that he had written a check to purchase explosives, which were ultimately used to kill his girlfriend. They went to his house and asked his wife for permission to search the house, including the checkbook that they both jointly used. Evidence was located in the checkbook to authorize charges.

The court upheld the search because the consent given by the wife included areas that were jointly occupied and used. The area of the search was commonly used between the husband and wife and was not under the exclusive control of the husband. *People v. Chism*, 390 Mich. 104 (1973).

Joint access or control: Disputed consent

Officers obtained consent to search a home from one spouse but were denied consent from the other spouse, who was also present. They found drugs, which they sought to use against the refusing spouse. The Court held that a "disputed invitation" cannot overcome the protections guaranteed by the Fourth Amendment. As a result, evidence gathered against a refusing party cannot be used against them. *Georgia v. Randolph*, 547 U.S. 103 (2006).

Officers were investigating an arson. They went to the suspect's house and arrested him after he invoked his *Miranda* rights. He was then placed in a patrol car. An officer then asked the suspect's roommate if the officer could enter the residence and use their phone. The roommate agreed, and when the officer entered, he saw evidence of the arson. The defendant claimed that by invoking *Miranda* he had effectively denied consent to search.

The Court held that mere invocation of rights does not constitute express objection to entry. The Court further noted that police are never under an obligation to seek out an absent tenant to gain approval of consent given by another. However, police may never remove a suspect for the purpose of preventing him from having an opportunity to object. *People v. Lapworth*, 273 Mich. App. 424 (2006).

Parental consent

Officers were looking for a runaway when they went to defendant's house. Defendant's mother allowed the officers to search the house for the runaway, including defendant's bedroom. In the bedroom they seized a pan on the floor containing four sandwich bags of marijuana.

The district court dismissed the charges on the basis that the mother did not have the authority to consent to the search of defendant's room. The court based its decision on a sign that read "Keep Out" and that the door was closed and defendant did not allow anyone into the room.

The Court of Appeals reversed. There was sufficient evidence presented to the officers that the mother had common authority over the bedroom. She had "ready access" to clean his room and gather his laundry. The sign by itself would not stop the consent, because kids routinely put similar signs on their doors, nor were there any indications that defendant had exclusive control over the room, such as locks where the parents had no keys. Even if the mother did not have actual authority to search, she had apparent authority to allow the search by the officers. *People v. Goforth*, 222 Mich. App. 306 (1997).

Apparent authority

A woman claimed her boyfriend assaulted her. She had a key to the apartment, and she referred to the residence as "our place." She opened the door and officers found cocaine in plain view on a table. The trial court held that the woman did not live there and, therefore, could not have given consent.

The Court held the entry was valid, because the officers at the time of the entry reasonably believed that the person who allowed them entry had common authority over the premises. *Illinois v. Rodriguez*, 497 U.S. 177 (1990).

Police were asked to do periodic checks on a residence because the former owner had died. Over an eight-month period, the officers made 33 checks. Unbeknownst to the officers, the house was sold. One day, an officer found a strange car in the garage. A LEIN check revealed the car was stolen. The court upheld the search because consent had been given and the officers had no reason to know that the consent was no longer valid. *People v. Grady*, 193 Mich. App. 721 (1992).

Requesting an attorney under *Miranda* does not invoke the Fourth Amendment for purposes of consent

Defendant was a suspect in the murder of a DNR officer. After being questioned for a while, the defendant stated, "I'm no match for you. I want to talk to an attorney." The officers then asked him for consent to search his home. He agreed and signed the waivers. He argued on appeal that the officers violated his Fifth and Sixth Amendment rights and that the evidence seized during the search should be suppressed.

The court held that the defendant was not in custody because he voluntarily came down to the station and was free to leave at any time. In addition, the Fifth Amendment covers testimonial evidence and evidence seized during the search was tangible, physical evidence. The court then found that the defendant's Fourth Amendment rights were not violated when police asked the defendant to sign a consent form after he asked for an attorney. The defendant's consent to the search was freely and voluntarily given. *People v. Marsack*, 231 Mich. App. 364 (1998).

Use of a fake warrant may invalidate consent

Officers went to defendant's house. When he opened the door, one of the detectives opened up a leather folder to get a business card. A form bearing the label of a search warrant was inside the folder. The officers then asked to come in and, as he stepped back, the officers entered. He was then asked if there were any drugs in the house. Defendant went to a freezer and got a bag of marijuana, which he gave to the officers.

Defendant testified that there was a warrant and that he could not refuse them the opportunity to search. Based on the testimony of the defendant and the officers, the Supreme Court held the consent was invalid, because it was not freely, voluntarily, or intelligently given. *People v. Farrow*, 461 Mich. 202 (1999),

"Knock and talk" is a valid procedure if done properly

Officers received information that defendant may have controlled substances on his property. Since there was not sufficient evidence to obtain a search warrant the officers decided to do a "knock and talk." (Going to the suspect house, engaging in conversation, and attempting to gain consent to search).

The court held in the context of a "knock and talk" the mere fact that the officers initiated contact with a citizen does not implicate constitutional protections. It is unreasonable to think that simply because one is at home that he or she is free from having the police come to his or her house and initiate a conversation. The fact that the police's motive for the contact is an attempt to secure permission to conduct a search does not change that reasoning. The police may still obtain consent to search, so long as it is freely, voluntarily, and intelligently given.

A "knock and talk" may, however, run afoul of constitutional protections against unreasonable search and seizure. Any time the police initiate a procedure, whether by search warrant or otherwise, the particular circumstances surrounding the incident are subject to judicial review to ensure compliance with general constitutional protections. Therefore, what happens within the context of a "knock and talk" and any resulting search is certainly subject to judicial review. For example, a person's Fourth Amendment right to be free of unreasonable searches and seizures may be implicated where a person does not feel free to leave or where consent to search is coerced." *People v. Frohriep*, 247 Mich. App. 692 (2001).

Officers received an anonymous tip that defendant was growing marijuana. During a helicopter fly-over, they observed pots and potting materials in the back yard of the house. This information was relayed to a ground crew, which went to the residence. The first officer to arrive proceeded around the side of the house into the back yard, where he observed marijuana plants growing in a lean-to attached to the back of the house. The officer then saw the defendant at the rear of the property entering the lean-to. When he refused to obey the officer's commands to stop, he was placed in handcuffs. Officers then went to the front of the house and knocked on the front door. The defendant's wife answered and officers did a protective sweep of the house and then took defendant's wife to a patrol car to be questioned. The wife eventually signed a consent form and 122 marijuana plants were seized.

The Court of Appeals suppressed the evidence by holding that this was not a valid "knock and talk." The officer who discovered the marijuana did not wait for the other officers to conduct the purported "knock and talk," but instead proceeded directly to the back of defendant's home. The police report stated that according to the anonymous tip, the marijuana was in a six-foot by four-foot container right behind defendant's house. The officer saw the marijuana plants inside the lean-to in a large container. At that point, defendant was coming out of the woods at the back of the property. The police did not first approach the front door of home, they did not proceed along a path that the public could be expected to travel in visiting defendant's home, nor did they simply approach defendant as he was standing in his yard to ask permission to "look around." Only after the marijuana was discovered did the officers go to the door of the home and knock, at which point the defendant's wife answered the door. The court held "[s]uch intrusions cannot be sanctioned under the guise of knock and talk and 'ordinary citizen contact'." *People v. Galloway*, 259 Mich. App. 634 (2003).

After receiving a tip that defendant was storing marijuana, officers went to his residence to conduct a "knock and talk." Defendant admitted them into his residence. The police informed defendant that they were police officers and that they had received a tip that marijuana was stored at the site. Although defendant did not deny that there was any marijuana, he denied the officer's request to search. Further, defendant asked the officers to leave. However, officers did not leave and began to question him further and subsequently narcotics and money were seized.

The court held, although police are free to employ the knock and talk procedure, they have no right to remain in a home without consent, absent some other legal justification. A person is seized for purposes of the Fourth Amendment when the police fail to promptly leave the person's home following the request that they do so, absent a legal basis for the police to remain independent of the person's consent. Therefore, the evidence was suppressed. *People v. Bolduc*, 263 Mich. App. 430 (2004).

TERRY ENCOUNTERS

Stop and frisk

Reasonable suspicion to believe a crime is afoot = **stop**

Reasonable suspicion to believe person is armed = **frisk**

KEY: Pat down for weapons for officer safety purposes, based on reasonable suspicion.

An officer with 39 years on the force observed three subjects he thought were "casing" a store for a robbery. The suspects would walk by the store, look in, and then pass by. When the officer stopped them, he was concerned that they may have weapons. He then patted down the outer surface of the defendant's clothing and felt a pistol.

The Court held the search was valid. A police officer who has reason to believe that he is dealing with an armed and dangerous individual, regardless of whether he has probable cause to arrest, may make a reasonable search for weapons, even though he is not absolutely certain that individual is armed. Reasonableness of the action depends not on his inchoate and unparticularized suspicion or hunch but on specific reasonable inferences, which he is entitled to draw from facts in light of his experience. *Terry v. Ohio*, 392 U.S. 1 (1968).

Officers were patrolling near a high school when they observed three juveniles on a sidewalk in front of the school. As the officers approached, one officer noticed a bulge in the waistband of one of the subjects. The officers patted the defendant down and found a loaded 9-mm pistol. The trial court suppressed the gun, but the Court of Appeals reversed.

The court held that no level of cause was needed to approach the individuals. Based on the officer's 4 1/2 of years experience and observations, sufficient reasonable suspicion existed that the subject may have been armed and potentially dangerous. *People v. Taylor*, 214 Mich. App. 167 (1995).

A pat-down search conducted merely as a routine precautionary measure for officer's personal safety is unreasonable under the Fourth Amendment.

A pistol was suppressed when, at the time of the pat-down, the defendant was not under arrest, nor was there probable cause to arrest, and the officer had no articulable suspicion that the defendant was armed.

The court held that officers cannot search people as a matter of routine, but must be able to articulate facts that lead the officer to suspect the individual is armed. *People v. Parham*, 147 Mich. App. 358 (1985).

Terry search of an auto

The test is whether the officer possesses an articulable and objectively reasonable belief that the suspect is potentially dangerous. A protective sweep for weapons can include the vehicle, if the officer has a sufficient reasonable belief. *Michigan v. Long*, 463 U.S. 1032 (1983).

An argument was witnessed by a security guard. One of the men ran up to the guard and stated that the other man had a gun and was going to kill him. The suspect then drove off in a car. Police were called, and as the guard was explaining to the officer what happened, the suspect's car drove by. The officers stopped the car and observed the driver reach over and place something in the glove box. The officers opened the glove box and found a gun.

Citing *Long*, the court held that the officers had an articulable and objectively reasonable belief that the defendant was armed and potentially dangerous and the seizure was valid. *People v. Vandiver*, 140 Mich. App. 484 (1985).

Ordering occupants from vehicles

The Fourth Amendment is not violated when officers order occupants from a lawfully stopped vehicle.

Drivers

During a valid traffic stop, a police officer ordered the driver out of the vehicle. As the driver exited, the officer noticed a large bulge under the driver's coat. The driver was frisked, and a gun was discovered.

The Court held that ordering the defendant out of the car was a minimal intrusion and did not violate the Fourth Amendment. Once an officer legitimately stops a vehicle, the officer has the right to order the driver out of the vehicle for any purpose. However, without supporting testimony that the suspect is potentially dangerous and may be armed, the police are prohibited from conducting a pat-down search. *Pennsylvania v. Mimms*, 434 U.S. 106 (1977).

Passengers

The court has also held that danger to an officer from a traffic stop is likely to be greater when there are passengers in addition to the driver in the stopped car. While there is not the same basis for ordering the passengers out of the vehicle as there is for ordering the driver out, the additional intrusion on the passenger is minimal. Therefore, an officer making a traffic stop may order passengers to get out of the car pending completion of the stop. *Maryland v. Wilson*, 519 U.S. 408 (1997).

Terry (investigatory) stops: reasonable suspicion

Officers can make a stop based on reasonable suspicion that a crime may be occurring. The stop must be no longer than is necessary to extinguish their suspicions or build up to probable cause.

Reasonable suspicion is not needed if the contact is voluntary

At 1:40 a.m. an officer observed a vehicle with Arkansas plates parked in a private driveway. The vehicle was running and its parking lights were on. The officer approached and observed the defendant sleeping in the driver's seat with a pillow over his head. The officer testified that he tapped on the window to make sure the driver was okay. When the driver woke up, the officer asked if he lived at the residence and he said no. The officer then asked for identification. As the driver exited the vehicle, the officer could see the grips of a handgun between the passenger seat and the center console.

The district court and circuit court dismissed the charges on the grounds that the officer did not have reasonable suspicion that criminal activity was afoot to justify the request for identification. The Court of Appeals reinstated the charges.

While the Michigan Supreme Court in *People v. Freeman*, 413 Mich. 492 (1982) suppressed evidence located when officers approached a parked car, ordered the occupant to exit, and produce identification because there was no reasonable suspicion for the detention, the Court of Appeals distinguished this case because here the officer "asked" for ID. Unlike the officer in *Freeman*, the arresting officer did not order defendant from his car. There was nothing on the record to suggest that intimidating circumstances compelled defendant to cooperate. The record showed that the officer "merely made a voluntary request to defendant to produce identification." The court held no suspicion was required for this contact. *People v. Shankle*, 227 Mich. App. 690 (1998).

Officers were dispatched to a housing complex, which was known to the police as a high crime and drug area, reference a loud gathering. Upon their arrival, they found a group of fifteen to twenty people drinking and talking loudly. Defendant was seated on stairs leading to one of the housing units. An officer approached defendant, and the two engaged in a general conversation about the party. At that point, a woman emerged from the attached housing unit and, using profane language, asked defendant who he was and why he was seated on her porch. After hearing this, the officer asked defendant if he lived in the housing complex. Defendant said that he did not, and the officer asked to see defendant's identification.

When defendant handed over his state identification card, the officer used his radio and started to run the subject via LEIN. Defendant's behavior immediately changed. He became obviously nervous and made furtive gestures toward a large pocket on the side of his pants. He began to walk away, despite the fact that the officer still held his identification card and was speaking to him. At that point, the officer and his partner walked alongside defendant, encouraging him to wait for the results of the LEIN inquiry. When defendant did not stop, one officer placed a hand on defendant's back and told him that he was not free to leave. The LEIN inquiry revealed an outstanding warrant for defendant's arrest. As the officer was placing defendant in handcuffs, a gun fell from defendant's waistband to the ground. Defendant argued that he had been stopped without any reasonable suspicion and that the gun should be suppressed.

The court held that the officer's initial encounter with defendant was consensual. The officer did not seize defendant when he asked whether defendant lived in the housing complex, nor did he seize defendant when he asked for identification. The Fourth Amendment was not implicated until the officer actually hindered defendant's attempt to leave the scene, thereby seizing him within the meaning of the Fourth Amendment. Specifically, this seizure occurred when the officer followed defendant as he tried to walk away, orally discouraged him from leaving, and, finally, put a hand on his back and told him to wait for the results of the LEIN inquiry. This point – when the officer physically hindered defendant's departure and instructed him to stay in the officer's presence – is when a reasonable person might have concluded that he was not free to leave. By this point, however, the officer had a reasonable suspicion to make an investigatory stop. *People v. Jenkins*, 472 Mich. 26 (2005).

The smell of intoxicants by themselves may provide the basis for an investigatory detention

During a traffic stop for a broken taillight, the officer detected a strong odor of intoxicants on the driver's breath. Based solely on the odor, the officer requested the driver to exit and perform sobriety tests. The driver was ultimately arrested. The court upheld the arrest.

The court held that the presence of an odor of intoxicants may give rise to a reasonable suspicion that the motorist has recently consumed alcoholic liquor, which may have affected his or her ability to operate a motor vehicle. *People v. Rizzo*, 243 Mich. App. 151 (2000).

Drug checkpoints are unconstitutional

The City of Indianapolis set up vehicle checkpoints on its roads in an effort to interdict unlawful drugs. The vehicles were systematically stopped and a drug dog would walk around them while an officer would ask the occupants a few questions.

The Supreme Court held that this practice violated the Fourth Amendment. The primary purpose of the Indianapolis narcotics checkpoints was to advance the general interest in crime control. The Court declined to suspend the usual requirement of individualized suspicion where the police seek to employ a checkpoint primarily for the ordinary enterprise of investigating crimes. Stops justified only by the generalized and ever-present possibility that interrogation and inspection may reveal that any given motorist has committed some crime are not permitted. *City of Indianapolis v. Edmond*, 531 U.S. 32 (2000).

Informational checkpoints may be constitutional

Police set up a highway checkpoint to obtain information from motorists about a hit-and-run accident occurring about one week earlier at the same location and time of night. Officers stopped each vehicle for 10 to 15 seconds, asked the occupants whether they had seen anything happen there the previous weekend, and handed each driver a flyer describing and requesting information about the accident. As defendant approached, his minivan swerved, nearly hitting an officer. The driver was ultimately arrested for O.W.I. He argued on appeal that the checkpoint was unconstitutional.

The Court held that the checkpoint stop did not violate the Fourth Amendment. The checkpoint in *Edmond* was designed to ferret out drug crimes committed by the motorists themselves. Here, the stop's primary law enforcement purpose was not to determine whether a vehicle's occupants were committing a crime, but to ask the occupants, as members of the public, for help in providing information about a crime in all likelihood committed by others.

Information-seeking highway stops are less likely to provoke anxiety or to prove intrusive, since they are likely brief, the questions asked are not designed to elicit self-incriminating information, and citizens will often react positively when police ask for help. In judging its reasonableness, hence, its constitutionality, the Court looks to the gravity of the public concerns served by the seizure, the degree to which the seizure advances the public interest, and the severity of the interference with individual liberty. The relevant public concern was grave, as the police were investigating a crime that had resulted in a human death, and the stop advanced this concern to a significant degree given its timing and location. Most important, the stops interfered only minimally with liberty of the sort the Fourth Amendment seeks to protect. Viewed objectively, each stop required only a brief wait in line and contact with police for only a few seconds. Viewed subjectively, the systematic contact provided little reason for anxiety or alarm, and there is no allegation that the police acted in a discriminatory or otherwise unlawful manner. *Illinois v. Lidster*, 540 U.S. 419 (2004).

Vehicle Terry stops

Officers saw a vehicle traveling without the use of headlights at 3:30 a.m. in a dark parking lot where stores were located. The vehicle was stopped, and the driver was arrested for O.W.I. The court held that the officers had sufficient reasonable suspicion to make the stop. *People v. Peebles*, 216 Mich. App. 661 (1996).

Plainclothes officers observed a Trans Am drive into the parking lot of a Holiday Inn. The vehicle drove up to a Ford Taurus, then the two vehicles drove off together. The vehicles pulled into a plaza about a mile from the Holiday Inn and went to an unlit parking area where the passenger of the Trans Am entered the Taurus. The driver of the Trans Am got out and looked around. After two to three minutes, the passenger returned to the Trans Am and the vehicles departed. A marked unit was called and stopped the Trans Am. Open intoxicants were found and a search incident the arrest revealed crack cocaine and marijuana.

The officer testified to the following: "Upon the basis of the meeting at the Holiday Inn, . . . together driving to the Tel-X Plaza, both vehicles parking separate, the drivers, one passenger getting out, the driver getting out and moving, I believe that there was... a possible drug transaction occurring."

The Court suppressed the evidence because the officer failed to articulate enough to justify the original traffic stop. All the court had was a "bald assertion" by the officer that the situation looked like a drug transaction.

The Court said the officers failed to indicate any of the following:

- Prior experience with the defendants.
- Whether the area was a high crime area.
- Did the suspect act evasively or engage in furtive gestures?
- Prior experiences that persons looping in the back of the Holiday Inn or similar lots were a carbon copy of drug activity.

- There was no extended surveillance.
- There was no tip concerning the activity.
- There was no testimony explaining the reason or type of undercover surveillance.

People v. LoCicero, 453 Mich. 496 (1996).

An officer responded to a bank robbery involving two black males. Near the scene, he drove to an apartment complex, which was a location that he believed would be a good place to hide a getaway car. The officer testified that during his nineteen years experience as a police officer he has investigated about 20 bank robberies, and it had been his experience that there usually was another person involved who drives the getaway car. Based on this, he was looking for more than two subjects in a car. As he pulled into the complex, a car with four black male occupants was pulling out of the driveway. The officer testified that "[A]s I was passing by them, I turned and looked over at them, and all four subjects looked directly ahead. They would not, any of them, look over at me." The officer found this very unusual because, based on his experience as a police officer, "people always look at the cops." The officer saw the car within ten or fifteen minutes of the dispatch regarding the bank robbery and he passed within six to eight feet of the car when they passed by each other at the entrance to the apartment complex. The officer called for back up and followed the car as it took a circular route instead of a more direct route that would have taken them directly by the bank. The vehicle was stopped and evidence of the robbery was located. The defendants argued that there was no reasonable suspicion to allow the stop.

The Michigan Supreme Court disagreed. The police stopped a car that contained at least three people in a situation where the police were looking for two bank robbers and expecting to find a getaway driver as well. Because the car had at least two black male occupants, its occupants were consistent with the description of the bank robbers. After the officer eliminated the direction north of the bank, he found the car leaving a secluded area close to the bank from what was a logical hiding place. The occupants of the car drew further suspicion by appearing to a trained law enforcement officer to be evasive by declining to look in the direction of his marked police car as it passed nearby. Finally, the car followed a circuitous route that avoided the site of the bank robbery before the traffic stop. While one or more of these factors in isolation may not have constituted reasonable suspicion to stop the car, the court held there was reasonable suspicion to justify the traffic stop in this case under the totality of the circumstances. *People v. Oliver*, 464 Mich. 184 (2001).

A trooper stopped a vehicle for speeding. Upon questioning, the driver stated that he was going to Cheboygan and was staying at the Holiday Inn. The trooper was aware that there was no Holiday Inn in Cheboygan and asked the driver to step from the vehicle for further questioning. The driver advised that he was from Detroit and was going to be staying in Cheboygan for a couple of days but he had no luggage. Upon further questioning, the driver admitted that he had been arrested for marijuana related offenses in the past. The passengers also provided inconsistent stories and a K-9 unit was called and drugs were located in the vehicle.

Defendant argued that the trooper had "unlawfully exceeded the initial stop when he asked defendant to step from the vehicle to answer questions when he only possessed a generalized hunch that criminal activity was afoot." Defendant further argued that the trooper had no reasonable suspicion of criminal activity to warrant the questioning and had insufficient grounds for pursuing an investigatory stop.

The Michigan Supreme Court held that the traffic stop was reasonable in both scope and duration. "The Fourth Amendment is not violated when an officer asks reasonable questions to obtain additional information about the underlying offense and the circumstances leading to its commission. For example, in addition to asking for necessary identification, an officer may ask questions relating to the driver's destination and travel plans. Implicit in this authority to ask questions is the authority to ask follow-up questions when the initial answers given are suspicious. Likewise, there is no constitutional prohibition against asking similar questions of any passengers in the vehicle. In response to questions about his travel plans defendant provided an explanation that was implausible. Therefore, the trooper was presented with suspicious circumstances that warranted further investigation." *People v. Williams* 472 Mich. 308 (2005).

Detaining pedestrians

Police learned that the defendant had paid $2,100 for two airplane tickets from Honolulu,

Hawaii, to Miami, Florida, with a roll of $20 bills. Miami was known as a source city for illegal drugs. He traveled under a name that did not match the name under which his telephone number was listed and he appeared nervous during the trip. The defendant only spent 48 hours in Miami and did not check any of his baggage during the flights.

Based on these facts, the Court felt there was reasonable suspicion to make the stop. Police may briefly detain a person for investigatory purposes if they have reasonable suspicion that criminal activity may be afoot even if the officer lacks probable cause. *United States v. Sokolow*, 490 U.S. 1 (1989).

Length of detention

An investigative detention must be temporary and last no longer than is necessary to achieve the purpose of the stop. In determining if the detention is too long, the court must examine whether police diligently pursued a means of investigation that was likely to confirm or dispel their suspicions quickly. *United States v. Sharpe*, 470 U.S. 675 (1985).

A witness saw three men moving something over a golf course at 3:00 a.m. When he confronted them, they took off running. An officer responded and found a pile of equipment and three sets of footprints leading toward an apartment complex. Based on this, and the witness description, the officer radioed to another officer to watch out for three white males. The defendants were located and stopped. The investigating officer followed the tracks to a locker facility and found that it had been broken into. The officer then checked and found that the boots of the three defendants matched the tracks he had been following. This took 20 minutes.

The court held that the detention was valid because the officers diligently investigated facts available to them, which led to the reasonable suspicion and eventually probable cause to make the arrest. *People v. Chambers*, 195 Mich. App. 118 (1992).

Officers stopped a car after receiving reliable information that it contained narcotics. After searching the car and its occupants for drugs, the officers placed the occupants into their patrol car and drove them to the police department. The drugs were ultimately located at the police station, after the defendant had been held, against her will, for over an hour.

The Sixth Circuit dismissed the charges, holding that the officers unreasonably seized defendant by placing her in the police car and questioning her, transporting her to the police station, detaining defendant while at the police station, and questioning her further once there. Although the officers properly relied upon the bulletin from the undercover officers indicating that defendant was suspected as being involved in drug trafficking, once defendant identified herself, answered the officer's questions, and consented to the pat-down, which did not reveal anything suspicious, the officers were required under the Fourth Amendment to allow defendant to go free. The officer's continued detention of defendant in the back of the locked patrol car ripened the investigatory stop into an arrest, and because the officers did not have probable cause to arrest defendant at that time, the seizure was illegal. *United States v. Butler*, 223 F.3d 368 (6th Cir. 2000).

Defendant was stopped for a vision obstruction, weaving within the lane of traffic and speeding. Upon contacting him, the officer requested to see his driver's license and vehicle information, which he produced. When he was checked in LEIN, there were several warrants for his arrest. Following his arrest for the warrants, the officer searched the car and found 261 grams of cocaine.

The defendant argued that since he cooperated with the officer in providing his information, the stop should have lasted no longer than what was necessary to issue a citation and release him. The officer should not have taken the additional time to file check him in LEIN.

The court disagreed, holding that a LEIN check is an unobtrusive investigative tool employed by the police to retrieve information regarding an individual's driving record and to determine whether there are any outstanding warrants for his arrest, all matters of public record. As such, a LEIN check does not involve an unlawful disregard for individual liberties. Accordingly, because this amount of time is a minimal invasion in light of the substantial government interest in arresting citizens wanted on outstanding warrants, the court found the officer's use of LEIN does not violate defendant's constitutional rights. *People v. Davis*, 250 Mich. App. 357 (2001).

Pat down of individuals before placing them in a patrol car

> A trooper contacted a man and woman walking on the freeway. He gave them a warning and then offered them a ride to the next exit. They agreed and, before being seated in the patrol car, they were patted down by the trooper. A gun was located.
>
> Since the officer had no authority to arrest the couple, and leaving them on the freeway would be dangerous and allow the offense to continue, the court held that the officer was justified in conducting a pat-down despite absence of any showing of specific and articulable facts that defendant was armed and dangerous. *People v. Otto*, 91 Mich. App. 444 (1979).

Fleeing from police may establish reasonable suspicion for a Terry stop

> The suspect fled upon seeing police vehicles converge on an area of Chicago known for drug trafficking. The officers stopped him and conducted a pat-down for weapons locating a pistol.
>
> The Court held a defendant's unprovoked flight from officers in an area of heavy narcotics trafficking supported reasonable suspicion that defendant was involved in criminal activity and justified a Terry stop. "[N]ervous, evasive behavior is a pertinent factor in determining reasonable suspicion." *Illinois v. Wardlow*, 528 U.S. 119 (2000).

Anonymous tip

> An anonymous caller reported that a young black male standing at a particular bus stop and wearing a plaid shirt was carrying a gun. Officers responded and observed three black males. Absent the tip, the officers had no reason to suspect any of the three of illegal conduct. The officers did not see a firearm or observe any unusual movements. The officers approached the subjects and frisked them, finding a gun on J.L., a juvenile.
>
> The court held that an anonymous tip that a person is carrying a gun is not, without more, sufficient to justify a police officer's stop and frisk of that person. Because the officers' suspicion that J.L. was carrying a weapon arose not from their own observations but solely from a call made from an unknown location by an unknown caller, the tip lacked sufficient indicia of reliability to provide reasonable suspicion to make a Terry stop. It provided no predictive information and, therefore, left the police without means to test the informant's knowledge or credibility. *Florida v. J.L.*, 529 U.S. 266 (2000).

Handcuffing during Terry stops

> Defendant parked his car across several visitor parking spaces at a Ford plant after traveling over the grass and causing damage to a front tire. After noticing the smell of alcohol on defendant's breath, security personnel called the Wixom police, who arrived in uniform and in fully marked police cars to investigate. As the police officers approached defendant, he appeared to be preparing for a fight, then became belligerent and approached a female officer with clenched fists. After momentarily following instructions to place his hands on the trunk of the vehicle, defendant pushed away then turned toward the officers. As a result, defendant was handcuffed. Defendant then began to fight, scream obscenities and threats, and became totally out of control. The fight lasted several minutes, during which time additional officers were called to assist. Defendant was eventually restrained, but continued to thrash violently and make threats for several hours thereafter. Officers searched the car after he was restrained and found a loaded 9-mm handgun, several dozen additional rounds of ammunition, and a number of documents in an unlocked briefcase in the trunk. Defendant claimed that he was placed under arrest as soon as the officers handcuffed him and that the arrest was illegal because the officers did not have probable cause.
>
> The court held that a defendant's restraint is not necessarily an arrest. Police conduct in trying to restrain defendant during the investigation may be a reasonable intrusion on defendant's liberty if the safety of the officers is at risk during their lawful attempt to investigate the situation. In this case, the defendant appeared intoxicated and led the officers to believe that he planned to fight them. He was aggressive and hostile, and the officers were unaware whether he possessed a weapon. They were not required to take unnecessary risks when dealing with defendant.

After the officers validly attempted to restrain defendant for safety reasons, he committed the charge of resisting and obstructing the officers. The police then had probable cause to arrest defendant. *People v. Green*, 260 Mich. App. 392 (2004).

Searches of probationers may be based on reasonable suspicion

Defendant was placed on probation for drug violations. Part of the probation order required him to submit to a search at any time, with or without a warrant, by any probation or law enforcement officer. Later, officers suspected that he was involved in a number of arsons against a power company. At one point, a detective who was investigating him observed a Molotov cocktail and other explosive devices in a pickup truck parked in his driveway. The detective then entered the apartment to search under the probation order. Inside the residence, the officer located incriminating evidence against the defendant. The trial court dismissed the charges holding that although the detective had "reasonable suspicion" to believe he was involved with incendiary materials, the search was for "investigatory" rather than "probationary purposes."

The United States Supreme Court reversed, holding that the Fourth Amendment's touchstone is reasonableness, and a search's reasonableness is determined by assessing, on one hand, the degree to which it intrudes upon an individual's privacy and, on the other, the degree to which it is needed to promote legitimate governmental interest. In this case, the defendant's status as a probationer subject to a search condition informs both sides of that balance—he was unambiguously informed of the search condition. Therefore, his reasonable expectation of privacy was significantly diminished. In assessing the governmental interest, it must be remembered that the very assumption of probation is that the probationer is more likely than others to violate the law. On balance, no more than reasonable suspicion was required to search the defendant's residence. "Although the Fourth Amendment ordinarily requires probable cause, a lesser degree satisfies the Constitution when the balance of governmental and private interest makes such a standard reasonable." *United States v. Knights*, 534 U.S. 112 (2001).

INVENTORIES

Vehicles

The inventory of a vehicle must be reasonable and completed in compliance with departmental policy.

A car was parked in a tow-away zone and impounded. During an inventory of the car, officers located marijuana in the glove compartment.

The Supreme Court held that routine inventory searches of automobiles lawfully impounded by the police are reasonable. *South Dakota v. Opperman*, 428 U.S. 364 (1976).

Officers arrested the driver for O.W.I. The passenger also was under the influence and unable to drive. The passenger asked if he could arrange for his wife to get the car. The officers refused and towed the vehicle. Before it was towed, the officers conducted an inventory search on the vehicle and found cocaine. The departmental policy stated that a vehicle could be impounded where it would be left unattended.

The court held that impounding the vehicle under these circumstances was reasonable. Obviously, the officers could not turn it over to the passenger and the police do not have to make alternative arrangements to avoid impoundment.

Police may make routine, warrantless searches of contents of any vehicle that lawfully comes into police custody as part of police caretaking. The purposes of an inventory search are to:

- Protect the owner's property while in police custody.
- Protect the police against claims or disputes over lost or stolen property.
- Protect the police from potential dangers.
- The search cannot be a pretext.

People v. Toohey, 438 Mich. 265 (1991)

Defendant was arrested for O.W.I. After the arrest, but before the arrival of the tow truck, the officer searched the vehicle and found a closed knapsack, opened it, and found controlled substances.

The Court held that because the department had a written inventory procedure for towing the vehicle, the search was valid. *Colorado v. Bertine*, 479 U.S. 367 (1987).

Florida Highway Patrol had no policy specifically requiring the opening of closed containers during a legitimate inventory search. The Court suppressed marijuana located in a suitcase in the trunk of the vehicle.

The court held that an inventory search must be conducted based on a department policy in order to restrict officer's discretion. *Florida v. Wells*, 495 U.S. 1 (1990).

Arrestee's personal effects

Defendant was arrested and brought to the police station for booking. He was required to empty his pockets and turn over the bag he was carrying at the time of arrest. The booking officer examined the contents of the bag and found amphetamine pills.

The Court ruled this was a valid inventory search. It did not fall under the search incident to arrest exception because the search was not done contemporaneous with the arrest. *Illinois v. Lafayette*, 462 U.S. 640 (1983).

EMERGENCIES

Elements:

Reasonable suspicion that an emergency exists.

Injury: Community care-taking function

During a fire call, fireman entered the defendant's residence and garage to extinguish the fire. In the process, they located a number of dead deer that had been illegally shot hanging in the garage. The court held that the fire was sufficient as an emergency to authorize the entry and, once inside, the deer could be seized as evidence. *People v. Chapman*, 73 Mich. App. 547 (1977)

Defendant was involved in a hit-and-run crash. A witness saw his plate and officers went to his house. They located a vehicle with front-end damage and observed a subject lying unconscious and bleeding in the house. Officers knocked and had dispatch attempt to make contact with telephone calls, with no response. Officers entered the residence to check on his well being. Subject was o.k., but intoxicated.

The court upheld the entry into the home and the arrest as valid under the emergency exception. *People v. Ohlinger*, 438 Mich. 477 (1991).

Officers were dispatched to "Belmar Motel, Room 33 or 34, desk clerk says shots fired." The officers went directly to Room 33, because it was closer and banged on the door. They observed a female looking through the curtains. She shut them and, after three to five minutes, opened the door. The officers entered and observed drug paraphernalia and the butt of a gun underneath the mattress.

The court held that police may enter a location if they have reasonable belief (suspicion) that a person inside is in need of immediate aid. In applying this to the facts of this case, the court held that the officers did not have reasonable suspicion that someone was in need. Therefore, the entry and search were invalid. *People v. Davis*, 442 Mich. 1 (1993).

Officers were dispatched to respond to a domestic disturbance in progress, possibly involving guns and knives. The officers knocked on the door, but no one answered. They then tried to gain entry, but the door was locked. They heard a lot of wrestling or moving around inside the house. A woman then answered the door and the officers entered. Once inside, they observed the defendant in the back bedroom and ordered him out. The officers then conducted a protective sweep and observed cocaine on the kitchen floor, in the front room, and on a tray in the bedroom.

The Court of Appeals upheld the entry into the home, the protective sweep of the home, and the seizure of the drugs. "[P]olice may enter a dwelling without a warrant when they reasonably believe that a person within is in need of immediate aid. They must possess specific and articulable facts that lead them to this conclusion. In addition, the entry must be limited to the justification therefore, and the officer may not do more than is reasonably necessary to determine whether a person is in need of assistance, and to provide that assistance." *People v. Beuschlein*, 245 Mich. App. 744 (2001).

Officers may enter a residence to prevent injury or restore order (e.g., to break up a fight). An officer's motivation for entry is irrelevant, as long as entry is reasonable as viewed by an objective person. *Brigham City v. Stuart*, 547 U.S. 398 (2006).

HOT PURSUIT

Elements:
Pursuit of a fleeing felon.
Exigent circumstances requiring immediate arrest.

If police have probable cause that a suspect has committed a felony and they are pursuing him to make an arrest, they have the right to enter a private building during pursuit. *Warden, Maryland Penitentiary v. Hayden*, 387 U.S. 294 (1967).

Undercover officers had probable cause to arrest defendant for drug dealing from observations they made as she was standing in front of her house. As the officers approached, she retreated into her house. The officers entered and while arresting her, the paper bag she had been carrying fell to the floor and envelopes, later determined to contain heroin, were seized.

The U.S. Supreme Court upheld the arrest and seizure of the evidence. Holding that, defendant could not thwart an otherwise proper arrest that had been set in motion in a public place by retreating into a private place, her residence. There was also a need to act quickly by the police to prevent the destruction of evidence and therefore the warrantless entry by the police into the house to make the arrest was justified as well as the subsequent search. *United States v. Santana*, 427 U.S. 38 (1976).

Warrantless misdemeanors: Police cannot enter under Michigan statute

Officers chased a subject into his house for fleeing and eluding, which was a misdemeanor at the time. The court held the arrest violated state law.

The court held that Michigan's statute allowing breaking and entering of outer or inner door of any building by a police officer to make an arrest applied only when the officer possessed a warrant or in cases of a felony without a warrant. The statute did not authorize nonconsensual entry into a person's home or other building for purpose of making a warrantless misdemeanor arrest. *People v. Reinhardt*, 141 Mich. App. 173 (1985). (See Chapter Nineteen, Laws of Arrest, for further information and explanation.)

Exigent circumstances needed for warrantless entry

After two days of intense investigation, New York detectives determined that Mr. Payton had murdered the manager of a gas station. At approximately 7:30 a.m. on a Saturday morning, six officers went to Payton's apartment without either an arrest warrant or a search warrant. Although music was coming from the apartment, there was no answer to their knocks. They used crowbars and forced entry into the residence. They were unable to find Payton, but they did locate and seize a thirty-caliber shell casing that was later admitted into evidence at Payton's trial. The U.S. Supreme Court held the entry was unlawful and suppressed the evidence.

The Court has consistently held that the "physical entry of the home is the chief evil against which the wording of the Fourth Amendment is directed." In this case, the entry was too substantial an invasion to allow without a warrant, in the absence of exigent circumstances, even when it is accomplished under statutory authority and when probable cause is present. For Fourth Amendment purposes, an arrest warrant founded on probable cause implicitly carries with it the limited authority to enter a dwelling in which the suspect lives when there is reason to believe the suspect is within. However, the officers in this case did not have an arrest warrant; therefore, the entry was improper. *Payton v. New York*, 445 U.S. 573 (1980).

A 10-1/2—year-old was taken from her apartment at knifepoint. She was taken to another apartment where she was forced to perform fellatio, and the defendant attempted penetration using petroleum jelly. About an hour and a half later, she was released and officers found her wandering outside. The officers broke into the apartment to arrest the defendant, but were unable to locate him. However, in the process they found the jar of petroleum jelly and seized it.

The court held that entering the apartment to look for the defendant fell under hot pursuit and the petroleum jelly was in plain view; thus, its seizure was proper. *People v. Lynn*, 91 Mich. App. 117 (1979).

Police were dispatched to a robbery/murder that had just occurred. A tracking dog led officers to a nearby house. The officers entered and discovered defendant and the murder weapon.

The court held that the entry was valid because the dog track constituted probable cause and the entry was within minutes of the murder; thus falling within the hot pursuit exception. *People v. Joyner*, 93 Mich. App. 554 (1979).

Officers investigated a double homicide that had occurred at 10:00 p.m. At 4:00 a.m., they received information that the suspect was in a motel room. At that point, the murder weapon, a shotgun, had not yet been recovered. The officers went to the room without a warrant and knocked and announced their presence. When there was no answer, they entered, locating the subject and the weapon lying on the bed.

The court held that the police were justified in concluding that the suspect's armed presence in the hotel endangered the lives of the other guests. Further, the police were justified in concluding that any delay in arresting the suspect while obtaining an arrest warrant would be unreasonable in light of the danger that he posed to the other guests. Therefore, there were exigent circumstances known to the police that excused them from taking time to obtain an arrest warrant. *People v. Snider*, 239 Mich. App. 393 (2000).

Non-exigent circumstances

Officers were investigating a B&E, during which the 65-year-old victim was physically assaulted, raped, and robbed in her home. Officers received a tip that Love may have been involved, and he was currently at his apartment. Several officers went to the home and entered it, searched it, and found evidence.

The court held the entry and search ware not valid, because there were no exigent circumstances. There was no concern that evidence would be lost or destroyed while the police obtained a warrant. Further, there was no threat that the defendant would escape, and if there was, the police could have prevented it by posting officers outside of the apartment while others obtained a warrant. *People v. Love*, 156 Mich. App. 568 (1986).

Police suspected Olson of being the driver of the getaway car used in a robbery-murder. After recovering the murder weapon and arresting the suspected murderer, they surrounded the home of two women with whom they believed Olson had been staying. When police telephoned the home and told one of the women that Olson should come out, a male voice was heard saying, "Tell them I left." Without seeking permission and with weapons drawn, they entered the home, found Olson hiding in a closet, and arrested him. Shortly thereafter, he made an inculpatory statement.

The Court held that an entry may be justified by hot pursuit of a fleeing felon, the imminent destruction of evidence, the need to prevent a suspect's escape, or the risk of danger to the police or others. However, in the absence of hot pursuit, there must be at least probable cause to believe that one or more of the other factors were present and, in assessing the risk of danger, the gravity of the crime and likelihood that the suspect is armed should be considered. In this case, although a grave crime was involved, Olson was known not to be the murderer and the murder weapon had been recovered. There was no suggestion of danger to the women; several police squads surrounded the house, it was evident that the suspect was not leaving; and if he came out of the house he would have been promptly apprehended. In light of all of these factors, the court held that the police should have obtained a warrant before they entered the home. *Minnesota v. Olson*, 495 U.S. 91 (1990).

Third party residence: Police may not enter solely under the authority of an arrest warrant

DEA agents had an arrest warrant for a subject with the last name of Lyons. They received information from an informant that he was at Steagald's house. They went to the residence and entered without a search warrant or consent. The officers did not find Lyons, but did seize cocaine and subsequently charged Steagald for possession of cocaine.

The Court suppressed the evidence. The Court reasoned that, when issuing an arrest warrant, the magistrate does not generally consider privacy interests of third parties as is the case when a search warrant is issued. The arrest warrant issued for Lyons offered no protection to Steagald's expectation of privacy, he was not even contemplated by the magistrate at the time of issuance. The Court held the entry was unlawful. An arrest warrant may only be used to search the residence of the person for whom the warrant is issued. For other third-party residences, police must obtain a search warrant, unless another exemption to the search warrant requirement exists. *Steagald v. United States*, 451 U.S. 204 (1982).

Officers entered a third-party residence to arrest a fugitive. A scuffle between the police and the occupants of the home ensued and the officers charged the occupants with R and O.

The court dismissed the charges because the officers did not first seek a search warrant before entry into the house. *People v. Stark*, 120 Mich. App. 350 (1982).

ADMINISTRATIVE SEARCHES

Searches conducted pursuant to a statutory scheme to regulate a particular industry or business.

Generally, there is implied consent for the inspections.

The court uses a balancing test to determine if an administrative search is permissible, using the following factors:

1. The existence of express statutory authorization for search or seizure.
2. The importance of the governmental interest at stake.
3. The pervasiveness and longevity of industry regulation.
4. The inclusion of reasonable limitations on searches in statutes and regulations.
5. The government's need for flexibility in the time, scope, and frequency of inspections in order to achieve reasonable levels of compliance.
6. The degree of intrusion occasioned by a particular regulatory search.
7. The degree to which a business person may be said to have impliedly consented to warrantless searches as a condition of doing business, so that the search does not infringe upon reasonable expectations of privacy.

Some industries are pervasively regulated to ensure safety, such as fire codes, public health codes, and buildings. In this case, an inspector attempted to force his way into an apartment without a warrant to check for fire code violations.

The Court held that the entry was illegal without a warrant; but the standard for getting the warrant would be less than the probable cause needed for a search warrant. The inspectors should have sought a warrant based on reasonable legislative or administrative standards. *See v. Seattle*, 387 U.S. 541 (1967).

Department of natural resources

DNR officers attempted to board several licensed commercial fishing vessels on a number of different occasions to see if there was a violation of commercial fishing laws. Some, but not all, of the attempted boardings were with probable cause.

The Court held searches can be conducted without a showing of probable cause to determine if there has been a violation of a pervasively regulated industry. Searches must be done pursuant to a statutory scheme to regulate a particular industry or business that gives authority to search. Implied consent is given as a condition of doing business. In this case, the searches fit within the parameters of an administrative search. *Tallman v. DNR*, 421 Mich. 585 (1984).

Liquor inspections

Officers received a tip that defendant was selling cocaine out of a party store. The information was that cocaine was located in a wooden box with a smoked glass top on a shelf in the back of the store. The officers went to the store and found the box. When they were not given consent to open it, they obtained a search warrant to open the box and found cocaine.

The Court of Appeals held that the search locating the box was legal and, further, the officers did not need a warrant to open the box once it was found. The Liquor Control Act provides that a "commission investigator or law enforcement officer" can inspect licensed premises. The inspections must take place during regular business hours. The search fit within the parameters of the statutory authorization; therefore, it was proper. *People v. Jones*, 180 Mich. App. 625 (1989).

Junk yards

During an inspection of a salvage yard, officers discovered that the owner neither had a license nor the required records. The officers checked some of the parts and found that they were stolen.

The court held, since state law requires the inspection, the search was valid. *People v. Barnes*, 146 Mich. App. 37 (1985).

Fire scenes

Firefighters may enter a scene of a fire within a reasonable time after the fire has been extinguished without a warrant. The entry may be to ensure the fire is extinguished and there is no pending danger.

The Court held an entry to fight a fire required no warrant and additional entries after the fire to investigate the cause may be made under the warrant procedures for administrative searches. In this case, because arson was suspected, the officials needed to obtain a warrant to gather evidence for the prosecution of the crime. *Michigan v. Tyler*, 436 U.S. 499 (1978).

Officers at the scene of a fire may enter to search for the origin of the fire, to prevent further damage. Once in the building, they need no warrant to remain for a reasonable time to investigate the cause of a blaze after it has been extinguished. However, reasonable expectations of privacy remain in the fire-damaged property. Therefore, additional investigations after the fire has been extinguished require a warrant or the identification of some new exigency. *Michigan v. Clifford*, 464 U.S. 287 (1984).

Other businesses or industries affected

- Precious metal and gem dealers
- Pawn shops
- Junk and scrap metal dealers
- Tobacco retailers and wholesalers

BORDER SEARCHES EXCEPTION

To protect the borders of the country, federal officers enforcing federal law may make routine searches of persons without probable cause or reasonable suspicion.

A checkpoint must be a fixed checkpoint or the functional equivalent. Roving checkpoints without probable cause are not proper. *Alemida-Sanchez v. United States*, 413 U.S. 266 (1973).

At a border checkpoint an inspector stopped a car and requested the driver to step out. The vehicle was taken to a secondary inspection station where the gas tank was tapped. It produced a different sound than expected, which piqued the inspector's interest. A mechanic was called in to remove the tank. He arrived 20 to 30 minutes later and after the tank was removed. The inspector located 37 kilograms of marijuana.

The Court held that the government's authority to conduct suspicion-less inspections at the border includes the authority to remove, disassemble, and reassemble a vehicle's parts. *United States v. Flores-Montano*, 541 U.S. 149 (2004).

24

LAWS OF EVIDENCE

INTRODUCTION

Definition of Evidence

Any means by which an issue, fact, or the truth of the matter is proved or disproved.

Purpose of the Rules of Evidence - MRE 102

To secure fairness, eliminate unjustifiable expense and delay, and to ascertain the truth.

General Descriptive Terms

Circumstantial Evidence: A group of facts that, when linked together, gives rise to a certain conclusion. Includes presumptions, inferences, habit, custom, and many types of physical evidence. It is equally competent with direct evidence, and its relative weight is for the fact-finder to decide.

Cumulative Evidence: Additional evidence tending to prove the same point. May be excluded from trial.

Demonstrative Evidence: Evidence used to illustrate something to the jury (i.e., photograph, sketches, maps, models of crime scene).

Direct Evidence: Evidence that, if believed, proves existence of fact in issue without inference or presumption (i.e., witness identification, written statements by suspect).

Real Evidence: Tangible items (i.e., fingerprint, document, gun).

Testimonial Evidence: Evidence received from a witness. Witness testifies to what he or she directly saw or indirectly saw as to habit, custom, circumstantial evidence, etc.

Judging Credibility and Weight of Evidence

> Weight and credibility are questions for the jury to decide alone. The judge decides the admissibility of the evidence. *Knowles v. People*, 15 Mich. 408 (1867).

The jury, or the judge in a bench trial, must:

- Decide what the facts of this case are.
- Decide which witnesses are credible and how important their testimony is.

The jury does not have to accept or reject everything a witness says, jury members are free to believe all, none, or part of any person's testimony.

In deciding which testimony to believe, the trier of fact should rely on his or her own common sense and everyday experience. However, the believability of a witness shall not be predicated on any bias or prejudice based on the race, gender, or national origin of the witness.

There is no fixed set of rules for determining whether a witness should be believed. The court

263

provides lay jurors the following factors to help them determine whether they should believe a witness. CJI2d 6.

- Was the witness able to see or hear clearly?
- How long was the witness watching or listening?
- Was anything else going on that might have distracted the witness?
- Does the witness seem to have a good memory?
- How does the witness look and act while testifying? Does the witness seem to be making an honest effort to tell the truth, or does the witness seem to evade the questions or argue with the lawyers?
- Does the witness's age or maturity affect how you judge his or her testimony?
- Does the witness have any bias or prejudice or any personal interest in how this case is decided?
- Have there been any promises, threats, suggestions, or other influences that affect how the witness testifies?
- In general, does the witness have any special reason to tell the truth, or any special reason to lie?
- All in all, how reasonable does the witness's testimony seem when you think about all the other evidence in the case?

PROOF
Burden of Proof

- **Burden of Producing Evidence:** Party has to produce enough evidence so that reasonable people viewing the evidence in the light most favorable to that party could find in that party's favor.
- **Burden of Persuasion:** A party must persuade the trier of fact to accept his or her argument.

Standard of Proof

- **Criminal Trial**—*Beyond a reasonable doubt:* A reasonable doubt is a fair, honest doubt growing out of the evidence or lack of evidence. It is not merely an imaginary or possible doubt, but a doubt based on reason and common sense. A reasonable doubt is just that—-a doubt that is reasonable, after a careful and considered examination of the facts and circumstances of this case. (CJI 2d 3.2).
- **Civil Trial, Informal Hearings, Formal Hearings**—*Preponderance of the evidence:* Evidence that, as a whole, shows the fact sought to be proven is more probable than not. It is the greater weight of the evidence. This also is the standard used for evidentiary hearings.
- **Stricter Civil Standard**—*Clear and convincing:* This standard requires the trier of fact to have less doubt and a firmer conviction about decision than the usual civil standard of preponderance of the evidence. Party is usually relying upon a theory that is disfavored upon policy grounds (i.e., Mental Commitment Hearings).

CORPUS DELICTI
Definition

- "Body of the crime"— substance of the crime.
- Each element of the crime must be proven beyond a reasonable doubt.
- Evidentiary rule where each individual element of crime must be proven.

Burden of Proof

- On prosecutor.
- An extrajudicial confession by itself cannot establish the corpus delecti.

A voluntary confession, made extra-judicially, is only received as evidence of guilt and by itself cannot establish guilt.

> Carolyn Kenyon disappeared without a trace in 1985. In 1990 police were investigating the defendant when he confessed to killing Kenyon. He stated that he had cut the body up and thrown it into a dumpster. Other than the confession, the prosecution produced no other evidence.
>
> Defendant's conviction for second degree murder was reversed. Evidence of the murder must exist independent of the confession. *People v. McMahan*, 451 Mich. 543 (1996).

RES GESTAE

The *res gestae* include circumstances, facts, and declarations that surround the commission of a crime. The evidence should be contemporaneous with the crime and serve to illustrate its character.

Res gestae witness

Definition

- An eyewitness to a criminal event whose testimony will aid in developing a full disclosure of all the facts.
- Also includes all witnesses having contact with the defendant reasonably contemporaneous with the crime, whose testimony tends to show the state of mind in which the criminal act was done.

Purpose of res gestae witness rule

- Shield defendant from false accusations.
- Prevent suppression of testimony favorable to accused.
- Ensure disclosure of all circumstances.

People v. Norwood, 123 Mich. App. 287 (1983).

Requirements—MCL 767.40a

- Prosecutor must list all known witnesses.
- Prosecutor must advise defense who will be called 30 days prior to trial.
- Prosecutor and police must use due diligence in assisting defense in locating any witnesses required by the defense. Due diligence is defined as doing everything reasonable, not everything possible.

> The prosecuting attorney or investigative law enforcement agency shall provide to the defendant, or defense counsel, upon request, reasonable assistance, including investigative assistance, as may be necessary to locate and serve process upon a witness. *People v. Koonce*, 466 Mich. 515 (2002).

CHAIN OF CUSTODY

Definition

The one who offers real evidence must account for the custody of the evidence from the moment it reaches his or her custody until the moment it is offered into evidence.

Purpose

To ensure the integrity of evidence and that it is, in fact, the item or evidence that is a part of the criminal charges being litigated.

Effect

Chain of custody goes toward the weight of evidence and not admissibility.

> A perfect chain of custody is not always required. Items of evidence may be admitted where the absence of a mistaken exchange, contamination, or tampering has been established to a reasonable degree of probability or certainty. *People v. White*, 208 Mich. App. 126 (1994).

JUDICIAL NOTICE—MRE 201

Definition

Judicial Notice is an evidentiary shortcut. The court accepts certain facts without requiring formal proof. It is only permissible when the matter is not subject to reasonable dispute because the issue is:

- Generally known within the territorial jurisdiction of the court, or
- Capable of accurate and ready determination by sources whose accuracy cannot reasonably be questioned.

Example: City of Lansing is located in Ingham County and the State of Michigan.

Effect

- Civil Trial: A jury must accept as conclusive.
- Criminal Trial: A jury may, but is not bound to, accept as conclusive.

> Judicial notice was taken regarding the reliability of bloodstain interpretation evidence. The court held that a trial court may take judicial notice of the general acceptance of certain forensic evidence by the scientific community. *People v. Haywood*, 209 Mich. App. 217 (1995).
>
> It was improper for the trial judge to take judicial notice of the time it takes the toilet to cycle because the fact was not generally known within the court's jurisdiction and was not readily ascertainable. *People v. United States Currency*, 158 Mich. App. 126 (1986).

PRESUMPTIONS AND INFERENCES

Presumption

The finding of one basic fact gives rise to the existence of the presumed fact.
- In a civil trial, the jury is bound to accept a presumption (MRE 301). However, the presumption may be rebutted by the opposing party.
- In a criminal trial, the jury is not bound to accept a presumption. The jury may, but need not, infer the existence of a presumed fact. The prosecution still bears the burden of proof beyond a reasonable doubt of all elements. —MRE 302

Presumption of innocence

A defendant is presumed innocent. Each element of the prosecutor's case must be proven beyond a reasonable doubt before conviction.

> MCL 750.535 states the presumption that a dealer who receives property with an altered registration number has knowingly received stolen property. This does not violate the presumptions of innocence where the prosecution must still prove all the elements beyond a reasonable doubt. *People v. Gallagher*, 404 Mich. 429 (1979).
>
> In a prosecution for stalking, evidence that the defendant continued to engage in repeated contact without consent after being asked to stop gives rise to a rebuttable presumption that the continuation of conduct caused the victim to feel frightened, intimidated, threatened, harassed, or molested. *People v. White*, 212 Mich. App. 298 (1995).

Inference

Deductions or conclusions that, with reason and common sense, lead the jury to draw from the facts already established.

> Where there was testimony that a battered child was in exclusive custody of the defendant at the time the child suffered the injuries, the jury could infer that the defendant caused the injuries. *People v. Barnard*, 93 Mich. App 590 (1979).

ADMISSIBILITY OF EVIDENCE

Relevancy of Evidenc—MRE 402

- All relevant evidence is admissible.
- All irrelevant evidence is not admissible.

Definition of Relevant Evidence—MRE 401

Evidence having any tendency to make the existence of any fact that is of consequence to the determination of the action more probable or less probable than it would be without the evidence.

- **Probative:** Must be able to help prove the matter.
  Example: Witness testifies that he saw Adam near the place where Bob was stabbed at the time of the stabbing. This evidence by itself cannot prove that Adam stabbed Bob, but is relevant.
- **Material:** Must tend to prove a matter that is in issue. Evidence must be relevant to a material issue to be admissible.

  Example: In an O.W.I. case, it would be immaterial to prove that the subject's license was suspended at the time of the stop.

> Evidence that the defendant borrowed a set of books titled *How to Kill*, which discussed different ways to kill people and suggested that the witness help murder someone was relevant to premeditation. *People v. Burgess*, 153 Mich. App. 715 (1986).
>
> Evidence that the crime was committed at an abandoned crack house had no probative value and was highly prejudicial. *People v. Spearman*, 195 Mich. App. 434 (1992).

Prejudicial Effect vs. Probative Value—MRE 402

Although relevant, evidence may be excluded if its probative value is substantially outweighed by the danger of:

- *Unfair* prejudice.

> Defendant in a gruesome murder admitted guilt and only contested his sanity. Therefore, photographs of the victim, a bloodstained sheet, and other items used in the attack had little, if any, probative value. *People v. Murphy*, 100 Mich. App. 413 (1980).

- *Confusion* of the issues

> In a civil suit founded on police brutality, evidence that drug paraphernalia was found at the scene was properly excluded because the danger of confusion outweighed the probative value. *Gainey v. Sieloff*, 163 Mich. App. 538 (1987).

- *Misleading* the jury, or
- By considerations of undue delay, waste of time, or needless presentation of cumulative evidence.

> The trial court properly excluded as cumulative the testimony of officials, including several commissioners, district court judges, mayors, police chiefs, and county sheriffs. *Wayne County Sheriff v. Wayne County Commissioners*, 148 Mich. App. 601 (1983).

BEST EVIDENCE RULE (ORIGINAL DOCUMENT RULE)

The Original Document is Required to Ensure Reliability—MRE 1001

To prove the content of a writing, recording, or photograph, the original writing, recording, or photograph is required, except as otherwise provided by the rules or by the statute.

KEY:

- When the actual contents of the document are an issue in controversy.
- Only when the contents have to be proven.

Definitions—MRE 1001

- **Writings and recordings (MRE 1001(1)):** Letters, words, or numbers set down in handwriting, typewriting, photostatting, electronic recording, or other form.
- **Photographs (MRE 1001(2)):** Still photographs, X-ray films, videotapes, and motion pictures.
- **Originals (MRE 1001(4)):** The writing or recording itself or any counterpart intended to have the same effect by a person executing or issuing it; photos include any negative or print from any computer printout.
- **Duplicates (MRE 1001(4)):** Counterpart produced by same impression as photocopy of the original that accurately reproduces original. Under MRE 1003, duplicates are admissible to the same extent as the original, *unless*:
  - Authenticity of original is in dispute, or
  - Would be unfair to admit the duplicate (partial document).

> The trial court properly admitted a filtered copy of a tape recording after the court determined it to be an accurate reproduction of the original. The difficulty in understanding the tape justified filtering out the background noise. *People v. Schram*, 98 Mich. App. 292 (1980).

Admissibility of Other Evidence of Contents—Mre 1004

Secondary evidence

If it is shown that there is a genuine original, then secondary evidence of its contents is permissible under the following circumstances:

- All originals are lost or destroyed.
- Original cannot be obtained by judicial process (i.e., outside court's subpoena power).
- Original is in possession of opponent who will not produce it.
- Document is relevant to a collateral issue and not closely related to the basic issue being tried.
- Public records may be proven by certified copy. MRE 1005

> The court properly admitted testimony regarding the content of threatening letters that had been destroyed. The destruction of the letters did not occur because of negligence or bad faith on the part of either the complainant or prosecutor. *People v. Thompson*, 111 Mich. App. 324 (1981).

HEARSAY RULE

Definition—MRE 801

Hearsay is an out of court statement, oral or written, made by someone other than the witness while testifying and offered for the purpose of proving the truth of the matter asserted.

For example, an officer responds to an accident. Upon arrival, a witness informs the officer that one of the drivers ran a red light, which caused the accident. It would be hearsay for the officer to testify in court as to what the witness observed. The officer can base his report and enforcement action on what the witness told him. However, if there is a trial, the witness must describe their observations in their own words so the jury may determine the credibility of the witness.

Nonverbal conduct may be hearsay if intended as an assertion.

Verbal acts are not hearsay. For example, "this is a stick-up" is part of the act and thus not considered a statement.

> The victim began to cry when she saw the suspect's picture in a mug book. Crying does not qualify as a statement because it was not intended as an assertion. *People v. Gwinn*, 111 Mich. App. 223 (1981).

Generally, hearsay statements are not admissible except as provided by the Rules of Evidence. Some specific situations, however, neutralize the dangers of hearsay, and the court has carved out some exceptions to the rule. There are some situations where the hearsay rule does not apply. Those include:

- Exclusion from the definition of hearsay and thus admissible.
- Hearsay but admissible any time.
- Hearsay but admissible if the declarant is not available to testify.

> A police officer properly testified as to a radio dispatcher stating robbery was in progress at a particular location, not to prove truth of statement, but rather to prove why officer proceeded to that location. *People v. Jackson*, 113 Mich. App. 620 (1982).
>
> A police radio dispatch indicating someone was screaming and honking a car horn was used as substantive proof the victim resisted the defendant's sexual advances. The testimony was inadmissible as hearsay. Also, the witness who reported the screaming was not available for trial. *People v. Eady*, 409 Mich. 356 (1980).

Confrontation clause (Sixth Amendment)

> It violates the defendant's Sixth Amendment right to confront witnesses to admit the testimony of a person unless the defendant has the opportunity to cross-examine the witness. This only applies if the statements are testimonial in nature. Non-testimonial statements (statements that fall into one of the categories below) are admissible. *Davis v. Washington*, 547 U.S. 813 (2006).

Statements That are Not Considered Hearsay—MRE 801(d)

A prior statement of a witness

This includes any statement by a witness at a trial and one of the following:

- A prior inconsistent statement that was given under oath.
- A prior consistent statement to rebut a charge of recent fabrication, improper influences, or motive. Used to bolster the witness's credibility (i.e., the defense claims at trial that the witness is changing his or her story). The police officer testifies that witness reported the same account when the investigation began.
- A prior identification made by an eyewitness who is testifying at trial; i.e., line-up, photo display, or show-up.

Admission by party opponent

A party's own statement that is being offered against him or her. This does not include guilty pleas to misdemeanor traffic offenses and admissions of responsibility for civil infractions.

> An officer could testify that the defendant had stated he had no need to rob because he made a lot of money selling drugs and that he had just been robbed of $80,000 worth of heroin. *People v. Smith*, 120 Mich. App. 429 (1982).
>
> The defendant's statement to his mother that he was going to kill her was not hearsay because the statement was offered against the defendant and was his own statement. *People v. Kowalak*, 215 Mich. App. 554 (1996).

Statement not made by a party, but one to which he or she has manifested belief

> Defendant was a Salvation Army truck driver and went to the victim's house to pick up a donation. The next day, the victim noticed her ring was missing. She reported it and the detective called the defendant and asked him to come to the station. The defendant never appeared.
>
> At trial, the prosecutor stated that defendant must be guilty of the crime because he did not accept the invitation to discuss the crime with the detective. The conviction was reversed. *People v. Greenwood*, 209 Mich. App. 470 (1995).
>
> The Fifth Amendment does not preclude use of testimony concerning defendant's behavior and demeanor after a valid waiver of rights. A suspect's lack of responsiveness during the interview with police was not evidence of silence. Rather, it was admissible as nonverbal, nonassertive conduct. *People v. McReavy*, 436 Mich. 197 (1990).

Statement by a co-conspirator during the course and in furtherance of the conspiracy

> A codefendant made a statement to the police that implicated the defendant. Since this statement was made immediately after and at the scene of the drug transfer, it was sufficiently connected to the conspiracy to be admissible. *People v. Johnson*, 103 Mich. App. 825 (1981).

Statement by a person made within the scope of his employment and made during the time of employment

Hearsay Exceptions Where Availability of Declarant Does Not Matter—MRE 803

Present sense impression—MRE 803(1)

A statement describing or explaining an event or condition made *while the declarant was perceiving the event or condition, or immediately thereafter* (i.e., "Look at those fools speeding." or "That guy looks drunk.")

> During a 911 call, the victim stated, "I have just had the living s- beat out of me." Her live-in boyfriend was subsequently arrested and charged with domestic violence. The victim then requested that the charges be dropped and refused to testify. The question presented to the court was whether the 911 tape could be entered as a present sense impression exception to the hearsay rule.
>
> Although for differing reasons, the Supreme Court held that the tape was admissible. Three of the justices held the statement was admissible if there was corroborating evidence to substantiate the assault took place. In this case, the investigating officer took pictures of the victim's injuries, which verified the statement by the victim that she had been assaulted. *People v. Hendrickson*, 459 Mich. 229 (1998).

Excited utterance—MRE 803(2)

A statement relating to *a startling event or condition made while the declarant was under the stress of excitement caused by the event or condition* (i.e., "My wife shot me!").

> An out-of-court statement by a child made one month after alleged sexual misconduct did not fit within the excited utterance exception because it was not sufficiently established that declarant spoke while still under the stress caused by the startling event. *People v. Straight*, 430 Mich. 418 (1988).
>
> A statement that a 16-year-old son made to his mother 10 hours after being sexually assaulted was an excited utterance where it was shown that he was still under the stress of the event. *People v. Smith*, 456 Mich. 543 (1998).

Then existing mental, emotional, or physical condition—MRE 803(3)

Use of a present mental state may be allowed as circumstantial evidence that the mental state continued into the future and that the declarant at some future time acted in accordance with the mental state. For example, "I plan to travel to Lansing tomorrow."

Includes intent, plan, motive, design, mental feelings, pain, and body health.

> In a first-degree murder prosecution, a page from the victim's appointment book was admissible under the state-of-mind exception to the hearsay rule as a declaration of where the victim intended to go. *People v. Howard*, 226 Mich. App. 528 (1997).

Recorded recollection—MRE 803(5)

A record of something that the witness once had knowledge about, but now has insufficient recollection. Record must have been made or adopted by the witness when the matter was fresh in his memory (i.e., list of stolen property in a complaint).

Present memory refreshed—MRE 612

A witness may use any writing or object to refresh his or her memory when testifying. If the witness refreshes his or her memory while testifying, the adverse party is entitled to have the writing or object produced. If the witness refreshes his or her memory before testifying, the court, at its discretion, can determine if justice so requires that an adverse party is entitled to have the writing or object produced. For example, a police officer may have to review his or her notes during testimony. If the notes were used to refresh the memory, the defense would have access to review the notes.

Terms and conditions of production and use:

- Party can inspect the object.
- Party can cross-examine the witness regarding the object.
- Party can introduce into evidence those portions relating to the testimony of the witness.

Business records or regularly conducted activity—MRE 803(6)

Bank records, business records, etc., are admissible as long as regularly recorded as part of the business activity.

> Plainclothes officers shot a father while in the process of arresting his son in the driveway of the home. The father came out of his house with his gun not knowing that the officers were officers. Because the reports were made under the circumstances of highly probable civil and criminal litigation and department discipline, they were not admissible. *Solomon v. Shuell*, 435 Mich. 104 (1990).
>
> The report of a medical exam in a CSC case was not admissible where the report was prepared solely for litigation purposes and thus lacked trustworthiness. *People v. Huyser*, 221 Mich. App. 293 (1997).

Statements made for purposes of medical treatment or medical diagnosis in connection with treatment—MRE 803(4)

An inherent truthfulness exists when a person describes a pain, symptom, or problem to medical personnel. The statement can be made to a nurse, ambulance driver, doctor, etc.

> A statement to a doctor by a 5-year-old in which she identified the defendant as the perpetrator of a sexual assault upon her was both trustworthy and reasonably necessary for her medical treatment and diagnosis. *People v. Meerboer*, 439 Mich. 310 (1992).

Public records—MRE 803 (8)(B)

There are records, reports, statements, or data compilations of public agencies setting forth activities of the agency or matters observed pursuant to a duty imposed by law. This does not include criminal matters observed by police officers and other law enforcement personnel.

> The trial court did not err by admitting a police report concerning the location of another suspect at the time of the offense. A police report of routine matters observed by police officers made in a non-adversarial setting, as opposed to matters observed by police officers at a scene of a crime or while investigating a crime, is admissible under MRE 803 (8)(B). (*People v. Stacy*, 192 Mich. App. 19 [1992]).

Child's statement about sexual act (Tender Years Rule)—MRE 803(A)

A statement describing a sexual act performed on the declarant by defendant or accomplice is admissible, if it corroborates testimony given by the declarant during the same proceeding and:

- Declarant is under the age of 10 when statement is made.
- Statement is spontaneous and not manufactured.
- Statement is made immediately after the incident; or fear or some other reason excuses any delay.

> A delay of several days in reporting an incident was excusable because the complainant feared reprisal by the defendant. In this case, a father placed his finger in his 9-year-old daughter's vagina. *People v. Hammons*, 210 Mich. App. 554 (1995).

Exceptions Where Declarant is Unavailable—MRE 804

Unavailable defined

- Declarant refuses to testify.
- Declarant lacks sufficient memory to testify.
- Where party has been unable to locate the declarant after due diligence.
- Death, physical or mental illness, or infirmity to the declarant.
- Where the statement is exempt under a privilege: attorney/client, doctor/patient, right against self-incrimination.

Former testimony

Former testimony is when a witness at another hearing gives a statement and the opposing side has a prior opportunity and similar motive to cross-examine. For example, a murder trial is overturned on appeal ten years after the trial. During that time, a witness at the trial passed away. That testimony at the second trial could be admissible under former testimony.

> Where witness was not available, the trial court properly admitted his testimony in a retrial for B & E. The former testimony had been taken at trial where the defendant and counsel had a similar motive and opportunity to examine the witness. *People v. Murray*, 106 Mich. App. 257 (1981).

Dying declaration

Requires the following 4 elements:

1. The declarant was conscious of impeding death.
2. Death ensued.
3. The statements were being admitted against the one who killed the declarant.
4. The statement relates to the circumstances of the killing.

> A dying declaration did not occur where a statement was made a month after the shooting and that the victim was recuperating at the time it was made. *People v. Parney*, 98 Mich. App. 571 (1979).

In criminal cases, dying declarations are only allowed in homicide cases. In civil cases, they are allowed in all proceedings.

Statement against interest

Statement made by declarant and against pecuniary or criminal interest of declarant. A reasonable person in declarant's position would not have made the statement unless he or she believed it to be true. Also, the declarant does not need to be a party to the case as in admissions in MRE 801.

> A police officer was allowed to testify to the contents of a telephone call that the officer listened to involving an informant and the defendant arranging the sale of drugs. *People v. Lucas*, 188 Mich. App. 554 (1991).

> Statements that an unavailable declarant made were admissible because they were made against his penal interest. In this case, the declarant stated that there was blood in his bathtub and that he cleaned up the house where the murder occurred. The statements were made voluntarily and to a person he considered a friend. *People v. Kehoe*, 237 Mich. App. 508 (1999).

> The defendant was convicted of murder. The key evidence was a statement that his codefendant, Andre Freeman, had made. Freeman told his ex-girlfriend that he and Beasley went to the victim's house to purchase drugs. At the residence, they found more drugs than expected and decided to take advantage of the situation by shooting the woman and man at the residence. The ex-girlfriend testified that Freeman told her this information because he had to get it off his chest and that she was the only one he could talk to.

> Beasley argued on appeal that the ex-girlfriend's statement to Freeman was not admissible against him. The Court of Appeals disagreed. "Freeman's statement was voluntarily given to Townsend (his ex-girlfriend), who was someone to whom Freeman would likely speak truthfully. Furthermore, Freeman sought out Townsend to initiate the making of the statement. In addition, as stated earlier, Freeman's statement was clearly against his penal interest, and does not shift the blame but makes reference to defendant only in the context of his narration of the events of the incident." *People v. Beasley*, 239 Mich. App. 548 (2000).

Bottom line is to record the facts and circumstances surrounding all statements. Circumstances may allow the prosecutor to use evidence that would have otherwise gone unheard.

Hearsay statements in domestic violence cases—MCL 768.27c

Statements made by victims of domestic violence are admissible in court, even if the victim is not present, if the victim's statement:

- Is made to a law enforcement officer,
- Describes the infliction or threat of physical injury,
- Is made at or near the time of the infliction or threat of physical injury, and
- Is made under circumstances indicating trustworthiness

TESTIMONY

Competency—MRE 601

Every person is competent to be a witness, unless the court finds he or she does not have:

- Sufficient physical or mental capacity; or
- Sense of obligation to testify truthfully and understandably.

Personal Knowledge—MRE 602

The witness may not testify unless he or she has personal knowledge of the crime. Evidence to prove personal knowledge may, but need not, consist of testimony of the witness.

Oath or Affirmations—MRE 603

The witness must declare that he or she will testify truthfully by oath or affirmation, administered in a form calculated to awaken his or her conscience and impress upon his or her mind with a duty to do so.

Sequestration of Witnesses—MRE 615

A party must request that a witness be sequestered. This ensures that other witnesses do not taint the witness's testimony. For example, two officers are subpoenaed to testify on an O.W.I. arrest that they made together. One officer will testify while the other is sequestered and will wait outside the courtroom.

Persons who cannot be sequestered include:

- A party who is a natural person (i.e., defendant).
- An officer or employee of a party who is not a natural person, but designated as a representative.
- A person essential to the presentation of the case (i.e., prosecutor may need AU: There is a verb missing here. The prosecutor may what?the investigating officer to help present the case).

OPINION EVIDENCE

Lay Opinion—MRE 701

A lay opinion is rationally based on the perception of a witness. The opinion is helpful for a clear understanding of the incident.

> Witnesses were allowed to give opinions about the visible intoxication of the defendant. *Heyler v. Dixson*, 160 Mich. App. 130 (1987).
>
> A police officer, who was not an expert in drug enforcement, was allowed to give an opinion based on his observations of the defendant selling crack cocaine. *People v. Daniel*, 207 Mich. App. 47 (1994).

Expert Opinion—MRE 702

A witness may be qualified as an expert, which would allow him or her to give an expert opinion on a certain issue. The expertise of the witness will assist the trier of fact in understanding the evidence or determining a fact in issue. For example, police officers may be experts if they have special training to qualify them as experts.

> An officer trained in accident reconstruction was qualified as an expert to give an opinion about results of tests that he had performed after an accident. *Osner v. Boughner*, 180 Mich. App. 248 (1989).

IMPEACHMENT

Definition

To impeach is to attack the credibility of a witness.

Who may impeach—MRE 607

Any party, including the party calling him or her, may attack the credibility of a witness.

Impeachment by Character Evidence—MRE 608

Opinion or reputation

- This includes evidence about a witness's reputation for truth and veracity from someone who is familiar with the witness in the community where he or she lives. For example, "He's lived in our neighborhood for four years. Everyone knows he is dishonest."
- A party's present personal opinion of witness's ability to tell the truth. There must be a reasonable basis for the opinion. For example, "I've worked with Jones for five years and he has lied to me a number of times."

Prior bad acts

Specific instances of conduct involving honesty or dishonesty. This is under the discretion of the court.

Impeachment by Evidence of Conviction—MRE 609

Evidence that a witness has been convicted of a crime shall not be admitted unless elicited from the witness or established by public record and all of the following:

- The crime contained an element of dishonesty, false statement, or theft;
- The crime was punishable for more than one year or death;
- The court determines the evidence has significant probative value on the issue of credibility; and
- The court determines the probative value of the evidence outweighs its prejudicial effect.

A conviction is not admissible if a period of 10 years has elapsed since the date of:

- conviction, or
- release from confinement.

> Because armed robbery contains an element of theft, evidence of such prior conviction is admissible under MRE 609, if it satisfies the balancing test. *People v. Cross*, 202 Mich. App. 138 (1993).

CHARACTER EVIDENCE

Generally, evidence of a person's character is not admissible to prove he acted similarly on a particular occasion. MRE 404 (a). Exceptions to this rule include the following:

- The defendant may introduce evidence of his or her good character to prove it was unlikely he or she committed the crime. The prosecution may then prove bad character.
- The defendant may introduce evidence of the victim's character. If the defendant raises self-defense in homicide, he or she may show the victim's reputation for violence. The prosecution may counter with evidence indicating the victim was peaceful. This does not apply to the victim in a CSC case.
- In a CSC case, evidence of the victim's past sexual relationship with the defendant is admissible, as well as specific instances of sexual activity showing source of semen, pregnancy, or disease.

Other Crimes, Wrongs, or Acts—MRE 404 (b)

Evidence of other crimes, wrongs, or acts is not admissible to prove a person acted similarly. It may be admissible to prove motive, opportunity, intent, preparation, scheme, plan, or system in doing an act, knowledge, identity, absence of mistake, or accident.

> The policy underlying MRE 404(b) is the desire to avoid the danger of conviction based on the defendant's history of other misconduct rather than on evidence of his or her conduct in the

case at issue. *People v. Golochowicz*, 413 Mich. 298 (1982).

MRE 404(b) only limits evidence of other acts introduced solely to show criminal propensity. Evidence of other acts may be introduced for any other purpose provided that it is logically relevant to a disputed material issue and is not substantially more prejudicial than probative. *People v. VanderVliet*, 444 Mich. 52 (1993).

Evidence of uncharged prior sexual abuse of defendant's half sister over a period of years by defendant was admissible in his trial for criminal sexual conduct involving his minor, adopted daughter. This evidence was admissible because it was offered to rebut his claim of fabrication by the victim's mother and explains why the victim was questioned regarding her father's conduct. *People v. Starr*, 457 Mich. 490 (1998).

Evidence that there had been previous altercations between the victim and defendant was admissible to contradict the argument that the altercation was an accident. *People v. Morris*, 139 Mich. App. 550 (1984).

Evidence of prior bad acts

During a CSC trial, the victim's sister was allowed to testify to similar activity by the defendant. The defendant's alleged assault of the complainant and alleged abuse of his stepdaughter shared sufficient common features to infer a plan, scheme, or system to do the acts. *People v. Sabin*, 463 Mich. 43 (2000).

During a trial for CSC 2nd between a teacher and a student, the prosecutor was allowed to enter into evidence the defendant had previously engaged in sexual penetration of a student as it showed a common plan in approaching and molesting his victims. *People v. Knapp*, 244 Mich. App. 361 (2001).

Evidence of assaults against the defendant's former girlfriends was admissible to establish common scheme, plan, or system in perpetrating a particular type of physical assault. *People v. Hine*, 467 Mich. 242 (2002).

Testimony of several girls that the defendant allowed his pants to fall down in front of them, or that the defendant otherwise exposed his genitals, was admissible because this evidence was relevant to the defendant's plan, scheme, or system. All three complainants described incidents in which the defendant's overalls fell to the floor while they were present. The frequency with which this happened in front of girls was relevant to show the improbability that the defendant's overalls accidentally fell and exposed his genitals and supported an inference that the defendant's actions were part of a system of desensitizing girls to sexual misconduct. *People v. Ackerman*, 257 Mich. App. 434 (2003).

Prior bad acts against minors—MCL 768.27a

If a defendant is accused of committing a listed offense against a person under the age of 18, evidence that the defendant committed another listed offense against a minor is admissible and may be considered for its bearing on any matter to which it is relevant. A "listed offense" is any offense that would require registration on Michigan's sex offender registry.

Prior bad acts – domestic violence—MCL 768.27b

If a defendant is accused of an offense involving domestic violence, evidence of the defendant's commission of other acts of domestic violence is admissible for any purpose for which it is relevant, if it is not otherwise excluded under Michigan rule of evidence 403, if the other acts were committed within the previous 10 years.

Rape shield statute—MCL 750.520j

(1) Evidence of specific instances of the victim's sexual conduct, opinion evidence of the victim's sexual conduct, and reputation evidence of the victim's sexual conduct shall not be admitted under sections 520b to 520g unless and only to the extent that the judge finds that the following proposed evidence is material to a fact at issue in the case and that its inflammatory or prejudicial nature does not outweigh its probative value:

  (a) Evidence of the victim's past sexual conduct with the actor.
  (b) Evidence of specific instances of sexual activity showing the source or origin of semen, pregnancy, or disease.

(2) If the defendant proposes to offer evidence described in subsection (1)(a) or
  (b) The defendant within 10 days after the arraignment on the information shall file a

written motion and offer of proof. The court may order an in camera hearing to determine whether the proposed evidence is admissible under subsection (1). If new information is discovered during the course of the trial that may make the evidence described in subsection (1)(a) or (b) admissible, the judge may order an in camera hearing to determine whether the proposed evidence is admissible under subsection (1).

The rape shield statute not only bars evidence of the complainant's sexual activities before the alleged rape, it also bars evidence of all sexual activity by the complainant not incident to the alleged rape. Evidence that the complainant had consented to sex with a stranger seven hours after the rape was not admissible to show she had consented to sex with the defendant. *People v. Stull*, 127 Mich. App. 14 (1983).

If a victim's statement regarding sex does not constitute specific sexual conduct, it is not precluded from admission by the rape shield statute. In this case, the victim made a statement earlier in the day to a friend that she was ready to have sex. Later that night, she had a sexual encounter with the defendant that she argued was rape, while his defense was consent. The statement to the friend was admissible on the issue of consent. *People v. Ivers*, 459 Mich. 320 (1998).

The rape shield statute bars evidence of all sexual activity by the complainant that is not incident to the alleged rape, except evidence of the victim's past sexual conduct with the defendant. Past sexual conduct includes acts that occur between the alleged rape and trial. *People v. Adair*, 452 Mich. 473 (1996).

The rape shield statute barred evidence that the complainant was a topless dancer and had been seen with prostitutes. *People v. Powell*, 201 Mich. App. 516 (1993).

Method to prove character—MRE 405

Character may be proven by reputation or opinion.

A county jail correctional officer was allowed to testify about a defense witness's reputation for untruthfulness among county jail employees. *People v. Bieri*, 153 Mich. App. 696 (1986).

Habit—MRE 406

Habit is a regular response to a repeated specific situation, a regular practice of meeting a particular kind of situation with a specific type of conduct, a set pattern, or evidence of something that is done routinely or has been performed on countless occasions. *Cook v. Rontal*, 109 Mich. App. 220 (1981).

PRIVILEGES—MRE 501

Certain confidential communications are considered privileged and cannot be used against a person. Only the holder can waive the privilege. The purpose of maintaining privileged communication is to encourage parties under certain circumstances to have open communication without concern of reprisal. Types of privileges are listed below.

Communications that take place in the presence of a third party are not privileged. The privilege protects only confidential communications. *People v. Biggs*, 202 Mich. App. 450 (1993).

Attorney-Client

Admission of a police officer's testimony that incriminating evidence had been seized from the defense counsel's office did not violate defendant's attorney-client privilege. *People v. Nash*, 418 Mich. 196 (1983).

Either the client or attorney may assert the privilege, but only the client may waive it. *Kubiak v. Hurr*, 143 Mich. App. 465 (1985).

There was no attorney/client privilege where a defendant chose to communicate with counsel by speaking in a manner that could be overheard by a third person rather than covering his mouth and quietly whispering or communicating in writing. *People v. Compeau*, 244 Mich. App. 595 (2001).

Spouses—MCL 600.2162

There are two types of privileges between a husband and wife. There is the spousal privilege and the confidential communications privilege.

> The defendant and the witness were married two weeks after the crime occurred and the time of the communications. They were divorced almost a year before trial. Because they had not yet married at the time of the communications, the communications privilege did not apply. Because they were divorced at the time of the trial, the spousal privilege did not apply. *People v. Zak*, 184 Mich. App. 1 (1990).

In a criminal prosecution, a party may consent to testify against his or her spouse. Thus the testifying party holds the privilege.

MCL 600.2162(2) provides:

"In criminal prosecution, a husband shall not be examined as a witness for or against his wife without his consent, or a wife for or against her husband without her consent."

MCL 600.2162(7) provides:

"A married person or a person who has been married previously shall not be examined in a criminal prosecution as to any communication made between that person and his or her spouse or former spouse during the marriage without consent of the person to be examined."

This privilege does not apply to the following actions: divorce, bigamy, crimes against the spouse or children, desertion or abandonment, certain property actions, and cases involving invalid marriages.

Physician-Patient—MCL 600.2157

Obtaining blood results from the hospital may violate doctor-patient privilege.

> In a drug prosecution, the defendant's doctor was not precluded from testifying about the defendant's altered prescription. Legitimate confidential communications are protected, but not communications that further an unlawful purpose. *People v. Johnson*, 111 Mich. App. 383 (1981).

> The prosecutor could not subpoena blood results of a mother whose house burned down while she was intoxicated, killing her three children. The Court of Appeals denied the subpoena on the basis of the physician-patient privilege. *People v. Childs*, 243 Mich. App. 360 (2000).

Psychologist-Patient—MCL 333.18237

> The purpose of the psychologist-patient privilege statute is to protect the confidential nature of the psychologist-patient relationship. *People v. Lobaito*, 133 Mich. App. 577 (1984).

Clergy—MCL 600.2156

> The privilege of the confessional belongs to the penitent. *People v. Lipsczinska*, 212 Mich. 484 (1920).

Traffic crash reports—MCL 257.624

Answers required by statute are not admissible.

Domestic violence victim or sexual assault victim-counselor—MCL 600.2157a(2)

A confidential communication, or any report, working paper, or statement made in connection with a consultation between a victim and a sexual assault or domestic violence counselor, is not admissible as evidence in any civil or criminal proceeding without the prior written consent of the victim.

Informants

> Disclosure of an informant's identity must be determined according to the circumstances of each case. The trial court should require production of the informant and conduct a hearing in chambers out of the presence of the defendant, if the government invokes the informer's privilege following a defense request for disclo-

sure and the accused is able to demonstrate a possible need for the informer's testimony. At the hearing, the court can examine the informant to determine whether any testimony could be offered that would be helpful to the defense. If the testimony would be helpful to the defense, the informant's identity will be revealed to the defense. A record should be made of the hearing with the contents sealed, and access must be limited to appellate review. *People v. Underwood*, 447 Mich. 695 (1994).

Social worker—MCL 333.18513

A social worker may be an affiant on a search warrant. The social worker privilege does not apply to actions taken under the child protection law. *People v. Wood*, 447 Mich. 80 AU: Date missing for this case. (1994).

Self-incrimination—MCL 600.2154

A witness cannot be forced to give an answer that has a tendency of incriminating him- or herself of a crime.

Polygraph results or reports (MCL 338.1728)

A polygraph result or the refusal to take a polygraph may not be used by the prosecution.

The mention of taking a polygraph by a witness during trial may require a mistrial. *People v. Nash*, 244 Mich. App. 93 (2000).

Accountant-Client—MCL 339.732

The privilege ceases to operate when the advice sought refers to future wrongdoing. The privilege does protect past wrongdoing. *People v. Paasche*, 207 Mich. App. 698 (1994).

EXCLUSIONARY RULE

The purpose of the exclusionary rule is to deter police activity that violates the rights of a citizen. Illegally seized evidence may not be introduced at trial.

Evidence gained by violating defendant's federal Constitutional rights will not be admitted into evidence in a criminal proceeding. *Weeks v. United States*, 232 U.S. 383 (1914).

Fourth Amendment standards are applied to the states via the Fourteenth Amendment. The exclusionary rule is applicable to the states. *Mapp v. Ohio*, 367 U.S. 643 (1961).

The Michigan Supreme Court also applies the exclusionary rule against evidence seized in violation of the Michigan Constitution. *People v. Margelis*, 217 Mich. 423 (1922).

"Fruit of the poisonous tree" doctrine

Evidence obtained after illegal governmental action will be excluded. This includes not only materials subject to the Exclusionary Rule, but also subsequent confessions, admissions, identifications, and testimony obtained as a result of the primary taint. The "fruit" of the illegality will be excluded. *Wong Sun v. United States*, 371 US 471 (1963).

25

O.W.I. LAW

O.W.I. STATUTE—MCL 257.625(1)

A person shall not operate a vehicle upon a highway or other place open to the general public or generally accessible to motor vehicles, including an area designated for the parking of vehicles, if the person is operating while intoxicated.

Operating while intoxicated means either of the following:

- The person is under the influence of alcoholic liquor, a controlled substance, or a combination of alcoholic liquor and a controlled substance.
- The person has an alcohol content of 0.08 grams or more per 100 milliliters of blood, per 210 liters of breath, or per 67 milliliters of urine.

Definition, Under the Influence

Under the influence of alcohol means that, because of drinking alcohol, the defendant's ability to operate a motor vehicle in a normal manner was substantially lessened. To be under the influence, a person does not have to be inebriated to the point of falling down. Conversely, just because the person has consumed alcohol does not prove, by itself, that the person is under the influence of alcohol. The test is whether, because of drinking alcohol, the defendant's mental or physical condition was *significantly affected* to the point that the ability to operate a vehicle in a normal manner is impacted.

What Does It Mean To Operate?

- Operate or Operating means being in actual physical control of a vehicle, regardless of whether the person is licensed. MCL 257.35a.
- Operator means any person who is in actual physical control of a motor vehicle upon a highway. MCL 257.36.

Defendant was found slumped over the steering wheel in the lane of a drive-through restaurant. The vehicle's engine was running, the vehicle was in gear, and the defendant's foot was on the brake. The court held that the driver was operating the vehicle because he put the van in a position posing a significant risk of collision and had not returned it to a position of safety. *People v. Wood*, 450 Mich. 359 (1995).

Defendant was a passenger in a vehicle driven by his girlfriend, with whom he was arguing. The defendant grabbed the steering wheel, causing the vehicle to veer off the road and strike a jogger. The jogger was severely injured and the defendant was charged with felonious driving. The Court held the Vehicle Code's definition of operate neither requires exclusive nor complete control of a vehicle; nor does it require "control over all the functions necessary to make the vehicle operate." In order to operate a vehicle under the Vehicle Code, "actual physical control" is all that is required, which the Court defined as the "power to guide the vehicle." Under that definition, grabbing a steering wheel is enough to exert the control required by the Vehicle Code. *People v. Yamat*, 475 Mich. 49 (2006).

The statute covers areas open to the public, though not open necessarily to vehicular travel. For instance, the lawn of a girl's dormitory at Wayne State University is a place open to the public and an arrest for O.W.I on the lawn is valid. *People v. Tracy*, 18 Mich. App. 529 (1969).

An officer observed a vehicle drifting within the lane and driving on the lane markers. The weather was dry and there was no rain or ice on the paved road. The driver of the car activated his left turn signal, traveling past numerous driveways and one side street. He traveled approximately two-tenths of a mile before finally turning. He was stopped and subsequently arrested for O.W.I. The court upheld the stop. Erratic driving can give rise to reasonable suspicion of unlawful intoxication to justify an investigatory stop by a police officer. *People v. Christie*, 206 Mich. App 304 (1994).

Responding to an anonymous call, a police officer discovered the defendant asleep in his truck at the county fairgrounds. The truck was wedged on a parking log, with the tires barely touching the ground. Defendant was found asleep in the front seat, covered by a sleeping bag. The truck's engine was not running, the automatic transmission was in park, and the keys to the truck were inside defendant's pocket. The police officer woke up the defendant, observed that he smelled strongly of intoxicants and was confused and unaware of his surroundings. Defendant explained that he had been at a bar earlier that evening, had too much to drink, and drove to the fairgrounds to sleep because he was too intoxicated to drive home. Defendant explained that he struck the parking log while trying to leave the fairgrounds and, after unsuccessfully attempting to free the truck from the log, he turned off the engine and went to sleep. The police officer arrested defendant for O.W.I. The defendant argued that the arrest was illegal.

The court held that the officer's arrest of the valid because an officer may arrest a person without a warrant if the officer has reasonable cause to believe a misdemeanor punishable by more than 92 days' imprisonment occurred, and reasonable cause to believe the person committed it. First offense O.W.I. is a misdemeanor punishable by imprisonment for not more than 93 days. Therefore, an officer does not have to observe a defendant operating a vehicle for the defendant to be arrested and prosecuted for O.W.I. under this exception. The officer must have reasonable cause to believe that the crime of O.W.I. had been committed, and that defendant committed it.

In this case, the defendant admitted to the police officer that he drove on public roadways to the fairgrounds to sleep off the effects of having too much to drink. According to defendant, he struck the parking log while attempting to leave the fairgrounds and turned off the engine and went to sleep after he was unable to dislodge his truck. This is different than the defendant not driving the vehicle, but rather using the vehicle as a shelter, rather than a motor vehicle, in a parking lot. *People v. Stephen*, 262 Mich. App. 213 (2004).

UNLAWFUL BODILY ALCOHOL CONTENT (UBAC)— MCL 257.625(1)(b)

Elements

A person shall not operate a vehicle upon a highway or other place open to the public whose bodily alcohol content is 0.08 grams or more per:

- 100 milliliters of blood,
- 210 liters of breath, or
- 67 milliliters of urine.

IMPAIRED DRIVING— MCL 257.625(3)

Elements

1. A person shall not operate a vehicle upon a highway or other place open to the public or generally accessible to vehicles including parking lots, within this state,
2. Whose ability to operate is *visibly impaired*, due to the consumption of alcoholic liquor or a controlled substance, or a combination of both.

Definition, Impaired

To prove that the defendant operated while impaired, the prosecutor must prove beyond a reasonable doubt that the defendant drove with less ability than would an ordinary, careful driver due to the consumption of alcohol. The defendant's driving ability must have lessened to the point that another person would have noticed it. CJI2d 15.4.

OPERATING WITH THE PRESENCE OF DRUGS (OWPD)— MCL 257.625(8)

A person shall not operate a vehicle upon a highway or other place open to the general public or generally accessible to motor vehicles, including an area designated for the parking of vehicles, if the person has in his or her body any amount of a controlled substance listed in schedule 1 under MCL 333.7212 or of a controlled substance described in MCL 333.7214.

> Defendant was the driver of a vehicle that was involved in a traffic crash that killed one person and severely injured two others. Defendant's blood was drawn pursuant to a search warrant. Results indicated the presence of carboxy THC, a metabolite of THC, the active ingredient in marijuana.
>
> The court held that even though carboxy THC is not a controlled substance, it is a derivative of marijuana. Since the statute classifies both the drug and its derivatives under schedule 1, the presence of carboxy THC falls within the prohibition of operating with any presence of drugs. Further, the prosecutor does not have to prove that a driver knew he or she might be intoxicated; nor does the prosecutor have to prove intoxication or impairment; the prosecutor need only prove that a driver had any amount of a controlled substance in his or her body, regardless of the amount of time elapsed between arrest and testing. *People v. Derror*, 475 Mich. 316 (2006).

O.W.I. AT THE SCENE OF AN ACCIDENT/PASSED OUT BEHIND THE WHEEL—MCL 257.625A(1)

A peace officer may arrest a person without a warrant under either of the following circumstances:

- The peace officer has reasonable cause to believe the person was, at the time of an accident *in this state,* the operator of a vehicle involved in the accident and was operating the vehicle in violation of MCL 257.625.
- The person is found in the driver's seat of a vehicle parked or stopped on a highway or street within this state if any part of the vehicle intrudes into the roadway and the peace officer has reasonable cause to believe the person was operating the vehicle in violation of MCL 257.625.

> Whether an accident has occurred, for purposes of applying the implied consent statute, depends on an examination of all the circumstances surrounding the incident. Factors include:
>
> - Whether there was a collision.
> - Whether personal injury or property damage resulted.
> - Whether the incident was either undesirable for or unexpected by any of the parties involved.
>
> *People v. Keskimaki*, 446 Mich. 240 (1994).

Subpoena Of Blood Tests

MCL 257.625a (6)(e) authorizes the prosecutor to obtain blood results from the hospital if a person involved in an accident is suspected of O.W.I. The prosecutor may use a subpoena and does not need to obtain a search warrant.

> The results of blood tests taken at the request of medical facilities for purposes of medical treatment may be obtained by law enforcement officers and be used at trial to prove blood alcohol levels. *People v. Perlos*, 436 Mich. 305, (1990).
>
> The subpoena of blood results taken by a medical facility is not limited to persons who are arrested, but may apply to anyone involved in a traffic crash. *People v. Aldrich*, 246 Mich. App. 101 (2001).

PENALTIES—MCL 257.625(9)

1st conviction O.W.I/UBAC and Impaired	93 days Court may order **immobilization**
2nd conviction within 7 years	1 year misdemeanor Vehicle is subject to forfeiture; if not forfeited, must be immobilized under MCL 257.904d
3rd conviction during lifetime	5 year felony Vehicle is subject to forfeiture; if not forfeited, must be immobilized under MCL 257.904d

What Constitutes Prior Convictions

- All drug and alcohol violations under MCL 257.625 (except allowing an intoxicated person to operate a vehicle under MCL 257.625(2)).
- Murder, manslaughter, and negligent homicide with a vehicle.
- Child endangerment.
- Commercial motor vehicle violations under MCL 257.625m.
- Attempted violations and similar laws from other states are also included.
- Only one, zero tolerance violation can be used to enhance.
- Only one conviction can be used for violations arising out of the same transaction.

.02/ZERO TOLERANCE

Elements—MCL 257.625(6)

1. A person who is less than 21 years of age shall not operate a vehicle upon a highway or other place open to the general public or generally accessible to motor vehicles, including an area designated for the parking of vehicles, within this state,
2. If the person has any bodily alcohol content. Bodily alcohol content is defined:
   - A blood alcohol content of not less than 0.02 grams or more than 0.08 grams.
   - Any presence of alcohol within a person's body resulting from the consumption of alcoholic liquor, other than consumption of alcoholic liquor as part of a generally recognized religious ceremony.

Penalties—MCL 257.625(10)

First conviction	Misdemeanor Up to 360 hours of community service Up to $250 fine 30 days restricted license
Second conviction, if violation occurs within 7 years of 1 or more prior convictions	Misdemeanor Up to 60 days of community service Up to $500 fine Up to 93 days in jail 90 days to 1 year license suspension

A person arrested for violating MCL 257.625(6) may be lodged until it is safe to be released. Attorney General's Opinion No. 6824 (1994).

Commercial Motor Vehicle Drivers—MCL 257.625(m)

A person shall not operate a commercial vehicle with a bodily alcohol content of 0.04 or more. (Operating with a bodily alcohol content of 0.08 or higher falls under O.W.I., MCL 257.625.)
Penalties:

Refusal to take PBT for commercial driver	93 day misdemeanor
First conviction impaired driving of a commercial vehicle	93 day misdemeanor
Second conviction within 7 years	1 year misdemeanor
Third conviction within 10 years	1 to 5 year felony

O.W.I., IMPAIRED, OR O.W.P.D. CAUSING DEATH—MCL 257.625(4)

Elements

1. A person who operates a vehicle upon a highway or other place open to the public or generally accessible to motor vehicles, including the area designated for the parking of vehicles, and

2. And who is in violation of either subsection (1), (3), or (8) (O.W.I., impaired, or O.W.P.D.), and
3. *Causes the death* of another person.

Violation is a felony, punishable by 15 years imprisonment.

Second Degree Murder

> After a fatal traffic accident, defendant was charged with second degree murder. He argued he did not have sufficient malice for the charge. The court held the mens rea for second degree murder does not mandate a finding of specific intent to harm or kill. The intent to do an act in obvious disregard of life-endangering consequences is a malicious intent. Second degree murder is a general-intent crime to which voluntary intoxication is not an available defense.
>
> In this case, the court found there was sufficient evidence to bind the defendant over. First, he tried to evade the police as they drove by on patrol giving the inference that he was aware of his intoxication. Despite this intoxication, he drove recklessly down a main road and, after nearly striking another vehicle, he continued driving. He then sped through a red light before striking the victim.
>
> In two related cases, there was also sufficient evidence to establish second degree murder charges. In *Baker*, the defendant's blood-alcohol content was 0.18 percent. He drove in excess of the speed limit, ran a red light, and drove through an intersection where he would have seen three vehicles if he had been driving properly. He missed two, but struck the third, killing two people.
>
> Finally, the court also found sufficient evidence in the *Hoskinson* case. Here, defendant was highly intoxicated and, while leaving the bar, backed twice into the same vehicle. This could infer that he should have known that he should not be driving. Still, he drove at a high rate of speed through a residential area. He swerved to miss a car stopped at a stop sign, ran through a stop sign and nearly hit another car. The occupants of his vehicle told him he was driving too fast and should slow down. He then collided with a vehicle, drove over a curb, across some grass, and struck the victim. The passengers then jumped out and told him he had hit the child. He continued to drive for several blocks before stopping. *People v. Goecke*, 457 Mich. 442 (1998).
>
> Second degree murder charges were upheld where the defendant had a history of blacking out when drinking, knew he may drive irresponsibly if he drank alcohol, and still went to the bar and drank before driving his vehicle the wrong way on the freeway. *People v. Werner*, 254 Mich. App. 528 (2002).

O.W.I., IMPAIRED, OR O.W.P.D. CAUSING SERIOUS IMPAIRMENT OF A BODY FUNCTION— MCL 257.625(5)

Elements

1. A person, whether licensed or not, who operates a vehicle upon highway or other place open to public or generally accessible to motor vehicles, including areas designated for the parking of vehicles, and
2. Who is in violation of subsection (1), (3), or (8) (O.W.I., Impaired, or O.W.P.D.), and
3. *Causes a serious impairment* of a bodily function to another person.

Violation is a felony, punishable by 5 years imprisonment.

Definition

Serious impairment of a bodily function is defined as

- Loss of a limb or use of a limb.
- Loss of a hand, foot, finger, or thumb or loss of their use.
- Loss of an eye or ear or loss of their use.
- Loss or substantial impairment of a bodily function.
- Serious visible disfigurement.
- A comatose state that lasts for more than three days.
- Measurable brain damage or mental impairment.
- A skull fracture or other serious bone fracture.
- Subdural hemorrhage or subdural hematoma.
- Loss of an organ. MCL 257.58c.

CHILD ENDANGERMENT—MCL 257.625(7))

Applies to a person who violates MCL 257.625 (1), (3), (4), (5), or (8), with another person less than 16 years old in vehicle at time of offense. (O.W.I., Impaired, causing death, causing serious impairment, or O.W.P.D.)

Penalties:

First conviction	1 year misdemeanor
Second conviction within 7 years or third conviction	Felony/immobilization

Child endangerment is included in the implied consent law.

If a person violates the zero tolerance statute, MCL 257.625(6), with someone less than 16 years old in the vehicle:

Penalties:

First conviction	93 day misdemeanor
Second conviction within 7 years or third conviction	1 year misdemeanor

PERMITTING PERSON UNDER INFLUENCE TO DRIVE—MCL 257.625(2)

Elements

1. The *owner of a vehicle or a person in charge* or in control of a vehicle,
2. Shall *not authorize or knowingly permit* the vehicle to be operated upon the highway or other place open to the public or generally accessible to motor vehicles,
3. By a person who is impaired or under the influence of alcoholic liquor or a controlled substance, or a combination of alcoholic liquor and a controlled substance, or who has a UBAC.

Penalties:

No aggravating factors	93 day misdemeanor
If operation results in serious impairment	2 year felony
If operation results in death	5 year felony

CONFISCATION OF REGISTRATION PLATE—MCL 257.904c

If a person is being arrested for a second alcohol violation or third DWLS, the Secretary of State will advise the officer via LEIN that the driver is a repeat offender. The officer must then do the following:

- Immediately confiscate the vehicle's registration plate and destroy it (ownership of the vehicle does not matter).
    - **Exceptions:** tribal, rental, trailer, manufacture, dealer, U.S. government, out-of-state, or IRP plates.
- The officer must issue a temporary plate and place it on the vehicle. The temporary plate expires on the same date as the original plate.
- The plate shall not be seized if the Secretary of State computer system is not functioning.
- At the station:
    - A copy of the paper plate must be attached to the warrant request and print cards.
    - The SOS screen for confiscated plate must be completed and, if there was no plate on the vehicle, the VIN number shall be entered.

IMMOBILIZATION—MCL 257.904c

If a vehicle stopped by an officer is supposed to be immobilized, SOS will notify the officer of the dates of immobilization and the offender's driver license number. If the vehicle is being operated in violation of an immobilization order, the vehicle shall be impounded.

- **Exception**: If the vehicle is immobilized under tether technology that immobilizes the offender only and the offender is not driving.

The penalty for tampering with or removing an immobilization device is a 93 day misdemeanor. MCL 257.904e.

IGNITION INTERLOCKS—MCL 257.625l

As part of a restricted license, SOS may require ignition interlocks to be installed.

The following violations are 6 month misdemeanors:

- Requesting another person to blow into the interlock device.
- Blowing into another's interlock device.
- Tampering with the device in any way.

REGISTRATION DENIAL

SOS will cancel and deny registration for following offenders:

- 3rd offense drunk driving.
- 4th offense DWLS/DWLR.

Obtaining a car during suspension:

- A person cannot buy, lease, or otherwise acquire a motor vehicle during a period of suspension, revocation, or denial.
- Violation is a 93 day misdemeanor.

Recouping Costs—MCL 257.625(13)

The court may order a defendant to pay costs for the arrest, investigation, emergency response, and prosecution of charges of O.W.I.

IMPLIED CONSENT— MCL 257.625(c)

A person who operates a vehicle is considered to have given consent to chemical tests of his or her blood, breath, or urine for the purposes of determining the amount of alcohol or presence of a controlled substance for all the following offenses:

- Murder or manslaughter resulting from the operation of a motor vehicle, if reasonable cause to believe the driver was O.W.I. or impaired.
- Felonious driving, if reasonable cause to believe the driver was O.W.I. or impaired.
- Negligent homicide, if reasonable cause to believe the driver was O.W.I. or impaired.
- O.W.I.
- O.W.I. causing death.
- O.W.I. causing serious injury.
- Unlawful Blood Alcohol Content.
- Impaired Driving.
- O.W.P.D.
- 0.02/Zero Tolerance.
- Child Endangerment.
- Commercial motor vehicle - refusing to take the PBT.
- Commercial motor vehicle - 0.04 - 0.07 BAC.

Exception to Implied Consent to Withdrawal of Blood—MCL 257.625C(2)

- Hemophiliacs, diabetics, or persons requiring the use of anticoagulants under the direction of a physician are not considered to have given consent to the withdrawal of blood.

PRELIMINARY BREATH TESTS (PBTs)—MCL 257.625a

Basis of Arrest:

- On reasonable cause, an officer may require a person to submit to a PBT.
- An arrest may be based wholly or in part on a PBT result.
- Results may be used in court for the following reasons:
    - To assist the court or hearing officer in determining a challenge to the validity of an arrest.
    - As evidence of the defendant's breath alcohol content, if offered by the defendant, to rebut testimony elicited on cross-examination of a defense witness that the defendant's breath alcohol content was higher at the time of the charged offense than when a chemical test was administered.
    - As evidence of the defendant's breath alcohol content, if offered by the prosecution, to rebut testimony elicited on cross-examination of a prosecution witness that the defendant's breath alcohol content was lower at the time of the charged offense than when a chemical test was sections.

Penalty for Refusal to Submit to a Pbt— MCL 257.625a(2)(D)

- Civil infraction.
- 93 day misdemeanor for commercial motor vehicle drivers.

CHEMICAL TESTS—MCL 257.625a(6)

A chemical test may be administered at the request of the police officer who has reasonable grounds to believe a person has committed a crime described in MCL 257.625c.

> The defendant was involved in an accident and taken to a hospital. Police determined she had been drinking, but did not arrest her. The officer asked for a blood sample, which she voluntarily provided. Since she was not under arrest, implied consent rights were not read.
>
> The court held that implied consent rights are only triggered once arrested. Here, defendant

> was never arrested before the request for blood. The case was remanded to determine if consent was voluntary. *People v. Borchard-Ruhland*, 460 Mich. 278 (1999).
>
> It is not a denial of a defendant's due process rights to deny the defendant's request for a blood test after defendant has refused to take a requested breath test. *People v. Dewey*, 172 Mich. App. 367 (1988).

A person arrested shall be advised of his or her **chemical test rights.** If a person submits to a test requested by a police officer, he or she shall be given a reasonable opportunity to have a person of his or her own choosing administer one of the chemical tests described within a reasonable time of detention. If the person seeks his or her own test, he or she is responsible for obtaining an analysis of the test.

> A police department's policy was reasonable where defendant was given an opportunity to seek an independent blood test and offered a ride within reason to a hospital of his choosing. *People v. Craun*, 159 Mich. App 564 (1987).
>
> Dismissal of an O.W.I. charge is not appropriate where a person is denied the opportunity to obtain exculpatory evidence with an independent test. However, the jury may be given an instruction informing them that the defendant was denied an opportunity to obtain an independent test. The jury may decide what weight to give the denial of such a test. *People v. Anstey*, 476 Mich. 436 (2006).

If a person refuses to take a chemical test requested by a police officer, it will not be given without a court order, but the officer may seek to obtain a court order.

The following are the duties of a peace officer if a person refuses to take the test or results reveal *unlawful alcohol content.*

- Immediately confiscate the person's license or permit.
- Issue a temporary license or permit.
- Immediately forward a copy of the refusal form to the SOS.
- Notify the SOS of the temporary license via LEIN.
- Destroy the person's license or permit.

Duties of a peace officer if a *blood or urine test is taken* include the following:

- Immediately confiscate the person's license or permit and issue a temporary license.
- Wait for the results to return from the lab.
- If the results show an unlawful alcohol content, the officer shall destroy the license.
- If there is not an unlawful alcohol content, the officer shall notify the person and immediately return the license or permit via first class mail. MCL 257.625g.

Unlawful Alcohol Content Applies to— MCL 257.625g(4)

- 0.02/Zero tolerance legislation.
- 0.04 - .08 BAC and commercial motorvehicle drivers.
- 0.08 BAC or more.

Administering the Test

An administrative rule for Breathalyzer tests requires that the defendant be observed by the operator for 15 minutes prior to the test to prevent the defendant from smoking, regurgitating, or placing anything in his or her mouth.

Compare

> The case where the defendant was observed on a videotape for 35 minutes before the test was administered during which the camera's view was blocked at different times. The test was held to be invalid because he was not watched for the full 15 minutes before the test. *People v. Boughner*, 209 Mich. App. 397 (1995).

With

> The case where, prior to performing a breath test on a suspected drunk driver, the officer testified that he continually observed the subject for 18 minutes, except for the few seconds it took him to check the time on the machine. During that time a corrections officer watched the defendant.
>
> Defendant argued that, under the administrative rules and the case of *People v. Boughner*, the results of the test should not be admissible. The court disagreed and held that, even though this may have been a technical violation, it was a harmless error.

The facts of *Boughner* were quite different according to the court. "In *Boughner*, a thirty-five-minute videotape of the defendant showed that the operator of the Breathalyzer machine observed the defendant for no more than eight minutes before the test was given, the operator did not observe the defendant continually, even for the eight minutes, and throughout the thirty-five-minutes before the test was administered, the defendant's hand was either at his face or mouth and this court was unable to determine if the defendant actually placed anything in his mouth." *People v. Wujkowski*, 230 Mich. App. 181 (1998).

Request for an Attorney Prior to the Test

The great weight of authority establishes that there is no right to counsel under the U.S. Constitution or Michigan Constitution before taking of a Breathalyzer test. Thus, for a defendant deciding whether to take a Breathalyzer test, neither of these provisions entitles a defendant to successfully protest police refusal to permit an OWI suspect and his attorney to privately confer over that decision. *Ann Arbor v. McCleary*, 228 Mich. App. 674 (1998). However, it may be unreasonable under due process analysis to refuse him or her a reasonable opportunity to contact a lawyer. *Hall v. SOS*, 60 Mich. App. 431 (1975).

Denial of the right to consult with counsel before an accused decides to take the Breathalyzer test does not violate the Sixth Amendment. *However*, the mere allowing of a reasonable phone call to counsel prior to administering the test would be a more commendable practice on the part of the police. *Holmberg v. 54-A Judicial Dist. Judge*, 60 Mich. App. 757 (1975).

KEY: If officer denies the driver the opportunity to call his or her attorney, it will not effect the criminal charges, but may effect the DLAD hearing.

DLAD HEARING—MCL 257.625f(4)

If a person received a refusal for taking a chemical test, he or she has the right to a hearing with the Driver's License Appeal Division to determine if the refusal was properly taken. During this hearing, the officer acts as the prosecutor.

The hearing shall cover the following issues:
- Whether the police officer had reasonable grounds to believe that the person had committed a crime.
- Whether the person was placed under arrest for the crime.
- If the person refused to submit to the test upon request of the officer, whether the refusal was reasonable.
- Whether the person was advised of the chemical test rights required by MCL 257.625a(6). (Submit a copy of the refusal when testifying to this portion.)

MIRANDA RIGHTS AND THE O.W.I. ARREST

Miranda warnings are required when a person is in custody and subject to interrogation. Custody requires that the person be placed under arrest or his or her freedom of movement significantly deprived.

Generally, traffic stops do not involve custody for purposes of *Miranda*. Once an arrest is made, however (i.e., O.W.I.), *Miranda* warnings are required before questioning. *Berkemer v. McCarty*, 468 U.S. 420 (1984).

Failure of a police officer to give *Miranda* warnings prior to conducting roadside questioning as to whether defendant had been drinking and how much he had been drinking does not mandate suppression of the defendant's answers. Even if the officer intends to arrest a driver from the outset, this does not automatically trigger the *Miranda* rule because an officer's unarticulated plan had no bearing on the question whether a suspect was "in custody" at a particular time. The only relevant inquiry was how a reasonable person in defendant's position would have understood his or her situation. *People v. Chinn*, 141 Mich. App. 92 (1985).

FORCING ENTRY INTO THE RESIDENCE

Under MCL 764.21, officers may not forcibly enter a residence for a warrantless misdemeanor arrest if consent or some other lawful means is not present. *People v. Reinhardt*, 141 Mich. App. 173 (1985).

Officers responded to a hit-and-run accident where witnesses observed the driver driving away holding his head. They went to the registered owner's house and, after knocking on his front door, observed him lying in the house with a cut to his forehead. They knocked on the windows and had dispatch call the residence. When the subject did not respond, the officers entered. The court upheld the entry and subsequent arrest for the following reasons:

- A police officer may enter a dwelling without a warrant where it is reasonably believed that a person inside is in need of *medical assistance.*
- The entry must be limited to the reason for its justification.
- The officer must be motivated primarily by a perceived need to render assistance and may do no more than is reasonably necessary to determine whether assistance is required and render it.

Once lawfully inside the residence, the officer may make an arrest without a warrant that is authorized by law and, absent a reason for exclusion, the evidence obtained is admissible. *People v. Ohlinger*, 438 Mich. 477 (1991).

JUVENILE LAW

DIFFERENCES IN TERMINOLOGY

Juvenile proceedings are not considered criminal in nature. "Labeling theory" purports that if we label a juvenile as a criminal then he or she will grow up to be a criminal. "Labeling theory" is a large part of the basis for the Juvenile Justice and Delinquency Prevention Act (see below). Thus, it is important to know the differences in terminology between juvenile proceedings and criminal proceedings. The focus of the juvenile process is not to punish, as in the adult system, but to rehabilitate. Some examples of the different terminology are:

- An offender is a *delinquent,* not a *criminal.*
- Officers will seek a *petition,* not request an *arrest warrant.*
- Juveniles are *apprehended,* not *arrested.*
- Juveniles must be *forthwith* turned over to their parents or the court, whereas an adult has to be brought to the court without *unnecessary delay.*
- The juvenile's guilt or innocence is determined in *adjudication,* not at a *trial.*
- After adjudication, the court will have a *disposition,* not a *sentencing.*

Status Offender

A status offender is a person who commits an act that is a violation because of the person's special status, such as the person's age. Certain offenses would not be an offense if an adult committed the act. For example, if a 15-year-old skips school, he would be considered a truant and could fall under the jurisdiction of the court. However, if a 20-year-old skips his college classes, the court would not take notice.

"[A] juvenile status offense is an offense which is illegal only because of the offender's age (under eighteen) and which is not serious." *United States v. Cole*, 418 F.3d 592 (6th Cir. 2005)

Examples of status offenders include the following:

- Runaways
- Curfew violators
- Truants
- Minors in possession of alcohol

JURISDICTION OF THE FAMILY DIVISION OF THE CIRCUIT COURT— MCL 712A.2

Exclusive, Original Jurisdiction Over any Children Who Are Less Than 17 Years Old and Who

- Violate any ordinance or law. Exceptions include civil infractions and where the prosecutor charges the juvenile as an adult for a specific juvenile violation.
- Run away.
- Do not attend school.
- Are repeatedly disobedient to reasonable and lawful demands of parents, guardians, or custodians.

Exclusive Jurisdiction Over any Child Less Than 18 Years Old Who Has Been Abused or Neglected

Concurrent Jurisdiction Over Children Between 17 and 18 Years Old Who

- Are repeatedly addicted to drugs or alcohol.
- Repeatedly associate with criminals.
- Are willfully disobedient to reasonable demands of parents.
- Are willfully and with knowledge in a house of prostitution or ill-fame.

Other Jurisdiction

May accept jurisdiction of children under 18 years old who are subject to a custody battle as a result of a divorce.

Civil Infractions

MCL 257.741 gives District Courts jurisdiction over minors for purposes of civil infractions.

Under MCL 712A.2e, the Family Division of the Circuit Court may agree with the District Court to waive jurisdiction for all civil infractions to the District Court.

CUSTODY

A Police Officer May Take any Child into Custody Without A Court Order When

- The child is found violating any criminal law or criminal ordinance. MCR 3.933, MCL 712A.14.
- The child's surroundings endanger the child's health, safety, or welfare. MCR 3.963, MCL 712A.14.
- The child is violating or has violated a personal protection order or foreign protection order. MCL 600.2950 (11).

Upon Such Custody

- Officers must immediately attempt to notify the parent, guardian, or custodian if that person can be found. MCL 712A.14(1), MCR 3.933.
- While awaiting the arrival of the parents, the child must be completely isolated from verbal, visual, or physical contact with any adult prisoner. MCL 712A.14(1), MCL 712A.16(1), MCR 3.933.
- Unless immediate detention is required, juveniles shall be released once the parent or guardian makes a written promise that the juvenile will appear in court. Immediate detention is allowed under the following circumstances:
    - Due to the nature of the violation, releasing the juvenile would not serve the best interest of the juvenile or the public.
    - No parent or guardian can be located, or
    - The parent or guardian refuses to take custody.

MCL 712A.14(1), MCR 3.933 A (3).

- If the child is not released to the parents, the child shall be immediately brought before the court for a preliminary hearing. If a complaint is authorized the court shall order where the child shall be placed. MCL 712A.14(2), MCR 3.934.
- For civil infractions, the officer may issue a citation and release. MCR 3.933.

Juvenile Justice and Delinquency Prevention Act (JJDPA)—42 U.S.C. 5601-5633

The federal JJDPA establishes the following mandates:

- *Deinstitutionalization of status offenders:* A juvenile status offender cannot be placed in a secure institution, except those found in contempt of a court order and full due process protections are afforded.
- *Sight and sound separation:* There must be total sight and sound separation between juveniles and adults held in the same facility.
- *Jail removal initiative:* All juveniles shall be removed from the adult jails, except those who are transferred to the adult court and against whom criminal felony charges have been filed.
- *Six-hour rule:* Federal and state guidelines permit locking juveniles in adult facilities for a maximum of *six hours, for processing purposes only.* This applies only to those juveniles who are charged with a crime. The sight and sound rule still applies.

This rule *does not apply to status offenders* and abused or neglected children because they cannot be locked up at all. *Status offenders must be kept under constant supervision or visual contact at all times during their detention.* Soft restraints may be used if necessary.

The six-hour time frame starts the moment that juvenile is placed in a locked setting or cuffed to a stationary object. The clock does not start when a juvenile is placed in a police vehicle, unless locked in a vehicle parked in a sallyport. (*Michigan Guide to Compliance with Laws Governing the Placement of*

Juveniles in Secure Facilities, Mich. Comm. On Juvenile Justice [Jan. 2000])

Detention Facilities—MCL 712A.16

If a juvenile under the age of 17 years is taken into custody or detained, the juvenile shall not be confined in any police station, prison, jail, lock-up, or reformatory or transported with, or compelled or permitted to associate or mingle with, criminal or dissolute persons . . . the court may order a juvenile 15 years of age or older whose habits or conduct are considered a menace to other juveniles, or who may not otherwise be safely detained, placed in a jail or other place of detention for adults, but in a room or ward separate from adults and for not more than 30 days, unless longer detention is necessary for the service of process.

Juveniles under 17 years of age may not have contact with adult prisoners. There is an exception allowing a court to order that a dangerous juvenile over 15 years of age be jailed in an adult facility.

Escape by Juvenile from Facility or Residence—MCL 712A.18j

(1) *If a juvenile escapes from a facility or residence in which he or she has been placed for a violation described in section 2(a)(1) of this chapter, other than his or her own home or the home of his or her parent or guardian, the individual at that facility or residence who has responsibility for maintaining custody of the juvenile at the time of the escape shall immediately notify 1 of the following of the escape or cause 1 of the following to be immediately notified of the escape:*

   (a) *If the escape occurs in a city, village, or township that has a police department, the police department of that city, village, or township.*
   (b) *Except as provided in subdivision (a), 1 of the following:*
      (i) *The sheriff department of the county in which the escape occurs.*
      (ii) *The department of state police post having jurisdiction over the area in which the escape occurs.*

(2) *A police agency that receives notification of an escape under subsection (1) shall enter that notification into the law enforcement information network without undue delay.*
(3) *As used in this section, "escape" means to leave without lawful authority or to fail to return to custody when required.*

WAIVER OF JURISDICTION
Non-Automatic Waiver Offenses—MCL 712A.4

Under certain circumstances, a prosecutor may request the Family Division of the Circuit Court to waive jurisdiction of a child to the adult court system. Generally, the child must be at least 14 years old. The judge will then decide whether to retain jurisdiction over the child or transfer said child to the adult court. In making this decision, the court will look at a number of factors including the following:

- The child's prior record, physical and mental maturity, and pattern of living.
- The seriousness of the offense charged.
- Whether the offense is part of a repetitive pattern.
- If the child's behavior is likely to render the child dangerous to the public.
- If waiving the child would be in the best interest of the public.

Automatic Waiver—MCL 712A.2

Under the automatic waiver the prosecutor will decide whether to authorize a complaint and warrant instead of a petition charging an enumerated life offense. Once this is done, the juvenile becomes subject to the jurisdiction of the court of general criminal jurisdiction automatically. Generally, the child has to be at least 14 years old and must have committed a very serious offense such as murder, first degree CSC, armed robbery, carjacking, kidnapping, serious assaults, or a controlled substance violation where the amount was 650 grams or more.

TRANSFER OF JURISDICTION—MCR 3.926

When a minor is brought before a juvenile court in a county other than where the minor resides, the court may transfer the case to the court in the county of residence prior to trial.

RIGHTS OF A CHILD
Preliminary Hearing—MCR 3.935

- A hearing to determine if probable cause exists that the child committed the offense.
- The hearing must be within 24 hours of detention, excluding Sundays or holidays, or the juvenile must be released.

Admission or Confession

For many years the test for admitting a confession of a juvenile was a per se rule that, if the parent or guardian was not present during the interrogation, the confession was automatically suppressed. This test has now given way to the *totality of the circumstances test,* which is similar to the test used for adult confessions. This is a balancing test, which requires that the court weigh various factors.

- The Michigan Supreme Court has accepted "totality of the circumstances" test for juvenile confessions. *People v. Hana*, 443 Mich. 202 (1993).
- Under the totality of the circumstance test for a juvenile confession, the court must consider:
    - Whether Miranda requirements were met and whether the juvenile clearly understood his or her rights and properly waived them.
    - The degree of police compliance with applicable statutes and court rules.
    - The presence of an adult parent, custodian, or guardian.
    - The juvenile defendant's personal background.
    - The juvenile's age, education, intelligence level, and extent of prior experience with police.
    - The length of detention before statement was made.
    - The repeated and prolonged nature of the questioning.
    - Whether the accused was injured, intoxicated, ill, physically abused, threatened with abuse, or deprived of food, sleep, or medical attention.

Note: the court specifically held that the "failure to take defendant immediately and forthwith before the juvenile division of the probate court does not per se require suppression of the statement." *People v. Good*, 186 Mich. App. 180 (1990).

Defendant, an 11-year-old, was charged with first degree murder. During a police interrogation where his mother was present, the juvenile confessed to the shooting. Under the totality of the circumstances, the court upheld the admissibility of the confession.

The officers asked the defendant to explain the rights that they had read to him. In reference to his right to an attorney, he stated, "That-that when the police talk to me I can talk with my lawyer with the police." Also, "If we don't got no money, the court give me one." Finally, as to the fact that his statement may be used against him, he replied, "If you say something you go to court for it." In ruling the confession was admissible, the court also found that it was of "great significance," that the defendant's mother was present for and participated in the entire Miranda-waiver process. *People v. Abraham*, 234 Mich. App. 640 (1999).

FINGERPRINTING, PHOTOGRAPHING, IDENTIFICATION PROCEDURES—MCL 28.243

A court may permit a juvenile to be fingerprinted and photographed when in court custody. MCR 3.936

- The identification must be placed in separate confidential file, capable of being located and destroyed on court order. MCR 3.923
- The court shall examine the court files to determine if fingerprints have been taken as required by law. If the prints have not been taken, the court shall either order the child to submit him- or herself to the police department that arrested him or her, or order him or her committed to the custody of the sheriff for the taking of the prints.

Officers must fingerprint juveniles immediately upon arrest for a felony or a misdemeanor violation of state law for which the maximum possible penalties exceed 92 days imprisonment or a fine of $1,000, or both, or for criminal contempt of a Michigan personal protection order, or criminal contempt for a violation of a foreign protection order. MCL 28.243.

The fingerprint cards and records thereof must be destroyed if the juvenile is not petitioned, is adjudicated and found to be outside of the provisions of the probate code, or is charged as an adult and found not guilty. MCL 28.243

HEARING PHASES

Trial Phase

Includes the following:

- Determines child's guilt or innocence.
- The child has the right to a jury. MCR 3.911.

- The child has the right to an attorney. MCR 3.915.
- The trial must be held within six months after the petition is filed, unless adjourned for good cause, if child is in custody. If the child is detained, the trial must be within 63 days after the child is taken into custody. If longer than 63 days, the court shall order the juvenile released pending trial. MCR 3.942
- Proof beyond a reasonable doubt. MCR 3.942

Dispositional Phase

Measures taken by the court after adjudication (similar to the sentencing phase in adult cases). MCR 3.943, MCL 712A.18.

- After a juvenile has been convicted, the court must conduct a juvenile sentencing hearing, unless the hearing is waived.
- If convicted as an adult, a dispositional hearing is still required to determine if the subject should be sentenced as an adult or juvenile, unless he or she must automatically be sentenced as an adult. MCR 3.955
- If the juvenile is to be sentenced as an adult, the burden is on the prosecuting attorney to prove by a preponderance of the evidence that such a sentence is in the best interest of the public. MCR 3.955.
- No right to jury at this phase. MCR 3.911. (a juvenile only has a right to a jury at a trial).

27

LAWS ON USE OF FORCE

It is important that police officers know the use of force laws because the improper use of force can open up both criminal and civil liability.

MICHIGAN STANDARD

An officer may use such force as he or she deems necessary in forcibly arresting an offender or in preventing his or her escape after an arrest. *Firestone v. Rice*, 71 Mich. 377 (1888).

An officer may use that force necessary to apprehend a criminal, but neither law nor morality can tolerate the use of needless violence, even upon the worst criminals. *People v. McCord*, 76 Mich. 200 (1889).

"Both officers and private persons seeking to prevent a felon's escape must exercise reasonable care to prevent the escape of the felon without doing personal violence, and it is only where killing him is necessary to prevent this escape, that the killing is justified. . . . If a killing is not justifiable, it is either murder or manslaughter." *People v. Gonsler*, 251 Mich. 443 (1930).

Although Michigan has a fleeing felon rule, under the Fourth Amendment, a police officer's use of deadly force is limited to those situations where the officer has probable cause to believe that the felon poses a threat of serious physical harm to either himself or others. *Washington v. Starke*, 173 Mich. App. 230 (1988).

There is serious liability where one takes a life while arresting a subject on mere suspicion alone. "One who kills an actual felon in trying to arrest him, without knowing or believing him to be guilty, commits murder, especially if the person attempting to make the arrest is not an officer." *People v. Burt*, 51 Mich. 199 (1883).

FEDERAL STANDARD

A peace officer may use deadly force:

- In defense of his or her own life,
- In defense of another, or
- In pursuit of a fleeing felon. (*Tennessee v. Garner*, 471 U.S. 1 (1985)).

> The courts take an objective view when deciding use of force cases. The question is whether the officer's actions are "objectively reasonable" in light of the facts and circumstances confronting them, regardless of their underlying intent or motivation. *Graham v. Conner*, 490 U.S. 386 (1989).

In the case of *Graham v. Connor*, 490 U.S. 386 (1989), the United States Supreme Court applied the reasonableness standard of the Fourth Amendment to use of force actions by police. Reasonableness is determined by balancing "the nature and quality of the intrusion" against "the countervailing governmental interests." Factors include:

- The severity of the crime at issue,
- Whether the suspect poses an immediate threat to the safety of officers and others,
- Whether the suspect is actively resisting arrest or attempting to evade arrest by flight.

Reasonableness is "judged from the prospective of a reasonable officer *on the scene,* rather than with the 20/20 vision hindsight." *Graham v. Connor*, 490 U.S. 386 (1989).

- The reasonableness standard must make an allowance for the fact that police officers are often forced to make split-second judgments in circumstances that are tense, uncertain, and rapidly evolving.
- An officer's use of force will be judged *at the moment* the force is used.

Example: At night an officer is dispatched to a suspicious situation at an abandoned house. He walks inside and sees an individual pointing a gun at him. The officer draws his gun and shoots the individual. In the aftermath, it turns out that the gun was a toy and that the individual was a 12-year-old. Although tragic, the use of force may be appropriate based on the facts the officer had at the time of the shooting.

> "An officer's evil intentions will not make a Fourth Amendment violation out of an objectively reasonable use of force; nor will an officer's good intentions make an objectively unreasonable use of force constitutional." *Graham v. Connor*, 490 U.S. 386 (1989).

Example: An officer knows that the person confronting him is 6'5" tall, has just used PCP, is a martial arts expert, may have a concealed weapon, and has just brutally attacked another officer without provocation. All of this is relevant because they are the facts and circumstances confronting the officer. The officer may be very angry with the subject for the injury to the fellow officer. This anger is irrelevant to the analysis because it is the officer's subjective intent.

MICHIGAN LAW ON THE USE OF DEADLY FORCE

Deadly Force Defined

"That force which could result in the loss of human life." Michigan Attorney General Opinion No. 5068 (1976). This may include batons, saps, flashlights, brass knuckles, and even an officer's fists.

> Police were dispatched to an apartment after several calls from a screaming woman about a man with a knife and a gun. Officers arrived and entered the apartment. Butler, who had a guitar in one hand and a butcher knife in the other, confronted an officer. Butler advanced toward the officer in a threatening manner. The officer repeatedly told Butler to drop the knife. When Butler got within two to five feet, the officer shot him twice.
>
> The court held that the police officer was protected by governmental immunity because he was acting during the course of employment, he reasonably believed that he was acting within the scope of his employment, he acted in good faith, and he was performing a discretionary act. In regards to the "scope of employment" analysis, it was held to be undisputed that the officer possessed the authority to use deadly force in certain circumstances. *Butler v. City of Detroit*, 149 Mich. App. 708 (1986).
>
> Pursuant to a court writ, Officers went to the O'Brien residence to assist in removing a pickup truck. While the tow truck driver was attempting to hook up the truck, O'Brien was observed standing in the doorway carrying a rifle in the port arms position. He yelled, "Leave my truck alone! Get out of here!" He then retreated into his house. He never pointed the gun at any officers or verbally threatened to use it.
>
> After a nearly six-hour stand-off, an officer broke a window to see inside. O'Brien responded by firing approximately 10 shots. At that point, the

chief issued a "shoot to kill order." Subsequently, a sharpshooter shot O'Brien in the neck as he was standing in his kitchen.

The Court held the excessive force issue was settled out of court. The court did hold, however, that the police violated the plaintiff's Fourth Amendment rights because they should have attempted to obtain either a search warrant or an arrest warrant. The officers argued that there were exigent circumstances. The court ruled that the exigent circumstances no longer existed once the house was surrounded. However, the court also ruled that the police were protected by qualified immunity. Even though there was a Fourth Amendment violation, an objectively reasonable officer could believe that there was an exigency. *O'Brien v. City of Grand Rapids*, 23 F.3d 990 (6th Cir. 1994).

On October 19, 1990, the plaintiff was experiencing a manic episode, which made him extremely volatile. He broke into the Forest View Hospital by smashing out a window to the reception area. He then began smashing windows and whatever was in his path while yelling that he was the "baddest [expletive] around." Someone called 911, and deputies from the Kent County Sheriff's Department responded.

Officers entered the hospital armed with ASP batons. The plaintiff took a boxer's stance and began approaching the officers while verbally threatening them. The officers swung and hit plaintiff a number of times, including two strikes to the head. One deputy was picked up and thrown to the floor. The plaintiff even removed a drinking fountain from the wall. Eventually, eight officers were able to subdue and handcuff him.

Applying the objective standard, the court held that the officers did not use excessive force against the plaintiff. Further, "Once the plaintiff started and continued the fight, the officers had no constitutional duty to retreat or to submit." *Nicholson v. Kent County Sheriff's Dept.*, 839 F. Supp. 508 (W.D. Mich. 1993).

Troopers were dispatched to investigate a report of shots being fired. The caller also advised that a man was walking nearby with a long gun. The troopers stated they located Roxbury walking down the street carrying a gun. One trooper yelled very loudly, "State Police — drop the gun." Defendant reportedly then raised the gun and pointed it directly at an officer. Three troopers then responded by firing several times. Roxbury died a short time thereafter.

The plaintiff countered that Roxbury was obviously intoxicated and walking down the street singing and carrying a large bottle of beer. The plaintiff also claimed that, even though Roxbury did have an unloaded shotgun, he was not threatening anyone and was carrying it with the barrel down.

Summary judgment was denied because there were facts that had to go to the jury for determination. The key question was whether there was a *material issue of fact* as to reasonableness of the officers' actions. A judge at summary judgment cannot decide issues of fact. At trial, the jury returned a verdict in favor of the troopers. *Roxbury v. Michigan State Police*, 838 F. Supp 1204 (1992).

Officers responded to a residence where there was a suicidal subject. He had cut his arms in a number of places and was carrying a knife. Officers attempted to communicate with him, but he refused to communicate. He also mentioned a gun, and his father confirmed that there were guns in the house. He exited the house but then went back inside. When he reentered the house, officers followed him into the breezeway. At one point, he approached an officer, who sprayed him with mace. The mace was not effective, and the subject was able to reenter the house.

Approximately 15 minutes after the officers' arrival, the subject approached the officers holding two knives. Officers testified that his right arm was raised above his shoulder and a knife was in his hand. Officers told him to drop the knives. When he was between six to nine feet from the officers, two officers shot and killed him.

The trial court granted summary judgment to the officers. The Sixth Circuit Court of Appeals reversed. "The discovery depositions, affidavits, exhibits, and other material demonstrates clearly that the two sides do not agree on the facts. The police claim Thomas threatened to get a gun and then charged at them through the kitchen door with the knives on the porch. The Sovas deny this version of what happened. They claim Thomas never said anything about a gun and was shot before he ever stepped out of the kitchen doorframe. Our resolution of this case therefore turns upon whether it was proper

> for the District Court to grant the officers qualified immunity in the face of such a factual dispute. . . . This court has established that summary judgment is *inappropriate* where there are contentious factual disputes over the reasonableness of the use of deadly force." In short, the jury must decide factual issues.
>
> The Court did uphold the summary judgments granted to the police department because "a plaintiff who sues a city and its police department for constitutional violations under 42 U.S.C. § 1983 must establish that a governmental policy or custom caused the alleged injury" and the plaintiff failed to meet that burden. The suit against the officers was eventually settled out of court. *Sova v. The City of Mt. Pleasant*, 142 F.3d 898 (6th Cir. 1998).

FLEEING FELONS

Tennessee v. Garner

In the case of *Tennessee v. Garner*, 471 U.S. 1 (1985), officers responded to a "prowler" complaint. One officer went to the rear of the house, heard a door slam, and saw someone run across the backyard. The suspect stopped at a 6-foot high fence. The officer could see the suspect's face and hands and was reasonably sure that the suspect was not armed. The officer walked toward the suspect and yelled, "[P]olice, halt." The suspect then began to climb the fence. The officer then shot and killed the suspect. There was a purse and ten dollars from the house on the suspect's body.

The United States Supreme Court stated that were very few felonies, all of which were punishable by death, when the fleeing felon rule was established. There are now many more felonies, and many of today's felonies are not considered to be dangerous. The Court found that the fleeing felon statute was unconstitutional as it applied to the facts in this case.

Garner requirements: Deadly force and fleeing felon

"Where the officer has probable cause to believe that the suspect poses a threat of serious physical harm, either to the officer or others, it is not constitutionally unreasonable to prevent escape by using deadly force." *Tennessee v. Garner*, 471 U.S. 1 (1985). Examples include:

- The suspect threatened the officer with a weapon, or
- The officer has probable cause to believe that the suspect has committed a crime involving the infliction or threatened infliction of serious physical harm.

If feasible, some warning should be given.

The use of deadly force must be reasonably *necessary* to prevent the suspect's escape and alternative steps are not likely to lead to the safe control of the subject. "We conclude that such force may not be used unless it is necessary to prevent the escape. . . . " *Tennessee v. Garner*, 471 U.S. 1 (1985).

Fleeing Vehicles

> An officer attempted to stop a vehicle for speeding, and the driver fled. The pursuit was on a two-lane road and, at times, was at speeds over 85 mph. The driver crossed the centerline multiple times, ran red lights, and, at one point, went through a parking lot and struck a police car. The pursuit ended when the officer rammed the suspect vehicle, causing it to leave the road and overturn. The driver was rendered quadriplegic and sued the officer.
>
> The Court analyzed the case under the *Garner* reasonableness standard, which is adopted from the Fourth Amendment, and held that the fleeing driver's actions posed a risk to innocent bystanders, including police officers, and this risk outweighed his Fourth Amendment rights. The driver was the one who created a substantial risk to others, and it was reasonable for the officer to use force to stop him. This is the rule even when the officer's actions place a fleeing motorist at risk of serious injury or death. The Court also held that pursuing officers have no constitutional obligation to terminate a pursuit in order to protect innocent bystanders from a fleeing motorist; termination of a pursuit does not guarantee a driver will drive more safely, whereas ramming a fleeing vehicle will end the pursuit, thus making it safer for everyone (except the fleeing driver). *Scott v. Harris*, 550 U.S. 372 (2007).
>
> Note: The plaintiff's account of this incident conflicted with the officers' account. The Court held that there was no "genuine" dispute of the facts because the pursuit was recorded on patrol-car video, which the Court was able to review. The pursuit video is available as of April 24, 2009, at YOUTUBE by searching *Scott v. Harris*.

Case Law in Michigan on Fleeing Felons

Deadly force was justified to prevent the escape of a suspect who was attempting to escape from the scene of a robbery attempt. The suspect was armed with a knife and had demonstrated his willingness to use the knife against store clerks during the robbery. While he was attempting to flee, the suspect either slipped, fell, or lunged at one of the clerks and was subsequently shot in the head by an officer. *Newcomb v. City of Troy*, 719 F Supp. 1408 (E.D. Mich., 1989).

Two victims were waiting for a bus when the suspects drove up. The passenger in the suspect vehicle brandished a gun, and the victims were robbed. The victims escaped and found two Southfield officers. Later the officers observed the vehicle in the parking lot. The passenger pointed a gun at a woman who was walking to her car. The officers surrounded the car, and the passenger pointed the gun at one of the officers. The officers fired into the car. The driver exited the car and began to run away. The officers shot and killed him.

The estate brought suit against the officers for excessive force and against the police department for failing to adequately train their officers and for having an unconstitutional deadly force policy.

The Court of Appeals asked the following questions:

> "Would objectively reasonable officers have realized that Ellington, in fact, was not armed?"
>
> "Did the officers have probable cause to believe that Ellington posed a threat of serious bodily harm to them or to others?"
>
> "Did Ellington commit, or was he in the process of committing, a crime involving the infliction of serious physical harm?"
>
> "Was deadly force necessary to prevent Ellington's escape?"
>
> "Was Ellington given warning, or was one necessary under the circumstances?"

The court sent the case back to the jury to determine if an objective police officer should have perceived Ellington as unarmed or as "nondangerous." *Washington v. Newsome*, 977 F.2d 991 (6th Cir. 1992).

PRIVATE CITIZEN USE OF DEADLY FORCE

A split Michigan Supreme Court held that the rule from *Tennessee v. Garner* is not applicable to a private citizen because *Garner* is a Fourth Amendment case and, thus, only applies to governmental agents. Since the fleeing-felon rule still exists, it is up to the legislature, not the Court, to change law. *People v. Couch*, 436 Mich. 414 (1990).

The use of deadly force by a private citizen is justified when the following occur:

> The evidence must show that a felony actually occurred."
>
> The fleeing suspect against whom the force was used must be the person who committed the felony."
>
> The use of deadly force must have been '*necessary*' to ensure the apprehension of the felon." *People v. Hampton*, 194 Mich. App. 593 (1992).

USE OF FORCE IN SELF DEFENSE

The Self-Defense Act—MCL 780.971–780.974

Using force

A person may use deadly force with no duty to retreat if *all* of the following conditions exist:

- The person is not engaged in a crime.
- The person is in a place he or she has a legal right to be.
- The person honestly and reasonably believes deadly force is necessary.
- The deadly force is used to prevent imminent death, great bodily harm, or sexual assault of the person using force or another person.

MCL 780.972.

A person may use less than deadly force if *all* of the following conditions exist:

- The person is not engaged in a crime.
- The person is in a place where he or she has a legal right to be.
- The person honestly and reasonably believes force is necessary.

- The person uses force to prevent the imminent use of unlawful force against himself or another person.
- The person only uses the amount of force that is necessary. *People v. Deason*, 148 Mich. App. 27 (1985).

MCL 780.972.

Presumptions: Honest and Reasonable Belief—MCL 780.951

There is a rebuttable presumption that a person using force has an honest and reasonable belief that imminent death, great bodily harm, or sexual assault will occur if the person using force honestly and reasonably believes the person against whom force is used is any of the following:

- In the process of breaking and entering a dwelling or business.
- In the process of committing a home invasion.
- Has committed a breaking and entering or home invasion and is still present in the dwelling or business.
- Is attempting to unlawfully remove a person from a dwelling, business, or vehicle against his or her will.

The presumption does not apply in the following circumstances:

- The person against whom force was used had a legal right to be in the dwelling, business, or vehicle.
- The person being removed from a dwelling, business, or vehicle was a child in the lawful custody of the person removing the child.
- The person using force was engaged in a crime or was using the business, dwelling, or vehicle to further a crime.
- The person against whom force was used was a police officer attempting to enter a dwelling, business, or vehicle in the performance of the officer's duties.
- The person against whom force was used had a domestic relationship with the person using force and the person using force had a history of domestic violence as the aggressor.

Duty of Prosecution—MCL 780.961

If the prosecutor believes that force was unjustified (i.e., it was not self-defense), the prosecutor must present evidence to that effect at the time of warrant issuance, preliminary examination, and trial.

Duty to Retreat—MCL 780.973

Whether the person could have safely retreated may be considered by the jury in determining whether the use of deadly force was reasonable.

However, there is no duty to retreat if:

- The person is being attacked in his or her own home,
- The person reasonably believes that the attacker is about to use a deadly weapon, or
- The person is attacked suddenly, fiercely, and violently.

CJ12d 7.16.

CIVIL LAW AND LIABILITY

CIVIL LAW

Civil law is that body of principles that determines private rights and liabilities.

Civil Law Compared to Criminal Law

Civil law

Laws governing private rights and remedies, designed to adjudicate differences between private persons. Civil law is a truth-seeking process where constitutional limitations against self-incrimination and unreasonable search and seizure have little application.

Criminal law

Criminal acts are wrongs committed against society and not only against the individual. Criminal prosecutions are limited by constitutional protections against self-incrimination and unreasonable search and seizure. An act may be both a crime and a civil wrong.

CIVIL LITIGATION

Discovery for Civil Litigation

Discovery (MCR 2.301 et seq.) is a pretrial method used to obtain facts and information about the case from the other party including:

- Depositions,
- Interrogatories,
- Production of documents or things,
- Permission to enter on lands or other property,
- Physical or mental examinations, and
- Requests for admissions.

Scope of discovery—MCR 2.302

- Parties may obtain discovery regarding any matter, not privileged, *that is relevant* to the subject matter involved in the pending action.
- It does not matter that the information being sought will be inadmissible at trial, as long as it appears "*reasonably calculated*" to lead to discovery of admissible evidence.
- If the information or item sought is privileged, then it cannot be discovered (e.g., self-incrimination, attorney-client, physician-patient, and husband-wife).

Types of discovery

- A **deposition** (MCR 2.303) is an interview under oath. A deposition can be taken of any person, whether a party to the action or not. A deposition provides examination and cross-examination of a person, face to face, without time to deliberate carefully and fashion a response. A plaintiff cannot take a defendant's deposition until the defendant has had a reasonable amount of time to consult an attorney.

If a deposition is taken before a suit is filed, the person requesting the discovery must serve notice and a copy of the petition on the deponent. If an action is filed, the deposition may be taken without a petition (leave of court). Notice to the deponent or attorney is sufficient, but petitioner may also obtain a subpoena for deponent and his or her records.

Depositions may be used in later court proceedings:

- To impeach a witness.
- When deponent is an expert witness.
- When the witness is dead.
- When the witness is unable to attend the trial.
- When the witness refuses to testify.
- When the witness has a lack of memory.

If a party decides to use part of a deposition, an adverse party can require any other part of the deposition to be admitted.

- **Interrogatories** (MCR 2.309) are written questions, submitted to a party who is to answer them as part of discovery under oath and signs a sworn statement that the answers are true. Interrogatories can only be required from a party of an action. Answers or objections to interrogatories must be returned within 28 days of receiving them. (42 days if served with the complaint.)
- **Sanctions** (MCR 2.313). There are sanctions for failure to cooperate in discovery. A party can request a court order to complete discovery. Failure to comply with a court order can bring the following:
    - A default judgment may be entered or the case may be dismissed,
    - A contempt order, which may include a fine or imprisonment, could be imposed, or
    - The information sought could be found in favor of the party seeking discovery.

Summons—MCR 2.102

A **summons** is a writing used to notify a person of an action that was commenced against him or her. Upon a complaint being filed, the court clerk issues a summons. A summons contains the following:

- Lists the court with jurisdiction.
- Discloses the allegations within the complaint.
- Reveals the names and addresses of the parties.
- Tells the time in which the defendant is required to respond.
- Gives notice that, if the respondent fails to answer the complaint within the time allowed, judgment may be entered against him or her.

Service of Process—MCR 2.103 et seq.

Any legally competent adult, who is not a party to the action, may serve civil process in civil actions. Proof of service may be made by:

- A written acknowledgment by the person served.
- A certificate stating the facts of service if served by a court officer, sheriff, or attorney.

Service may be made by:

- *State court*
    - Delivering a summons and copy of complaint to the defendant personally, or
    - Sending a copy of the summons and complaint by registered or certified mail, return receipt requested, and delivery restricted to the defendant.
- *Federal court*
    - Delivering a summons to the defendant personally, or
    - By first class mail.

Mediation

Process of settling differences between persons before taking case to trial.

CIVIL LIABILITY

Crime Compared to Tort

A civil wrong, or **tort**, differs from what has been discussed up to this point as criminal. A **crime** is an offense against society that results in punishment, whereas a tort is a wrong against another person. A person convicted of a crime may be sentenced to jail, whereas a person found responsible for a tort will be ordered to financially compensate that person for the injury.

Under a civil wrong, a person may sue the person who injured him or her for money damages. Generally, the courts will only allow the amount of damages recoverable to the actual amount of injury sustained. Sometimes, the court will allow punitive damages. These damages go beyond the actual injury and have the purpose of punishing the person responsible for the injury.

A crime can also result in civil litigation. For example, a person could strike another in the face, breaking his nose. The state would seek criminal charges for aggravated assault, and the person injured could sue to recover the costs of the injury.

Three Theories of Tort Affecting Law Enforcement

There are three theories of torts that generally affect law enforcement. They include intentional torts, negligence and constitutional torts.

- An *intentional tort* is an act that is done with purpose. A typical example is where the officer strikes someone without justification.
- Officers can also be held to be *negligent* in their actions, but in Michigan, officers must be shown to have been grossly negligent before they are held to be liable.
- A *constitutional tort* is when the officer violates a person's constitutional rights. The officer will not be liable if he or she was acting in good faith.

INTENTIONAL TORTS

Intentional Torts Typically Affecting Law Enforcement

False arrest or false imprisonment. Examples include falsely procuring an arrest warrant, failure to confirm a warrant, and what has sometimes been called an "attitude arrest."

Battery. An example is where an officer kicks or hits another person without justification.

Intentional infliction of mental distress. An example of this is where officers beat a person in front of a family member. The family member can file suit for emotional distress resulting from witnessing the beating.

Typical Defenses to Intentional Torts

There are many possible defenses to an intentional tort, including the following:

- *Action was justified:* e.g., the person was attacking the officer at the time he was struck.
- *Reasonable mistake:* An officer may reasonably feel he is being attacked when, in fact, he was not, or an officer makes an arrest based on mistaken facts, but the mistake was reasonable at the time.
- *Consent:* The person consented to the act, e.g. the person consented to go to the police station.

- *Self-defense*
- *Defense of others*
- *Defense of property*
- *Recapture of chattels (reclaiming property).*
- *Necessity:* e.g., shooting of a dog that is rabid
- *Legal process:* e.g., officer carrying out legal duties such as an arrest warrant

NEGLIGENCE TORTS

Negligence Actions Require Four Elements

Duty

Public duty doctrine: Unless there is a *special relationship*, officers do not owe a duty to any one individual.

- Before an individual can bring suit against a police officer, a special relationship must exist between the injured party and the officer. To demonstrate a special relationship, the plaintiff must show:
  - The police officer *made assurances* of protection verbally or demonstratively.
  - The police officer knew that, without his or her action, harm could come to the victim.
  - The police officer was in *direct contact* with the victim.
  - The *victim relied* on the officer's assurances of protection. *White v. Beasley*, 453 Mich. 308 (1996)

> Officers did not establish a special relationship with plaintiffs when the officers did not arrest suspects after they called 911 to report a suspicious situation. During the investigation, the officers took the suspects in the patrol car and parked across the street from the plaintiff's house. No arrests were made and later in the evening, the plaintiff's house was firebombed. The Court of Appeals applied the four factors under White and dismissed the suit. *Smith v. Jones*, 246 Mich. App. 270 (2001).

Breach

The officer breached the duty owed to the plaintiff.

Causation (connection)

The breach caused the injury.

Injury

An injury resulted.

Elements in Action

A trooper cocked his revolver while in the process of arresting a driver after a high-speed chase. The driver was not cooperative and the officer placed his left hand on the driver's left shoulder. The driver suddenly swung his left elbow around and struck the officer. The driver's movement placed the side of his head against the muzzle of the gun. The gun discharged and the driver was killed.

Duty: A duty was created when placing plaintiff under arrest.

Breach: The officer may have breached that duty when he arrested plaintiff with a cocked revolver.

Legal cause: The cocking of the revolver caused the weapon to accidentally discharge.

Injury: Plaintiff died.

McMillian v. Vliet, 422 Mich. 570 (1985).

Negligence during Pursuits

State standard

MCL 691.1405 states in part that, "[government] agencies shall be liable for bodily injury and property damage resulting from negligent operation by any officer, . . . or employee of the government agency, of a motor vehicle of which the government agency is owner. . . ."

The Michigan Supreme Court has limited officer liability in this context as it applies negligence liability in police pursuits.

The court held that the police owe a duty to innocent passengers, but not to passengers who are themselves wrongdoers whether they help bring about the pursuit or encourage flight. "A passenger who seeks to recover for injuries allegedly caused by a negligent police pursuit bears the burden of proving personal innocence as a precondition to establishing the duty element of a cause of action."

An officer's physical handling of a motor vehicle during a police chase can constitute "negligent operation . . . of a motor vehicle" within the motor vehicle exception. However, a plaintiff must demonstrate that his or her injuries were the result of the actual operation of the police cars. If the police cars did not hit the plaintiff, cause another vehicle or object to hit the plaintiff, or force the vehicle occupying the plaintiff off the road or into another vehicle or object, the motor vehicle exception to governmental immunity does not apply.

An officer's decision to pursue a vehicle does not constitute the negligent operation of a motor vehicle.

Finally, actions of individual police officers must be the proximate cause of the plaintiff's injuries in order for the individual officer to be liable. The actions of one officer during a pursuit do not make all officers in the pursuit subject to liability. *Robinson v. Detroit*, 462 Mich. 439 (2000).

Federal standard

Two officers observed two subjects on a motorcycle traveling at a high rate of speed. The officers turned on their emergency lights and yelled for the cyclist to stop. The driver maneuvered around the patrol cars and sped away. The officers activated their emergency equipment and chased the motorcycle. The chase ended when the motorcycle tipped over. One officer slammed on his brakes, but was unable to avoid striking the passenger and caused his death.

The family of the decedent brought a suit in federal court for violating his constitutional rights. The Supreme Court applied the "shock-the-conscience" standard (an extremely high standard of review) for determining liability. "In the circumstances of a high-speed chase aimed at apprehending a suspected offender, where unforeseen circumstances demand an instant judgment on the part of the officer who feels the pulls of competing obligations, only a purpose to cause harm unrelated to the legitimate object of arrest will satisfy the shock-the-conscience standard."

The Court also refused to apply the Fourth Amendment to this type of situation. "The Amendment covers only 'searches and seizures,' neither of which took place here. No one suggests that there was a search, and this Court's cases foreclose finding a seizure, since Smith did not terminate Lewis's freedom of movement through means intentionally applied." *County of Sacramento v. Lewis*, 523 U.S. 833 (1998).

Immunity to Negligent Torts—MCL. 691.1407

Individual tort immunity for negligence actions

Judges, legislators, and highest level executive officials at all levels of government have **absolute immunity** if acting within scope of authority.

Lower-level officials and employees (police officers) are granted immunity if:

- They are acting or reasonably believe they are acting within scope of authority.
- The agent is engaged in a governmental function (see below).
- The conduct is not *grossly negligent* (not so reckless as to demonstrate a substantial lack of concern for whether an injury results).

Governmental agent immunity

Agent must be performing a governmental function:

- Expressly or impliedly mandated or authorized by constitution, statute, local charter or ordinance, or other law.
- Governmental function includes any activity for the purpose of public safety, which is performed on public or private property by a sworn law enforcement officer within the scope of the law enforcement officer's authority.
- Government function must not fall under a statutory exception to immunity
    - Maintaining highways in reasonable repair. MCL 691.1402.
    - Negligent operation of government vehicles. MCL 691.1405.
    - Dangerous/defective conditions of public buildings. MCL 691.1406.
- Operation of police department is governmental function for immunity purposes. *Isabella County v. Michigan*, 181 Mich. App. 99 (1989).
- Intentional torts of governmental employees are not within exercise or discharge of governmental function and are not entitled to governmental immunity. *Odom v. Wayne County*, 482 Mich. 459 (2008).

Fireman's Rule

Traditionally, police officers were precluded from filing civil suits against someone who injured them while they were performing their duty as a police officer. On-duty injuries at one time were considered "part of the job."

> The Michigan Supreme Court held that the fireman's rule is not "a license to act with impunity, without regard for the officer's well being." A suit based on an act that is alleged to have been *wanton, reckless, or grossly negligent,* is not precluded by the fireman's rule. In this case, while directing traffic, Officer Gibbons was struck by a reckless driver. The court held that being struck by a reckless driver is not a risk inherent in a police officer's duties. *Gibbons v. Caraway*, 455 Mich. 314 (1997).
>
> Trooper Fields was on a traffic stop on I-94 when he was struck by a vehicle driven by the defendant. The lawsuit was dismissed on the grounds of the fireman's rule. The Michigan Supreme Court reversed. The Court held that in instances where the "negligent conduct of the defendant did not result in the officer's presence at the scene of the injury, the fireman's rule does not apply." *Harris-Fields v. Syze*, 461 Mich. 188 (1999).

CONSTITUTIONAL TORTS— 42 U.S.C. 1983

Definition

Any *person* who, *acting under color of law* subjects any other person to the deprivation of any rights, privileges, or immunities secured by the Constitution and laws, is liable to the party injured.

Person

- A state or state agency is not a "person" and cannot be sued under this section.
- Cities and municipalities can be persons if it is shown that they have a custom or policy of violating constitutional rights.
- Individual officers are considered persons.

Acting under color of law

Police officers are generally acting under color of state law.

Deprive a person of rights, privileges, or immunities secured by the Constitution

The purpose of the Constitution is to protect people from the state, not from one another. *Rogers v. Port Huron*, 833 F. Supp 1212 (E.D. Mich. 1994).

General Claims under 42 USC 1983

- Excessive Force—Fourth Amendment.
- Cruel and Unusual Punishment—Eighth Amendment.
- False Arrest—Fourth Amendment.

- Freedom of Speech—First Amendment.
- Violation of the Equal Protection of Laws—Fourteenth Amendment.
- Violation of Due Process—Fourteenth Amendment.
- Illegal Search and Seizure—Fourth Amendment.

Immunity to 42 USC 1983 Actions

Absolute immunity is given to judges, legislators, and prosecutors when they are performing their respective functions. *Schorn v. Larose*, 829 F. Supp. 215 (6th Cir. Mich. 1993) **Qualified immunity** is given to other governmental officials when they:

- *Act in good faith,* and
- *Reasonably believe their actions are constitutional.*
- State immunity acts are not controlling for violations under § 1983 claims. *Howlett v. Rose*, 496 U.S. 356 (1990).

> General rule of qualified immunity from civil liability is intended to provide government officials the ability to "reasonably" anticipate when their conduct may give rise to liability. Where rule is applicable, officers can know that they will not be liable as long as their actions are "reasonable" under current American law. *Anderson v. Creighton*, 483 U.S. 635 (1987).

> The Sixth Circuit denied qualified immunity to a police officer who arrested a man who drove by a group of abortion protesters and yelled obscenities out the window. Because the vehicle was traveling at a fast rate of speed and was located quite a distance away from the protesters, the court would not classify the statement as "fighting words." Thus, the speech was protected under the First Amendment. *Sandul v. Larion*, 119 F. 3d 1250 (6th Cir. 1997).

> Officers are provided qualified immunity when an officer reasonably believes that his or her conduct complies with the law. The relevant, dispositive inquiry is whether it would be clear to a reasonable officer that the conduct was lawful in the situation he confronted. *Pearson v. Callahan*, 555 U.S. __(2009).

> Government officials in general, and police officers in particular, may not exercise their authority for personal motives, particularly in response to real or personal slights to their dignity. The fighting words doctrine may be limited in the case of communications addressed to a properly trained police officer because police officers are expected to exercise great restraint in their response than the average citizen. *Greene v. Barber*, 310 F. 3d 889 (6th Cir. 2002).

> A search warrant that failed to describe the persons or things to be seized was invalid on its face, notwithstanding that requisite particularized description was provided in search warrant application. Residential search that was conducted pursuant to this facially invalid warrant could not be regarded as "reasonable," though items to be seized were described in search warrant application, and though officers conducting search exercised restraint in limiting scope of search to that indicated in application.

> The officer who had prepared and executed warrant was not entitled to qualified immunity from liability. *Groh v. Ramirez*, 540 U.S. 551 (2004).

Theories of Liability under 42 U.S.C. § 1983

Intentional torts

Negligence

§1983 requires *gross negligence or recklessness*; generally ordinary negligence or carelessness does not cause liability under 42 U.S.C. 1983. *Daniels v. Williams*, 474 U.S. 327 (1986).

Good Faith Defense

Defense applies where officer acts in "*good faith.*" Courts look at subjective (officer's belief) of probable cause.

> The good faith defense will apply even if probable cause is absent, so long as the officer has a "good faith" belief his actions are lawful. *Pierson v Ray*, 386 U.S. 547 (1967).

> Government officials performing discretionary functions generally are shielded from liability for civil damages as long as their conduct does not violate clearly established statutory or constitutional rights of which a reasonable person would have known. If the court finds that the officer did violate this test, he or she may plead a "good faith" defense. An officer pleading a good faith defense where a clearly established right has been violated must claim extraordinary circumstances and prove that he or she neither knew nor should have known that he or she was violating clearly established statutory or constitutional rights. *Harlow v. Fitzgerald*, 457 U.S. 800 (1982).

29

CRIME VICTIM'S RIGHTS ACT

DEFINITIONS UNDER THE CRIME VICTIM'S RIGHTS ACT

Victim—MCL 780.752

Includes one of the following:

- An individual who suffers direct or threatened physical, financial, or emotional harm as a result of the commission of a crime, serious misdemeanor, or juvenile offense.
- Sole proprietorships, partnerships, corporations, associations, governmental agencies, or any other legal entity that has suffered direct physical or financial harm as a result of a crime, serious misdemeanor or juvenile offense.

> The intent behind the CVRA permits narcotics enforcement teams as victims to obtain restitution of buy money lost to a defendant's criminal act of selling controlled substances. *People v. Crigler*, 244 Mich. App. 420 (2001).

- The following relations of a deceased victim if the relation is not the defendant:
    - The spouse.
    - A child 18 years of age or older if sub paragraph (A) does not apply.
    - A parent if subparagraphs (A) and (B) do not apply.
    - A guardian or custodian of a child of deceased if the child is less than 18 years old and (A) through (C) do not apply.
    - A sibling if subparagraphs (A) to (D) do not apply.
    - A grandparent if subparagraphs (A) to (E) do not apply.
- A parent, guardian, or custodian of a victim who is less than 18 years of age and who is neither the defendant nor incarcerated if the parent, guardian, or custodian so chooses.
- A parent, guardian, or custodian, of a victim who is so mentally incapacitated that he or she cannot meaningfully understand or participate in the legal process if he or she is neither the defendant nor incarcerated.
- If a victim is physically unable to exercise the privileges and rights under this article, the victim may designate one of the following to act in place of the victim during the duration of the disability if he or she is neither the defendant nor incarcerated:
    - The spouse.
    - A child 18 years or older.
    - A parent.
    - A sibling.

307

- A grandparent.
- Or any other person 18 years or older.

Crimes as Defined Under the Act

A crime is a violation of a penal law of this state for which the offender may be punished by imprisonment for more than one year, or an offense expressly designated as a felony.

Serious Misdemeanors—MCL 780.811

Serious misdemeanors under the act include the following:

- MCL 750.81—Assault and battery.
- MCL 750.81a—Assault, infliction of serious injury.
- MCL 750.115—Breaking and entering, or illegal entry.
- MCL 750.136b(6)—Child abuse in the fourth degree.
- MCL 750.145—Contributing to the neglect or delinquency of a minor.
- MCL 750.145d—Using the Internet or a computer to make a prohibited communication.
- MCL 750.233—Intentionally aiming a firearm without malice.
- MCL 750.234—Discharging a firearm intentionally aimed at a person.
- MCL 750.235—Discharge of an intentionally aimed firearm resulting in injury.
- MCL 750.335a—Indecent exposure.
- MCL 750.411h—Stalking.
- MCL 257.601b—Injuring a worker in a work zone.
- MCL 257.617a—Leaving the scene of a personal injury accident.
- MCL 257.625 & .625a—O.W.I. & impaired driving, if the violation involves an accident resulting in injury or death to another person or damage to another's property.
- MCL 324.80176—(Marine Safety Act) Operating a vessel while under the influence of or impaired by alcoholic liquor or a controlled substance, or with an unlawful blood alcohol content, if the violation involves an accident resulting in damage to another individual's property or physical injury or death to any individual.
- MCL 436.1701—Selling or furnishing alcoholic liquor to an individual less than 21 years of age if the violation results in physical injury or death to any individual.
- A local ordinance substantially corresponding to the above.

Juvenile Offense

A juvenile is a child within the jurisdiction of the family division of the circuit court. An offense is either a crime or serious misdemeanor as described above.

REQUIREMENTS UNDER THE ACT FOR LAW ENFORCEMENT

Initial Contact—MCL 780.753

Within 24 hours after initial contact between the victim of a reported "crime," "serious misdemeanor," or "juvenile offense," the law enforcement agency having the responsibility for investigating the incident shall give the victim the following information:

- The availability of emergency and medical services, if applicable.
- The availability of victim's compensation benefits and the address of the crime victim's compensation board.
- The address and phone number of the prosecuting attorney whom the victim should contact to obtain information about **victim's rights.**
- The following statement: "If you would like to be notified of an arrest in your case or the release of the person arrested, or both, you should call [law enforcement agency's telephone number] and inform them. If you are not notified of an arrest in your case, you may call [law enforcement agency's telephone number] for the status of the case at anytime."

Property—MCL 780.754

The law enforcement agency investigating a "crime," "serious misdemeanor," or "juvenile offense" shall promptly return to the victim property belonging to the victim that is taken in the course of the investigation, except:

- Contraband.
- When the ownership of the property is in dispute.
- Any weapons used in the commission of a crime or other evidence that the prosecutor certifies that there is a need to retain the evidence in lieu of a photograph or other means of memorializing its possession by the agency.

Arraignment for a Crime—MCL 780.755

Within 24 hours of defendant's arraignment for a "crime," the arresting agency must:

- Give the victim notice of the availability of pretrial release.
- Supply the telephone number of the sheriff or juvenile facility.
- Provide notice that the victim may contact the sheriff to determine if defendant has been released.
- Promptly notify the victim of the arrest or pretrial release, or both, if the victim requests or has requested the information.

Arrest for a Serious Misdemeanor—MCL 780.815

Not later than 72 hours after the arrest of the defendant for a "serious misdemeanor," the investigating agency shall give to the victim:

- Notice of the availability of pretrial release for the defendant,
- The phone number of the sheriff, and
- Notice that the victim may contact the sheriff to determine whether the defendant has been released from custody.
- Promptly notice of the arrest or pretrial release, or both, if the victim requests or has requested the information.

List of Victims of Serious Misdemeanor or Juvenile Offense—MCL 780.812

A law enforcement officer investigating a "serious misdemeanor" or "juvenile offense" involving a victim shall include with the complaint, appearance ticket, traffic citation, or petition filed with the court a separate written statement including the name, address, and phone number of each victim. This separate statement shall not be a matter of public record.

APPENDIX

Approved, SCAO

Original - Return
1st copy - Witness
2nd copy - File
3rd copy - Extra

STATE OF MICHIGAN JUDICIAL DISTRICT JUDICIAL CIRCUIT COUNTY PROBATE	SUBPOENA Order to Appear and/or Produce	CASE NO.

Court address | Court telephone no.

Police Report No. (if applicable)

Plaintiff(s)/Petitioner(s)
☐ People of the State of Michigan
☐ _____

v

Defendant(s)/Respondent(s)

☐ Civil ☐ Criminal | Charge

☐ Probate   In the matter of _____

In the Name of the People of the State of Michigan. TO:

If you require special accommodations to use the court because of disabilities, please contact the court immediately to make arrangements.

YOU ARE ORDERED:

☐ 1. to appear personally at the time and place stated below: You may be required to appear from time to time and day to day until excused.

☐ The court address above ☐ Other:

Day	Date	Time

☐ 2. Testify at trial / examination / hearing.

☐ 3. Produce/permit inspection or copying of the following items: _____

_____

_____

☐ 4. Testify as to your assets, and bring with you the items listed in line 3 above.

☐ 5. Testify at deposition.

☐ 6. MCL 600.6104(2), 600.6116, or 600.6119 prohibition against transferring or disposing of property is attached.

☐ 7. Other: _____

☐ 8.
Person requesting subpoena	Telephone no.
Address	
City	State	Zip

NOTE: If requesting a debtor's examination under MCL 600.6110, or an injunction under item 6. this subpoena must be issued by a judge. For a debtor examination, the affidavit of debtor examination on the other side of this form must also be completed. Debtor's assets can also be discovered through MCR 2.305 without the need for an affidavit of debtor examination or issuance of this subpoena by a judge.

FAILURE TO OBEY THE COMMANDS OF THE SUBPOENA OR APPEAR AT THE STATED TIME AND PLACE MAY SUBJECT YOU TO PENALTY FOR CONTEMPT OF COURT.

Court use only
☐ Served ☐ Not served

Date | Judge/Clerk/Attorney | Bar no.

MC 11 (6/04) **SUBPOENA, Order to Appear and/or Produce**   MCL 600.1455, 600.1701, 600.6110, 600.6119, MCR 2.506

SUBPOENA

Case No. _____

PROOF OF SERVICE

TO PROCESS SERVER: You must make and file your return with the court clerk. If you are unable to complete service, you must return this original and all copies to the court clerk.

CERTIFICATE / AFFIDAVIT OF SERVICE / NON-SERVICE

☐ **OFFICER CERTIFICATE** OR ☐ **AFFIDAVIT OF PROCESS SERVER**

I certify that I am a sheriff, deputy sheriff, bailiff, appointed court officer, or attorney for a party [MCR 2.104(A)(2)], and that: (notarization not required)

Being first duly sworn, I state that I am a legally competent adult who is not a party or an officer of a corporate party, and that: (notarization required)

☐ I served a copy of the subpoena, together with _____ (including any required fees) by
Attachment

☐ personal service   ☐ registered or certified mail (copy of return receipt attached)   on:

Name(s)	Complete address(es) of service	Day, date, time

☐ I have personally attempted to serve the subpoena and required fees, if any, together with _____
on the following person and have been unable to complete service.   Attachment

Name(s)	Complete address(es) of service	Day, date, time

Service fee	Miles traveled	Mileage fee	Total fee
$		$	$

Signature _____

Title _____

Subscribed and sworn to before me on _____, _____ County, Michigan.
                                       Date

My commission expires: _____   Signature: _____
                        Date   Deputy court clerk/Notary public

Notary public, State of Michigan, County of _____

ACKNOWLEDGMENT OF SERVICE

I acknowledge that I have received service of the subpoena and required fees, if any, together with _____
                                                                                                    Attachment
_____ on _____
                              Day, date, time
_____ on behalf of _____ .
Signature

AFFIDAVIT FOR JUDGMENT DEBTOR EXAMINATION

I request that the court issue a subpoena which orders the party named on this form to be examined under oath before a judge concerning the money or property of:
for the following reasons:

Signature _____

Subscribed and sworn to before me on _____, _____ County, Michigan.
                                       Date

My commission expires: _____   Signature: _____
                        Date   Deputy court clerk/Notary public

Notary public, State of Michigan, County of _____

MCR 2.105

Approved, SCAO

	Information - Circuit court Original complaint - Court Warrant - Court	Bind over/Transfer - Circuit/Juvenile court Complaint copy - Prosecutor Complaint copy - Defendant/Attorney
STATE OF MICHIGAN **JUDICIAL DISTRICT** **JUDICIAL CIRCUIT**	**INFORMATION** **FELONY**	**CASE NO.** **DISTRICT** **CIRCUIT**

District Court ORI: MI-   Circuit Court ORI: MI-

	Defendant's name and address	Victim or complainant
THE PEOPLE OF THE STATE OF MICHIGAN v		
		Complaining witness
Co-defendant(s)		Date: On or about

City/Twp./Village	County in Michigan	Defendant TCN	Defendant CTN	Defendant SID	Defendant DOB
Police agency report no.	Charge			Maximum penalty	
Witnesses		☐ Oper./Chauf. ☐ CDL	Vehicle Type	Defendant DLN	

STATE OF MICHIGAN, COUNTY OF
IN THE NAME OF THE PEOPLE OF THE STATE OF MICHIGAN: The prosecuting attorney for this County appears before the court and informs the court that on the date and at the location described, the defendant:

and against the peace and dignity of the State of Michigan.

Prosecuting Attorney

By: _____

Date

MCL 764.1 et seq., MCL 766.1 et seq., MCL 767.1 et seq., MCR 6.110

MC 200   (7/05)   **FELONY SET, Information**

Approved, SCAO

Information - Circuit court
Original complaint - Court
Warrant - Court

Bind over/Transfer - Circuit/Juvenile court
Complaint copy - Prosecutor
Complaint copy - Defendant/Attorney

STATE OF MICHIGAN JUDICIAL DISTRICT JUDICIAL CIRCUIT	COMPLAINT FELONY	CASE NO. DISTRICT CIRCUIT

District Court ORI: MI-   Circuit Court ORI: MI-

THE PEOPLE OF THE STATE OF MICHIGAN	v	Defendant's name and address	Victim or complainant
			Complaining witness

Co-defendant(s) | Date: On or about

City/Twp./Village	County in Michigan	Defendant TCN	Defendant CTN	Defendant SID	Defendant DOB

Police agency report no.	Charge	Maximum penalty

Witnesses	☐ Oper./Chauf. ☐ CDL	Vehicle Type	Defendant DLN

STATE OF MICHIGAN, COUNTY OF _____ .

The complaining witness says that on the date and at the location described, the defendant, contrary to law,

The complaining witness asks that defendant be apprehended and dealt with according to law.

Warrant authorized on _____ by: _____ Date	Complaining witness signature
Prosecuting official	Subscribed and sworn to before me on _____ . Date
☐ Security for costs posted	Judge/Magistrate/Clerk Bar no.

MCL 764.1 et seq., MCL 766.1 et seq., MCL 767.1 et seq., MCR 6.110

MC 200 (7/05) **FELONY SET, Complaint**

Approved, SCAO

	Information - Circuit court Original complaint - Court Warrant - Court	Bind over/Transfer - Circuit/Juvenile court Complaint copy - Prosecutor Complaint copy - Defendant/Attorney
STATE OF MICHIGAN **JUDICIAL DISTRICT** **JUDICIAL CIRCUIT**	**WARRANT** **FELONY**	**CASE NO.** **DISTRICT** **CIRCUIT**

District Court ORI: MI-   Circuit Court ORI: MI-

THE PEOPLE OF THE STATE OF MICHIGAN	v	Defendant's name and address	Victim or complainant
			Complaining witness
Co-defendant(s)			Date: On or about

City/Twp./Village	County in Michigan	Defendant TCN	Defendant CTN	Defendant SID	Defendant DOB
Police agency report no.	Charge			Maximum penalty	
Witnesses		☐ Oper./Chauf. ☐ CDL	Vehicle Type	Defendant DLN	

STATE OF MICHIGAN, COUNTY OF _____ .
To any peace officer or court officer authorized to make arrest: The complaining witness has filed a sworn complaint in this court stating that on the date and the location described, the defendant, contrary to law,

Upon examination of the complaining witness, I find that the offense charged was committed and that there is probable cause to believe that defendant committed the offense. THEREFORE, IN THE NAME OF THE PEOPLE OF THE STATE OF MICHIGAN, I order you to arrest and bring defendant before the _____ District Court immediately.

☐ The defendant may be released before arraignment if $ _____ is posted as interim bail by _____
                                                                                                                        Date

Date _____ (SEAL)   Judge/Magistrate _____   Bar no.
See return on reverse side.

MCL 764.1 et seq., MCL 766.1 et seq., MCL 767.1 et seq., MCR 6.110

MC 200 (7/05) **FELONY SET, Warrant**

RETURN

As ordered in this warrant, the defendant was arrested on _____ at _____
                                                                Date   Time

at _____ .
   Place of arrest

_____   _____
Date   Peace Officer

Approved, SCAO

Original complaint - Court
Warrant - Court

2nd Complaint copy - Prosecutor
3rd Complaint copy - Defendant

STATE OF MICHIGAN JUDICIAL DISTRICT	COMPLAINT MISDEMEANOR	CASE NO.

ORI MI-_____ Court address_____ Court telephone no._____

THE PEOPLE OF
☐ The State of Michigan
☐ _____

Defendant's name and address

v

Victim or complainant

Complaining witness

Co-defendant(s)

Date: On or about

City/Twp./Village	County in Michigan	Defendant TCN	Defendant CTN	Defendant SID	Defendant DOB

Police agency report no.	Charge	Maximum penalty

Witnesses	☐ Oper./Chauf. ☐ CDL	Vehicle Type	Defendant DLN

STATE OF MICHIGAN, COUNTY OF _____ .

The complaining witness says that on the date and at the location described, the defendant, contrary to law,

The complaining witness asks that defendant be apprehended and dealt with according to law.

(Peace Officers only) I declare that the statements above are true to the best of my information, knowledge, and belief.

Warrant authorized on _____ by: _____ Date	Complaining witness signature_____
Prosecuting official_____	Subscribed and sworn to before me on _____ Date
	Judge/Court clerk/Magistrate

DC 225 (7/05) **COMPLAINT, MISDEMEANOR**

Approved, SCAO	Original complaint - Court Warrant - Court	2nd Complaint copy - Prosecutor 3rd Complaint copy - Defendant
STATE OF MICHIGAN **JUDICIAL DISTRICT**	**WARRANT** **MISDEMEANOR**	**CASE NO.**

ORI
MI-
Court address Court telephone no.

THE PEOPLE OF ☐ The State of Michigan ☐ _____	Defendant's name and address v	Victim or complainant
		Complaining witness
Co-defendant(s)		Date: On or about

City/Twp./Village	County in Michigan	Defendant TCN	Defendant CTN	Defendant SID	Defendant DOB
Police agency report no.	Charge			Maximum penalty	
Witnesses		☐ Oper./Chauf. ☐ CDL	Vehicle Type	Defendant DLN	

STATE OF MICHIGAN, COUNTY OF _____ .
To any peace officer or court officer authorized to make an arrest: The complaining witness has filed a sworn complaint in this court stating that on the date and the location described, the defendant, contrary to law,

Upon examination of the complaint, I find probable cause to believe defendant committed the offense set forth.
THEREFORE, IN THE NAME OF THE PEOPLE OF THE STATE OF MICHIGAN, I order you to arrest and bring defendant before the court immediately, or the defendant may be released when a cash bond is posted in the amount of $ _____ for personal appearance before the court.

_____   (SEAL)   _____   _____
Date   Judge/Magistrate   Bar no.

By virtue of this warrant the defendant has been taken into custody as ordered.

_____   _____
Date   Peace officer

DC 225 (7/05) **WARRANT, MISDEMEANOR**

Approved, SCAO

STATE OF MICHIGAN ___ JUDICIAL DISTRICT ___ JUDICIAL CIRCUIT	WARRANT MISDEMEANOR ☐ Traffic ☐ Nontraffic	CASE NO. COURT ORI

Court address | Court telephone no.

THE PEOPLE OF
☐ The State of Michigan
☐ _____

v

Defendant

TO: Any peace officer or court officer authorized to make an arrest.

Upon examination of the citation, I find probable cause to believe the defendant committed the offense set forth.

THEREFORE, IN THE NAME OF THE PEOPLE OF THE STATE OF MICHIGAN, I command you to arrest and bring defendant before the court immediately, or defendant may be released when a cash interim bond is posted in the amount of $_____ for personal appearance before the court.

⇨ COPY OF CITATION ⇨

_____
Date

_____
Judge/Magistrate

(SEAL)

Authorized on _____ by: _____
          Date
_____
Prosecuting official

By virtue of this warrant, the defendant has been taken into custody as commanded.

_____
Date

_____
Arresting official

DC 226 (5/07) **WARRANT, MISDEMEANOR, TRAFFIC/NONTRAFFIC**   MCR 6.615

Instructions for Preparing Affidavit and Search Warrant

This packet consists of seven parts. TYPE OR PRESS HARD.

*Alternate procedures may be required for these items when using electromagnetic means for issuing warrants.

1. In paragraph one FULLY describe the person, place, or thing to be searched and give its EXACT location.

2. In paragraph two FULLY describe the property that is to be searched for and seized.

3. In paragraph three set forth the facts and observations that establish probable cause. If additional pages are necessary, continue on form MC 231a.

4. *Present to prosecuting official for review if required locally.

5. *Present the original of the affidavit and search warrant to the judge/magistrate for review.

6. *Swear to the contents of the affidavit and sign it before the judge/magistrate.

7. Have the judge/magistrate sign both the original of the affidavit and the search warrant.

8. Print names of judge/magistrate and affiant on all copies of the affidavit and/or search warrant where the signatures have not been reproduced by the carbons.

9. Separate packet, retaining carbons to make duplicate tabulations later.

10. *Leave original affidavit and last copy of warrant with the issuing judge/magistrate.

11. *Execute search warrant at location given.

12. Complete the tabulation (list) of property taken in the presence of the person(s) from whom it is seized, if present, or any other person (including another officer).

13. Have person before whom the tabulation is completed sign the tabulation as witness.

14. *Leave a copy of the search warrant and completed tabulation with the person(s) from whom the property was taken, if present, or at the premises.

15. *Return the original search warrant and complete tabulation to the issuing court indicating the date returned and name of the person(s) served.

Approved, SCAO

Original affidavit - Issuing court
1st copy - Prosecutor

AFFIDAVIT FOR SEARCH WARRANT

Please type or press hard.　　　See the other side for instructions.　　Police Agency Report Number: _____

_____ , affiant(s), state that:

1. The person, place, or thing to be searched is described as and is located at:

2. The PROPERTY to be searched for and seized, if found, is specifically described as:

3. The FACTS establishing probable cause or the grounds for search are:

This affidavit consists of _____ pages.

Review on _____
　　　　　　　　Date
by _____
　　Prosecuting official

_____
Affiant

Subscribed and sworn to before me on _____
　　　　　　　　　　　　　　　　　　　　　Date
_____ Court

_____
Judge/Magistrate

MC 231 (3/08) AFFIDAVIT FOR SEARCH WARRANT

Approved, SCAO

Original warrant - Return to issuing court
1st copy - Prosecutor
2nd copy - Serve
3rd copy - Issuing judge

SEARCH WARRANT

TO THE SHERIFF OR ANY PEACE OFFICER:

Police Agency
Report Number: _____

_____ , has sworn to the affidavit regarding the following:

1. The person, place, or thing to be searched is described as and is located at:

2. The PROPERTY to be searched for and seized, if found, is specifically described as:

IN THE NAME OF THE PEOPLE OF THE STATE OF MICHIGAN: I have found that probable cause exists and you are commanded to make the search and seize the described property. Leave a copy of this warrant and a tabulation (a written inventory) of all property taken with the person from whom the property was taken or at the premises. You are further commanded to promptly return this warrant and tabulation to the court.

Issued: _____   _____
          Date   Judge/Magistrate   Bar no.

RETURN AND TABULATION

Search was made _____ and the following property was seized:
                        Date

☐ Continued on other side.

_____
Officer

Copy of warrant and tabulation served on: _____
                                                 Name

Tabulation filed: _____
                Date

MC 231 (3/08) AFFIDAVIT AND SEARCH WARRANT

Approved, SCAO

Original affidavit - Issuing court
1st copy - Prosecutor

AFFIDAVIT FOR SEARCH WARRANT
PAGE _____ OF _____ PAGES

MC 231a (6/04) **AFFIDAVIT FOR SEARCH WARRANT (continuation)**

Complete items A through D using the instructions. Fill out the form by tabbing to each item or moving the mouse to each item. Select check box items with the mouse.
Approved, SCAO

*NOTE: THE INFORMATION IN ITEM D IS ABOUT THE RESPONDENT, NOT THE PETITIONER.
Original - Court
1st copy - Law enforcement agency (file) (green)
2nd copy - Respondent (blue)
3rd copy - Petitioner (pink)
4th copy - Return (yellow)
5th copy - Return (goldenrod)

STATE OF MICHIGAN JUDICIAL CIRCUIT COUNTY	(A)	PERSONAL PROTECTION ORDER ☐ EX PARTE (DOMESTIC RELATIONSHIP)	(B)	CASE NO.

Court address / Court telephone no.
ORI
MI-

(C) Petitioner's name

Address and telephone no. where court can reach petitioner

v

*Respondent's name, address, telephone no., and DLN

(D) Height | Weight | Race * | Sex * | Date of birth or Age* | Hair color | Eye color | Other identifying information

*These items **must** be filled in for the police/sheriff to enter on LEIN; the other items are not required but are helpful. **Needed for NCIC entry.

Date: _____ Judge: _____ ☐ no hearing. ☐ **after hearing.

☐ 1. A petition requested respondent be prohibited from entry onto the premises, and either the parties are married, petitioner has property interest in the premises, or respondent does not have a property interest in the premises.
☐ 2. Petitioner requested an ex parte order which should be entered without notice because irreparable injury, loss, or damage will result from the delay required to give notice or notice itself will precipitate adverse action before the order can be issued.
** ☐ 3. Respondent poses a credible threat to the physical safety of the petitioner and/or a child of the petitioner.
☐ 4. The respondent ☐ **is the spouse or former spouse of the petitioner, had a child in common with the petitioner, or is residing or had resided in the same household as the petitioner. ☐ has or had a dating relationship with the petitioner.
5. _____ is prohibited from:
   ☐ a. entering onto property where petitioner lives.
   ☐ b. entering onto property at _____.
** ☐ c. assaulting, attacking, beating, molesting, or wounding _____.
   ☐ d. removing minor children from petitioner who has **legal** custody, except as allowed by custody or parenting time order provided removal of the children does not violate other conditions of this order. An existing custody order is dated _____. An existing parenting time order is dated _____.
** ☐ e. stalking as defined under MCL 750.411h and MCL 750.411i which includes but is not limited to:
      ☐ following petitioner or appearing within his/her sight.   ☐ appearing at petitioner's workplace or residence.
      ☐ sending mail or other communications to petitioner.   ☐ contacting petitioner by telephone.
      ☐ approaching or confronting petitioner in a public place or on private property.
      ☐ entering onto or remaining on property owned, leased, or occupied by petitioner.
      ☐ placing an object on or delivering an object to property owned, leased, or occupied by petitioner.
   ☐ f. interfering with petitioner's efforts to remove his/her children/personal property from premises solely owned/leased by respondent.
** ☐ g. threatening to kill or physically injure _____.
   ☐ h. interfering with petitioner at his/her place of employment or education or engaging in conduct that impairs his/her employment or educational relationship or environment.
   ☐ i. having access to information in records concerning a minor child of petitioner and respondent that will reveal petitioner's address, telephone number, or employment address or that will reveal the child's address or telephone number.
** ☐ j. purchasing or possessing a firearm.
6. As a result of this order, federal and/or state law may prohibit you from possessing or purchasing ammunition or a firearm (including a rifle, pistol, or revolver).
7. Violation of this order subjects respondent to immediate arrest and to the civil and criminal contempt powers of the court. If found guilty, respondent shall be imprisoned for not more than 93 days and may be fined not more than $500.00.
8. **This order is effective when signed, enforceable immediately, and remains in effect until** _____.
   This order is enforceable anywhere in this state by any law enforcement agency when signed by a judge, and upon service, may also be enforced by another state, an Indian tribe, or a territory of the United States. If respondent violates this order in a jurisdiction other than this state, respondent is subject to enforcement and penalties of the state, Indian tribe, or United States territory under whose jurisdiction the violation occurred.
9. The court clerk shall file this order with _____ who will enter it into the LEIN.
10. Respondent may file a motion to modify or terminate this order. For ex parte orders, the motion must be filed within 14 days after being served with or receiving actual notice of the order. Forms and instructions are available from the clerk of court.
11. A motion to extend the order must be filed 3 days before the expiration date in item 8 or else a new petition must be filed.

Date and time issued _____   Judge _____   Bar no. _____

CC 376 (1/08) **PERSONAL PROTECTION ORDER (Domestic Relationship)** MCL 600.2950, MCR 3.705, MCR 3.706, 18 USC 922(g)(8)(c)

Complete items A through D using the instructions. Fill out the form by tabbing to each item or moving the mouse to each item. Select check box items with the mouse.
Approved, SCAO

Original - Court
1st copy - Law enforcement agency (file) (green)
2nd copy - Respondent (blue)

3rd copy - Petitioner (pink)
4th copy - Return (yellow)
5th copy - Return (goldenrod)

| STATE OF MICHIGAN JUDICIAL CIRCUIT COUNTY | (A) | PERSONAL PROTECTION ORDER AGAINST STALKING (NONDOMESTIC) ☐ EXPARTE | (B) | CASE NO. |

Court address
ORI
MI-

Court telephone no.

(C) Petitioner's name

Address and telephone no. where court can reach petitioner

v

Respondent's name, address, and telephone no.

Address and telephone no. where court can reach respondent

(D) Full name of respondent (type or print) *

Driver's license number (if known)

| Height | Weight | Race * | Sex * | Date of birth or Age* | Hair color | Eye color | Other identifying information |

*These items **must** be filled in for the police/sheriff to enter on LEIN; the other items are not required but are helpful.

Date: _____ Judge: _____
Bar no.

1. This order is entered ☐ without a hearing. ☐ after hearing.

THE COURT FINDS:
☐ 2. A petition requesting an order to restrain conduct prohibited under MCL 750.411h and 750.411i has been filed under the authority of MCL 600.2950a.
☐ 3. Petitioner requested an ex parte order, which should be entered without notice because irreparable injury, loss, or damage will result from delay required to give notice or notice itself will precipitate adverse action before an order can be issued.
4. Respondent committed the following acts of willful, unconsented contact: (State the reasons for issuance.)

IT IS ORDERED:
5. _____ is prohibited from stalking as defined under
Full name of respondent
MCL 750.411h and MCL 750.411i, which includes but is not limited to
☐ following or appearing within sight of the petitioner.
☐ appearing at the workplace or the residence of the petitioner.
☐ approaching or confronting the petitioner in a public place or on private property.
☐ entering onto or remaining on property owned, leased, or occupied by the petitioner.
☐ sending mail or other communications to the petitioner.
☐ contacting the petitioner by telephone.
☐ placing an object on or delivering an object to property owned, leased, or occupied by the petitioner.
☐ threatening to kill or physically injure the petitioner.
☐ purchasing or possessing a firearm.
☐ other: _____
6. Violation of this order subjects the respondent to immediate arrest and to the civil and criminal contempt powers of the court. If found guilty, respondent shall be imprisoned for not more than 93 days and may be fined not more than $500.00.
7. **This order is effective when signed, enforceable immediately, and remains in effect until** _____ .
This order is enforceable anywhere in this state by any law enforcement agency when signed by a judge, and upon service, may also be enforced by another state, an Indian tribe, or a territory of the United States. If respondent violates this order in a jurisdiction other than this state, respondent is subject to enforcement and penalties of the state, Indian tribe, or United States territory under whose jurisdiction the violation occurred.
8. The court clerk shall file this order with _____ who will enter it into the LEIN.
9. Respondent may file a motion to modify or terminate this order. For ex parte orders, the motion must be filed within 14 days after being served with or receiving actual notice of the order. Forms and instructions are available from the clerk of court.
10. A motion to extend the order must be filed 3 days before the expiration date in item 7, or else a new petition must be filed.

Date and time issued _____   Judge _____

CC 380 (3/08) PERSONAL PROTECTION ORDER AGAINST STALKING (Nondomestic)   MCL 600.2950a, MCR 3.705, MCR 3.706

Approved, SCAO

Original - Court file
Copies as needed

STATE OF MICHIGAN JUDICIAL CIRCUIT COUNTY	PROOF OF SERVICE/ORAL NOTICE REGARDING PERSONAL PROTECTION ORDER	CASE NO.

Court address Court telephone no.

Petitioner's name	v	Respondent's name, address, and telephone no.
Address and telephone no. where court can reach petitioner		

AFFIDAVIT OF SERVICE

I certify that on this date I personally served _____
Respondent name

at _____
Address or location of service

with a copy of the personal protection order issued on _____ by the _____
Date

Circuit Court.

_____ _____
Officer signature   Law enforcement agency

_____ _____
Name (type or print)   ID no.   Address

_____
City, state, zip   Telephone no.

Subscribed and sworn to before me on _____, _____County, Michigan.
Date

My commission expires: _____ Signature: _____
Date   Deputy court clerk/Notary public

Notary public, State of Michigan, County of _____

PROOF OF ORAL NOTICE

I certify that on this date I orally notified _____ of
Respondent name

the existence of a personal protection order issued on _____ by the _____
Date

Circuit Court. I also certify that the respondent was advised of the following:
- the specific conduct enjoined.
- the penalties for violating the order.
- where the respondent could obtain a copy of the personal protection order.

_____ _____
Date   Officer signature

_____
Name (type or print)   ID no.

_____
Law enforcement agency

_____
Address

_____
City, state, zip   Telephone no.

MCL 600.2950(22), MCL 600.2950a(19), MCR 3.706(E)

CC 386 (6/04) PROOF OF SERVICE/ORAL NOTICE REGARDING PERSONAL PROTECTION ORDER

MICR ARREST CHARGE CODES

RI-1 (Rev. 04/08)
Michigan State Police

FILE CLASS OFFENSE/ARREST CHARGES	ARR CHG	FILE CLASS OFFENSE/ARREST CHARGES	ARR CHG	FILE CLASS OFFENSE/ARREST CHARGES	ARR CHG	FILE CLASS OFFENSE/ARREST CHARGES	ARR CHG
01000 - Sovereignty		Felony Death by Drunk Driving:		**11008 - Sexual Contact Forcible**		**13003 - Intimidation/Stalking**	
Treason	0101	Snowmobile	5466	Forcible Contact - CSC 4th Deg.	1178	Intimidation	1316	**22001 - Burglary - Forced Entry**	
Treason Misprision	0102	ORV	5476			Tx. Used for Harassment, Threats	1380	Burglary - Safe/Vault	2201
Espionage	0103	Boat	5486	**12000 - Robbery**		Aggravated Stalking (Felony)	1381	Forced Entry - Residence	2202
Sabotage	0104	Vehicle	8046	Business - Gun	1201	Stalking (Misdemeanor)	1382	Forced Entry - Non-Residence	2203
Sedition	0105	Let Intoxicated Person Operate M/V		Business - Other Weapon	1202	Stalking a Minor (Felony)	1383	Banking Type Institution	2207
Selective Service	0106	Causing Death (Alcohol)	8034	Business - Strong Arm	1203	Computer/Internet Used for		Unoccupied Bldg. or	
Sovereignty (Other)	0199	Let Intoxicated Person Operate M/V		Street - Gun	1204	Harassment, Threats	1384	Other Structure	2275
02000 - Military		Causing Death (Drugs)	8035	Street - Other Weapon	1205	Other Electronic Medium Used for		Burglary - (Other)	2299
Desertion	0201	Felony Death While Under		Street - Strong Arm	1206	Harassment, Threats	1385	**22002 - Burglary - Entry Without**	
AWOL	0297	Controlled Substance	8039	Residence - Gun	1207	Threat to Bomb	5215	**Force (Intent to Commit)**	
Military (Other)	0299	Felony Death from Fleeing Vehicle	8175	Residence - Other Weapon	1208	Threat to Burn	5216	No Forced Entry - Residence	2204
		Let Suspended Person Operate		Residence - Strong Arm	1209			No Forced Entry - Non-Residence	2205
03000 - Immigration		Causing Death	8268	Forcible - Purse Snatching	1210	**14000 - Abortion**		**22003 - Burglary - Entry Without**	
Illegal Entry	0301	**09004 - Justifiable Homicide**		Banking Type Institution	1211	Abortion Act on Other	1401	**Authority, With or Without**	
False Citizenship	0302			Motor Vehicle (Carjacking)	1270	Abortion Act on Self	1402	**Force (No Intent)**	
Smuggling Aliens	0303	**10001 - Kidnapping/Abduction**		Attempted Robbery - Unarmed	1297	Submission to Abortional Act	1403	Entering Without Permission	2298
Immigration (Other)	0399	Kidnap Minor for Ransom	1001	Attempted Robbery - Armed	1298	Abortifacient		**22004 - Poss. of Burglary Tools**	
		Kidnap Adult for Ransom	1002	Robbery (Other)	1299	Selling, Manufacturing, etc.	1404	Possession Burglary Tools	2206
09001 - Murder/Non-negligent		Kidnap Minor to Sexually Assault	1003	**13001 - Nonaggravated Assault**		Abortion (Other)	1499	**23001 - Larceny - Pocketpicking**	
Manslaughter (Voluntary)		Kidnap Adult to Sexually Assault	1004	A & B/Simple Assault	1313			Pocketpicking	2301
Willful Killing:		Kidnap Minor	1005			**20000 - Arson**			
Family - Gun	0901	Kidnap Adult	1006			Business - Endangered Life	2001	**23002 - Larceny - Purse Snatching**	
Other Weapon	0902	Kidnap Hostage for Escape	1007			Residence - Endangered Life	2002	Purse Snatching - No Force	2302
Non-family - Gun	0903	Abduct - No Ransom or Assault	1008			Business - Defraud Insurer	2003	**23003 - Larceny - Theft from Bldg.**	
Other Weapon	0904	Kidnap - Hijack Aircraft	1009	**13002 - Agg./Felonious Assault**		Residence - Defraud Insurer	2004	From Bldg. (Library, Office,	2005
Public Official - Gun	0905	Human Trafficking	1010	Family - Gun	1301	Arson - Business	2005	etc. - Used by Public)	2006
Other Weapon	0906	Human Trafficking Causing Injury	1011	Family - Other Weapon	1302	Arson - Residence	2006	From Bank Type Institution	2311
Police Officer - Gun	0907	Kidnapping (Other)	1099	Family - Strong Arm	1303	Setting Fire - Woods & Prairies	2007	**23004 - Larceny - Theft from Coin**	
Other Weapon	0908	**10002 - Parental Kidnapping**		Non-family - Gun	1304	Pub. Bldg. (Incl. Hotel/Motel)		**Operated Machine/Device**	
Willful Killing - Gun	0911	Parental Kidnap MCL750.350A[1]	1072	Non-family - Other Weapon	1305	Endangered Life	2008	From Coin Machines (Includes	2307
Willful Killing - Other Weapon	0912			Non-family - Strong Arm	1306	Arson - Public Building	2009	Telephone Coin Box)	
Human Trafficking Causing Death	0913	**11001 - Sexual Penetration**		Public Official - Gun	1307	Burning of Real Property	2072	**23005 - Larceny - Theft from**	
Homicide (Other)	0999	Penis/Vagina - CSC 1st Degree	1171	Public Official - Other Weapon	1308	Burning of Personal Property	2073	**Motor Vehicle**	
		11002 - Sexual Penetration		Public Official - Strong Arm	1309	Burning Insured Prop. (Own)	2097	Personal Property from Vehicle	2305
09002 - Neg. Homicide/		Penis/Vagina - CSC 3rd Degree	1172	Police Officer - Gun	1310	Preparation to Burn	2098	**23006 - Larceny - Theft of Motor**	
Manslaughter (Involuntary)		**11003 - Sexual Penetration**		Police Officer - Other Weapon	1311	Arson (Other)	2099	**Vehicle Parts/Accessories**	
Weapon	0910	Oral/Anal - CSC 1st Degree	1173	Police Officer - Strong Arm	1312			Parts and Accessories from Vehicle	2304
Deliver Controlled Substance		**11004 - Sexual Penetration**		Murder Attempt	1371	**21000 - Extortion**		Strip Stolen Vehicle	2407
Causing Death	0996	Oral/Anal - CSC 3rd Degree	1174	Mayhem	1393	Threat to:		**23007 - Larceny - Other**	
Assisted Suicide	0997	**11005 - Sexual Penetration**		Assault, Intent to Commit Felony	1394	Injure Person	2101	From Shipment	2306
		Object - CSC 1st Degree	1175	Assault, Intent to Maim	1395	Damage Property	2102	From Yards (Grounds surrounding	2309
09003 - Negligent Homicide		**11006 - Sexual Penetration**		Assault Less Than Murder	1396	Injure Reputation	2103	a building)	
Veh./Boat/Snowmobile		Object - CSC 3rd Degree	1176	Assault with Intent to Murder	1397	Accuse Person of Crime	2104	From Mails	2310
Negligent Homicide - Vehicle	0909	**11007 - Sexual Contact Forcible**		Assault (Other)	1177	Threat of Informing of Violation	2105		
Negligent Homicide (Other)	0998	Forcible Contact - CSC 2nd Deg.	1177	Fleeing Resulting in Assault	3601	Extortion (Other)	2199		
		Sex Offense Against Child - Fondle	8176						

Quick Reference Card 1 of 4

MICR ARREST CHARGE CODES

RI-1 (Rev. 04/08)
Michigan State Police

FILE CLASS OFFENSE/ARREST CHARGES	ARR CHG	FILE CLASS OFFENSE/ARREST CHARGES	ARR CHG	FILE CLASS OFFENSE/ARREST CHARGES	ARR CHG	FILE CLASS OFFENSE/ARREST CHARGES	ARR CHG
From Interstate Shipment	2312	Forgery (Other)	2589	Banking Type Institution	2703	Amphetamine - Use	3574
Obstruct Corr. (Postal Violation)	2313	Counterfeiting (Other)	2599	Pub. Property (Federal, State, City)	2704	Barbiturate - Manufacture	3580
Theft of U.S. Govt. Property	2314			Postal	2705	Barbiturate - Sell	3581
Larceny from U.S. Govt. Reserve	2315	**26001 - Fraud - False Pretense/**		Misappropriate Funds	2798	Barbiturate - Possess	3582
Larceny Gas Self-Service Station	2379	**Swindle/Confidence Game**		Embezzlement (Other)	2799	Barbiturate (Other)	3583
Larceny (Other)	2399	Confidence Game/Fortune Telling	2601			Barbiturate - Use	3584
Aircraft Theft (Taking/Using)	2410	Swindle	2602	**28000 - Stolen Property**		LSD - Manufacture	3585
24001 - Motor Vehicle Theft		Mail Fraud	2603	Sale of Stolen Property	2801	LSD - Sell	3586
Theft and Sale	2401	False Statements	2607	Interstate Transportation of		LSD - Possess	3587
Theft and Strip	2402	Fraud (Larceny) by Conversion	2674	Receiving	2803	LSD - Use	3588
Theft - Use in Other Crime	2403	Fraudulently Obtaining of Goods		Possessing	2804	LSD (Other)	3589
Vehicle Theft	2404	Offered for Sale	2675	Concealing	2805	Crack - Sell	3590
Theft by Bailee - Fail to Return	2405	Defrauding Hotels, Restaurants,		Stolen Property (Other)	2899	Crack - Smuggle	3591
Possess Stolen Vehicle	2408	Innkeepers, etc.	2677			Crack - Possess	3592
Unauthorized Use (Incl. Joy Riding)	2411	Fraudulently Obtaining Gasoline		Opium or Derivative - Sell	2901	Crack (Other)	3593
Stolen (Other)	2499	(Attendant Delivered)	2679	Opium or Derivative - Smuggle	2902	Crack - Use	3594
		29000 - Damage to Property		Opium or Derivative - Possess	2903	Drug, Illegal Use of	3595
24002 - M/V as Stolen Property		Business Property	2695	Opium or Derivative - (Other)	2904	Ephedrine/Pseudo > 12 grams poss	3596
Poss./Receive Stolen Vehicle/Parts	2406	Private Property	2699	Opium or Derivative - Use	2905	Delivery Imitation Controlled Subs.	3597
Interstate Transport Stolen Vehicle	2409	Public Property		Cocaine - Sell	2906	Narc. Drugs, Fraud Procurement of	3598
Theft and Sale	2472	Business Property with Explosives		Cocaine - Smuggle	2995	Dangerous Drugs (Other)	3599
Theft and Strip (Incl. Chop Shop)	2473	Private Property with Explosives		Cocaine - Possess	2996		
Theft and Use	2474	Public Property with Explosives		Cocaine (Other)	2997	**35002 - Narcotic Equipment**	
Unauthorized Use (Incl. Joy Riding)	2475	Destruction of Tombs/Memorials		Cocaine - Use	2998	Violations	3550
Motor Veh. as Stolen Prop. (Other)	2498	Throwing Stone, etc.,		Synthetic Narcotic - Sell	2999	Operating/Maintaining Meth Lab	3551
		at Train or Motor Vehicle	2605	Synthetic Narcotic - Smuggle		Opr/Maint Meth Lab in Presense	
24003 - Motor Vehicle Fraud		Computer Used in Commission of Crime		Synthetic Narcotic - Possess		of Minor	3552
Obt. Money/Goods - False Pretense	2470	Destroy, Injure Prop. of Police		Synthetic Narcotic - (Other)		Opr/Maint Meth Lab Involving	
Concealing Identity Motor Vehicle	2471	or Fire Department	2604	Synthetic Narcotic - Manufacture		Firearm/Harmful Device	3553
Acquire M/V During Denial	2496	Damage to Property (Other)	2609	Methamphetamine - Deliver		Opr/Maint Meth Lab Near	
Motor Vehicle Fraud (Other)	2497	Pers Ident Info Obt/Poss/Trans W/I	2610	Methamphetamine - Possess		Specified Places	3554
				Methamphetamine - Use		Opr/Maint Meth Lab involving	
25000 - Forgery/Counterfeiting		**26004 - Fraud - Welfare Fraud**		Methamphetamine - Manufacture		Hazardous Waste	3555
Forgery of Checks	2501	Obtain Welfare	2678	Ecstasy - Deliver	3071		
Forgery of Other Object	2502			Ecstasy - Possess	3072		
Counterfeiting of Any Object	2503	**26005 - Fraud - Wire Fraud**		Ecstasy - Use	3077		
Pass Forged - Any Object	2504	Fraud by Wire	2608	Ecstasy - Manufacture			
Pass Counterfeited - Any Object	2505			Marijuana - Sell	3073	**36001 - Sexual Penetration -**	
Possess Forged - Any Object	2506	**26006 - Fraud - Bad Checks**		Marijuana - Smuggle	3074	**Nonforcible - Blood/Affinity**	
Poss. Counterfeited - Any Object	2507	Non-Sufficient Funds Checks	2606	Marijuana - Possess	3078	(CSC 1st/3rd degree)	3691
Poss. Tools, Plates, Etc., for		No-Account Check	2676	Marijuana - Producing			
Forgery or Counterfeiting	2508	Uttering & Publishing Check	2693	Marijuana (Use)	3080	**36002 - Sexual Penetration**	
Transport Forged - Any Object	2509			Amphetamine - Manufacture		**Nonforcible - Other**	
Transport Counterfeit - Any Object	2510	**27000 - Embezzlement**		Amphetamine - Sell	3075	(CSC 1st/3rd degree)	3692
Transport Tools, Plates, Etc. for		Business Property	2701	Amphetamine - Possess	3076		
Forgery or Counterfeiting	2511	Interstate Shipment	2702	Amphetamine (Other)	3079	**36003 - Peeping Tom**	
						Peeping Tom	3611

30001 - Retail Fraud-Misrepresent
Misrepresentation 1st Degree — 3071 (wire fraud section note)

35001 - Violation of Controlled Substance Act
Hallucinogen - Manufacture — 3501
Hallucinogen - Distribute — 3502
Hallucinogen - Sell — 3503
Hallucinogen - Possess — 3504
Hallucinogen (Other) — 3505
Hallucinogen - Use — 3506
Heroin - Sell/Manufacture — 3510
Heroin - Smuggle — 3511
Heroin - Possess — 3512
Heroin (Other) — 3513
Heroin - Use — 3514
Opium or Derivative - Sell — 3520
Opium or Derivative - Smuggle — 3521
Opium or Derivative - Possess — 3522
Opium or Derivative - (Other) — 3523
Opium or Derivative - Use — 3524
Cocaine - Sell — 3530
Cocaine - Smuggle — 3531
Cocaine - Possess — 3532
Cocaine (Other) — 3533
Cocaine - Use — 3534
Synthetic Narcotic - Sell — 3540
Synthetic Narcotic - Smuggle — 3541
Synthetic Narcotic - Possess — 3542
Synthetic Narcotic - (Other) — 3543
Synthetic Narcotic - Manufacture — 3544
Methamphetamine - Deliver — 3545
Methamphetamine - Possess — 3546
Methamphetamine - Use — 3547
Methamphetamine - Manufacture — 3548
Ecstasy - Deliver — 3549
Ecstasy - Possess — 3556
Ecstasy - Use — 3557
Ecstasy - Manufacture — 3558
Marijuana - Sell — 3559
Marijuana - Smuggle — 3560
Marijuana - Possess — 3561
Marijuana - Producing — 3562
Marijuana (Use) — 3563
Amphetamine - Manufacture — 3564
Amphetamine - Sell — 3565
Amphetamine - Possess — 3570
Amphetamine (Other) — 3571
 — 3572
 — 3573

Quick Reference Card 2 of 4

MICR ARREST CHARGE CODES

Ri-1 (Rev. 04/08)
Michigan State Police

FILE CLASS OFFENSE/ARREST CHARGES	ARR CHG
36004 - Sex Offense - Other	
Indecent Exposure	3605
Bestiality	3606
Seduction of Adult	3608
Gross Indecency	3696
Sex Offense (Other)	3699
37000 - Obscenity	
Obscene Material - Mfg./Publish	3701
Obscene Material - Sell	3702
Obscene Material - Mailing	3703
Obscene Material - Possess	3704
Obscene Material - Distribute	3705
Obscene Material - Transport	3706
Obscene Communication	3707
Obscenity (Other)	3799
38001 - Family - Abuse/Neglect Nonviolent	
Cruelty Toward Child/Nonviolent	3802
Cruelty Toward Spouse/Nonviolent	3803
Neglect Child	3806
Cruelty/Neglect (Other)	3898
38002 - Family - Nonsupport	
Neglect Family/Nonsupport Felony	3801
Non-Payment of Alimony	3807
Non-Support of Parents	3808
38003 - Family - Other	
Bigamy - Polygamy	3804
Contributing to Delinquency of Minor (Excluding Alcohol)	3805
Failing to Report Child Abuse	3871
Family Offense (Other)	3899
39001 - Gambling - Betting/Wagering	
Card Game - Playing	3903
Dice Game - Playing	3906
Lottery - Planning	3917
Gambling (Other)	3999

FILE CLASS OFFENSE/ARREST CHARGES	ARR CHG
39002 - Gambling - Operating/ Promoting/Assisting	
Bookmaking	3901
Card Game - Operating	3902
Card Game	3904
Dice Game - Operating	3905
Dice Game	3907
Lottery - Operating	3915
Lottery - Runner	3916
Lottery	3918
Transmit Wager Information	3920
Establish Gambling Places	3921
License/Rule Violations	3970
Gambling Activities Felony	3971
Gambling Activities Misdemeanor	3972
39003 - Gambling - Equip. Violations	
Gambling Device - Possess	3908
Gambling Device - Transport	3909
Gambling Device Not Registered	3910
Gambling Device	3911
Gambling Goods - Possess	3912
Gambling Goods - Transport	3913
Gambling Goods	3914
39004 - Gambling - Sports Tampering	
Sports Tampering	3919
40001 - Commercialized Sex Prostitution	
Prostitution - Homosexual	4003
Prostitution	4004
40002 - Commercialized Sex - Assist/Promoting Prostitution	
Keeping House of Ill Fame	4001
Procure for Prostitute - Pimping	4002
Frequent House of Ill Fame	4005
Transport Female Interstate for Immoral Purpose	4006
Commercial Sex (Other)	4099

FILE CLASS OFFENSE/ARREST CHARGES	ARR CHG
41001 - Liquor License-Establishment	
Violation of Liquor Control Laws	4171
41002 - Liquor Violations - Other	
Manufacture	4101
Sell	4102
Transport (Open Container, etc.)	4103
Poss. of Alcohol (Liquor in MV)	4104
Minor Misrepresenting Age	4105
Minor in Possession in MV	4195
Minor Poss/Cons/Purch; Attempts	4196
Minor Refusing PBT, Non-Driving	4197
Furnishing Alcohol to a Minor	4198
Liquor Violations (Other)	4199
42000 - Drunkenness - Except OUIL	
Drunkenness (All Criminal)	4299
48000 - Obstructing Police	
Resisting Officer	4801
Obstructing Criminal Investigation	4802
Making False Report	4803
Evidence Destroying	4804
Witness - Dissuading	4805
Witness - Deceiving	4806
Refusing to Assist Officer	4807
Compounding Crime	4808
Unauth. Communication/Prisoner	4809
Illegal Arrest	4810
Crossing Police Lines	4811
Failure to Report Crime	4812
Failing to Move On	4813
False Personation/Wearing Badge or Uniform of State Policeman	4872
False Personation of Police Officer	4873
Police Radio in Vehicle	4874
Police Radio Receiver in a MV	4876
Fleeing or Eluding (Felony)	4877
Obstructing Police and/or Fireman	4898
Obstructing Police (Other)	4899

FILE CLASS OFFENSE/ARREST CHARGES	ARR CHG
49000 - Escape/Flight	
Escape - Prison	4901
Flight to Avoid Prosecution, etc.	4902
Absconding, Flee or Elude	4903
Aiding Prisoner Escape	4904
Harboring (Escapee or Fugitive)	4971
Escape - County Jail/Work Farm	4975
Escape Mental Institution - Crim.	
Breaking While En Route - Awaiting Court	4976
Escape - Youth Home, Youth Training Camp, etc.	4991
Fugitive	4998
Escape/Flight (Other)	4999
50000 - Obstructing Justice	
Bail - Secured Bond	5001
Bail - Personal Recognizance	5002
Perjury	5003
Subornation of Perjury	5004
Contempt of Court	5005
Obstructing Justice	5006
Obstructing Court Order	5007
Judicial Officer Misconduct	5008
Contempt of Congress	5009
Contempt of Legislature	5010
Parole Violation	5011
Probation Violation	5012
Conditional Release Violation	5013
Mandatory Release Violation	5014
Failure to Appear	5015
Violation of Preliminary Injunctive Order (Peace Bond)	5070
Failure to Register (Sex Offender)	5089
Failure to Comply with Reporting Duties (Sex Offender)	5090
Failure to Sign Registration (Sex Offender)	5091
Student Safety Zone - Work/Loitering Violation	5092
Obstruct (Other)	5099

FILE CLASS OFFENSE/ARREST CHARGES	ARR CHG
51000 - Bribery	
Bribe - Giving	5101
Bribe - Offering	5102
Bribe - Receiving	5103
Bribe (Other)	5104
Conflict of Interest	5105
Gratuity - Giving	5106
Gratuity - Offering	5107
Gratuity - Receiving	5108
Gratuity (Other)	5109
Kickback - Giving	5110
Kickback - Offering	5111
Kickback - Receiving	5112
Kickback (Other)	5113
Bribery (Other)	5199
52001 - Weapons Offense - Concealed	
Altering Identification	5201
Carrying Concealed	5202
Carrying Prohibited	5203
Safety Inspection & Reg. Violation	5210
Possession of Weapon	5212
Selling & Purchase Violations	5214
Short Barreled Shotgun or Rifle Mfg., Sell, Offer Sale, Possess	5273
Possession of Firearm in Commission of Crime	5275
Carrying Pistol-Free Zone	5287
Concealed Pistol Permit Violations	5288
Firearm in Auto (CCW)	5295
Possession or Use of Firearm While Under Influence of Liquor/Drugs	5297
Weapons Concealed (Other)	5289
52002 - Weapons Off - Explosives	
Explosives (Bombs) - Teaching Use	5204
Explosives (Bombs) - Transporting	5205
Explosives (Bombs) - Using	5206
Incendiary Device - Possess	5207
Incendiary Device - Using	5208
Explosives - Mfg., Sale, Furnish	5209
Explosives (Bombs) Posses	5279
	5281

Quick Reference Card 3 of 4

MICR ARREST CHARGE CODES

RI-1 (Rev. 04/08)
Michigan State Police

FILE CLASS OFFENSE/ARREST CHARGES	ARR CHG	FILE CLASS OFFENSE/ARREST CHARGES	ARR CHG	FILE CLASS OFFENSE/ARREST CHARGES	ARR CHG	FILE CLASS OFFENSE/ARREST CHARGES	ARR CHG
Fireworks - Possess, Sale, Use or Furnish	5282	Let Intoxicated Person Operate M/V Causing Serious Injury (Alcohol)	8036	Ability Impaired by Drugs, Voluntary - Boat	5473	Persons Under 18 Years of Age in Possess/Use - Tobacco Products	5570
Illegal Poss./Use of Blank Pistol	5283	Let Intoxicated Person Operate M/V Causing Serious Injury (Drugs)	8037	OUI of Alcohol - Boat	5481	Aircraft Safety Violator	5581
Weapons Explosives (Other)	5296	OUI Alcohol	8041	Permitted Persons UI of Alcohol to Operate - Boat	5482	Viol. of Boat & Navigation Laws	5582
52003 - Weapons Offense - Other		Permitted Persons Under Influence of Alcohol to Operate	8042	Ability Impaired by Alcohol, Voluntary - Boat	5483	Animals - Cruelty to	5586
Weapons, Firing (Include Careless, Reckless, Heedless Use)	5213	Ability Impaired by Alcohol, Vol	8043	"Per Se" Viol. of Operating with B.A.C. of .10% or More -Boat	5484	Littering by Medical Waste	5587
Weapons Offense (Other)	5299	Operating with B.A.C. of .10% or mor	8044	Anhydrous Ammonia Container - Unauthorized Tampering		Tax/Revenue (Other)	5588
		Felony Long Term Incap. Injury	8047	Anhydrous Ammonia Possess/transport	5589	**62000 - Conservation**	
53001 - Disorderly Conduct		Com. Drv. B.A.C. of .04%-.07%	8048	Inhalation of Chemical Agent:	5591	Out of Season, Over Limit, Etc.:	
Disorderly Conduct	5311	B.A.C. of Not Less Than 0.02% or more than 0.07% for Person		OUI-Controlled Substance Aircraft/Locomotive	5491	Animals	6201
Disturbing the Peace	5312	Under 21Years of Age	8050	Violation of Smokeless Tobacco Products Law	5492	Fish	6202
Affray, Jostling, Roughing Crowd	5374	OUIL-Dispose of Vehicle to Avoid Forfeiture	8053	Violation of Smoking Laws	5493	Birds	6203
Indecent, Immoral, Obscene or Vulgar Language	5375	OUI-Controlled Substance Aircraft/Locomotive	5421	Agricultural Violator	5498	License - Stamp Violation	6204
Disorderly Conduct (Other)	5393	Off Road Vehicle	5422	Environment Health & Safety Violations (Other)	5499	Uncased Gun in Vehicle (Conservation Violation)	6205
		Permitted Persons UI of Controlled Subs. to Operate Off Rd. Veh.		OUI-Intoxicating Liquor Aircraft/Locomotive		Hunting While Intoxicated	6272
53002 - Public Peace - Other		Ability Impaired-Controlled Subs Off Road Vehicle		Permitted Persons UI Intoxicating Liquor Opr. Aircraft/Locomotive	5495	Littering on Public or Private Property	6273
Anarchism	5301	OUI-Intoxicating Liquor Off Road Vehicle	5302	Ability Impaired-Intoxicating Liquor Aircraft/Locomotive	5423	Civil Rights - All Violation:	6274
Riot - Inciting	5302	Permitted Persons UI of Intoxicating Liquor to Operate Off Rd. Veh.	5304	Unlawful Blood Alcohol Content Aircraft/Locomotive	5424	Snowmobile Violations (Except Trespass)	6276
Riot - Engaging In	5303	Ability Impaired-Intoxicating Liquor Voluntary - Snowmobile	5305	Operating W/I 8Hrs. of Consuming Intox. Liquor/Controlled Subs.	5425	**56000 - Civil Rights**	
Riot - Interfere Fireman	5304	Off Road Vehicle	5306		5426	Off Road Vehicle Violations	6277
Riot - Interfere Officer	5305		5307			Violation DNR Directors Order	6280
Riot - (Other)	5306	Operating with B.A.C. .10% or more Off Road Vehicle	5308	**55000 - Health and Safety**		Violation DNR Conservation Order	6281
Assembly - Unlawful	5307		5309	Drugs - Adulterated	5427	Viol. DNR Administrative Rule	6282
False Fire Alarm	5308	Operating UI Causing Serious Injury Snowmobile	5372	Drugs - Misbranded	5428	Viol. County Parks/Airport Rules/ Regulations	6283
Harassing Communications	5309	OUI of Drugs - Snowmobile	5399	Drugs - (Other)	5451	Viol. Conservation Laws (Other)	6299
Telephone Used for Obscene Calls	5372	Permitted Persons UI Drugs Operate - Snowmobile		Food - Adulterated	5452	**57001 - Trespass - Other**	
Public Peace (Other)	5399	Ability Impaired by Drugs. Voluntary - Snowmobile	8011	Food - Misbranded	5453	Trespass - Other	5496
54001 - Hit & Run M/V Accident		OUI of Alcohol - Snowmobile	8012	Food - (Other)	5212	Trespass - Hunting & Fishing On Private Lands	5497
Failed to Stop and Identify	8011	Permitted Persons UI Alcohol to Operate - Snowmobile	8013	Cosmetics - Adulterated	5461	**57002 - Invasion of Privacy - Other**	
Failed to Give Assistance	8012	Ability Impaired by Alcohol Voluntary - Snowmobile		Cosmetics - Misbranded	5462	Divulge Eavesdrop Information	5701
Accident, Failed to Report	8013	"Per Se" Violation of Operating with B.A.C. of .10% or More -Snowmobile	8028	Large Carnivore Law Violations	5559	Divulge Eavesdrop Order	5702
54002 - OUI of Liquor or Drugs			8029	Dog Law Violations	5463	Divulge Message Contents	5703
Operating with BAC of .08% or more	8028	Felony Long Term Incapacitating Injury - Snowmobile	8030	Animals at Large	5464	Eavesdropping (Other)	5704
Operating while in the Presence of Drugs (OWPD)	8029	OUI of Drugs - Boat	8031	Viol. of Underground Storage Tank Regulatory Act	5467	Eavesdrop Equipment	5705
Child Endangerment (Occupant Less Than 16)	8030	Permitted Persons UI of Drugs to Operate - Boat	8032	Viol. of Above Ground Storage Tank Regulatory Act	5471	Opening Sealed Communicatior	5706
OUI of Drugs	8031	Ability Impaired by Drugs, Vol.	8033	Sell/Give/Furnish Tobacco Products Persons Under 18 Years of Age	5472	Wiretap, Failure to Report	5708
Permitted Persons UI Drugs Operate	8032					Invade Privacy (Other)	5799
Ability Impaired by Drugs, Vol.	8033						

FILE CLASS OFFENSE/ARREST CHARGES	ARR CHG
61000 - Tax/Revenue	
Income Tax	6101
Sales Tax	6102
Liquor Tax	6103
Fuel Tax	6104
Cigarette Tax	6173
Tax/Revenue (Other)	6199
58000 - Smuggling	
Smuggle Contraband	5520
Smuggle Contraband into Prison County Jail	5521
Smuggle to Avoid Paying Duty	5560
Smuggling (Other)	5561
59000 - Election Laws	
Violation of Election Laws	5562
60000 - Antitrust	
Antitrust	5569
63000 - Vagrancy	
Curfew	5313
Loitering	5314
Vagrancy (Other)	6399
70000 - Juvenile Runaway	
Runaway	7070
73000 - Miscellaneous Criminal	
Miscellaneous Arrest	7399
75000 - Solicitation (All Crimes Except Prostitution)	
Solicitation	7571
77000 - Conspiracy (All Crimes)	
Conspiracy	7771
Conspiracy By Computer	7772

Quick Reference Card 4 of 4

GLOSSARY

14-Day Rule A preliminary examination must be held within 14 days of an arraignment and may be adjourned for good cause only.

180-Day Rule An inmate of the Department of Corrections must be brought before the court for trial within 180 days.

Absolute Immunity Immunity given to judges, legislators, and prosecutors when they are performing their respective functions.

Accessory After the Fact A person who knowingly helps a felon avoid discovery, arrest, trial, or punishment.

Actus Rea The guilty act or otherwise stated as a wrongful deed rendering the actor criminally liable, if combined with the mens rea.

Adjudication The trial phase of a juvenile criminal proceeding.

*Administration of Oath The affiant for a search warrant must swear or affirm that the information contained in the affidavit is true to the best of his or her belief while holding up his or her right hand.

Administrative Searches Exception to the Search Warrant Rule. A search pursuant to a statutory scheme to regulate a particular industry or business. The business must be a pervasively regulated industry and the search is to ensure compliance to the regulations.

Admission A partial admittance to crime involvement.

Adulterated Food Food that a person has placed pins, needles, razor blades, glass, or any other harmful substance in it.

Affidavit for a Search Warrant An application for a search warrant that contains facts that establish probable cause.

Aggravated Assault An assault and battery where physical injury occurs requiring immediate medical attention or that causes disfigurement or impairment.

Aggravated Stalking Stalking that also is in violation of a court order, where there is a previous stalking conviction, or where there was a credible threat against the victim or the victim's family.

Aiding and Abetting Anyone who intentionally assists someone else in committing a crime is as guilty as the person who directly commits it and can be convicted of that crime as an aider and abettor.

Alcoholic Liquor More than 1/2 of 1% of alcohol per volume.

*Anticipatory Search Warrant A search warrant that is signed by a judge in anticipation of certain specific events occurring. If the events do not occur, the warrant is not valid.

Arraignment The first appearance of the defendant before a judge or magistrate following his or her arrest. The defendant is formally advised of charges, an attorney may be appointed and bond is set.

Arrest The taking, seizing, or detaining another person by either touching or putting hands on that person, or by any act that indicates an intention to take him or her into custody and subjects the person arrested to the actual control and will of the person making the arrest and must be so understood by the person arrested.

Arson Willfully or maliciously, without just cause or excuse, starting a fire or doing anything that could result in the starting of a fire.

Assault An attempt to commit a battery, or an illegal act that caused victim to reasonably fear a battery. Defendant must, at the time of the assault, have the ability, appeared to have the ability, or thought he or she had the ability to commit a battery.

Assault with a Dangerous Weapon An assault where the suspect is armed with a dangerous weapon.

Assault with the Intent to Do Great Bodily Harm Less Than Murder An assault with the intent to cause great bodily harm, but not the intent to kill. Actual injury is not necessary.

Assault with the Intent to Maim An assault with the intent to maim or disfigure that includes cutting out or maiming the tongue, putting out or destroying an eye, cutting or slitting or mutilating the nose or lips, or cutting off or disabling a limb, organ, or member.

Assault with the Intent to Murder An assault where the suspect intended to kill the victim without justification.

Attempt Defendant intended to commit a crime and took some action toward committing the offense but failed in completing it. An attempt goes beyond mere preparation to the point where the crime would have been completed if it had not been interrupted by outside circumstances.

Authority

Actual Authority A person who has access and control over a premise.

Apparent Authority If a person did not have the actual authority to give consent to search, the search will still be valid if the officer at the time of the entry reasonably believed that the person who is allowing him or her entry had common authority over the premises.

***Automobile Exception** An exception to the search warrant rule where exigent circumstances automatically occur with a vehicle due to its mobility. If an officer possesses probable cause to believe that a vehicle contains contraband, the vehicle can be searched without a warrant. Also referred to as Probable Cause and Exigent Circumstances.

Battery A forceful, violent or offensive touching of the person or something closely connected with the victim.

Billy A small bludgeon that may be carried in a pocket.

Blackjack A lead slug attached to a narrow strip, usually leather.

Bludgeon A short club usually weighted at one end or bigger at one end and designed to be a weapon.

Bodily Alcohol Content

***Body Armor** Clothing or a device designed to protect an individual's body from injury by a firearm.

Body Cavity Search Body cavity searches are searches that include the physical intrusion into the body cavity to discover any object concealed therein. A body cavity is defined as the interior of the human body, stomach, rectal cavity, and vagina of females.

Bomb or Bombshell A hollow container filled with gunpowder or other explosive designed to be set off with fuse or other device.

***Border Searches** An exception to the search warrant rule that applies to federal officers enforcing federal law at the U.S. border or a functional equivalent of the U.S. border.

Breaking Force, however slight, used to enter a building regardless of whether anything was actually broken. Examples include opening a closed door, raising a window, or removing a screen.

Burden of Persuasion A party must persuade the trier of fact to accept his or her argument.

Burden of Producing Evidence A party must produce enough evidence so a reasonable person viewing the evidence in the light most favorable to that party could find in that party's favor.

Burden of Proof Clear and convincing evidence generally requires the trier of fact to have less doubt and a firmer conviction about decision than the usual civil standard. Party is usually relying upon a theory that is disfavored upon policy grounds; i.e. Mental Commitment Hearings.

Caregiver of a Vulnerable Adult An individual who directly cares for or has physical custody of a vulnerable adult.

Carjacking The taking of a motor vehicle from another person by force or violence, by threat of force or violence or putting the victim in fear. The vehicle was taken from the victim, a passenger, or other person with lawful possession.

Chain of Custody The party offering real evidence must account for the custody of the evidence from the moment in which it reaches his or her custody until the moment in which it is offered into evidence.

Challenge for Cause The exclusion of a prospective juror based on some prejudice or interest.

Chemical Irritants Solids, liquids, or gases that, through their chemical or physical properties alone or in combination with other substances, can be used to produce an irritant effect in humans, animals, or plants.

Chemical Tests Rights Rights given to a driver suspected of consuming alcoholic liquor or a controlled substance prior to the administration of a breath, blood, or urine chemical test.

Child Abandonment The exposure of a child under the age of 6, in any street, field, house, or other place, with intent to injure or wholly to abandon it.

*Child Abuse Suspect Either a parent or guardian of a child, or a person who has care, custody, or authority over the child.

Child (in a child abuse case) A person less than 18 years old.

Child Kidnapping Maliciously, forcibly, or fraudulently enticing away a child under 14 years of age with the intent to detain or conceal the child.

*Child Neglect Harm or threatened harm to a child's health or welfare by a parent, legal guardian, or any other person responsible for the child's health or welfare that occurs through negligent treatment, including the failure to provide adequate food, clothing, shelter, or medical care, or placing a child at an unreasonable risk to the child's health or welfare by failure of the parent, legal guardian, or other person responsible for the child's health or welfare, to intervene to eliminate that risk when that person is able to do so and has, or should have, knowledge of the risk.

Child Sexually Abusive Activity Applies where a child engages in a listed sexual act, under the Child Pornography statute.

Child Sexually Abusive Material Developed or undeveloped photograph, film, slide, electronic visual image, computer diskette, recording, book, magazine, or other visual or print medium containing a child involved in a listed sexual act.

Civil Laws Laws concerned with private rights and remedies and designed to adjudicate differences between private persons.

Competency Every person is competent to be a witness unless the court finds he or she does not have sufficient physical or mental capacity or sense of obligation to testify truthfully and understandably.

Complaint Consists of the essential facts constituting the offense charged.

Confession The complete admittance to the involvement in a crime.

Consent An exception to the search warrant rule where a person voluntarily waives his or her Fourth Amendment rights in a protected area. The courts will apply a totality of the circumstance tests in determining if the consent was valid.

Conspiracy The collaboration and agreement between 2 or more persons to plan and commit a crime.

Controlled Substances

Schedule 1 has a high potential for abuse and has no accepted medical use.

Schedule 2 has a high potential for abuse, an accepted medical use, and abuse may lead to severe psychic or physical dependence.

Schedule 3 has potential for abuse, but less than schedules 1 and 2, has currently accepted medical use, and abuse may lead to moderate or low physical dependence or high psychological dependence.

Schedule 4 has low potential for abuse, current medical use, and abuse may lead to limited physical dependence or psychological dependence compared to schedule 3.

Schedule 5 has low potential for abuse, current medical use, and limited physical dependence or psychological dependence compared to schedule 4.

Analogue A substance with a similar chemical structure to that of a schedule 1 or 2 controlled substance and has a narcotic, stimulant, depressant, or hallucinogenic effect on the nervous system.

Corporeal Lineups Physical lineups involving the suspect and others with similar physical characteristics.

Corpus Delicti The "body of the crime" or substance of the crime. Each element of the crime must be proven beyond a reasonable doubt.

Counterfeit To make an unauthorized copy, imitation, or forgery of something with the intent to deceive or cheat someone by using the copy, imitation, or forgery as if it were real.

*Counterfeit Substance A controlled substance that bears the trademark, trade name, or other identifying marks of a manufacturer other than the person who in fact manufactured the substance.

Credible Threat A threat to kill another individual or inflict physical injury upon another individual that is made in any manner or context that causes the individual hearing or receiving the threat to reasonably fear for his or her safety or the safety of another individual.

Crime An act against society that results in punishment.

Criminal Laws Laws concerned with wrongs committed against society and not only against the individual.

Curtilage Area around a home that is protected under the Fourth Amendment. In determining what falls under the curtilage, the courts will look at the proximity of area to the home, the area in an enclosure surrounding the home, the nature of the area's use, and steps taken to protect the area from observation.

Custody (under Miranda) The suspect is under arrest, or the suspect's freedom has been deprived in any significant way.

*Dangerous Stabbing Instruments Stabbing weapons that are carried as dangerous weapons and could cause serious physical injury or death.

Dating Relationship Frequent, intimate associations primarily characterized by the expectation of affectional involvement. Does not include a casual relationship or an ordinary fraternization between two individuals in a business or social context.

Deadly Force That force that could result in the loss of human life. This may include the use of batons, saps, flashlights, brass knuckles, and, according to the Civil Rights Commission, even the officer's fists.

Defense Attorney An attorney who safeguards guaranteed rights of the accused.

*Defrauding an Innkeeper To stay at a hotel, motel, inn, restaurant, or café as a guest and a suspect, with the intent to defraud, procured food, entertainment, or accommodation without paying and credit was not given by express agreement.

*Degrees of Affinity Relationships by marriage.

Delinquent A juvenile offender.

*Delivery of a Controlled Substance The transfer or attempt to transfer of a controlled substance to another person, where there is knowledge of the controlled substance and the intent to transfer said substance to another person.

Deposition An interview under oath.

Discovery The pretrial methods used to obtain facts and information about the case from the other party.

Dispositional Phase The sentencing phase for juvenile offenders.

District Court The court responsible for misdemeanor trials, civil suits under $25,000, and pretrial hearings for felonies and circuit court misdemeanors.

Domestic Relationship For purposes of the Domestic Violence Statute, a relationship that includes spouse or former spouse, resident or former resident of the same household, or persons who have had a child in common.

Domestic Violence An assault or assault and battery that occurs within a domestic relationship.

Double Jeopardy Being tried twice for the same crime; does apply to crimes arising out of the same criminal transaction even if the crime occurs in different counties.

Due Process Notice and an opportunity to be heard. A person has the right to defend in an orderly proceeding adapted to the nature of the case, and the guarantee of due process requires that every person have the protection of his or her day in court and the benefit of general law.

*Duplicates Counterparts produced by the same impression as Xerox original, which accurately reproduces the original.

Dwelling (for home invasion) A structure or shelter used permanently or temporarily as a place of abode, including an appurtenant structure attached to it.

Dwelling House (under arson) A dwelling house that is an occupied or unoccupied building that is actually lived in or could reasonably have been lived in at the time of the fire.

Dying Declaration A statement that was made by the declarant who was conscious of impeding death, the death ensued, the statements were being admitted against the one who killed the declarant, and the statement relates to the circumstances of the killing.

Embezzlement The taking of money or property from a victim with whom the suspect had a relationship of trust.

*Emergency Exception Situations may allow officers to enter Fourth Amendment protected areas where they have reasonable (belief) suspicion that an emergency exists.

Entering For breaking and entering charges, entry of any part of the suspect's body into the building is sufficient.

Entering Without Breaking Applies where a suspect enters without breaking into a structure other than a dwelling and, at the time had the intent to commit a felony or larceny therein.

Entrapment Occurs if (1) the police engage in impermissible conduct that would induce an otherwise law-abiding person to commit a crime in similar circumstances, or (2) the police engage in conduct so reprehensible that it cannot be tolerated by the court.

Equal Protection No person or class of persons shall be denied the same protection of the laws that is enjoyed by other persons or other classes in like circumstances in their lives, liberty, property, and in their pursuit of happiness.

*Ethnic Intimidation A person caused or threatened to cause physical contact with a victim or damaged, destroyed or defaced or threatened damage, destruction, or defacement of property of the victim because of the race, color, religion, gender, or national origin of the victim, with the intent to intimidate or harass.

Evidence Any means by which an issue, fact, or the truth of the matter is proved or disproved. Circumstantial evidence is a group of facts, that when linked together, give rise to a certain conclusion. Includes presumptions, inferences, habit, custom and many types of physical evidence.

- **Circumstantial Evidence**
- **Cumulative Evidence** is additional evidence tending to prove the same point.
- **Demonstrative Evidence** is evidence used to illustrate something to the jury (i.e. photograph, sketches, maps, models of crime scene, etc.)
- **Direct Evidence** is evidence that, if believed, proves existence of fact in issue without inference or presumption.
- **Real Evidence**
- **Testimonial Evidence**

Excited Utterance A statement relating to a starling event or condition made while the declarant was under the stress of excitement caused by the event or condition, e.g., "My wife shot me!"

Exclusionary Rule A rule to deter illegal police activity and states that illegally seized evidence may not be introduced at trial.

Executive Branch (enforcement arm of government) The branch responsible for making treaties, appointing federal judges, and enforcing laws.

Expert Opinion Opinion evidence given by a witness that is qualified as an expert in a certain area. The expertise of the witness will assist the trier of fact in understanding the evidence or determining a fact in issue.

Extortion Applies where the suspect threatens to injure the victim, victim's property, victim's family (mother, father, husband, wife, or child) or falsely accusing the victim of a crime. The threat must be stated or written down. By making the threat, the suspect intended either to get money or make the victim do something or refrain from doing something against his or her will.

Federal Circuit Court of Appeals The courts where cases are appealed to after adjudication at the federal district court level.

Federal District Courts The trial courts for the federal system.

Felony An offense for which the offender may be punished by death or by imprisonment in state prison. "Felony" also means a violation of a penal law of this state for which the offender may be punished by death or by imprisonment for more than 1 year or an offense expressly designated by law to be a felony.

*Felony Murder Applies when a suspect commits murder while perpetrating or attempting to perpetrate arson, CSC first, second, or third degrees, child abuse first degree, major controlled substance offense, robbery, home invasion first or second degrees, larceny of any kind, extortion, kidnapping, or carjacking.

*Financial Transaction Device An electronic funds card or ATM card, a credit card, a debit card, a point of sale card, or any other instrument, code number, PIN number, means of access to a credit or deposit account, or a driver's license or identification card that can be used either alone or with another device, to obtain money, cash, credit, goods, services, or anything else of value, certify or guarantee that the device holder has available funds on deposit to honor a draft or check or to provide the device holder with access to an account in order to deposit, withdraw, or transfer funds to obtain information about a deposit account.

Firearms Weapons from which a dangerous projectile may be propelled by an explosive or by gas or air.

*Fleeing from Police Fleeing generally does not constitute a seizure for Fourth Amendment purposes. Fleeing from police may be a factor in allowing for an investigative detention.

Foreign Protection Order (FPO) Injunction or other order issued by another state, Indian tribe or United States territory. Does not include foreign countries.

Force or Coercion Applies under the CSC law where the defendant either used physical force or did something to make the victim reasonably afraid of present or future danger.

Forgery Applies where a document is falsely made, altered, or forged by the suspect who exposed some party to loss or risk of loss.

*Former Testimony A hearsay exception where a witness at another hearing gave a statement and the opposing side had a prior opportunity and similar motive to cross-examine.

*Forty-Eight Hour Rule Officers must secure a judicial determination of probable cause within forty-eight hours of a warrantless arrest in all but the most extraordinary situations.

Fresh Pursuit An officer from another state may pursue felons into Michigan and make an arrest with the same arrest powers as those of Michigan peace officers. Once an arrest is made, the subject must be brought before a Michigan magistrate.

*Fruit of the Poisonous Tree Doctrine Any evidence obtained through illegal means will be suppressed.

Gambling When money or other valuable items are directly or indirectly taken, received, or accepted from a person with the agreement and understanding that they would be paid or delivered to another person contingent upon the result of any race, contest, game, or upon the happening of any uncertain event.

*General Intent The intent to do the act that the law prohibits. It is not necessary for the prosecution to prove that the defendant intended the precise harm or the precise result, which occurred.

Good Faith Exception As long as the police did not act illegally and in good faith, the evidence should be admissible. The Michigan courts have not yet accepted this exception.

*Habit A regular response to a repeated specific situation, a regular practice of meeting a particular kind of situation with a specific type of conduct, a set pattern or evidence of something that is done routinely or has been performed on countless occasions.

Harassment Under the stalking laws is conduct directed toward a victim that includes, but is not limited to, repeated or continuing unconsented contact that would cause a reasonable individual to suffer emotional distress and that actually causes the victim to suffer emotional distress.

Harmful Biological Substances Bacteria, viruses or other microorganisms or toxic substances derived from microorganism that can cause death, injury or disease in humans, animals or plants.

Harmful Chemical Substances Solids, liquids, or gases that, alone or in combination with one or more other chemical substances, can cause death, injury, or disease in humans, animals, or plants.

Harmful Radioactive Materials Materials that are radioactive and can cause death, injury, or disease in humans, animals, or plants.

Hazing An intentional, knowing, or reckless act by a person acting alone or acting with others that is directed against an individual and that the person knew or should have known endangers the physical health or safety of the individual, and that is done for the purpose of pledging, being initiated into, affiliating with, participating in, holding office in, or maintaining membership in any organization.

Hearsay An out-of-court statement, oral or written, made other than by the witness while testifying, offered for the purpose of proving the truth of the matter asserted.

*Homicide   The killing of another human being.

*Hot Pursuit   Authorizes an officer to pursue a person suspected of committing a felony into a residence without a warrant where there are exigent circumstances.

*Ignition Interlocks   Devices attached to the ignition of a vehicle that will check a person's alcohol content before the vehicle can be started.

*Imitation Controlled Substances   A substance that is not a controlled substance, but by its color, shape, size, or markings would lead a reasonable person to believe it is a controlled substance.

Immobilization   When a vehicle is held for a repeat offender violation under O.W.I. or DWLS violations.

Impaired Driving   Because of drinking alcohol, a person drove with less ability than would an ordinary careful driver. The person's driving ability must have lessened to the point that another person would have noticed it.

Impeachment   Attacking the credibility of a witness.

Implied Consent   A person implies he or she will consent to a breath test if he or she is driving a motor vehicle and is suspected of drinking intoxicants.

Indictment   An accusation in writing issued by a grand jury and similar to a complaint or information.

*Inevitable Discovery   Any evidence obtained illegally may still be admissible if police were actively pursuing the evidence and the evidence would have been found anyway as a result of an ongoing investigation.

Inferences   Deductions or conclusions that, with reason and common sense, lead the jury to draw from the facts already established.

Informational/Voluntary Contacts between police and citizens where no level of suspicion is needed.

Information and Belief   The belief something is true, but it is not based on firsthand knowledge.

Injuries to a Fetus or Embryo   Certain acts are prohibited when they result in injury or death to a fetus or an embryo.

Intentional Torts   One form of liability facing police officers where they intentionally cause injury to another person. (i.e., assault and battery).

Interim Bond   Bond that is posted if a person is arrested without a warrant for a misdemeanor or ordinance punishable by imprisonment for not more than 1 year or by a fine or both and the person arrested cannot be brought before a judge or magistrate immediately. Bond may be denied under a number of different circumstances.

Interrogation   Express questioning, or any words or actions that the police know or reasonably should know are likely to elicit an incriminating response.

Interrogatories   Written questions submitted to a party in a civil action who is to answer them under oath.

Intimate Part   The primary genital area, groin, inner thigh, buttock, or breast of a human being.

*Inventory Search   Police may make routine, warrantless searches of contents of any vehicle that lawfully comes into police custody as part of police care taking and as long as the search is in compliance with departmental policy.

Investigatory Detention   A lawful detention where the officer has reasonable suspicion that a crime is afoot.

Involuntary Manslaughter   Applies where a person acted in a grossly negligent manner or at the time of the act had the intent to hurt or injure another and these actions resulted in the death of another person.

*Joint Access or Control   A person who possesses authority over premises or effects with one or more other persons has common authority to give consent. There must be a showing of mutual use of the property by persons generally having joint access or control so that each person has a right to permit inspection in his or her own right.

Judicial Branch (interprets laws and treaties)   The branch of government that has jurisdiction in reviewing constitutional questions and treaties and interpreting the laws of the United States.

Judicial Notice   An evidentiary short cut whereby the court accepts certain facts without requiring formal proof. (i.e., the City of Lansing is in Ingham County.)

Jurisdiction Applies to the types of cases a court has the power to hear.

Kidnapping Applies where a person forcibly confines or imprisons the victim against his or her will without legal authority and, during confinement, the suspect forcibly moved or caused the victim to be moved from one place to another for the purpose of kidnapping.

Knock and Announce Officers have the authority to break in or out of a building after giving notice of their authority and purpose and being refused admittance.

Larceny Taking of another's property with the intent to steal or permanently deprive that person of that property.

Larceny from the Person Applies when the offense of larceny is committed by stealing from the person of another (pickpocket).

Lay Opinion A rational opinion based on the perception of a witness. The opinion is helpful for a clear understanding of the incident.

Legislative Branch (lawmakers) The branch responsible for making laws.

***Length of Detention** An investigative detention must be temporary and last no longer than is necessary to effectuate the purpose of the stop. In determining if the detention is too long, the court must examine whether police diligently pursued a means of investigation that was likely to confirm or dispel their suspicions quickly.

Lesser Included Crimes Crimes consisting of different degrees, where the fact finder may find the accused not guilty of the offense in the degree charged, but may find the accused person guilty of a lesser included offense, or of an attempt to commit that offense.

Listed Sexual Act Under the Child Pornography Law the listed sexual acts include sexual intercourse, erotic fondling, sadomasochistic abuse, masturbation, passive sexual involvement, sexual excitement, or erotic nudity.

Litter Includes rubbish, refuse, waste, material, garbage, offal, paper, glass, cans, bottles, trash, debris, or other foreign substances.

Machine Guns Guns that fire more than one round with single pull of the trigger.

***Magistrate** Magistrates assist the district court judge. They hear informal civil infraction hearings, issue search and arrest warrants, and set bail and accept bond.

***Malicious Use of Phones** Applies when a person maliciously uses any service provided by a communications common carrier with intent to terrorize, frighten, intimidate, threaten, harass, molest or annoy any other person, or to disturb the peace and quiet of any other person.

***Manufacture** To produce or process a controlled substance.

Mens Rea Guilty mind.

Mental Anguish Applies under CSC and means extreme pain, extreme distress, or extreme suffering, either at the time of the incident or later as a result of it.

Mentally Incapable When a person suffers from a mental disease or defect, which renders that person temporarily or permanently incapable of appraising the nature of his or her conduct.

Mentally Incapacitated When a person is temporarily incapable of appraising or controlling his or her conduct due to the influence of a narcotic, anesthetic, or other substance administered to that person without his or consent, or due to any other act committed upon that person without his or her consent.

Metallic Knuckles Pieces of metal designed to be worn over the knuckles in order to protect them in striking a blow or to make the blow more effective.

Misdemeanor A violation of a penal law of this state that is not a felony or a violation of an order, rule, or regulation of a state agency that is punishable by imprisonment or a fine that is not a civil fine.

***Misdemeanor Stalking** When a suspect has two or more willful, separate, and non-continuous acts of unconsented contact with the victim. These contacts would cause a reasonable individual to feel terrorized, frightened, intimidated, threatened, harassed, and molested and cause the victim to feel terrorized, frightened, intimidated, threatened, harassed, and molested.

Motion in Limine A written motion preventing certain prejudicial questions being asked at trial.

Muffler or Silencer A device used to muffle the sound of a firing gun.

*Negligence

Gross Negligence Means more than carelessness. The injury could have been avoided by using ordinary care. Willfully disregarding the dangerousness of the actions.

Ordinary Negligence Means not taking reasonable care under the circumstances. A sensible person would have known that the actions could have caused injury.

Slight Negligence Doing something that is not usually dangerous.

Negligent Homicide
A person was operating a motor vehicle in a negligent manner, which caused an accident that resulted in the death of another person.

No Account Check
Occurs when a person writes or delivers a check, draft, or money order that was drawn on a bank where the person did not have an account. The person must also have the intent to cheat or defraud someone.

Non-Sufficient Funds (NSF)
Occurs when a person writes or delivers a check, draft, or money order that was drawn on a bank and at the time, the person knew there was not enough money or credit to pay the amount in full. The person must also have the intent to defraud or cheat someone.

*Notice to Appear
An appearance ticket that may be issued in lieu of custodial arrest for minor offenses of 93 day misdemeanors or less.

*Oaths or Affirmations
Declarations by a witness that the information he or she will provide will be truthful.

Omission
Under the child abuse law, willfully failing to provide food, clothing, or shelter necessary for the welfare of the child or to abandon the child.

*Open Fields
Includes areas beyond the curtilage of the dwelling and are not protected by the Fourth Amendment.

*Open View
What a person knowingly exposes to the public, even in his or her own home, is not protected under the Fourth Amendment.

Operate or Operating
Applies to O.W.I. and means being in actual physical control of a vehicle. Operator means any person who is in actual physical control of a motor vehicle upon a highway.

O.W.I.
Because of drinking alcohol, the defendant's ability to operate a motor vehicle in a normal manner was substantially lessened.

*Pandering
Applies to a person who entices a woman to become a prostitute.

*Parental Discipline
Reasonable discipline by a parent, including physical force, is not against the law.

Parental Kidnapping
For parental kidnapping, a parent or guardian must take and keep a child for more than 24 hours with the intent to keep or conceal the child from another parent or legal guardian who had legal custody or visitation at the time.

*Pat-Down
Officers may pat the outer clothing of a person the officer has reasonable suspicion to believe may be armed and potentially dangerous. The purpose of the search is to look for weapons.

*Peace Bonds
A district or municipal judge may require a person to post a security to keep the peace.

Perjury
Occurs when a person knowingly makes a false statement that is material to the case after taking a recognized oath.

Personal Injury
Under the CSC law, personal injury is bodily injury, disfigurement, mental anguish, chronic pain, pregnancy, disease or loss or impairment of a sexual or reproductive organ.

Personal Protection Order (PPO)
An injunctive order issued by the circuit court restraining or enjoining individuals from certain conduct.

Petition
A request for court action against a juvenile.

Physically Helpless
Under the CSC law, physically helpless applies to a person who was unconscious, asleep, or for any other reason was physically unable to communicate an unwillingness to act.

Pistols
Include loaded or unloaded firearms, 30 inches or less in length, or by their construction or appearance conceals them as firearms.

*Plain Feel
An object may be seized without a warrant during the course of a pat-down if the officer's sense of touch makes it immediately apparent that the object, though not threatening in nature, is contraband.

*Plain View Officers may seize items where they have a legitimate reason for being in an area protected by the Fourth Amendment and have probable cause to believe the items are contraband or incriminating evidence.

Plea Bargaining The process where accused and prosecutor work out an agreement as to the disposition of a case.

*Possession Possession applies where a person knowingly possesses an object and either has physical control of the object or has the right to control the object.

Possession of Burglary Tools Tools that are adapted and designed for breaking and entering and expressly planned to be used for that purpose.

*Preemptory Challenges A limited challenge where a juror is excused from duty for not stated reason.

Preliminary Breath Tests (PBT) Hand held instruments utilized to determine if a person has alcohol in his or her system. Examples for use include minor in possessions and O.W.I. investigations.

Preliminary Examination The purpose of this hearing is to determine if probable cause exists to believe a crime has been committed and to determine if probable cause exists that defendant committed the offense.

*Premeditation An element for first degree murder where the suspect deliberately killed another human being. It must be shown that the suspect had time for a "second thought" before the killing.

*Preparation to Burn A person willfully and maliciously, without just cause or excuse, placed in or around the property a flammable or explosive device.

Preponderance of the Evidence A standard where the evidence shows that the fact sought to be proven is more probable than not.

Pre-sentence Investigation An investigation by the probation department prior to sentencing. The investigation will review the defendant's criminal record, investigating officers' comments, and other factors to make a recommendation to the judge for sentencing.

Present Memory Refreshed A witness may use any writing or object to refresh his or her memory when testifying. If the witness refreshes his or her memory, the adverse party is entitled to have the writing or object produced. If the witness refreshes his or her memory before testifying, the court at its discretion can determine if justice so requires that an adverse party is entitled to have the writing or object produced.

Presumption A rule of law where the finding of one basic fact gives rise to the existence of the presumed fact.

Presumption of Innocence A defendant is presumed innocent. Each element of the prosecutor's case must be proven beyond a reasonable doubt before conviction.

Pretext Stops Traffic stops for traffic violations when an officer has another underlying motive to pull the vehicle over. As long as the officer has probable cause that a violation has occurred, the stop will be reasonable under the Fourth Amendment.

*Prior Convictions for O.W.I. Include all drug and alcohol violations under MCL 257.625. (Except allowing an intoxicated person to operate a vehicle under MCL 257.625[2].) murder, manslaughter, and negligent homicide with a vehicle, commercial motor vehicle violations under MCL 257.625m, attempted violations and similar laws from other states are also included, only one zero tolerance violation can be used to enhance.

Privilege Certain confidential communications cannot be used against a person. (e.g., attorney/client)

Probable Cause A practical, non-technical concept, not a point, but a zone in which reasonable mistakes can be made. Police have probable cause to arrest an individual when the facts and circumstances within their knowledge and of which they have reasonably trustworthy information are sufficient to warrant that a prudent person would believe that the suspect had committed or was committing an offense. Probable cause to issue a search warrant means considering facts in a common sense and realistic manner and where there is a fair probability that contraband or evidence of a crime would be found at the place being searched. Under Michigan law, probable cause and reasonable cause are the same.

Probable Cause and Exigent Circumstances Officers may search when they possess probable cause that items sought to be seized are in a specific location and at the time of the search there are exigent circumstances that require the officers to search without a warrant.

Procedural Due Process Safeguards to one's liberty and property mandated by the Constitution. Procedural due process is how the rights are protected from governmental action.

***Property**

   ***Personal property** includes property that is not a building, or permanently attached to a building and is movable (i.e. cars, clothing, furniture, etc.).

   ***Real property** includes buildings and items that are permanently attached to the buildings (i.e., bar, barn, gas station, store).

Prosecuting Attorney The chief law enforcement officer in a county, who authorizes complaints and represents state and county in all civil and criminal matters in county courts.

Protective Custody A peace officer may take a person into custody who can reasonably be expected in the near future to intentionally or unintentionally injure him or herself or another and who has engaged in an act or made significant threats that are supportive of this expectation.

Protective Sweeps Allows officers to search areas for persons that may harm the officers while they are attempting to do their lawful duties. The sweep, if justified by the circumstances, is nevertheless not a full search of the premises, but may extend only to a cursory inspection of those spaces where a person may be found. The sweep lasts no longer than is necessary to dispel the reasonable suspicion of danger and in any event no longer than it takes to complete the arrest and depart the premises.

Prurient Interest A shameful or morbid interest in nudity, sex, or excretion.

Public Duty Doctrine A liability doctrine under negligence that states that officers do not owe a duty to the public unless a special relationship exists.

Publishing Publishing means to declare, by words or actions, that a forged document is genuine.

Qualified Immunity Immunity given to governmental officials for violating constitutional rights when they act in good faith and reasonably believe their actions are constitutional.

Rape Shield Statute A statute that protects a victim from having to testify about sexual activity not incident to the alleged incident.

Reasonable Cause *See* Probable Cause.

***Reasonable Doubt** A fair, honest doubt growing out of the evidence or lack of evidence. It is not merely an imaginary or possible doubt, but a doubt based on reason and common sense. A reasonable doubt is just that — a doubt that is reasonable, after a careful and considered examination of the facts and circumstances of this case.

***Reasonable Expectation of Privacy** Privacy rights that society and the courts are prepared to recognize as reasonable.

Reasonable Suspicion A lower level then probable cause. Officers need to have an articulable and objectively reasonable belief to justify the action (i.e., used in Terry stops and pat-downs).

Recorded Recollection A record of something that a witness once had knowledge about, but now has insufficient recollection. Record must have been made or adopted by the witness when the matter was fresh in his or her memory (i.e., list of stolen property in a complaint.)

***Relevant Evidence** Evidence having any tendency to make the existence of any fact that is of consequence to the determination of the action more probable or less probable than it would be without the evidence.

Res Gestae Includes circumstances, facts, and declarations which surround the commission of a crime. The evidence should be contemporaneous with the crime and serve to illustrate its character.

Res Gestae Witness An eyewitness to a criminal event whose testimony will aid in developing a full disclosure of all the facts. Also includes all witnesses having contact with the defendant reasonably contemporaneous with the crime, whose testimony tends to show the state of mind in which the criminal act was done.

***Retail Fraud** A larceny of property by theft, price switching, or through a refund scam. The property must be offered for sale and the incident must occur inside a store or in the immediate area around the store while it is open to the public.

Rifles Firearms designed and intended to be fired from the shoulder, that fire a single fixed metallic cartridge through a rifle bore, and with a single pull of the trigger.

Riots Five or more persons working together who are engaged in violent conduct and intentionally or recklessly creating a serious risk of causing public terror or alarm.

Robbery

Armed Robbery Larceny where the victim is assaulted by a suspect who is armed with a dangerous weapon or an object used or fashioned in a manner to lead the person who was assaulted to reasonably believe it was a dangerous weapon, or where suspect indicates that he has a weapon.

Unarmed Robbery Occurs when a person who is unarmed forcibly takes property from another. The property must have been moved and the suspect had the intent to permanently deprive the victim of the property.

Sand Club or Sandbag A narrow bag filled with sand and used as a bludgeon.

Scope of Discovery Parties in civil actions are able to obtain discovery regarding any matter, not privileged, that is relevant to the subject matter involved in the pending action.

Search Incident to Arrest Officers may, incident to a lawful custodial arrest, search for weapons and evidence that is within the reach of the person being arrested. The search must occur contemporaneously with the arrest.

Search Warrant Rule Searches with a warrant are presumed legal, whereas searches without a warrant are presumed illegal.

*Secondary Evidence Other forms of evidence may be allowed under the best evidence rule where it shows that the originals have been lost or destroyed.

*Sequestration of Witness Occurs where a witness is isolated from the trial proceedings prior to testifying.

Serious Mental Harm to a Child Under the child abuse law includes injury to a mental condition that results in visible signs of impairment in a child's judgment, behavior, ability to recognize reality, or ability to cope with ordinary demands of life.

Serious Mental Harm to a Vulnerable Adult Under the vulnerable adult abuse law occurs when there is substantial alteration of mental functioning that is manifested in a visibly demonstrable manner.

Serious Physical Harm to a Child Under the child abuse law includes any physical injury to a child that seriously impairs the child's health or physical well-being, including, but not limited to, brain damage, a skull or bone fracture, subdural hemorrhage or hematoma, dislocation, sprain, internal injury, poisoning, burn or scald, or severe cut.

Serious Physical Harm to a Vulnerable Adult An injury that threatens the life of a vulnerable adult, causes substantial bodily disfigurement, or seriously impairs the functioning or well-being of the vulnerable adult.

Sexual Contact Includes the intentional touching of the victim's or actor's intimate parts or the intentional touching of the clothing covering the immediate area of the victim's or actor's intimate parts, if that intentional touching can reasonably be construed as being for the purpose of sexual arousal or gratification, done for a sexual purpose, or in a sexual manner for: (i) Revenge. (ii) To inflict humiliation. (iii) Out of anger.

Sexual Penetration Includes sexual intercourse, cunnilingus, fellatio, anal intercourse or any other intrusion, however slight, of any part of a person's body or of any object into the genital or anal opening of another person's body, but emission of semen is not required.

Short-Barreled Rifles Rifles with one or more barrels less than 16 inches or overall length less than 26 inches.

Short-Barreled Shotguns Shotguns with 1 or more barrels less than 18 inches, or overall length less than 26 inches.

Shotguns Firearms that are designed and intended to be fired from the shoulder. They fire a fixed shotgun shell that contains either ball shot or a single projectile through a smooth bore. The gun fires with a single pull of the trigger.

*Show-Ups One-on-one confrontations done either physically or by photograph between a witness and a person meeting the description of a perpetrator of a crime. The show-up must occur promptly after the crime.

*Sodomy Occurs when a person commits an abominable and detestable crime against nature with another person or an animal.

Solicitation to Commit a Felony A person, through words or actions, offered, promised or gave money, services, or anything of value (or forgave or promised to forgive a debt or obligation owed) to another person. The person intended that what he or she said or did would cause the felony to be committed.

*Specific Intent To convict persons of certain crimes that have a specific intent, the prosecution must prove not only that the defendant did certain acts, but that he or she did the acts with the intent to cause a particular result. (i.e., the intent to commit a felony or larceny.)

*Staleness Probable cause must exist when a search warrant is sought and executed. If officers wait too long to execute a search warrant, the probable cause may become stale.

Stalking A willful course of conduct involving repeated or continuing harassment of another individual that would cause a reasonable person to feel terrorized, frightened, intimidated, threatened, harassed, or molested, and that actually causes the victim to feel terrorized, frightened, intimidated, threatened, harassed, or molested.

*Standing A person with standing has an expectation of privacy to challenge a search.

*Statement Against Interest A statement made by declarant and against his or her pecuniary or criminal interest. A reasonable person in declarant's position would not have made the statement unless he or she believed it to be true.

Status Offender A juvenile who commits an act that is a violation because of the juvenile's age. (i.e. runaways and truants.)

Stop and Frisk Officers may stop a person when they have reasonable suspicion to believe that a crime is afoot and may frisk the person for weapons when they have reasonable suspicion to believe the person is armed and potentially dangerous.

Strip Searches Searches that include the removal of clothing exposing underclothing, breasts, buttocks, or genitalia of another person. These searches are limited to certain situations and have specific requirements.

Stun Guns Portable devices or weapons from which an electric current, impulse, wave, or beam may be directed; they are designed to temporarily incapacitate, injure, or kill.

Substantive Due Process A Constitutional guarantee that no person will be arbitrarily or unreasonably deprived of life, liberty, or property without due process of law. The essence of substantive due process is the protection from arbitrary and unreasonable governmental action.

Summons A judicial notice used to notify a person that an action has commenced against him or her.

Tabulation and Receipt All property taken from a residence during the execution of a search warrant must be tabulated. The tabulation must be done in the presence of at least one other person. The officer must leave a copy of the tabulation at the place searched and another copy must be presented to the court.

Terry (Investigatory) Stops Officers may detain persons on reasonable suspicion that a crime may be occurring. The stop must be no longer than is necessary to extinguish their suspicions or build up to probable cause.

*Threat for Extortion A threat that does not have to be said in certain words, but it can be made in general or vague terms without exactly stating what kind of injury is being threatened. It can be made by suggestion, but a threat must be definite enough to be understood by a person of ordinary intelligence as a threat of injury.

*Three NSF Checks Within 10 Days Occurs when a person writes or delivers three checks, drafts, or money orders within 10 days. The checks were drawn on a bank account that, at the time, did not have enough money or credit to pay the amount in full. The person also had the intent to defraud or cheat someone.

Tort A civil wrong against another person.

Transient Merchant Any person, firm, association, or corporation engaging temporarily in a retail sale of goods, wares, or merchandise, in any place in this state and who, for the purpose of conducting business, occupies any lot, building, room or structure of any kind.

*Unauthorized Use of an Automobile Occurs when a person knowingly uses someone else's vehicle without authority. (Also see Unlawfully Driving Away an Automobile.)

*Unavailable Under the Hearsay Rule Occurs under the hearsay rule where the declarant refuses to testify, lacks sufficient memory to testify, or cannot be located after due diligence. This also includes if the declarant is dead, has a physical or mental illness or infirmity, or when the statement is exempt under a privilege (i.e., attorney/client, right against self-incrimination, etc.)

United States Supreme Court The Supreme Court of the land that has appellate jurisdiction from

*U.S. Court of Appeals May review constitutional issues from state supreme courts. The court also has original jurisdiction in suits between states.

Unlawful Bodily Alcohol Content (UBAC) 0.08 grams or more of alcohol per 100 milliliters of blood, 210 liters of breath, or 67 milliliters of urine.

*Unlawful Entry Breaking and entering without permission.

*Unlawfully Driving Away an Automobile Occurs when a person takes possession of a vehicle belonging to someone else without authority.

Utter and Publish Offering something forged as if it is real. It does not matter if the document is accepted or not.

Uttering To offer a forged instrument.

Venue The geographic areas a court may preside over.

Victim's Rights Certain rights mandated by statute that law enforcement must provide to victims of certain crimes.

Voir Dire Examination The questioning of prospective jurors to determine their suitability to sit as jurors.

Voluntary Manslaughter Occurs when a person acted out of passion or anger brought about by adequate cause and acted before he or she had a reasonable time to calm down.

Vulnerable Adult Applies to a person 18 years old or older who, because of age, has a developmental disability, mental illness, or physical handicap requiring supervision or personal care or lacks the personal and social skills required for living independently and is placed in an adult foster care family home or an adult foster care small group home.

*Vulnerable Targets Places described under the laws dealing with explosives such as daycare centers, healthcare facilities, a building open to the general public, a church or other place of religious worship, or a school, k-12 or a college or university.

Warrant for Arrest Document issued by a judge if the information contained in the complaint is sufficient to substantiate the offense charged.

*Warrantless Misdemeanors Under MCL 764.21, officers may not enter a residence to effectuate an arrest for a warrantless misdemeanor arrest.

*Weapon-Free School Zone Penalties are increased for certain weapons violations that occur in a school zone. Under this section, the term "school" includes public, private, denominational, or parochial schools for grades 1 through 12. The school property includes buildings, playing fields, or property used for school purposes. Vehicles are also included if used to transport students to or from school property.

*Wingspan of Control Applies to where an officer can search while making a lawful custodial arrest. The officer may search the area within reach of the person being arrested.

INDEX

A

Abandonment, privacy and, 222
Absolute immunity, 305
Accessory after the fact, 14
    aiding and abetting *versus*, 14
Accidents, arrests without warrant and, 175–76
Accountant-client privilege, 277
Actus reus, 8
Administrative rules, 12
Administrative searches, 261–62
    department of natural resources, 261
    fire scenes, 262
    junk yards, 261–62
    liquor inspections, 261
Admissibility, of evidence, 266–67
Admissions, 189–209
    advisement of rights, 200
    ambiguous or limited assertion of rights, 199–200
    confessions *versus*, 190
    considerations, 189–90
    Fifth Amendment, 189, 196–98
    interrogation, 193–95
    juveniles and, 206–7
    Miranda warnings, 190–93
    questioning by persons other than law enforcement, 207–8
    remedies for violation of rights, 208–9
    right to remain silent, 195–96
    Sixth Amendment, 198–99
    voluntariness standard, 203–6
    waiver of rights, 201–3
Adulterated food, 73
Advisement of rights, 200
    failure, 200
Affidavit for search warrant, 229
Aggravated assault, 18–19
Aggravated stalking, 60–61
    defined, 30
    domestic violence and, 30
Aiding and abetting, 13–14
    accessory after the fact *versus*, 14
    inducement, 13
    prostitution, 43
Airplanes, privacy and, 221
Alcoholic liquor
    consuming on school property, 161
    defined, 157
    furnishing to minors, 157–58
    minors possessing, 158–61
    possessing or consuming in public, 161
    violations, minors and, 25

Ambiguous or limited assertion of rights, 199–200
    request for counsel, 199–200
    requests to talk to non-attorney, 200
    right to remain silent, 199
Amendments, Constitutional, 2
    Eighth, 2
    Fifth, 2
    First, 2
    Fourteenth, 2
    Fourth, 2
    Ninth, 2
    Second, 2
    Seventh, 2
    Sixth, 2
    Tenth, 2
    Third, 2
Androgenic anabolic steroids, 115
Anhydrous ammonia, unlawful containers for, 116
Animals
    confiscation and forfeiture of, 163
    cruelty to, 162–67
    dog bites, 167
    fighting, 162–63
    police, 167
    service dogs, beating or impeding, 165–66
    willfully killing/torturing, 166
Ann Arbor v. McCleary, 287
Anonymous tip, terry stops and, 256
Apparent authority, 248
Appeal process, in state courts, 5–6
Arizona v. Fulminante, 209
Arizona v. Gant, 240
Arizona v. Hicks, 245
Arizona v. Mauro, 195
Arizona v. Roberson, 197
Arkansas v. Sullivan, 227
Armed robbery, 53–54
    assault with intent to, 21
Arraignment, 5, 6
    Crime Victim's Rights Act and, 309
    on the information, 7
Arrest
    authority, 154
    Crime Victim's Rights Act and, 309
    defined, 173
    entry into residence for, 184–86
    in home, 239
    laws of, 173–87
    personal protection orders and, 32
    pretext, 226–27
    probable cause for, 241
    resisting, 178–79

Arrestee, rights of, 181
Arrest powers, domestic violence and, 29
Arrests, without warrants
    accidents and O.W.I., 175–76
    basic crimes, 175
    domestic violence, 176
    narcotics, 176
    personal protection orders, 176–77
    private person's authority to, 178, 181
    protective custody, 177–78
    retail fraud, 176
    school property, 176
    violation of child protective order, 177
    violation of condition of release, 177
Arrest warrants, arrests pursuant to, 174–75
Arson, 75–78
    defined, 78
    disobeying firefighter during riot, 78
    dwelling house, 75–76
    insured property, 76–77
    personal property, 76
    preparation to burn, 77–78
    willfully or negligently setting fire, 78
Assaults, 17–22
    aggravated, 18–19
    and battery, 17–18
    with dangerous weapon, 20
    domestic, 18
    upon FIA worker, 19
    with intent to commit felony, 21
    with intent to do bodily harm, 21
    with intent to maim, 21
    with intent to murder, 20
    with intent to rob, armed, 21
    with intent to rob, unarmed, 21
    killing, harming, or interfering with police or search and rescue dog or horse, 20
    peace officer, EMT, firefighter, or search and rescue team, 19–20
    on third person, 21
    torture, 21–22
Attempts, 14
    elements, 14
    impossibility and, 14
Attorney-client privilege, 275
Attorney general opinions, 12
Atwater v. City of Lago Vista, 241
Authority, 174
    apparent, 248
    outside jurisdiction, 179–80
    private person's, to arrest without warrant, 178, 181
Auto theft, 85–88
    alteration of VINs, 86–87
    chop shop, 88
    tampering or meddling with vehicle, 87–88
    UDAA *versus* unauthorized use, 86
    unauthorized use, 85–86
    unlawfully driving away, 85

B

Bank robbery, 83
Belief, 6
Berkemer v. McCarty, 192
Best evidence rule, 267
Beyond a reasonable doubt, 8
Bill of Rights, 1–2
    preamble of, 1–2
Billy, 124
Biological substances, 120–21
    manufacturing, delivering, possessing, using, 121
Blackjack, 123
Blood
    implied consent and, 285
    search warrants for, 233
Bludgeon, 124
Body armor, 156
Body cavity search, 183
Bombs
    fake, 119
    placing, 119
    as unlawful weapon, 123
Bombshell, 123
Bond, 183–84
    interim, 183
    requirements, 7
Bond appearance, personal protection orders and, 32–33
Bond v. United States, 219
Booking procedures, 195
Border searches exception, 262
Bram v. United States, 204
Breaking and entering, 81–82
Breaking and entering, unlawful entry, 81–82
Breathalyzer, 286
Brewer v. Williams, 195, 208
Bribery, 139–42
    appraisers, 140–41
    arbitrators, 140–41
    athletes, 141–42
    auditors, 140–41
    executors, 140–41
    jurors, 140–41
    officials of public institutions, 141
    peace officers, 141
    public officials, 139–40
Brigham City v. Stuart, 258
Bright v. Littlefield, 178
Brinegar v. United States, 174
Brown v. Mississippi, 204
Buckley v. Fitzsimmons, 36
Burden of persuasion, 264
Burden of proof, 264
Burglary, 81–84
    bank, safe, vault robbery, 83
    breaking and entering, 81–82
    coin operated device, 83–84
    coin or depository box, 83

entering without breaking, 82
using explosives, 83
home invasion, 82
possession of tools, 83
Butler v. City of Detroit, 296

C

California v. Carney, 243
California v. Gilbert, 211
California v. Greenwood, 221
California v. Hodari D., 228
Caregiver, defined, 57
Carjacking, 54
Carkendall v. People, 76
Chain of custody, 265
Challenge for cause, 7
Chambers v. Maroney, 243
Character evidence
    habit, 275
    impeachment by, 273
    method to prove character, 275
    prior bad acts, 274
    rape shield statute, 274–75
Check law violations, 97–99
    no account check, 98
    non-sufficient funds, 97–98
    three NSF checks within 10 days, 98–99
Chemical irritant, 121
Chemical substances, 120–21
    manufacturing, delivering, possessing, using, 121
Chemical test rights, 286
Chemical tests, O.W.I. and, 285–87
Child
    defined under law, 22
    rights of, 291–92
Child abuse, 22–25
    child abandonment, 23
    definition, 22–23
    failure to report, 24–25
    first degree, 23
    fourth degree, 23
    leaving unattended in vehicle, 24
    parental discipline, 23
    reporting requirements, 24
    sale of children, 24
    second degree, 23
    third degree, 23
Child endangerment, 284
Child kidnapping, 50
Child protective order, violation of, 177
Child sexually abusive activity, 26
Child sexually abusive material, 26–28
    definitions, 26–27
    distributing or promoting, 27
    film developers/computer technicians and, 28
    possession of, 28
    producing, 27
Chimel v. California, 182, 239

Chop shop, 88
Circuit courts, 5
Circumstantial evidence, 263
Citation, search subsequent to, 240
Citizenship
    obligations of, 4
    rights of, 4
City of Grand Rapids v. Williams, 168
City of Indianapolis v. Edmond, 253
City of Westland v. Okopski, 168
Civil law, 301
    criminal law *versus,* 301
Civil liability, 302–3
    crime *versus* tort, 302–3
    theories of tort, 303
Civil litigation, 301–2
    discovery for, 301
    discovery types, 301–2
    mediation, 302
    scope of discovery, 301
    service of process, 302
    summons, 302
Civil trial, 264
Clergy privilege, 276
Coercion, defined, 38
Coercive police activity, 203
Colorado v. Bertine, 257
Colorado v. Connelly, 203
Colorado v. Spring, 202
Complaint, 6
Computer crimes, 69–72
    attempts to defraud, 70
    penalties, 71–72
    prohibited access to computer, 71
    use of computers, to commit crimes, 69–70
Concealed pistol licenses (CPL), 126, 133–34
    exemptions for, 127
    requirements, 126
Concealed weapons
    carrying, 124–27
    exceptions to MCL, 125–26
Confessions, 189–209
    admissions *versus,* 190
    advisement of rights, 200
    ambiguous or limited assertion of rights, 199–200
    considerations, 189–90
    Fifth Amendment, 189, 196–98
    interrogation, 193–95
    juveniles and, 206–7, 292
    Miranda warnings, 190–93
    questioning by persons other than law enforcement, 207–8
    remedies for violation of rights, 208–9
    right to remain silent, 195–96
    Sixth Amendment, 198–99
    violation of *Miranda* and, 197
    voluntariness standard, 203–6

Confiscation
    of goods, 162
    of registration plate, 284
Congress, 3
Connecticut v. Barrett, 201
Consent, 34, 246–50
    apparent authority, 248
    fake warrant and, 249
    implied, 285
    joint access or control, 247–48
    knock and talk, 249–50
    limited and revoked, 247
    parental, 248
    requesting attorney, 249
    scope of search, 247
Consideration, defined, 157
Conspiracy, 14–15
    agreement for, 14–15
    elements, 14
Constitution. *See* U.S. Constitution
Constitutional law, 1–4
    Declaration of Independence, 1
    due process, 3
    equal protection, 3
    federal government branches, 2–3
    U.S. Constitution, 1–2
Constitutional torts, 303, 305–6
    color of law, 305
    defined, 305
    general claims, 305–6
    good faith defense, 306
    immunity to, 306
    theories of liability, 306
Contributing to the delinquency of a minor, 25
Controlled substances, 111–18
    analogue, 116
    androgenic anabolic steroids, 115
    counterfeit, 116
    date rape drugs, 114–15
    delivery of relating in death, 48
    drug-free school zones, 117–18
    drug paraphernalia, 115
    imitation, 115
    inhalants, 116
    licensing requirement, 117
    manufacture, delivery, possession of, 111–13
    medical marihuana, 118
    penalties for manufacturing, 114
    possession of ephedrine, 116
    prescription misuse, 115
    sale of nitrous oxide, 116–17
    schedules, 111
    unlawful containers of anhydrous ammonia, 116
    use of, 113–14
Conversations, private, 225
Cook v. Rontal, 275
Coolidge v. New Hampshire, 217
Corporeal lineups, 212–13
    fairness and suggestivity in, 212–13
    right to line up, 213
    right to self-incrimination and, 212
Corpus delicti, 8
    confessions and, 206
    evidence and, 264
Corrections officers, questioning by, 208
Counterfeiting, 100–101
    defined, 100
    possession of bills, 100
    possession of coins, 100
    tools for, 100–101
County of Riverside v. McLaughlin, 181, 228
County of Sacramento v. Lewis, 304
Court appearance, personal protection orders and, 32–33
Court functions, 5–12
Court of Appeals, 5
Court opinions
    citations, 11
    of Michigan law, 10
Crane v. Kentucky, 206
Credible threat, 30
Crimes
    computer, 69–72
    defined, 8–9, 302
    defined under Crime Victim's Rights Act, 308
    financial, 97–104
    of indecency, 40–42
    lesser included, 9
    prosecution of, 178
    public interest, 155–72
    tort *versus,* 302–3
Crimes against persons, 57–73
    adulterated food, 73
    computer crimes, 69–72
    eavesdropping, 63–66
    ethnic intimidation, 58–59
    hazing, 62–63
    identity theft, 66–69
    obscene, harassing, or threatening phone calls, 66
    poisoning, 73
    stalking, 59–62
    vulnerable adult abuse, 57–58
Crimes against property, 105–9
    possession of stolen property, 105–6
    trespass, 106–9
Crime scenes, 224–25
Crime Victim's Rights Act, 307–9
    arraignment and, 309
    arrest and, 309
    crimes as defined under, 308
    definitions under, 307–8
    juvenile offenses, 308, 309
    property and, 308
    requirements under, 308–9
    serious misdemeanors, 308
Criminal Jury Instructions (CJI), 12
Criminal law
    actus reus, 8
    basic concepts of, 8–10

civil law *versus*, 301
corpus delicti, 8
crime, 8–9
felony, 9
general intent, 8
lesser included crimes, 9
mens rea, 8
misdemeanor, 9
specific intent, 8
statute of limitations, 9–10
Criminal sexual conduct, 37–40
definitions, 37–38
first degree, 38–39
force or coercion, 38
fourth degree, 40
married persons and, 40
mental anguish, 37
personal injury, 37
resistance, 40
second degree, 39
sexual contact, 37
sexual penetration, 37
third degree, 39–40
Criminal trial, 264
Cruel, defined, 23
Cruelty to animals, 162–67
beat or impede service dog, 165–66
dog bites, 167
fighting animals, 162–63
police animal, 167
willfully killing/torturing, 166
Cumulative evidence, 263
Curtilage, search and seizure and, 223–24
determining, 223
search warrant and, 232
technical trespass, 223–24
Custodial traffic arrests, 184
Custody, 174, 290–91
Miranda warnings and, 190–93

D

Dangerous weapon, assault with, 20
Date rape drugs, 114–15
gamma-butyrolactone, 114
gamma hydroxybutyrate, 114
Dating relationship, 29, 31
Davis v. United States, 200
Davis v. Washington, 268
Dawson v. Austin, 229
Deadly force
defined, 180
fleeing felon and, 180
Michigan law on use of, 296–98
private citizen use of, 299
Deception, confessions and, 205–6
Declaration of Independence, 1
Defense attorney, 6
Defrauding innkeeper, 101–2
Demonstrative evidence, 263

Deposition, 301
Destruction of property, 75–80
arson, 75–78
malicious, 78–80
Detention
during execution of search warrant, 236
for juveniles, 291
length of, 255
pending issuance of search warrant, 236
Direct evidence, 263
Discovery, 301
scope of, 301
types of, 301–2
Disorderly conduct, 168–70
disorderly person, 168–69
disturbing the peace, 169–70
at funerals, 169
District court magistrate, 6
District courts, 5
Disturbing the peace, 169–70
DLAD hearing, 287
Dog bites, 167
Dogs, privacy and, 221
Domestic assault and battery, 18
Domestic relationships, 18
Domestic violence, 29–36
aggravated assault, 31
aggravated stalking, 30
arrest powers, 29–30
arrests without warrant, 176
assault and battery, 31
authority to enter scene of, 34–35
exception to interim bond, 183–84
foreign protection order, 33–34
hearsay and, 272
interim bond, 30
liability, 36
Michigan personal protection orders, 31–33
preparing report, 35–36
prior bad acts, 274
stalking, 30
substantive crimes associated with, 30–31
victim-counselor privilege, 276
victim's rights, 35
Double jeopardy, 7
Draper v. United States, 175
Drug checkpoints, 252–53
Drug-free school zones, 117–18
Duckworth v. Eagan, 200
Due process, 3
procedural, 3
substantive, 3
Dunaway v. New York, 191
Duty to retreat, 300
Dwelling house
accompanying arestees into, 239
arson and, 75–76
riotously destroying, 170
Dying declaration, hearsay rule and, 271

E

Eavesdropping, 63–66
- definitions, 63
- divulgence of unlawfully obtained information, 64
- installation of device for, 63–64
- upon private conversation, 63
- surveillance of individual having reasonable expectation of privacy, 64
- tampering with electronic communication, 65–66
- trespassing for, 63
- video taping in movie theaters, 64–65

Edwards v. Arizona, 195, 196
Eighth Amendment, 2
Electronic tracking device, privacy and, 220
Embezzlement, 95–96
- by police officer, 96
- by public official, 96

Embryo, injury to, 22
Emergencies, 258
- injury, 258

Emergency circumstances, authority to enter domestic violence scene under, 34–35
EMT worker
- assault on, 19
- impersonation of, 138

Enforcement
- of foreign protection order, 33–34
- of personal protection orders, 31–32

Entering without breaking, 82
Entrapment, 8
Entry into residence, for arrest, 184–86
- breaking open door, 184
- exigent circumstances and, 185–86
- protective sweeps, 186
- routine felony arrests and, 184
- third party residence and, 184–85
- warrantless misdemeanors and, 184

Ephedrine, possession of, 116
Equal protection, 3
Erotic fondling, defined, 26
Erotic nudity, defined, 26–27
Escape, 144–46
- aiding, 144
- cellular telephone to prisoner, 146
- concealing or harboring fugitive, 146
- while awaiting court hearing, 145
- from jail, 145
- from juvenile facility, 144, 291
- from lawful custody, 145–46
- from prison, 144–45
- pursuit and, 146
- from work program, 145

Ethnic intimidation, 58–59
Evidence. *See also* Proof
- admissibility of, 179, 266–67, 267
- arrestee swallowing, 240–41
- best evidence rule, 267
- burden of producing, 264
- chain of custody, 265
- character, 273–75
- circumstantial, 263
- clear and convincing, 8
- *corpus delicti*, 264
- credibility and weight of, 263–64
- cumulative, 263
- defined, 263
- demonstrative, 263
- descriptive terms, 263
- direct, 263
- exclusionary rule, 277
- hearsay rule, 267–72
- impeachment, 273
- judicial notice, 265
- laws of, 263–77
- material, 266
- opinion, 272–73
- prejudicial effect *versus* probative value, 266–67
- preponderance of, 8
- presumptions and inferences, 266
- privileges, 275–77
- probative, 266
- purpose of rules of, 263
- real, 263
- relevancy of, 266
- *res gestae*, 264–65
- testimonial, 263
- testimony, 272

Exclusionary rule, 217–18
- evidence, 277
- good faith exception, 217–18
- knock and announce and, 187

Executive branch, 3
Executive orders, 12
- citations, 12

Exemption, from arrest, 181
Exigent circumstances, 241–44
- residence, 243–44
- vehicle-automobile exception, 242
- vehicle destroyed by fire, 243
- warrantless entry and, 259–60

Expert opinion, 272–73
Explosives, 119–20
- burglary using, 83
- concealment of, 119
- fake bombs, 119
- as implements of terrorism, 119
- manufacturing, carrying, buying, selling, or furnishing, 120
- placing bombs, 119
- placing injurious substances, 120
- possession of, 120
- in public place, 120
- vulnerable targets, 120

Extortion, 55
- completion of, 55
- threat for, 55

F

Fair market value, 78–79
  test, 76
False exchange, 93
False reports, 142–44
  abducted or missing child, 143–44
  ambulance, 143
  bomb threat, 143
  police, 142–43
  police dispatch center, 143
False representations, 138–39
  as FIA worker, 138–39
  of fire or EMS equipment, 139
  of law enforcement equipment, 139
  as public utility employee, 138
Federal Circuit Court of Appeals, 5
Federal court system, organization of, 5–6
Federal district courts, 5
Federal government
  branches of, 2–3
  executive branch, 3
  judicial branch, 3
  legislative branch, 2–3
Federal law, exemption from registration requirements, 135
Fellers v. United States, 198
Felony, 9
  assault with intent to commit, 21
  firearms during commission of, 130
  murder, 47
  solicitation to commit, 15
  soliciting minor to commit, 26
Fetus, injury to, 22
FIA worker
  assault upon, 19
  false representation of, 138–39
Fifth Amendment, 2, 7, 196–98, 199
  admissions and confessions and, 189
Financial crimes, 97–104
  check law violations, 97–99
  counterfeiting, 100–101
  defrauding an innkeeper, 101–2
  financial transaction device, 102–4
  forgery, 99
  uttering and publishing, 99–100
Financial transaction device, 102–4
  defrauding with, 103–4
  possession of fraudulent or altered, 103
  possession with intent to use, deliver, circulate, or sell, 102–3
  revoked or canceled, 103
  violations, 102
Finding, 8
Fingerprinting, juveniles, 292
Fingerprint requirements, laws of arrest and, 179
Firearms, 122–35
  aiming firearm without malice, 131
  altering serial numbers on, 129
  brandishing in public, 129
  carrying concealed weapon, 124–27
  carrying dangerous weapons with unlawful intent, 127–28
  carrying while under the influence, 127
  concealed pistol licenses, 126
  definitions, 122–23
  discharge at emergency or law enforcement vehicle, 132
  discharge in dwelling, 132
  discharge of, with malice, 131
  discharge of, without malice, 131
  exceptions to violations, 128–29
  exemptions for concealed pistol license, 127
  felon in possession of, 132–33
  forfeiture of, 135
  hunting with, intoxicated, 131
  long gun violations, 128
  notice of suspension, 127
  operability requirements, 133
  pistol-free zones, 126–27
  pistol registration requirements, 133–35
  possession by minor, 129
  possession during commission of felony, 130
  possession of shotgun or rifle, 123
  possession of stolen, 106
  possession while intoxicated, 131
  prohibited places to possess, 130
  reckless or wanton use of, 131–32
  self-defense, 126
  selling, 129–30
  signaling device, 132
  spring guns, 130
  stun gun, 123
  transporting in vehicles, 128
  unlawful weapons, 123–24
  from vehicle, 132
  weapon-free school zone, 129
Firefighter
  assault on, 19
  disobeying during riot, 78, 171
  impersonation of, 138
Fireman's rule, 305
Fire scenes, administrative searches and, 262
Firestone v. Rice, 295
Fireworks, 121–22
First Amendment, 2
Fleeing and eluding, 152–54
  first degree, 154
  use of force and, 298–99
  fourth degree, 153
  police, 228
  second degree, 154
  terry stops and, 256
  third degree, 153
  vehicles and, 298
Flippo v. West Virginia, 225
Florida v. Jimeno, 247

Florida v. J.L., 256
Florida v. Meyers, 243
Florida v. Riley, 221
Florida v. Royer, 192
Florida v. Wells, 258
Florida v. White, 242
Force, 174
    caselaw on use of, 180
    defined, 38
    to effectuate arrests, 180
Foreign protection order (FPO), 33–34
    enforcement of, 33–34
    good faith immunity for enforcement of, 34
Forgery, 99
Formal hearings, 264
Former testimony, 271
48-hour rule, 228
Foster v. California, 214
14-Day Rule, 7
Fourteenth Amendment, 2
Fourth Amendment, 2, 217, 218–20, 233
    applying, 218–20
    expectation of privacy and, 219
    governmental conduct and, 218–19
    laws of arrest and, 173
    physical manipulation invokes, 219–20
    warrantless searches and, 241
Frasier v. Cupp, 205
Fraud
    confessions and, 205–6
    retail, 93–95, 176
    vulnerable adult, 58
Fresh pursuit, 181

G

Gainey v. Sieloff, 267
Gambling, 155–56
    frequently places of, 156
    house, 155–56
    selling posts and registered bets, 156
Garbage, privacy and, 221
Gauthier v. Alpena County Prosecutor, 115
General intent, 8
General warrants, 232
Georgia v. Randolph, 248
Gilbert v. California, 213
Good faith defense, 306
Good faith exception, 217–18
Goods, confiscation of, 162
Graham v. Connor, 180, 296
Greene v. Barber, 306
Groh v. Ramirez, 232, 306
Gross indecency, 42
Gross negligence, 48–49

H

Hall v. SOS, 287
Handcuffing, Terry stops and, 256–57
Harassing phone calls, 66

Harassment, 30
Harlow v. Fitzgerald, 306
Harmful biological substance, 120
Harmful chemical substance, 120
Harmful radioactive material, 121
Harmful substances, 121
    false exposure to, 121
Harmless error, violation of rights and, 209
Harris-Fields v. Syze, 305
Hazing, 62–63
Hearing phases, for juveniles, 292–93
Hearsay rule, 267–72
    business records, 270
    child's statement about sexual act, 270–71
    in domestic violence, 272
    dying declaration, 271
    exceptions, 269
    excited utterance, 269
    former testimony, 271
    medical diagnosis and, 270
    mental, emotional, physical condition, 269–70
    present memory refreshed, 270
    public records, 270
    recorded recollection, 270
    statement against interest, 271–72
    statement by co-conspirator, 269
Helicopters, privacy and, 221
Heyler v. Dixson, 272
Hoffa v. United States, 193
Hoffman v. Warden, 178
Holding, 8
Hollis v. Baker, 175
Holmberg v. 54-A Judicial Dist. Judge, 287
Home invasion, 82
    first degree, 82
    second degree, 82
    third degree, 82
Homicide, 47–49
    first degree, 47–48
    manslaughter, 48–49
    negligent, 49
    second degree, 48
Horton v. California, 245
Hospital rooms, privacy and, 222
Hot pursuit, 259–61
    exigent circumstances, 259–60
    non-exigent circumstances, 260
    third party residence, 260–61
    warrantless misdemeanors, 259
Howlett v. Creighton, 306
Hudson v. Michigan, 187, 234
Human trafficking, 50–51
    facilitating, 51
Hunting, intoxicated, 131

I

Identity theft, 66–69
    Identity Protection Act, 66–67
    penalties, 68–69

prosecuting, 69
secretly capturing, 69
unlawfully obtaining, 68
unlawful use, 68
Ignition interlocks, 284
Illinois v. Caballes, 221
Illinois v. Lafayette, 258
Illinois v. Lidster, 253
Illinois v. McArthur, 236
Illinois v. Perkins, 208
Illinois v. Rodriguez, 34, 248
Illinois v. Wardlow, 256
Imitation controlled substance, 115
Immobilization, O.W.I. and, 284
Immunity
absolute, 305
qualified, 306
Impaired driving, 280–81
Impeachment, 273
by character evidence, 273
by evidence of conviction, 273
Impersonation, 137–38
disguising with intent to intimidate, 138
EMT, 138
firefighter, 138
police officer, 137–38
unauthorized wearing of uniform or badge, 138
Implied consent, 285
Inchoate offenses, 13–16
accessory after the fact, 14
aiding and abetting, 13–14
attempts, 14
conspiracy, 14–15
solicitation to commit a felony, 15
Indecency, crimes of, 40–42
gross indecency, 42
indecent exposure, 41
lewd and lascivious behavior, 41
obscene language, 42
sodomy, 40–41
Indecent exposure, 41
Indictment, 6
Inference, 266
Informal hearings, 264
Informants, privilege and, 276–77
Informational checkpoints, terry stops and, 253
Informational/voluntary contact, 173
Ingram v. City of Columbus, 235
Inhalants, use of, 116
Injury, confessions and, 204
Injury to fetus/embryo, 22
Inmates, questioning by, 208
Inspections, liquor, 157
Insured property, arson and, 76–77
Intent, 174
Intentional torts, 303
defenses to, 303
Interim bond, 30, 183, 240
exception to, for domestic violence, 183–84

Interrogation, 193–95
defined, 194
held not to be, 195
held to be, 194–95
normal arrest and booking procedures, 195
police communication *versus*, 195–96
silence and demeanor during, 196
voluntary statement and, 195
Interrogatories, 302
Intimate part, defined, 37
Inventories, 257–58
personal effects, 258
vehicles, 257–58
Investigatory detention, 173
Involuntary manslaughter, 48
Isabella County v. Michigan, 305

J
Jail cell, privacy and, 222
Joint access/control, consent and, 247–48
Judges, 6
Judicial branch, 3
Judicial notice, 265
Judicial system
defense attorney, 6
district court magistrate, 6
judges, 6
jury, 6
prosecuting attorney, 6
roles within, 6
Junk yards, administrative searches and, 261–62
Jurisdiction, 3, 6
of family division of circuit court, 289–90
officer's authority outside, 179–80
transfer of, 291
waiver of, 291
Jury, 6
misleading, 267
tampering, 147–48
Justice, obstruction of, 148–49
Juvenile Justice and Delinquency Prevention Act (JJDPA), 290–91
Juvenile law, 289–93
confessions, 292
confessions and, 206–7
under Crime Victim's Rights Act, 308, 309
custody, 290–91
fingerprinting, photographing, identification procedures, 292
hearing phases, 292–93
jurisdiction of family division of circuit court, 289–90
rights of child, 291–92
terminology differences, 289
transfer of jurisdiction, 291
waiver of jurisdiction, 291

K
Katz v. United States, 217, 219, 220
Kaupp v. Texas, 209

Kidnapping, 49–51
  child, 50
  human trafficking, 50–51
  parental, 50
  unlawful imprisonment, 49–50
Knock and announce, 186–87
  exclusionary rule and, 187
  Fourth Amendment and, 186
  search warrants and, 233–36
Knock and talk, consent and, 249–50
Knowles v. Iowa, 240
Knowles v. People, 263
Kubiak v. Hurr, 275
Kuhlmann v. Wilson, 208
Kyllo v. United States, 221

L

Larceny, 88–93
  in building, 89–90
  by conversion, 91–92
  by false pretense, 92–93
  at fire, 90
  of firearms, 90
  of livestock, 90
  lost property, 93
  from motor vehicle, 90–91
  of rental property, 91
  by trick, 92
  from vacant dwelling, 90
Lawful self-defense, 29
Laws
  civil, 301
  Constitutional, 1–4
  of evidence, 263–77
  juvenile, 289–93
  O.W.I., 279–88
  sources of, 12
  sources of Michigan, 10–12
  on suspect identification, 211–16
Laws of arrest, 173–87
  accessibility of evidence, 179
  arrestee's rights, 181
  arrests pursuant to arrest warrants, 174–75
  arrests without warrant, 175–78
  bond, 183–84
  custodial traffic arrests, 184
  entry into residence for arrest, 184–86
  exemptions from arrest, 181
  fingerprint requirements, 179
  force to effectuate, 180
  Fourth Amendment, 173
  fresh pursuit, 181
  knock and announce, 186–87
  LEIN check requirements, 179
  length of duration during investigatory stop, 174
  levels of contact between police and citizens, 173
  officer's authority outside jurisdiction, 179–80
  prosecution of crimes, 178
  resisting arrest, 178–79
  search incident to arrest, 181–83
  valid, 174
Laws on use of force, 295–300
  federal standard, 295–96
  fleeing felons, 298–99
  Michigan law on use of deadly force, 296–98
  Michigan standard, 295
  private citizen use of deadly force, 299
  self defense, 299–300
Lay opinion, 272
Ledbetter v. Edwards, 206
Legal terminology, 6–8
Legislative branch, 2–3
  Congress, 3
  Senate, 2
LEIN check requirements, laws of arrest and, 179
Leonard v. Robinson, 170
Lesser included crimes, 9
Lewd and lascivious behavior, 41
Lewis v. Legrow, 64
Liability
  civil, 302–3
  domestic violence and, 36
  state tort actions, 36
Liquor law violations, 156–61
  consuming on school property, 161
  definitions, 157
  furnishing to minors, 157–58
  inspections, 157, 261
  license requirements, 156
  minors in possession of alcoholic liquor, 158–61
  possessing or consuming in public, 161
Listed sexual act, defined, 27
Litigation
  civil, 301–2
  examples of, 234–35
Littering, 171–72
  defined, 171
  throwing in front of vehicle, 171
  throwing objects at vehicles, 172
  wreckers, 171
LoJi Sales, Inc. v. New York, 233
Long gun violations, 128

M

Machine gun, 123
Maim, assault with intent to, 21
Malcomson v. Scott, 178
Malicious destruction of property, 78–80
  fair market value, 78–79
  of personal property, 79
  to police or fire department, 80
  to real property, 80
  to school bus, 80
Manslaughter, 48–49
  gross negligence, 48–49
  involuntary, 48
  voluntary, 48
Mapp v. Ohio, 217, 277

Marbury v. Madison, 3
Marihuana
   medical, 118
   plain smell and, 246
Maryland v. Buie, 186, 227
Maryland v. Pringle, 241
Maryland v. Wilson, 251
Massachusetts v. Sheppard, 217
Masturbation, defined, 27
Material evidence, 266
Mathis v. United States, 193
Mechanical knife, 128
Mediation, 302
Medical marihuana, 118
Mens rea, 8
Mental anguish, 37
Mentally disabled, defined, 38
Mentally incapable, defined, 37
Mentally incapacitated, defined, 37
Metallic knuckles, 124
Michigan Constitution, 3–4
   U.S. Constitution *versus,* 218
Michigan Court of Appeals opinion, effect of, 11
Michigan law, sources of, 10–12
   administrative rules, 12
   attorney general opinions, 12
   citations, 10, 11, 12
   court opinions, 10
   executive orders, 12
   statutes, 10
Michigan Medical Marihuana Act, 118
Michigan personal protection orders, 31–33
Michigan Supreme Court opinion, effect of, 11
Michigan v. Clifford, 262
Michigan v. Long, 218, 251
Michigan v. Mosley, 195
Michigan v. Summers, 236
Mincey v. Arizona, 204, 224
Minnesota v. Carter, 225
Minnesota v. Murphy, 189
Minnesota v. Olson, 185, 225, 260
Minnick v. Mississippi, 197
Minors, violations involving, 25–28
   in a bar, 25
   alcohol consumption and, 25
   contributing to delinquency of, 25
   firearms, 129
   furnishing liquor to, 157–58
   in house of prostitution, 43
   possession of alcoholic liquor, 158–61
   prior bad acts, 274
   sexually abusive material, 26–28
   soliciting for immoral purposes, 26
   soliciting to commit felony, 26
   tobacco, 25
Miranda v. Arizona, 201
Miranda warnings, 190–93
   consent to search and, 197–98
   custody and, 190–93
   O.W.I. arrest and, 287
   requirements, 190
   violation of, 197
Misdemeanors, 9
   under Crime Victim's Rights Act, 308
   stalking, 59–60
   unauthorized strip search as, 183
Missouri v. Seibert, 200
Molotov cocktails, 121
Montejo v. Louisiana, 198
Moore v. Illinois, 211
Moran v. Burbine, 201, 202
Motion in limine, 7
Moving objects, plain view and, 245
Muffler, 123. *See also* Silencer
Murder
   assault with intent to, 20
   felony, 47
   second degree, 48, 283

N
Narcotics, arrests without warrant, 176
Negligence torts, 303–5
   breach, 303
   causation, 303
   duty, 303
   fireman's rule, 305
   immunity to, 305
   injury, 303
   during pursuits, 304
Negligent homicide, 49
Newcomb v. City of Troy, 299
New Jersey v. T.L.O., 219
New York v. Class, 221
New York v. Quarles, 209
Nicholson v. Kent County Sheriff's Dept., 297
Ninth Amendment, 2
Nitrous oxide, sale of, 116–17
No account check, 98
Non-attorney, requests to talk to, 200
Non-sufficient funds, 97–98
North Carolina v. Butler, 201
Notice to appear, 181

O
O'Brien v. City of Grand Rapids, 297
Obscene language, 42
Obscene phone calls, 66
Obstruction, 151–52
   of justice, 148–49
   person performing lawful duty, 151–52
Odom v. Wayne County, 305
Ohio v. Robinette, 246
Oliver v. United States, 223
Omission, 23
180-Day Rule, 7
Open fields, privacy and, 222–23
Operating while intoxicated (O.W.I.). *See* O.W.I. law
Operating with the presence of drugs (OWPD), 281

Opinion evidence, 272–73
  expert opinion, 272–73
  lay opinion, 272
Opinions, 8
  attorney general, 12
  court, 10–11
Oregon v. Bradshaw, 197
Oregon v. Mathiason, 190
Original document rule. *See* Best evidence rule
Orozco v. Texas, 192
Osner v. Boughner, 273
O.W.I., arrests without warrant and, 175–76
O.W.I. law, 279–88
  causing serious impairment, 283
  chemical tests, 285–87
  child endangerment, 284
  commercial motor vehicle drivers and, 282
  confiscation of registration plate, 284
  defined, 279
  DLAD hearing, 287
  forcing entry into residence, 287–88
  ignition interlocks, 284
  immobilization, 284
  impaired, or causing death, 282–83
  impaired driving, 280–81
  implied consent, 285
  Miranda rights and, 287
  operating with presence of drugs, 281
  penalties, 282
  permitting person under influence to drive, 284
  preliminary breath tests, 285
  registration denial, 285
  at scene of accident, 281
  statute, 279–80
  unlawful bodily alcohol content, 280
  .02/zero tolerance, 282

P

Pandering, 43–44
Papachristou v. City of Jacksonville, 169
Parental consent, 248
Parental kidnapping, 50
Passive sexual involvement, defined, 27
Pat downs, terry stops and, 256
Patterson v. Illinois, 198
Payton v. New York, 184, 259
Peace bonds, 154
  arrest authority, 154
  complaint, 154
  issuance of warrant by court, 154
Peace officer
  arrestee rights and, 181
  assault on, 19
Pearson v. Callahan, 306
Peddler license violations, 162
  restrictions on items sold, 162
  transient merchant, 162
Pedestrians, detaining, 254–55
Pennsylvania v. Labron, 242
Pennsylvania v. Mimms, 251
Pennsylvania v. Muniz, 195
People v. Abraham, 207, 292
People v. Abramski, 153
People v. Ackerman, 274
People v. Adair, 275
People v. Adams, 200, 213, 214
People v. Aguwa, 100
People v. Aldrich, 281
People v. Alfafara, 245
People v. Anderson, 20, 102, 208, 212, 214, 215
People v. Anstey, 286
People v. Armstrong, 40
People v. Attebury, 209
People v. Ayers, 77
People v. Barbat, 34
People v. Barkley, 128, 229
People v. Barnard, 266
People v. Barnes, 262
People v. Battles, 124
People v. Beam, 163
People v. Beasley, 272
People v. Beckman, 168
People v. Belanger, 87
People v. Belknap, 73
People v. Bender, 202
People v. Bergman, 95
People v. Beuschlein, 258
People v. Bieri, 275
People v. Biggs, 275
People v. Biller, 124
People v. Bishop, 169
People v. Bladel, 197
People v. Blasius, 244
People v. Blunt, 121
People v. Bobo, 196
People v. Bolduc, 250
People v. Bommarito, 141
People v. Bono, 42
People v. Boomer, 42
People v. Borchard-Ruhland, 286
People v. Borrelli, 143
People v. Boughner, 286
People v. Bowles, 47
People v. Bradford, 98
People v. Brown, 19, 42, 133, 202
People v. Bugaiski, 167
People v. Bullis, 14
People v. Bullock, 4, 242
People v. Burgenmeyer, 130
People v. Burgess, 266
People v. Burt, 180, 295
People v. Butler, 198
People v. Butts, 95
People v. Carlson, 38
People v. Carrier, 41
People v. Carter, 243
People v. Cartwright, 227
People v. Cassadime, 100

People v. Cavanaugh, 89
People v. Chambers, 173, 255
People v. Champion, 246
People v. Chapman, 183, 240, 258
People v. Chappelle, 98
People v. Chavis, 143
People v. Cheatham, 201
People v. Childs, 276
People v. Chinn, 192
People v. Chism, 248
People v. Christie, 280
People v. Cipriano, 203
People v. Clark, 48, 220
People v. Clarkson, 100
People v. Cleveland, 204
People v. Cohen, 102
People v. Coleman, 236
People v. Collins, 103, 225
People v. Compeau, 275
People v. Conte, 205
People v. Cook, 99
People v. Coomer, 203
People v. Cortez, 236
People v. Couch, 299
People v. Courts, 222
People v. Cox, 169
People v. Craig, 84
People v. Craun, 286
People v. Criger, 307
People v. Crippen, 38
People v. Cross, 273
People v. Crusoe, 197
People v. Currelley, 214
People v. Custer, 223, 246
People v. Czerwinski, 128
People v. Dagwan, 247
People v. Dandy, 106
People v. Daniel, 272
People v. Daoud, 201
People v. Davis, 35, 54, 78, 214, 255, 258
People v. Dean, 216
People v. Deason, 300
People v. DeKorte, 57
People v. DeLisle, 203
People v. Derror, 281
People v. Devine, 168
People v. Dewey, 286
People v. Dinsmore, 221
People v. Dixon, 183, 240
People v. Doane, 186, 235
People v. Dombe, 169
People v. Dorrington, 83
People v. Dowdy, 37
People v. Drake, 42
People v. Duffield, 178
People v. Dunlap, 195
People v. Dunn, 205
People v. Dunnigan, 205
People v. Eady, 268

People v. Eaton, 214
People v. Eaves, 113
People v. Edwards, 192
People v. Egelston, 101
People v. Eisenberg, 178
People v. Ewing, 79, 205
People v. Farrow, 249
People v. Favreau, 168
People v. Feldman, 203
People v. Fennell, 166
People v. Ferguson, 83
People v. Fetterley, 234
People v. Finney, 81
People v. Fishel, 106
People v. Fisher, 192
People v. Fortuin, 106
People v. Freeman, 173, 179, 251
People v. Frohriep, 249
People v. Gagnon, 168
People v. Gallagher, 266
People v. Galloway, 250
People v. Garcia, 170
People v. Gardner, 124
People v. Garvin, 242
People v. Gatski, 108
People v. Giacalone, 182, 239
People v. Gillman, 81
People v. Girard, 27, 28
People v. Giuchici, 195, 199
People v. Givans, 207
People v. Godboldo, 202
People v. Goecke, 48, 283
People v. Goforth, 248
People v. Goldston, 218
People v. Golochowicz, 274
People v. Gonsler, 295
People v. Gonzales, 174, 228
People v. Good, 206, 292
People v. Goold, 40
People v. Grady, 248
People v. Grandberry, 125
People v. Granderson, 200
People v. Gray, 216
People v. Grayer, 153
People v. Green, 54, 153, 257
People v. Greene, 150
People v. Greenwood, 196, 269
People v. Gregg, 23
People v. Griffis, 87
People v. Guthrie, 73
People v. Gwinn, 268
People v. Hack, 27
People v. Hadesman, 91
People v. Haisha, 213
People v. Hall, 189, 207, 213
People v. Hamblin, 79
People v. Hamilton, 203
People v. Hammond, 99
People v. Hammons, 37, 271

People v. Hampton, 211, 231, 299
People v. Haney, 226
People v. Hanna, 233
People v. Hardiman, 113
People v. Hardy, 204
People v. Harmelin, 192
People v. Harmon, 27
People v. Harrington, 198
People v. Harris, 197
People v. Harrison, 214
People v. Harvey, 186, 235
People v. Hassenfratz, 124
People v. Hawkins, 218
People v. Hayward, 86
People v. Haywood, 265
People v. Henderson, 165
People v. Hendrickson, 269
People v. Henry, 132, 222
People v. Henson, 98
People v. Hernandez-Garcia, 125
People v. Herndon, 48, 222
People v. Hickman, 212
People v. Hicks, 53, 199, 205
People v. Hider, 214
People v. Hill, 3, 27, 78, 190, 192
People v. Hillard, 103
People v. Hine, 274
People v. Holley, 149
People v. Holloway, 182
People v. Holtschlag, 73
People v. Hornsby, 214
People v. Houze, 223
People v. Howard, 270
People v. Hoy, 168
People v. Hryshko, 140
People v. Hudson, 58
People v. Hunter, 113
People v. Huyser, 270
People v. Ish, 206
People v. Ivers, 275
People v. Jackson, 76, 101, 232, 237, 268
People v. Jacobson, 98
People v. Jagotka, 238
People v. Jenkins, 252
People v. Johnson, 47, 156, 200, 214, 269, 276
People v. Jolly, 54
People v. Jones, 20, 42, 93, 96, 112, 138, 145, 176, 222, 261
People v. Jordan, 204
People v. Joyner, 186, 260
People v. Kachar, 214, 216
People v. Kalchik, 231
People v. Karoll, 142
People v. Kaslowski, 231
People v. Kay, 20
People v. Kazmierczak, 246
People v. Kehoe, 271
People v. Keller, 174
People v. Kelly, 175

People v. Keskimaki, 281
People v. Kim, 170
People v. Kimble, 54
People v. King, 145
People v. Kirstein, 142
People v. Knapp, 20, 39, 274
People v. Koonce, 265
People v. Kotesky, 102
People v. Kowalak, 268
People v. Kowalski, 195
People v. Kratz, 41
People v. Krokker, 236
People v. Kurylczyk, 214, 215
People v. Labelle, 247
People v. Lapworth, 248
People v. Lawrence, 145
People v. Lay, 73
People v. Lee, 214
People v. Leversee, 202
People v. Levine, 243
People v. Libbett, 216
People v. Lillis, 221
People v. Lino, 42
People v. Lipsczinska, 276
People v. Lively, 147
People v. Lobaito, 276
People v. LoCiero, 254
People v. Long, 93
People v. Lopez, 156
People v. Love, 185, 260
People v. Lowenstein, 228
People v. Lucas, 14, 271
People v. Lundberg, 178
People v. Lynn, 259
People v. Mackey, 232
People v. Mackle, 37
People v. Magyar, 47
People v. Malone, 34
People v. Mamon, 222
People v. Mankin, 146
People v. Manning, 204
People v. Marbury, 191
People v. Margelis, 277
People v. Marsack, 198, 249
People v. Mash, 170
People v. Mason, 92
People v. Mass, 112
People v. Matusik, 89
People v. Mayes, 145, 186, 235
People v. Maynor, 23
People v. McAllister, 214
People v. McCarty, 78
People v. McClain, 90
People v. McCord, 180, 295
People v. McCrady, 47
People v. McDonald, 141
People v. McElhaney, 198
People v. McGhee, 232

People v. McGill, 38
People v. McKenzie, 215
People v. McKim, 91
People v. McMahan, 206, 264
People v. McReavy, 196, 269
People v. Meerboer, 270
People v. Mell, 41
People v. Mendez, 191
People v. Miller, 112, 126, 216
People v. Mitchell, 106, 229
People v. Moore, 129, 245
People v. Morey, 44, 45
People v. Morris, 274
People v. Moselar, 48
People v. Mosley, 147
People v. Murphy, 266
People v. Murray, 271
People v. Musser, 82
People v. Nankervis, 142
People v. Nash, 275, 277
People v. Neal, 41
People v. Nimeth, 124
People v. Noel, 81
People v. Nowack, 78
People v. Nunez, 230
People v. Nutt, 7, 106
People v. Ohlinger, 35, 175, 258, 288
People v. O'Keefe, 169
People v. Oliver, 180
People v. Omell, 207
People v. Otto, 256
People v. Owen, 106
People v. Paasche, 277
People v. Paintman, 197, 201
People v. Parham, 251
People v. Parney, 271
People v. Pasha, 125
People v. Patterson, 90
People v. Peach, 98
People v. Peals, 133
People v. Peebles, 253
People v. Peerenboom, 192
People v. Pena, 21, 55
People v. Percin, 141
People v. Perlos, 281
People v. Perry, 37
People v. Philabaun, 152
People v. Philbaun, 19
People v. Phillips, 38
People v. Pinnix, 221
People v. Plummer, 48
People v. Porterfield, 208
People v. Powell, 222, 247, 275
People v. Pratt, 106
People v. Premo, 38
People v. Purofoy, 216
People v. Quinn, 128
People v. Rabin, 77

People v. Ramos, 146
People v. Ramsey, 90
People v. Raper, 195
People v. Reeves, 76
People v. Reinhardt, 184, 259, 287
People v. Reynolds, 124
People v. Richardson, 53
People v. Richter, 204
People v. Riggs, 27, 199
People v. Rizzo, 252
People v. Roark, 193
People v. Robinson, 13, 49, 204
People v. Rodgers, 54
People v. Ross, 47, 83
People v. Russo, 229, 230
People v. Rutherford, 54
People v. Sabin, 274
People v. Schram, 267
People v. Schultz, 112
People v. Schutter, 59
People v. Scott, 91
People v. Secrest, 237
People v. Sexton, 191
People v. Shankle, 173, 252
People v. Shaw, 227
People v. Sheets, 20, 145
People v. Sherman-Huffman, 23
People v. Shipley, 130
People v. Shipp, 85, 213
People v. Simpson, 78
People v. Singer, 168
People v. SLL, 207
People v. Sloan, 229
People v. Slocum, 195
People v. Small, 54
People v. Smith, 20, 86, 145, 205, 225, 268
People v. Smock, 76
People v. Smola, 220
People v. Snider, 185, 244, 260
People v. Spalding, 145
People v. Spearman, 266
People v. Spencer, 199
People v. Stacy, 197, 270
People v. Stark, 185, 261
People v. Starr, 274
People v. Stephen, 175, 280
People v. Stevens, 20, 59, 205
People v. Stewart, 237
People v. Stone, 64, 124
People v. Straight, 269
People v. Stull, 275
People v. Sturgis, 7
People v. Susalla, 99
People v. Sykes, 92
People v. Taugher, 92
People v. Taylor, 54, 76, 222, 250
People v. Tejeda, 229
People v. Terry, 54

People v. Thomas, 20, 209
People v. Thompson, 89, 146
People v. Threatt, 32
People v. Tierney, 224
People v. Tolbert, 113
People v. Tombs, 27, 72
People v. Toohey, 257
People v. Tracy, 233, 280
People v. Turner, 216
People v. Uhl, 81
People v. Underwood, 277
People v. United States Currency, 265
People v. VanderVliet, 274
People v. Vandiver, 251
People v. VanDriver, 20
People v. Vasquez, 20
People v. Vaughn, 214
People v. Venticinque, 87
People v. Ventura, 20, 179
People v. Vronko, 41
People v. Wade, 243
People v. Wagner, 34
People v. Wallach, 202
People v. Walters, 89
People v. Ward, 21, 220
People v. Warren, 45, 96
People v. Weinberg, 170
People v. Weiss, 179
People v. Werner, 283
People v. Westra, 232
People v. White, 265, 266
People v. Whitehead, 228
People v. Whitfield, 230
People v. Wilbourne, 89
People v. Wilkens, 27
People v. Wilkins, 39
People v. Williams, 15, 89, 126, 146, 191, 214, 236, 254
People v. Wilson, 83, 91, 132, 221
People v. Wofford, 48
People v. Wolfe, 175
People v. Wood, 154, 279
People v. Woods, 37
People v. Wujkowski, 287
People v. Yamat, 280
People v. Young, 213
People v. Zahn, 190
People v. Zak, 276
Peremptory challenge, 7
Perjury, 146–50
   in court, 146–47
   inhibiting witness, 149–50
   jury tampering, 147–48
   obstruction of justice, 148–49
   subornation of, 147
Personal effect, inventory, 258
Personal injury, defined, 37
Personal property
   arson, 76
   fair market value test, 76

Personal protection orders, 5
   arrest and, 32
   arrests without warrant, 176–77
   bond/court appearance and, 32–33
   enforcement of, 31–32
   Michigan, 31–33
   serving, 32
Persuasion, burden of, 264
Photo display, 214–15
Photographic lineups, 214–15
Photographing, juveniles, 292
Physical abuse, confessions and, 204
Physical harm, 23, 57
Physically helpless, defined, 38
Physician-patient privilege, 276
Pierson v. Ray, 306
Pistol, 122
   exemptions to registration requirements, 134–35
   registration requirements, 133–35
   in vehicle, 124
Pistol-free zones, 126–27
Plain feel, 245–46
Plain smell, 246
Plain view, 244–46
   moving objects and, 245
   plain feel, 245–46
   plain smell, 246
Plea bargaining, 7, 205
Poisoning, 73
Police animals, 167
Police communication, interrogation *versus,* 195–96
Police dog, assault on, 20
Police horse, assault on, 20
Police officers
   authority outside jurisdiction, 179–80
   embezzlement by, 96
   impersonation of, 137–38
   taking weapon from, 150–51
Police scanners, 161–62
Polygraph, 198
   privilege, 277
Pre-arraignment delay, 203–4
Preliminary breath tests (PBT), 285
Preliminary examination, 7
Preponderance of evidence, 8
Prescription misuse, 115
Pre-sentence investigation, 7
Presumption, 266
   of innocence, 266
Pretext arrests, 226–27
Pretext stops, 226
Pretrial motions, 7
Price switching, 93
Prior bad acts, evidence of, 274
Privacy, expectation of, 220–23
   abandonment, 222
   aiding vision, 220
   dogs, use of, 221
   electronic tracking device and, 220

garbage, 221
helicopter/airplane, 221
hospital rooms, 222
jail cell, 222
open fields, 222–23
registration plates, 222
rest areas, 221
standing on patrol car, 220
thermal imaging, 221
vehicle identification numbers, 221
workplace, 222
Private conversations, 225
Privileges, 275–77
accountant-client, 277
attorney-client, 275
clergy, 276
domestic violence or sexual assault victim-counselor, 276
informants, 276–77
physician-patient, 276
polygraph, 277
psychologist-patient, 276
self-incrimination, 277
social worker, 277
spouse, 276
traffic crash reports, 276
Probable cause, 7, 173, 241–44
for arrest, 241
defined, 174
motor homes, 243
search at police station, 243
for search warrant, 229–30
Probative evidence, 266
Procedural due process, 3
Promises, confessions and, 204–5
Proof, 264
burden of, 264
standard of, 264
Property
crimes against, 105–9
Crime Victim's Rights Act and, 308
destruction of (See Destruction of property)
disposition of, 238
seized, safety of, 238
stolen, possession of, 105–6
Prosecuting attorney, 6
Prosecution, duty of, 300
Prostitution, 42–45
accepting earnings from, 44–45
aiding and abetting, 43
minor in house of, 43
pandering, 43–44
penalties for, 43
permitting place of, 43
soliciting for, 42
solicitor for, 43
Protective custody, arrests without warrant, 177–78
Protective service workers, questioning by, 208
Protective sweeps, 186, 227–28

Prurient interest, 27
Psychologist-patient privilege, 276
Pubic interest crimes, 155–72
Public duty doctrine, 303
Public interest crimes
body armor, 156
cruelty to animals, 162–67
disorderly conduct, 168–70
gambling, 155–56
liquor law violations, 156–61
littering, 171–72
peddler license violations, 162
police scanners, 161–62
riots, 170–71
Public records, hearsay rule and, 270
Public safety, violation of rights and, 209
Publishing, 99–100
Purchaser, 122

Q
Qualified immunity, 306

R
Radioactive substances, 120–21
manufacturing, delivering, possessing, using, 121
Rakas v. Illinois, 225
Rape shield statute, 274–75
Real evidence, 263
Reasonable cause, 7
for search warrant, 229–30
Reasonable suspicion, 8, 173, 186
terry encounters and, 257
terry stops and, 251–53
Reasonable time, 195
Reckless act, defined, 57
Reckless failure to act, defined, 57
Recreational trespass, 107–8
Registration, of sex offenders, 45
Registration denial, O.W.I. and, 285
Registration plates, privacy and, 222
Reimbursement order, 71
Report
of child abuse, failure to, 24–25
of child abuse, requirements for, 24
preparing domestic violence, 35–36
Res Gestae, 264–65
purpose of witness rule, 265
requirements, 265
witness, 265
Residence, forcing entry into, 287–88
Resistance, 40
Resisting, 151–52
Rest areas, privacy and, 221
Retail fraud, 93–95, 176
first degree, 93–94
possession of device to shield merchandise from detection, 95
second degree, 94
third degree, 94, 95

Retreat, duty to, 300
Rhode Island v. Innis, 195
Richardson v. Bonds, 174
Richard v. Wisconsin, 234
Rifle, 122–23
    possession of, 123
Rights
    advisement of, 200
    of arrestee, 181
    of child, 291–92
    to lineup, 214
    reassertion of, 203
    remedies for violation of, 208–9
    waiver of, 201–3
Right to counsel. *See also* Sixth Amendment
    suspect identification and, 211–12
Right to remain silent, 195–96, 199
    silence and demeanor during interrogation, 196
    tacit admission, 196
Riots, 170–71
    destroying dwelling house during, 170
    disobeying firefighters or emergency personnel, 171
    inciting, 170
    refusal to aid officer, 170
Robbery, 53–55
    armed, 53–54
    assault with intent to, 21
    carjacking, 54
    extortion, 55
    larceny from person, 53
    unarmed, 53
Robbins v. California, 217
Robinson v. Detroit, 304
Roxbury v. Michigan State Police, 297
Ruling, 8
Russell v. United States, 213

S

Sanchez v. United States, 262
Sanctions, 302
Sandbag, 124
Sand club, 124
Sandul v. Larion, 306
Schedules, of controlled substances, 111
Schneckloth v. Bustamonte, 246
School property
    arrests without warrant, 176
    consuming alcoholic liquor on, 161
Scott v. Harris, 298
Scott v. Illinois, 198
Scott v. United States, 174
Search and rescue team, assault on, 19
Search and seizure, 3–4, 217–38
    crime scenes, 224–25
    curtilage around residence, 223–24
    exclusionary rule, 217–18
    fleeing from police and, 228
    48-hour rule, 228
    Fourth Amendment, 217, 218–20
    Michigan *versus* U.S. Constitution, 218
    open view, 220–23
    pretext arrests, 226–27
    pretext stops, 226
    private conversations, 225
    protective sweeps, 227–28
    search warrant requirements, 228–38
    search warrant rule, 217
    standing, 225
Search incident to arrest, 181–83
    accompanying arrestees into dwelling, 182
    body cavity search, 183
    strip search, 182–83
    vehicles, 182
Search incident to lawful arrest, 239–41
    accompanying arrestees into dwelling, 239
    arrestee swallowing evidence, 240–41
    arrest in home, 239
    interim bond, 240
    probable cause, 241
    search subsequent to citation, 240
    vehicles, 239–40
Search warrant requirements, 228–38
    administration of oath, 229
    affidavit for, 229
    anticipatory, 230–31
    for blood, 233
    detention during execution of, 236
    detentions pending issuance, 236
    disposition of property, 238
    file tabulation with court, 238
    general, 232
    items to search for, 231
    judge's signature, 229
    knock and announce, 233–36
    leave copy, 237–38
    mistakes and, 231–32
    named/unnamed persons, 231
    neutral and detached magistrate, 228–29
    penalties with, 238
    place to be searched, 232–33
    private citizens on executions, 237
    probable/reasonable cause, 229–30
    safe keeping of property for trial, 238
    scope of search, 236
    search of persons at scene, 236–37
    staleness, 230
    tabulation and receipt, 237
Search warrant rule, 217
Second Amendment, 2
Security guards, questioning by, 207–8
See v. Seattle, 261
Self-defense, 126
    lawful, 29
    spray, 124
    use of force in, 299–300
Self-Defense Act, 299–300

Self-incrimination, 3, 277
   lineups and, 213
Seller, 122
Senate, 2
Sentencing requirements, 7
Serious mental harm
   to child, 23
   defined, 57
Serious physical harm
   to child, 22–23
   defined, 57
Service dogs, beating or impeding, 165–66
Service of process, 302
Seventh Amendment, 2
Sex offenders, registration of, 45
   address verification, 45
   institutes of higher learning, 45
   moving, 45
   prosecution and, 45
   school safety zones and, 45
Sex offense, 37–45
   crimes of indecency, 40–42
   criminal sexual conduct, 37–40
   prostitution, 42–45
   registration of sex offenders, 45
Sexual contact, defined, 37
Sexual excitement, defined, 27
Sexual intercourse, defined, 27
Sexual penetration, defined, 37
Shotgun, 122
   possession of, 123
Show-ups, 215–16
   on-the-scene exception, 216
Signaling device, 132
Silencer, 123
Simmons v. United States, 213
Sixth Amendment, 2
   informant in jail, 199
   length of right, 199
   polygraph, 198
   right to counsel, 198–99
   waiver after request for attorney, 199
6th Circuit Court of Appeals opinion, effect of, 11
Smith v. Hubbell, 147
Smith v. Jones, 303
Social worker privilege, 277
Sodomy, 40–41
Solicitation to commit a felony, 15
   elements, 15
Soliciting
   child for immoral purposes, 26
   minor to commit felony, 26
   for prostitution, 42
Solomon v. Shuell, 270
South Dakota v. Opperman, 257
Sova v. The City of Mt. Pleasant, 298
Specific intent, 8
Spousal privilege, 276

Spring guns, 130
Staleness, of search warrant, 230
Stalking, 59–62
   aggravated, 60–61
   defined, 30
   domestic violence and, 30
   misdemeanor, 59–60
   posting message as, 61–62
Standard of proof, 264
Standing, 225
Stansbury v. California, 191
State court system
   appeal process in, 5–6
   circuit courts, 5
   district courts, 5
   organization of, 5–6
Status offender, 289
Statute of limitations, 9–10
Statutes
   citations, 10
   of Michigan law, 10
Steagald v. United States, 185, 261
Steele v. United States, 232
Stolen property, possession of, 105–6
   firearms, 106
Stop and frisk, 250–51
Stovall v. Denno, 211
Stricter civil standard, 264
Strip search, 182–83
Stun gun, 123
Submission, defined, 174
Substantive due process, 3
Summons, 302
Supreme Court, 3, 5
   opinion, effect of, 11
Suspect identification, laws on, 211–16
   corporeal lineups, 212–13
   identification methods, 211–12
   inanimate objects, 216
   of juveniles, 292
   photographic lineups/photo display, 214–15
   remedy for improper procedures, 216
   show-ups, 215–16

T

Tabulation
   filing with court, 238
   of search, 237
Tallman v. DNR, 261
Tampering
   with electronic communication, 65–66
   jury, 147–48
   with motor vehicle, 87
Technical trespass, 223–24
Telephone calls, obscene, harassing, and threatening, 66
Tender years rule, 270–71
Tennessee v. Garner, 180, 295, 298, 299
Tenth Amendment, 2

Terrorism, explosives as implements of, 119
Terry encounters, 250–57
   anonymous tip, 256
   detaining pedestrians, 254–55
   drug checkpoints, 252–53
   fleeing from police, 256
   handcuffing, 256–57
   informational checkpoints, 253
   length of detention, 255
   ordering occupants from vehicles, 251
   pat downs, 256
   reasonable suspicion and, 251–53, 257
   search of auto, 251
   smell of intoxicants, 252
   stop and frisk, 250–51
   vehicle, 253–54
Terry v. Ohio, 11, 250
Testimonial evidence, 263
Testimony, 272
   competency, 272
   oath or affirmations, 272
   personal knowledge, 272
   sequestration of witnesses, 272
Texas v. Brown, 245
Texas v. Cobb, 198
Theft crimes, 85–96
   auto, 85–88
   embezzlement, 95–96
   larceny, 88–93
   retail fraud, 93–95
Thermal imaging, privacy and, 221
Third Amendment, 2
Third party residence, hot pursuit and, 260–61
Third person, assault on, 21
Thompson v. Louisiana, 224
Thornton v. United States, 182, 240
Threatening phone calls, 66
Threats, confessions and, 204
Tobacco violations, minors and, 25
Tort
   constitutional, 303, 305–6
   crime *versus*, 302–3
   intentional, 303
   negligence, 303–5
   theories affecting, 303
Torture, 21–22
   of animals, 166
Transient merchant, 162
Trespass, 106–9
   on key facilities, 108–9
   on land of another, 106–7
   recreational, 107–8
   on state correctional facility, 107
   technical, 223–24
Tricks, confessions and, 205–6

U
Unarmed robbery, 53
Unconsented contact, 30

United States v. Banks, 187, 235
United States v. Butler, 255
United States v. Cole, 289
United States v. Dickerson, 196
United States v. Dionisio, 189, 213
United States v. Drayton, 247
United States v. Dunn, 222, 223
United States v. Flores-Montano, 262
United States v. Flowal, 220
United States v. Freeman, 226
United States v. Grubbs, 231
United States v. Karo, 220
United States v. Keszthelyi, 238
United States v. Knights, 257
United States v. Knotts, 220
United States v. Leon, 217
United States v. Matlock, 248
United States v. Mezzanatto, 205
United States v. Patane, 193
United States v. Place, 221
United States v. Ramirez, 235
United States v. Recio, 15
United States v. Robinson, 226
United States v. Ross, 236, 242
United States v. Salvucci, 225
United States v. Santana, 259
United States v. Sharp, 174
United States v. Sharpe, 255
United States v. Sokolow, 255
United States v. Wade, 189, 211, 213
United States v. Whitmore, 168
Unlawful alcohol content, 286
Unlawful bodily alcohol content (UBAC), 280
Unlawful entry, 81–82
Unlawful imprisonment, 49–50
Unlawful purpose, 121
U.S. Constitution, 1–2
   amendments to, 2
   Bill of Rights, 1–2
   Fourteenth Amendment, 2
   main provisions of, 1
   Michigan Constitution *versus*, 3–4, 218
   police officers and, 4
Uttering, 99–100

V
Vehicle identification numbers, privacy and, 221
Venue, 6
Victim, 307–8
Victim's rights, domestic violence and, 35
Video taping, in movie theaters, 64–65
Violation of child protective order, arrests without warrant, 177
Violation of condition of release, arrests without warrants, 177
Violation of rights, remedies for, 208–9
   exceptions, 209
   harmless error, 209
   public safety, 209

Violence, domestic, 29–36
Voir dire examination, 7
Voluntariness standard, 203–6
　coercive police activity, 203
　corpus delicti, 206
　deception, trick, or fraud, 205–6
　determination of, 203
　injury, 204
　physical abuse, 204
　plea bargaining, 205
　pre-arraignment delay, 203–4
　promises, 204–5
　threats, 204
　totality of circumstances, 203
Voluntary manslaughter, 48
Vulnerable adult
　abuse, 57–58
　defined, 57
Vulnerable adult abuse, 57–58
　definitions, 57
　first degree, 57
　fourth degree, 58
　fraud, 58
　second degree, 57–58
　third degree, 58
Vulnerable targets, 120

W

Waiver of jurisdiction, 291
Waiver of rights, 201–3
　knowledge of subjects, 202
　mental condition and, 201
　reasonable time and, 202
　reassertion of rights, 203
　valid, 201
　validity of, 202
　writing and, 201
Warden, Maryland Penitentiary v. Hayden, 259
Warrant for arrest, 6
Warrantless searches, 239–62
　administrative searches, 261–62
　border searches exception, 262
　consent, 246–50
　emergencies, 258
　exigent circumstances, 241–44
　hot pursuit, 259–61
　inventories, 257–58
　plain view, 244–46
　probable cause, 241–44
　search incident to lawful arrest, 239–41
　terry encounters, 250–57
Warrants, 174–75
　arrests without, 175–78
　fake, 249
　issuance by court, 154
Washington v. Newsome, 299
Washington v. Starke, 295
Wayne County Prosecutor v. Recorder's Court Judge, 241
Wayne County Sheriff v. Wayne County Commissioners, 267
Weapon-free school zone, 129
Weapons, 122–35. *See also* Firearms
　carrying concealed, 124–27
　carrying dangerous with unlawful intent, 127–28
　exceptions to violations, 128–29
　forfeiture of, 135
　mechanical knife, 128
　taking from officer, 150–51
　unlawful, 123–24
Weeks v. United States, 277
Werner v. Hartfelder, 180
White v. Beasley, 36
Whren v. United States, 226
Wilson v. Arkansas, 186, 233
Wilson v. Layne, 237
Witness, inhibiting, 149–50
Wong Sun v. United States, 179, 277
Workplace, privacy and, 222
Wyoming v. Houghton, 242

Z

.02/Zero tolerance, 282